Access™ 2007 Programming by Example with VBA, XML, and ASP

Julitta Korol

Wordware Publishing, Inc.

Library of Congress Cataloging-in-Publication Data

Korol, Julitta.
   Access 2007 programming by example with VBA, XML, and ASP / by Julitta Korol.
     p. cm.
   Includes index.
   ISBN-13: 978-1-59822-042-1
   ISBN-10: 1-59822-042-X (pbk.)
   1. Microsoft Access. 2. Database management. 3. Microsoft Visual Basic
   for applications   4. XML (Document markup language)   5. Active server
   pages   I. Title.
   QA76.9.D3K65733 2007
   005.75'65--dc22   2007044561
                                      CIP

Printed in the United States of America

ISBN-13: 978-1-59822-042-1
ISBN-10: 1-59822-042-X
10 9 8 7 6 5 4 3 2 1
0711

All inquiries for volume purchases of this book should be addressed to Wordware Publishing, Inc., at the above address. Telephone inquiries may be made by calling:

(972) 423-0090

Contents

Part II — Access VBA Programming with DAO and ADO

Part III — Programming with the Jet Data Definition Language

Part V — Taking Your VBA Programming Skills to the Web

Part VI — Working with New Features in Access 2007

Acknowledgments

Nobody works alone. In order for this book to become a reality, I had to enlist the help of numerous individuals. For example, while I was sleeping, far away in Hawaii Tana-Lee Rebhan was proofreading and testing all the hands-on exercises and custom projects that had just been written. She was the first person to see what went into this book, and her honest comments made me change a number of things to make this book easier to understand from a reader's standpoint.

After several months of hard work by our Julittana team, the book was finally finished, and the manuscript was sent over to the folks at Wordware Publishing. Martha McCuller had her hands full doing the first edit and designing hundreds of pages of not-so-easy technical stuff. Martha's edits helped make this book even friendlier. While Martha was busy editing and designing, Denise McEvoy was setting up desktop publishing and Alan McCuller was designing the book cover. These two people have used the best of their artistic skills to make this book visually pleasing. And when the page proofs were ready, Beth Kohler, senior editor, took over. I cannot begin to tell you how important Beth's final edits and comments were to the success of this book. She checked spelling and punctuation, standardized grammar, made sure that cross-references matched, and ensured the right placement of heading levels. This entire book project was coordinated by Tim McEvoy. I appreciate very much Tim's dedication and hard work in getting this book published, as well as his patience and understanding of all the obstacles that one faces in every endeavor, not just writing a book. Thanks, everyone, for your contribution to the book! I couldn't have done it without your help.

Introduction

For many years now, Microsoft Access has allowed users to design and develop Windows-based database applications, and Access continues to be the world's most popular database. This book is for people who have already mastered the use of Microsoft Access databases and now are ready for the next step — programming. *Access 2007 Programming by Example with VBA, XML, and ASP* takes non-programmers through detailed steps of creating Access databases from scratch and then shows them how to retrieve and manage their data programmatically using various programming languages and techniques. With this book in hand, users can quickly build the toolset required for developing their own database solutions. This book proves that, given the right approach, programming an Access database from scratch and controlling it via programming code can be as easy as designing and maintaining databases with Access built-in tools. This book gives a practical overview of many programming languages and techniques necessary in programming, maintaining, and retrieving data from today's Access databases.

Prerequisites

You don't need any programming experience to use *Access 2007 Programming by Example with VBA, XML, and ASP*. The only prerequisite is that you already know how to manually design an Access database and perform database tasks by creating and running various types of queries. This book also assumes that you know how to create more complex forms with embedded subforms, combo boxes, and other built-in controls. If you don't have these skills, there are countless books on the market that can teach you step-by-step how to build simple databases or use the sample Northwind database that comes with Microsoft Access. If you do meet these criteria, this book will take you to the Access programming level by example. You will gain working knowledge immediately by performing concrete tasks and without having to read long descriptions of concepts. True learning by example begins with the first step, followed by the next step, and the next one, and so on. By the time you complete all of the steps in a hands-on exercise or a custom project, you should be able to effectively apply the same technique again and again in your own database projects.

How This Book Is Organized

This book is divided into six parts (32 chapters) that progressively introduce you to programming Microsoft Access databases.

Part I introduces you to Access 2007 VBA programming. Visual Basic for Applications (VBA) is the programming language for Microsoft Office

Access. In this part of the book, you acquire the fundamentals of VBA that you will use over and over again in building real-life Microsoft Access database applications.

Part I consists of the following nine chapters:

Chapter 1 — Writing Procedures in Modules
In this chapter you learn about the types of Access procedures that you can write and learn how and where they are written.

Chapter 2 — The Visual Basic Editor (VBE)
In this chapter you learn almost everything you need to know about working with the Visual Basic Editor window, commonly referred to as VBE. Some of the programming tools that are not covered here are discussed and put to use in Chapter 9.

Chapter 3 — Variables, Data Types, and Constants
This chapter introduces basic VBA concepts that allow you to store various pieces of information for later use.

Chapter 4 — Passing Arguments to Procedures and Functions
In this chapter you find out how to provide additional information to your procedures and functions before they are run.

Chapter 5 — Decision Making with VBA
Here you learn how to control your program flow with a number of different decision-making statements.

Chapter 6 — Repeating Actions in VBA
Here you learn how to repeat the same actions by using looping structures.

Chapter 7 — Working with Arrays
In this chapter you learn about static and dynamic arrays and how to use them for holding various values.

Chapter 8 — Custom Collections and Class Modules
This chapter shows how to create and use your own objects and collections of objects.

Chapter 9 — Debugging VBA Procedures and Handling Errors
In this chapter you begin using built-in debugging tools to test your programming code and trap errors.

The skills obtained in Part I of this book are fairly portable. They can be utilized in programming other Microsoft Office applications that also use VBA as their native programming language (Excel, Word, PowerPoint, and Outlook).

Part II introduces you to two sets of programming objects known as Data Access Objects (DAO) and ActiveX Data Objects (ADO) that enable Microsoft Office Access and other client applications to access and manipulate data. In this part of the book, you learn how to use DAO and ADO objects in your VBA code to connect to a data source; create, modify, and secure database objects; and read, add, update, delete, and replicate data.

Part II consists of the following nine chapters:

Chapter 10 — Data Access Technologies in Microsoft Access
In this chapter you get acquainted with two database engines (Jet/ACE) that

Office Access 2007 uses, as well as several object libraries that provide objects, properties, and methods for your VBA procedures.

Chapter 11 — Creating and Accessing Database Tables and Fields
This chapter demonstrates how to create, copy, link, and delete database tables programmatically by using objects from the DAO and ADO object libraries. You also learn how to write code to add and delete fields as well as create listings of existing tables in a database and fields in a table.

Chapter 12 — Setting Up Primary Keys, Indexes, and Table Relationships
In this chapter you learn how to write VBA code to add primary keys and indexes to your database tables using objects, properties, and methods from the DAO and ADO object libraries. You also learn how to use objects from the ADOX library to create relationships between your tables.

Chapter 13 — Finding and Reading Records
Here you practice various methods of using programming code to open a set of database records, commonly referred to as a recordset. You learn how to move around in a recordset, and find, filter, and sort the required records, as well as read their contents. This chapter covers both DAO and ADO Recordsets.

Chapter 14 — Working with Records
This chapter teaches you essential database operations such as adding, updating, and deleting records. You also learn how to render your database records into three popular formats (Excel, Word, and a text file).

Chapter 15 — Creating and Running Queries with DAO/ADO
In this chapter you learn how to use VBA code instead of the Query Design view to create and run various types of database queries.

Chapter 16 — Using Advanced ADO/DAO Features
This chapter explains several advanced ADO/DAO features such as how to disconnect a recordset from a database, save it in a disk file, clone it, and shape it. You also learn about database transactions.

Chapter 17 — Implementing Database Security
In this chapter you learn about two types of security in Microsoft Access databases: share-level security that applies to both older (MDB) and new (ACCDB) Access databases, and user-level security that can only be used in MDB files.

Chapter 18 — Database Replication
In this chapter you learn how to make a database available in various geographical locations by using database replication. The information presented in this chapter can only be used with Access databases created in the older MDB file format, as database replication is not supported in the new ACCDB file format introduced in Access 2007.

You will find the skills obtained in Part II of this book essential in accessing, manipulating, and securing Access databases.

Part III introduces you to the Data Definition Language (DDL), an important component of the Structured Query Language (SQL). Like ADO and

DAO, which were introduced in Part II, DDL is used for defining database objects (tables, views, stored procedures, primary keys, indexes, and constraints) and managing database security. In this part of the book, you learn how to use DDL statements with Jet/ACE databases, ADO, and the Jet OLE DB Provider.

Part III consists of the following five chapters:

Chapter 19 — Creating, Modifying, and Deleting Tables and Fields
  In this chapter you learn special Data Definition Language commands for creating a new Access database, as well as creating, modifying, and deleting tables. You also learn commands for adding, modifying, and deleting fields and indexes.

Chapter 20 — Enforcing Data Integrity and Relationships between Tables
  Here you learn how to define rules regarding the values allowed in table fields to enforce data integrity and relationships between tables.

Chapter 21 — Defining Indexes and Primary Keys
  Here you learn DDL commands for creating indexes and primary keys.

Chapter 22 — Database Security
  In this chapter you learn how to use DDL commands to manage security in the Microsoft Access database. You learn how to quickly create, modify, and remove a database password, and how to manage user-level accounts.

Chapter 23 — Views and Stored Procedures
  This chapter shows you how to work with two powerful database objects known as views and stored procedures. You learn how views are similar to Select queries, and how stored procedures can perform various actions similar to Access Action queries and Select queries with parameters.

The skills you learn in Part III of this book will allow you to create, manipulate, and secure your Microsoft Access databases using SQL DDL statements. Numerous Access SQL/DDL statements and concepts introduced here are important in laying the groundwork for moving into the client/server environment (porting your Microsoft Access database to SQL Server).

Part IV introduces you to responding to events that occur in Access forms and reports. The behavior of Microsoft Access objects such as forms, reports, and controls can be modified by writing programming code known as an event procedure or an event handler. In this part of the book, you learn how you can make your forms, reports, and controls perform useful actions by writing event procedures in class modules.

Part IV consists of the following four chapters:

Chapter 24 — Using Form Events
  In this chapter you learn the types of events that can occur on a Microsoft Access form and write event procedures to handle various form events.

Chapter 25 — Using Report Events
  In this chapter you learn about many events that are triggered when the Access report is run. You write your own event procedures to specify what happens when the report is opened, activated/deactivated, or closed.

Chapter 26 — Events Recognized by Controls

In this chapter you work with a custom application and learn how to write event procedures for various controls that are placed on an Access form.

Chapter 27 — More about Event Programming

This chapter teaches advanced concepts in event programming. You learn how to respond to events in standalone class modules to make your code more manageable and portable to other objects. You also learn how to create and raise your own events.

The skills acquired in Part IV of this book will allow you to enhance and alter the way users interact with your database application.

Part V introduces you to programming Microsoft Access databases for Internet access. Gone are the times when working with Access required the presence of the Microsoft Access application on a user's desktop. Thanks to the development of Internet technologies, you can now publish both static and dynamic Access data to the web. In this part of the book, you learn how Active Server Pages (ASP) and Extensible Markup Language (XML) are used with Microsoft Access to develop database solutions for the World Wide Web.

Part V consists of the following two chapters:

Chapter 28 — Access and Active Server Pages

In this chapter you learn how to use the Microsoft developed Active Server Pages (ASP) technology to view, insert, delete, and modify records stored in a Microsoft Access database from a web browser. Before you go on to explore numerous examples of database access presented in this chapter, you are walked through the installation of the Internet Information Services (IIS) for Windows 2000/XP. (See the downloadable files for installation/configuration steps in Windows Vista.)

Chapter 29 — XML Features in Access 2007

In this chapter you learn how to use the Extensible Markup Language (XML) with Access. You learn how to manually and programmatically export Access data to XML files as well as import an XML file to Access and display its data in a table. You also learn how to use stylesheets and transformations to present Access data to users in a desired format.

The skills acquired in Part V of the book will make your Access applications Internet and intranet ready. You are now able to connect to, read from, and write to Access databases from within a web browser using two important Microsoft technologies.

Part VI introduces you to working with new features in Access 2007. Whether you have used Access for years, or you are just starting to use Access with this version, find out how you can put to use new features and enhancements in areas such as the user interface, tables, forms, reports, templates, and macros.

Part VI consists of the following three chapters:

Chapter 30 — Programming the User Interface

Here you learn how to use VBA, macros, and XML to customize the new user interface in Access 2007. You learn about the features found in the initial Microsoft Office Access screen, Office Button menu, Quick Access toolbar, Navigation pane, and the Ribbon.

Chapter 31 — Tables, Forms, and Reports
In this chapter you master new features and enhancements that Access 2007 added to tables, forms, and reports. For instance, you learn about using complex data types (multi-value fields, the attachment field, and enhancements to a memo field), form and report layouts, and new filtering and rich text formatting features.

Chapter 32 — Macros and Templates
This chapter contains an easy-to-follow introduction to creating and working with macros in Access 2007. You learn about embedded macros, temporary variables, macro actions, macro error handling, and debugging. Additionally, you learn about the new ACCDT file format in Access 2007, which is used in the creation of database templates. You also learn about built-in and custom templates and examine the structure of a template file.

The skills acquired in Part VI of the book will allow you to customize database applications according to the needs of your end users, store more types of data in an Access database, design more effective and visually appealing forms and reports, as well as take advantage of templates and macros.

How to Work with This Book

This book has been designed as a tutorial and should be followed chapter by chapter.

As you read each chapter, perform the tasks you read about. Be an active learner by getting totally involved in the book's hands-on exercises and custom projects. When you get totally involved, you learn things by doing rather than studying, and you learn faster. Do not move on to new information until you've fully grasped the current topic. Allow your brain to sort things out and put them in proper perspective before you move on. Take frequent breaks between your learning sessions, as some chapters in this book cover lots of material. Do not try to do everything in one sitting. It's always better to divide the material into smaller units than attempt to master all there is to learn at once. However, never stop in the middle of a hands-on exercise; finish it before taking a break. Having learned a particular technique or command, try to think of ways to apply it to your own work. As you work with this book, create small sample procedures for yourself based on what you've learned up to a particular point. These procedures will come in handy when you need to review the subject in the future or simply need to steal some ready-made code.

Source Files

You've probably noticed there is no companion CD with this book. All source files for the exercises and projects can be downloaded from www.wordware.com/files/access07.

PART I

Introduction to Access 2007 VBA Programming

Visual Basic for Applications (VBA) is the programming language for Microsoft Office Access.

In this part of the book, you acquire the fundamentals of VBA that you will use over and over again in building real-life Microsoft Office Access database applications.

Chapter 1

Writing Procedures in Modules

This chapter's objective is to introduce you to writing programming code using the built-in language of Microsoft Access — Visual Basic for Applications (commonly referred to as VBA). By writing your own code you can extend the functionality of existing Microsoft Access database applications or create your own applications from scratch. VBA is a language embedded in all the Microsoft Office applications. Therefore, what you learn in this book about Access programming can be utilized in writing programs that control Excel, Word, Outlook, or Microsoft Project. Your job as a programmer (at least during the course of this book) will boil down to writing various procedures. A *procedure* is a group of instructions that allows you to accomplish specific tasks when your program runs. When you place instructions (programming code) in a procedure, you can call this procedure whenever you need to perform that particular task. Although many tasks can be automated in Office Access 2007 by using macro actions, such as opening forms and reports, finding records, and executing queries, you will need VBA skills to perform advanced customizations.

Procedure Types

VBA has the following types of procedures: subroutine procedures, function procedures, event procedures, and property procedures. You create and store procedures in modules. Each procedure in the same module must have a unique name; however, procedures in different modules can have the same name. Let's learn a bit about each procedure type so that you can quickly recognize them when you see them in books, magazine articles, or on the Internet.

■ **Subroutine procedures** (also called subroutines or subprocedures)

Subroutine procedures perform useful tasks, but never return values. They begin with the keyword Sub and end with the keywords End Sub. *Keywords* are words that carry a special meaning in VBA. Let's look at the simple subroutine ShowMessage that displays a message to the user:

```
Sub ShowMessage()
    MsgBox "This is a message box in VBA."
End Sub
```

Notice a pair of empty parentheses after the procedure name. The instruction that we want the procedure to execute is placed on a separate line between the Sub and End Sub keywords. This instruction will be executed when the procedure is run. You may place one or more instructions and even complex control structures within a subroutine procedure. Instructions are also called *statements*. The above procedure will always display the same message when executed. MsgBox is a built-in VBA function often used for programming user interactions (see Chapter 4 for more information on this function). To execute the above subroutine programmatically, you need to write the following line of code:

```
Call ShowMessage()
```

If you'd like to write a more universal procedure that can display a different message each time the procedure is executed, you will need to write a subroutine that takes arguments. *Arguments* are values that are needed for a procedure to do something. You place arguments within the parentheses after the procedure name. Let's look at the following procedure that also displays a message to the user; however, this time we can pass any text string to display:

```
Sub ShowMessage2(strMessage)
    MsgBox strMessage
End Sub
```

The above subprocedure requires one text value before it can be run; strMessage is the arbitrary argument name. It can represent any text you want. Therefore, if you pass it the text "Today is Monday" that's the text the user will see when the procedure is executed. If you don't pass the value to this procedure, VBA will display an error.

If your subprocedure requires more than one argument, list the arguments within the parentheses and separate them with commas. For example, let's improve the above procedure by passing it a text string containing a user name:

```
Sub ShowMessage3(strMessage, strUserName)
    MsgBox strUserName & ",  your message is: " &  strMessage
End Sub
```

Notice how the & operator is used for concatenating text strings inside the VBA procedure. If we pass to the above subroutine the text "Keep on learning." as the strMessage argument and "John" as the strUserName argument, the procedure will display the following text in a message box:

```
John, your message is: Keep on learning.
```

To call the above subroutine in a program, you can write the following line of code:

```
Call ShowMessage3("Keep on learning.", "John")
```

Notice that when calling a procedure with arguments, the arguments are enclosed in parentheses. The arguments are listed in the same order in which they are specified in the procedure definition. See exceptions to this rule and discover more information about passing arguments to subprocedures and functions in Chapter 4.

▪ **Function procedures** (functions)

Functions perform specific tasks and can return values. They begin with the keyword Function and end with the keywords End Function. Let's look at a simple function that adds two numbers:

```
Function addTwoNumbers()
    Dim num1 As Integer
    Dim num2 As Integer

    Num1 = 3
    Num2 = 2
    addTwoNumbers = Num1 + Num2
End Function
```

The above function procedure always returns the same result, which is the value 5. The Dim statements inside this function procedure are used to declare variables that the function will use. A *variable* is a name that is used to refer to an item of data. Because we want the function to perform a calculation, we specify that the variables will hold integer values. Variables and data types used in Office Access 2007 are covered in detail in Chapter 3.

The variable definition is followed by the variable assignment in which we assign specific numbers to the variables Num1 and Num2. Finally, we perform the calculation by adding together the values held in both variables: Num1 + Num2. To return the result of our calculation, we set the function name to the value or the expression we want to return:

```
addTwoNumbers = Num1 + Num2
```

Although the above function example returns a value, not all functions have to return values. Functions, like subroutines, can perform a number of actions without returning any values.

Similar to procedures, functions can accept arguments. For example, to make our addTwoNumbers function more versatile, we can rewrite it as follows:

```
Function addTwoNumbers2(num1 As Integer, num2 As Integer)
    addTwoNumbers2 = Num1 + Num2
End Function
```

Now we can pass any two numbers to the above function to add them together. For example, we can write the following statement to display the result of the function in a message box:

```
msgBox("Total=" & addTwoNumbers2(34,80))
```

You will learn more about writing and calling functions in Chapter 4.

■ **Event procedures**

Event procedures are automatically executed in response to an event initiated by the user or program code, or triggered by the system. Events, event properties, and event procedures are introduced later in this chapter. They are also covered in Part IV of this book.

■ **Property procedures**

Property procedures are used to get or set the values of custom properties for forms, reports, and class modules. The three types of property procedures (Property Get, Property Let, and Property Set) begin with the Property keyword followed by the property type (Get, Let, or Set), the property name, and a pair of empty parentheses, and end with the End Property keywords. Here's an example of a property procedure that retrieves the value of an author's royalty:

```
Property Get Royalty()
    Royalty = (Sales * Percent) — Advance
End Property
```

Property procedures are covered in detail in Chapter 8.

Module Types

As mentioned earlier, procedures are created and stored in modules. Similar to the previous version, Office Access 2007 has two types of modules: standard and class.

Standard Modules

Standard modules are used to hold subprocedures and function procedures that can be run from anywhere in the application because they are not associated with any particular form or report. In the previous section, we looked at the types of procedures that may be entered in a standard module.

Writing Procedures in a Standard Module

Since we already have a couple of procedures to try out, let's do a quick hands-on exercise to learn how to open standard modules, write procedures, and execute them.

◎ **Hands-On 1-1: Working in a Standard Module**

1. Create a folder on your hard drive named **C:\Acc07_ByExample**.

2. Open Office Access 2007 and click **Blank Database** (see Figure 1-1). Name the file **Chap01.accdb** and change its location to the **C:\Acc07_ByExample** folder. Click the **Create** button to create the specified database.

Introduction to Access 2007 VBA Programming

Figure 1-1: Creating a blank Office Access 2007 database.

3. To launch the programming environment in Office Access 2007, select the **Database Tools** tab and click **Visual Basic** (see Figure 1-2). You can also press **Alt+F11** to activate Visual Basic from any Access 2007 database view.

Figure 1-2: Switching to a Visual Basic development environment.

4. Insert a standard module by choosing **Module** from the **Insert** menu (see Figure 1-3).

Figure 1-3: Inserting a standard module.

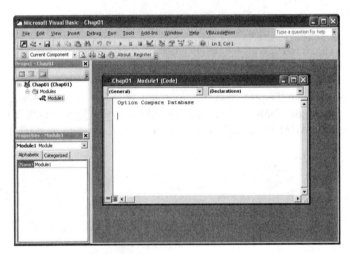

Figure 1-4: Standard module.

Each module begins with a declaration section that lists various settings and declarations that apply to every procedure in the module. Option Compare specifies how string comparisons are evaluated in the module — whether the comparison is case sensitive or insensitive. By default, Access VBA uses:

```
Option Compare Database
```

This is a case-insensitive comparison that respects the sort order of the database. This means that "a" is the same as "A". If you delete the Option Compare Database statement, the default string comparison setting for the module is Option Compare Binary (used for case-sensitive comparisons where "a" is not the same as "A").

Following the declaration section is the procedure section, which holds the module's procedures. You can begin writing your procedures at the cursor position within the Module1 (Code) window.

5. In the Module1 (Code) window, enter the code of all subroutines and function procedures that we discussed earlier in this chapter (see Figure 1-5).

Notice that Access inserts a horizontal line after each End Sub or End Function keyword to make it easier to identify each procedure. The Procedure drop-down box at the top-right corner of the Module Code window displays the name of the procedure in which the insertion point is currently located.

Figure 1-5: Standard module with subprocedures and functions.

Executing Your Procedures and Functions

Now that you've filled the standard module with these procedures and functions, let's see how you can run them. There are many ways of running your code. In the next hands-on exercise, you will learn to run your code from the:

- Run menu (Run Sub/UserForm)
- Toolbar button (Run Sub/UserForm)
- Keyboard (F5)
- Immediate window

⊚ Hands-On 1-2: Running Procedures and Functions

1. Place the insertion point anywhere within the ShowMessage procedure. The Procedure box in the top-right corner of the Module1 (Code) window should display ShowMessage. Choose **Run Sub/UserForm** from the **Run** menu.

   Access runs the selected procedure and displays the message box with the text "This is a message box in VBA." Click OK to close the message box. Try running this procedure again, this time by pressing the F5 key on the keyboard. Click OK to close the message box. Now, run this procedure for the third time by clicking the Run Sub/UserForm button (■) on the toolbar. This button has the same tooltip as the the Run Sub/UserForm (F5) option on the Run menu.

➔ **Note:** Procedures that require arguments cannot be executed directly using the methods you employed in step 1 above. You need to type some input values for these procedures to run. A perfect place to do this is in the Immediate window, which is covered in detail in Chapter 2. For now, let's open this window and see how you can use it to run the remaining procedures.

2. Select **Immediate Window** from the **View** menu.

   Access opens a small window and places it just below the Module1 (Code) window. You can size and reposition this window as needed. Figure 1-6 shows statements that you will run from the Immediate window in steps 3-6 below.

3. Type the following in the Immediate window and press **Enter** to execute.

   ```
   ShowMessage2 "I'm learning VBA."
   ```

   Access executes the procedure and displays the message in a message box. Click OK to close the message box. Notice that to execute the ShowMessage2 procedure, you need to type the procedure name, a space, and the text you want to display. The text string has to be surrounded by double quotation marks.

   In a similar way you can execute the ShowMessage3 procedure by providing not one but two required text strings. For example, on a new line in the Immediate window, type the following statement and press Enter to execute:

   ```
   ShowMessage3 "Keep on learning.", "John"
   ```

   When you press the Enter key, Access executes the ShowMessage3 procedure and displays the text "John, your message is: Keep on learning." Click OK to close this message box.

➔ **Note:** You can also use the Call statement to run a procedure in the Immediate window. When using this statement you must place the values of arguments within parentheses, as shown below:

   ```
   Call ShowMessage3("Keep on learning.", "John")
   ```

Function procedures are executed using different methods. Step 4 below demonstrates how to quickly call the addTwoNumbers function

4. On a new line in the Immediate window, type a question mark followed by the name of the function procedure and press **Enter**:

```
?addTwoNumbers
```

Access should display the result of this function (the number 5) on the next line in the Immediate window.

5. Now run the addTwoNumbers2 procedure. Type the following instruction in the Immediate window and press **Enter**:

```
?addTwoNumbers2(56, 24)
```

Access displays the result of adding these two numbers on the next line.

6. If you'd rather see the function result in a message box, type the following instruction in the Immediate window and press **Enter**:

```
msgBox("Total=" & addTwoNumbers2(34,80))
```

Access displays a message box with the text "Total = 114".

 Note: See Chapter 2 for more information on running your procedures and functions from the Immediate window.

```
Immediate                                                    [x]
ShowMessage2 "I'm learning VBA."
Call ShowMessage3("Keep on learning.", "John")
?addTwoNumbers
 5
?addTwoNumbers2(56, 24)
 80
msgBox("Total=" & addTwoNumbers2(34,80))
```

Figure 1-6: Running procedures and functions in the Immediate window.

Now that you've familiarized yourself a bit with standard modules, let's move on to the class module that you can use in Access programming.

Class Modules

Class modules come in three varieties: standalone class modules, form modules, and report modules.

■ **Standalone class modules** — These modules are used to create your own custom objects with their own properties and methods. You create a standalone class module by choosing Insert | Class Module in the Microsoft Visual Basic window. Access will create a default class module named Class1 and will list it in the Class modules folder in the Project Explorer window. You will work with standalone class modules in Chapter 8.

■ **Form modules and report modules** — Each Access form can contain a form module, and each report can contain a report module. These modules are special types of class modules that are saved automatically whenever you save the form or report.

All newly created forms and reports are lightweight by design, because they don't have modules associated with them when they're first created. Therefore, they load and display faster than forms and reports with modules. These lightweight forms and reports have their Has Module property set to No (see Figure 1-7). When you open a form or report in Design view and click the View Code button in the Tools section of the Design tab, Access creates a form or report module. The Has Module property of a form or report is automatically set to Yes to indicate that the form or report now has a module associated with it. Note that this happens even if you have not written a single line of VBA code. Access opens a module window and assigns a name to the module that consists of three parts: the name of the object (e.g., form or report), an underscore character, and the name of the form or report. For example, a newly created form that has not been saved is named Form_Form1, a form module in the Customers form is named Form_Customers, and the report module in the Customers report is named Report_Customers.

Figure 1-7: When you begin designing a new form in the Microsoft Office Access user interface, the form does not have a module associated with it. Notice that the Has Module property on the form's property sheet is set to No.

As with report modules, form modules store event procedures for events recognized by the form and its controls, as well as general function procedures and subprocedures. You can also write Property Get, Property Let, and Property Set procedures to create custom properties for the form or report.

The procedures stored in their class modules are available only while you are using that particular form or report.

Figure 1-8: Microsoft Office Access organizes database modules in folders. Form and report modules are listed in the Microsoft Office Access Class Objects folder. Standard modules can be found under the Modules folder. The Class Modules folder organizes standalone class modules.

Events, Event Properties, and Event Procedures

In order to customize your database applications or to deliver products that fit your users' specific needs, you'll be doing quite a bit of event-driven programming. Access 2007 is an *event-driven* application. This means that whatever happens in an Access application is the result of an event that Access has detected. *Events* are things that happen to objects, and can be triggered by the user or by the system, such as clicking a mouse button, pressing a key, selecting an item from a list, or changing a list of items available in a list box. As a programmer, you will often want to modify the application's built-in response to a particular event. Before the application processes the user's mouse clicks and key presses in the usual way, you can tell the application how to react to the activity. For example, if a user clicks a Delete button on your form, you can display a custom delete confirmation message to ensure that the user selected the intended record for deletion.

For each event defined for a form, form control, or report, there is a corresponding *event property*. If you open any Microsoft Access form in Design view and choose Properties in the Tools

Figure 1-9: Event properties for an Access form are listed on the Event tab in the property sheet.

section of the Design tab, and then click the Event tab of the property sheet, you will see a long list of events your form can respond to (see Figure 1-9).

Forms, reports, and the controls that appear on them have various event properties you can use to trigger desired actions. For example, you can open or close a form when a user clicks a command button, or you can enable or disable controls when the form loads.

To specify how a form, report, or control should respond to events, you can write *event procedures*. In your programming code, you may need to describe what should happen if a user clicks on a particular command button or makes a selection from a combo box. For example, when you design a custom form you should anticipate and program events that can occur at run time (while the form is being used). The most common event is the Click event. Every time a command button is clicked, it triggers an event procedure to respond to the Click event for that button.

When you assign your event procedure to an event property, you set an *event trap*. Event trapping gives you considerable control in handling events because you basically interrupt the default processing that Access would normally carry out in response to the user's key press or mouse click. If a user clicks a command button to save a form, whatever code you've written in the Click event of that command button will run. The event programming code is stored as a part of a form, report, or control and is triggered only when user interaction with a form or report generates a specific event; therefore, it cannot be used as a standalone procedure.

Why Use Events?

By using events you can make your applications dynamic and interactive. To handle a specific event, you need to select the appropriate event property on the property sheet, and then write an event handling procedure. Access will provide its own default response to those events you have not programmed. Events cannot be defined for tables and queries.

Walking Through an Event Procedure

The following hands-on exercise shows you how to get started with writing event procedures. Your task is to change the background color of a text box control on a form when the text box is selected, and return the default background color when you tab or click out of that text box.

⊚ Hands-On 1-3: Writing an Event Procedure

1. Copy the **HandsOn_01_3.accdb** database from the downloaded **Acc07_HandsOn** folder to your **C:\Acc07_ByExample** folder. This file contains the Customers table and the Customers form from the Northwind database that comes with Office Access 2007.

2. Open the database **C:\Acc07_ByExample\HandsOn_01_3.accdb**. Upon loading, Access displays a security warning message. In order to use this file, click the **Options** button in the message bar, select **Enable this content**, and click **OK**.

> ➜ **Note:** The last section of this chapter explains how you can use trusted locations to keep Access 2007 from disabling your VBA code upon opening a database.

3. Open the Customers form in Design view. To do this, you can right-click the **Customers** form and choose **Design View** from the shortcut menu, as shown in Figure 1-10.

4. Click the **ContactName** text box control on the form, then click the **Event** tab in the property sheet. Make sure that the property sheet displays ContactName in the control drop-down box.

The list of event procedures available for the text box control appears.

5. Click in the column next to the **On Got Focus** event name, then click the **Build** button ([...]). This will bring up the Choose Builder dialog box, as shown in Figure 1-12.

Figure 1-10: Opening the Customers form in Design view.

6. Select **Code Builder** in the Choose Builder dialog box and click **OK**. This will display a VBA code module in the Visual Basic Editor window (see Figure 1-13). This window (often referred to as VBE) is discussed in detail in Chapter 2.

Figure 1-12: To write VBA programming code for your event procedure, choose Code Builder in the Choose Builder dialog box.

Figure 1-11: Use the Build button, which is displayed as an ellipsis (...), to create an event procedure. This button is not available unless an event is selected.

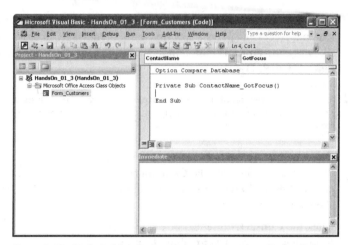

Figure 1-13: Code Builder displays the event procedure Code window with a blank event procedure for the selected object. Here you can enter the code Access will run when the specified GotFocus procedure is triggered.

Take a look at Figure 1-13. Access creates a skeleton of the GotFocus event procedure. The name of the event procedure consists of three parts: the object name (ContactName), an underscore character (_), and the name of the event (GotFocus) occurring to that object. The word Private indicates that the event procedure cannot be triggered by an event from another form. The word Sub in the first line denotes the beginning of the event procedure. The words End Sub in the last line denote the end of the event procedure. The statements to be executed when the event occurs are written between these two lines.

Notice that each procedure name ends with a pair of empty parentheses( ). Words such as Sub, End, or Private have special meaning to Visual Basic and are called *keywords* (reserved words). Visual Basic displays keywords in blue, but you can change the color of your keywords from the Editor Format tab in the Options dialog box (choose Tools | Options in the Visual Basic Editor window). All VBA keywords are automatically capitalized.

At the top of the Code window (see Figure 1-13), there are two drop-down list boxes. The one on the left is called Object. This box displays the currently selected control (ContactName). The box on the right is called Procedure. If you position the mouse over one of these boxes, the tooltip indicates the name of the box. By clicking on the down-arrow to the right of the Procedure box, a list of all possible event procedures associated with the object type selected in the Object box will be displayed. You can close the drop-down list box by clicking anywhere in the unused portion of the Code window.

7. To change the background color of a text box control to green, enter the following statement between the existing lines:

```
Me.ContactName.BackColor = 65280
```

Notice that when you type each period, Visual Basic displays a list containing the possible item choices. This feature, called List Properties/Methods, is a part of Visual Basic's on-the-fly syntax and programming assistance, and is covered in Chapter 2. When finished, your first event procedure should look as follows:

```
Private Sub ContactName_GotFocus()
    Me.ContactName.BackColor = 65280
End Sub
```

The statement you just entered tells Visual Basic to change the background color of the ContactName text box to green when the cursor is moved into that control. You can also specify the color by using the RGB function, like this:

```
Me.ContactName.BackColor = RGB(0, 255, 0)
```

The above statement is equivalent to the statement you used earlier in the ContactName_GotFocus event procedure.

RGB Colors

Color values are combinations of red, green, and blue components. The RGB function has the following syntax:

```
RGB(red, green, blue)
```

The intensity of red, green, and blue can range from 0 to 255. Here are some frequently used colors:

White	255, 255, 255	Dark Green	0, 128, 0
Black	0, 0, 0	Cyan	0, 255, 255
Gray	192, 192, 192	Dark Cyan	0, 128, 128
Red	255, 0, 0	Blue	0, 0, 255
Dark Red	128, 0, 0	Dark Blue	0, 0, 128
Yellow	255, 255, 0	Magenta	255, 0, 255
Dark Yellow	128, 128, 0	Dark Magenta	128, 0, 128
Green	0, 255, 0		

8. In the Visual Basic window, choose **File | Close and Return to Microsoft Office Access**. Notice that [Event Procedure] now appears next to the On Got Focus event property in the property sheet for the selected ContactName text box control (see Figure 1-14).

Figure 1-14: [Event Procedure] in the property sheet denotes that the text box's On Got Focus event has an event procedure associated with it.

9. To test your GotFocus event procedure, switch from the Design view of the Customers form to Form view.

10. Click in the **Contact Name** text box and notice the change in the background color.

11. Now, click on any other text box control.

    Notice that the Contact Name text box does not return to the original color. So far, you've only told Visual Basic what to do when the specified control receives the focus. If you want the background color to change when the focus moves to another control, there is one more event procedure to write — On Lost Focus.

12. To create the LostFocus procedure, return your form to Design view and click the **Contact Name** control. In the property sheet for this control, select the **Event** tab, then click the **Build** button to the right of the On Lost Focus event property. In the Choose Builder dialog box, select **Code Builder**.

13. To change the background color of a text box control to whatever it was before, enter the following statement inside the ContactName_LostFocus event procedure:

```
Me.ContactName.BackColor = 13434879
```

The completed On Lost Focus procedure looks like this:

```
Private Sub ContactName_LostFocus()
    Me.ContactName.BackColor = 13434879
End Sub
```

14. In the Visual Basic window, choose **File | Close and Return to Microsoft Office Access**. Notice that [Event Procedure] now appears next to the On Lost Focus event property in the property sheet for the selected Contact-Name text box control.

15. Repeat steps 9-11 to test both of the event procedures you have written.

16. When you are done, close the database files you have worked with in this chapter.

➥ **Note:**   Because objects recognize a sequence of events, it's important to understand what actions fire the events and the order in which the events occur. In Part IV of this book, you'll learn what events can be used for a particular task to make your application smarter.

Compiling Your Procedures

The VBA code you write in the Visual Basic Editor Code window is automatically compiled by Microsoft Access before you run it. The syntax of your VBA statements is first thoroughly checked for errors, and then your procedures are converted into executable format. If an error is discovered during the compilation process, Access stops compiling and displays an error message. It also highlights the line of code that contains the error. The compiling process can take from seconds to minutes or longer, depending on the number of procedures written and the number of modules used.

To ensure that your procedures have been compiled, you can explicitly compile them after you are done programming. You can do this by choosing Debug | Compile in the Visual Basic Editor window.

Microsoft Access saves all the code in your database in its compiled form. Compiled code runs more quickly when you open it in the future. You should always save your modules after you compile them. In Chapter 9 you will learn how to test and troubleshoot your VBA procedures.

Placing a Database in a Trusted Location

The new security features in Access 2007 make it more complicated for users to work with databases that include VBA code and other executable content such as Action queries that add, modify, or delete data, DDL (Data Definition Language) queries that create and alter tables, SQL Pass-Through queries, and ActiveX controls, as well as certain unsafe expressions and macro commands.

When an Access database is opened in Access 2007, by default, Access turns off all potentially unsafe code or content and displays a security warning message just under the Ribbon (Figure 1-15).

To use the disabled components of the database, a user must click the Options button on the message bar. This will bring up the Security Alert dialog box (Figure 1-16). By default, the "Help protect me from unknown content (recommended)" option button is selected. To enable the disabled content only for the current session, users need to select the "Enable this content" option button and then click OK. These steps will need to be repeated each time the database is opened. If users select not to trust the database — in other words, they ignore the security warning message — they will still be able to view the data in the database and use components that Access has not disabled.

Figure 1-15: The Security Warning message bar in Access 2007.

Figure 1-16: The Security Alert dialog box allows you to temporarily enable database content.

To make it easy to work with Access databases in this book, you will not want to bother with enabling content each time you open a database. To trust your databases permanently, you can place them in a trusted location — a folder on your local or network drive that you mark as trusted.

Notice the Open the Trust Center hyperlink at the bottom of the Security Alert dialog box. This hyperlink will open the Trust Center where you can set up a trusted folder. You can also access the Trust Center from the Microsoft Office button as demonstrated in Hands-On 1-4.

⊚ Hands-On 1-4: Placing an Access Database in a Trusted Location

1. To start the Trust Center, in the Microsoft Access window, click the **Microsoft Office** button, and then click the **Access Options** button.

2. In the left pane of the Access Options dialog box, click **Trust Center**, and then click **Trust Center Settings** in the right pane.

3. In the left pane of the Trust Center dialog box, click **Trusted Locations**.

4. Click the **Add new location** button.

5. In the Path text box, type the path and folder name of the location on your local drive that you want to set up as a trusted source for opening files. Let's enter **C:\Acc07_ByExample** to designate this folder as a trusted location for this book's database programming exercises (Figure 1-17).

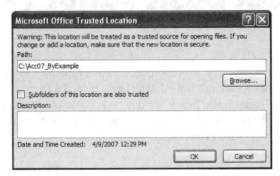

Figure 1-17: Setting a Trusted Location folder for this book's programming examples.

6. Click **OK** to close the Trusted Location dialog box.

7. The Trusted Locations list in the Trust Center dialog box now includes the C:\Acc07_ByExample folder as a trusted source. Files put in a trusted location can be opened without being checked by the Trust Center security feature. Click **OK** to close the Trust Center dialog box.

8. Click **OK** to close the Access Options dialog box.

Chapter Summary

In this chapter, you got a hands-on introduction to writing VBA procedures in Access 2007 standard and class modules. You learned about subroutine procedures, function procedures, property procedures, and event procedures. You also learned different ways of executing subroutines and functions. The main hands-on exercise in this chapter walked you through writing two event procedures in a form's class module for a text control placed in an Access form. You finished this chapter by setting up a trusted location to keep Access 2007 from disabling your VBA code upon opening a database.

This chapter has given you a glimpse of the Microsoft Visual Basic programming environment built into Access. The next chapter will take you deeper into this interface, showing you various windows and shortcuts that you can use to program faster and with fewer errors.

Chapter 2

The Visual Basic Editor (VBE)

Now that you know how to write subprocedures and functions in standard modules and event procedures in modules placed behind a form, we'll spend some time in the Visual Basic Editor window to become familiar with the multitude of tools it offers to simplify your programming tasks. With the tools located in the Visual Basic Editor window, you can:

- Write your own VBA procedures
- Create custom forms
- View and modify object properties
- Test and debug VBA procedures and locate errors

You can enter the VBA programming environment in either of the following ways:

- By selecting the Database Tools tab, then Visual Basic in the Macro group
- From the keyboard, by pressing Alt+F11

Understanding the Project Explorer Window

The Project Explorer window, located on the left side of the Visual Basic Editor window, provides access to modules behind forms and reports via the Microsoft Office Access Class Objects folder (see Figure 2-1). The Modules folder lists only standard modules that are not behind a form or report.

In addition to the Microsoft Office Access Class Objects and Modules folders, the VBA Project Explorer window can contain a Class Modules folder. Class modules are used for creating your own objects, as demonstrated in Chapter 8. Using the Project Explorer window, you can easily move between modules currently loaded into memory.

Figure 2-1: The Project Explorer window provides easy access to your VBA procedure code.

You can activate the Project Explorer window in one of three ways:

■ From the View menu by selecting Project Explorer

■ From the keyboard by pressing Ctrl+R

■ From the Standard toolbar by clicking the Project Explorer button ( ) as shown in Figure 2-2

➡ **Note:** If the Project Explorer window is visible but not active, activate it by clicking the Project Explorer title bar.

Buttons on the Standard toolbar (Figure 2-2) provide a quick way to access many Visual Basic features.

Project Explorer (Ctrl+R)

Figure 2-2: Use the toolbar buttons to quickly access frequently used features in the VBE window.

The Project Explorer window (see Figure 2-3) contains three buttons:

■ **View Code** — Displays the Code window for the selected module

■ **View Object** — Displays the selected form or report in the Microsoft Office Access Class Objects folder. This button is disabled when an object in the Modules or Class Modules folder is selected.

■ **Toggle Folders** — Hides and unhides the display of folders in the Project Explorer window

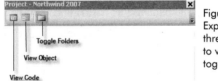

Figure 2-3: The VBE Project Explorer window contains three buttons that allow you to view code or objects and toggle folders.

Understanding the Properties Window

The Properties window allows you to review and set properties for the currently selected Access class or module. The name of the selected object is displayed in the Object box located just below the Properties window title bar. The Properties window displays the current settings for the selected object. Object properties can be viewed alphabetically or by category by clicking on the appropriate tab.

■ **Alphabetic tab** — Lists all properties for the selected object alphabetically. You can change the property setting by selecting the property name, then typing or selecting the new setting.

■ **Categorized tab** — Lists all properties for the selected object by category. You can collapse the list so that you see only the category names or you can expand a category to see the properties. The plus (+) icon to the left of the category name indicates that the category list can be expanded. The minus (–) indicates that the category is currently expanded.

The Properties window can be accessed in the following ways:

■ From the View menu by selecting Properties Window

■ From the keyboard by pressing F4

■ From the Standard toolbar by clicking the Properties Window button (🖆) located to the right of the Project Explorer button

Figure 2-4 displays the properties of the E-mail Address text box control located in the Form_Order Details form in the Northwind 2007 sample Access database. In order to access properties for a form control, you need to perform the steps as outlined in Hands-On 2-1 below.

◎ Hands-On 2-1: Using Properties Window to View Control Properties

1. Copy the **Northwind 2007** sample database from the Acc07_HandsOn folder to your **C:\Acc07_ByExample** folder. Recall from Chapter 1 that we made this folder a trusted location, so Access should not prompt you to enable the database content when you load this file in the next step.

2. Open Microsoft Office Access 2007 and load the **C:\Northwind 2007.accdb** file. Log in to the database as **Andrew Cencini**.

3. When Northwind 2007 opens, press **Alt+F11** to activate the Visual Basic Editor window.

4. In the Project Explorer window, click the **Toggle Folders** button (🗀) and select the **Microsoft Office Access Class Objects** folder. Highlight the **Form_Order Details** form (Figure 2-4) and click the **View Object** button (▤). This will open the selected form in Design view.

5. Press **Alt+F11** to return to the Visual Basic Editor. The Properties window will be filled with the properties for the Form_Order Details form. To view the properties of the E-mail Address text box control on this form, as shown in Figure 2-4, select **E-mail Address** from the drop-down list located below the Properties window title bar.

Figure 2-4: You can edit object properties in the Properties window, or you can edit them in the property sheet when a form or report is open in Design view.

Understanding the Code Window

The Code window is used for Visual Basic programming as well as for viewing and modifying the code of existing Visual Basic procedures. Each VBA module can be opened in a separate Code window.

There are several ways of activating the Code window:

■ From the Project Explorer window, choose the appropriate module and then click the View Code button (📰)

■ From the Microsoft Visual Basic menu bar, choose View | Code

■ From the keyboard, press F7

At the top of the Code window there are two drop-down list boxes that allow you to move quickly within the Visual Basic code. In the Object box on the left side of the Code window, you can select the object whose code you want to view.

Figure 2-5: The Object drop-down box lists objects that are available in the module selected in the Project Explorer window.

The box on the right side of the Code window lets you select a procedure to view. When you open this box, the names of all procedures located in a module are listed alphabetically. If you select a procedure in the Procedure box, the cursor will jump to the first line of that procedure.

Figure 2-6: The Procedure drop-down box lists events to which the object selected in the Object drop-down box can respond. If the selected module contains events written for the highlighted object, the names of these events appear in bold type.

By choosing Window | Split or dragging the split bar down to a selected position in the Code window, you can divide the Code window into two panes, as shown in Figure 2-7.

Figure 2-7: By splitting the Code window you can view different sections of a long procedure or a different procedure in each window pane.

Setting up the Code window for the two-pane display is useful for copying, cutting, and pasting sections of code between procedures in the same module. To return to a one-window display, drag the split bar all the way to the top of the Code window or choose Window | Split again.

There are two icons at the bottom of the Code window (Figure 2-7). The Procedure View icon changes the display to only one procedure at a time in the Code window. To select another procedure, use the Procedure drop-down box. The Full Module View icon changes the display to all the procedures in the selected module. Use the vertical scroll bar in the Code window to scroll through the module's code. The Margin Indicator bar is used by the Visual Basic Editor to display helpful indicators during editing and debugging.

Other Windows in the VBE

In addition to the Code window, there are several other windows that are frequently used in the Visual Basic environment, such as the Immediate, Locals, Watch, Project Explorer, Properties, and Object Browser windows. The Docking tab in the Options dialog box (select Tools | Options in the Visual Basic Editor window) displays a list of available windows and allows you to choose which windows you want to be dockable.

Figure 2-8: You can use the Docking tab in the Options dialog box to control which windows are currently displayed in the Visual Basic programming environment.

On-the-Fly Syntax and Programming Assistance

Writing procedures in Visual Basic requires that you use hundreds of built-in instructions and functions. Because most people cannot memorize the correct syntax of all the instructions available in VBA, the IntelliSense technology provides you with syntax and programming assistance on demand while you are entering instructions. While working in the Code window, you can have special tools pop up and guide you through the process of creating correct VBA code. The Edit toolbar in the VBE window contains several buttons that let you enter correctly formatted VBA instructions with speed and ease. If the Edit toolbar isn't currently docked in the Visual Basic Editor window, you can turn it on by choosing View | Toolbars.

Figure 2-9: The Edit toolbar provides timesaving buttons while entering VBA code.

List Properties/Methods

Each object can contain one or more properties and methods. When you enter the name of the object in the Code window followed by a period that separates the name of the object from its property or method, a pop-up menu may appear. This menu lists the properties and methods available for the object that precedes the period. To turn on this automated feature, choose Tools | Options. In the Options dialog box, click the Editor tab, and make sure the Auto List Members check box is selected. While entering the VBA instructions, Visual Basic suggests properties and methods that can be used with the particular object, as demonstrated in Figure 2-10.

Figure 2-10: When Auto List Members is selected, Visual Basic suggests properties and methods that can be used with the object as you are entering the VBA instructions.

To choose an item from the pop-up menu, start typing the name of the property or method you want to use. When the correct item name is highlighted, press Enter to insert the item into your code and start a new line, or press the Tab key to insert the item and continue writing instructions on the same line. You can also double-click the item to insert it in your code. To close the pop-up menu without inserting an item, press Esc. When you press Esc to remove the pop-up menu, Visual Basic will not display the menu for the same object again.

To display the Properties/Methods pop-up menu again, you can:

■ Press Ctrl+J

■ Use the Backspace key to delete the period, then type the period again

■ Right-click in the Code window, and select List Properties/Methods from the shortcut menu

■ Choose Edit | List Properties/Methods

■ Click the List Properties/Methods button (▦) on the Edit toolbar

Parameter Info

Some VBA functions and methods can take one or more arguments (or parameters). If a Visual Basic function or method requires an argument, you can see the names of required and optional arguments in a tip box that appears just below the cursor as soon as you type the open parenthesis or enter a space. The Parameter Info feature (see Figure 2-11) makes it easy for you to supply correct arguments to a VBA function or method. In addition, it reminds you of two other things that are very important for the function or method to work correctly: the order of the arguments and the required data type of each argument. For example, if you enter in the Code window the instruction DoCmd.OpenForm and type a space after the OpenForm method, a tip box appears just below the cursor. Then as soon as you supply the first argument and enter the comma, Visual Basic displays the next argument in bold. Optional arguments are surrounded by square brackets [ ]. To close the Parameter Info window, all you need to do is press Esc.

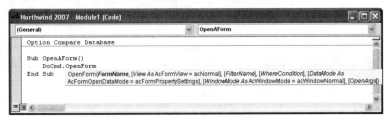

Figure 2-11: A tip window displays a list of arguments used by a VBA function or method.

To open the tip box using the keyboard, enter the instruction or function, followed by the left parenthesis, then press Ctrl+Shift+I. You can also click the

Parameter Info button (🔧) on the Edit toolbar or choose Edit | Parameter Info from the menu bar.

You can also display the Parameter Info box when entering a VBA function. To try this out quickly, choose View | Immediate Window, then type the following in the Immediate window:

```
Mkdir(
```

You should see the MkDir(Path As String) tip box just below the cursor. Now, type "C:\NewFolder" followed by the ending parenthesis. When you press Enter, Visual Basic will create a folder named NewFolder in the root directory of your computer. Activate Explorer and check it out!

List Constants

If there is a check mark next to the Auto List Members setting in the Options dialog box (Editor tab), Visual Basic displays a pop-up menu listing the constants that are valid for the property or method. A *constant* is a value that indicates a specific state or result. Access and other members of the Microsoft Office suite have a number of predefined, built-in constants.

Suppose you want to open a form in Design view. In Microsoft Access, a form can be viewed in Design view (acDesign), Datasheet view (acFormDS), PivotChart view (acFormPivotChart), PivotTable view (acFormPivotTable), Form view (acNormal), and Print Preview (acPreview). Each of these options is represented by a built-in constant. Microsoft Access constant names begin with the letters ac. As soon as you enter a comma and a space following your instruction in the Code window (e.g., DoCmd.OpenForm "Products",), a pop-up menu will appear with the names of valid constants for the OpenForm method.

Figure 2-12: The List Constants pop-up menu displays a list of constants that are valid for the property or method typed.

The List Constants menu can be activated by pressing Ctrl+Shift+J or by clicking the List Constants button (🔣) on the Edit toolbar.

Quick Info

When you select an instruction, function, method, procedure name, or constant in the Code window and then click the Quick Info button ( ) on the Edit toolbar (or press Ctrl+I), Visual Basic will display the syntax of the highlighted item as well as the value of its constant. The Quick Info feature can be turned on or off using the Options dialog box (Tools | Options). To use the feature, click the Editor tab in the Options dialog box, and make sure there is a check mark in the box next to Auto Quick Info.

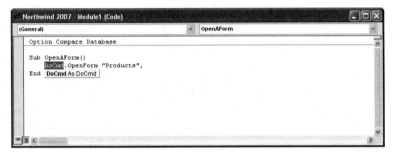

Figure 2-13: The Quick Info feature provides a list of function parameters, as well as constant values and VBA statement syntax.

Complete Word

Another way to increase the speed of writing VBA procedures in the Code window is with the Complete Word feature. As you enter the first few letters of a keyword and click the Complete Word button ( ) on the Edit toolbar, Visual Basic will complete the keyword entry for you. For example, if you enter the first three letters of the keyword DoCmd (DoC) in the Code window, then click the Complete Word button on the Edit toolbar, Visual Basic will complete the rest of the command. In the place of DoC you will see the entire instruction, DoCmd.

If there are several VBA keywords that begin with the same letters, when you click the Complete Word button on the Edit toolbar Visual Basic will display a pop-up menu listing all of them. To try this, enter only the first three letters of the word Application (App), then press the Complete Word button on the toolbar. You can then select the appropriate word from the pop-up menu.

Indent/Outdent

The Editor tab in the Options dialog box contains many settings you can turn on to make automated features available in the Code window.

Figure 2-14: The Options dialog box lists features you can turn on and off to fit the VBA programming environment to your needs.

When the Auto Indent option is turned on, Visual Basic automatically indents the selected lines of code using the Tab Width value. The default entry for Auto Indent is four characters (Figure 2-14). You can easily change the tab width by typing a new value in the text box. Why would you want to use indentation in your code? Indentation makes your VBA procedures more readable and easier to understand. Indenting is especially recommended for entering lines of code that make decisions or repeat actions.

Let's see how you can indent and outdent lines of code using the Form_InventoryList form in the Northwind database that you opened in the previous hands-on exercise.

◎ Hands-On 2-2: Using the Indent/Outdent Feature

1. In the Project Explorer window in the Microsoft Office Access Class Objects folder, double-click on **Form_Inventory List**. The Code window should now show the CmdPurchase_Click event procedure written for this form.

2. In the Code window, select the block of code beginning with the keyword **If** and ending with the keywords **End If**.

3. Click the **Indent** button ( ) on the Edit toolbar or press **Tab** on the keyboard. The selected block of code will move four spaces to the right. You can adjust the number of spaces to indent by choosing **Tools | Options** and entering the appropriate value in the Tab Width box on the Editor tab.

4. Now, click the **Outdent** button ( ) on the Edit toolbar or press **Shift+Tab** to return the selected lines of code to the previous location in the Code window. The Indent and Outdent options are also available from Visual Basic Editor's Edit menu.

Comment Block/Uncomment Block

The apostrophe placed at the beginning of a line of code denotes a comment. Besides the fact that comments make it easier to understand what the procedure does, comments are also very useful in testing and troubleshooting VBA procedures. For example, when you execute a procedure, it may not run as expected. Instead of deleting the lines of code that may be responsible for the problems encountered, you may want to skip the lines for now and return to them later. By placing an apostrophe at the beginning of the line you want to avoid, you can continue checking the other parts of your procedure. While commenting one line of code by typing an apostrophe works fine for most people, when it comes to turning entire blocks of code into comments, you'll find the Comment Block and Uncomment Block buttons on the Edit toolbar very handy and easy to use.

To comment a few lines of code, select the lines and click the Comment Block button (▦). To turn the commented code back into VBA instructions, click the Uncomment Block button (▦). If you don't select a block of text, when you click the Comment Block button the apostrophe is added only to the line of code where the cursor is currently located.

Using the Object Browser

If you want to move easily through the myriad of VBA elements and features, examine the capabilities of the Object Browser. This special built-in tool is available in the Visual Basic Editor window.

To access the Object Browser, use any of the following methods:

- Press F2
- Choose View | Object Browser
- Click the Object Browser button (▦) on the toolbar

The Object Browser allows you to browse through the objects available to your VBA procedures, as well as view their properties, methods, and events. With the aid of the Object Browser, you can quickly move between procedures in your database application, and search for objects and methods across various type libraries.

The Object Browser window is divided into several sections. The top of the window displays the Project/Library drop-down list box with the names of all currently available libraries and projects.

A *library* is a special file that contains information about the objects in an application. New libraries can be added via the References dialog box (select Tools | References). The entry for <All Libraries> lists the objects of all libraries installed on your computer. While the Access library contains objects specific to using Microsoft Office Access, the VBA library provides access to three objects (Debug, Err, and Collection) as well as a number of built-in functions and constants that give you flexibility in programming. You can send output to the Immediate window, get information about run-time errors, work with the Collection object, manage files, deal with text strings, convert data types, set date and time, and perform mathematical operations.

Below the Project/Library drop-down list box is a search box (Search Text) that allows you to quickly find information in a particular library. This field remembers the last four items you searched for. To find only whole words, right-click anywhere in the Object Browser window, then choose Find Whole Word Only from the shortcut menu. The Search Results section of the Object Browser displays the Library, Class, and Member elements that meet the criteria entered in the Search Text box. When you type the search text and click the Search button, Visual Basic expands the Object Browser window to show the search results. You can hide or show the Search Results section by clicking the button located to the right of the binoculars. In the lower section of the Object Browser window, the Classes list box displays the available object classes in the selected library. If you select the name of the open database (e.g., Northwind) in the Project/Library list box, the Classes list will display the objects as listed in the Explorer window.

In Figure 2-15, the Form_Inventory List object class is selected. When you highlight a class, the list on the right side (Members) shows the properties, methods, and events available for that class. By default, members are listed alphabetically. You can, however, organize the Members list by group type (properties, methods, or events) using the Group Members command from the Object Browser shortcut menu (right-click anywhere in the Object Browser window to display this menu).

Project/Library List box

Search text box

Search Results are shown here

Code template

Figure 2-15: The Object Browser window allows you to browse through all the objects, properties, and methods available to the current VBA project.

If you select the Northwind 2007 project in the Project/Library list box, the Members list box will list all the procedures available in this project. To examine a procedure's code, double-click its name. If you select a VBA library in the Project/Library list box, you will see the Visual Basic built-in functions and constants. If you need more information on the selected class or member, click the question mark button located at the top of the Object Browser window.

The bottom of the Object Browser window displays a code template area with the definition of the selected member. If you click the green hyperlink text in the code template, you can jump to the selected member's class or library in the Object Browser window. Text displayed in the code template area can be copied and pasted to a Code window. If the Code window is visible while the

Object Browser window is open, you can save time by dragging the high-lighted code template and dropping it into the Code window. You can easily adjust the size of the various sections of the Object Browser window by drag-ging the dividing horizontal and vertical lines.

Let's put the Object Browser to use in VBA programming. Assume that you want to write a VBA procedure to control a check box placed on a form and would like to see the list of properties and methods that are available for work-ing with check boxes.

⊚ Hands-On 2-3: Using the Object Browser

1. In the Visual Basic Editor window, press **F2** to display the Object Browser.
2. In the Project/Library list box (see Figure 2-15), click the drop-down arrow and select the **Access** library.
3. Type **checkbox** in the Search Text box and click the **Search** button (🔍). Make sure you don't enter a space in the search string.

   Visual Basic begins to search the Access library and displays the search results. By analyzing the search results in the Object Browser window, you can find the appropriate VBA instructions for writing your VBA proce-dures. Looking at the Members list, you can quickly determine that you can enable or disable a check box by setting the Enabled property. To get detailed information on any item found in the Object Browser, select the item and press F1 to activate online help.

Using the VBA Object Library

While the Access library contains objects specific to using Microsoft Access, the VBA Object Library provides access to many built-in VBA functions grouped by categories. These functions are general in nature. They allow you to manage files, set the date and time, interact with users, convert data types, deal with text strings, or perform mathematical calculations. In the following exercise, you will see how to use one of the built-in VBA functions to create a new subfolder without leaving Access.

⊚ Hands-On 2-4: Using Built-in VBA Functions

1. In the Visual Basic Editor window with the open Northwind 2007 data-base, choose **Insert | Module** to create a new standard module.
2. In the Code window, enter **Sub NewFolder()** as the name of the procedure and press **Enter**. Visual Basic will enter the ending keywords: End Sub.
3. Press **F2** to display the Object Browser.
4. Click the drop-down arrow in the Project/Library list box and select **VBA**.
5. Enter **file** in the Search Text box and press **Enter**.
6. Scroll down in the Members list box and highlight the **MkDir** method.

7. Click the **Copy** button in the Object Browser window to copy the selected method name to the Windows clipboard.

8. Close the Object Browser and return to the **Code** window. Paste the copied instruction inside the **NewFolder** procedure.

9. Now, enter a space, followed by **"C:\Study"**. Be sure to enter the name of the entire path and the quotation marks. The NewFolder procedure is shown below.

```
Sub NewFolder()
    MkDir "C:\Study"
End Sub
```

10. Choose **Run | Run Sub/UserForm** to run the NewFolder procedure.

After you run the NewFolder procedure, Visual Basic creates a new folder on drive C called Study. To see the folder, activate Windows Explorer. After creating a new folder, you may realize that you don't need it after all. Although you could easily delete the folder while in Windows Explorer, how about getting rid of it programmatically?

The Object Browser contains many other methods that are useful for working with folders and files. The RmDir method is just as simple to use as the MkDir method. To remove the Study folder from your hard drive, replace the MkDir method with the RmDir method and rerun the NewFolder procedure. Or create a new procedure called RemoveFolder, as shown below:

```
Sub RemoveFolder()
    RmDir "C:\Study"
End Sub
```

When writing procedures from scratch, it's a good idea to consult the Object Browser for names of the built-in VBA functions.

Using the Immediate Window

The Immediate window is a sort of VBA programmer's scratch pad. Here you can test VBA instructions before putting them to work in your VBA procedures. It is a great tool for experimenting with your new language. The Immediate window allows you to type VBA statements and test their results immediately without having to write a procedure. Use it to try out your statements. If the statement produces the expected result, you can copy the statement from the Immediate window into your procedure (or you can drag it right onto the Code window, if it is visible).

To activate the Immediate window, choose View | Immediate Window in the Visual Basic Editor.

The Immediate window can be moved anywhere on the Visual Basic Editor window, or it can be docked so that it always appears in the same area of the screen. The docking setting can be turned on and off from the Docking tab in the Options dialog box (Tools | Options).

To access the Immediate window you can also press Ctrl+G while in the Visual Basic Editor window. To close the Immediate window, click the Close button in the top-right corner of the window.

The following hands-on exercise demonstrates how to use the Immediate window to check instructions and get answers.

◎ Hands-On 2-5: Experiments in the Immediate Window

1. Switch to the VBE window by pressing **Alt+F11**.

2. Press **Ctrl+G** to activate the Immediate window, or choose **View | Immediate Window.**

3. In the Immediate window, type the instruction shown below, and press **Enter**:

```
DoCmd.OpenForm "Inventory List"
```

4. If you entered the above VBA statement correctly, Visual Basic opens the Inventory List form, assuming the Northwind database is open.

5. Enter the following instruction in the Immediate window:

```
Debug.Print Forms![Inventory List].RecordSource
```

When you press **Enter**, Visual Basic indicates that Inventory is the RecordSource for the Inventory List form. Every time you type an instruction in the Immediate window and press Enter, Visual Basic executes the statement on the line where the insertion point is located. If you want to execute the same instruction again, click anywhere in the line containing the instruction and press Enter. For more practice, rerun the statements shown in Figure 2-16. Start from the instruction displayed in the first line of the Immediate window. Execute the instructions one by one by clicking in the appropriate line and pressing Enter.

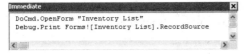

Figure 2-16: Use the Immediate window to evaluate and try Visual Basic statements.

So far you have used the Immediate window to perform some actions. The Immediate window also allows you to ask questions. Suppose you want to find out the answers to "How many controls are in the Inventory List form?" or "What's the name of the current application?" When working in the Immediate window, you can easily get answers to these and other questions.

In the preceding exercise, you entered two instructions. Let's return to the Immediate window to ask some questions. Access remembers the instructions entered in the Immediate window even after you close this window. The contents of the Immediate window are automatically deleted when you exit Microsoft Access.

Hands-On 2-6: Asking Questions in the Immediate Window

1. Click in a new line of the Immediate window and enter the following statement to find out the number of controls in the Inventory List form:

   ```
   ?Forms![Inventory List].Controls.Count
   ```

   When you press **Enter**, Visual Basic enters the number of controls on a new line in the Immediate window.

2. Click in a new line of the Immediate window, and enter the following statement:

   ```
   ?Application.Name
   ```

   When you press **Enter**, Visual Basic enters the name of the active application on a new line in the Immediate window.

3. In a new line in the Immediate window, enter the following instruction:

   ```
   ?12/3
   ```

   When you press **Enter**, Visual Basic shows the result of the division on a new line. But what if you want to know the result of 3 + 2 and 12 * 8 right away? Instead of entering these instructions on separate lines, you can enter them on one line as in the following example:

   ```
   ?3+2:?12*8
   ```

   Notice the colon separating the two blocks of instructions. When you press the Enter key, Visual Basic displays the results 5 and 96 on separate lines in the Immediate window.

      Here are a couple of other statements you may want to try out on your own in the Immediate window:

   ```
   ?Application.GetOption("Default Database Directory")
   ?Application.CodeProject.Name
   ```

   Instead of using the question mark, you may precede the statement typed in the Immediate window with the Print command, like this:

   ```
   Print Application.CodeProject.Name
   ```

   To delete the instructions from the Immediate window, highlight all the lines and press **Delete**.

4. In the Visual Basic Editor window, choose **File | Close and Return to Microsoft Office Access**.

5. Close the Northwind 2007.accdb database.

Note: In Chapter 1 you learned how to run subprocedures and functions from the Immediate window. You will find other examples of running procedures and functions from this window in the subsequent chapters.

Chapter Summary

Programming in Access 2007 requires a working knowledge of objects and collections of objects. In this chapter you explored features of the Visual Basic Editor window that can assist you in writing VBA code. Here are some important points:

■ When in doubt about objects, properties, or methods in an existing VBA procedure, highlight the instruction in question and fire up the online help by pressing F1.

■ When you need on-the-fly programming assistance while typing your VBA code, use the shortcut keys or buttons available on the Edit toolbar.

■ If you need a quick listing of properties and methods for every available object, or have trouble locating a hard-to-find procedure, go with the Object Browser.

■ If you want to experiment with VBA and see the results of VBA commands immediately, use the Immediate window.

In the next chapter you will learn how you can remember values in your VBA procedures by using various types of variables and constants.

Chapter 3

Variables, Data Types, and Constants

In Chapter 2, you used the question mark to have Visual Basic return some information in the Immediate window. Unfortunately, outside the Immediate window, when you write Visual Basic procedures, you can't use the question mark. So how do you obtain answers to your questions in VBA procedures? To find out what a particular VBA instruction (statement) has returned, you must tell Visual Basic to memorize it. This is done by using variables. This chapter introduces you to many types of variables, data types, and constants that you can and should use in your VBA procedures.

What Is a Variable?

A *variable* is a name used to refer to an item of data. Each time you want to remember the result of a VBA instruction, think of a name that will represent it. For example, if you want to keep track of the number of controls on a particular form, you can make up a name such as NumOfControls, TotalControls, or FormsControlCount.

The names of variables can contain characters, numbers, and punctuation marks except for the following:

    , # $ % & @ !

The name of a variable cannot begin with a number or contain a space. If you want the name of the variable to include more than one word, use the underscore (_). Although a variable name can contain as many as 254 characters, it's best to use short and simple names. Using short names will save you typing time when you need to reuse the variable in your Visual Basic procedure. Visual Basic doesn't care whether you use uppercase or lowercase letters in variable names; however, most programmers use lowercase letters. When the variable name is comprised of more than one word, most programmers capitalize the first letter of each word, as in the following: NumOfControls, First_Name.

> ### Reserved Words Can't Be Used for Variable Names
>
> You can use any label you want for a variable name except for the reserved words that VBA uses. Visual Basic function names and words that have a special meaning in VBA cannot be used as variable names. For example, words such as Name, Len, Empty, Local, Currency, or Exit will generate an error message if used as a variable name.

Give your variables names that can help you remember their roles. Some programmers use a prefix to identify the variable's type. A variable name preceded with "str," such as strName, can be quickly recognized within the procedure code as the one holding the text string.

What Are Data Types?

When you create Visual Basic procedures you have a purpose in mind: You want to manipulate data. Because your procedures will handle different kinds of information, you should understand how Visual Basic stores data.

The *data type* determines how the data is stored in the computer's memory. For example, data can be stored as a number, text, date, object, etc. If you forget to tell Visual Basic the data type, it is assigned the Variant data type. The *Variant* type has the ability to figure out on its own what kind of data is being manipulated and then take on that type. The Visual Basic data types are shown in Table 3-1. In addition to the built-in data types, you can define your own data types, known as user-defined data types. Because data types take up different amounts of space in the computer's memory, some of them are more expensive than others. Therefore, to conserve memory and make your procedure run faster, you should select the data type that uses the fewest bytes but at the same time is capable of handling the data that your procedure has to manipulate.

Table 3-1: VBA data types

Data Type	Storage Size	Range
Byte	1 byte	0 to 255
Boolean	2 bytes	True or False
Integer	2 bytes	–32,768 to 32,767
Long (long integer)	4 bytes	–2,147,483,648 to 2,147,483,647
Single (single-precision floating-point)	4 bytes	–3.402823E38 to –1.401298E–45 for negative values; 1.401298E–45 to 3.402823E38 for positive values
Double (double-precision floating-point)	8 bytes	–1.79769313486231E308 to –4.94065645841247E–324 for negative values; 4.94065645841247E–324 to 1.79769313486232E308 for positive values
Currency (scaled integer)	8 bytes	–922,337,203,685,477.5808 to 922,337,203,685,477.5807

Data Type	Storage Size	Range
Decimal	14 bytes	+/–79,228,162,514,264,337,593,543,950,335 with no decimal point; +/–7.9228162514264337593543950335 with 28 places to the right of the decimal; smallest nonzero number is +/–0.0000000000000000000000000001
Date	8 bytes	January 1, 100, to December 31, 9999
Object	4 bytes	Any Object reference
String (variable-length)	10 bytes + string length	0 to approximately 2 billion
String (fixed-length)	Length of string	1 to approximately 65,400
Variant (with numbers)	16 bytes	Any numeric value up to the range of a Double
Variant (with characters)	22 bytes + string length	Same range as for variable-length String
User-defined (using Type)	Number required by elements	The range of each element is the same as the range of its data type.

Creating Variables

You can create a variable by declaring it with a special command or by just using it in a statement. When you declare your variable, you make Visual Basic aware of the variable's name and data type. This is called *explicit variable declaration*.

Advantages of Explicit Variable Declaration

Explicit variable declaration:

- Speeds up the execution of your procedure. Since Visual Basic knows the data type, it reserves only as much memory as is absolutely necessary to store the data.

- Makes your code easier to read and understand because all the variables are listed at the very beginning of the procedure.

- Helps prevent errors caused by misspelling a variable name. Visual Basic automatically corrects the variable name based on the spelling used in the variable declaration.

If you don't let Visual Basic know about the variable prior to using it, you are implicitly telling VBA that you want to create this variable. *Implicit variables* are automatically assigned the Variant data type (see Table 3-1). Although implicit variable declaration is convenient (it allows you to create variables on the fly and assign values to them without knowing in advance the data type of the values being assigned), it can cause several problems.

Disadvantages of Implicit Variable Declaration

- If you misspell a variable name in your procedure, Visual Basic may display a run-time error or create a new variable. You are guaranteed to waste some time troubleshooting problems that could easily have been avoided had you declared your variable at the beginning of the procedure.
- Since Visual Basic does not know what type of data your variable will store, it assigns it a Variant data type. This causes your procedure to run slower, because Visual Basic has to check the data type every time it deals with your variable. And because Variant variables can store any type of data, Visual Basic has to reserve more memory to store your data.

Declaring Variables

You declare a variable with the Dim keyword. Dim stands for "dimension." The Dim keyword is followed by the variable's name and type.

Suppose you want the procedure to display the age of an employee. Before you can calculate the age, you must feed the procedure the employee's date of birth. To do this, you declare a variable called dateOfBirth, as follows:

```
Dim dateOfBirth As Date
```

Notice that the Dim keyword is followed by the name of the variable (dateOfBirth). If you don't like this name, you are free to replace it with another word, as long as the word you are planning to use is not one of the VBA keywords. You specify the data type the variable will hold by including the As keyword followed by one of the data types from Table 3-1. The Date data type tells Visual Basic that the variable dateOfBirth will store a date.

To store the employee's age, you declare the variable as follows:

```
Dim intAge As Integer
```

The intAge variable will store the number of years between today's date and the employee's date of birth. Since age is displayed as a whole number, the intAge variable has been assigned the Integer data type. You may also want your procedure to keep track of the employee's name, so you declare another variable to hold the employee's first and last name:

```
Dim strFullName As String
```

Since the word Name is on the VBA list of reserved words, using it in your VBA procedure would guarantee an error. To hold the employee's full name, we used the variable strFullName and declared it as the String data type because the data it will hold is text. Declaring variables is regarded as good programming practice because it makes programs easier to read and helps prevent certain types of errors.

Informal (Implicit) Variables

Variables that are not explicitly declared with Dim statements are said to be implicitly declared. These variables are automatically assigned a data type called Variant. They can hold numbers, strings, and other types of information. You can create an informal variable by assigning some value to a variable name anywhere in your VBA procedure. For example, you implicitly declare a variable in the following way: intDaysLeft = 100.

Now that you know how to declare your variables, let's write a procedure that uses them.

◎ Hands-On 3-1: Using Variables

The procedure code for this chapter's hands-on exercises is located in the C:\Acc07_HandsOn folder in a text file named HandsOn_03.txt. Instead of typing in the programming code as instructed in each hands-on exercise, you can save time by copying the required procedure from this text file.

1. Start Microsoft Office Access 2007 and create a new Microsoft Office Access 2007 database named **Chap03.accdb** in your **C:\Acc07_ByExample** folder.

2. Once your new database is opened, press **Alt+F11** to switch to the Visual Basic Editor window.

3. Choose **Insert | Module** to add a new standard module, and notice Module1 under the Modules folder in the Project Explorer window.

4. In the Module1 (Code) window, enter the code of the **AgeCalc** procedure shown below. (You may copy this procedure from the HandsOn_03.txt file in the Acc07_HandsOn folder.)

```
Sub AgeCalc()
    ' variable declaration
    Dim strFullName As String
    Dim dateOfBirth As Date
    Dim intAge As Integer

    ' assign values to variables
    strFullName = "John Smith"
    dateOfBirth = #1/3/1967#

    ' calculate age
    IntAge = Year(Now()) - Year(dateOfBirth)

    ' print results to the Immediate window
    Debug.Print strFullName & " is " & intAge & " years old."
End Sub
```

Notice that in the AgeCalc procedure the variables are declared on separate lines at the beginning of the procedure. If you want, you can declare several variables on the same line, separating each variable name with a comma, as shown in the example below:

```
Dim strFullName As String, dateOfBirth As Date, intAge As Integer
```

When you list all your variables on one line, the Dim keyword appears only once at the beginning of the variable declaration line.

5. If the Immediate window is not open, press **Ctrl+G** or choose **View | Immediate Window**. Since the example procedure writes the results to the Immediate window, you should ensure that this window is open prior to executing step 6 below.

6. To run the AgeCalc procedure, click any line between the Sub and End Sub keywords and press **F5**.

What Is the Variable Type?

You can find out the type of a variable used in your procedure by right-clicking the variable name and selecting Quick Info from the shortcut menu.

When Visual Basic executes the variable declaration statements, it creates the variables with the specified names and reserves memory space to store their values. Then specific values are assigned to these variables. To assign a value to a variable, you begin with a variable name followed by an equal sign. The value entered to the right of the equal sign is the data you want to store in the variable. The data you enter here must be of the type stated in the variable declaration. Text data should be surrounded by quotation marks and the date by # characters.

Using the data supplied by the dateOfBirth variable, Visual Basic calculates the age of an employee and stores the result of the calculation in the variable called intAge. Then, the full name of the employee and the age are printed to the Immediate window using the instruction Debug.Print.

Concatenation

You can combine two or more strings to form a new string. The joining operation is called concatenation. You saw an example of concatenated strings in the AgeCalc procedure above. Concatenation is represented by an ampersand character (&). For instance, "His name is " & strFirstName will produce a string like: His name is John or His name is Michael. The name of the person is determined by the contents of the strFirstName variable. Notice that there is an extra space between "is" and the ending quotation mark: "His name is ". Concatenation of strings can also be represented by a plus sign (+); however, many programmers prefer to restrict the plus sign to numerical operations to eliminate ambiguity.

Specifying the Data Type of a Variable

If you don't specify the variable's data type in the Dim statement, you end up with the *untyped* variable. Untyped variables in VBA are always assigned the Variant data type. Variant data types can hold all the other data types (except for user-defined data types). This feature makes Variant a very flexible and popular data type. Despite this flexibility, it's highly recommended that you create typed variables. When you declare a variable of a certain data type, your VBA procedure runs faster because Visual Basic does not have to stop to analyze the variable to determine its type.

Visual Basic can work with many types of numeric variables. Integer variables can only hold whole numbers from –32,768 to 32,767. Other types of numeric variables are Long, Single, Double, and Currency. The Long variables can hold whole numbers in the range –2,147,483,648 to 2,147,483,647. As opposed to Integer and Long variables, Single and Double variables can hold decimals.

String variables are used to refer to text. When you declare a variable of the String data type, you can tell Visual Basic how long the string should be. For instance, Dim strExtension As String * 3 declares the fixed-length String variable named strExtension that is three characters long. If you don't assign a specific length, the String variable will be *dynamic*. This means that Visual Basic will make enough space in computer memory to handle whatever text length is assigned to it.

After a variable is declared, it can only store the type of information that you stated in the declaration statement.

Assigning string values to numeric variables or numeric values to string variables results in the error message "Type Mismatch" or causes Visual Basic to modify the value. For example, if your variable was declared to hold whole numbers and your data uses decimals, Visual Basic will disregard the decimals and use only the whole part of the number.

Let's use the MyNumber procedure in Hands-On 3-2 below as an example of how Visual Basic modifies the data according to the assigned data types.

◎ Hands-On 3-2: Understanding the Data Type of a Variable

This hands-on exercise uses the C:\Acc07_ByExample\Chap03.accdb database that you created in Hands-On 3-1.

1. In the Visual Basic Editor window, choose **Insert | Module** to add a new module.

2. Enter the procedure code for **MyNumber** (as shown below) in the new module's Code window. (You can copy the procedure code from the **HandsOn_03.txt** file in the **Acc07_HandsOn** folder.)

```
Sub MyNumber()
    Dim intNum As Integer

    intNum = 23.11
    MsgBox intNum
End Sub
```

3. To run the procedure, click any line between the Sub and End Sub keywords and press **F5** or choose **Run | Run Sub/UserForm**.

When you run the above procedure, Visual Basic displays the contents of the variable intNum as 23, and not 23.11, because the intNum variable was declared as an Integer data type.

Using Type Declaration Characters

If you don't declare a variable with a Dim statement, you can still designate a type for it by using a special character at the end of the variable name. For example, to declare the FirstName variable as String, you append the dollar sign to the variable name as shown:

```
Dim FirstName$
```

The above is the same as Dim FirstName As String. Other type declaration characters are shown in Table 3-2.

Notice that the type declaration characters can only be used with six data types. To use the type declaration character, append the character to the end of the variable name.

Table 3-2: Type declaration characters

Data Type	Character
Integer	%
Long	&
Single	!
Double	#
Currency	@
String	$

Declaring Typed Variables

The variable type can be indicated by the As keyword or by attaching a type symbol. If you don't add the type symbol or the As command, VBA will default the variable to the Variant data type.

◎ Hands-On 3-3: Using Type Declaration Characters in Variable Names

This hands-on exercise uses the Chap03.accdb database that you created in Hands-On 3-1.

1. In the Visual Basic window, choose **Insert | Module** to add a new module.

2. Enter the **AgeCalc2** procedure code in the new module's Code window. (You can copy the procedure code from the **HandsOn_03.txt** file in the **Acc07_HandsOn** folder.)

```
Sub AgeCalc2()
    ' variable declaration
    Dim FullName$
    Dim DateOfBirth As Date
    Dim age%

    ' assign values to variables
    FullName$ = "John Smith"
    DateOfBirth = #1/3/1967#

    ' calculate age
    age% = Year(Now()) - Year(DateOfBirth)

    ' print results to the Immediate window
    Debug.Print FullName$ & " is " & age% & " years old."
End Sub
```

3. To run the procedure, click any line between the Sub and End Sub keywords and press **F5** or choose **Run | Run Sub/UserForm**.

Assigning Values to Variables

Now that you know how to correctly name and declare variables, it's time to start using them.

◎ Hands-On 3-4: Assigning Values to Variables

This hands-on exercise uses the C:\Acc07_ByExample\Chap03.accdb database that you created in Hands-On 3-1.

1. In the Visual Basic window, choose **Insert | Module** to add a new module.

2. Enter the code of the **CalcCost** procedure in the new module's Code window. (You can copy the procedure code from the **HandsOn_03.txt** file in the **Acc07_HandsOn** folder.)

```
Sub CalcCost()
    slsPrice = 35
    slsTax = 0.085
    cost = slsPrice + (slsPrice * slsTax)
    strMsg = "The calculator total is " & "$" & cost & "."
    MsgBox strMsg
End Sub
```

3. To run the procedure, click any line between the Sub and End Sub keywords and press **F5** or choose **Run | Run Sub/UserForm**.

The CalcCost procedure uses four variables: slsPrice, slsTax, cost, and strMsg. Because none of these variables have been explicitly declared, they all have the same data type — Variant. The variables slsPrice and slsTax were created by assigning some values to the variable names at the beginning of the procedure. The cost variable was assigned the value resulting from the calculation slsPrice + (slsPrice * slsTax). The cost calculation uses the values supplied by the slsPrice and slsTax variables. The strMsg variable puts together a text message to the user. This message is then displayed with the MsgBox function.

When you assign values to variables, you follow the name of the variable with the equal sign. After the equal sign you enter the value of the variable. This can be text surrounded by quotation marks, a number, or an expression. While the values assigned to the variables slsPrice, slsTax, and cost are easily understood, the value stored in the strMsg variable is a little more involved. Let's examine the content of the strMsg variable:

```
strMsg = "The calculator total is " & "$" & cost & "."
```

- The string "The calculator total is " begins and ends with quotation marks. Notice the extra space before the ending quotation mark.

- The & symbol allows one string to be appended to another string or to the contents of a variable and must be used every time you want to append a new piece of information to the previous string.

- The $ character is used to denote the type of currency. Because it is a character, it is surrounded by quotation marks.

- The & symbol attaches another string.

- The cost variable is a placeholder. The actual cost of the calculator will be displayed here when the procedure runs.

- The & symbol attaches yet another string.

- The period (.) is a character and must be surrounded by quotation marks. When you require a period at the end of the sentence, you must attach it separately when it follows the name of a variable.

Variable Initialization

Visual Basic automatically initializes a new variable to its default value when it is created. Numerical variables are set to zero (0), Boolean variables are initialized to False, string variables are set to the empty string (""), and Date variables are set to December 30, 1899.

Notice that the cost displayed in the message box has three decimal places. To display the cost of a calculator with two decimal places you need to use a function. VBA has special functions that allow you to change the format of data. To change the format of the cost variable you should use the Format function. This function has the following syntax:

```
Format(expression, format)
```

where *expression* is a value or variable you want to format and *format* is the type of format you want to apply.

◎ Hands-On 3-4: (Continued)

4. Change the calculation of the cost variable in the CalcCost procedure, as shown below:

```
cost = Format(slsPrice + (slsPrice * slsTax), "0.00")
```

5. To run the modified procedure, click any line between the Sub and End Sub keywords and press **F5** or choose **Run | Run Sub/UserForm**.

After having tried the CalcCost procedure, you may wonder why you should bother declaring variables if Visual Basic can handle undeclared variables so well. The CalcCost procedure is very short, so you don't need to worry about how many bytes of memory will be consumed each time Visual Basic uses the Variant variable. In short procedures, however, it is not the memory that matters but the mistakes you are bound to make when typing variable names. What will happen if the second time you use the cost variable you omit the "o" and refer to it as cst?

```
strMsg = "The calculator total is " & "$" & cst & "."
```

And what will you end up with if, instead of slsTax, you use the word tax in the formula?

```
cost = Format(slsPrice + (slsPrice * tax), "0.00")
```

When you run the procedure with the above errors introduced, Visual Basic will not show the cost of the calculator because it does not find the assignment statement for the cst variable. And because Visual Basic does not know the sales tax, it displays the price of the calculator as the total cost. Visual Basic does not guess. It simply does what you tell it to do. This brings us to the next section, which explains how to make sure that errors of this sort don't occur.

 Note: Before you continue with this chapter, be sure to replace the names of the variables cst and tax with cost and slsTax.

Forcing Declaration of Variables

Visual Basic has an Option Explicit statement that you can use to automatically remind you to formally declare all your variables. This statement has to be entered at the top of each of your modules. The Option Explicit statement will cause Visual Basic to generate an error message when you try to run a procedure that contains undeclared variables.

◎ Hands-On 3-5: Forcing Declaration of Variables

1. Return to the Code window where you entered the **CalcCost** procedure (see Hands-On 3-4).

2. At the top of the module window (in the first line), enter

   ```
   Option Explicit
   ```

   and press **Enter**. Visual Basic will display the statement in blue.

3. Position the insertion point anywhere within the CalcCost procedure and press **F5** to run it. Visual Basic displays the error message: "Compile error: Variable not defined."

4. Click **OK** to exit the message box. Visual Basic selects the name of the variable, slsPrice, and highlights in yellow the name of the procedure, Sub CalcCost(). The title bar displays "Microsoft Visual Basic — Acc2003_Chap03 [break] — [Module4 (Code)]." The Visual Basic break mode allows you to correct the problem before you continue. Now you have to formally declare the slsPrice variable.

5. Enter the declaration statement

   ```
   Dim slsPrice As Currency
   ```

   on a new line just below Sub CalcCost() and press **F5** to continue. When you declare the slsPrice variable and rerun your procedure, Visual Basic will generate the same compile error as soon as it encounters another variable name that was not declared. To fix the remaining problems with the variable declaration in this procedure, choose **Run | Reset** to exit the break mode.

6. Enter the following declarations at the beginning of the CalcCost procedure:

   ```
   ' declaration of variables
   Dim slsPrice As Currency
   Dim slsTax As Single
   Dim cost As Currency
   Dim strMsg As String
   ```

7. To run the procedure, click any line between the Sub and End Sub keywords and press **F5** or choose **Run | Run Sub/UserForm**. Your revised CalcCost procedure (see CalcCost2 in the companion files) looks like this:

```
Sub CalcCost2() ' revised CalcCost procedure
    ' declaration of variables
    Dim slsPrice As Currency
    Dim slsTax As Single
    Dim cost As Currency
    Dim strMsg As String

    slsPrice = 35
    slsTax = 0.085
```

```
cost = Format(slsPrice + (slsPrice * slsTax), "0.00")
strMsg = "The calculator total is " & "$" & cost & "."

    MsgBox strMsg
End Sub
```

The Option Explicit statement you entered at the top of the module (see step 2) forced you to declare variables. Because you must include the Option Explicit statement in each module where you want to require variable declaration, you can have Visual Basic enter this statement for you each time you insert a new module.

To automatically include Option Explicit in every new module you create, follow these steps:

1. Choose **Tools | Options**.

2. Make sure the **Require Variable Declaration** check box is selected in the Options dialog box (Editor tab).

3. Choose **OK** to close the Options dialog box.

From now on, every new module will be added with the Option Explicit statement in line 1. If you want to require variables to be explicitly declared in a module you created prior to enabling Require Variable Declaration in the Options dialog box, you must enter the Option Explicit statement manually by editing the module yourself.

More about Option Explicit

Option Explicit forces formal (explicit) declaration of all variables in a particular module. One big advantage of using Option Explicit is that misspellings of variable names will be detected at compile time (when Visual Basic attempts to translate the source code to executable code). The Option Explicit statement must appear in a module before any procedures.

Understanding the Scope and Lifetime of Variables

Variables can have different ranges of influence in a VBA procedure. *Scope* defines the availability of a particular variable to the same procedure or other procedures. A variable's scope can be procedure-level or module-level. In addition to scope, variables have a *lifetime*. The lifetime of a variable determines how long a variable retains its value.

Procedure-Level (Local) Variables

From this chapter you already know how to declare a variable using the Dim statement. The position of the Dim statement in the module determines the scope of a variable. Variables declared with the Dim statement within a VBA procedure have a *procedure-level* scope. Procedure-level variables can also be declared by using the Static statement (see "Understanding and Using Static Variables" later in this chapter).

Procedure-level variables are frequently referred to as *local* variables, which can only be used in the procedure where they were declared. Undeclared variables always have a procedure-level scope.

A variable's name must be unique within its scope. This means that you cannot declare two variables with the same name in the same procedure. However, you can use the same variable name in different procedures. In other words, the CalcCost procedure can have the slsTax variable, and the ExpenseRep procedure in the same module can have its own variable called slsTax. Both variables are independent of each other.

Local Variables: with Dim or Static?

When you declare a local variable with the Dim statement, the value of the variable is preserved only while the procedure in which it is declared is running. As soon as the procedure ends, the variable dies. The next time you execute the procedure, the variable is reinitialized.

When you declare a local variable with the Static statement, the value of the variable is preserved after the procedure in which the variable was declared has finished running. Static variables are reset when you quit the Microsoft Access application or when a run-time error occurs while the procedure is running.

Module-Level Variables

Often you want the variable to be available to other VBA procedures in the module after the procedure in which the variable was declared has finished running. This situation requires that you change the variable's scope to *module-level*.

Module-level variables are declared at the top of the module (above the first procedure definition) by using the Dim or Private statement. These variables are available to all of the procedures in the module in which they were declared, but are not available to procedures in other modules.

For instance, to make the slsTax variable available to any other procedure in the module, you could declare it by using the Dim or Private statement:

```
Option Explicit
Dim slsTax As Single      ' module-level variable declared with Dim statement

Sub CalcCost()
    ...Instructions of the procedure...
End Sub
```

Notice that the slsTax variable is declared at the top of the module, just below the Option Explicit statement and before the first procedure definition. You could also declare the slsTax variable like this:

```
Option Explicit
Private slsTax As Single  ' module-level variable declared with Private
                          ' statement
```

```
Sub CalcCost()
    ...Instructions of the procedure...
End Sub
```

There is no difference between module-level variables declared with Dim or Private statements.

Before you can see how module-level variables actually work, you need another procedure that also uses the slsTax variable.

◎ Hands-On 3-6: Understanding Module-Level Variables

This hands-on exercise requires the prior completion of Hands-On 3-4 and 3-5.

1. In the Code window, in the same module where you entered the revised CalcCost procedure (CalcCost2), cut the declaration line **Dim slsTax As Single** and paste it at the top of the module sheet, below the Option Explicit statement.

2. Enter the code of the **ExpenseRep** procedure shown below in the same module where the CalcCost2 procedure is located. (You can copy the procedure code from the **HandsOn_03.txt** file in the **Acc07_HandsOn** folder.)

```
Sub ExpenseRep()
    Dim slsPrice As Currency
    Dim cost As Currency

    slsPrice = 55.99
    cost = slsPrice + (slsPrice * slsTax)

    MsgBox slsTax
    MsgBox cost
End Sub
```

The ExpenseRep procedure declares two Currency type variables: slsPrice and cost. The slsPrice variable is then assigned a value of 55.99. The slsPrice variable is independent of the slsPrice variable declared within the CalcCost2 procedure.

The ExpenseRep procedure calculates the cost of a purchase. The cost includes the sales tax. Because the sales tax is the same as the one used in the CalcCost2 procedure, the slsTax variable has been declared at the module level. After Visual Basic executes the CalcCost2 procedure, the contents of the slsTax variable equals 0.085. If slsTax were a local variable, upon the termination of the CalcCost2 procedure, the contents of this variable would be empty. The ExpenseRep procedure ends by displaying the value of the slsTax and cost variables in two separate message boxes.

After running the CalcCost2 procedure, Visual Basic erases the contents of all the variables except for the slsTax variable, which was declared at a module level. As soon as you attempt to calculate the cost by running the ExpenseRep procedure, Visual Basic retrieves the value of the slsTax variable and uses it in the calculation.

3. Click anywhere inside your revised CalcCost or CalcCost2 procedure and press **F5** to run it.

4. As soon as the CalcCost (CalcCost2) procedure finishes executing, run the ExpenseRep procedure.

Public (Global) Variables

In the previous section, you learned that by declaring a variable with the Dim or Private keyword at the top of the module, you can make it available to other procedures in that module. If you want the variable to be available to all procedures in all modules in the current Microsoft Access database as well as in any Visual Basic for Applications modules that your code references, you will need a module-level variable with a Public scope, which can be declared with the Public statement like this:

```
Option Explicit
Public gslsTax As Single

Sub CalcCost()
    ...Instructions of the procedure...
End Sub
```

The gslsTax variable declared at the top of the module with the Public statement will now be available to any Visual Basic for Applications modules that your code references.

A variable declared in the declaration section of a module using the Public keyword is also called a *global variable*. This variable can be seen by all procedures in the database's modules. It is customary to use the prefix "g" to indicate a public module-level variable.

When using global variables, it's important to keep in mind the following:

- The value of the global variable can be changed anywhere in your program. An unexpected change in the value of a variable is a common cause of problems. Be careful not to write a block of code that modifies a global variable. If you need to change the value of a variable within your application, make sure you are using a local variable.

- Values of all global variables declared with the Public keyword are cleared when Access encounters an error. If you are using the Access 2007 database format (ACCDB), use the new TempVars collection for your global variable needs (see the next section).

- Don't put your global variable declaration in a form class module. Variables in the code module behind the form are never global even if you declare them as such. You must use a standard code module (Insert | Module) to declare variables to be available in all modules and forms. Variables declared in a standard module can be used in the code for any form.

- Use constants as much as possible whenever your application requires global variables. Constants are much more reliable because their values are unchangeable. Constants are covered later in this chapter.

> **Public Variables and the Option Private Module Statement**
> Variables declared using the Public keyword are available to all procedures in all modules across all applications. To restrict a public module-level variable to the current database, include the Option Private Module statement in the declaration section of the standard or a class module in which the variable is declared.

Understanding and Using Temporary Variables

In the previous section you learned that you can declare a global variable with the Public keyword and use it throughout your entire application. You also learned that these variables can be quite problematic, especially when you or another programmer accidentally changes the value of the variable or your application encounters an error and the values of the variables you have initially set for your application to use are completely wiped out. To avoid such problems, many programmers resort to using a separate global variables form to hold their global variables. And if they need certain values to be available the next time the application starts, they create a separate database table to store these values. A *global variables form* is simply a blank Access form where you can place both bound and unbound controls. Bound controls are used to pull the data from the table where global variables have been stored. You can use unbound controls on a form to store values of global variables that are not stored in a separate table. Simply set the ControlSource property of the unbound control by typing a value in it or use a VBA procedure to set the value of the ControlSource. The form set up as a global variables form must be open while the application is running for the values of the bound and unbound controls to be available to other forms, reports, and queries in the database. A global variables form can be hidden if the values of the global variables are pulled from a database table or set using VBA procedures or macro actions.

In Microsoft Office Access 2007, if your database is in the new ACCDB format, instead of using a database table or a global variables form, use the new TempVars collection to store the Variant values you want to reuse. TempVars stands for *temporary variables*. Temporary variables are global. You can refer to them in VBA modules, event procedures, queries, expressions, add-ins, and in any referenced databases. Access 2007 allows you to define up to 255 temporary variables at one time. These variables remain in memory until you close the database (unless you remove them when you are finished working with them). Unlike the public variables, the temporary variable values are not cleared when an error occurs.

Creating a Temporary Variable with a TempVars Collection Object

Let's look at several examples of using the TempVars collection introduced in Access 2007. Assume your application requires three variables named gtvUserName, gtvuserFolder, and gtvEndDate.

To try this out, open the Immediate window and type the statements listed below. The variable is created as soon as you press Enter after each statement.

```
TempVars("gtvUserName").Value = "Julitta Korol"

TempVars("gtvUserFolder").Value = Environ("HOMEPATH")

TempVars("gtvEndDate").Value = Format(now(),"mm/dd/yyyy")
```

Notice that to create a temporary variable all you have to do is specify its value. If the variable does not already exist, Access adds it to the TempVars collection. If the variable exists, Access modifies its value.

You can explicitly add a global variable to the TempVars collection by using the Add method, like this:

```
TempVars.Add "gtvCompleted", "true"
```

Retrieving Names and Values of TempVar Objects

Each TempVar object in the TempVars collection has Name and Value properties that you can use to access the variable and read its value from any procedure. By default, the items in the collection are numbered from zero (0), the first item being zero, the second item being one, the third two, and so on. Therefore, to find the value of the second variable in the TempVars you have entered (gtvUserFolder), type the following statement in the Immediate window:

```
?TempVars(1).Value
```

When you press Enter, you will see the location of the user's private folder on the computer. In this case, it is your private folder. The folder information was returned by passing the "HOMEPATH" parameter to the built-in Environ function. Functions and parameter passing is covered in Chapter 4.

You can also retrieve the value of the variable from the TempVars collection by using its name, like this:

```
?TempVars("gtvUserFolder").Value
```

You can iterate through the TempVars collection to see the names and values of all global variables that you have placed in it. To do this from the Immediate window you need to use the colon operator (:) to separate lines of code. Type the following statement to try this out:

```
For Each gtv in TempVars : Debug.Print gtv.Name & ":" & gtv.Value : Next
```

When you press Enter, the Debug.Print statement will write to the Immediate window a name and value for each variable that is currently stored in the TempVars collection:

```
gtvUserName:Julitta Korol
gtvUserFolder:\Documents and Settings\Julitta
gtvEndDate:03/17/2007
gtvCompleted:true
```

The For Each…Next statement is covered in detail in Chapter 6. The "gtv" is an object variable used as an iterator. You can use any variable name as an iterator as long as it is not a VBA keyword. An iterator allows you to traverse through all the elements of a collection. Object variables are discussed later in this chapter. For more information on working with collections, see Chapter 8.

Using Temporary Global Variables in Expressions

You can use temporary global variables anywhere expressions can be used. For example, you can set the value of the unbound text box control on a form to display the value of your global variable by activating the property sheet and typing the following in the ControlSource property of the text box:

```
=[TempVars]![gtvCompleted]
```

You can also use a temporary variable to pass selection criteria to queries:

```
SELECT * FROM Orders WHERE Order_Date = TempVars!gtvEndDate
```

Removing a Temporary Variable from a TempVars Collection Object

When you are done using a variable, you can remove it from the TempVars collection with the Remove method, like this:

```
TempVars.Remove "gtvUserFolder"
```

To check the number of the TempVar objects in the TempVars collection, use the Count property in the Immediate window:

```
?TempVars.Count
```

Finally, to quickly remove all global variables (TempVar objects) from the TempVars collection, simply use the RemoveAll method, like this:

```
TempVars.RemoveAll
```

The TempVars Collection Is Exposed to Macros

The following three macro actions have been added to Access 2007 to allow macro users to set and remove TempVar objects:

- SetTempVar — Sets a TempVar to a given value. You must specify the name of the temporary variable and the expression that will be used to set the value of this variable. Expressions must be entered without an equal sign (=).
- RemoveTempVar — Removes the TempVar from the TempVars collection. You must specify the name of the temporary variable you want to remove.
- RemoveAllTempVars — Clears the TempVars collection.

The values of TempVar objects can be used in the arguments and in the condition columns of macros. For more information on macro programming in Access 2007, see Part VI of this book.

Understanding and Using Static Variables

A variable declared with the Static keyword is a special type of local variable. *Static variables* are declared at the procedure level. Unlike the local variables declared with the Dim keyword, static variables remain in existence and retain their values when the procedure in which they were declared ends.

The CostOfPurchase procedure (see Hands-On 3-7) demonstrates the use of the Static variable allPurchase. The purpose of this variable is to keep track of the running total.

⊚ Hands-On 3-7: Using Static Variables

This hands-on exercise uses the C:\Acc07_ByExample\Chap03.accdb database that you created in Hands-On 3-1.

1. In the Visual Basic window, choose **Insert | Module** to add a new module.
2. Enter the **CostOfPurchase** procedure code shown below in the new module's Code window. (You can copy the procedure code from the **HandsOn_03.txt** file in the **Acc07_HandsOn** folder.)

```
Sub CostOfPurchase()
    ' declare variables
    Static allPurchase
    Dim newPurchase As String
    Dim purchCost As Single

    newPurchase = InputBox("Enter the cost of a purchase:")
    purchCost = CSng(newPurchase)
    allPurchase = allPurchase + purchCost

    ' display results
    MsgBox "The cost of a new purchase is: " & newPurchase
    MsgBox "The running cost is: " & allPurchase
End Sub
```

The above procedure begins with declaring a Static variable named allPurchase and two local variables named newPurchase and purchCost. The InputBox function allows you to get a user's input while the procedure is running. The InputBox function used in this procedure displays a dialog box and waits for the user to enter a value. As soon as the user inputs the value and clicks OK, Visual Basic assigns the value to the newPurchase variable. Because the result of the InputBox function is always a string, the newPurchase variable was declared as the String data type. Because you cannot use strings in mathematical calculations, the next instruction uses a *type conversion* function (CSng) to translate the text value into a numeric value, which is stored in the variable purchCost of the Single data type. The CSng function requires only one argument: the value you want to translate.

The next instruction, allPurchase = allPurchase + purchCost, adds the new value supplied by the InputBox function to the current purchase value. When you run this procedure for the first time, the value of the allPurchase variable is the same as the value of the purchCost variable. When you run the procedure the second time, the value of the static variable is increased by the new value entered in the dialog box. You can run the CostOfPurchase procedure as many times as you want. The allPurch variable will keep the running total for as long as the project is open.

3. To run the procedure, position the insertion point anywhere within the CostOfPurchase procedure and press **F5**.

4. When the dialog box appears, enter a number. For example, type **100** and press **Enter**. Visual Basic displays the message "The cost of a new purchase is: 100."

5. Click **OK** in the message box. Visual Basic displays the second message "The running cost is: 100."

6. Rerun the same procedure.

7. When the input box appears, enter another number. For example, type **50** and press **Enter**. Visual Basic displays the message "The cost of a new purchase is: 50."

8. Click **OK** in the message box. Visual Basic displays the second message "The running cost is: 150."

9. Run the procedure a couple of times to see how Visual Basic keeps track of the running total.

> **Type Conversion Functions**
> To learn more about the CSng function (and other type conversion functions), position the insertion point anywhere within the word CSng and press F1.

Understanding and Using Object Variables

The variables you've learned about so far are used to store data, which is the main reason for using "normal" variables in your procedures. There are also special variables that refer to the Visual Basic objects. These variables are called *object variables*. Object variables don't store data; they store the location of the data. You can use them to reference databases, forms, and controls as well as objects created in other applications. Object variables are declared in a similar way as the variables you already know. The only difference is that after the As keyword, you enter the type of object your variable will point to. For instance:

```
Dim myControl As Control
```

The statement above declares the object variable called myControl of type Control.

```
Dim frm As Form
```

This statement declares the object variable called frm of type Form.

You can use object variables to refer to objects of a generic type such as Application, Control, Form, or Report, or you can point your object variable to specific object types such as TextBox, ToggleButton, CheckBox, CommandButton, ListBox, OptionButton, Subform or Subreport, Label, BoundObjectFrame or UnboundObjectFrame, and so on. When you declare an object variable, you also have to assign it a specific value before you can use it in your procedure. You assign a value to the object variable by using the Set keyword followed by the equal sign and the value that the variable refers to. For example:

```
Set myControl = Me!CompanyName
```

The above statement assigns a value to the object variable called myControl. This object variable will now point to the CompanyName control on the active form. If you omit the word Set, Visual Basic will display the error message "Run-time error 91: Object variable or With block variable not set."

Again, it's time to see a practical example. The HideControl procedure in Hands-On 3-8 below demonstrates the use of the object variables frm and myControl.

◎ Hands-On 3-8: Working with Object Variables

1. Close the currently open Access database **Chap03.accdb**. When prompted to save changes in the modules, click **OK**. Save the modules with the suggested default names Module1, Module2, and so on.

2. Copy the **HandsOn_03_8.accdb** database from the **C:\Acc07_HandsOn** folder to your **C:\Acc07_ByExample** folder. This database contains a Customer table and a simple Customer form imported from the Northwind.mdb sample database that shipped with previous versions of Microsoft Office Access.

3. Open Microsoft Office Access and load the **C:\Acc07_ByExample\ HandsOn_03_8.accdb** database file.

4. Open the **Customers** form in Form view.

5. Press **Alt+F11** to switch to the Visual Basic Editor window.

6. Choose **Insert | Module** to add a new module.

7. Enter the **HideControl** procedure code shown below in the new module's Code window. (You can copy the procedure code from the **C:\Acc07_ HandsOn\HandsOn_03.txt** file.)

```
Sub HideControl()
    ' this procedure is run against the open Customers form
    Dim frm As Form
    Dim myControl As Control
    Set frm = Forms!Customers
    Set myControl = frm.CompanyName
    myControl.Visible = False
End Sub
```

8. To run the procedure, click any line between the Sub and End Sub keywords and press **F5** or choose **Run | Run Sub/UserForm**.

The procedure begins with the declaration of two object variables called frm and myControl. The object variable frm is set to reference the Customers form. For the procedure to work, the referenced form must be open. Next, the myControl object variable is set to point to the CompanyName control located on the Customers form.

Instead of using the object's entire address, you can use the shortcut — the name of the object variable. For example, the statement

```
Set myControl = frm.CompanyName
```

is the same as

```
Set myControl = Forms!Customers.CompanyName
```

The purpose of this procedure is to hide the control referenced by the object variable myControl. After running the HideControl procedure, switch to the Microsoft Access window containing the open Customers form. The CompanyName control should not be visible on the form.

 Note: To make the CompanyName text box visible again, modify the last line of this procedure by setting the Visible property of myControl to True and rerun the procedure.

Advantages of Using Object Variables

The advantages of object variables are:

- They can be used instead of the actual object.
- They are shorter and easier to remember than the actual values they point to.
- You can change their meaning while your procedure is running.

When the object variable is no longer needed, you should assign Nothing to it. This frees up memory and system resources:

```
Set frm = Nothing
Set myControl = Nothing
```

Finding a Variable Definition

When you find an instruction that assigns a value to a variable in a VBA procedure, you can quickly locate the definition of the variable by selecting the variable name and pressing Shift+F2. Alternately, you can choose View | Definition. Visual Basic will jump to the variable declaration line. To return your mouse pointer to its previous position, press Ctrl+Shift+F2 or choose View | Last Position. Let's try it out.

◎ Hands-On 3-9: Finding a Variable Definition

This hands-on exercise requires prior completion of Hands-On 3-8.

1. Locate the code of the procedure **HideControl** you created in Hands-On 3-8.
2. Locate the statement **myControl.Visible** = .
3. Right-click the **myControl** variable name and choose **Definition** from the shortcut menu.
4. Press **Ctrl+Shift+F2 to** return to the previous location in the procedure code (myControl.Visible =).

What Type Is This Variable?

Visual Basic has a built-in VarType function that returns an integer indicating the variable's type. Let's see how you can use this function in the Immediate window.

◎ Hands-On 3-10: Asking Questions about the Variable Type

1. Open the Immediate window (**View | Immediate Window**) and type the following statements that assign values to variables:

```
age = 28
birthdate = #1/1/1981#
firstName = "John"
```

2. Now, ask Visual Basic what type of data each variable holds:

```
?varType(age)
```

When you press **Enter**, Visual Basic returns 2. The number 2 represents the Integer data type.

```
?varType(birthdate)
```

Now Visual Basic returns 7 for Date. If you make a mistake in the variable name (let's say you type birthday instead of birthdate), Visual Basic returns zero (0).

```
?varType(firstName)
```

Visual Basic tells you that the value stored in the firstName variable is a String (8).

Table 3-3: Values returned by the VarType function

Constant	Value	Description
vbEmpty	0	Empty (uninitialized)
vbNull	1	Null (no valid data)
vbInteger	2	Integer
vbLong	3	Long integer
vbSingle	4	Single-precision floating-point number
vbDouble	5	Double-precision floating-point number
vbCurrency	6	Currency value
vbDate	7	Date value
vbString	8	String
vbObject	9	Object
vbError	10	Error value
vbBoolean	11	Boolean value
vbVariant	12	Variant (used only with arrays of variants)
vbDataObject	13	Data access object
vbDecimal	14	Decimal value
vbByte	17	Byte value
vbUserDefinedType	36	Variants that contain user-defined types
vbArray	8192	Array

Using Constants in VBA Procedures

The value of a variable can change while your procedure is executing. If your procedure needs to refer to unchanged values over and over again, you should use constants. A *constant* is like a named variable that always refers to the same value. Visual Basic requires that you declare constants before you use them.

You declare constants by using the Const statement, as in the following examples:

```
Const dialogName = "Enter Data" As String
Const slsTax = 8.5
Const Discount = 0.5
Const ColorIdx = 3
```

A constant, like a variable, has a scope. To make a constant available within a single procedure, you declare it at the procedure level, just below the name of the procedure. For instance:

```
Sub WedAnniv()
    Const Age As Integer = 25
    ...instructions...
End Sub
```

If you want to use a constant in all the procedures of a module, use the Private keyword in front of the Const statement. For instance:

```
Private Const dsk = "B:" As String
```

The Private constant has to be declared at the top of the module, just before the first Sub statement.

If you want to make a constant available to all modules in your application, use the Public keyword in front of the Const statement. For instance:

```
Public Const NumOfChar = 255 As Integer
```

The Public constant has to be declared at the top of the module, just before the first Sub statement.

When declaring a constant, you can use any one of the following data types: Boolean, Byte, Integer, Long, Currency, Single, Double, Date, String, or Variant.

Like variables, constants can be declared on one line if separated by commas. For instance:

```
Const Age As Integer = 25, City As String = "Denver", PayCheck As Currency =
350
```

Using constants makes your VBA procedures more readable and easier to maintain. For example, if you refer to a certain value several times in your procedure, instead of using a value, use a constant. This way, if the value changes (for example, the sales tax goes up), you can simply change the value in the declaration of the Const statement instead of tracking down every occurrence of the value.

Intrinsic Constants

Both Microsoft Access and Visual Basic for Applications have a long list of predefined (intrinsic) constants that do not need to be declared. These built-in constants can be looked up using the Object Browser window, which was discussed in detail in Chapter 2.

Let's open the Object Browser to take a look at the list of constants in Access.

◎ Hands-On 3-11: Exploring Access's Constants

1. In the Visual Basic Editor window, choose **View | Object Browser**.

2. In the Project/Library list box, click the drop-down arrow and select the **Access** library.

3. Enter **constants** as the search text in the Search Text box and either press **Enter** or click the **Search** button. Visual Basic shows the results of the search in the Search Results area. The right side of the Object Browser window displays a list of all built-in constants available in the Microsoft Access Object Library. Notice that the names of all the constants begin with the prefix "ac."

Figure 3-1: Use the Object Browser to look up any intrinsic constant.

4. To look up VBA constants, choose **VBA** in the Project/Library list box. Notice that the names of the VBA built-in constants begin with the prefix "vb."

Hands-On 3-12 illustrates how to use the intrinsic constants acFilterByForm and acFilterAdvanced to disable execution of filtering on a form.

◎ Hands-On 3-12: Using Intrinsic Constants in a VBA Procedure

This hands-on exercise uses the HandsOn_03_8.accdb database file used in Hands-On 3-8.

1. Open the **Customers** form in Design view.

2. In the property sheet, click the **Event** tab. Make sure that **Form** is selected in the drop-down box on the top of the property sheet.

3. Click to the right of the **On Filter** property and select the **Build** button (...).

4. In the Choose Builder dialog box, select **Code Builder** and click **OK**.

5. In the Code window, enter the **Form_Filter** event procedure code as shown below. (You can copy the procedure code from the **HandsOn_ 03.txt** file in the **Acc07_HandsOn** folder.)

```
Private Sub Form_Filter(Cancel As Integer, FilterType As Integer)
    If FilterType = acFilterByForm Or _
    FilterType = acFilterAdvanced Then
        MsgBox "You need authorization to filter records."
        Cancel = True
    End If
End Sub
```

6. Press **Alt+F11** to switch back to Design view in the Customers form.

7. Right-click the Customers form tab and choose **Form View**. You can also use the Views section of the Design tab to activate the Form view.

8. Choose **Home | Sort & Filter | Advanced Filter Options | Filter By Form**.

Access displays the message "You need authorization to filter records." The same message appears when you choose Advanced Filter/Sort from the Advanced Filter Options.

Grouping Constants with the Enum Type

If your application needs to use a set of related constants, consider declaring them with an enumerated data type. VBA has an enumerated data type (Enum) that you can use to define your constant values. The following code entered in a standard module creates an Enum that defines various status types:

```
Public Enum StatusType
    Rejected = 0
    MoreInfo = 1
    Approved = 2
    Completed = 3
End Enum
```

Notice that the Enum statement is always followed by the name of the enumeration. Within the Enum statement you simply list the names of constants you need to use. You can assign values to the constants using the equal sign (=). If you don't assign values, the first constant in the enumeration will be given the value zero (0), the second constant the value 1, and so on. The values assigned within the Enum statement are constant and can't be changed at run time.

To end the enumeration, use the End Enum statement.

The StatusType enumeration will be visible throughout the entire VBA project. Enum types are Public by default. To limit the visibility of the Enum type to the module in which it was declared, use the Private keyword.

Once you have defined your custom Enum object, you can refer to the specific constant by typing the name of the enumeration followed by a dot operator and the name of the constant. As soon as you enter the Enum name followed by a period, Visual Basic will display a list of available constants, as shown in Figure 3-2.

The following VBA procedure shows how to use the constants listed in the StatusType enumeration. You can enter this procedure in the same standard module where you have defined the Enum StatusType.

```
Sub GetStatusType()
    Dim result As Integer
    result = InputBox("Please enter a number from 0 to 3", "Status Type", 0)

    If result = StatusType.MoreInfo Then
        MsgBox ("Please provide more details on a separate form.")
    ElseIf result = StatusType.Rejected Then
        MsgBox ("Please apply again next year.")
    ElseIf result >= StatusType.Approved Then
        MsgBox ("Thank you for applying.")
    End If
End Sub
```

The above VBA procedure uses two popular built-in functions (InputBox and MsgBox) that allow interaction with the procedure's end users. These functions are covered in detail in the next chapter. The InputBox function prompts the user to type a number for the status type. Zero (0) is specified as the default value. When the user enters the value and clicks OK in the input box, the supplied value will be stored in a local variable named result. The remaining code of the GetStatusType procedure uses the If...Then...ElseIf conditional statement (see Chapter 5) to determine which message text should be displayed to the user. The MsgBox function used in this example specifies just a simple text message. Before a specific message is displayed, the value in the result variable is compared to the value of the enumerated constant.

By using enumerated data types instead of hard-coding values, you make your programming code easier to understand and reduce the chance of accidental errors.

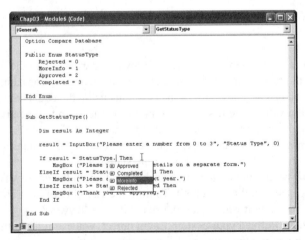

Figure 3-2: VBA provides a list of constants to choose from after you type your custom Enum name followed by a dot operator.

Chapter Summary

This chapter introduced several new VBA concepts. You found in it information about data types, variables, and constants. You learned how to declare various types of variables and constants. You also saw the difference between a variable and a constant.

In the next chapter, you will expand your knowledge of Visual Basic for Applications by using procedures and functions with arguments. In addition, you will learn about functions that allow your VBA procedures to interact with the user.

Chapter 4

Passing Arguments to Procedures and Functions

As you already know from Chapter 1, VBA procedures (both subroutines and functions) often require arguments to perform certain tasks. In this chapter, you learn various methods of passing arguments to procedures and functions.

Writing a Function Procedure

Function procedures can perform calculations based on data received through arguments. When you declare a function procedure, you list the names of arguments inside a set of parentheses, as shown in Hands-On 4-1.

⊚ Hands-On 4-1: Writing a Function Procedure with Arguments

1. Start Microsoft Office Access 2007 and create a new database named **Chap04.accdb** in your **C:\Acc07_ByExample** folder.

2. Once your new database is opened, press **Alt+F11** to switch to the Visual Basic Editor window.

3. Choose **Insert | Module** to add a new standard module and notice that Module1 appears under the Modules folder in the Project Explorer window.

4. In the Module1 (Code) window, enter the code of the **JoinText** function procedure as shown below. (You may copy this procedure from the **C:\Acc07_HandsOn\HandsOn_04.txt** file.)

```
Function JoinText(k, o)
    JoinText = k + " " + o
End Function
```

Note that there is a space character in quotation marks concatenated between the two arguments of the JoinText function's result: JoinText = k + " " + o.

A better way of adding a space is by using one of the built-in functions as shown below:

```
JoinText = k + Space(1) + o
```

or:

```
JoinText = k + Chr(32) + o
```

The Space function returns a string of spaces as indicated by the number in the parentheses. The Chr function returns a string containing the character associated with the specified character code.

Other control characters you may need to use when writing your VBA procedures are listed below:

Tab	Chr(9)
Line Feed	Chr(10)
Carriage Return	Chr(13)

You can execute a function procedure from the Immediate window, or you can write a subroutine to call the function. See Hands-On 4-2 and 4-3 for instructions on how to run the JoinText function procedure using these two methods.

◎ Hands-On 4-2: Executing a Function Procedure from the Immediate Window

This hands-on exercise requires prior completion of Hands-On 4-1.

1. Choose **View | Immediate Window** or press **Ctrl+G**, and enter the following statement:

```
?JoinText("function", " procedure")
```

Notice that as soon as you type the opening parenthesis, Visual Basic displays the arguments that the function expects. Type the value of the first argument, enter the comma, and supply the value of the second argument. Finish off by entering the closing parenthesis.

2. Press **Enter** to execute the above statement from the Immediate window. When you press Enter, the string "function procedure" appears in the Immediate window.

You can also execute a function procedure programmatically, as demonstrated in Hands-On 4-3.

◎ Hands-On 4-3: Executing a Function Procedure from a Subroutine

This hands-on exercise requires prior completion of Hands-On 4-1.

1. In the same module where you entered the JoinText function procedure, enter the following **EnterText** subroutine:

```
Sub EnterText()
    Dim strFirst As String, strLast As String, strFull As String

    strFirst = InputBox("Enter your first name:")
    strLast = InputBox("Enter your last name:")
    strFull = JoinText(strFirst, strLast)

    MsgBox strFull
End Sub
```

2. Place the cursor anywhere inside the code of the EnterText procedure and press **F5** to run it.

As Visual Basic executes the statements of the EnterText procedure, it uses the InputBox function to collect the data from the user, then stores the data (the values of the first and last names) in the variables strFirst and strLast. Then these values are passed to the JoinText function. Visual Basic substitutes the variables' contents for the arguments of the JoinText function and assigns the result to the name of the function (JoinText). When Visual Basic returns to the EnterText procedure it stores the function's value in the strFull variable. The MsgBox function then displays the contents of the strFull variable in a message box. The result is the full name of the user (first and last name separated by a space).

More about Arguments

Argument names are like variables. Each argument name refers to whatever value you provide at the time the function is called. You write a subroutine to call a function procedure. When a subroutine calls a function procedure, it passes it the required arguments as variables. Once the function does something, the result is assigned to the function name. Notice that the function procedure's name is used as if it were a variable.

Specifying the Data Type for a Function's Result

Like variables, functions can have types. The data type of your function's result can be a String, Integer, Long, etc. To specify the data type for your function's result, add the As keyword and the name of the desired data type to the end of the function declaration line. For example:

```
Function MultiplyIt(num1, num2) As Integer
```

If you don't specify the data type, Visual Basic assigns the default type (Variant) to your function's result. When you specify the data type for your function's result, you get the same advantages as when you specify the data type for your variables — your procedure uses memory more efficiently, and therefore runs faster.

Let's take a look at an example of a function that returns an integer, although the arguments passed to it are declared as Single in a calling subroutine.

◎ Hands-On 4-4: Calling a Function from a Procedure

1. In the Visual Basic Editor window, choose **Insert | Module** to add a new module.

2. Enter the following **HowMuch** subroutine in the Code window:

```
Sub HowMuch()
    Dim num1 As Single
    Dim num2 As Single
    Dim result As Single

    num1 = 45.33
    num2 = 19.24
    result = MultiplyIt(num1, num2)

    MsgBox result
End Sub
```

3. Enter the following **MultiplyIt** function procedure in the Code window below the HowMuch subroutine:

```
Function MultiplyIt(num1, num2) As Integer

    MultiplyIt = num1 * num2

End Function
```

4. Click anywhere within the HowMuch procedure and press **F5** to run it.

Because the values stored in the variables num1 and num2 are not whole numbers, to ensure that the result of the multiplication is a whole number, you may want to assign the Integer type to the result of the function. If you don't assign the data type to the MultiplyIt function's result, the HowMuch procedure will display the result in the data type specified in the declaration line of the result variable. Instead of 872, the result of the multiplication will be 872.1492.

To make the MultiplyIt function more useful, instead of hard-coding the values to be used in the multiplication, you can pass different values each time you run the procedure by using the InputBox function.

5. Take a few minutes to modify the HowMuch procedure on your own, following the example of the EnterText subroutine that was created in Hands-On 4-3.

6. To pass a specific value from a function to a subroutine, assign the value to the function name. For example, the NumOfDays function shown below passes the value of 7 to the subroutine DaysInAWeek.

```
Function NumOfDays()
    NumOfDays = 7
End Function

Sub DaysInAWeek()
    MsgBox "There are " & NumOfDays & " days in a week."
End Sub
```

Subroutines or Functions: Which Should You Use?

Create a subroutine when you:

- Want to perform some actions.
- Want to get input from the user.
- Want to display a message on the screen.

Create a function when you:

- Want to perform a simple calculation more than once.
- Must perform complex computations.
- Must call the same block of instructions more than once.
- Want to check if a certain expression is true or false.

Passing Arguments by Reference and by Value

In some procedures, when you pass arguments as variables, Visual Basic can suddenly change the value of the variables. To ensure that the called function procedure does not alter the value of the passed arguments, you should precede the name of the argument in the function's declaration line with the ByVal keyword. Let's practice this with an example.

◎ Hands-On 4-5: Passing Arguments to Subroutines and Functions

1. In the Visual Basic Editor window, choose **Insert | Module** to add a new module.

2. In the Code window, type the **ThreeNumbers** subroutine and the **MyAverage** function procedure as shown below.

```
Sub ThreeNumbers()
    Dim num1 As Integer, num2 As Integer, num3 As Integer

    num1 = 10
    num2 = 20
    num3 = 30

    MsgBox MyAverage(num1, num2, num3)
    MsgBox num1
    MsgBox num2
    MsgBox num3
End Sub

Function MyAverage(ByVal num1, ByVal num2, ByVal num3)
    num1 = num1 + 1
    MyAverage = (num1 + num2 + num3) / 3
End Function
```

3. Click anywhere within the ThreeNumbers procedure and press **F5** to run it.

The ThreeNumbers procedure assigns values to three variables, and then calls the MyAverage function to perform and return the average of the numbers stored in these variables. The function's arguments are the names of the variables: num1, num2, and num3. Notice that all variable names are preceded with the ByVal keyword. Also, notice that prior to the calculation of the average, the MyAverage function changes the value of the num1 variable. Inside the function procedure, the num1 variable equals 11 (10 + 1). Therefore, when the function passes the calculated average to the ThreeNumbers procedure, the MsgBox function displays the result as 20.3333333333333 and not 20, as expected. The next three functions show the contents of each of the variables. The values stored in these variables are the same as the original values assigned to them: 10, 20, and 30.

What will happen if you omit the ByVal keyword in front of the num1 argument in the MyAverage function's declaration line? The function's result will still be the same, but the content of the num1 variable displayed by the MsgBox num1 is now 11. The MyAverage function has not only returned an unexpected result (20.3333333333333 instead of 20), but also has modified the original data stored in the num1 variable. To prevent Visual Basic from permanently changing the values supplied to the function, use the ByVal keyword.

Know Your Keywords: ByRef and ByVal

Because any of the variables passed to a function procedure (or a subroutine) can be changed by the receiving procedure, it is important to know how to protect the original value of a variable. Visual Basic has two keywords that give or deny the permission to change the contents of a variable: ByRef and ByVal.

By default, Visual Basic passes information to a function procedure (or a subroutine) by reference (ByRef keyword), referring to the original data specified in the function's argument at the time the function is called. So, if the function alters the value of the argument, the original value is changed. You will get this result if you omit the ByVal keyword in front of the num1 argument in the MyAverage function's declaration line. If you want the function procedure to change the original value, you don't need to explicitly insert the ByRef keyword, because passed variables default to ByRef.

When you use the ByVal keyword in front of an argument name, Visual Basic passes the argument by value, which means that Visual Basic makes a copy of the original data. This copy is then passed to a function. If the function changes the value of an argument passed by value, the original data does not change — only the copy changes. That's why when the MyAverage function changed the value of the num1 argument, the original value of the num1 variable remained the same.

Using Optional Arguments

At times, you may want to supply an additional value to a function. Let's say you have a function that calculates the price of a meal per person. Sometimes, however, you'd like the function to perform the same calculation for a group of two or more people. To indicate that a procedure argument isn't always required, you precede the name of the argument with the Optional keyword. Arguments that are optional come at the end of the argument list, following the names of all the required arguments. Optional arguments must always be the Variant data type. This means that you can't specify the optional argument's type by using the As keyword.

In the preceding section, you created a function to calculate the average of three numbers. Suppose that sometimes you would like to use this function to calculate the average of two numbers. You could define the third argument of the MyAverage function as optional. To preserve the original MyAverage function, let's create the Avg function to calculate the average for two or three numbers.

◎ Hands-On 4-6: Using Optional Arguments

1. In the Visual Basic Editor window, choose **Insert | Module** to add a new module.

2. Type the following **Avg** function procedure in the Code window:

```
Function Avg(num1, num2, Optional num3)
    Dim totalNums As Integer

    totalNums = 3
    If IsMissing(num3) Then
        num3 = 0
        totalNums = totalNums - 1
    End If
    Avg = (num1 + num2 + num3) / totalNums
End Function
```

3. Call this function from the Immediate window by entering the following instruction and pressing **Enter**:

```
?Avg(2, 3)
```

As soon as you press Enter, Visual Basic displays the result: 2.5.

4. Now, type the following instruction and press **Enter**:

```
?Avg(2, 3, 5)
```

This time the result is: 3.3333333333333.

As you've seen, the Avg function allows you to calculate the average of two or three numbers. You decide what values and how many values (two or three) you want to average. When you start typing the values for the function's arguments in the Immediate window, Visual Basic displays the name of the optional argument enclosed in square brackets.

Let's take a few minutes to analyze the Avg function. This function can take up to three arguments. Arguments num1 and num2 are required. Argument num3 is optional. Notice that the name of the optional argument is preceded by the Optional keyword. The Optional argument is listed at the end of the argument list. Because the types of the num1, num2, and num3 arguments are not declared, Visual Basic treats all three arguments as Variants.

Inside the function procedure, the totalNums variable is declared as an Integer and then assigned a beginning value of 3. Because the function has to be capable of calculating an average of two or three numbers, the handy built-in function IsMissing checks for the number of supplied arguments. If the third (optional) argument is not supplied, the IsMissing function puts the value of zero (0) in its place, and deducts the value of 1 from the value stored in the totalNums variable. Hence, if the optional argument is missing, totalNums is 2. The next statement calculates the average based on the supplied data, and the result is assigned to the name of the function.

Using the IsMissing Function

The IsMissing function called from within Hands-On 4-6 allows you to determine whether or not the optional argument was supplied. This function returns the logical value of True if the third argument is not supplied, and returns False when the third argument is given. The IsMissing function is used here with the decision-making statement If…Then (discussed in Chapter 5). If the num3 argument is missing (IsMissing), then Visual Basic supplies a zero (0) for the value of the third argument (num3 = 0), and reduces the value stored in the argument totalNums by 1 (totalNums = totalNums – 1).

Testing a Function Procedure

To test whether a custom function does what it was designed to do, write a simple subroutine that will call the function and display its result. In addition, the subroutine should show the original values of arguments. This way, you'll be able to quickly determine when the argument value was altered. If the function procedure uses optional arguments, you'll also need to check those situations in which the optional arguments may be missing.

Built-in Functions

VBA comes with many built-in functions that can be looked up in the Visual Basic online help. To access an alphabetical listing of all VBA functions, choose Help | Microsoft Visual Basic Help in the Visual Basic Editor window. In the Table of Contents, choose Visual Basic for Applications Language Reference | Visual Basic Language Reference | Functions.

One of the features of a good program is its interaction with the user. When you work with Microsoft Access, you interact with the application by using various dialog boxes such as message boxes and input boxes. When you write your own procedures, you can use the MsgBox function to inform the users about an unexpected error or the result of a specific calculation. So far you have seen a simple implementation of this function. In the next section, you will find out how to control the appearance of your message. Then you will learn how to get information from the user with the InputBox function.

Using the MsgBox Function

The MsgBox function you have used thus far was limited to displaying a message to the user in a simple, one-button dialog box. You closed the message box by clicking the OK button or pressing the Enter key. You can create a simple message box by following the MsgBox function name with the text enclosed in quotation marks. In other words, to display the message "The procedure is complete." you use the following statement:

```
MsgBox "The procedure is complete."
```

You can try the above instruction by entering it in the Immediate window. When you type this instruction and press Enter, Visual Basic displays the message box shown in Figure 4-1.

Figure 4-1: To display a message to the user, place the text as the argument of the MsgBox function.

The MsgBox function allows you to use other arguments that make it possible to determine the number of buttons that should be available in the message box or to change the title of the message box from the default. You can also assign your own help topic. The syntax of the MsgBox function is shown below.

```
MsgBox (prompt [, buttons] [, title], [, helpfile, context])
```

Notice that while the MsgBox function has five arguments, only the first one, prompt, is required. The arguments listed in square brackets are optional.

When you enter a long text string for the prompt argument, Visual Basic decides how to break the text so it fits the message box. Let's do some exercises in the Immediate window to learn various text formatting techniques.

◎ Hands-On 4-7: Formatting the Message Box

1. In the Visual Basic Editor window, activate the Immediate window and enter the following instruction. Be sure to enter the entire text string on one line, and then press **Enter**.

```
MsgBox "All done. Now open ""Test.doc"" and place an empty CD in the CD-ROM
drive. The following procedure will copy this file to the CD."
```

As soon as you press **Enter**, Visual Basic shows the resulting dialog box. If you get a compile error, click **OK**. Then, make sure that the name of the file is surrounded by double quotation marks (""Test.doc"").

Figure 4-2: This long message will look more appealing to the user when you take the text formatting into your own hands.

When the text of your message is particularly long, you can break it into several lines using the VBA Chr function. The Chr function's argument is a number from 0 to 255, which returns a character represented by this number. For example, Chr(13) returns a carriage return character (this is the same as pressing the Enter key), and Chr(10) returns a linefeed character (this is useful for adding spacing between the text lines).

2. Modify the instruction entered in the previous step in the following way:

```
MsgBox "All done." & Chr(13) & "Now open ""Test.doc"" and place" & Chr(13) &
"an empty CD in the CD-ROM drive." & Chr(13) & "The following procedure will
copy this file to the CD."
```

Figure 4-3: You can break a long text string into several lines by using the Chr(13) function.

You must surround each text fragment by quotation marks. Quoted text embedded in a text string requires an additional set of quotation marks, as in """Test.doc"". The Chr(13) function indicates a place where you'd like to start a new line. The concatenate character (&) is used to combine the strings. When you enter exceptionally long text messages on one line, it's easy to make a mistake. An underscore (_) is a special line continuation character in VBA that allows you to break a long VBA statement into several lines. Unfortunately, the line continuation character cannot be used in the Immediate window.

3. Add a new module by choosing **Insert | Module**.

4. In the Code window, enter the **MyMessage** subroutine as shown below. Be sure to precede each line continuation character with a space.

```
Sub MyMessage()
    MsgBox "All done." & Chr(13) _
    & "Now open ""Test.doc"" and place" & Chr(13) _
    & "an empty CD in the CD-ROM drive." & Chr(13) _
    & "The following procedure will copy this file to the CD."
End Sub
```

5. Position the insertion point within the code of the MyMessage procedure and press **F5** to run it.

When you run the MyMessage procedure, Visual Basic displays the same message as the one illustrated in Figure 4-3.

As you can see, the text entered on several lines is more readable, and the code is easier to maintain. To improve the readability of your message, you may want to add more spacing between the text lines by including blank lines. To do this, use two Chr(13) or two Chr(10) functions, as shown in the following step.

6. Enter the following **MyMessage2** procedure:

```
Sub MyMessage2()
    MsgBox "All done." & Chr(10) & Chr(10) _
    & "Now open ""Test.doc"" and place" & Chr(13) _
    & "an empty CD in the CD-ROM drive." & Chr(13) & Chr(13) _
    & "The following procedure will copy this file to the CD."
End Sub
```

7. Position the insertion point within the code of the MyMessage2 procedure and press **F5** to run it.

Figure 4-4: You can increase the readability of your message by increasing spacing between selected text lines.

Now that you have mastered the text formatting techniques, let's take a closer look at the next argument of the MsgBox function. Although the buttons argument is optional, it's frequently used. The buttons argument specifies how many and what types of buttons you want to appear in the message box. This argument can be a constant or a number (see Table 4-1). If you omit this argument, the resulting message box includes only the OK button, as you've seen in the preceding examples.

Table 4-1: The MsgBox buttons argument settings

Constant	Value	Description
Button settings		
vbOKOnly	0	Displays only an OK button. This is the default.
vbOKCancel	1	OK and Cancel buttons
vbAbortRetryIgnore	2	Abort, Retry, and Ignore buttons
vbYesNoCancel	3	Yes, No, and Cancel buttons
vbYesNo	4	Yes and No buttons
vbRetryCancel	5	Retry and Cancel buttons
Icon settings		
vbCritical	16	Displays the Critical Message icon
vbQuestion	32	Displays the Question Message icon
vbExclamation	48	Displays the Warning Message icon
vbInformation	64	Displays the Information Message icon
Default button settings		
vbDefaultButton1	0	The first button is default
vbDefaultButton2	256	The second button is default
vbDefaultButton3	512	The third button is default
vbDefaultButton4	768	The fourth button is default

Constant	Value	Description
Message box modality		
vbApplicationModal	0	The user must respond to the message before continuing to work in the current application.
vbSystemModal	4096	On Win16 systems, this constant is used to prevent the user from interacting with any other window until he or she dismisses the message box. On Win32 systems, this constant works like the vbApplicationModal constant (see above) with the following exception: The message box always remains on top of any other programs you may have running.
Other MsgBox display settings		
vbMsgBoxHelpButton	16384	Adds the Help button to the message box
vbMsgBoxSetForeground	65536	Specifies the message box window as the foreground window
vbMsgBoxRight	524288	Text is right aligned
vbMsgBoxRtlReading	1048576	Text appears as right-to-left reading on Hebrew and Arabic systems

When should you use the buttons argument? Suppose you want the user of your procedure to respond to a question with Yes or No. Your message box may then require two buttons. If a message box includes more than one button, one of them is considered a default button. When the user presses Enter, the default button is selected automatically.

Because you can display various types of messages (critical, warning, information), you can visually indicate the importance of the message by including the graphical representation (icon). In addition to the type of message, the buttons argument can include a setting to determine if the message box must be closed before the user switches to another application. It's quite possible that the user may want to switch to another program or perform another task before he responds to the question posed in your message box. If the message box is application modal (vbApplicationModal), then the user must close the message box before continuing to use your application.

For example, consider the following message box:

```
MsgBox "How are you?", vbOKOnly + vbApplicationModal, "Application Modal"
```

If you type the above in the Immediate window and press Enter, a message box will pop up and you won't be able to work with your currently open Microsoft Office Access application until you respond to the message box.

On the other hand, if you want to keep the message box visible while the user works with other open applications, you must include the vbSystemModal setting in the buttons argument, like this:

```
MsgBox "How are you?", vbOKOnly + vbSystemModal, "System Modal"
```

 Note: Use the vbSystemModal constant when you want to ensure that your message box is always visible (not hidden behind other windows).

The buttons argument settings are divided into five groups: button settings, icon settings, default button settings, message box modality, and other MsgBox display settings (see Table 4-1). Only one setting from each group can be included in the buttons argument. To create a buttons argument you can add up the values for each setting you want to include. For example, to display a message box with two buttons (Yes and No), the question mark icon, and the No button as the default button, look up the corresponding values in Table 4-1, and add them up. You should arrive at 292 (4 + 32 + 256).

To see the message box using the calculated message box argument, enter the following statement in the Immediate window:

```
MsgBox "Do you want to proceed?", 292
```

The resulting message box is shown in Figure 4-5.

Figure 4-5: You can specify the number of buttons to include, their text, and an icon in the message box by using the optional buttons argument.

When you derive the buttons argument by adding up the constant values, your procedure becomes less readable. There's no reference table where you can check the hidden meaning of 292. To improve the readability of your MsgBox function, it's better to use the constants instead of their values. For example, enter the following revised statement in the Immediate window:

```
MsgBox "Do you want to proceed?", vbYesNo + vbQuestion + vbDefaultButton2
```

The above statement produces the result shown in Figure 4-5. The following example shows how to use the buttons argument inside the Visual Basic procedure.

◉ Hands-On 4-8: Using the MsgBox Function with Arguments

1. In the Visual Basic Editor window, choose **Insert | Module** to add a new module.

2. In the Code window, enter the **MsgYesNo** subroutine as shown below.

```
Sub MsgYesNo()
    Dim question As String
    Dim myButtons As Integer

    question = "Do you want to open a new report?"
    myButtons = vbYesNo + vbQuestion + vbDefaultButton2
    MsgBox question, myButtons
End Sub
```

3. Run the MsgYesNo procedure by pressing **F5**.

In the above subroutine, the question variable stores the text of your message. The settings for the buttons argument are placed in the myButtons variable. Instead of using the names of constants, you can use their values, as in the following:

```
myButtons = 4 + 32 + 256
```

The question and myButtons variables are used as arguments for the MsgBox function. When you run the procedure, you see a result similar to the one shown in Figure 4-5. Note that the No button is selected, indicating that it's the default button for this dialog box. If you press Enter, Visual Basic removes the message box from the screen. Nothing happens because your procedure does not have any instructions following the MsgBox function. To change the default button, use the vbDefaultButton1 setting instead.

The third argument of the MsgBox function is title. While this is also an optional argument, it's very handy because it allows you to create procedures that don't provide visual clues to the fact that you programmed them with Microsoft Access. Using this argument, you can set the title bar of your message box to any text you want.

Suppose you want the MsgYesNo procedure to display the text "New report" in its title. The following MsgYesNo2 procedure demonstrates the use of the title argument.

```
Sub MsgYesNo2()
    Dim question As String
    Dim myButtons As Integer
    Dim myTitle As String

    question = "Do you want to open a new report?"
    myButtons = vbYesNo + vbQuestion + vbDefaultButton2
    myTitle = "New report"
    MsgBox question, myButtons, myTitle
End Sub
```

The text for the title argument is stored in the myTitle variable. If you don't specify the value for the title argument, Visual Basic displays the default text "Microsoft Access." Notice that the arguments are listed in the order determined by the MsgBox function.

If you would like to list the arguments in any order, you must precede the value of each argument with its name, as shown below:

```
MsgBox title:=myTitle, prompt:=question, buttons:=myButtons
```

The last two MsgBox arguments, helpfile and context, are used by more advanced programmers who are experienced with using help files in the Windows environment. The helpfile argument indicates the name of a special help file that contains additional information you may want to display to your VBA application user. When you specify this argument, the Help button will be added to your message box. When you use the helpfile argument, you must also use the context argument. This argument indicates which help subject in the specified help file you want to display. Suppose HelpX.hlp is the help file you created and 55 is the context topic you want to use. To include this information in your MsgBox function, you would use the following instruction:

```
MsgBox title:=myTitle, _
    prompt:=question, _
    buttons:=myButtons, _
```

```
helpfile:= "HelpX.hlp", _
context:=55
```

The above is a single VBA statement broken down into several lines using the line continuation character.

Returning Values from the MsgBox Function

When you display a simple message box dialog with one button, clicking the OK button or pressing the Enter key removes the message box from the screen. However, when the message box has more than one button, your procedure should detect which button was pressed. To do this, you must save the result of the message box in a variable. Table 4-2 shows values that the MsgBox function returns.

Table 4-2: Values returned by the MsgBox function

Button Selected	Constant	Value
OK	vbOK	1
Cancel	vbCancel	2
Abort	vbAbort	3
Retry	vbRetry	4
Ignore	vbIgnore	5
Yes	vbYes	6
No	vbNo	7

The MsgYesNo3 procedure is a revised version of MsgYesNo2. It shows how you can find out which button the user chose.

◎ Hands-On 4-9: Returning Values from the MsgBox Function

1. In the Visual Basic Editor window, choose **Insert | Module** to add a new module.

2. In the Code window, enter the code of the **MsgYesNo3** procedure as shown below:

```
Sub MsgYesNo3()
    Dim question As String
    Dim myButtons As Integer
    Dim myTitle As String
    Dim myChoice As Integer

    question = "Do you want to open a new report?"
    myButtons = vbYesNo + vbQuestion + vbDefaultButton2
    myTitle = "New report"
    myChoice = MsgBox(question, myButtons, myTitle)
    MsgBox myChoice
End Sub
```

3. Position the insertion point within the MsgYesNo3 procedure and press **F5** to run it.

In the above procedure, you assigned the result of the MsgBox function to the variable myChoice. Notice that the arguments of the MsgBox function are now listed in parentheses:

```
myChoice = MsgBox(question, myButtons, myTitle)
```

When you run the MsgYesNo3 procedure, a two-button message box is displayed. By clicking on the Yes button, the statement MsgBox myChoice displays the number 6. When you click the No button, the number 7 is displayed.

MsgBox Function — With or without Parentheses?

Use parentheses around the MsgBox function argument list when you want to use the result returned by the function. By listing the function's arguments without parentheses, you tell Visual Basic that you want to ignore the function's result. Most likely, you will want to use the function's result when the message box contains more than one button.

Using the InputBox Function

The InputBox function displays a dialog box with a message that prompts the user to enter data. This dialog box has two buttons: OK and Cancel. When you click OK, the InputBox function returns the information entered in the text box. When you select Cancel, the function returns the empty string (""). The syntax of the InputBox function is as follows:

```
InputBox(prompt [, title] [, default] [, xpos] [, ypos] [, helpfile, context])
```

The first argument, prompt, is the text message you want to display in the dialog box. Long text strings can be entered on several lines by using the Chr(13) or Chr(10) functions. (See examples of using the MsgBox function earlier in this chapter.) All the remaining InputBox arguments are optional.

The second argument, title, allows you to change the default title of the dialog box. The default value is "Microsoft Access."

The third argument of the InputBox function, default, allows the display of a default value in the text box. If you omit this argument, the empty text box is displayed.

The following two arguments, xpos and ypos, let you specify the exact position where the dialog box should appear on the screen. If you omit these arguments, the input box appears in the middle of the current window. The xpos argument determines the horizontal position of the dialog box from the left edge of the screen. When omitted, the dialog box is centered horizontally. The ypos argument determines the vertical position from the top of the screen. If you omit this argument, the dialog box is positioned vertically approximately one-third of the way down the screen. Both xpos and ypos are measured in special units called *twips*. One twip is the equivalent of approximately 0.0007 inches.

The last two arguments, helpfile and context, are used in the same way as the corresponding arguments of the MsgBox function discussed earlier in this chapter.

Now that you know the meaning of the InputBox arguments, let's see some examples of using this function.

◎ Hands-On 4-10: Using the InputBox Function

1. In the Visual Basic Editor window, choose **Insert | Module** to add a new module.

2. In the Code window, type the **Informant** subroutine shown below:

```
Sub Informant()
    InputBox prompt:="Enter your place of birth:" & Chr(13) _
    & " (e.g., Boston, Great Falls, etc.) "
End Sub
```

3. Position the insertion point within the Informant procedure and press **F5** to run it.

   The above procedure displays a dialog box with two buttons. The input prompt is displayed on two lines (see Figure 4-6). Similar to using the MsgBox function, if you plan on using the data entered by the user in the dialog box, you should store the result of the InputBox function in a variable.

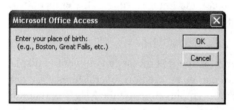

Figure 4-6: A dialog box generated by the Informant procedure.

4. Now, in the same module, enter the code of the **Informant2** procedure as shown below:

```
Sub Informant2()
    Dim myPrompt As String
    Dim town As String

    Const myTitle = "Enter data"
    myPrompt = "Enter your place of birth:" & Chr(13) _
    & "(e.g., Boston, Great Falls, etc.)"
    town = InputBox(myPrompt, myTitle)

    MsgBox "You were born in " & town & ".", , "Your response"
End Sub
```

5. Position the insertion point within the Informant2 procedure and press **F5** to run it.

   Notice that the Informant2 procedure assigns the result of the InputBox function to the town variable.

This time, the arguments of the InputBox function are listed in parentheses. Parentheses are required if you want to use the result of the InputBox function later in your procedure. The Informant2 subroutine uses a constant to specify the text to appear in the title bar of the dialog box. Because the constant value remains the same throughout the execution of your procedure, you can declare the input box title as a constant. However, if you'd rather use a variable, you still can.

When you run a procedure using the InputBox function, the dialog box generated by this function always appears in the same area of the screen. To change the location of the dialog box, you must supply the xpos and ypos arguments, explained earlier.

6. To display the dialog box in the top left-hand corner of the screen, modify the InputBox function in the Informant2 procedure as follows:

```
town = InputBox(myPrompt, myTitle, , 1, 200)
```

Notice that the argument myTitle is followed by two commas. The second comma marks the position of the omitted default argument. The next two arguments determine the horizontal and vertical position of the dialog box. If you omit the second comma after the myTitle argument, Visual Basic will use the number 1 as the value of the default argument. If you precede the values of arguments by their names (for example, prompt:=myPrompt, title:=myTitle, xpos:=1, ypos:=200), you won't have to remember to place a comma in the place of each omitted argument.

What will happen if, instead of the name of a town, you enter a number? Because users often supply incorrect data in the input box, your procedure must verify that the data the user entered can be used in further data manipulations. The InputBox function itself does not provide a facility for data validation. To validate user input, you must use other VBA instructions, which are discussed in the next chapter.

Converting Data Types

The result of the InputBox function is always a string. So if a user enters a number, its *string* value must be converted to a *numeric* value before your procedure can use the number in mathematical computations. Visual Basic is able to automatically convert many values from one data type to another.

◎ Hands-On 4-11: Converting Data Types

1. In the Visual Basic Editor window, choose **Insert | Module** to add a new module.

2. In the Code window, enter the **AddTwoNums** procedure as shown below:

```
Sub AddTwoNums()
    Dim myPrompt As String
    Dim value1 As String
```

```
Dim mySum As Single

Const myTitle = "Enter data"

myPrompt = "Enter a number:"
value1 = InputBox(myPrompt, myTitle, 0)
mySum = value1 + 2

    MsgBox mySum & " (" & value1 & " + 2)"
End Sub
```

3. Place the cursor anywhere inside the code of the AddTwoNums procedure and press **F5** to run it.

The above procedure displays the dialog box shown in Figure 4-7. Notice that this dialog box has two special features that are obtained by using the InputBox function's optional arguments: title and default value. Instead of the default title "Microsoft Access," the dialog box displays a text string as defined by the contents of the myTitle constant. The zero (0) entered as the default value in the edit box suggests that the user enter a number instead of text. Once the user provides the data and clicks OK, the input is assigned to the variable value1.

```
value1 = InputBox(myPrompt, myTitle, 0)
```

Figure 4-7: To suggest that the user enter a specific type of data, you may want to provide a default value in the edit box.

The data type of the variable value1 is String. You can check the data type easily if you follow the above instruction with this statement:

```
MsgBox varType(value1)
```

When Visual Basic runs the above line, it will display a message box with the number 8. Recall that this number represents the String data type. The next line,

```
mySum = value1 + 2
```

adds 2 to the user's input and assigns the result of the calculation to the variable mySum. And because the value1 variable's data type is String, prior to using this variable's data in the computation, Visual Basic goes to work behind the scenes to perform the data type conversion. Visual Basic has the brains to understand the need for conversion. Without it, the two incompatible data types (text and number) would generate a Type Mismatch error.

The procedure ends with the MsgBox function displaying the result of the calculation and showing the user how the total was derived.

Define a Constant

To ensure that all the title bars in a particular VBA procedure display the same text, assign the title text to a constant. By following this tip, you will save yourself the time of typing the title text in more than one place.

Avoid a Type Mismatch Error

If you attempt to run the AddTwoNums procedure in older versions of Microsoft Access (prior to version 2000), you will get a Type Mismatch error when Visual Basic tries to execute the following line of code:

```
mysum = value1 + 2
```

To avoid the Type Mismatch error, use the built-in CSng function to convert the string stored in the value1 variable to a Single type number. You would write the following statement:

```
mysum = CSng(value1) + 2
```

Using Master Procedures and Subprocedures

When your VBA procedure gets larger, it may be difficult to maintain its many lines of code. To make your program easier to write, understand, and change, you should use a structured approach. When you create a structured program, you break a large problem into small problems that can be solved one at a time. In VBA, you do this by creating a master procedure and one or more subordinate procedures. Because both master procedures and subordinate procedures are subroutines, you declare them with the Sub keyword. The master procedure can call the required subroutines and pass arguments to them. It may also call functions.

The following hands-on exercise demonstrates the AboutUser procedure. The procedure requests the user's full name, then extracts the first and last name from the fullName string. The last statement displays the user's last name followed by a comma and the first name. As you read further, this procedure will be broken down into several tasks to demonstrate the concept of using master procedures, subprocedures, and functions.

◎ Hands-On 4-12: Breaking Up Large Procedures

1. In the Visual Basic Editor window, choose **Insert | Module** to add a new module.

2. In the Code window, enter the code of the **AboutUser** procedure as shown below:

```
Sub AboutUser()
    Dim fullName As String
    Dim firstName As String
    Dim lastName As String
```

```
    Dim space As Integer

    ' get input from user
    fullName = InputBox("Enter first and last name:")

    ' get first and last name strings
    space = InStr(fullName, " ")
    firstName = Left(fullName, space - 1)
    lastName = Right(fullName, Len(fullName) - space)

    ' display last name, first name
    MsgBox lastName & ", " & firstName
End Sub
```

3. Position the insertion point within the code of the AboutUser procedure and press **F5** to run it.

   The AboutUser procedure can be divided into smaller tasks. The first task is obtaining the user's full name. The next task requires that you divide the user-supplied data into two strings: last name and first name. These tasks can be delegated to separate functions (for example: GetLast and GetFirst). The last task is displaying a message showing the reordered full name string.

   Now that you know what tasks you should focus on, let's see how you can accomplish each task.

4. In the Visual Basic Editor window, choose **File | Save Chap04**.

5. In the Save dialog box, click **Yes** to save changes to all the listed modules. Click **OK** to confirm the default module name in each Save As prompt.

6. In the Visual Basic Editor window, choose **Insert | Module** to add a new module.

7. Choose **File | Save Chap04** and type the new module name, **MasterProcedures**, in the Save As dialog box. Click **OK** when done.

8. Enter the following **AboutUserMaster** procedure in the MasterProcedures module window:

```
Sub AboutUserMaster()
    Dim first As String, last As String, full As String

    Call GetUserName(full)

    first = GetFirst(full)
    last = GetLast(full)

    Call DisplayLastFirst(first, last)
End Sub
```

The master procedure shown above controls the general flow of your program by calling appropriate subprocedures and functions. The master procedure begins with variable declarations. The first statement, Call GetUserName(full), calls the GetUserName subroutine (see step 9 below), and passes an argument to it — the contents of the full variable. Because the variable full is not assigned any value prior to the execution of the Call statement, it has the value of an empty string (""). Notice that the name of the subprocedure is preceded by the Call statement. Although you are not required to use the Call keyword when calling a procedure, you must use it when the call to the procedure requires arguments. The argument list must be enclosed in parentheses.

9. In the MasterProcedures module, enter the following **GetUserName** subroutine:

```
Sub GetUserName(fullName As String)

    fullName = InputBox("Enter first and last name:")

End Sub
```

The GetUserName procedure demonstrates two very important Visual Basic programming concepts: how to pass arguments to a subprocedure and how to pass values back from a subprocedure to a calling procedure.

In the master procedure in step 8, you called the GetUserName procedure and passed one argument to it — the variable full. This variable is received by a fullName parameter declared in the GetUserName subprocedure's Sub statement. Because the variable full contained an empty string, when Visual Basic called the GetUserName subprocedure, the fullName parameter received the same value — an empty string (""). When Visual Basic displays the dialog box and gets the user's full name, the name is assigned to the fullName parameter. A value assigned to a parameter is passed back to the matching argument after the subprocedure is executed. Therefore, when Visual Basic returns to the master procedure, the full variable will contain the user's full name.

Arguments passed to a subprocedure are received by *parameters*. Notice that the parameter name (fullName) is followed by the declaration of the data type (As String). Although the parameter's data type must agree with the data type of the matching argument, different names may be used for an argument and its corresponding parameter.

10. In the MasterProcedures module, enter the following **GetFirst** function procedure:

```
Function GetFirst(fullName As String)
    Dim space As Integer

    space = InStr(fullName, " ")
    GetFirst = Left(fullName, space - 1)
End Function
```

The second statement in the master procedure (see step 8), first = GetFirst(full), passes the value of the full variable to the GetFirst function. This value is received by the function's parameter — fullName. To extract the first name from the user-provided fullName string, you must find the location of the space separating the first name and last name. Therefore, the function begins with a declaration of a local variable — space. The next statement uses the VBA built-in function InStr to return the position of a space character (" ") in the fullName string. The obtained number is then assigned to the variable space. Finally, the Left function is used to extract the specified number of characters (space −1) from the left side of the fullName string. The length of the first name is one character less than the value stored in the variable space. The result of the function (user's first name) is then assigned to the function's name. When Visual Basic returns to the master procedure, it places the result in the variable first.

11. In the MasterProcedures module, enter the following **GetLast** function procedure:

```
Function GetLast(fullName As String)
    Dim space As Integer

    space = InStr(fullName, " ")
    GetLast = Right(fullName, Len(fullName) - space)
End Function
```

The third statement in the master procedure (see step 8), last = GetLast(full), passes the value of the full variable to the GetLast function. This function's purpose is to extract the user's last name from the user-supplied fullName string. The GetLast function uses the built-in Len function to calculate the total number of characters in the fullName string. The Right function extracts the specified number of characters (Len(fullName) − space) from the right side of the fullName string. The obtained string is then assigned to the function name and is stored in the variable last upon returning to the master procedure.

12. In the MasterProcedures module, enter the following **DisplayLastFirst** subroutine:

```
Sub DisplayLastFirst(firstName As String, lastName As String)

    MsgBox lastName & ", " & firstName

End Sub
```

The fourth statement in the master procedure (see step 8), Call DisplayLastFirst(first, last), calls the DisplayLastFirst subroutine and passes two arguments to it: first and last. To receive these arguments, the DisplayLastFirst subprocedure is declared with two matching parameters: firstName and lastName. Recall that different names can be used for arguments and their corresponding parameters. The DisplayLastFirst subprocedure then displays the message box showing the user's last name followed by a comma and the first name.

13. Position the insertion point within the code of the AboutUserMaster procedure and press **F5** to run it.

14. Choose **File | Save Chap04** to save changes to the module.

15. Choose **File | Close and Return to Microsoft Office Access**.

16. Close the Chap04.accdb database and exit Microsoft Office Access.

Arguments vs. Parameters

- An argument is a variable, constant, or expression that is passed to a subprocedure.
- A parameter is a variable that receives a value passed to a subprocedure.

Advantages of Using Subprocedures

- It's easier to maintain several subprocedures than one large procedure.
- A task performed by a subprocedure can be used by other procedures.
- Each subprocedure can be tested individually before being placed in the main program.
- Different people can work on individual subprocedures that constitute a larger procedure.

Chapter Summary

In this chapter, you learned the difference between subroutine procedures that perform actions and function procedures that return values. You saw examples of function procedures called from another Visual Basic procedure. You learned how to pass arguments to functions, and determine the data type of a function's result. You increased your repertoire of VBA keywords with the ByVal, ByRef, and Optional keywords. Finally, you learned how subprocedures can pass values back to the calling procedures with the help of parameters.

After working through this chapter, you should be able to create some custom functions of your own that are suited to your specific needs. You should also be able to interact easily with your users by employing the MsgBox and InputBox functions.

Chapter 5

Decision Making with VBA

You can make decisions in your VBA procedures by using conditional expressions inside the special control structures. A *conditional expression* is an expression that uses a relational operator (see Table 5-1), a logical operator (see Table 5-2), or a combination of both. When Visual Basic encounters a conditional expression in your program, it evaluates the expression to determine whether it is true or false.

Table 5-1: Relational operators in VBA

Operator	Description
=	Equal to
<>	Not equal to
>	Greater than
<	Less than
>=	Greater than or equal to
<=	Less than or equal to

Table 5-2: Logical operators in VBA

Operator	Description
AND	All conditions must be true before an action can be taken.
OR	At least one of the conditions must be true before an action can be taken.
NOT	If a condition is true, NOT makes it false. If a condition is false, NOT makes it true.

Boolean Expressions

Conditional expressions and logical operators are also known as *Boolean*. George Boole was a nineteenth-century British mathematician who made significant contributions to the evolution of computer programming. Boolean expressions can be evaluated as true or false.

For example:

One meter equals 10 inches.	False
Two is less than three.	True

If...Then Statement

The simplest way to get some decision making into your VBA procedure is by using the If...Then statement. Suppose you want to choose an action depending on a condition. You can use the following structure:

```
If condition Then statement
```

For example, a quiz procedure might ask the user to guess the number of weeks in a year. If the user's response is other than 52, the procedure should display the message "Try Again."

⊚ Hands-On 5-1: Using the If...Then Statement

1. Start Microsoft Office Access 2007 and create a new Microsoft Office Access 2007 database named **Chap05.accdb** in your **C:\Acc07_ByExample** folder.

2. Once your new database is opened, press **Alt+F11** to switch to the Visual Basic Editor window.

3. Choose **Insert | Module** to add a new standard module.

4. In the Module1 Code window, enter the **SimpleIfThen** procedure shown below. (You may copy this procedure from the **C:\Acc07_HandsOn\ HandsOn_05.txt** file.)

```
Sub SimpleIfThen()
    Dim weeks As String

    weeks = InputBox("How many weeks are in a year:", "Quiz")
    If weeks<>52 Then MsgBox "Try Again"
End Sub
```

The SimpleIfThen procedure stores the user's answer in the weeks variable. The variable's value is then compared with the number 52. If the result of the comparison is true (that is, if the value stored in the variable weeks is not equal to 52), Visual Basic will display the message "Try Again."

5. Run the SimpleIfThen procedure and enter a number other than **52**.

6. Rerun the SimpleIfThen procedure and enter the number **52**. When you enter the correct number of weeks, Visual Basic does nothing. The procedure ends. It would be nice to also display a message when the user guesses right.

7. Enter the following instruction on a separate line before the End Sub keywords:

```
If weeks = 52 Then MsgBox "Congratulations!"
```

8. Run the SimpleIfThen procedure again and enter the number **52**. When you enter the correct answer, Visual Basic does not execute the Try Again statement. When the procedure is executed, the statement to the right of the

Then keyword is ignored if the result from evaluating the supplied condition is false. As you recall, a VBA procedure can call another procedure. Let's see if it can also call itself.

9. Modify the first If statement in the SimpleIfThen procedure as follows:

```
If weeks <> 52 Then MsgBox "Try Again" : SimpleIfThen
```

We added a colon and the name of the SimpleIfThen procedure to the end of the existing If...Then statement. If the user enters the incorrect answer, he will see a message, and as soon as he clicks the OK button in the message box, he will get another chance to supply the correct answer. The user will be able to keep on guessing for a long time. In fact, he won't be able to exit the procedure gracefully until he supplies the correct answer. If he clicks Cancel, he will have to deal with the unfriendly "Type Mismatch" error message. For now, you may want to revise your SimpleIfThen procedure as follows:

```
Sub SimpleIfThen2()
    Dim weeks As String

    On Error GoTo VeryEnd
    weeks = InputBox("How many weeks are in a year:", "Quiz")
    If weeks <> 52 Then MsgBox "Try Again" : SimpleIfThen2
    If weeks = 52 Then MsgBox "Congratulations!"
VeryEnd:
End Sub
```

If Visual Basic encounters an error, it will jump to the VeryEnd label placed at the end of the procedure. The statements placed between On Error GoTo VeryEnd and the VeryEnd label are ignored. Later in this chapter you will find other examples of trapping errors in your VBA procedures.

10. Run the SimpleIfThen2 procedure a few times by supplying incorrect answers. The error trap that you added to your procedure will allow you to quit guessing without having to deal with the ugly error message.

Multi-Line If...Then Statement

Sometimes you may want to perform several actions when the condition is true. Although you could add other statements on the same line by separating them with colons, your code will look clearer if you use the multi-line version of the If...Then statement, as shown below:

```
If condition Then
    statement1
    statement2
    statementN
End If
```

For example, you could modify the SimpleIfThen procedure to include additional statements.

◎ Hands-On 5-2: Using the Multi-Line If...Then Statement

1. Insert a new module and enter the **SimpleIfThen3** procedure as shown below:

```
Sub SimpleIfThen3()
    Dim weeks As String
    Dim response As String

    On Error GoTo VeryEnd
    weeks = InputBox("How many weeks are in a year?", "Quiz")
    If weeks <> 52 Then
        response = MsgBox("This is incorrect. Would you like to try again?", _
        vbYesNo + vbInformation + vbDefaultButton1, _
        "Continue Quiz?")
        If response = vbYes Then
            Call SimpleIfThen3
        End If
    End If
VeryEnd:
End Sub
```

2. Run the SimpleIfThen3 procedure and enter any number other than 52.

In the above example, the statements between the Then and the End If keywords don't get executed if the variable weeks is equal to 52. Notice that the multi-line If...Then statement must end with the keywords End If. How does Visual Basic make a decision? Simply put, it evaluates the condition it finds between the If...Then keywords.

Two Formats of the If...Then Statement

The If...Then statement has two formats: a single-line format and a multi-line format. The short format is good for statements that fit on one line, like:

```
If secretCode <> "01W01" Then MsgBox "Access denied"
```

or

```
If secretCode = "01W01" Then alpha = True : beta = False
```

In the above examples, secretCode, alpha, and beta are the names of variables. In the first example, Visual Basic displays the message "Access denied" if the value of the secretCode variable is not equal to 01W01. In the second example, Visual Basic will set the value of the variable alpha to True and the value of the variable beta to False when the secretCode value is equal to 01W01. Notice that the second statement to be executed is separated from the first one by a colon. The multi-line If...Then statement is more clear when there are more statements to be executed when the condition is true, or when the statement to be executed is extremely long.

Decisions Based on More Than One Condition

The SimpleIfThen procedure you worked with earlier evaluated only a single condition in the If...Then statement. This statement, however, can take more than one condition. To specify multiple conditions in an If...Then statement, you use the logical operators AND and OR (see Table 5-2 at the beginning of the chapter). Here's the syntax with the AND operator:

```
If condition1 AND condition2 Then statement
```

In the above syntax, both condition1 and condition2 must be true for Visual Basic to execute the statement to the right of the Then keyword. For example:

```
If sales = 10000 AND salary < 45000 Then SlsCom = sales * 0.07
```

In this example, *condition1* is sales = 10000, and *condition2* is salary < 45000. When AND is used in the conditional expression, both conditions must be true before Visual Basic can calculate the sales commission (SlsCom). If any of these conditions is false or both are false, Visual Basic ignores the statement after Then. When it's good enough to meet only one of the conditions, you should use the OR operator. Here's the syntax:

```
If condition1 OR condition2 Then statement
```

The OR operator is more flexible. Only one of the conditions has to be true before Visual Basic can execute the statement following the Then keyword. Let's look at this example:

```
If dept = "S" OR dept = "M" Then bonus = 500
```

In the above example, if at least one condition is true, Visual Basic assigns 500 to the bonus variable. If both conditions are false, Visual Basic ignores the rest of the line.

Now, let's look at a complete procedure example. Suppose you can get a 10% discount if you purchase 50 units of a product priced at $7.00. The IfThenAnd procedure demonstrates the use of the AND operator.

◎ Hands-On 5-3: Using the If...Then...AND Conditional Statement

1. Insert a new module and enter the following **IfThenAnd** procedure in the module's Code window:

```
Sub IfThenAnd()
    Dim price As Single
    Dim units As Integer
    Dim rebate As Single

    Const strMsg1 = "To get a rebate you must buy an additional "
    Const strMsg2 = "Price must equal $7.00"

    units = 234
    price = 7

    If price = 7 And units >= 50 Then
```

```
        rebate = (price * units) * 0.1
        MsgBox "The rebate is: $" & rebate
    End If

    If price = 7 And units < 50 Then
        MsgBox strMsg1 & "50 - units."
    End If

    If price <> 7 And units >= 50 Then
        MsgBox strMsg2
    End If

    If price <> 7 And units < 50 Then
        MsgBox "You didn't meet the criteria."
    End If
End Sub
```

2. Run the IfThenAnd procedure.

The IfThenAnd procedure shown above has four If...Then statements that are used to evaluate the contents of two variables: price and units. The AND operator between the keywords If...Then allows more than one condition to be tested. With the AND operator, all conditions must be true for Visual Basic to run the statements between the Then...End If keywords.

Indenting If Block Instructions

To make the If blocks easier to read and understand, use indentation. Compare the following:

```
If condition Then          If condition Then
    action1                    action
End If                     End If
```

Looking at the If...Then block statement on the right side, you can easily see where the block begins and where it ends.

If...Then...Else Statement

Now you know how to display a message or take an action when one or more conditions are true or false. What should you do, however, if your procedure needs to take one action when the condition is true and another action when the condition is false? By adding the Else clause to the simple If...Then statement, you can direct your procedure to the appropriate statement depending on the result of the test.

The If...Then...Else statement has two formats: single-line and multi-line. The single-line format is as follows:

```
If condition Then statement1 Else statement2
```

The statement following the Then keyword is executed if the condition is true, and the statement following the Else clause is executed if the condition is false. For example:

```
If sales > 5000 Then Bonus = sales * 0.05 Else MsgBox "No Bonus"
```

If the value stored in the variable sales is greater than 5000, Visual Basic will calculate the bonus using the following formula: sales * 0.05. However, if the variable sales is not greater than 5000, Visual Basic will display the message "No Bonus."

The If...Then...Else statement should be used to decide which of two actions to perform. When you need to execute more statements when the condition is true or false, it's better to use the multi-line format of the If...Then...Else statement:

```
If condition Then
    statements to be executed if condition is True
Else
    statements to be executed if condition is False
End If
```

Notice that the multi-line (block) If...Then...Else statement ends with the End If keywords. Use the indentation shown above to make this block structure easier to read.

```
If Me.Dirty Then
    Me!btnUndo.Enabled = True
Else
    Me!btnUndo.Enabled = False
End If
```

In the above example, if the condition (Me.Dirty) is true, Visual Basic will execute the statements between Then and Else, and will ignore the statement between Else and End If. If the condition is false, Visual Basic will omit the statements between Then and Else, and execute the statement between Else and End If. The purpose of this procedure fragment is to enable the Undo button when the data on the form has changed and keep the Undo button disabled if the data has not changed. Let's look at the procedure example.

⊚ Hands-On 5-4: Using the If...Then...Else Conditional Statement

1. Insert a new module and enter the following **WhatTypeOf Day** procedure in the module's Code window:

```
Sub WhatTypeOfDay()
    Dim response As String
    Dim question As String
    Dim strMsg1 As String, strMsg2 As String
    Dim myDate As Date

    question = "Enter any date in the format mm/dd/yyyy:" _
               & Chr(13)& " (e.g., 11/22/2007)"
    strMsg1 = "weekday"
    strMsg2 = "weekend"
    response = InputBox(question)
    myDate = Weekday(CDate(response))

    If myDate >= 2 And myDate <= 6 Then
```

```
        MsgBox strMsg1
    Else
        MsgBox strMsg2
    End If
End Sub
```

2. Run the WhatTypeOfDay procedure.

   The above procedure asks the user to enter any date. The user-supplied string is then converted to the Date data type with the built-in CDate function. Finally, the Weekday function converts the date into an integer that indicates the day of the week (see Table 5-3). The integer is stored in the variable myDate. The conditional test is performed to check whether the value of the variable myDate is greater than or equal to 2 (>=2) and less than or equal to 6 (<=6). If the result of the test is true, the user is told that the supplied date is a weekday; otherwise, the program announces that it's a weekend.

3. Run the procedure a few more times, each time supplying a different date. Check the Visual Basic answers against your desktop or wall calendar.

Table 5-3: The Weekday function values

Constant	Value
vbSunday	1
vbMonday	2
vbTuesday	3
vbWednesday	4
vbThursday	5
vbFriday	6
vbSaturday	7

If...Then...ElseIf Statement

Quite often you will need to check the results of several different conditions. To join a set of If conditions together, you can use the ElseIf clause. Using the If...Then...ElseIf statement, you can evaluate more conditions than is possible with the If...Then...Else statement that was the subject of the preceding section. Here's the syntax of the If...Then...ElseIf statement:

```
If condition1 Then
    statements to be executed if condition1 is True
ElseIf condition2 Then
    statements to be executed if condition2 is True
ElseIf condition3 Then
    statements to be executed if condition3 is True
ElseIf conditionN Then
    statements to be executed if conditionN is True
Else
    statements to be executed if all conditions are False
End If
```

The Else clause is optional; you can omit it if there are no actions to be executed when all conditions are false.

ElseIf Clause

Your procedure can include any number of ElseIf statements and conditions. The ElseIf clause always comes before the Else clause. The statements
in the ElseIf clause are executed only if the condition in this clause is true.

Let's look at the following procedure fragment:

```
If myNumber = 0 Then
    MsgBox "You entered zero."
ElseIf myNumber > 0 Then
    MsgBox "You entered a positive number."
ElseIf myNumber < 0 Then
    MsgBox "You entered a negative number."
End if
```

This example checks the value of the number entered by the user and stored in
the variable myNumber. Depending on the number entered, an appropriate
message (zero, positive, negative) is displayed. Notice that the Else clause is
not used. If the result of the first condition (myNumber = 0) is false, Visual
Basic jumps to the next ElseIf statement and evaluates its condition
(myNumber > 0). If the value is not greater than zero, Visual Basic skips to the
next ElseIf and the condition myNumber < 0 is evaluated.

Nested If...Then Statements

You can make more complex decisions in your VBA procedures by placing an
If...Then or If...Then...Else statement inside another If...Then or
If...Then...Else statement. Structures in which an If statement is contained
inside another If block are referred to as *nested* If statements. To understand
how nested If...Then statements work, it's time for another hands-on exercise.

⊚ Hands-On 5-5: Using Nested If...Then Statements

1. In the database **Chap05.accdb**, create a blank form by choosing **Blank
   form** in the Forms section of the Create tab (Microsoft Office Access 2007
   window). Access will open the new form in Layout view. Switch to Design
   view.

2. Use the text box control in the Controls section of the Design tab to add
   two text boxes to the form (see Figure 5-1).

Figure 5-1: Placing text box controls on an Access form for Hands-On 5-5.

3. Change the label in front of the first text box to **User**, and the label in front of the second text box to **Password**.

4. Click the **Property Sheet** button in the Tools section of the Design tab.

5. Click the Unbound text box to the right of the User label. In the property sheet on the Other tab, set the Name property of this control to **txtUser**. Click the Unbound text box to the right of the Password label. In the property sheet on the All tab, set the Name property of this text box to **txtPwd** (see Figure 5-2).

6. In the property sheet on the Data tab, type **Password** next to the Input Mask property of the txtPwd text box control.

7. Click the **Button** (Form Control) in the Controls section of the Design tab, and add a button to the form. When the Command Button Wizard dialog box appears, click **Cancel**. With the Command button selected, set the Caption and Name properties of this button by typing the following values in the property sheet next to the shown property name (Figure 5-3):

Name property: **cmdOK**
Caption property: **OK**

8. Right-click the **OK** button and choose **Build Event** from the shortcut menu. In the Choose Builder dialog box, select **Code Builder** and click **OK**.

9. Enter the code for the cmdOK_Click event procedure as shown below. To make the cmdOK_Click procedure easier to understand, the conditional statements are shown with different formatting (bold and underlined).

```
Private Sub cmdOK_Click()
    If txtPwd = "FOX" Then
        MsgBox "You are not authorized to run this report."
    ElseIf txtPwd = "DOG" Then
        If txtUser = "John" Then
            MsgBox "You are logged on with restricted privileges."
        ElseIf txtUser = "Mark" Then
            MsgBox "Contact the Admin now."
        ElseIf txtUser = "Anne" Then
            MsgBox "Go home."
        Else
            MsgBox "Incorrect user name."
        End If
    Else
        MsgBox "Incorrect password or user name"
    End If
    Me.txtUser.SetFocus
End Sub
```

Figure 5-2: Setting the Name property of the text box control for Hands-On 5-5.

Figure 5-3: Setting the Command button properties for Hands-On 5-5.

10. Choose **File | Close and Return to Microsoft Office Access**.

11. Save your form as **frmTestNesting**. When prompted to save standard modules you created in earlier exercises, save these objects with default names.

12. Switch to Form view. Enter any data in the User and Password text boxes, then click **OK**.

The procedure first checks if the txtPwd text box on the form holds the text string "FOX." If this is true, the message is displayed, and Visual Basic skips over the ElseIf and Else clauses until If finds the matching End If (see the bolded conditional statement).

If the txtPwd text box holds the string "DOG," then we use a nested If...Then...Else statement (underlined) to check if the content of the txtUser text box is set to John, Mark, or Anne, and display the appropriate message. If the user name is not one of the specified names, then the condition is false and we jump to the underlined Else to display a message stating that the user entered an incorrect user name.

The first If block (in bold) is called the *outer* If statement. This outer statement contains one *inner* If statement (underlined).

Nesting Statements

Nesting means placing one type of control structure inside another control structure. You will see more nesting examples with the looping structures discussed in Chapter 6.

Select Case Statement

To avoid complex nested If statements that are difficult to follow, you can use the Select Case statement instead. The syntax of this statement is as follows:

```
Select Case testExpression
    Case expressionList1
        statements if expressionList1 matches testExpression
    Case expressionList2
        statements if expressionList2 matches testExpression
    Case expressionListN
        statements if expressionListN matches testExpression
    Case Else
        statements to be executed if no values match testExpression
End Select
```

You can place any number of cases to test between the keywords Select Case and End Select. The Case Else clause is optional. Use it when you expect that there may be conditional expressions that return False. In the Select Case statement, Visual Basic compares each expressionList with the value of testExpression.

Here's the logic behind the Select Case statement. When Visual Basic encounters the Select Case clause, it makes note of the value of testExpression. Then it proceeds to test the expression following the first Case clause. If the value of this expression (expressionList1) matches the value stored in testExpression, Visual Basic executes the statements until another Case clause is encountered, and then jumps to the End Select statement. If, however, the expression tested in the first Case clause does not match testExpression, Visual Basic checks the value of each Case clause until it finds a match. If none of the Case clauses contain the expression that matches the value stored in testExpression, Visual Basic jumps to the Case Else clause and executes the statements until it encounters the End Select keywords. Notice that the Case Else clause is optional. If your procedure does not use Case Else, and none of the Case clauses contain a value matching the value of testExpression, Visual Basic jumps to the statements following End Select and continues executing your procedure.

Let's look at the example of a procedure that uses the Select Case statement. As you already know, the MsgBox function allows you to display a message with one or more buttons. The result of the MsgBox function can be assigned to a variable. Using the Select Case statement you can decide which action to take based on the button the user pressed in the message box.

⊚ Hands-On 5-6: Using the Select Case Statement

1. Press **Alt+F11** to switch to the Visual Basic Editor window.

2. Insert a new module and enter the following **TestButtons** procedure in the module's Code window:

```
Sub TestButtons()
    Dim question As String
```

```
Dim bts As Integer
Dim myTitle As String
Dim myButton As Integer

question = "Do you want to preview the report now?"
bts = vbYesNoCancel + vbQuestion + vbDefaultButton1
myTitle = "Report"
myButton = MsgBox(prompt:=question, buttons:=bts, Title:=myTitle)

Select Case myButton
    Case 6
        DoCmd.OpenReport "Sales by Year", acPreview
    Case 7
        MsgBox "You can review the report later."
    Case Else
        MsgBox "You pressed Cancel."
End Select
End Sub
```

3. Run the TestButtons procedure three times, each time selecting a different button. (Since there is no Sales by Year report in the current database, an error message will pop up when you select Yes. Click **End** to exit the error message.)

The first part of the TestButtons procedure displays a message with three buttons: Yes, No, and Cancel. The value of the button selected by the user is assigned to the variable myButton.

If the user clicks Yes, the variable myButton is assigned the vbYes constant or its corresponding value 6. If the user selects No, the variable myButton is assigned the constant vbNo or its corresponding value 7. Lastly, if Cancel is pressed, the contents of the variable myButton equals vbCancel, or 2.

The Select Case statement checks the values supplied after the Case clause against the value stored in the variable myButton. When there is a match, the appropriate Case statement is executed.

The TestButtons procedure will work the same if you use constants instead of button values:

```
Select Case myButton
    Case vbYes
        DoCmd.OpenReport "Sales by Year", acPreview
    Case vbNo
        MsgBox "You can review the report later."
    Case Else
        MsgBox "You pressed Cancel."
End Select
```

You can omit the Else clause. Simply revise the Select Case statement as follows:

```
Select Case myButton
    Case vbYes
        DoCmd.OpenReport "Sales by Year", acPreview
    Case vbNo
```

```
    MsgBox "You can review the report later."
Case vbCancel
    MsgBox "You pressed Cancel."
End Select
```

Capture Errors with Case Else

Although using Case Else in the Select Case statement isn't required, it's always a good idea to include one just in case the variable you are testing has an unexpected value. The Case Else is a good place to put an error message.

Using Is with the Case Clause

Sometimes a decision is made based on whether the test expression uses the greater than, less than, equal to, or some other relational operator (see Table 5-1). The Is keyword lets you use a conditional expression in a Case clause. The syntax for the Select Case clause using the Is keyword is shown below.

```
Select Case testExpression
    Case Is condition1
        statements if condition1 is true
    Case Is condition2
        statements if condition2 is true
    Case Is conditionN
        statements if conditionN is true
End Select
```

Let's look at an example:

```
Select Case myNumber
    Case Is <= 10
        MsgBox "The number is less than or equal to 10."
    Case 11
        MsgBox "You entered 11."
    Case Is >= 100
        MsgBox "The number is greater than or equal to 100."
    Case Else
        MsgBox "The number is between 12 and 99."
End Select
```

Assuming that the variable myNumber holds 120, the third Case clause is true, and the only statement executed is the one between Case Is >= 100 and the Case Else clause.

Specifying a Range of Values in a Case Clause

In the preceding example you saw a simple Select Case statement that uses one expression in each Case clause. Many times, however, you may want to specify a range of values in a Case clause. You do this by using the To keyword between the values of expressions, as in the following example:

```
Select Case unitsSold
    Case 1 To 100
        Discount = 0.05
    Case Is <= 500
        Discount = 0.1
    Case 501 To 1000
        Discount = 0.15
    Case Is >1000
        Discount = 0.2
End Select
```

Let's analyze the above Select Case block with the assumption that the variable unitsSold currently has a value of 99. Visual Basic compares the value of the variable unitsSold with the conditional expression in the Case clauses. The first and third Case clauses illustrate how to use a range of values in a conditional expression by using the To keyword.

Because unitsSold equals 99, the condition in the first Case clause is true; thus, Visual Basic assigns the value 0.05 to the variable Discount. Well, how about the second Case clause, which is also true? Although it's obvious that 99 is less than or equal to 500, Visual Basic does not execute the associated statement Discount = 0.1. The reason for this is that once Visual Basic locates a Case clause with a true condition, it doesn't bother to look at the remaining Case clauses. It jumps over them and continues to execute the procedure with the instructions that may follow the End Select statement.

To get more practice with the Select Case statement, let's use it in a function procedure. As you recall from Chapter 4, function procedures allow you to return a result to a subroutine. Suppose a subroutine has to display a discount based on the number of units sold. You can get the number of units from the user and then run a function to figure out which discount applies.

⊚ Hands-On 5-7: Using the Select Case Statement in a Function

1. Insert a new module and enter the following **DisplayDiscount** procedure in the Code window:

```
Sub DisplayDiscount()
    Dim unitsSold As Integer
    Dim myDiscount As Single

    unitsSold = InputBox("Enter the number of sold units:")
    myDiscount = GetDiscount(unitsSold)
    MsgBox myDiscount
End Sub
```

2. In the same module, enter the following **GetDiscount** function procedure:

```
Function GetDiscount(unitsSold As Integer)
    Select Case unitsSold
        Case 1 To 200
            GetDiscount = 0.05
        Case 201 To 500
            GetDiscount = 0.1
```

```
Case 501 To 1000
    GetDiscount = 0.15
Case Is > 1000
    GetDiscount = 0.2
End Select
End Function
```

3. Place the insertion point anywhere within the code of the DisplayDiscount procedure and press **F5** to run it.

   The DisplayDiscount procedure passes the value stored in the variable unitsSold to the GetDiscount function. When Visual Basic encounters the Select Case statement, it checks whether the value of the first Case clause expression matches the value stored in the unitsSold parameter. If there is a match, Visual Basic assigns a 5% discount (0.05) to the function name, and then jumps to the End Select keywords. Because there are no more statements to execute inside the function procedure, Visual Basic returns to the calling procedure, DisplayDiscount. Here it assigns the function's result to the variable myDiscount. The last statement displays the value of the retrieved discount in a message box.

4. Choose **File | Save Chap05** to save changes to the modules.

5. Choose **File | Close and Return to Microsoft Office Access**.

6. Close the **Chap05.accdb** database and exit Microsoft Office Access.

 Note: You may want to delete Table1 prior to closing the Chap05.accdb database.

Specifying Multiple Expressions in a Case Clause

You may specify multiple conditions within a single Case clause by separating each condition with a comma:

```
Select Case myMonth
    Case "January", "February", "March"
        Debug.Print myMonth & ": 1st Qtr."
    Case "April", "May", "June"
        Debug.Print myMonth & ": 2nd Qtr."
    Case "July", "August", "September"
        Debug.Print myMonth & ": 3rd Qtr."
    Case "October", "November", "December"
        Debug.Print myMonth & ": 4th Qtr."
End Select
```

Multiple Conditions within a Case Clause

The commas used to separate conditions within a Case clause have the same meaning as the OR operator used in the If statement. The Case clause is true if at least one of the conditions is true.

Chapter Summary

Conditional statements, introduced in this chapter, let you control the flow of your VBA procedure. By testing the truth of a condition, you can decide which statements should be run and which should be skipped over. In other words, instead of running your procedure from top to bottom, line by line, you can execute only certain lines. Here are a few guidelines to help you determine what kind of conditional statement you should use:

- If you want to supply only one condition, the simple If...Then statement is the best choice.

- If you need to decide which of two actions to perform, use the If...Then...Else statement.

- If your procedure requires two or more conditions, use the If...Then...ElseIf or Select Case statements.

- If your procedure has many conditions, use the Select Case statement. This statement is more flexible and easier to comprehend than the If...Then...ElseIf statement.

Sometimes decisions have to be repeated. The next chapter teaches you how your procedures can perform the same actions over and over again.

Chapter 6

Repeating Actions in VBA

Now that you've learned how conditional statements can give your VBA procedures decision-making capabilities, it's time to get more involved. Not all decisions are easy. Sometimes you will need to perform a number of statements several times to arrive at a certain condition. On other occasions, however, after you've reached the decision, you may need to run the specified statements as long as a condition is true or until a condition becomes true. In programming, performing repetitive tasks is called *looping*. VBA has various looping structures that allow you to repeat a sequence of statements a number of times. In this chapter, you learn how to loop through your code.

Visual Basic has two types of Do loop statements that repeat a sequence of statements either as long as or until a certain condition is true: Do...While and Do...Until.

Using the Do...While Statement

The Do...While statement lets you repeat an action as long as a condition is true. This statement has the following syntax:

```
Do While condition
    statement1
    statement2
    statementN
Loop
```

When Visual Basic encounters this loop, it first checks the truth value of the condition. If the condition is false, the statements inside the loop are not executed, and Visual Basic will continue to execute the program with the first statement after the Loop keyword or will exit the program if there are no more statements to execute. If the condition is true, the statements inside the loop are run one by one until the Loop statement is encountered. The Loop statement tells Visual Basic to repeat the entire process again as long as the testing of the condition in the Do...While statement is true.

Let's see how you can put the Do...While loop to good use in Microsoft Access. You will find out how to continuously display an input box until the user enters the correct password. The following hands-on exercise demonstrates this.

⊚ Hands-On 6-1: Using the Do...While Statement

1. Start Microsoft Office Access 2007 and create a new Microsoft Office Access 2007 database named **Chap06.accdb** in your **C:\Acc07_ ByExample** folder.

2. Once your new database is opened, press **Alt+F11** to switch to the Visual Basic Editor window.

3. Choose **Insert | Module** to add a new standard module.

4. In the Module1 Code window, enter the **AskForPassword** procedure shown below. (You may copy this procedure from the **C:\Acc07_ HandsOn\HandsOn_06.txt** file.)

```
Sub AskForPassword()
    Dim pWord As String

    pWord = ""
    Do While pWord <> "DADA"
        pWord = InputBox("What is the Report password?")
    Loop
        MsgBox "You entered the correct Report password."
End Sub
```

5. Run the AskForPassword procedure.

In the above procedure, the statement inside the Do...While loop is executed as long as the variable pWord is not equal to the string DADA. If the user enters the correct password (DADA), Visual Basic leaves the loop and executes the MsgBox statement after the Loop keyword.

To allow the user to exit the procedure gracefully and cancel out of the input box if he does not know the correct password, you should add the following statement on an empty line before the Loop keyword:

```
If pWord = "" Then Exit Do
```

The Exit Do statement tells Visual Basic to exit the Do loop if the variable pWord does not hold any value (please see the section titled "Exiting Loops Early" later in this chapter). This statement tells Visual Basic to exit the Do loop if the variable pWord does not hold any value. Therefore, when the input box appears, the user can leave the text field empty and click OK or Cancel to stop the procedure. Without the above statement, the procedure will keep on asking the user to enter the password until the correct value is supplied.

To forgo displaying the informational message when the user has not provided the correct password, you may want to use the conditional statement If...Then that you learned in the previous chapter. Below is the revised AskForPassword procedure:

```
Sub AskForPassword2()
    Dim pWord As String

    pWord = ""
```

```
Do While pWord <> "DADA"
    pWord = InputBox("What is the Report password?")
    If pWord = "" Then
        MsgBox "You did not enter a password."
        Exit Do
    End If
Loop

If pWord <> "" Then
    MsgBox "You entered the correct Report password."
End If
End Sub
```

What Is a Loop?

A *loop* is a programming structure that causes a section of program code to execute repeatedly. VBA provides several structures to implement loops in your procedures: Do...While, Do...Until, For...Next, and For Each...Next.

Another Approach to the Do...While Statement

The Do...While statement has another syntax that lets you test the condition at the bottom of the loop:

```
Do
    statement1
    statement2
    statementN
Loop While condition
```

When you test the condition at the bottom of the loop, the statements inside the loop are executed at least once. Let's try this in the next hands-on exercise.

Hands-On 6-2: Using the Do...While Statement with a Condition at the Bottom of the Loop

1. In the Visual Basic Editor window, insert a new module and type the **SignIn** procedure as shown below:

```
Sub SignIn()
    Dim secretCode As String

    Do
        secretCode = InputBox("Enter your secret code:")
        If secretCode = "sp1045" Then Exit Do
    Loop While secretCode <> "sp1045"
End Sub
```

2. Run the SignIn procedure.

   Notice that by the time the condition is evaluated, Visual Basic has already executed the statements one time. In addition to placing the condition at the end of the loop, the SignIn procedure shows again how to exit the loop when a condition is reached. When the Exit Do statement is encountered, the loop ends immediately.

To exit the loop in the SignIn procedure without entering the password, you may revise it as follows:

```
Sub SignIn2()
    Dim secretCode As String

    Do
        secretCode = InputBox("Enter your secret code:")
        If secretCode = "sp1045" Or secretCode = "" Then Exit Do
    Loop While secretCode <> "sp1045"
End Sub
```

Avoid Infinite Loops

If you don't design your loop correctly, you can get an *infinite loop* — a loop that never ends. You will not be able to stop the procedure by using the Escape key. The following procedure causes the loop to execute endlessly because the programmer forgot to include the test condition:

```
Sub SayHello()
    Do
        MsgBox "Hello."
    Loop
End Sub
```

To stop the execution of the infinite loop, you must press Ctrl+Break. When Visual Basic displays the message box "Code execution has been interrupted," click End to end the procedure.

Using the Do...Until Statement

Another handy loop is Do...Until, which allows you to repeat one or more statements until a condition becomes true. In other words, Do...Until repeats a block of code as long as something is false. Here's the syntax:

```
Do Until condition
    statement1
    statement2
    statementN
Loop
```

Using the above syntax, you can now rewrite the previously written AskForPassword procedure as shown in the following hands-on exercise.

◎ Hands-On 6-3: Using the Do...Until Statement

1. In the Visual Basic Editor window, insert a new module and type the **AskForPassword3** procedure:

```
Sub AskForPassword3()
    Dim pWord As String
```

```
pWord = ""
Do Until pWord = "DADA"
    pWord = InputBox("What is the Report password?")
Loop
End Sub
```

2. Run the AskForPassword3 procedure.

The first line of this procedure says: Perform the following statements until the variable pWord holds the value DADA. As a result, until the correct password is supplied, Visual Basic executes the InputBox statement inside the loop. This process continues as long as the condition pWord = "DADA" evaluates to false.

You could modify the procedure as shown below to allow the user to cancel the input box without supplying the password.

```
Sub AskForPassword4()
    Dim pWord As String

    pWord = ""
    Do Until pWord = "DADA"
        pWord = InputBox("What is the Report password?")
        If pWord = "" Then Exit Do
    Loop
End Sub
```

Variables and Loops

All variables that appear in a loop should be assigned default values before the loop is entered.

Another Approach to the Do...Until Statement

Similar to the Do...While statement, the Do...Until statement has a second syntax that lets you test the condition at the bottom of the loop:

```
Do
    statement1
    statement2
    statementN
Loop Until condition
```

If you want the statements to execute at least once, no matter what the value of the condition, place the condition on the line with the Loop statement. Let's try out the following example that prints 27 numbers to the Immediate window.

Hands-On 6-4: Using the Do...Until Statement with a Condition at the Bottom of the Loop

1. In the Visual Basic Editor window, insert a new module and type the **PrintNumbers** procedure shown below:

```
Sub PrintNumbers()
    Dim num As Integer

    num = 0
    Do
        num = num + 1
        Debug.Print num
    Loop Until num = 27
End Sub
```

2. Make sure the Immediate window is open in the Visual Basic Editor window (choose **View | Immediate Window**).

3. Run the PrintNumbers procedure.

   The variable num is initialized at the beginning of the procedure to zero (0). When Visual Basic enters the loop, the content of the variable num is increased by one, and the value is written to the Immediate window with the Debug.Print statement. Next, the condition tells Visual Basic that it should execute the statements inside the loop until the variable num equals 27.

Counters

A *counter* is a numeric variable that keeps track of the number of items that have been processed. The PrintNumbers procedure shown above declares the variable num to keep track of numbers that were printed. A counter variable should be initialized (assigned a value) at the beginning of the program. This ensures that you always know the exact value of the counter before you begin using it. A counter can be incremented or decremented by a specified value.

For...Next Statement

The For...Next statement is used when you know how many times you want to repeat a group of statements. The syntax of a For...Next statement looks like this:

```
For counter = start To end [Step increment]
    statement1
    statement2
    statementN
Next [counter]
```

The code in the brackets is optional. *Counter* is a numeric variable that stores the number of iterations. *Start* is the number at which you want to begin counting. *End* indicates how many times the loop should be executed. For example, if you want to repeat the statements inside the loop five times, use the following For statement:

```
For counter = 1 To 5
    statements
Next
```

When Visual Basic encounters the Next statement, it will go back to the beginning of the loop and execute the statements inside the loop again, as long as the counter hasn't reached the end value. As soon as the value of counter is greater than the number entered after the To keyword, Visual Basic exits the loop. Because the variable counter automatically changes after each execution of the loop, sooner or later the value stored in the counter exceeds the value specified in end.

By default, every time Visual Basic executes the statements inside the loop, the value of the variable counter is increased by one. You can change this default setting by using the Step clause. For example, to increase the variable counter by three, use the following statement:

```
For counter = 1 To 5 Step 3
    statements
Next counter
```

When Visual Basic encounters the above statement, it executes the statements inside the loop twice. The first time the loop runs, the counter equals 1. The second time the loop runs, the counter equals 4 (1+3). The loop does not run a third time, because now the counter equals 7 (4+3), causing Visual Basic to exit the loop.

Note that the Step increment is optional. Optional statements are always shown in square brackets (see the syntax at the beginning of this section). The Step increment isn't specified unless it's a value other than 1. You can place a negative number after Step in order to decrement this value from the counter each time it encounters the Next statement. The name of the variable (counter) after the Next statement is also optional; however, it's good programming practice to make your Next statements explicit by including the counter variable's name.

How can you use the For...Next loop in Microsoft Access? Suppose you want to get the names of the text boxes located on an active form. The procedure in the next hands-on exercise demonstrates how to determine if a control is a text box and how to display its name if a text box is found.

⊚ Hands-On 6-5: Using the For...Next Statement

1. Import the **Customers** table from the **Northwind 2007.accdb** database located in the Acc07_HandsOn folder. To do this, choose **File | Close and Return to Microsoft Office Access**. Click **Access** in the Import section of the External Data tab. In the File name text box of the Get External Data dialog box, enter **C:\Acc07_HandsOn\Northwind 2007.accdb** and click **OK**. In the Import Objects dialog box, select the **Customers** table and click **OK**. Click **Close** to exit the Get External Data dialog box.

2. Now, create a simple **Customers** form based on the Customers table. To do this, select the Customers table in the navigation pane by clicking on its name. Next, click the **Form** button in the Forms section of the Create tab. Access creates a form as shown in Figure 6-1.

Figure 6-1: Automatic data entry form created by Microsoft Access 2007.

3. Press **Alt+F11** to switch to the Visual Basic Editor window and insert a new module.

4. In the module's Code window, enter the **GetTextBoxNames** procedure as shown below:

```
Sub GetTextBoxNames()
    Dim myForm As Form
    Dim myControl As Control
    Dim c As Integer

    Set myForm = Screen.ActiveForm
    Set myControl = Screen.ActiveControl

    For c = 0 To myForm.Count - 1
        If TypeOf myForm(c) Is TextBox Then
            MsgBox myForm(c).Name
        End If
    Next c
End Sub
```

The conditional statement (If…Then) nested inside the For…Next loop tells Visual Basic to display the name of the active control only if it is a text box.

5. Run the GetTextBoxNames procedure.

Paired Statements

For and Next must be paired. If one is missing, Visual Basic generates the following error message: "For without Next."

For Each...Next Statement

When your procedure needs to loop through all of the objects of a collection or all of the elements in an array (arrays are the subject of the next chapter), the For Each...Next statement should be used. This loop does not require a counter variable. Visual Basic can figure out on its own how many times the loop should execute. The For Each...Next statement looks like this:

```
For Each element In Group
    statement1
    statement2
    statementN
Next [element]
```

Element is a variable to which all the elements of an array or collection will be assigned. This variable has to be of the Variant data type for an array and of the Object data type for a collection. *Group* is the name of a collection or an array. Let's now see how to use the For Each...Next statement to print the names of the controls in the Customers form to the Immediate window.

◎ Hands-On 6-6: Using the For Each...Next Statement

This hands-on exercise requires the completion of steps 1-2 of Hands-On 6-5.

1. Ensure that the Customers form you created in Hands-On 6-5 is still open in Form view.

2. Switch to the Visual Basic Editor window and insert a new module.

3. In the Code window, enter the **GetControls** procedure as shown below:

```
Sub GetControls()
    Dim myControl As Control
    Dim myForm As Form

    DoCmd.OpenForm "Customers"
    Set myForm = Screen.ActiveForm

    For Each myControl In myForm
        Debug.Print myControl.Name
    Next
End Sub
```

4. Run the GetControls procedure.

5. To see the results of the procedure you just executed, press **Ctrl+G** in the Visual Basic Editor window to open the Immediate window or choose **View | Immediate Window**.

Exiting Loops Early

Sometimes you might not want to wait until the loop ends on its own. It's possible that a user will enter the wrong data, a procedure will encounter an error, or perhaps the task will complete and there's no need to do additional looping. You can leave the loop early without reaching the condition that normally terminates it. Visual Basic has two types of Exit statements:

■ The Exit For statement is used to end either a For...Next or a For Each...Next loop early.

■ The Exit Do statement immediately exits any of the VBA Do loops.

The following hands-on exercise demonstrates how to use the Exit For statement to leave the For Each...Next loop early.

◎ Hands-On 6-7: Early Exit from a Loop

1. In the Visual Basic Editor window, choose **Insert | Module**.

2. In the module's Code window, enter the **GetControls2** procedure as shown below:

```
Sub GetControls2()
    Dim myControl As Control
    Dim myForm As Form

    DoCmd.OpenForm "Customers"
    Set myForm = Screen.ActiveForm

    For Each myControl In myForm
        Debug.Print myControl.Name
        If myControl.Name = "Address" Then Exit For
    Next
End Sub
```

3. Run the GetControls2 procedure.

The GetControls2 procedure examines the names of the controls in the open Customers form. If Visual Basic encounters the control named "Address," it exits the loop.

Exiting Procedures

If you want to exit a subroutine earlier than normal, use the Exit Sub statement. If the procedure is a function, use the Exit Function statement instead.

Nested Loops

So far in this chapter you have tried out various loops. Each procedure demonstrated the use of an individual looping structure. In programming practice, however, one loop is often placed inside another. Visual Basic allows you to "nest" various types of loops (For and Do loops) within the same procedure. When writing nested loops, you must make sure that each inner loop is completely contained inside the outer loop. Also, each loop has to have a unique counter variable. When you use nesting loops, you can often execute specific tasks more effectively.

The GetFormsAndControls procedure shown in the following hands-on exercise illustrates how one For Each…Next loop is nested within another For Each…Next loop.

◎ Hands-On 6-8: Using Nested Loops

1. Import the **Employees** table from the **Northwind 2007.accdb** database located in the Acc07_HandsOn folder. To do this, choose **File | Close and Return to Microsoft Office Access**. Click **Access** in the Import section of the External Data tab. In the File name text box of the Get External Data dialog box, enter **C:\Acc07_HandsOn\Northwind 2007.accdb** and click **OK**. In the Import Objects dialog box, select the **Employees** table and click **OK**. Click **Close** to exit the Get External Data dialog box.

2. Now, create a simple **Employees** form based on the Employees table. To do this, select the Employees table in the navigation pane by clicking on its name. Next, click the **Form** button in the Forms section of the Create tab. Access creates a simple Employees data entry form.

3. Leave the Employees form in Form view and press **Alt+F11** to switch to the Visual Basic Editor window.

4. Choose **Insert | Module** to add a new module. In the module's Code window, enter the **GetFormsAndControls** procedure as shown below:

```
Sub GetFormsAndControls()
    Dim accObj As AccessObject
    Dim myControl As Control

    For Each accObj In CurrentProject.AllForms
        Debug.Print accObj.Name & " Form"
        If Not accObj.IsLoaded Then
            DoCmd.OpenForm accObj.Name
        End If
        For Each myControl In Forms(accObj.Name).Controls
            Debug.Print Chr(9) & myControl.Name
        Next
        DoCmd.Close
    Next
End Sub
```

5. Run the GetFormsAndControls procedure.

The GetFormsAndControls procedure shown above uses two For Each...
Next loops to print the name of each currently open form and its controls to
the Immediate window. To enumerate through the form's controls, the form
must be open. Notice the use of the Access built-in function IsLoaded. The
procedure will only open the form if it is not yet loaded. The control names
are indented in the Immediate window using the Chr(9) function. This is
like pressing the Tab key once. To get the same result, you can replace
Chr(9) with a VBA constant: vbTab.

After reading the names of the controls, the form is closed and the next
form is processed in the same manner. The procedure ends when no more
forms are found in the AllForms collection of CurrentProject.

6. Choose **File | Save Chap06** to save changes to the modules.

7. Choose **File | Close and Return to Microsoft Office Access**.

8. Close the Chap06.accdb database and exit Microsoft Office Access.

Chapter Summary

In this chapter you learned how to repeat certain groups of statements in VBA
procedures by using loops. While working with several types of loops, you
saw how each loop performs repetitions in a slightly different way. As you
gain experience, you'll find it easier to choose the appropriate flow control
structure for your task.

In the following chapters of this book, there are many additional examples
of using loops. In the next chapter, for instance, you will see how, by using
arrays and nested loops, you can create your own VBA procedure to pick your
lottery numbers. The next chapter also shows you how to code procedures that
require a large number of variables.

Chapter 7

Working with Arrays

In previous chapters you worked with many VBA procedures that used variables to hold specific information about an object, property, or value. For each single value you wanted your procedure to manipulate, you declared a variable. But what if you have a series of values? If you had to write a VBA procedure to deal with larger amounts of data, you would have to create enough variables to handle all of the data. Can you imagine the nightmare of storing currency exchange rates for all the countries in the world in your program? To create a table to hold the necessary data, you'd need at least three variables for each country: country name, currency name, and exchange rate. Fortunately, Visual Basic has a way to get around this problem. By clustering the related variables together, your VBA procedures can manage a large amount of data with ease. In this chapter, you'll learn how to manipulate lists and tables of data with arrays.

In Visual Basic, an *array* is a special type of variable that represents a group of similar values that are of the same data type (String, Integer, Currency, Date, etc.). The two most common types of arrays are one-dimensional arrays (lists) and two-dimensional arrays (tables).

A one-dimensional array is sometimes referred to as a *list*. A shopping list, a list of the days of the week, or lists of employees are examples of one-dimensional arrays. A one-dimensional array is simply a numbered list. Each value in the list has an index. Below is a diagram of a list that contains six elements (items):

item(1)	
item(2)	
item(3)	
item(4)	
item(5)	
item(6)	

Notice that the column representing the one-dimensional array is currently empty. If you want to fill this array with data, instead of six individual labels, simply use one variable name followed by a number in parentheses. In the diagram above, item represents a variable name and the numbers in parentheses — (1), (2), (3), (4), (5), and (6) — identify individual elements of the array.

All elements of the array must be of the same data type. In other words, one array cannot store both strings and integers. Below are two examples of one-dimensional arrays: a one-dimensional array, cities, is populated with text

(String data type, $), and a one-dimensional array, lotto, contains six lottery numbers (Integer data type, %).

One-dimensional array named cities$ (of String data type)	
cities(1)	Baltimore
cities(2)	Atlanta
cities(3)	Boston
cities(4)	Washington
cities(5)	New York
cities(6)	Trenton

One-dimensional array named lotto% (of Integer data type)	
lotto(1)	25
lotto(2)	4
lotto(3)	31
lotto(4)	22
lotto(5)	11
lotto(6)	5

As you can see, the contents assigned to each array element match the variable type. If you want to store values of different data types in the same array, you must declare the array as Variant.

Two-dimensional arrays are tables of data represented in rows and columns. The position of each element in a table is determined by its row and column number. Below is a diagram of an empty two-dimensional array.

rows ↓	1	2	3	←columns
1	(1, 1)	(1, 2)	(1, 3)	
2	(2, 1)	(2, 2)	(2, 3)	
3	(3, 1)	(3, 2)	(3, 3)	
4	(4, 1)	(4, 2)	(4, 3)	
5	(5, 1)	(5, 2)	(5, 3)	

Notice how items in a two-dimensional array are identified with row and column indexes. In this diagram, the first element of the array is located in the first row and the first column (1, 1). The last element of the array is positioned in the fifth row and the third column (5, 3).

Let's now populate this array with some values. The two-dimensional array below stores the name of a country or region, its currency, and the U.S. dollar equivalent.

Two-dimensional array named exchange (of Variant data type)		
Japan (1, 1)	Japanese Yen (1, 2)	118.87 (1, 3)
Australia (2, 1)	Australian Dollar (2, 2)	1.1654 (2, 3)
Canada (3, 1)	Canadian Dollar (3, 2)	1.0582 (3, 3)
Norway (4, 1)	Norwegian Krone (4, 2)	5.8776 (4, 3)
Europe (5, 1)	Euro (5, 2)	0.7323 (5, 3)

Although VBA arrays can have up to 60 dimensions, most people find it difficult to picture dimensions beyond 3D. A three-dimensional array is a collection of tables where each table has the same number of rows and columns. Each element of a three-dimensional array is identified by three pieces of data: row, column, and table.

What Is an Array Variable?

An *array* is a group of variables that have a common name. While a typical variable can hold only one value, an *array variable* can store a large number of individual values. You refer to a specific value in the array by using the array name and an index number.

Declaring Arrays

Because an array is a variable, you must declare it the same way you declare other variables — by using the Dim statement. When you declare an array variable you set aside the required memory space to hold its values.

Let's take a look at some examples of array declarations:

```
Dim cities(6) As String
Dim daysOfWeek(7) As String
Dim lotto(6) As Integer
Dim exchange(5, 3) As Variant
```

Notice that the names of variables are followed by numbers in parentheses. One-dimensional arrays require one number between parentheses. This number specifies the maximum number of elements that can be stored in a list. The name of a two-dimensional array is always followed by two numbers; the first number is the row index and the second number is the column index. In the example above, the exchange array can hold a maximum of 15 values (5 * 3 = 15).

The last part in the array declaration is the definition of the data type the array will hold. An array can hold any of the following data types: Integer, Long, Single, Double, Variant, Currency, String, Boolean, Byte, and Date.

When you declare an array, Visual Basic automatically reserves enough memory space for it. The amount of memory allocated depends on the array's size and data type. When you declare a one-dimensional array named lotto with six elements, Visual Basic sets aside 12 bytes — two bytes for each element of the array (recall that the size of the Integer data type is 2, hence 12 = 2 * 6). The larger the array, the more memory space is required to store the data. Because arrays can eat up a lot of memory and impact your computer's performance, it is recommended that you declare arrays with only as many elements as you think you'll use.

Array Upper and Lower Bounds

By default, Visual Basic assigns zero (0) to the first element of the array. Therefore, the number 1 represents the second element of the array, number 2 the third, and so on. With numeric indexing starting at 0, the one-dimensional array cities(6) contains seven elements numbered from 0 to 6. If you'd rather start counting your array's elements at 1, you can explicitly specify a lower bound of the array by using an Option Base 1 statement. This instruction must be placed in the declaration section at the top of the VBA module, before any Sub statements. If you don't specify Option Base 1 in a procedure that uses arrays, Visual Basic assumes that the statement Option Base 0 is to be used, and begins indexing your array's elements at 0.

You can have the array indexing start at a number other than 0 or 1. To do this, you must specify the bounds of an array when declaring the array variable. The bounds of an array are its lowest and highest indexes. Let's take a look at the following example:

```
Dim cities(3 To 6) As Integer
```

The above statement declares a one-dimensional array with four elements. The numbers enclosed in parentheses after the array name specify the lower (3) and upper (6) bounds of the array. The first element of this array has the number 3, the second 4, the third 5, and the fourth 6. Notice the keyword To between the lower and upper index numbers.

The Range of the Array

The spread of the elements specified by the Dim statement is called the *range* of the array. For example: Dim mktgCodes(5 To 15).

Using Arrays in VBA Procedures

After you declare an array, you must assign values to its elements. Assigning values to the array's elements is often referred to as "filling an array" or "populating an array." Let's try a VBA procedure that uses a one-dimensional array to display a list of six American cities.

◎ Hands-On 7-1: Using a One-Dimensional Array

1. Start Microsoft Office Access 2007 and create a new Microsoft Office Access 2007 database named **Chap07.accdb** in your C:\Acc07_ ByExample folder.

2. Once your new database is opened, press **Alt+F11** to switch to the Visual Basic Editor window.

3. Choose **Insert | Module** to add a new standard module.

4. In the Module1 Code window, enter the **FavoriteCities** procedure shown below. (You may copy this procedure from the **C:\Acc07_HandsOn**

HandsOn_07.txt file.) Be sure to enter the Option Base 1 statement before this procedure.

```
Option Base 1

Sub FavoriteCities()
    ' declare the array
    Dim cities(6) As String

    ' assign the values to array elements
    cities(1) = "Baltimore"
    cities(2) = "Atlanta"
    cities(3) = "Boston"
    cities(4) = "Washington"
    cities(5) = "New York"
    cities(6) = "Trenton"

    ' display the list of cities
    MsgBox cities(1) & Chr(13) & cities(2) & Chr(13) _
        & cities(3) & Chr(13) & cities(4) & Chr(13) _
        & cities(5) & Chr(13) & cities(6)
End Sub
```

5. Choose **Run | Run Sub/UserForm** to execute the FavoriteCities procedure.

    Before the FavoriteCities procedure begins, the default indexing for an array is changed. Notice that the position of the Option Base 1 statement is at the top of the module window before the Sub statement. This statement tells Visual Basic to assign the number 1 instead of the default 0 to the first element of the array. The array cities is declared with six elements of the String data type. Each element of the array is then assigned a value. The last statement in this procedure uses the MsgBox function to display the list of cities in a message box. When you run this procedure, each city name will appear on a separate line (see Figure 7-1). You can change the order of the displayed data by switching the index values.

Figure 7-1: You can display the elements of a one-dimensional array with the MsgBox function.

6. Click **OK** to close the message box.

7. Modify the **FavoriteCities** procedure so that it displays the names of the cities in reverse order (from 6 to 1).

> ## Initial Value of an Array Element
> Until a value is assigned to an element of an array, the element retains its default value. Numeric variables have a default value of zero (0), and string variables have a default value of empty string ("").

Arrays and Looping Statements

Several looping statements you learned earlier (For...Next and For Each...Next) will come in handy now that you're ready to perform such tasks as populating an array or displaying the elements of an array. It's time to combine the skills you've learned so far.

How can you rewrite the FavoriteCities procedure so that it shows the name of each city in a separate message box? The FavoriteCities2 procedure in the following hands-on exercise replaces the last statement of the original procedure with the For Each...Next loop.

◉ Hands-On 7-2: Using Arrays and Loops

1. In the Visual Basic Editor window, insert a new module.
2. Enter the following **FavoriteCities2** procedure in the Code window:

```
Option Base 1

Sub FavoriteCities2()
    ' declare the array
    Dim cities(6) As String
    Dim city As Variant

    ' assign the values to array elements
    cities(1) = "Baltimore"
    cities(2) = "Atlanta"
    cities(3) = "Boston"
    cities(4) = "Washington"
    cities(5) = "New York"
    cities(6) = "Trenton"

    ' display the list of cities in separate messages
    For Each city In cities
        MsgBox city
    Next
End Sub
```

3. Choose **Run | Run Sub/UserForm** to execute the FavoriteCities2 procedure.

Notice that the For Each...Next loop uses the variable city of the Variant data type. As you recall from Chapter 6, the For Each... Next loop allows you to loop through all of the objects in a collection or all of the elements of an array and perform the same action on each object or element. When you run the FavoriteCities2 procedure, the loop will execute as many times as there are elements in the array.

In Chapter 4 you practiced passing arguments as variables to subroutines and functions. The procedure CityOperator in the next hands-on exercise demonstrates how you can pass elements of an array to another procedure.

◎ Hands-On 7-3: Passing Elements of an Array to Another Procedure

1. In the Visual Basic Editor window, insert a new module.

2. Enter the following two procedures (**CityOperator** and **Hello**) in the module's Code window:

```
Option Base 1

Sub CityOperator()
    ' declare the array
    Dim cities(6) As String

    ' assign the values to array elements
    cities(1) = "Baltimore"
    cities(2) = "Atlanta"
    cities(3) = "Boston"
    cities(4) = "Washington"
    cities(5) = "New York"
    cities(6) = "Trenton"

    ' call another procedure and pass
    ' the array as argument
    Hello cities()
End Sub

Sub Hello(cities() As String)
    Dim counter As Integer

    For counter = 1 To 6
    MsgBox "Hello, " & cities(counter) & "!"
    Next
End Sub
```

3. Execute the CityOperator procedure (choose **Run | Run Sub/UserForm**).

Notice that the declaration of the Hello procedure includes an array type argument named cities(). Passing array elements from one subroutine to another subroutine or function procedure allows you to reuse the same array in many procedures without unnecessary duplication of the program code.

Passing Arrays between Procedures

When an array is declared in a procedure, it is local to this procedure and unknown to other procedures. However, you can pass the local array to another procedure by using the array's name followed by an empty set of parentheses as an argument in the calling statement. For example, the statement Hello cities() calls the procedure named Hello and passes to it the array cities.

You can put your newly acquired knowledge about arrays and loops to work in real life. If you're an avid lotto player who is getting tired of picking your own lucky numbers, have Visual Basic do the picking. The Lotto procedure below populates an array with six numbers from 1 to 51.

◉ Hands-On 7-4: Using Arrays and Loops in Real Life

1. In the Visual Basic Editor window, insert a new module.

2. Enter the following **Lotto** procedure in the module's Code window:

```
Sub Lotto()
    Const spins = 6
    Const minNum = 1
    Const maxNum = 51
    Dim t As Integer          ' looping variable in outer loop
    Dim i As Integer          ' looping variable in inner loop
    Dim myNumbers As String   ' string to hold all picks
    Dim lucky(spins) As String ' array to hold generated picks

    myNumbers = ""
    For t = 1 To spins
        Randomize
        lucky(t) = Int((maxNum - minNum + 1) * Rnd + minNum)

        ' check if this number was picked before
        For i = 1 To (t - 1)
            If lucky(t) = lucky(i) Then
                lucky(t) = Int((maxNum - minNum + 1) * Rnd + minNum)
                i = 0
        End If
        Next i
        MsgBox "Lucky number is " & lucky(t), , "Lucky number " & t
        myNumbers = myNumbers & " -" & lucky(t)
    Next t
    MsgBox "Lucky numbers are " & myNumbers, , "6 Lucky Numbers"
End Sub
```

3. Execute the Lotto procedure (choose **Run | Run Sub/UserForm**) to get the computer-generated lottery numbers.

   The Randomize statement initializes the random number generator. The instruction Int((maxNum – minNum + 1) * Rnd + minNum) uses the Rnd function to generate a random value from the specified minNum to maxNum. The Int function converts the resulting random number to an integer. Instead of assigning constant values for minNum and maxNum, you can use the InputBox function to get these values from the user.

The inner For...Next loop ensures that each picked number is unique — it may not be any one of the previously picked numbers. If you omit the inner loop and run this procedure multiple times, you'll likely see some occurrences of duplicate numbers.

Using a Two-Dimensional Array

Now that you know how to programmatically produce a list (a one-dimensional array), it's time to take a closer look at how you can work with tables of data. The following hands-on exercise creates a two-dimensional array that will hold three country or region names, currency names, and exchange rates.

◎ Hands-On 7-5: Using a Two-Dimensional Array

1. In the Visual Basic Editor window, insert a new module.

2. Enter the following **Exchange** procedure in the module's Code window:

```
Sub Exchange()
    Dim t As String
    Dim r As String
    Dim Ex(3, 3) As Variant

    t = Chr(9)  ' Tab
    r = Chr(13) ' Enter

    Ex(1, 1) = "Japan"
    Ex(1, 2) = "Japanese Yen"
    Ex(1, 3) = 102.76
    Ex(2, 1) = "Europe"
    Ex(2, 2) = "Euro"
    Ex(2, 3) = 0.744734
    Ex(3, 1) = "Canada"
    Ex(3, 2) = "Canadian Dollar"
    Ex(3, 3) = 1.20892

    MsgBox "Country " & t & t & "Currency" & t & t & "Value per US$" _
        & r & r _
        & Ex(1, 1) & t & t & Ex(1, 2) & t & Ex(1, 3) & r _
        & Ex(2, 1) & t & t & Ex(2, 2) & t & t & Ex(2, 3) & r _
        & Ex(3, 1) & t & t & Ex(3, 2) & t & t & Ex(3, 3), , _
        "Exchange"
End Sub
```

3. Execute the Exchange procedure (choose **Run | Run Sub/UserForm**).

When you run the Exchange procedure, you will see a message box with the information presented in three columns (see Figure 7-2).

Figure 7-2: The text displayed in a message box can be custom formatted. (These are fictitious exchange rates for demonstration only.)

4. Click **OK** to close the message box.

Static and Dynamic Arrays

The arrays introduced thus far are static. A *static array* is an array of a specific size. You use a static array when you know in advance how big the array should be. The size of the static array is specified in the array's declaration statement. For example, the statement Dim Fruits(10) As String declares a static array called Fruits that is made up of 10 elements.

But what if you're not sure how many elements your array will contain? If your procedure depends on user input, the number of user-supplied elements might vary every time the procedure is executed. How can you ensure that the array you declare is not wasting memory?

You may recall that after you declare an array, VBA sets aside enough memory to accommodate the array. If you declare an array to hold more elements than what you need, you'll end up wasting valuable computer resources. The solution to this problem is making your arrays dynamic. A *dynamic array* is an array whose size can change. You use a dynamic array when the array size will be determined each time the procedure is run.

Fixed-Dimension Arrays

A static array contains a fixed number of elements. The number of elements in a static array will not change once it has been declared.

A dynamic array is declared by placing empty parentheses after the array name. For example:

```
Dim Fruits() As String
```

Before you use a dynamic array in your procedure, you must use the ReDim statement to dynamically set the lower and upper bounds of the array.

The ReDim statement redimensions arrays as the procedure code executes. The ReDim statement informs Visual Basic about the new size of the array. This statement can be used several times in the same procedure. Let's see how your procedure could use a dynamic array.

⊚ Hands-On 7-6: Using a Dynamic Array

1. Insert a new module and enter the following **DynArray** procedure in the module's Code window:

```
Sub DynArray()
    Dim counter As Integer
    Dim myArray() As Integer       ' declare a dynamic array
    ReDim myArray(5)               ' specify the initial size of the array
    Dim myValues As String

    ' populate myArray with values
    For counter = 1 To 5
        myArray(counter) = counter + 1
        myValues = myValues & myArray(counter) & Chr(13)
    Next

    ' change the size of myArray to hold 10 elements
    ReDim Preserve myArray(10)

    ' add new values to myArray
    For counter = 6 To 10
        myArray(counter) = counter * counter
        myValues = myValues & myArray(counter) & Chr(13)
    Next counter

    MsgBox myValues
    For counter = 1 To 10
        MsgBox myArray(counter)
    Next counter
End Sub
```

2. Execute the DynArray procedure (choose **Run | Run Sub/UserForm**).

In the DynArray procedure, the statement Dim myArray() As Integer declares a dynamic array called myArray. Although this statement declares the array, it does not allocate any memory to the array. The first ReDim statement specifies the initial size of myArray and reserves for it 10 bytes of memory to hold its five elements. As you know, every Integer value requires 2 bytes of memory. The For...Next loop populates myArray with data and writes the array's elements to the variable myValues. The value of the variable counter equals 1 at the beginning of the loop.

The first statement in the loop (myArray(counter) = counter +1) assigns the value 2 to the first element of myArray. The second statement (myValues = myValues & myArray(counter) & Chr(13)) enters the current value of myArray's element followed by a carriage return (Chr(13)) into the variable myValues. The statements inside the loop are executed five times. Visual Basic places each new value in the variable myValues and proceeds to the next statement: ReDim Preserve myArray(10).

Normally, when you change the size of the array, you lose all the values that were in that array. When used alone, the ReDim statement reinitializes the array. However, you can append new elements to an existing array by following the ReDim statement with the Preserve keyword. In other words, the

Preserve keyword guarantees that the redimensioned array will not lose its existing data.

The second For...Next loop assigns values to the sixth through tenth elements of myArray. This time the values of the array's elements are obtained by multiplication: counter * counter.

Dimensioning Arrays

Arrays must be dimensioned in a Dim or ReDim statement before they are used. This means that you can't assign a value to an array element until you have declared the array with the Dim or ReDim statement.

Array Functions

You can manipulate arrays with five built-in VBA functions: Array, IsArray, Erase, LBound, and UBound. The following sections demonstrate the use of each of these functions in VBA procedures.

The Array Function

The Array function allows you to create an array during code execution without having to first dimension it. This function always returns an array of Variants. Using the Array function you can quickly place a series of values in a list.

The CarInfo procedure in the following hands-on exercise creates a fixed-size, one-dimensional, three-element array called auto.

⊚ Hands-On 7-7: Using the Array Function

1. Insert a new module and enter the following **CarInfo** procedure in the module's Code window:

```
Option Base 1

Sub CarInfo()
    Dim auto As Variant

    auto = Array("Ford", "Black", "1999")
    MsgBox auto(2) & " " & auto(1) & ", " & auto(3)

    auto(2) = "4-door"
    MsgBox auto(2) & " " & auto(1) & ", " & auto(3)
End Sub
```

2. Run the CarInfo procedure and examine the results.

When you run the above procedure, you get two message boxes. The first one displays the following text: "Black Ford, 1999". After changing the value of the second array element, the second message box will say: "4-door Ford, 1999".

Note: Be sure to enter Option Base 1 at the top of the module before running the CarInfo procedure. If this statement is missing in your module, Visual Basic will display run-time error 9 — "Subscript out of range."

The IsArray Function

The IsArray function lets you test whether a variable is an array. The IsArray function returns True if the variable is an array or False if it's not an array. Let's do another hands-on exercise.

◎ Hands-On 7-8: Using the IsArray Function

1. Insert a new module and enter the code of the **IsThisArray** procedure in the module's Code window as shown below:

```
Sub IsThisArray()
    ' declare a dynamic array
    Dim tblNames() As String
    Dim totalTables As Integer
    Dim counter As Integer
    Dim db As Database

    Set db = CurrentDb

    ' count the tables in the open database
    totalTables = db.TableDefs.Count

    ' specify the size of the array
    ReDim tblNames(1 To totalTables)

    ' enter and show the names of tables
    For counter = 1 To totalTables - 1
        tblNames(counter) = db.TableDefs(counter).Name
        Debug.Print tblNames(counter)
    Next counter

    ' check if this is indeed an array
    If IsArray(tblNames) Then
        MsgBox "The tblNames is an array."
    End If
End Sub
```

2. Run the IsThisArray procedure to examine its results.

When you run the above procedure, the list of tables in the current database is written to the Immediate window. A message box displays whether the tblNames array is indeed an array.

The Erase Function

When you want to remove the data from an array, you should use the Erase function. This function deletes all the data held by static or dynamic arrays. In addition, the Erase function reallocates all of the memory assigned to a dynamic array. If a procedure has to use the dynamic array again, you must use the ReDim statement to specify the size of the array. The next hands-on exercise demonstrates how to erase the data from the array cities.

◎ Hands-On 7-9: Removing Data from an Array

1. Insert a new module and enter the code of the **FunCities** procedure in the module's Code window as shown below:

```
' start indexing array elements at 1
Option Base 1

Sub FunCities()
    ' declare the array
    Dim cities(1 To 5) As String

    ' assign the values to array elements
    cities(1) = "Las Vegas"
    cities(2) = "Orlando"
    cities(3) = "Atlantic City"
    cities(4) = "New York"
    cities(5) = "San Francisco"

    ' display the list of cities
    MsgBox cities(1) & Chr(13) & cities(2) & Chr(13) _
        & cities(3) & Chr(13) & cities(4) & Chr(13) _
        & cities(5)

    Erase cities

    ' show all that was erased
    MsgBox cities(1) & Chr(13) & cities(2) & Chr(13) _
        & cities(3) & Chr(13) & cities(4) & Chr(13) _
        & cities(5)
End Sub
```

2. Run the FunCities procedure to examine its results.

3. Click **OK** to close the message box.

   Visual Basic should now display an empty message box, because all values are deleted from the array by the Erase function.

4. Click **OK** to close the empty message box.

The LBound and UBound Functions

The LBound and UBound functions return whole numbers that indicate the lower bound and upper bound indices of an array.

◎ Hands-On 7-10: Finding the Lower and Upper Bounds of an Array

1. Insert a new module and enter the code of the **FunCities2** procedure in the module's Code window as shown below:

```
Sub FunCities2()
    ' declare the array
```

```
Dim cities(1 To 5) As String

' assign the values to array elements
cities(1) = "Las Vegas"
cities(2) = "Orlando"
cities(3) = "Atlantic City"
cities(4) = "New York"
cities(5) = "San Francisco"

' display the list of cities
MsgBox cities(1) & Chr(13) & cities(2) & Chr(13) _
    & cities(3) & Chr(13) & cities(4) & Chr(13) _
    & cities(5)

' display the array bounds
MsgBox "The lower bound: " & LBound(cities) & Chr(13) _
    & "The upper bound: " & UBound(cities)
End Sub
```

2. Run the FunCities2 procedure.

   When determining the lower and upper bound indices of a two-dimensional array, you must specify the dimension number: 1 for the first dimension and 2 for the second dimension.

3. Click **OK** to close the message box that displays the favorite cities.

4. Click **OK** to close the message box that displays the lower and upper bound indices.

To determine the upper and lower indices in a two-dimensional array, you may want to add the following statements at the end of the Exchange procedure that was prepared in Hands-On 7-5 (add these lines just before the End Sub keywords):

```
MsgBox "The lower bound (first dimension) is " _
    & LBound(Ex, 1) & "."
MsgBox "The upper bound(first dimension) is " _
    & UBound(Ex, 1) & "."
MsgBox "The lower bound (second dimension) is " _
    & LBound(Ex, 2) & "."
MsgBox "The upper bound(second dimension) is " _
    & UBound(Ex, 2) & "."
```

Errors in Arrays

When working with arrays, it's easy to make a mistake. If you try to assign more values than there are elements in the declared array, Visual Basic will display the error message "Subscript out of range" (see Figure 7-3).

Figure 7-3: This error was caused by an attempt to access a nonexistent array element.

Suppose you declared a one-dimensional array that consists of three elements and you are trying to assign a value to the fourth element. When you run the procedure, Visual Basic can't find the fourth element, so it displays the above error message. If you click the Debug button, Visual Basic will highlight the line of code that caused the error (see Figure 7-4).

Figure 7-4: The statement that triggered the error shown in Figure 7-3 is highlighted.

The error "Subscript out of range" is often triggered in procedures using loops. The procedure Zoo1 shown in Hands-On 7-11 serves as an example of such a situation.

Hands-On 7-11: Understanding Errors in Arrays

1. Insert a new module and enter the following **Zoo1** and **Zoo2** procedures in the module's Code window:

```
Sub Zoo1()
    ' this procedure triggers an error "Subscript out of range"
    Dim zoo(3) As String
    Dim i As Integer
    Dim response As String

    i = 0
    Do
        i = i + 1
        response = InputBox("Enter a name of animal:")
        zoo(i) = response
    Loop Until response = ""
End Sub

Sub Zoo2()
    ' this procedure avoids the error "Subscript out of range"
    Dim zoo(3) As String
    Dim i As Integer
    Dim response As String

    i = 1
    Do While i >= LBound(zoo) And i <= UBound(zoo)
        response = InputBox("Enter a name of animal:")
        If response = "" Then Exit Sub
        zoo(i) = response
```

```
        Debug.Print zoo(i)
          i = i + 1
      Loop

    End Sub
```

2. Run the Zoo1 procedure and enter your favorite animal names when prompted. Do not cancel the procedure until you see the error.

   While executing this procedure, when the variable i equals 4, Visual Basic will not be able to find the fourth element in a three-element array, so the error message will appear.

3. Click the **Debug** button in the error message.

   Visual Basic will highlight the code that caused the error.

4. Position the cursor over the variable (i) in the highlighted line of code to view the variable's value.

   Visual Basic displays: *i=4*

   Notice that at the top of the Zoo1 procedure zoo has been declared as an array containing only three elements:

```
Dim zoo(3) As String
```

   Since Visual Basic could not find the fourth element, it displayed the "Subscript out of range" error.

   The Zoo2 procedure demonstrates how, by using the LBound and UBound functions introduced in the preceding section, you can avoid errors caused by an attempt to access a nonexistent array element.

5. Choose **Run | Reset** to terminate the debugging session and exit the procedure. You will learn more about debugging procedures in Chapter 9.

Another frequent error you may encounter while working with arrays is a Type Mismatch error. To avoid this error, keep in mind that each element of an array must be of the same data type. Therefore, if you attempt to assign to an element of an array a value that conflicts with the data type of the array, you will get a Type Mismatch error during the code execution. If you need to hold values of different data types in an array, declare the array as Variant.

Parameter Arrays

Earlier in this book you learned that values can be passed between subroutines or functions as required or by optional arguments. If the passed argument is not absolutely required for the procedure to execute, the argument's name is preceded by the keyword Optional. Sometimes, however, you don't know in advance how many arguments you want to pass. A classic example is addition. One time you may want to add two numbers together, another time you may want to add three, ten, or fifteen numbers.

Using the keyword ParamArray, you can pass an array consisting of any number of elements to your subroutines and function. The following hands-on exercise uses the AddMultipleArgs function to add as many numbers as you may require. This function begins with the declaration of an array myNumbers. Notice the use of the ParamArray keyword.

The array must be declared as type Variant, and it must be the last argument in the procedure definition.

⊚ Hands-On 7-12: Working with Parameter Arrays

1. Insert a new module and enter the following **AddMultipleArgs** function procedure in the module's Code window:

```
Function AddMultipleArgs(ParamArray myNumbers() As Variant)
    Dim mySum As Single
    Dim myValue As Variant

    For Each myValue In myNumbers
        mySum = mySum + myValue
    Next
    AddMultipleArgs = mySum
End Function
```

2. Choose **View | Immediate Window** and type the following instruction, then press **Enter** to execute it:

```
?AddMultipleArgs(1, 23.24, 3, 24, 8, 34)
```

When you press Enter, Visual Basic returns the total of all the numbers in the parentheses: 93.24. You can supply an unlimited number of arguments. To add more values, enter additional values in the parentheses after the function name in the Immediate window and press Enter. Notice that each function argument must be separated by a comma.

3. Choose **File | Save Chap07** to save changes to the modules.

4. Choose **File | Close and Return to Microsoft Office Access**.

5. Close the Chap07.accdb database and exit Microsoft Office Access.

Chapter Summary

In this chapter you learned how, by creating an array, you can write procedures that require a large number of variables. You worked with examples of procedures that demonstrated how to declare and use a one-dimensional array (list) and a two-dimensional array (table). You also learned the difference between static and dynamic arrays. This chapter ended by introducing you to five built-in VBA functions that are frequently used with arrays (Array, IsArray, Erase, LBound, and UBound), as well as the ParamArray keyword. You now know all the control structures that can make your code more intelligent: conditional statements, loops, and arrays.

In the next chapter you will learn how to use collections instead of arrays to manipulate large amounts of data.

Chapter 8

Custom Collections and Class Modules

You are not limited to using objects built into Microsoft Office Access. VBA allows you to create your own objects and collections of objects, complete with their own methods and properties. In this chapter, you learn how to work with collections, including how to declare a custom Collection object. You also learn how to use class modules to create user-defined objects.

Terminology

Before diving into theory and the hands-on examples of this chapter, let's start by going over several terms that will be used throughout this chapter.

Collection — An object that contains a set of related objects.

Class — A definition of an object that includes its name, properties, methods, and events. The class acts as a sort of object template from which an instance of an object is created at run time.

Class module — A module that contains the definition of a class, including its property and method definitions.

Event — An action recognized by an object, such as a mouse click or a key press, for which you can define a response. Events can be triggered by a user action, a VBA statement, or the system.

Event procedure — A procedure that is automatically executed in response to an event triggered by the user, program code, or the system.

Form module — A module that contains the VBA code for all event procedures triggered by events occurring in a user form or its controls. A form module is a type of class module.

Instance — A specific object that belongs to a class is referred to as an *instance of the class*. When you create an instance, you create a new object that has the properties and methods defined by the class.

Module — A structure containing subroutine and function procedures that are available to other VBA procedures and are not related to any object in particular.

Working with Collections

Collections are objects that contain other similar objects. For example, a Microsoft Access database has a collection of tables, and each table has a collection of fields and indexes. In Microsoft Excel, all open workbooks belong to the collection of workbooks, and all the sheets in a particular workbook are the members of the worksheets collection. In Microsoft Word, all open documents belong to the collection of documents, and each paragraph in a document is a member of the paragraphs collection.

No matter what collection you want to work with, you can do the following:

▪ Insert new items into the collection by using the Add method.

The following example uses the Immediate window to create a new collection named myTestCollection and adds three items to the collection:

```
set myTestCollection = New Collection    [Enter]
    myTestCollection.Add "first member"   [Enter]
    myTestCollection.Add "second member"  [Enter]
    myTestCollection.Add "third member"   [Enter]
```

▪ Determine the number of items in the collection by using the Count property.

For example, when you enter this statement in the Immediate window:

```
?myTestCollection.Count                  [Enter]
```

it returns the total number of items in myTestCollection.

▪ Refer to a specific object in a collection by using an index value.

For example, to find out the names of the collection members, you can type the following statement in the Immediate window:

```
?myTestCollection.Item(1)                [Enter]
```

Because the Item method is a default method of the collection, you may omit it from the statement, as shown below:

```
?myTestCollection(1)                     [Enter]
```

▪ Remove an object from a collection by using the Remove method.

For example, to remove the first object from myTestCollection, enter the following statement:

```
myTestCollection.Remove 1                [Enter]
```

▪ Cycle through every object in the collection by using the For Each...Next loop.

For example, to remove all objects from myTestCollection, enter the following looping structure in the Immediate window:

```
For Each m in myTestCollection : myTestCollection.Remove 1 : Next    [Enter]
```

Note that a colon is used to separate one statement from the next. You can
write two or more statements on a single line by separating them with a
colon (:). This is very convenient when testing statements in the Immediate
window. Because collections are reindexed, the above statement will
remove the first member of the collection on each iteration. Upon pressing
Enter, myTestCollection should have zero objects. However, to be sure,
enter the following statement in the Immediate window:

```
?myTestCollection.Count            [Enter]
```

While writing your own VBA procedures, you may come across a situation
where there's no built-in collection to handle the task at hand. The solution is
to create a custom collection. From the previous chapter you already know
how to work with multiple items of data by using dynamic or static arrays.
Because collections have built-in properties and methods that allow you to
add, remove, and count their elements, you will find that it's much easier to
work with collections than arrays.

Declaring a Custom Collection

To create a user-defined collection, you should begin by declaring an object
variable of the Collection type. This variable is declared with the New keyword in the Dim statement, as shown below:

```
Dim collection Fruits As New Collection
```

Adding Objects to a Custom Collection

After you've declared the Collection object, you can insert new items into the
collection by using the Add method. The objects with which you populate your
collection do not have to be of the same data type. The Add method looks as
follows:

```
object.Add item[, key, before, after]
```

For example, the following statement adds a new item to the previously
declared Fruits collection:

```
Fruits.Add "apples"
```

You are only required to specify object and item. Object is the collection name
(Fruits). This is the same name that was used in the declaration of the Collec-
tion object. Item ("apples") is the object you want to add to the collection
(Fruits).

Although the other arguments are optional, they are quite useful. It's important to understand that the items in a collection are automatically assigned
numbers starting with 1. However, they can also be assigned a unique key
value. Instead of accessing a specific item with an index (1, 2, 3, and so on) at
the time an object is added to a collection, you can assign a key for that object.
For instance, to identify an individual in a collection of students or employees,
you could use Social Security numbers as a key. If you want to specify the

position of the object in the collection, you should use either the before or after argument (do not use both). The before argument is the object before which the new object is added. The after argument is the object after which the new object is added.

The NewEmployees procedure in the following hands-on exercise declares the custom Collection object called colEmployees.

◉ Hands-On 8-1: Creating a Custom Collection

1. Start Microsoft Office Access 2007 and create a new Microsoft Office Access 2007 database named **Chap08.accdb** in your **C:\Acc07_ ByExample** folder.

2. Once your new database is opened, press **Alt+F11** to switch to the Visual Basic Editor window.

3. Choose **Insert | Module** to add a new standard module.

4. In the Module1 Code window, enter the **NewEmployees** procedure shown below. (You may copy this procedure from the **C:\Acc07_HandsOn\ HandsOn_08.txt** file.) Be sure to enter the Option Base 1 statement before this procedure.

```
Option Base 1       ' ensure that there is only one Option Base 1 statement
                    ' at the top of the module
Sub NewEmployees()
    ' declare the employees collection
    Dim colEmployees As New Collection
    ' declare a variable to hold each element of a collection
    Dim emp As Variant

    ' Add 3 new employees to the collection
    With colEmployees
        .Add Item:="John Collins", Key:="128634456"
        .Add Item:="Mary Poppins", Key:="223998765"
        .Add Item:="Karen Loza", Key:="120228876", Before:=2
    End With

    ' list the members of the collection
    For Each emp In colEmployees
        Debug.Print emp
    Next

    MsgBox "There are " & colEmployees.Count & " employees."
End Sub
```

5. Choose **Run | Run Sub/UserForm** to execute the NewEmployees procedure.

Note that the control variable used in the For Each...Next loop must be Variant or Object. When you run the above procedure, you will notice that the order of employee names stored in the colEmployees collection (as displayed in the Immediate window) may be different from the order in which these employees were entered in the program code. This is the result of using the optional before argument with Karen Loza's entry. This argument's value tells Visual Basic to place Karen before the second item in the collection.

Removing Objects from a Custom Collection

Removing an item from a custom collection is as easy as adding an item. To remove an element, use the Remove method in the following format:

```
object.Remove index
```

The object is the name of the custom collection that contains the object you want to remove. The index is an expression specifying the position of the object in the collection.

To demonstrate the process of removing an item from a collection, let's work with the following hands-on exercise that modifies the NewEmployees procedure that you prepared in Hands-On 8-1.

⊚ Hands-On 8-2: Removing Objects from a Collection

This hands-on exercise requires the prior completion of Hands-On 8-1.

1. Add the following lines to the **NewEmployees** procedure just before the End Sub keywords:

```
' remove the third element from the collection
colEmployees.Remove 3
MsgBox colEmployees.Count & " employees remain."
```

2. Rerun the NewEmployees procedure.

Reindexing Collections

Collections are reindexed automatically when an item is removed. Therefore, to remove all items from a custom collection you can use 1 for the Index argument, as in the following example:

```
Do While myCollection.Count > 0
    myCollection.Remove Index:=1
Loop
```

Creating Custom Objects

There are two module commands available in the Visual Basic Editor's Insert menu: Module and Class Module. So far you've used a standard module to create subprocedures and function procedures. You'll use the class module for the first time in this chapter to create a custom object and define its properties and methods.

Creating a new, non-standard VBA object involves inserting a class module into your project and adding code to that module. However, before you do so you need a basic understanding of what a class is.

If you refer back to the terminology section earlier in this chapter, you will find out that the class is a sort of object template. A frequently used analogy is comparing an object class to a cookie cutter. Just like a cookie cutter defines what a particular cookie will look like, the definition of the class determines how a particular object should look and how it should behave. Before you can actually use an object class, you must first create a new *instance* of that class. Object instances are the cookies. Each object instance has the characteristics (properties and methods) defined by its class. Just as you can cut out many cookies using the same cookie cutter, you can create multiple instances of a class. You can change the properties of each instance of a class independently of any other instance of the same class.

A *class module* lets you define your own custom classes, complete with custom properties and methods. A *property* is an attribute of an object that defines one of its characteristics, such as shape, position, color, title, etc. A *method* is an action that the object can perform. You can create the properties for your custom objects by writing property procedures in a class module. The object methods are also created in a class module by writing subprocedures or function procedures.

After building your object in the class module, you can use it in the same way you use other built-in objects. You can also export the object class outside the VBA project to other VBA-capable applications.

Creating a Class

The following sections of this chapter walk you through the process of creating and working with a custom object called CEmployee. This object will represent an employee. It will have properties such as Id, FirstName, LastName, and Salary. It will also have a method to modify the current salary.

◎ Custom Project 8-1 (Step 1): Creating a Class Module

1. In the Visual Basic Editor window, choose **Insert | Class Module**.

2. In the Project Explorer window, highlight the **Class1** module and use the Properties window to rename the class module **CEmployee** (Figure 1-8).

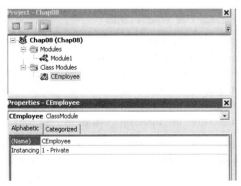

Figure 8-1: Use the Properties window to rename the module.

> **Naming a Class Module**
> Every time you create a new class module, give it a meaningful name. Set the name of the class module to the name you want to use in your VBA procedures using the class. The name you choose for your class should be easily understood and should identify the "thing" the object class represents. As a rule, the object class name is prefaced with an uppercase "C."

Variable Declarations

After adding and renaming the class module, the next step is to declare the variables that will hold the data you want to store in the object. Each item of data you want to store in an object should be assigned a variable. Class variables are called *data members* and are declared with the Private statement. Using the Private statement in a class module hides the data members and prevents other parts of the application from referencing them. Only the procedures within the class module in which the Private variables were defined can modify the value of these variables.

Because the name of a variable also serves as a property name, use meaningful names for your object's data members. It's traditional to preface the class variable names with m_ to indicate that they are data members of a class.

Custom Project 8-1 (Step 2): Declaring Class Members

1. Type the following declaration lines at the top of the **CEmployee** class module:

```
Option Explicit

' declarations
Private m_LastName As String
Private m_FirstName As String
Private m_Salary As Currency
Private m_ID As String
```

Notice that the name of each data member variable begins with the prefix m_.

Defining the Properties for the Class

Declaring the variables with the Private keyword guarantees that they cannot be accessed directly from outside the object. This means that the VBA procedures outside the class module will not be able to set or read data stored in those variables. To enable other parts of your VBA application to set or retrieve the employee data, you must add special property procedures to the CEmployee class module. There are three types of property procedures:

- **Property Let** — This type of procedure allows other parts of the application to set the value of a property.

- **Property Get** — This type of procedure allows other parts of the application to get or read the value of a property.

■ **Property Set** — This type of procedure is used instead of Property Let when setting the reference to an object.

Property procedures are executed when an object property needs to be set or retrieved. The Property Get procedure can have the same name as the Property Let procedure. You should create property procedures for each property of the object that can be accessed by another part of your VBA application.

The easiest of the three types of property statements to understand is the Property Get procedure. Let's examine the syntax of the property procedures by taking a close look at the Property Get LastName procedure.

Property procedures contain the following parts:

■ A procedure declaration line

■ An assignment statement

■ The End Property keywords

A procedure declaration line specifies the name of the property and the data type:

```
Property Get LastName() As String
```

LastName is the name of the property and As String determines the data type of the property's return value.

An assignment statement is similar to the one used in a function procedure:

```
LastName = m_LastName
```

LastName is the name of the property and *m_LastName* is the data member variable that holds the value of the property you want to retrieve or set. The m_LastName variable should be defined with the Private keyword at the top of the class module. Here's the complete Property Get procedure:

```
Property Get LastName() As String
    LastName = m_LastName
End Property
```

The Property Get procedure can return a result from a calculation, like this:

```
Property Get Royalty()
    Royalty = (Sales * Percent) - Advance
End Property
```

The End Property keywords specify the end of the property procedure.

Immediate Exit from Property Procedures

Just as the Exit Sub and Exit Function keywords allow you to exit early from a subroutine or a function procedure, the Exit Property keywords give you a way to immediately exit from a property procedure. Program execution will continue with the statements following the statement that called the Property Get, Property Let, or Property Set procedure.

Creating the Property Get Procedures

The CEmployee class object has four properties that need to be exposed to
VBA procedures that we will write later in a standard module named
EmpOperations. When working with the CEmployee object, you would certainly like to get information about the employee ID, first and last name, and
current salary.

⊚ Custom Project 8-1 (Step 3): Writing Property Get Procedures

1. Type the following Property Get procedures in the **CEmployee** class module, just below the declaration section that you entered in step 2 of this
   custom project:

```
Property Get ID() As String
    ID = m_ID
End Property

Property Get LastName() As String
    LastName = m_LastName
End Property

Property Get FirstName() As String
    FirstName = m_FirstName
End Property

Property Get Salary() As Currency
    Salary = m_Salary
End Property
```

Notice that each employee information type requires a separate Property Get
procedure. Each of the above Property Get procedures returns the current value
of the property. Notice also how a Property Get procedure is similar to a function procedure. Similar to function procedures, the Property Get procedures
contain an assignment statement. As you recall, in order to return a value from
a function procedure, you must assign it to the function's name.

Creating the Property Let Procedures

In addition to retrieving values stored in data members (private variables) with
Property Get procedures, you must prepare corresponding Property Let procedures to allow other procedures to change the values of these variables as
needed. The only time you don't define a Property Let procedure is when the
value stored in a private variable is meant to be *read-only*.

The example CEmployee class allows the user to assign values of the following data items by typing entries in the appropriate text boxes: last name,
first name, and salary. The employee ID will be assigned automatically with a
return value from a function procedure.

◎ Custom Project 8-1 (Step 4): Writing Property Let Procedures

1. Type the following Property Let procedures in the **CEmployee** class module below the Property Get procedures:

```
Property Let ID(ref As String)
    m_ID = ref
End Property

Property Let LastName(L As String)
    m_LastName = L
End Property

Property Let FirstName(F As String)
    m_FirstName = F
End Property

Property Let Salary(ByVal dollar As Currency)
    m_Salary = dollar
End Property
```

The Property Let procedures require at least one parameter that specifies the value you want to assign to the property. This parameter can be passed by *value* (see the ByVal keyword in Property Let Salary above) or by *reference* (ByRef is the default). If you need a refresher on the meaning of these keywords, see the section titled "Passing Arguments by Reference and by Value" in Chapter 4.

The data type of the parameter passed to the Property Let procedure must be exactly the same data type as the value returned from the Property Get or Set procedure with the same name. Notice that the Property Let procedures have the same names as the Property Get procedures prepared in the preceding section.

Defining the Scope of Property Procedures

You can place the Public, Private, or Static keyword before the name of a property procedure to define its scope. To indicate that the Property Get procedure is accessible to procedures in all modules, use the following statement format:

```
Public Property Get FirstName() As String
```

To make the Property Get procedure accessible only to other procedures in the module where it is declared, use the following statement format:

```
Private Property Get FirstName() As String
```

To preserve the Property Get procedure's local variables between procedure calls, use the following statement format:

```
Static Property Get FirstName() As String
```

If not explicitly specified using either Public or Private, property procedures are Public by default. Also, if the Static keyword is not used, the values of local variables are not preserved between procedure calls.

Creating the Class Methods

Apart from properties, objects usually have one or more methods. A *method* is an action that the object can perform. Methods allow you to manipulate the data stored in a class object. Methods are created with subroutines or function procedures. To make a method available outside the class module, use the Public keyword in front of the Sub or Function definition. The CEmployee object that you create in this chapter has one method that allows you to calculate the new salary. Assume that the employee salary can be increased or decreased by a specific percentage or amount.

◎ Custom Project 8-1 (Step 5): Writing Class Methods

1. Type the following **CalcNewSalary** function procedure in the **CEmployee** class module:

```
Public Function CalcNewSalary(choice As Integer, curSalary As Currency, _
    amount As Long) As Currency
    Select Case choice
        Case 1 ' by percent
            CalcNewSalary = curSalary + ((curSalary * amount) / 100)
        Case 2 ' by amount
            CalcNewSalary = curSalary + amount
    End Select
End Function
```

The CalcNewSalary function defined with the Public keyword in a class module serves as a method for the CEmployee class. To calculate a new salary, a VBA procedure from outside the class module must pass three arguments: choice, CurSalary, and amount. The choice argument specifies the type of the calculation. Suppose you want to increase the employee salary by 5% or by $5.00. Choice 1 will increase the salary by the specified percent, and choice 2 will add the specified amount to the current salary. The curSalary argument is the current salary figure for an employee, and the amount argument determines the value by which the salary should be changed.

About Class Methods

- Only those methods that will be accessed from outside of the class should be declared as Public. All others should be Private.
- Methods perform some operation on the data contained within the class.
- If a method needs to return a value, write a function procedure. Otherwise, create a subprocedure.

Creating an Instance of a Class

After typing all the necessary Property Get, Property Let, or function procedures for your VBA application in the class module, you are ready to create a new instance of a class, called an *object*. Before an object can be created, an object variable must be declared in a standard module to store the reference to the object. If the name of the class module is CEmployee, then a new instance of this class can be created with the following statement:

```
Dim emp As New CEmployee
```

The emp variable will represent a reference to an object of the CEmployee class. When you declare the object variable with the New keyword, VBA creates the object and allocates memory for it. However, the object isn't instanced until you refer to it in your procedure code by assigning a value to its property or by running one of its methods.

You can also create an instance of the object by declaring an object variable with the data type defined to be the class of the object. For example:

```
Dim emp As CEmployee
Set emp = New CEmployee
```

If you don't use the New keyword with the Dim statement (as shown above), VBA does not allocate memory for your custom object until your procedure actually needs it.

◎ Custom Project 8-1 (Step 6): Creating an Instance of a Class

1. Activate the Visual Basic Editor window and choose **Insert | Module** to add a standard module to your application.

2. Use the Properties window to change the name of the new module to **EmpOperations**.

3. Type the following declarations at the top of the EmpOperations module:

```
Option Explicit

Dim emp As New CEmployee
Dim CEmployee As New Collection
```

The first declaration statement (Dim) declares the variable emp as a new instance of the CEmployee class. The second statement declares a custom collection. The CEmployee collection will be used to store all employees' data.

Event Procedures in the Class Module

An *event* is basically an action recognized by an object. Custom classes recognize only two events: Initialize and Terminate. These events are triggered when an instance of the class is created (Initialize) and destroyed (Terminate). The Initialize event is generated when an object is created from a class (see the preceding section on creating an instance of a class). Because the statements included inside the Initialize event are the first ones to be executed for the object, before any properties are set or any methods are executed, the Initialize event is a good place to perform initialization of the objects created from the class.

The Class_Initialize procedure uses the following syntax:

```
Private Sub Class_Initialize()
    [code to perform tasks as the object is created goes here]
End Sub
```

The Terminate event occurs when all references to an object have been released. This is a good place to perform any necessary cleanup tasks. The Class_Terminate procedure uses the following syntax:

```
Private Sub Class_Terminate()
    [cleanup code goes here]
End Sub
```

To release an object variable from an object, use the following syntax:

```
Set objectVariable = Nothing
```

When you set the object variable to Nothing, the Terminate event is generated. Any code in this event is executed then.

Creating the User Interface

Implementing our custom CEmployee object requires that you design a form to enter and manipulate employee data.

⊚ Custom Project 8-1 (Step 7): Designing a User Form

1. Choose **File | Close and Return to Microsoft Office Access**.
2. Click the **Blank form** in the Forms section of the Create tab. Access will display a blank form in the Form view.
3. Switch to the form's Design view by choosing **Design View** from the Views section.
4. Save the form as **frmEmployeeSalaries**.
5. Use the tools in the Controls section of the Design tab to place controls on the form as shown in Figure 8-2.

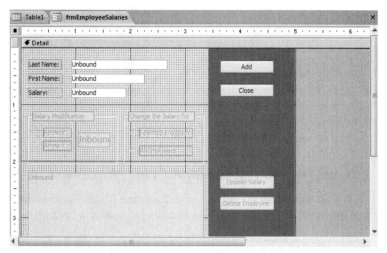

Figure 8-2: This form demonstrates the use of the CEmployee custom object.

6. Activate the property sheet and set the following properties for the form controls. To set the specified property, first click the control on the form to select it. Then, in the property sheet type the information as shown in the Setting column next to the property indicated in the Property column.

Object	Property	Setting
Label1	Caption	Last Name
Text box next to the Last Name label	Name	txtLastName
Label2	Caption	First Name
Text box next to the First Name label	Name	txtFirstName
Label3	Caption	Salary
Text box next to the Salary label	Name	txtSalary
Option group 1	Name Caption	frChangeSalary Salary Modification
Text box in the option group titled "Salary Modification"	Name	txtRaise
Option button 1	Name Caption	optPercent Percent
Option button 2	Name Caption	optAmount Amount
Option group 2	Name Caption	frSalaryMod Change the Salary for
Option button 3	Name Caption	optSelected Selected Employee
Option button 4	Name Caption	optAll All Employees
List box	Name Row Source Type Column Count Column Widths	lboxPeople Value List 4 0.5";0.9";0.7";0.5"

Object	Property	Setting
Command Button 1	Name	cmdAdd
	Caption	Add
Command Button 2	Name	cmdClose
	Caption	Close
Command Button 3	Name	cmdUpdate
	Caption	Update Salary
Command Button 4	Name	cmdDelete
	Caption	Delete Employee

◎ Custom Project 8-1 (Step 8): Writing Event Procedures

Now that the form is ready, you need to write few event procedures to handle various events, such as clicking a command button or loading the form.

1. Activate the Code window behind the form by choosing the **View Code** button in the Tools section of the Design tab.

2. Enter the following variable declarations at the top of the form's Code window:

```
Option Explicit

' variable declarations
Dim choice As Integer
Dim amount As Long
```

3. Type the following **UserForm_Initialize** procedure to enable or disable controls on the form:

```
Private Sub UserForm_Initialize()
    txtLastName.SetFocus
    cmdUpdate.Enabled = False
    cmdDelete.Enabled = False
    lboxPeople.Enabled = False
    frChangeSalary.Enabled = False
    frChangeSalary.Value = 0
    frSalaryMod.Enabled = False
    frSalaryMod.Value = 0
    txtRaise.Enabled = False
    txtRaise.Value = ""
End Sub
```

4. Type the **Form_Load** event procedure as shown below:

```
Private Sub Form_Load()
    Call UserForm_Initialize
End Sub
```

On loading the user form the UserForm_Initialize procedure will run.

5. Enter the following **cmdAdd_Click** procedure to add the employee to the collection:

```
Private Sub cmdAdd_Click()
    Dim strLast As String
    Dim strFirst As String
    Dim curSalary As Currency

    'Validate data entry
    If IsNull(txtLastName.Value) Or txtLastName.Value = "" _
        Or IsNull(txtFirstName.Value) Or txtFirstName.Value = "" _
        Or IsNull(txtSalary.Value) Or txtSalary.Value = "" Then
        MsgBox "Enter Last Name, First Name and Salary."
        txtLastName.SetFocus
        Exit Sub
    End If
    If Not IsNumeric(txtSalary) Then
        MsgBox "You must enter a value for the Salary."
        txtSalary.SetFocus
        Exit Sub
    End If
    If txtSalary < 0 Then
        MsgBox "Salary cannot be a negative number."
        Exit Sub
    End If

    'assign text box values to variables
    strLast = txtLastName
    strFirst = txtFirstName
    curSalary = txtSalary

    'enable buttons and other controls
    cmdUpdate.Enabled = True
    cmdDelete.Enabled = True
    lboxPeople.Enabled = True
    frChangeSalary.Enabled = True
    frSalaryMod.Enabled = True
    txtRaise.Enabled = True
    txtRaise.Value = ""
    lboxPeople.Visible = True

    'enter data into the CEmployees collection
    EmpOperations.AddEmployee strLast, strFirst, curSalary

    'update list box
    lboxPeople.RowSource = GetValues

    'delete data from text boxes
    txtLastName = ""
    txtFirstName = ""
    txtSalary = ""
    txtLastName.SetFocus
End Sub
```

The cmdAdd_Click procedure starts off with validating the user's input in
the Last Name, First Name, and Salary text boxes. If the user entered correct data, the text box values are assigned to the variables strLast, strFirst,
and strSalary. Next, a number of statements enable buttons and other

controls on the form so that the user can work with the employee data. The following statement calls the AddEmployee procedure in the EmpOperations standard module and passes the required parameters to it:

```
EmpOperations.AddEmployee strLast, strFirst, curSalary
```

Once the employee is entered into the collection, the employee data is added to the list box with the following statement:

```
lboxPeople.RowSource = GetValues
```

GetValues is the name of a function procedure in the EmpOperations module (see step 12 further on). This function cycles through the CEmployee collection to create a string of values for the list box row source.

The cmdAdd_Click procedure ends by clearing the text boxes, then setting the focus to the Last Name text box so the user can enter new employee data.

Figure 8-3: The list box control displays employee data as entered in the custom collection CEmployee.

6. Enter the following **cmdClose_Click** procedure to close the form:

```
Private Sub cmdClose_Click()
    DoCmd.Close
End Sub
```

7. Write the **Click** procedure for the cmdUpdate button as shown below:

```
Private Sub cmdUpdate_Click()
    Dim numOfPeople As Integer
    Dim colItem As Integer

    ' validate user selections
    If frChangeSalary.Value = 0 Or frSalaryMod.Value = 0 Then
        MsgBox "You must choose the appropriate option button in " & vbCr _
            & " the 'Salary Modification' and 'Change the Salary for' areas.", _
            vbOKOnly, "Insufficient selection"
        Exit Sub
    ElseIf Not IsNumeric(txtRaise) Or txtRaise = "" Then
        MsgBox "You must enter a number."
        txtRaise.SetFocus
```

```
        Exit Sub
    ElseIf frSalaryMod.Value = 1 And lboxPeople.ListIndex = -1 Then
        MsgBox "Click the employee name.", , "Missing selection in the List box"
        Exit Sub
    End If

    If frSalaryMod.Value = 1 And lboxPeople.ListIndex = -1 Then
        MsgBox "Enter data or select an option."
        Exit Sub
    End If
    ' get down to calculations
    amount = txtRaise
    colItem = lboxPeople.ListIndex + 1
    If frSalaryMod.Value = 1 And frChangeSalary.Value = 1 Then
        ' by percent, one employee
        choice = 1
        numOfPeople = 1
    ElseIf frSalaryMod.Value = 2 And frChangeSalary.Value = 1 Then
        ' by amount, one employee
        choice = 2
        numOfPeople = 1
    ElseIf frSalaryMod.Value = 1 And frChangeSalary.Value = 2 Then
        ' by percent, all employees
        choice = 1
        numOfPeople = 2
    ElseIf frSalaryMod.Value = 2 And frChangeSalary.Value = 2 Then
        ' by amount, all employees
        choice = 2
        numOfPeople = 2
    End If

    UpdateSalary choice, amount, numOfPeople, colItem
    lboxPeople.RowSource = GetValues
End Sub
```

When the user clicks the Update Salary button, the procedure checks to see whether the user selected appropriate option buttons and entered the adjusted figure in the text box. The update can be done for the selected employee or for all the employees listed in the list box control and collection. You can increase the salary by the specified percentage or amount. Depending on which options are specified, values are assigned to the variables choice, amount, numOfpeople, and colItem. These variables serve as parameters for the UpdateSalary procedure located in the EmpOperations module (see step 13 further on). The last statement in the cmdUpdate_ Click procedure sets the row source property of the list box control to the result obtained from the GetValues function located in the EmpOperations standard module.

Figure 8-4: The employee salary can be increased or decreased by the specified percentage or amount.

8. Enter the following **cmdDelete_Click** procedure:

```
Private Sub cmdDelete_Click()
    ' make sure an employee is highlighted in the list box control
    If lboxPeople.ListIndex > -1 Then
        DeleteEmployee lboxPeople.ListIndex + 1
        If lboxPeople.ListCount = 1 Then
            lboxPeople.RowSource = GetValues
            UserForm_Initialize
        Else
            lboxPeople.RowSource = GetValues
        End If
    Else
        MsgBox "Click the item you want to remove."
    End If
End Sub
```

The cmdDelete_Click procedure lets you remove an employee from the custom collection CEmployee. If you click an item in the list box and then click the Delete Employee button, the DeleteEmployee procedure is called. This procedure requires one argument that specifies the index number of the item selected in the list box. After the employee is removed from the collection, the row source of the list box control is reset to display the remaining employees. After removing the last employee from the collection, the UserForm_Initialize procedure is called to tackle the task of disabling controls that cannot be used until at least one employee is entered into the CEmployee collection.

9. Activate the **EmpOperations** module that you created earlier by double-clicking its name in the Project Explorer window. The top of the module should contain the following declaration lines:

```
Option Compare Database
Option Explicit
Dim emp As New CEmployee
Dim CEmployee As New Collection
```

10. In the EmpOperations standard module, enter the following **AddEmployee** procedure:

```
Sub AddEmployee(empLast As String, empFirst As String, _
    empSalary As Currency)
    With emp
        .ID = SetEmpId
        .LastName = empLast
        .FirstName = empFirst
        .Salary = CCur(empSalary)
        If .Salary = 0 Then Exit Sub
        CEmployee.Add emp
    End With
End Sub
```

The AddEmployee procedure is called from the cmdAdd_Click procedure attached to the form's Add button. This procedure takes three arguments. When Visual Basic reaches the With emp construct, a new instance of the CEmployee class is created. The LastName, FirstName, and Salary properties are set with the values passed from the cmdAdd_Click procedure. The ID property is set with the number generated by the result of the SetEmpId function (see the following step). Each time VBA sees the reference to the instanced emp object, it will call upon the appropriate Property Let procedure located in the class module. (The next section of this chapter demonstrates how to walk through this procedure step by step to see exactly when the Property procedures are executed.) The last statement inside the With emp construct adds the user-defined object emp to the custom collection called CEmployee.

11. In the **EmpOperations** standard module, enter the following **SetEmpId** function procedure:

```
Function SetEmpId() As String
    Dim ref As String

    Randomize
    ref = Int((99999 - 10000) * Rnd + 10000)
    SetEmpId = ref
End Function
```

This function's purpose is to assign a unique five-digit number to each new employee. To generate a random integer between two given integers where ending_number = 99999 and beginning_number = 10000, the following formula is used:

```
= Int((ending_number - beginning_number) * Rnd + beginning_number)
```

The SetEmpId function procedure also uses the Randomize statement to reinitialize the random number generator. For more information on using the Rnd and Integer functions, as well as the Randomize statement, search the online help.

12. Enter the **GetValues** function procedure as shown below. This function, which is called from the cmdAdd_Click, cmdUpdate_Click, and

cmdDelete_Click procedures, provides the values for the list box control to synchronize it with the current values in the CEmployee collection.

```
Function GetValues()
   Dim myList As String

   myList = ""
   For Each emp In CEmployee
      myList = myList & emp.ID & ";" & _
         emp.LastName & ";" & _
         emp.FirstName & "; $" & _
         Format(emp.Salary, "0.00") & ";"
   Next emp
   GetValues = myList
End Function
```

13. Enter the following **UpdateSalary** procedure:

```
Sub UpdateSalary(choice As Integer, myValue As Long, _
   peopleCount As Integer, colItem As Integer)
   Set emp = New CEmployee

   If choice = 1 And peopleCount = 1 Then
      CEmployee.Item(colItem).Salary = _
         emp.CalcNewSalary(1, CEmployee.Item(colItem).Salary, myValue)
   ElseIf choice = 1 And peopleCount = 2 Then
      For Each emp In CEmployee
         emp.Salary = emp.Salary + ((emp.Salary * myValue) / 100)
      Next emp
   ElseIf choice = 2 And peopleCount = 1 Then
      CEmployee.Item(colItem).Salary = _
         CEmployee.Item(colItem).Salary + myValue
   ElseIf choice = 2 And peopleCount = 2 Then
      For Each emp In CEmployee
         emp.Salary = emp.Salary + myValue
      Next emp
   Else
      MsgBox "Enter data or select an option."
   End If
End Sub
```

The UpdateSalary procedure is called from the cmdUpdate_Click procedure, which is assigned to the Update Salary button on the form. The click procedure passes four parameters that the UpdateSalary procedure uses for the salary calculations. When a salary for the selected employee needs to be updated by a percentage or amount, the CalcNewSalary method residing in the class module is called. For modification of salary figures for all the employees, we iterate over the CEmployee collection to obtain the value of the Salary property of each emp object, then perform the required calculation by using a formula. By entering a negative number in the form's txtRaise text box, you can decrease the salary by the specified percentage or amount.

14. Enter the **DeleteEmployee** procedure as shown below:

```
Sub DeleteEmployee(colItem As Integer)
    Dim getcount As Integer

    CEmployee.Remove colItem
End Sub
```

The DeleteEmployee procedure uses the Remove method to delete the selected employee from the CEmployee custom collection. Recall that the Remove method requires one argument, which is the position of the item in the collection. The value of this argument is obtained from the cmdDelete_ Click procedure. The class module procedures were called from the standard module named EmpOperations. This was done to avoid creating a new instance of a user-defined class every time we needed to call it.

Running the Custom Application

Now that you have finished writing the necessary VBA code, let's load frmEmployeeSalaries to enter and modify employee information.

Custom Project 8-1 (Step 9): Running the Custom Project

1. Choose **File | Save Chap08** to save all the objects in the VBA project.
2. Switch to the Microsoft Office Access window and activate **frmEmployeeSalaries** in the Form view.
3. Enter the employee last and first name and salary and click the **Add** button.

   The employee information now appears in the list box. Notice that an employee ID is automatically entered in the first column. All the disabled form controls are now enabled.
4. Enter data for another employee and click the **Add** button.
5. Enter information for at least three more people.
6. Increase the salary of the third employee in the list box by 10%. To do this, click the employee name in the list box, click the **Percent** option button, and type **10** in the text box in the Salary Modification section of the form. In the Change the Salary for section of the form, click the **Selected Employee** option button. Finally, click the **Update Salary** button to perform the update operation.
7. Now increase the salary of all the employees by **$5**.
8. Remove the fourth employee from the list box. To do this, select the employee in the list box and click the **Delete Employee** button.
9. Close frmEmployeeSalaries by clicking the **Close** button.

Watching the Execution of Your VBA Procedures

To help you understand what's going on when your code runs, and how the custom object works, let's walk through the cmdAdd_Click procedure. Treat this exercise as a brief introduction to the debugging techniques that are covered in detail in the next chapter.

◎ Custom Project 8-1 (Step 10): Custom Project Code Walkthrough

1. Open **frmEmployeeSalaries** in Design view and click **View Code** in the Tools section of the Design tab.

2. Select **cmdAdd** from the combo box at the top left of the Code window.

3. Set a breakpoint by clicking in the left margin next to the following line of code:

```
If IsNull(txtLastName.Value) Or txtLastName.Value = "" _
    Or IsNull(txtFirstName.Value) Or txtFirstName.Value = "" _
    Or IsNull(txtSalary.Value) Or txtSalary.Value = "" Then
```

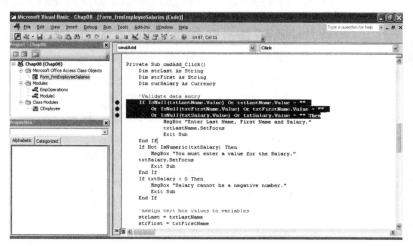

Figure 8-5: A red circle in the margin indicates a breakpoint. The statement with a breakpoint is displayed as white text on a red background.

4. Return to **frmEmployeeSalaries** in Design view and activate Form view to run the form.

5. Enter data in the Last Name, First Name, and Salary text boxes, and click the form's **Add** button. Visual Basic should now switch to the Code window because it came across the breakpoint in the first line of the cmdAdd_Click procedure.

6. Step through the code one statement at a time by pressing **F8**. Visual Basic runs the current statement and then automatically advances to the next statement and suspends execution. The current statement is indicated by a yellow arrow in the margin and a yellow background. Keep pressing **F8** to

execute the procedure step by step. After Visual Basic switches to the EmpOperations module to run the AddEmployee procedure and encounters the With emp statement, it will run the function to set the employee ID and will go out to execute the Property Let procedures in the CEmployee class module.

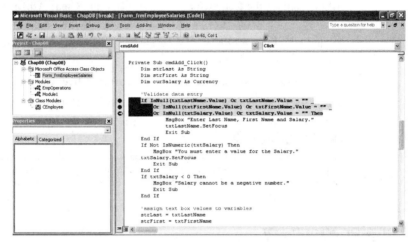

Figure 8-6: When Visual Basic encounters a breakpoint while running a procedure, it switches to the Code window and displays a yellow arrow in the margin to the left of the statement at which the procedure is suspended.

Figure 8-7: Setting the properties of your custom object is accomplished through the Property Let procedures.

7. Using the **F8** key, trace the execution of the cmdAdd_Click procedure to the end. When VBA encounters the end of the procedure (End Sub), the yellow highlighter will be turned off. At this time, switch back to the active form.

Note: To activate the form, you may need to first click the Table1 tab and then reselect the Employee Operations tab.

8. Enter data for a new employee, then click the **Add** button. When Visual Basic displays the Code window, choose **Debug | Clear All Breakpoints**. Now press **F5** to run the rest of the procedure without stepping through it.

9. In the Visual Basic Editor window, choose **File | Save Chap08** to save changes to the modules.

10. Choose **File | Close and Return to Microsoft Office Access**.

11. Close the Chap08.accdb database and exit Microsoft Office Access.

VBA Debugging Tools

Visual Basic provides a number of debugging tools to help you analyze how your application operates, as well as to locate the source of errors in your procedures. See the next chapter for details on working with these tools.

Chapter Summary

In this chapter you learned how to create and use your own objects and collections in VBA procedures. You used a class module to create a user-defined (custom) object. You saw how to define your custom object's properties using the Property Get and Property Let procedures. You also learned how to write a method for your custom object and saw how to make the class module available to the user with a custom form. Finally, you learned how to analyze your VBA application by stepping through its code.

As your procedures become more complex, you will need to start using special tools for tracing errors, which are covered in the next chapter.

Chapter 9

Debugging VBA Procedures and Handling Errors

In the course of writing or editing VBA procedures, no matter how careful you are, you're likely to make some mistakes. For example, you may misspell a word, misplace a comma or quotation mark, or forget a period or ending parenthesis. These kinds of mistakes are known as *syntax errors*. Fortunately, Visual Basic is quite helpful in spotting these kinds of errors. To have Visual Basic automatically check for correct syntax after you enter a line of code, choose Tools | Options in the Visual Basic window. Make sure the Auto Syntax Check setting is selected on the Editor tab.

Figure 9-1: The Auto Syntax Check setting on the Editor tab of the Options dialog box lets you pick up a lot of typos in your VBA procedures.

When Visual Basic finds a syntax error, it displays an error message box and changes the color of the incorrect line of code to red, or another color as indicated on the Editor Format tab in the Options dialog box.

If the explanation of the error in the error message isn't clear, you can click the Help button for more help. If Visual Basic cannot point you in the right direction, you must return to your procedure and carefully examine the offending instruction for missed letters, quotation marks, periods, colons, equal signs, and beginning and ending parentheses. Finding syntax errors can be aggravating and time consuming. Certain syntax errors can be caught only during the execution of the procedure. While attempting to run your procedure, Visual Basic can find errors that were caused by using invalid arguments or omitting instructions that are used in pairs, such as If...End statements and looping structures.

You've probably heard that computer programs are "full of bugs." In programming, errors are called bugs, and *debugging* is a process of eliminating errors from your programs. Visual Basic provides a myriad of tools for tracking down and eliminating bugs. The first step in debugging a procedure is to correct all syntax errors. In addition to syntax errors, there are two other types of errors: run-time and logic. *Run-time errors*, which occur while the procedure is running, are often caused by unexpected situations the programmer did not think of while writing the code. For example, the program may be trying to access a drive or a file that does not exist on the user's computer. Or it may be trying to copy a file to a floppy disk without first determining whether the user had inserted a floppy disk and closed the drive door.

The third type of error, a logic error, often does not generate a specific error message. Even though the procedure has no flaws in its syntax and runs without errors, it produces incorrect results. *Logic errors* happen when your procedure simply does not do what you want it to do. Logic errors are usually very difficult to locate. Those that happen intermittently are sometimes so well concealed that you can spend long hours, even days, trying to locate the source of the error.

Testing VBA Procedures

When testing your VBA procedure, use the following guidelines:

- If you want to analyze your procedure, step through your code one line at a time by pressing F8 or by choosing Debug | Step Into.
- If you suspect that an error may occur in a specific place in your procedure, use a breakpoint.
- If you want to monitor the value of a particular variable or expression used by your procedure, add a watch expression.
- If you are tired of scrolling through a long procedure to get to sections of code that interest you, set up a bookmark to quickly jump to the desired location.

Each of the above guidelines is demonstrated in a hands-on exercise in this chapter.

Stopping a Procedure

VBA offers four methods of stopping your procedure and entering into a so-called *break mode*:

- Pressing Ctrl+Break
- Setting one or more breakpoints

■ Inserting the Stop statement

■ Adding a watch expression

A break occurs when execution of your VBA procedure is temporarily suspended. Visual Basic remembers the values of all variables and the statement from which the execution of the procedure should resume when you decide to continue. You can resume a suspended procedure in one of the following ways:

■ Click the Run Sub/UserForm button on the toolbar

■ Choose Run | Run Sub/UserForm from the menu bar

■ Click the Continue button in the error message box (see Figure 9-2)

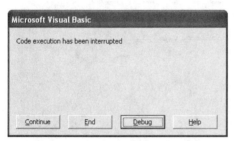

Figure 9-2: This message appears when you press Ctrl+Break while your VBA procedure is running.

The error message box shown in Figure 9-2 informs you that the procedure was halted. See the description of each button in Table 9-1.

Table 9-1: Error message box buttons

Button Name	Description
Continue	Click this button to resume code execution. This button will be grayed out if an error was encountered.
End	Click this button if you do not want to troubleshoot the procedure at this time. VBA will stop code execution.
Debug	Click this button to enter break mode. The Code window will appear, and VBA will highlight the line at which the procedure execution was suspended. You can examine, debug, or step through the code.
Help	Click this button to view the online help that explains the cause of this error message.

Using Breakpoints

If you know more or less where there may be a problem in your procedure code, you should suspend code execution at that location (on a given line). Set a breakpoint by pressing F9 when the cursor is on the desired line of code. When VBA gets to that line while running your procedure, it will display the Code window immediately. At this point you can step through the procedure code line by line by pressing F8 or choosing Debug | Step Into.

To see how this works, let's look at the following scenario. Assume that during the execution of the ListEndDates function procedure (see Custom Project 9-1) the following line of code could get you into trouble:

```
ListEndDates = Format(((Now() + intOffset) - 35) + 7 * row, "MM/DD/YYYY")
```

◎ Custom Project 9-1: Debugging a Function Procedure

The procedure code for this chapter's hands-on exercises is located in the
C:\Acc07_HandsOn folder in a text file named HandsOn_09.txt. Instead of
typing in the programming code as instructed in each hands-on or custom project you can save time by copying the required procedure from this text file.

1. Start Microsoft Office Access 2007 and create a new Microsoft Office
    Access 2007 database named **Chap09.accdb** in your **C:\Acc07_
    ByExample** folder.

2. Create the form shown in Figure 9-3.

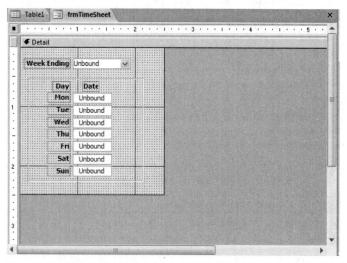

Figure 9-3: The combo box control shown on this form will be filled with
the result of the ListEndDates function.

3. Use the property sheet to set the following control properties:

Control Name	Property Name	Property Setting
combo box	Name Row Source Type Column Count	cboEndDate ListEndDates 1
text box controls	Name	txt1 txt2 txt3 txt4 txt5 txt6 txt7

4. Save the form as **frmTimeSheet**.

5. In the property sheet, select **Form** from the drop-down list box. Click the
    Event tab. Choose **[Event Procedure]** from the drop-down list next to the

On Load property, and then click the **Build** button (…). Complete the following **Form_Load** procedure when the Code window appears:

```
Private Sub Form_Load()
    With Me.cboEndDate
        .SetFocus
        .ListIndex = 5     ' Select current ending date
    End With
End Sub
```

6. Select the combo box control (cboEndDate) on the form. In the property sheet, click the **Event** tab. Choose **[Event Procedure]** from the drop-down list next to the **On Change** property, and then click the **Build** button (…). Enter the following code:

```
Private Sub cboEndDate_Change()
    Dim endDate As Date

    endDate = Me.cboEndDate.Value
    With Me
        .txt1 = Format(endDate - 6, "mm/dd")
        .txt2 = Format(endDate - 5, "mm/dd")
        .txt3 = Format(endDate - 4, "mm/dd")
        .txt4 = Format(endDate - 3, "mm/dd")
        .txt5 = Format(endDate - 2, "mm/dd")
        .txt6 = Format(endDate - 1, "mm/dd")
        .txt7 = Format(endDate - 0, "mm/dd")
    End With
End Sub
```

7. In the Visual Basic Editor window, choose **Insert | Module** to add a new standard module.

8. In the Properties window, change the Name property of Module1 to **TimeSheetProc**.

9. Enter the **ListEndDates** function procedure in the TimeSheetProc module:

```
Function ListEndDates(fld As Control, id As Variant, _
    row As Variant, col As Variant, code As Variant) As Variant
    Dim intOffset As Integer

    Select Case code
        Case acLBInitialize
            ListEndDates = True
        Case acLBOpen
            ListEndDates = Timer
        Case acLBGetRowCount
            ListEndDates = 11
        Case acLBGetColumnCount
            ListEndDates = 1
        Case acLBGetColumnWidth
            ListEndDates = -1
        Case acLBGetValue
            ' days till ending date
            intOffset = Abs((8 - Weekday(Now)) Mod 7)
```

```
' start 5 weeks prior to current week ending date
' (7 days * 5 weeks = 35 days before next ending date)
' and show 11 dates

        ListEndDates = Format(((Now() + intOffset) - 35) _
            + 7 * row, "MM/DD/YYYY")
    End Select
End Function
```

10. In the **ListEndDates** function procedure, click anywhere on the line containing the following statement:

```
ListEndDates = Format(((Now() + intOffset) - 35) + 7 * row, "MM/DD/YYYY")
```

11. Press **F9** (or choose **Debug | Toggle Breakpoint**) to set a breakpoint on the line where the cursor is located.

    When you set the breakpoint, Visual Basic displays a red dot in the margin. At the same time, the line that has the breakpoint will change to white text on a red background (see Figure 9-4). The color of the breakpoint can be changed on the Editor Format tab in the Options dialog box (Tools menu).

    Another way of setting a breakpoint is to click in the margin indicator to the left of the line on which you want to stop the procedure.

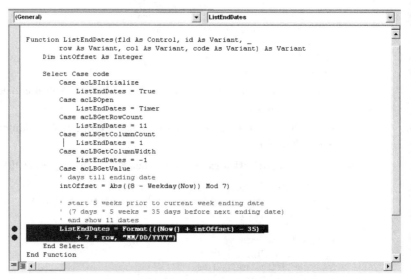

Figure 9-4: The line of code where the breakpoint is set is displayed in the color specified on the Editor Format tab in the Options dialog box.

12. Switch to the Microsoft Office Access application window and open the form **frmTimeSheet** that you prepared earlier in this project in the Form view.

    When you open the form, Visual Basic will call the ListEndDates function to fill the combo box, executing all the statements until it encounters the breakpoint you set in steps 10-11 above. Once the breakpoint is reached, the code is suspended and the screen displays the Code window (Figure 9-5) in break mode (notice the word "break" surrounded by square brackets in the Code window's title bar). Visual Basic displays a yellow arrow in the margin to the left of the statement at which the procedure was suspended. At the same time, the statement appears inside a box with a yellow background. The arrow and the box indicate the current statement, or the statement that is about to be executed. If the current statement also contains a breakpoint, the margin displays both indicators overlapping one another (the circle and the arrow).

Figure 9-5: When Visual Basic encounters a breakpoint, it displays the Code window. A yellow arrow appears in the margin to the left of the statement at which the procedure was suspended. Because the current statement also contains a breakpoint (indicated by a red circle), the margin displays both indicators overlapping one another (the circle and the arrow).

13. Finish running the ListEndDates function procedure by pressing **F5** to continue without stopping, or press **F8** to execute the procedure line by line.

When you step through your procedure code line by line by pressing F8, you can use the Immediate window to further test your procedure (see the section titled "Using the Immediate Window in Break Mode"). To learn more about stepping through a procedure, refer to the section titled "Stepping Through VBA Procedures" later in this chapter.

Visual Basic allows you to set any number of breakpoints in a procedure. This way you can suspend and continue the execution of your procedure as you please. You can press F5 to quickly move between the breakpoints. You can analyze the code of your procedure and check the values of variables while code execution is suspended. You can also perform various tests by typing statements in the Immediate window. Consider setting a breakpoint if you suspect that your procedure never executes a certain block of code.

Removing Breakpoints

When you finish running the procedure in which you had set breakpoints, Visual Basic does not automatically remove them. To remove the breakpoint, choose Debug | Clear All Breakpoints or press Ctrl+Shift+F9. All the breakpoints are removed. If you had set several breakpoints in a given procedure and would like to remove only some of them, click on the line containing the breakpoint you want to remove and press F9 (or choose Debug | Clear Breakpoint). You should clear the breakpoints when they are no longer needed. The breakpoints are automatically removed when you exit Microsoft Access.

 Note: Remove the breakpoint you set in Custom Project 9-1.

Using the Immediate Window in Break Mode

When the procedure execution is suspended, the Code window appears in break mode. This is a good time to activate the Immediate window and type VBA instructions to find out, for instance, the name of the open form or the value of a certain control. You can also use the Immediate window to change the contents of variables in order to correct values that may be causing errors. By now, you should be an expert when it comes to working in the Immediate window. Figure 9-6 shows the suspended ListEndDates function procedure and the Immediate window with the questions that were asked of Visual Basic while in break mode.

Figure 9-6: When code execution is suspended, you can find answers to a number of questions by entering appropriate statements in the Immediate window.

In break mode, you can hold the mouse pointer over any variable in a running procedure to see the variable's value. For example, in the ListEndDates function procedure shown in Figure 9-7, the breakpoint has been set on the statement just before the End Select keywords. When Visual Basic encounters this statement, the Code window appears in break mode. Because Visual Basic has already executed the statement that stores the value of the variable intOffset, you can quickly find out the value of this variable by resting the mouse pointer over its name. The name of the variable and its current value appear in a floating frame. To show the values of several variables used in a procedure at once, you should use the Locals window, which is discussed later in this chapter.

```
' days till ending date
intOffset = Abs((8 - Weekday(Now)) Mod 7)

' start 5 weeks prior to current week ending date
' (7 days * 5 weeks = 35 days before next ending date)
' and show 11 dates
ListEndDates = Format(((Now() + intOffset) - 35) _
            + 7 * row, "MM/DD/YYYY")   intOffset = 5
End Select
End Function
```

Figure 9-7: In break mode, you can find out the value of a variable by resting the mouse pointer on that variable.

Working in a Code Window in Break Mode

While in break mode, you can change code, add new statements, execute the procedure one line at a time, skip lines, set the next statement, use the Immediate window, and more. When Visual Basic is in break mode, all of the options on the Debug menu are available. You can enter break mode by pressing Ctrl+Break or F8, or setting a breakpoint. In break mode, if you change a certain line of code, VBA will prompt you to reset the project by displaying the message "This action will reset your project, proceed anyway?" Click OK to stop the program's execution and proceed editing your code, or Cancel to delete the new changes and continue running the code from the point where it was suspended. For example, change the variable declaration. As you press F5 to resume code execution, VBA will prompt you to reset your project.

Using the Stop Statement

Sometimes you won't be able to test your procedure right away. If you set up your breakpoints and then close the database file, the breakpoints will be removed; next time, when you are ready to test your procedure, you'll have to begin by setting up your breakpoints again. If you need to postpone the task of testing your procedure until later, you can take a different approach. Insert a Stop statement into your code wherever you want to halt a procedure.

Figure 9-8 shows the Stop statement before the With…End With construct. Visual Basic will suspend the execution of the cboEndDate_Change event procedure when it encounters the Stop statement and the screen will display the Code window in break mode. Although the Stop statement has exactly the same effect as setting a breakpoint, it does have one disadvantage. All Stop statements stay in the procedure until you remove them. When you no longer need to stop your procedure, you must locate and remove all the Stops.

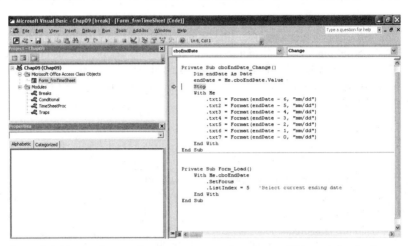

Figure 9-8: You can insert a Stop statement anywhere in your VBA procedure code. The procedure will halt when it gets to the Stop statement, and the Code window will appear with the code line highlighted.

Adding Watch Expressions

Many errors in procedures are caused by variables that assume unexpected values. If a procedure uses a variable whose value changes in various locations, you may want to stop the procedure and check the current value of that variable. Visual Basic offers a special Watches window that allows you to keep an eye on variables or expressions while your procedure is running. To add a watch expression to your procedure, select the variable whose value you want to monitor in the Code window, then choose Debug | Add Watch. The screen will display the Add Watch dialog box, as shown in Figure 9-9.

Figure 9-9: The Add Watch dialog box allows you to define conditions you want to monitor while a VBA procedure is running.

The Add Watch dialog box contains three sections, which are described in Table 9-2.

Table 9-2: Add Watch dialog box sections

Section	Description
Expression	Displays the name of a variable you have highlighted in your procedure. If you opened the Add Watch dialog box without selecting a variable name, type the name of the variable you want to monitor in the Expression text box.
Context	In this section, indicate the name of the procedure that contains the variable and the name of the module where this procedure is located.
Watch Type	Specifies how to monitor the variable. If you choose: • The Watch Expression option button, you can read the value of the variable in the Watch window while in break mode. • Break When Value Is True, Visual Basic will automatically stop the procedure when the variable evaluates to true (nonzero). • Break When Value Changes, Visual Basic will automatically stop the procedure each time the value of the variable or expression changes.

You can add a watch expression before running a procedure or after suspend-ing the execution of your procedure.

The difference between a breakpoint and a watch expression is that the breakpoint always stops a procedure in a specified location, but the watch stops the procedure only when the specified condition (Break When Value Is True or Break When Value Changes) is met. Watches are extremely useful when you are not sure where the variable is being changed. Instead of stepping through many lines of code to find the location where the variable assumes the specified value, you can put a watch breakpoint on the variable and run your procedure as normal. Let's see how this works.

◎ Hands-On 9-1: Working with the Watches Window

1. In the Visual Editor window, choose **Insert | Module** to insert a new stan-dard module.

2. Use the Properties window to change the name of the Module to **Breaks**.

3. In the Breaks Code window, type the following **WhatDate** procedure:

```
Sub WhatDate()
    Dim curDate As Date
    Dim newDate As Date
    Dim x As Integer

    curDate = Date
    For x = 1 To 365
        newDate = Date + x
    Next x
End Sub
```

The WhatDate procedure uses the For...Next loop to calculate the date that is *x* days in the future. You won't see any result when you run this procedure unless you insert the following instruction in the procedure code just before the End Sub keywords:

```
MsgBox "In " & x & " days, it will be " & NewDate
```

This time, however, you don't want to display the individual dates, day after day. Suppose that you want to stop the program when the value of the variable *x* reaches 211. In other words, you want to know what date will be 211 days from now. To get the answer, you could insert the following statement into your procedure before the Next x statement:

```
If x = 211 Then MsgBox "In " & x & " days it will be " & NewDate
```

But this time, you want to get the answer without introducing any new statements into your procedure. If you add watch expressions to the procedure, Visual Basic will stop the For...Next loop when the specified condition is met, and you'll be able to check the values of the desired variables.

Figure 9-10: Using the Watches window.

4. Choose **Debug | Add Watch**.

5. In the Expression text box, enter the following expression: **x = 211**.

6. In the Context section, choose **WhatDate** from the Procedure combo box and **Breaks** from the Module combo box.

7. In the Watch Type section, select the **Break When Value Is True** option button.

8. Click **OK** to close the Add Watch dialog box. You have now added your first watch expression.

9. In the Code window, position the insertion point anywhere within the name of the **curDate** variable.

10. Choose **Debug | Add Watch** and click **OK** to set up the default watch type with the **Watch Expression** option.

11. In the Code window, position the insertion point anywhere within the name of the **newDate** variable.

12. Choose **Debug | Add Watch** and click **OK** to set up the default watch type with the **Watch Expression** option.

After performing the above steps, the WhatDate procedure contains the following three watches:

x = 211	Break When Value Is True
curDate	Watch Expression
newDate	Watch Expression

13. Position the cursor anywhere inside the code of the WhatDate procedure and press **F5**.

Visual Basic stops the procedure when x = 211 (see Figure 9-10 above). Notice that the value of the variable x in the Watches window is the same as the value you specified in the Add Watch dialog box. In addition, the Watches window shows the value of the variables curDate and newDate. The procedure is in break mode. You can press F5 to continue, or you can ask another question: What date will be in 277 days? The next step shows how to do this.

14. Choose **Debug | Edit Watch** and enter the following expression: **x = 277**.

15. Display the Edit Watch dialog box by double-clicking the expression in the Watches window.

16. Click **OK** to close the Edit Watch dialog box. Notice that the Watches window now displays a new value of the expression. The x is now false.

17. Press **F5**. The procedure stops again when the value of x = 277. The value of curDate is the same; however, the newDate variable now contains a new value — a date that is 277 days from now. You can change the value of the expression again or finish the procedure.

18. Press **F5** to finish the procedure without stopping.

When your procedure is running and a watch expression has a value, the Watches window displays the value of the Watch expression. If you open the Watches window after the procedure has finished, you will see the error "<out of context>" instead of the variable values. In other words, when the watch expression is out of context, it does not have a value.

Removing Watch Expressions

To remove a watch expression, click on the expression you want to remove from the Watches window and press Delete. Remove all the watch expressions you defined in the preceding exercise.

Using Quick Watch

If you want to check the value of an expression not defined in the Watches window, you can use Quick Watch (see Figure 9-11).

To access the Quick Watch dialog box while in break mode, position the insertion point anywhere inside a variable name or an expression you want to watch and choose Debug | Quick Watch, or press Shift+F9.

Figure 9-11: The Quick Watch dialog box shows the value of the selected expression in a VBA procedure.

The Quick Watch dialog box contains an Add button that allows you to add the expression to the Watches window. Make sure that the WhatDate procedure does not contain any watch expressions. See the preceding section on how to remove a watch expression from the Watches window. Now, let's see how to take advantage of Quick Watch.

⊚ Hands-On 9-2: Using the Quick Watch Dialog Box

1. In the **WhatDate** procedure, position the insertion point on the name of the variable, **x**.
2. Choose **Debug | Add Watch**.
3. Enter the expression **x = 50**.
4. Choose the **Break When Value Is True** option button, and click **OK**.
5. Run the WhatDate procedure.

   Visual Basic will suspend procedure execution when x = 50. Notice that the Watches window does not contain either the newDate or curDate variables. To check the values of these variables, you can position the mouse pointer over the appropriate variable name in the Code window, or you can invoke the Quick Watch dialog box.

6. In the Code window, position the mouse inside the **newDate** variable and press **Shift+F9**, or choose **Debug | Quick Watch**.

   The Quick Watch dialog box shows the name of the expression and its current value.

7. Click **Cancel** to return to the Code window.
8. In the Code window, position the mouse inside the curDate variable and press **Shift+F9**, or choose **Debug | Quick Watch**.
9. The Quick Watch dialog box now shows the value of the variable curDate.

10. Click **Cancel** to return to the Code window.

11. Press **F5** to continue running the procedure.

Using the Locals Window and the Call Stack Dialog Box

If you want to keep an eye on all the declared variables and their current values during the execution of a VBA procedure, choose View | Locals Window before you run the procedure. While in break mode, Visual Basic will display a list of variables and their corresponding values in the Locals window (see Figure 9-12).

The Locals window contains three columns: Expression, Value, and Type.

The Expression column displays the names of variables that are declared in the current procedure. The first row displays the name of the module preceded by the plus sign. When you click the plus sign, you can check if any variables have been declared at the module level. Here the class module will show the system variable Me. In the Locals window, global variables and variables used by other projects aren't displayed.

The second column, Value, shows the current variable values. In this column, you can change the value of a variable by clicking on it and typing the new value. After changing the value, press Enter to register the change. You can also press Tab, Shift+Tab, up or down arrow, or click anywhere within the Locals window after you've changed the variable value.

Type, the third column, displays the type of each declared variable.

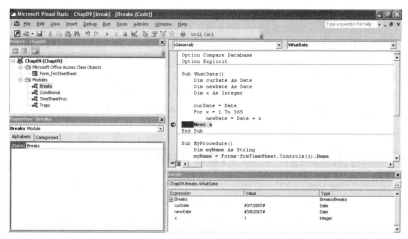

Figure 9-12: The Locals window displays the current values of all the declared variables in the current VBA procedure.

To observe the variable values in the Locals window, let's do the following hands-on exercise.

◎ Hands-On 9-3: Using the Locals Window

1. Choose **View | Locals Window**.
2. Click anywhere inside the **WhatDate** procedure and press **F8**.

   By pressing F8 you placed the procedure in break mode. The Locals window displays the name of the current module, the local variables, and their beginning values.
3. Press **F8** a few more times while keeping an eye on the Locals window.
4. Press **F5** to continue running the procedure.

   The Locals window also contains a button with an ellipsis (…). This button opens the Call Stack dialog box (see Figure 9-13), which displays a list of all active procedure calls. An *active procedure call* is a procedure that is started but not completed. You can also activate the Call Stack dialog box by choosing View | Call Stack. This option is only available in break mode.

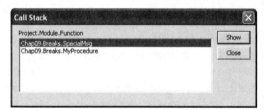

Figure 9-13: The Call Stack dialog box displays a list of procedures that are started but not completed.

The Call Stack dialog box is especially helpful for tracing nested procedures. Recall that a nested procedure is a procedure that is being called from within another procedure. If a procedure calls another, the name of the called procedure is automatically added to the Calls list in the Call Stack dialog box. When Visual Basic has finished executing the statements of the called procedure, the procedure name is automatically removed from the Call Stack dialog box. You can use the Show button in the Call Stack dialog box to display the statement that calls the next procedure listed in the Call Stack dialog box.

Stepping Through VBA Procedures

Stepping through the code means running one statement at a time. This allows you to check every line in every procedure that is encountered. To start stepping through the procedure from the beginning, place the cursor anywhere inside the code of your procedure and choose Debug | Step Into, or press F8. The Debug menu contains several options that allow you to execute a procedure in step mode (see Figure 9-14).

Figure 9-14: The Debug menu offers many commands for stepping through VBA procedures. Certain commands on this menu are only available in break mode.

When you run a procedure one statement at a time, Visual Basic executes each statement until it encounters the End Sub keywords. If you don't want Visual Basic to step through every statement, you can press F5 at any time to run the remaining code of the procedure without stepping through it.

⊚ Hands-On 9-4: Stepping Through a Procedure

1. Place the cursor anywhere inside the procedure you want to trace.

2. Press **F8** or choose **Debug | Step Into**.

   Visual Basic executes the current statement, then automatically advances to the next statement and suspends execution. While in break mode, you can activate the Immediate window, the Watches window, or the Locals window to see the effect of a particular statement on the values of variables and expressions. And, if the procedure you are stepping through calls other procedures, you can activate the Call Stack dialog box to see which procedures are currently active.

3. Press **F8** again to execute the selected statement. After executing this statement, Visual Basic will select the next statement, and again the procedure execution will be halted.

4. Continue stepping the procedure by pressing **F8**, or press **F5** to continue running the code without stopping.

5. You can also choose **Run | Reset** to stop the procedure at the current statement without executing the remaining statements.

   When you step over procedures (**Shift+F8**), Visual Basic executes each procedure as if it were a single statement. This option is particularly useful if a procedure contains calls to other procedures you don't want to step into because they have already been tested and debugged, or because you want to concentrate only on the new code that has not been debugged yet.

Stepping Over a Procedure

Suppose that the current statement in MyProcedure calls the SpecialMsg procedure. If you choose Debug | Step Over (Shift+F8) instead of Debug | Step Into (F8), Visual Basic will quickly execute all the statements inside the SpecialMsg procedure and select the next statement in the calling procedure, MyProcedure. All during the execution of the SpecialMsg procedure, Visual Basic continues to display the current procedure in the Code window.

◉ Hands-On 9-5: Stepping Over a Procedure

This hands-on exercise refers to the Access form named frmTimeSheet that you created in Custom Project 9-1 at the beginning of this chapter.

1. In the Visual Basic Editor window, choose **Insert | Module** to add a new standard module.

2. In the module's Code window, enter the **MyProcedure** and **SpecialMsg** procedures as shown below:

```
Sub MyProcedure()
    Dim myName As String

    myName = Forms!frmTimeSheet.Controls(1).Name

    ' choose Step Over to avoid stepping through the
    ' lines of code in the called procedure - SpecialMsg
    SpecialMsg myName
End Sub

Sub SpecialMsg(n As String)
    If n = "Label1" Then
        MsgBox "You must change the name."
    End If
End Sub
```

3. Add a breakpoint at the following statement:

```
SpecialMsg myName
```

4. Place the insertion point anywhere within the code of **MyProcedure** and press **F5** to run it.

   Visual Basic halts execution when it reaches the breakpoint.

5. Press **Shift+F8** or choose **Debug | Step Over**.

   Visual Basic runs the SpecialMsg procedure, then execution advances to the statement immediately after the call to the SpecialMsg procedure.

6. Press **F5** to finish running the procedure without stepping through its code.

   Now suppose you want to execute MyProcedure to the line that calls the SpecialMsg procedure.

7. Click anywhere inside the statement **SpecialMsg myName**.

8. Choose **Debug | Run to Cursor**.

   Visual Basic will stop the procedure when it reaches the specified line.

9. Press **Shift+F8** to step over the SpecialMsg procedure.

10. Press **F5** to execute the rest of the procedure without single stepping.

Stepping over a procedure is particularly useful when you don't want to analyze individual statements inside the called procedure (SpecialMsg).

Stepping Out of a Procedure

Another command on the Debug menu, Step Out (Ctrl+Shift+F8), is used when you step into a procedure and then decide that you don't want to step all the way through it. When you choose this option, Visual Basic will execute the remaining statements in this procedure in one step and proceed to activate the next statement in the calling procedure.

In the process of stepping through a procedure you can switch between the Step Into, Step Over, and Step Out options. The option you select depends on which code fragment you wish to analyze at a given moment.

Running a Procedure to Cursor

The Debug menu Run To Cursor (Ctrl+F8) command lets you run your procedure until the line you have selected is encountered. This command is really useful if you want to stop the execution before a large loop or you intend to step over a called procedure.

Setting the Next Statement

At times, you may want to rerun previous lines of code in the procedure or skip over a section of code that is causing trouble. In each of these situations, you can use the Set Next Statement option on the Debug menu. When you halt execution of a procedure, you can resume the procedure from any statement you want. Visual Basic will skip execution of the statements between the selected statement and the statement where execution was suspended.

Skipping Lines of Code

Although skipping lines of code can be very useful in the process of debugging your VBA procedures, it should be done with care. When you use the Next Statement option, you tell Visual Basic that this is the line you want to execute next. All lines in between are ignored. This means that certain things you may have expected to occur don't happen, which can lead to unexpected errors.

Showing the Next Statement

If you are not sure where procedure execution will resume, you can choose Debug | Show Next Statement, and Visual Basic will place the cursor on the line that will run next. This is particularly useful when you have been looking at other procedures and are not sure where execution will resume. The Show Next Statement option is available only in break mode.

Stopping and Resetting VBA Procedures

At any time while stepping through the code of a procedure in the Code window, you can press F5 to execute the remaining instructions without stepping through them, or choose Run | Reset to finish the procedure without executing the remaining statements. When you reset your procedure, all the variables lose their current values. Numeric variables assume the initial value of zero, variable-length strings are initialized to a zero-length string (""), and fixed-length strings are filled with the character represented by the ASCII character code 0, or Chr(0). Variant variables are initialized to Empty, and the value of Object variables is set to Nothing.

Understanding and Using Conditional Compilation

When you run a procedure for the first time, Visual Basic converts your VBA statements into the machine code understood by the computer. This process is called *compiling*. You can also perform the compilation of your entire VBA project before you run the procedure by choosing Debug | Compile (name of the current VBA project). You can tell Visual Basic to include or ignore certain blocks of code when compiling and running by using conditional compilation. Your procedure may behave differently depending on the condition you set. For example, conditional compilation is used to compile an application that will be run on different platforms (Windows or Macintosh, Win16 or Win32). Conditional compilation is also useful in localizing an application for different languages. The program code excluded during the conditional compilation is omitted from the final file, and thus it has no effect on the size or performance of the program.

Conditional compilation is enabled via special expressions called *directives*. First, you need to declare a Boolean (True, False) constant by using the #Const directive. Next, you check this constant inside the #If...Then... #Else directive. The portion of code that you want to compile conditionally must be surrounded by these directives. Notice that the If and Else keywords are preceded by a pound sign (#). If a portion of code is to be run, the value of the conditional constant has to be set to True (–1). Otherwise, the value of this constant should be set to False (0). You declare the conditional constant in the declaration section of the module. For example,

```
#Const User = True
```

declares the conditional constant named User.

In the hands-on exercise that follows, data is displayed in the Spanish language when the conditional constant named verSpanish is True. The WhatDay procedure calls the DayOfWeek function, which returns the name of the day based on the supplied date. To compile the program in the English language, all you have to do is change the conditional constant to False, and Visual Basic will jump to the block of instructions located after the #Else directive.

◎ Hands-On 9-6: Using Conditional Compilation

1. Insert a new module, and in the Properties window rename it **Conditional**.

2. Enter the **WhatDay** and **DayOfWeek** function procedures as shown below:

```
' declare a conditional compiler constant
#Const verSpanish = True

Sub WhatDay()
    Dim dayNr As Integer
    #If verSpanish = True Then
        dayNr = Weekday(InputBox("Entre la fecha, por ejemplo 01/01/2001"))
        MsgBox "Sera " & DayOfWeek(dayNr) & "."
    #Else
        WeekdayName
    #End If
End Sub

Function DayOfWeek(dayNr As Integer) As String
    DayOfWeek = Choose(dayNr, "Domingo", "Lunes", "Martes", _
        "Miercoles", "Jueves", "Viernes", "Sabado")
End Function

Function WeekdayName() As String
    Select Case Weekday(InputBox("Enter date, e.g., 01/01/2000"))
        Case 1
            WeekdayName = "Sunday"
        Case 2
            WeekdayName = "Monday"
        Case 3
            WeekdayName = "Tuesday"
        Case 4
            WeekdayName = "Wednesday"
        Case 5
            WeekdayName = "Thursday"
        Case 6
            WeekdayName = "Friday"
        Case 7
            WeekdayName = "Saturday"
    End Select
    MsgBox "It will be " & WeekdayName & "."
End Function
```

3. Run the WhatDay procedure.

Because the conditional compilation constant (verSpanish) is set to True at the top of the module, Visual Basic runs the Spanish version of the WhatDay procedure. It asks for the user's input in Spanish and displays the result in Spanish. To run the English version of the code, change the verSpanish constant to False, and rerun the procedure.

Figure 9-15: The conditional compilation constant can be declared either at the top of the module or in the Project Properties window, but never in both places.

Instead of declaring the conditional compiler constants at the top of a module, you can choose Tools | (Debugging) Properties (see Figure 9-15). When you use the Project Properties window, use the following syntax in the Conditional Compilation Arguments text box to enable the English version of the WhatDay procedure:

```
verSpanish = 0
```

If there are more conditional compilation constants, each of the constants must be separated by a colon.

4. Comment out the **#Const verSpanish** directive at the top of the module, and enter the conditional compilation constant in the Project Properties window as shown in Figure 9-15. Then run the WhatDay procedure to see how the Else branch of your program is now executed for English-speaking users.

Navigating with Bookmarks

In the process of analyzing or reviewing your VBA procedures you will often find yourself jumping to certain code areas. Using the built-in bookmark feature, you can easily mark the spots you want to navigate between.

To set up a bookmark:

1. Click anywhere in the statement you want to define as a bookmark.

2. Choose **Edit | Bookmarks | Toggle Bookmark** (or click the **Toggle Bookmark** button on the Edit toolbar).

    Visual Basic will place a blue, rounded rectangle in the left margin beside the statement (see Figure 9-16).

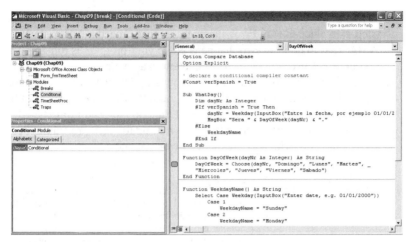

Figure 9-16: Using bookmarks, you can quickly jump between often-used sections of your procedures.

Once you've set up two or more bookmarks, you can jump between the marked locations of your code by choosing Edit | Bookmarks | Next Bookmark or simply click the Next Bookmark button on the Edit toolbar. You may also right-click anywhere in the Code window and select Next Bookmark from the shortcut menu. To go to the previous bookmark, select Previous Bookmark. You can remove bookmarks at any time by choosing Edit | Bookmarks | Clear All or by clicking the Clear All Bookmarks button on the Edit toolbar. To remove a single bookmark, click anywhere in the bookmarked statement and choose Edit | Bookmarks | Toggle Bookmark, or click the Toggle Bookmark button on the Edit toolbar.

Trapping Errors

No one writes bug-free programs the first time. For this reason, when you create VBA procedures you have to determine how your program will respond to errors. Many unexpected errors happen at run time. For example, your procedure may try to give a new file the same name as an open file.

Run-time errors are often discovered not by a programmer, but by the user who attempts to do something that the programmer has not anticipated. If an error occurs when the procedure is running, Visual Basic displays an error message and the procedure is stopped. Most often the error message that VBA displays is quite cryptic to the user.

You can keep users from seeing many run-time errors by including error-handling code in your VBA procedures. This way, when Visual Basic encounters an error, instead of displaying a default error message, it will show a much friendlier, more comprehensive error message, perhaps advising the user how to correct the error.

How do you implement error handling in your VBA procedure? The first step is to place the On Error statement in your procedure. This statement tells VBA what to do if an error happens while your program is running. In other words, VBA uses the On Error statement to activate an error-handling procedure that will trap run-time errors. Depending on the type of procedure, you can exit the error trap by using one of the following statements: Exit Sub, Exit Function, Exit Property, End Sub, End Function, or End Property.

You should write an error-handling routine for each procedure. See Table 9-3 for ways in which to use the On Error statement.

Table 9-3: On Error options

On Error Statement	Description
On Error GoTo Label	Specifies a label to jump to when an error occurs. This label marks the beginning of the error-handling routine. An *error handler* is a routine for trapping and responding to errors in your application. The label must appear in the same procedure as the On Error GoTo statement.
On Error Resume Next	When a run-time error occurs, Visual Basic ignores the line that caused the error and does not display an error message, but continues the procedure with the next line.
On Error GoTo 0	Turns off error trapping in a procedure. When VBA runs this statement, errors are detected but not trapped within the procedure.

Is This an Error or a Mistake?

In programming, mistakes and errors are not the same thing. A mistake — such as a misspelled or missing statement, a misplaced quotation mark or comma, or an assignment of a value of one type to a variable of a different (and incompatible) type — can be removed from your program through proper testing and debugging. But even though your code may be free of mistakes, errors can still occur. An error is a result of an event or operation that doesn't work as expected. For example, if your VBA procedure accesses a particular file on disk and someone deleted this file or moved it to another location, you'll get an error no matter what. An error prevents the procedure from carrying out a specific task.

Let's look at the example procedure in Hands-On 9-7. The OpenToRead procedure shown below demonstrates the use of the Resume Next and Error statements, as well as the Err object.

◎ Hands-On 9-7: Error Trapping Techniques

1. In the Visual Basic Editor window, insert a new module.

2. In the Code window, enter the following **OpenToRead** procedure.

Note: The purpose of the OpenToRead procedure is to read the contents of the user-supplied text file character by character. When the user enters a file-name, various errors can occur. For example, the filename may be wrong, the user may attempt to open a file from a CD, DVD, or diskette when there is no disk in the drive, or he may try to open a file that is already open. To trap these errors, the error-handling routine at the end of the OpenToRead procedure uses the Number property of the Err object. The Err object contains information about run-time errors. If an error occurs while the procedure is running, the statement Err.Number will return the error number.

```
Sub OpenToRead()
    Dim myFile As String
    Dim myChar As String
    Dim myText As String
    Dim FileExists As Boolean

    FileExists = True

    On Error GoTo ErrorHandler
    myFile = InputBox("Enter the name of file you want to open:")
    Open myFile For Input As #1
    If FileExists Then
        Do While Not EOF(1)        ' loop until the end of file
            myChar = Input(1, #1)   ' get one character
            myText = myText + myChar ' store in the variable myText
        Loop
        Debug.Print myText          ' print to the Immediate window
        ' Close the file - commenting out this instruction will cause
        ' error 52.
        Close #1
    End If
    Exit Sub

ErrorHandler:
    FileExists = False
    Select Case Err.Number
        Case 71
            MsgBox "The diskette drive is empty."
        Case 53
            MsgBox "This file can't be found on the specified drive."
        Case 75
            Exit Sub
        Case Else
            MsgBox "Error " & Err.Number & " :" & Err.Description
            Exit Sub
    End Select
    Resume Next
End Sub
```

If errors 71, 53, or 75 occur, Visual Basic will display the user-friendly messages given inside the Select Case block and then proceed to the Resume Next statement, which will send it to the line of code following the one that had caused the error. If another (unexpected) error occurs, Visual Basic will return its error code (Err.Number) and error description (Err.Description).

At the beginning of the procedure, the variable FileExists is set to True. If the program doesn't encounter an error, all the instructions inside the If FileExists Then block will be executed. However, if VBA encounters an error, the value of the FileExists variable will be set to False (see the first statement in the error-handling routine just below the ErrorHandler label).

If you comment the statement Close #1, Visual Basic will encounter the error on the next attempt to open the same file. Notice the Exit Sub statement before the ErrorHandler. Put the Exit Sub statement just above the error-handling routine. You don't want Visual Basic to carry out the error handling if there are no errors.

Procedure Testing

You are responsible for the code you produce. This means that before you give your procedure to others to test, you should test it yourself. After all, you understand best how it is supposed to work. Some programmers think testing their own code is some sort of degrading activity, especially when they work in an organization that has a team devoted to testing. *Don't make this mistake.* The testing process at the programmer level is as important as the code development itself. After you've tested the procedure yourself, you should give it to the users to test. Users will provide you with answers to questions such as: Does the procedure produce the expected results? Is it easy and fun to use? Does it follow the standard conventions? Also, it is a good idea to give the entire application to someone who knows the least about using this particular application, and ask them to play around with it and try to break it.

To better understand error trapping, let's perform another hands-on exercise.

◎ Hands-On 9-8: Understanding Error Trapping

This hands-on exercise requires prior completion of Hands-On 9-7.

1. Prepare a text file named **C:\Acc07_ByExample\Vacation.txt** using Windows Notepad. Enter any text you want in this file, or copy the Vacation.txt file from the C:\Acc07_HandsOn folder to your Acc07_ByExample folder.

2. Run the OpenToRead procedure three times in step mode, each time supplying one of the following:

   ■ The filename C:\Acc07_ByExample\Vacation.txt

   ■ A filename that does not exist on drive C

   ■ The name of any file that references your CD, DVD or diskette drive (when the drive slot is empty)

3. Comment the Close #1 statement and enter **C:\Acc07_ByExample\Vacation.txt** as the filename. Run the procedure twice. The second run will generate an error because the text file will be open.

Generating Errors to Test Error Handling

You can test the ways your program responds to run-time errors by causing them on purpose:

▪ Generate any built-in error by entering the following syntax:

```
Error error_number
```

For example, to display the error that occurs on an attempt to divide by zero (0), type the following statement in the Immediate window:

```
Error 11
```

When you press Enter, Visual Basic will display the error message saying, "Run-time error 11. Division by zero."

▪ To check the meaning of the generated error, use the following syntax:

```
Error(error_number)
```

For example, to find out what error number 7 means, type the following in the Immediate window:

```
?Error(7)
```

When you press Enter, Visual Basic returns the error description:

```
"Out of memory"
```

Chapter Summary

In this chapter, you learned how to test your VBA procedures to make sure they perform as planned. You debugged your code by stepping through it using breakpoints and watches, learned how to work with the Immediate window in break mode, found out how the Locals window can help you monitor the values of variables, and discovered how the Call Stack dialog box can be helpful for keeping track of where you are in a complex program. You also learned how to specify the parts of your procedure that you want to include or exclude upon compilation. Finally, you learned how to trap errors with error-handling routines. By using the built-in debugging tools, you can quickly pinpoint the problem spots in your procedures. Try to spend more time getting acquainted with these tools. Mastering the art of debugging can save you hours of trial and error.

This chapter completes Part I of this book — Introduction to Access 2007 VBA Programming.

PART II

Access VBA Programming with DAO and ADO

Microsoft Access offers programmers two data access object models for accessing and manipulating Access databases: Data Access Objects (DAO) and ActiveX Data Objects (ADO).

In this part of the book, you learn how to connect to Access databases and external data sources; create, modify, and secure database objects; and read, write, and manipulate data.

Chapter 10

Data Access Technologies in Microsoft Access

Microsoft Access has been effectively used by people all over the world for organizing and accessing data. While each new software release brought numerous changes in the design of the user interface and offered simpler ways of performing common database tasks, database access has evolved at a little slower pace.

This chapter begins with the introduction of the old (Jet) and the new (ACE) database engines and proceeds to an overview of Access versions and file formats supported by Microsoft Office Access 2007. This is followed by a review of data access methods that programmers and database developers can use to read, write, and manipulate data in Access databases (in MDB and the new ACCDB file formats). In addition, this chapter demonstrates various ways of opening both native Microsoft Jet databases as well as external data sources. You will also learn how to establish a connection to the currently open database, connect to an SQL Server, create a new database, set database properties, and handle database errors.

Understanding Database Engines: Jet/ACE

Since version 1.0 (1992), an integrated part of Microsoft Access has been its database engine, commonly referred to as *Microsoft Jet* (Joint Engine Technology (JET)) or *Jet database engine*. Microsoft Jet is a multi-user, relational database engine that provides support for the standard DBMS (Database Management System) functionality such as data definition, data manipulation, querying, security, and maintenance, as well as remote data access.

Jet stores data in the Microsoft Access database (MDB) file format according to the Indexed Sequential Access Method (ISAM). Queries are performed by the Jet query engine. A Replication engine is used to create copies (replicas) of database structures on multiple systems with periodic synchronization. Jet provides password-protected security and different levels of access via the user and group accounts. The user information is kept in a separate system database (MDW). Security is also built into the database tables in the form of object permissions.

The Microsoft Jet database engine enables you to access data that resides in Microsoft Jet databases (MDB files), external data sources (FoxPro, Borland dBASE, and Corel Paradox database files, Microsoft Excel and Lotus 1-2-3 files, MS Exchange Server files, text files, or HTML files), and Open Database Connectivity (ODBC) data sources (SQL Server, Oracle, or Sybase). To access external data via ODBC, you need a specific ODBC driver installed on the computer containing the data source.

The main component of the Microsoft Jet database engine is a dynamic link library file (.dll) installed in the \Windows\System32 folder (see Table 10-1). On the Windows platform, DLLs are libraries of common code that can be used by more than one application. The Jet DLL provides a simple interface to the data. If the data source is an .mdb file, then Jet reads and writes directly to the file. If the data source is external, Jet calls on the appropriate ODBC driver to perform the request.

Different versions of Access use different versions of Jet (see Table 10-1). In Access 2003 and earlier, Jet is included with Microsoft Windows and its upgrades are performed via separate Jet service packs. To keep your Jet database in good working condition, you must install the latest Jet update. (Find out how to obtain the latest service pack for the Microsoft Jet 4.0 database engine at http://support.microsoft.com/default.aspx?kbid=239114.)

In Office Access 2007, Microsoft has made many enhancements to the database engine, making it private for 2007 Microsoft Office suite applications. This private version of Jet, called the *Access Connectivity Engine* (ACE), uses the new file format with the extension .accdb and offers many useful features to Access users and developers alike (see Table 10-2).

Table 10-1: Database engine versions in Access 2007 and earlier

MS Access Version	Database Engine Used	Dynamic Link Library (DLL) File
Access 2007	ACE 12	ace.dll
Access 2003/2002/2000	Jet 4	msjet40.dll
Access 97	Jet 3.5	msjet35.dll

Understanding Access Versions and File Formats

In Office Access 2007 the default file format is ACCDB; however, users of Office Access 2007 can directly open and use Jet databases created in Access 2003/2002/2000. Jet databases created with Access 97 or earlier must be either enabled or converted for use in Office Access 2007. When an older database is enabled it is made compatible with Office Access 2007 so that you can make changes to the data. However, any design changes must be made in the version of Access that was used when the database was first created. When you opt to convert an Access 97 or earlier database to the Access 2007 ACCDB file format, you must first convert it to Access 2003, Access 2002, or Access 2000. Table 10-2 lists various file formats that are supported by Office Access 2007.

Access VBA Programming with DAO and ADO

Table 10-2: File formats supported in Access 2007

File Format	Description	Additional Notes
.accdb	New Office Access 2007 file format (default). This file format is not readable by Access versions prior to 2007. DO NOT use this file format if you need to support: • Replication • User-level security Note: You can use Access 2007 to create a replica of an .mdb database formatted in Access 2000 or Access 2002-2003 file format.	This file format can use the following new features: • Multi-value fields (create fields that hold multiple values) • Attachment data type (store pictures, graphics, and any type of file) • Rich text in memo fields • Total row in datasheets • Database and field templates • Split forms • Compatibility with Windows SharePoint Services 3.0 and Microsoft Office Outlook 2007
.accde	File extension for Access 2007 .accdb files that are in execute only mode. These files have all VBA source code removed. This file extension replaces the .mde file extension used in earlier versions of Access.	Users can only execute VBA code; they cannot view or modify it. In addition, users do not have permissions to make design changes to forms or reports. Note: You can make the .accde file from your Access database via the Database Tools group on the Database Tools tab.
.accdt	This is an Access Database Template file. Office Access 2007 comes with professionally designed database templates.	Templates provide you with predefined tables/table relationships, forms, reports, queries, and macros.
.accdr	This file extension denotes an Office Access 2007 database functioning in run-time mode.	To create a "locked-down" version of your Office Access 2007 database, simply change the file extension from .accdb to .accdr. To restore the full database functionality, do the reverse — change the file extension from .accdr to .accdb.
.mdb (Access 2000, Access 2002, Access 2003, Access 97)	Access database file format used in all earlier versions of Access (prior to 2007). Note: Office Access 2007 allows you to create files in either the Access 2000 format or the Access 2002-2003 format. These files will have the extension .mdb.	Use the .mdb file format if you need to support: • Replication • User-level security • Share the Access database with users who have not yet upgraded to Office Access 2007
.mde (Access 2000, Access 2002, Access 2003, Access 97)	An .mde file is a compiled version of an .mdb database without any VBA code. This change prevents a database user from reading or changing your VBA code. Users cannot edit the design of forms, reports, or modules.	An .accde file is the Office Access 2007 version of the .mde file in earlier versions of Access.

File Format	Description	Additional Notes
.adp	This is a file extension for a Microsoft Access Data Project file that lets you connect to an SQL Server database or the Microsoft Data Engine (MSDE) on your PC and create client/server applications. A project file does not contain any data or data definition objects such as tables, views, stored procedures, or user-defined functions. All database objects are stored in the SQL Server database. An .adp file stores only database front end forms, reports, and other application objects (macros, modules).	Access 2007 offers full support for the .adp file format. You can open and edit an existing .adp database that was created in an earlier version of Access or create a new .adp database. To create a new .adp database in Access 2007, select a blank database in the Getting Started screen and click the Folder button next to the File name box. Choose Microsoft Office Access Projects (*.adp) in the Save as type drop-down box and click OK.
.ade	This is a file format for a Microsoft Access project (.adp) file with all modules compiled and all editable source code removed. Similar to .mde files, projects stored in .ade file format prevent users from making design changes to the front end and gaining access to your VBA source code.	Access 2007 offers full support for the .ade file format. To create an .ade file from your Access Data Project (ADP), choose Database Tools | Make ADE.
.mdw (Access 2000, Access 2002, Access 2003, Access 97)	This file format is used by a workgroup information file. The .mdw files store information for secured .mdb databases.	There are no changes to the .mdw file format in Office Access 2007. The .mdw files created in earlier versions of Access (2000 through 2003) can be used by Office Access 2007 databases. When an .mdb database is opened in Access 2007, you can choose Database Tools | Users & Permissions | User-Level Security Wizard to create a new workgroup information file (.mdw).
.ldb	This is a locking file extension for the .mdb database. This file prevents users from writing data to pages that have been locked by other users and lets you determine which computer/user has a file or record locked. The .ldb file keeps track of user/computer names of the people who are currently logged into the .mdb. Note: You can view the information stored in this file by opening it with Windows Notepad.	A locking file is created automatically when the database is opened and is deleted automatically when the last user closes a shared database.

File Format	Description	Additional Notes
.laccdb	This is the file extension for a locking file used by Office Access 2007 (.accdb file format).	As with the .ldb file, the .laccdb file is created automatically when the database is opened and is deleted automatically when the last user closes a shared database. Note: Because different locking files are created for .mdb and .accdb databases in Office Access 2007, .mdb and .accdb files can be open in Office Access 2007 without causing conflicts in the locking file.

Understanding Library References

A Microsoft Access database consists of various types of objects stored in different object libraries. Libraries are components that provide specific functionality. They are listed in the References dialog box (Figure 10-1), which can be opened from the Visual Basic Editor window by selecting Tools | References. If you create an Access 2007 database in the default ACCDB file format, you will see the following default references in the References dialog box:

- Visual Basic For Applications

- Microsoft Access 12.0 Object Library

- OLE Automation

- Microsoft Office 12.0 Access database engine Object Library

Figure 10-1: The default object libraries for Access 2007.

Figure 10-2: The default object libraries for Access 2002-2003.

The VBA (Visual Basic for Applications) and Access libraries that appear on the top of the References dialog box are built in and Access will not allow you to remove them from the database. References that are not checked are listed alphabetically. The references that are checked are listed by priority. When your VBA procedure references an object, Visual Basic searches each referenced object library in the order in which the libraries are displayed in the References dialog box. If the referenced libraries have objects with the same name, Visual Basic uses the object definition provided by the library listed higher in the Available References list. You can change the priority of an object library by selecting its name and clicking the up or down arrow button in the References dialog box. To help Visual Basic resolve library references, specify the name of the library you intend to use. For example, to specify that the DAO Recordset should be used, declare it like this:

```
Dim rst As DAO.Recordset
```

To use the ADO Recordset, use the following declaration:

```
Dim rst As ADO.Recordset
```

You can reference additional libraries in your Access database if your VBA application requires features that are not provided by the default libraries. For example, if your VBA procedures need to access files and folders on the computer, you may want to check the box next to the Microsoft Scripting Runtime. Do not add references to libraries you don't plan to use as they consume memory and may make your Access VBA project more time-consuming to compile and harder to debug.

Missing Library

If the library is marked as Missing in the References dialog box, click the Browse button, and locate the correct library file. You can disable a missing reference by clearing the check box to the left of the reference labeled "Missing".

Library Does Not Show in the References Dialog Box

If the library you want to reference is not shown in the Available References list box, you may need to unregister and reregister it with Windows.

To unregister a library, close Access. Choose Run from the Start menu, and enter regsvr32-u followed by a space and the full path to the library file surrounded by quotation marks. For example:

```
regsvr32-u "C:\Program Files\Common Files\System\Ado\msjro.dll"
```

To register a library, choose Run from the Start menu, and enter regsvr32 followed by a space and the full path to the library file surrounded by quotation marks. For example:

```
regsvr32 "C:\Program Files\Common Files\System\Ado\msjro.dll"
```

The next time you open Access the library name should be listed in the References dialog box.

 Note: If you move a library file from where it was originally installed, be sure to reregister it with the operating system or things may not work as expected.

Because referencing a wrong library for the version of Access used can cause data corruption, it is important to know which library files were designed for a particular version of Access. The next section introduces you to library files that you will find useful in creating and manipulating MDB and ACCDB databases using VBA code.

Overview of Object Libraries in Microsoft Access

The object library contains information about its objects, properties, and methods. To work with the VBA programming examples included in this book, you will need to access objects from the libraries listed below.

The Visual Basic for Applications Object Library (VBA)

Objects contained in this library allow you to access your computer's file system, work with date and time functions, perform mathematical and financial computations, interact with users, convert data, and read text files. For Access 2000 through 2007, the VBA library is stored in the vbe6.dll file located in the C:\Program Files\Common Files\Microsoft Shared\VBA\VBA6 folder. Access 97 uses the vba33.dll file located in the C:\Program Files\Common Files\ Microsoft Shared\VBA folder.

The Microsoft Access 12.0 Object Library

This library provides objects that are used to display data and work with the Microsoft Access 2007 application. In Access 2007, the Access library is stored in the msacc.olb file and can be found in the C:\Program Files\Microsoft Office\Office12 folder. See the list below for the names and locations of Access library files in earlier versions of Access.

Access 2003 C:\Program Files Microsoft Office\Office11\msacc.olb

Access 2002 C:\Program Files Microsoft Office\Office10\msacc.olb

Access 2000 C:\Program Files Microsoft Office\Office\msacc9.olb

Access 97   C:\Program Files Microsoft Office\Office\msacc8.olb

The Microsoft Office 12.0 Access Database Engine Object Library

This library is the enhanced version of the DAO Object Library, built specifically for working with the new ACE database engine in Access 2007. The library is stored in the acedao.dll file in the C:\Program Files\Common Files\Microsoft Shared\Office12 folder. This library is used when you open an Access database in the default Access 2007 format (ACCDB). When you open an MDB file in Access 2007, the Microsoft DAO 3.6 Object Library is used. Both DAO and ACEDAO libraries are referenced with the "DAO" in object declarations, and therefore your existing VBA code should work in both versions.

The Microsoft Access DAO 3.6 Object Library

DAO provides programmatic access to Jet Access databases. It consists of a hierarchy of objects that supply methods and properties for designing and manipulating databases. The DBEngine object positioned at the top of the DAO object hierarchy is often referred to as the Jet engine and is used to reference the database engine as a whole. All the other objects and collections in the DAO object hierarchy fall under DBEngine. The DBEngine contains the following two collections of objects:

- The Errors collection, which stores a list of errors that have occurred in the DBEngine. These errors are represented by the Error objects and should not be confused with the Err object, which stores run-time errors generated in Visual Basic.

- The Workspaces collection (the default collection of the DBEngine object), which contains the Workspace objects and is used for database security in multi-user applications. The Workspace object is used in conjunction with User and Group objects.

Each open database is represented by the Database object. The Database object is used to reference a Microsoft Access database file (MDB) or another external database represented by an ODBC data source. The Databases collection contains all currently open databases. The Containers, QueryDefs, Relations, and TableDefs collections contain objects that are used to reference various components of the Database object. For example, the TableDef object represents a table or a linked table in a Microsoft Jet workspace. The QueryDef object represents a query in DAO. If values are supplied to a query, they are represented in DAO by a Parameter object. The Parameters collection contains all of the Parameter objects defined for a QueryDef object. The Relation object represents a relationship between fields in tables and queries. The Container object is used to access collections of saved objects that represent databases, tables, queries, and relationships.

The Recordsets collection contains all open Recordset objects. Each Recordset object represents a set of records within a database. You will use Recordset objects for retrieving, adding, editing, and deleting records from a database.

The Field object represents a field in a table, query, index, relation, or recordset. The Fields collection is the default collection of a TableDef, QueryDef, Index, Relation, and Recordset object.

Some DAO objects have a Properties collection. The Properties collection contains a separate object for each property of the DAO object that is referenced. You can use an object's Properties collection to enumerate its properties or to return their settings. You can also define your own custom properties on DAO objects.

The DAO Object Library is stored in the dao360.dll file located in the C:\Program Files\Common Files\Microsoft Shared\DAO folder. This library file can be used by Access MDB databases created in Access 2000 through 2007. Access 97 uses dao350.dll. In Access 2007, when you open an ACCDB file, the Microsoft Office 12.0 Access database engine Object Library is used.

The Microsoft ActiveX Data Objects 2.8 Library (ADO)

This library is stored in msado15.dll and can be found in the C:\Program Files\Common Files\System\ADO folder. ActiveX Data Objects (ADO) that are provided by this library allow you to access and manipulate data from a variety of sources through an OLE DB provider. ADO works with the technology known as *OLE DB*. This technology is object-based, but it is not limited to relational databases. OLE DB can access both relational and non-relational data sources such as directory services, mail stores, multimedia, and text files, as well as mainframe data (VSAM and MVS). You do not need any specific drivers installed on your computer to access external data with OLE DB because OLE DB does not use drivers; it uses data providers to communicate with data stores. *Data providers* are programs that enable access to data. OLE DB has many providers, such as Microsoft OLE DB Provider for SQL Server and Microsoft Jet 4.0 OLE DB Provider. There are also providers for Oracle, NT 5 Active Directory, and even a provider for ODBC.

Similar to DAO, ADO objects make it possible to establish a connection with a data source in order to read, insert, modify, and delete data. ADO offers to programmers many advanced features that are not available in DAO. For example, the ADO Connection object's State property lets you determine whether the connection is closed (adStateClosed), open and ready (adStateOpen), still trying to connect (adStateConnecting), processing a command (adStateExecuting), or fetching data (adStateFetching). The ADO Recordsets can be hierarchical, fabricated, disconnected, or persisted on disk.

ADO consists of three object models, each providing a different area of functionality (see Table 10-3). Because of this, only the objects necessary for a specific task need to be loaded at any given time.

Table 10-3: Components of ADO

Object Model	What It's Used For
ADODB — ActiveX Data Objects	Data manipulation
	Access and manipulate data through an OLE DB provider. With ADO objects you can connect to a data source and read, add, update, or delete data.
	Library Name: Microsoft ActiveX Data Objects 2.8 Library
	Library File: msado15.dll
	Library Folder: C:\Program Files\Common Files\System\ADO

Object Model	What It's Used For
ADOX — ADO Extensions for DDL and Security	Data definition and security
	With ADOX objects you can define data such as tables, views, indexes, or relationships, as well as create and modify user and group accounts, and grant and revoke permissions on objects.
	Library Name: Microsoft ADO Ext. 2.8 for DDL and Security (ADOX)
	Library File: msadox.dll
	Library Folder: C:\Program Files\Common Files\System\ADO
JRO — Jet and Replication Objects	Replication
	With JRO objects you can compact a Jet database, and create, modify, and synchronize replicas. JRO can be used only with Microsoft Jet databases.
	Library Name: Microsoft Jet and Replication Objects 2.6 Library (JRO)
	Library File: msjro.dll
	Library Folder: C:\Program Files\Common Files\System\ADO

ADO can be used from scripting languages such as Microsoft Visual Basic Scripting Edition (VBScript) or Microsoft JScript.

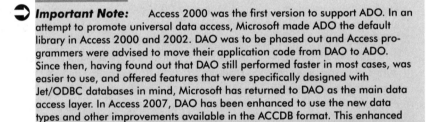

Important Note: Access 2000 was the first version to support ADO. In an attempt to promote universal data access, Microsoft made ADO the default library in Access 2000 and 2002. DAO was to be phased out and Access programmers were advised to move their application code from DAO to ADO. Since then, having found out that DAO still performed faster in most cases, was easier to use, and offered features that were specifically designed with Jet/ODBC databases in mind, Microsoft has returned to DAO as the main data access layer. In Access 2007, DAO has been enhanced to use the new data types and other improvements available in the ACCDB format. This enhanced version of DAO is offered as the Microsoft Office 12.0 Access database engine Object Library.

ADO Classic vs. ADO.NET

The classic ADO used in VBA in Office Access and other Microsoft Office applications is a completely different object model from ADO.NET used with the Microsoft .NET framework. ADO.NET is not built on ActiveX technology and its objects cannot be used directly in a VBA project.

Creating a Reference to the ADO Library

Prior to declaring variables as ADO objects in your VBA procedures, make sure that the reference to the library you are intending to use is set in the References dialog box. Hands-On 10-1 demonstrates how to create a reference to the Microsoft ActiveX Data Objects 2.x Object Library.

◎ Hands-On 10-1: Setting Up a Reference to ADO Object Libraries

1. Start Microsoft Office Access 2007 and create a new Microsoft Office Access 2007 database named **Chap10.accdb** in your **C:\Acc07_ByExample** folder.

2. Press **Alt+F11** to switch to the Visual Basic Editor window, and then choose **Tools | References**.

3. Scroll down the list of available references until you located the **Microsoft ActiveX Data Objects 2.8 (or earlier) Library**. Click the check box to the left of the name to select it.

4. Click **OK** to close the References dialog box.

All libraries that are checked in the References dialog box can be browsed using the Object Browser. This is a good way to get to know the names of objects that are available in a specific library and their various properties and methods (Figure 10-3).

Figure 10-3: Use the Object Browser to find the objects available in a specific library.

Understanding Connection Strings

Needless to say, to retrieve or write data to a database, you will need to open it. There are many ways to connect to a database or an external data source from Microsoft Access 2007. The first thing to know about establishing database connections from your VBA procedures is how to prepare and use connection strings.

A *connection string* is a string variable that tells your VBA application how to establish a connection to a data source. There are two types of connection strings:

- ODBC connection strings (used by ODBC drivers)
- OLE DB connection strings (used by the OLE DB provider)

The syntax of ODBC and OLE DB connection strings is very similar. The connection string consists of a series of keyword and value pairs separated by semicolons:

```
Keyword1=value; Keyword2=value
```

Please note that the connection string does not contain spaces before or after the equal sign (=). The parameters in the connection string may vary depending on the ODBC driver or OLE DB provider used and the data store that you are connecting to (e.g., Microsoft Access, SQL Server, and so forth).

For example, the following connection string will create an ODBC connection to an Access database called Northwind.mdb:

```
"Driver={Microsoft Access Driver (*.mdb)};"
"DBQ=C:\Acc07_ByExample\Northwind.mdb;"
```

In the above connection string, Driver specifies what type of database you're using. DBQ is the physical path to the database. If the Northwind.mdb file is protected with a password, you must provide additional information in the connection string:

```
"Driver={Microsoft Access Driver (*.mdb)};"
"DBQ=C:\Acc07_ByExample\Northwind.mdb;UID=admin;PWD=secret;"
```

UID specifies the user name. PWD specifies the user password.

To create an OLE DB connection to the same Access MDB database using standard security, the following connection string can be used:

```
"Provider=Microsoft.Jet.OLEDB.4.0;"
"Data Source=C:\Acc07_ByExample\Northwind.mdb;User Id=Admin;Password=;"
```

Provider identifies the OLE DB provider for your database; in this case, we want to use the JET OLE DB Provider. Data Source specifies the full path and filename of the MDB file.

To create an OLE DB connection to the SQL database called Northwind, use the following connection string:

```
"Provider=SQLOLEDB; Data Source=(local); Integrated Security=SSPI; Initial
Catalog=Northwind"
```

SQLOLEDB is the name of the OLE DB provider for SQL Server databases. The Data Source parameter specifies the name or address of the SQL Server. To connect with an SQL Server running on the same computer, use the keyword (local) in the Data Source. For trusted connection (Microsoft Windows NT integrated security), set the Integrated Security parameter to SSPI. Use the Initial Catalog parameter to specify which database you want to connect to.

 Note: If no Provider keyword is in the connection string, the OLE DB provider for ODBC (MSDASQL) is the default value. This provides backward compatibility with ODBC connection strings.

Using ODBC Connection Strings

When you choose to connect to a data source via the ODBC, you must specify the connection information. You do this by creating a DSN (Data Source Name) or DSN-less connection. *DSN* connections store the connection information in the Windows Registry or in a .dsn file. In a *DSN-less* connection, all connection information is specified in the connection string. The following subsections explain each ODBC connection type in detail.

Creating and Using ODBC DSN Connections

Windows uses an ODBC Data Source Administrator (Figure 10-4) to manage ODBC drivers and data sources available on the computer. If you are using Windows 2000 or Windows XP, you can access this tool by opening the Administrative Tools in the Control Panel and choosing the Data Sources (ODBC) icon.

The DSN contains information about database configuration, location, and user security. There are three types of DSNs:

- **User DSN** — A User DSN is stored locally in the Windows Registry and limits database connectivity to the user who creates it. In other words, if you create a User DSN under your user account, no other user will be able to see it or use it. Hands-On 10-2 demonstrates how to create this type of DSN so that you can run the example code on your computer.

- **File DSN** — A File DSN is a special type of a file that stores all the connection settings. File DSNs are saved by default in the Program Files\Common Files\Odbc\Data Sources folder. Because the connection parameters and values are stored in a file, they can be easily shared with other users. If other users require the same connection, simply send them the DSN file and you won't need to configure a DSN for each system.

- **System DSN** —A System DSN is stored locally in the Windows Registry and allows any logged on user, process, and service to see it or use it. System DSNs are often used in establishing connections to external data sources from Active Server Pages (ASP).

Figure 10-4: The ODBC Data Source Administrator allows you to set up appropriate connections with the required data provider via the User, System, or File DSN.

Hands-On 10-2 illustrates how to use the ODBC Data Source Administrator to create a User DSN named MyDbaseFile to access data in a dBASE database file (Customer.dbf) and use this data source name to programmatically open a dBASE file with ADO using the ODBC DSN connection.

◎ Hands-On 10-2: Creating and Using the ODBC DSN Connection to Read Data from a dBASE File

1. Copy the **Customer.dbf** file from the **C:\Acc07_HandsOn** folder to your **C:\Acc07_ByExample** folder.

2. Open the Control Panel, activate **Administrative Tools**, and double-click **Data Sources (ODBC)**.

    The ODBC Data Source Administrator dialog box appears, as shown in Figure 10-4.

3. With the **User DSN** tab selected, click the **Add** button.

4. Select **Microsoft dBASE driver (*.dbf)** and click **Finish**.

5. Enter **MyDbaseFile** as the Data Source Name and choose **dBase 5.0** for the database version, as shown in Figure 10-5. Make sure you clear the Use Current Directory check box, then click the **Select Directory** button.

Figure 10-5: Creating a Data Source Name (DSN) to access a dBASE file.

6. In the Select Directory dialog box, select the **C:\Acc07_ByExample** folder where the dBASE database .dbf file is located, and click the **OK** button.

7. Click **OK** to exit the ODBC dBASE Setup dialog box.

    The MyDbaseFile data source now appears in the list of User Data Sources in the ODBC Data Source Administrator dialog box.

8. Click **OK** to close the ODBC Data Source Administrator dialog box.

9. Activate the Visual Basic Editor window in the Chap10.accdb database and choose **Insert | Module**.

10. In the module's Code window, type the **Open_AndRead_dBaseFile** procedure as shown below or copy the procedure code from **C:\Acc07_HandsOn\HandsOn10.txt**:

```
Sub Open_AndRead_dBaseFile()
    Dim conn As ADODB.Connection
    Dim rst As ADODB.Recordset
```

```
Set conn = New ADODB.Connection
conn.Open "Provider=MSDASQL;DSN =MyDbaseFile;"

Debug.Print conn.ConnectionString

Set rst = New ADODB.Recordset
rst.Open "Customer.dbf", conn

Do Until rst.EOF
    Debug.Print rst.Fields(1).Value
    rst.MoveNext
Loop

rst.Close
Set rst = Nothing
conn.Close
Set conn = Nothing
End Sub
```

11. Choose **Run | Run Sub/UserForm** to execute the procedure.

The Open_AndRead_dBaseFile procedure uses the ADO Connection object to establish a connection with the data source. Prior to using ADO objects in your VBA procedures, make sure that the References dialog box contains the reference to the ActiveX Data Objects Library (see Hands-On 10-1). The procedure begins by declaring an object variable of Connection type, like this:

```
Dim conn As ADODB.Connection
```

 Note: The Connection object variable can be declared at procedure level or at module level. By declaring the variable at the top of the module, you can reuse it in multiple procedures in your module.

To handle data retrieval, an object variable of Recordset type is also declared:

```
Dim rst As ADODB.Recordset
```

Before you can use the declared ADO Connection object, you must initialize the object variable by using the Set keyword:

```
Set conn = New ADODB.Connection
```

At this point you can proceed to opening the data source by using the ADO Connection object's Open method. The required database connection information is passed to the Open method in the connection string, like this:

```
conn.Open "Provider=MSDASQL;DSN=MyDbaseFile;"
```

MSDASQL is the Microsoft OLE DB Provider for all ODBC data sources. The names of common data providers used with ADO are listed in Table 10-4. The Provider property of the ADO Connection object is used in the connection string as the provider name. DSN is the name of the data source that you specified for your connection settings in the ODBC Data Source Administrator dialog box. Since MSDASQL is the default provider for ODBC, it's okay to simply leave it off, like this:

```
conn.Open "DSN=MyDbaseFile;"
```

Using the ConnectionString property of the ADO Connection object you can obtain exact connection settings from the DSN. The following connection string is written to the Immediate window:

```
Provider=MSDASQL.1;Extended Properties="DSN=MyDbaseFile;DefaultDir=
C:\ACC07_BYEXAMPLE;DriverId=533;FIL=dBase 5.0;MaxBufferSize=
2048;PageTimeout=600;"
```

Table 10-4: Common data providers used with ADO

Provider Name	Provider Property	Description
Microsoft ACE	Microsoft.ACE.OLEDB.12.0	Used for Access 2007 databases in .accdb file format. By default, this provider opens databases in Read/Write mode.
Microsoft Jet	Microsoft.Jet.OLEDB.4.0	Used for Jet 4.0 databases (in .mdb file format). By default, this provider opens databases in Read/Write mode.
Microsoft SQL Server	SQLOLEDB	Used to access SQL Server 6.5, 7.0, and 2000 databases.
Oracle	MSDAORA	Used to access Oracle databases.
ODBC	MSDASQL	Used to access ODBC data sources without a specific OLE DB provider. This is the default provider for ADO.
Active Directory Service	ADSDSOObject	Used to access Windows NT 4.0 directory services, Novell directory services, and LDAP-compliant directory services.
Index Server	MSIDXS	Read-only access to web data.

Once the connection to the dBASE database is open, to gain access to its data, the procedure initializes the rst object variable using the Set keyword:

```
Set rst = New ADODB.Recordset
```

ADO Recordsets are covered in detail in Chapter 13. The ADO Recordset object's Open method is used to open the Customer.dbf file, like this:

```
rst.Open "Customer.dbf", conn
```

When you open the recordset, you need to specify at the minimum the data you want to retrieve (Customer.dbf) and how to connect to that data (conn). Once the recordset is open, you can start reading its data. The Do Until loop will iterate through the recordset until the EOF (End of File) is reached. Each time in the loop, VBA will write to the Immediate window the value of the first field. When the procedure ends you should see in the Immediate window the names of all customers from the Customer.dbf file.

When you are done reading the records, the recordset uses the Close method to close the recordset and destroy the rst object variable by setting it to Nothing:

```
Set rst = Nothing
```

The above statement completely releases the resources used by the Recordset object. The same should be done with the Connection object variable (conn) when it is no longer needed:

```
conn.Close
Set conn = Nothing
```

Creating and Using DSN-less ODBC Connections

It is possible that your VBA application that relies on database access via ODBC DSN (Data Source Name) may suddenly fail because the DSN was modified or deleted. Therefore, it may be a better idea to use a so-called DSN-less connection. Instead of setting up a DSN, simply specify your ODBC driver name and all driver-specific information in your connection string. Different types of databases can require that you specify different parameters. Because the ODBC DSN setup is not required, this type of connection is called "DSN-less." Here's how you can rewrite the procedure in Hands-On 10-2 to use a DSN-less ODBC connection:

```
Sub Open_AndRead_dBaseFile()
    Dim conn As ADODB.Connection
    Dim rst As ADODB.Recordset

    Set conn = New ADODB.Connection
    conn.Open "Driver={Microsoft dBase Driver (*.dbf));" & _
        "DBQ=" & CurrentProject.Path & "\"

    Debug.Print conn.ConnectionString

    Set rst = New ADODB.Recordset
    rst.Open "Customer.dbf", conn

    Do Until rst.EOF
        Debug.Print rst.Fields(1).Value
        rst.MoveNext
    Loop

    rst.Close
    Set rst = Nothing
    conn.Close
    Set conn = Nothing
End Sub
```

In the DSN-less connection shown above, we pass to the Open method of the Connection object a connection string that specifies how a driver connects to a data source. In this example, Driver specifies that you want to use the dBASE database file. Notice that the value of the driver is entered between curly brackets {}. This value should exactly match the name of the ODBC driver as listed in the ODBC Data Source Administrator dialog box. DBQ informs the ADO Connection object about the physical path to the file. The remaining code of this procedure is identical to the code used in a DSN connection (Hands-On 10-2).

Table 10-5: ODBC connection strings for common data sources

Data Source Driver	ODBC Connection String (used in DSN-less connections)
Microsoft Access 2007 (accessing .mdb or .accdb files from Access 2007)	"Driver={Microsoft Access Driver (*.mdb, *.accdb)}; DBQ=path to mdb/accdb file;UID=admin;PWD=;"
Microsoft Access (accessing .mdb files from Access 2003/2002/2000 /97)	*Using standard security:* "Driver={Microsoft Access Driver (*.mdb)}; DBQ=C:\filepath\myDb.mdb;UID=admin;PWD=;" *Using user-level security (workgroup information file):* "Driver={Microsoft Access Driver (*.mdb)}; DBQ=C:\filepath\myDb.mdb;SystemDB=C:\filepath\myDb.mdw; UID=myUserName;PWD=myPassword;"
Microsoft Excel 2007 (accessing .xls, .xlsx, .xlsm, and .xlsb files from Excel 2007)	"Driver={Microsoft Excel Driver (*.xls, *.xlsx, *.xlsm, *.xlsb)}; DBQ=path to xls/xlsx/xlsm/xlsb file;"
Microsoft Excel (accessing .xls files from Excel 2003/2002/2000/97)	"Driver={Microsoft Excel Driver (*.xls)}; DBQ=C:\filepath\Spreadsheet.xls;"
dBASE	"Driver={Microsoft dBASE Driver (*.dbf)}; DBQ=C:\filepath;"
Text	"Driver={Microsoft Text Driver (*.txt, *.csv)}; DefaultDir=C:\filepath\myText.txt;"
Microsoft SQL Server	*Using Trusted Connection security:* "Driver={SQL Server}; Server=myServerName; Database=myDatabaseName; UID=;PWD=;" *Using standard security:* "Driver={SQL Server}; Server=myServerName; Trusted_Connection=no; Database=myDatabaseName; UID=myUserName;PWD=myPassword;"
Oracle	"Driver={Microsoft ODBC for Oracle}; Server=OracleServer.World; UID=myUserName;PWD=myPassword;"

Using OLE DB Connection Strings

In numerous VBA procedures in this chapter we'll use an OLE DB provider to communicate with a data source. See Table 10-4 earlier in this chapter for the names of common OLE DB providers used with ADO. Table 10-6 below shows OLE DB connection strings for common data sources.

Table 10-6: OLE DB connection strings for common data sources

Data Source	OLE DB Connection String
Microsoft Access 2007	"Provider=Microsoft.ACE.OLEDB.12.0; Data Source=C:\Acc07_ByExample\Northwind 2007.accdb"
Microsoft Access (prior to 2007)	"Provider=Microsoft.Jet.OLEDB.4.0; Data Source=C:\Acc07_ByExample\Northwind.mdb;"
Microsoft Excel 2007	"Provider=Microsoft.ACE.OLEDB.12.0; Data Source=C:\Acc07_ByExample\Report2007.xlsx; Extended Properties=""Excel 12.0;HDR=Yes"";"
Microsoft Excel (prior to 2007)	"Provider=Microsoft.Jet.OLEDB.4.0; Data Source=C:\Acc07_ByExample\Report.xls; Extended Properties=""Excel 8.0;HDR=Yes"";"
Microsoft SQL Server	"Provider=SQLOLEDB;Data Source=myServerName;Network Library=DBMSSOCN;Initial Catalog=Pubs;"
Oracle	"Provider=MSDAORA;Data Source=myTable;"

Connection String via a Data Link File

If you are using the Windows operating system and are looking for an easy way to create and test a connection string that uses an ODBC driver or OLE DB provider, you may want to use the Data Link Properties dialog box, which is shown in Figure 10-6.

A universal data link file (.udl) is a text file containing the connection information. Hands-On 10-3 demonstrates how to create the .udl file to connect to a Microsoft Access 2007 database. You can use the same technique to create a valid connection string to other external data sources as long as the ADO provider is installed on your computer.

◉ Hands-On 10-3: Creating and Using a Universal Data Link File

1. In Windows Explorer, select the **C:\Acc07_ByExample** folder. Choose **File | New** and select **Text document**.

2. A new file named New Text Document.txt appears in the Acc07_ByExample folder. Rename this file **ConnectToAccdb.udl**.

    When changing the filename, be sure to type the new extension (.udl) as indicated.

3. Windows will display a warning message that changing the file extension can cause the file to become unusable. Ignore this message and click **OK**.

   Windows creates an empty universal data link file. Notice that the file size is 0 bytes.

4. Double-click the **ConnectToAccdb.udl** file.

   Windows opens the Data Link Properties dialog box containing the following four tabs:

Data Link Tab	Description
Provider	Lists the names of the ADO providers installed on your computer. The provider name you select must be appropriate for the data source you want to use. For example, if you select Microsoft Jet 4.0 OLE DB provider, you must select an Access database in MDB format.
Connection	Allows you to define a data source name for the selected provider type. The entries shown here are specific to the provider type selected via the Provider tab. The Connection tab is active by default when you activate the Data Link Properties dialog box.
Advanced	Allows you to view and set other initialization properties for your data connection.
All	Allows you to review and edit all OLE DB initialization properties available for the selected OLE DB provider.

5. Click the **Provider** tab and select **Microsoft Office 12.0 Access Database Engine OLE DB Provider**, as shown in Figure 10-6.

6. Click the **Next** button or activate the **Connection** tab.

   The entries shown on the Connection tab are related to the type of provider you selected in step 5 above.

7. In the Data Source box, type the location and filename of the Access 2007 database you want to connect to: **C:\Acc07_ByExample\Northwind 2007.accdb**.

8. Click the **Test Connection** button to test whether you can connect to the specified database using the chosen data provider.

9. Click **OK** to the message box "Test connection succeeded."

   If you misspelled a filename or Windows cannot locate the file in the specified folder, you will get an error.

Access VBA Programming with DAO and ADO

Figure 10-6: The Provider tab in the Data Link Properties dialog box lists the names of the ADO providers installed on your computer.

Figure 10-7: Using Data Link Properties to define a data source name for the selected provider type. Be sure to enter .accdb as the extension for the Access 2007 database (the Data Source text box's size is too short to capture the entire path for this snapshot).

At this point your connection string is ready to use.

10. Click **OK** to close the Data Link Properties dialog box.

When writing a VBA procedure to connect to the Northwind 2007.accdb database, you can simply pass the .udl filename to the Connection object's Open method:

```
Dim conn As ADODB.Connection
Set conn As New ADODB.Connection

conn.Open "File Name=C:\Acc07_ByExample\ConnectToAccdb.udl;"
```

When you use .udl files to store connection information, it is very easy to switch your procedure's data source without having to make changes to your code. Simply double-click the .udl file and make desired modifications in the Data Link Properties dialog box.

If you'd rather use the connection string in your VBA procedure, then go ahead and copy the string from the .udl file. You can open this file in Notepad in one of the following ways:

■ Right-click the .udl filename and choose Open With, then select Notepad.

   If Notepad is not available in the shortcut menu, select Choose Program, then choose Notepad, and click OK.

■ Make a copy of the .udl file. Change the .udl extension of the created copy to .txt. Double-click the file to open it in Notepad.

Figure 10-8: You can obtain the connection string from the universal data link (UDL) file by opening the file in Windows Notepad.

Opening Microsoft Access Databases

In this section you will learn how to use DAO and ADO to open Access ACCDB and MDB databases in read/write mode and in read-only mode. You will also learn how to open Access databases that have been protected with database passwords or user-level security.

Opening a Microsoft Jet Database in Read/Write Mode with DAO

The easiest way to open an existing Microsoft Access database from a VBA procedure is by using the Microsoft Access database engine's OpenDatabase method. This method requires that you provide at least one parameter — the name of the existing database. When you open the database with the OpenDatabase method, you should remember to close it. The Close method removes the database from the Databases collection.

Hands-On 10-4 demonstrates how to open an Access database in ACCDB or MDB format using the DAO's OpenDatabase method. This example will list containers and documents in the open database. Each Database object has a Containers collection that consists of built-in Container objects. The Containers collection is used for storing Microsoft Access's own objects. The Jet engine creates the following Container objects: Databases, Tables, and Relations. Other Container objects are created by Microsoft Access (Forms, Reports, Macros, and Modules).

The following table lists the Container objects and the type of information they contain.

Table 10-7: Container objects

Container Name	Type of Information Stored
Databases	Saved databases
Tables	Saved tables and queries
Relations	Saved relationships
Forms	Saved forms
Modules	Saved modules
Reports	Saved reports
Scripts	Saved scripts

Each Container object contains a Documents collection. Each document in this collection represents an object that can be found in an Access database. For example, the Forms container stores a list of all saved forms in a database, and each form is represented by a Document object. You cannot create new Container and Document objects; you can only retrieve the information about them.

◎ Hands-On 10-4: Opening a Database with DAO in Read/Write Mode

1. In the **Chap10.accdb** database that you created in Hands-On 10-1 (in the Visual Basic Editor window), choose **Insert | Module** to add a new module to the current VBA project.

2. In the module's Code window, type the **openDB_DAO** procedure shown below, or copy the procedure code from **C:\Acc07_HandsOn\ HandsOn10.txt**.

```
Sub openDB_DAO()
    Dim db As DAO.Database
    Dim dbName As String
    Dim c As Container
    Dim doc As Document

    dbName = InputBox("Enter a name of an existing database:", "Database Name")

    If dbName = "" Then Exit Sub
    If Dir(dbName) = "" Then
        MsgBox dbName & " was not found."
        Exit Sub
    End If

    Set db = OpenDatabase(dbName)
    With db
        ' list the names of the Container objects
        For Each c In .Containers
            Debug.Print c.Name & " container:" & _
                c.Documents.Count
            ' list the document names in the specified Container
            If c.Documents.Count > 0 Then
                For Each doc In c.Documents
                    Debug.Print vbTab & doc.Name
                Next doc
            End If
        Next c
        .Close
    End With
End Sub
```

3. Position the insertion point anywhere within the code of openDB_DAO and press **F5** or choose **Run | Run Sub/UserForm** to execute the procedure.

   When you run this procedure you are prompted to enter the name of the Access database.

4. Enter **C:\Acc07_HandsOn\Northwind 2007.accdb** or **C:\Acc07_HandsOn\Northwind.mdb** and press **OK**.

The procedure uses the OpenDatabase method of the DBEngine object to open the specified database in the default workspace. The database is opened as shared with read/write access. By supplying additional arguments to the OpenDatabase method you could open the database exclusively (a database opened exclusively can be accessed by a single user at a time) or as read-only.

The openDB_DAO procedure uses a For Each...Next loop to retrieve the names of all the Container objects in the opened database. If the specified container is not empty, the inner For Each... Next loop will print the name of each Document object in the Immediate window.

Opening a Microsoft Jet Database in Read/Write Mode with ADO

You can also use the ADO to open a Microsoft Access database for shared access (read/write). To connect to an older Microsoft Access database in the MDB format, use the Microsoft.Jet.OLEDB.4.0 provider. To connect to an Access 2007 database in the ACCDB format, use the Microsoft.ACE.OLEDB.12.0 Provider. The names of common data providers used with ADO are listed in Table 10-4 earlier in this chapter.

To specify the data source name, use the Connection object's ConnectionString property. As discussed earlier in this chapter, connection strings describe how to access data. Here's a code fragment that specifies the minimum required connection information:

```
With conn
    .Provider = "Microsoft.Jet.OLEDB.4.0;"
    .ConnectionString = "Data Source=" & CurrentProject.Path & "\Northwind.mdb"
End With
```

In the example above, the data source includes the full path to the database file you are going to open. Change the Provider string to "Microsoft.ACE.OLEDB.12.0" if you are planning to open an Access 2007 database:

```
With conn
    .Provider = "Microsoft.ACE.OLEDB.12.0;"
    .ConnectionString = "Data Source=" & CurrentProject.Path & _
        "\Northwind 2007.accdb"
End With
```

Once you've specified the minimum connection information, you may proceed to opening the database.

Use the Connection object's Open method to open the connection to a data source:

```
conn.Open
```

ADO syntax is quite flexible. A connection to a database can also be opened like this:

```
conn.Open "Provider = Microsoft.Jet.OLEDB.4.0;" & "Data Source=" & _
    CurrentProject.Path & "\Northwind.mdb"
```

As you can see in the code fragment above, the provider name and the data source (in this example, path to the database) are supplied as arguments when you call a Connection object's Open method.

Or you could open the database connection like this:

```
With conn
    .Provider = "Microsoft.ACE.OLEDB.12.0;"
    .Mode = adModeReadWrite
    .ConnectionString = "Data Source=" & CurrentProject.Path & _
        "\Northwind 2007.accdb"
    .Open
End With
```

By default, the Connection object's Open method opens a database for shared access. You can use the Connection object's Mode property to explicitly specify the type of access to a database. The Mode property must be set prior to opening the connection because it is read-only once the connection is open. Connections can be opened read-only, write-only, or read/write. You can also specify whether other applications should be prevented from opening a connection. The value for the Mode property can be one of the constants/values specified in Table 10-8.

Table 10-8: Intrinsic constants of the Connection object's Mode property

Constant Name	Value	Type of Permission
adModeUnknown	0	Permissions have not been set yet or cannot be determined. This is the default setting.
adModeRead	1	Read-only permissions
adModeWrite	2	Write-only permissions
adModeReadWrite	3	Read/write permissions
adModeShareDenyRead	4	Prevents others from opening the connection with read permissions
adModeShareDenyWrite	8	Prevents others from opening the connection with write permissions
adModeShareExclusive	12	Prevents others from opening the connection
adModeShareDenyNone	16	Prevents others from opening the connection with any permissions

Hands-On 10-5 demonstrates how to use ADO to open an Access database for shared access (read/write).

⊚ Hands-On 10-5: Opening a Database with ADO in Read/Write Mode

1. In the Visual Basic Editor window, choose **Insert** | **Module** to add a new module to the currently open **Chap10.accdb** database.

2. In the module's Code window, type the **openDB_ADO** procedure shown below, or copy the procedure code from **C:\Acc07_HandsOn\Hands-On10.txt**.

```
Sub openDB_ADO()
    Dim conn As ADODB.Connection
    Dim strDb As String

    On Error GoTo ErrorHandler

    strDb = CurrentProject.Path & "\Northwind 2007.accdb"
    Set conn = New ADODB.Connection

    With conn
        .Provider = "Microsoft.ACE.OLEDB.12.0;"
        .Mode = adModeReadWrite
        .ConnectionString = "Data Source=" & strDb
        .Open
    End With

    If conn.State = adStateOpen Then
        MsgBox "Connection was opened."
    End If

    conn.Close
    Set conn = Nothing
    MsgBox "Connection was closed."

    Exit Sub
ErrorHandler:
    MsgBox Err.Number & ": " & Err.Description
End Sub
```

3. Position the insertion point anywhere within the code of the openDB_ADO procedure and press **F5** or choose **Run** | **Run Sub/UserForm** to execute the procedure.

```
If conn.State = adStateOpen Then
    MsgBox "Database connection was established."
End If
```

The ADO Connection object's State property returns a value that describes if the connection is open, closed, connecting, executing, or retrieving data (see Table 10-9).

Table 10-9: Intrinsic constants of the Connection object's State property

Constant	Value	Description
adStateClosed	0	Connection is closed.
adStateOpen	1	Connection is open.
adStateConnecting	2	Connection is connecting.

Constant	Value	Description
adStateExecuting	4	Connection is executing a command.
adStateFetching	8	Connection is retrieving data.

If an error occurs during the procedure execution (for example, when a database with the specified name/path cannot be found), the statement On Error GoTo ErrorHandler will pass the program control to the error-handling code located at the ErrorHandler label at the bottom of the procedure. Errors that occur in ADO are reported to the VBA Err object. You can find out the details about the error that occurred by using various properties of the Err object (Name, Description, Source, HelpFile, or HelpContext). The code in the error handler will execute only if an error occurs. If the procedure executes without an error, the Exit Sub statement will cause the procedure to finish without running the error code. You will find more information on database errors near the end of this chapter.

Opening a Microsoft Access Database in Read-Only Mode with DAO

You can open a Microsoft Access database in read-only mode by providing settings for optional arguments in the OpenDatabase method. The procedure listed below opens a database for shared, read-only access. When the second argument of the OpenDatabase method is set to False, the database is opened in shared mode. This is the default setting. If the value of this argument is True, the database is opened in exclusive mode (other users are prevented from opening the database). The third argument of the OpenDatabase method specifies if you want to open the database with read/write (default) or read-only access. To open the database in read-only mode, set the value of this argument to True as demonstrated in the procedure below.

```
Sub openDB_DAOReadOnly()
    Dim db As DAO.Database
    Dim t As Variant
    Dim strNames As String

    strNames = ""

    ' Open for shared read-only access

    Set db = DBEngine.OpenDatabase(CurrentProject.Path & _
            "\Northwind 2007.accdb", False, True)

    For Each t In db.TableDefs
        strNames = strNames & t.Name & vbCrLf
    Next
    MsgBox "The following tables were found:" & _
            vbCrLf & strNames
    db.Close
End Sub
```

Opening a a Microsoft Jet Database in Read-Only Mode with ADO

If you'd like to open a database for read-only access, simply set the ADO Connection object's Mode property to the adModeRead constant (see Table 10-8 earlier).

Opening a Microsoft Jet Database Secured with a Password

Using passwords to secure the database or objects in the database is known as share-level security. When you set a password on the database, users will be required to enter a password in order to gain access to the data and database objects. Keep in mind that passwords are case-sensitive. You must use Data Access Objects (DAO) or ActiveX Data Objects (ADO) to programmatically open a password-protected Microsoft Access database. When using DAO to change a password of an existing Microsoft Access database in a VBA procedure, follow these steps:

1. Open the database in exclusive mode by setting the second argument of the OpenDatabase method to True.

2. To set a database password, use the NewPassword property of the Database object. This property requires that you first specify the old password and then the new one. Passwords can be up to 20 characters long and can include any characters except the ASCII character 0 (Null). To specify that the database does not have a password, use a zero-length string ("") in the first parameter of the NewPassword property. To clear the password, use the zero-length string for the second parameter of the New Password property.

To open a password-protected database using DAO, you must specify the database password in the Connect parameter of the OpenDatabase method as shown in Hands-On 10-6.

> **⊚ Hands-On 10-6: Setting a Database Password and Opening a Password-Protected Database with DAO**

1. In the Visual Basic Editor window, choose **Insert | Module** to add a new module to the currently open Chap10.accdb database.

2. In the module's Code window, type the **setPass_AndOpenDB_withDAO** procedure shown below, or copy the procedure code from **C:\Acc07_ HandsOn\HandsOn10.txt**.

```
Sub setPass_AndOpenDB_withDAO()
    Dim db As DAO.Database
    Dim strDb As String

    strDb = "C:\Acc07_ByExample\Northwind 2007.accdb"
```

```
' strDb = "C:\Acc07_ByExample\Northwind.mdb"

' open the database in exclusive mode to set database password
Set db = DBEngine.OpenDatabase(strDb, True)
db.NewPassword "", "secret"
MsgBox "Access Database version: " & Int(db.Version)
db.Close

' open password protected database
Set db = DBEngine.OpenDatabase(Name:=strDb, _
        Options:=False, _
        ReadOnly:=False, _
        Connect:=";PWD=secret")

MsgBox "Password protected database was successfully opened."
db.Close
MsgBox "Password protected database has been closed."

' remove password protection from the database
Set db = DBEngine.OpenDatabase(Name:=strDb, _
        Options:=True, _
        ReadOnly:=False, _
        Connect:=";PWD=secret")
db.NewPassword "secret", ""
MsgBox "Password protection was removed."
db.Close
End Sub
```

3. Position the insertion point anywhere within the code of the setPass_ AndOpenDB_withDAO procedure and press **F5** or choose **Run | Run Sub/UserForm** to execute the procedure.

When you run the above procedure, Access displays the version number of the Microsoft Jet or Microsoft Access database engine using the Version property of DBEngine. The version number consists of the version number, a period, and the release number. The procedure uses the VBA Int function to display only the integer portion of the number. Microsoft Office Access 2007 files use the Microsoft Access database engine 12.0. Databases created in versions 2000, 2002, and 2003 use Microsoft Jet 4.0. Microsoft Access 97 uses Microsoft Jet 3.5.

 Note: If a VBA procedure uses a method or a property that requires two or more parameters, you can make the procedure more readable by specifying the names of the parameters, like this:

```
Set db = DBEngine.OpenDatabase(Name:=strDb, _
                Options:=False, _
                ReadOnly:=False, _
                Connect:=";PWD=secret")
```

Use the Microsoft Visual Basic help to find the names of methods/properties and the names of the required and optional parameters.

Hands-On 10-7 demonstrates how to use ADO to set a database password for a Microsoft Access database in the MDB format and then open it using the new password. This technique will not work for the Access 2007 databases in the ACCDB format. To set a database password on an MDB database file, use the JRO JetEngine object's CompactDatabase method and specify the Password parameter. The JRO JetEngine object is a member of the Microsoft Jet and Replication Objects (JRO) Library.

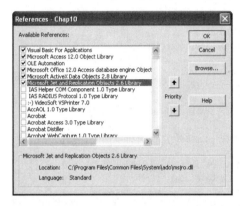

Figure 10-9: Before writing procedures that set or change the database password using ADO, you must set a reference to the Microsoft Jet and Replication Objects Library. To do this, choose Tools | References in the Visual Basic Editor window and select the required library in the list of Available References.

ⓐ Hands-On 10-7: Setting a Database Password and Opening a Password-Protected Database with ADO

1. In the Visual Basic Editor window, choose **Tools** | **References** and select the **Microsoft Jet and Replication Objects Library** as shown in Figure 10-9, then click **OK**.

2. In the Visual Basic Editor window, choose **Insert** | **Module** to add a new module to the currently open Chap10.accdb database.

3. In the module's Code window, type the **setPass_AndOpenDB_withADO** procedure shown below, or copy the procedure code from **C:\Acc07_HandsOn\HandsOn10.txt**.

```
Sub setPass_AndOpenDB_withADO()
    Dim jetEng As JRO.JetEngine
    Dim conn As ADODB.Connection
    Dim strCompactFrom As String
    Dim strCompactTo As String
    Dim strPath As String

    strPath = CurrentProject.Path & "\"

    strCompactFrom = "Northwind.mdb"
    strCompactTo = "Northwind_P.mdb"

    On Error GoTo ErrorHandler

    Set jetEng = New JRO.JetEngine

    ' Compact the database specifying
    ' the new database password
    jetEng.CompactDatabase "Data Source=" & _
```

```
        strPath & strCompactFrom & ";", _
        "Data Source=" & strPath & strCompactTo & ";" & _
        "Jet OLEDB:Database Password=welcome"

    MsgBox "The database file " & strPath & strCompactTo & _
        " has been protected with password."
    Set jetEng = Nothing

    ' now open the password-protected MDB database
    Set conn = New ADODB.Connection
    With conn
        .Provider = "Microsoft.Jet.OLEDB.4.0;"
        .ConnectionString = "Data Source=" & _
            strPath & strCompactTo & ";" & _
            "Jet OLEDB:Database Password=welcome;"
        .Open
    End With

    If conn.State = adStateOpen Then
        MsgBox "Password protected database was opened."
    End If

    conn.Close
    MsgBox "Password protected database was closed."

    Set conn = Nothing
    Exit Sub
ErrorHandler:
    If Err.Number = -2147217897 Then
        Kill strPath & strCompactTo
    ElseIf Err.Number = -2147467259 Then
        MsgBox "Make sure to close the " & strCompactFrom & _
            " database file prior to compacting it."
        Exit Sub
    Else
        MsgBox Err.Number & ": " & Err.Description
        Exit Sub
    End If
    Resume
End Sub
```

4. Position the insertion point anywhere within the code of the setPass_
   AndOpenDB_withADO procedure and press **F8** or choose **Debug | Step
   Into** to execute the procedure one line at a time. Keep pressing **F8** until the
   procedure ends.

The procedure demonstrated above uses the JetEngine object's Compact-
Database method to compact a Microsoft Jet database (MDB) and password
protect it. By compacting the database, you can greatly improve the database
performance and reduce its file size. The CompactDatabase method requires
that you provide the name of the MDB file you want to compact and the name
for the resulting compacted file. There are a number of connection properties
that you can use with the CompactDatabase method. This procedure illustrates
how to use the Jet OLEDB:Database Password property to set the password for

the compacted database. The database password is set using the following code:

```
jetEng.CompactDatabase "Data Source=" & _
    strPath & strCompactFrom & ";", _
    "Data Source=" & strPath & strCompactTo & ";" & _
    "Jet OLEDB:Database Password=welcome"
```

You must close the database before attempting to compact it or Visual Basic will generate error -2147467259. The ErrorHandler code is used to trap errors that may occur during the procedure execution. For example, if the specified database file cannot be found in the specified path, Visual Basic will display the error number and error description and will immediately exit the procedure. If you run this procedure more than once, Visual Basic will encounter the error -2147217897: database already exists. To allow the procedure to run again, use the VBA Kill statement. This statement tells VBA to delete the file. The Resume statement will pass the procedure execution back to the line of code that caused the error and Visual Basic will proceed to execute this line and other lines of code that follow.

Notice that to open a Microsoft Jet database (an MDB file) secured with a password, you must specify the Jet OLEDB:Database Password property as part of the Connection object's ConnectionString property, like this:

```
With conn
    .Provider = "Microsoft.Jet.OLEDB.4.0;"
    .ConnectionString = "Data Source=" & _
        strPath & strCompactTo & ";" & _
        "Jet OLEDB:Database Password=welcome;"
    .Open
End With
```

Opening a Microsoft Jet Database with User-Level Security

Office Access 2007 does not provide user-level security for databases that are created in the new file format (ACCDB and ACCDE). The following discussion and Hands-On 10-8 apply only to Access databases in the MDB file format.

User-level security secures the code and objects in your database so that users can't accidentally modify or change them. With this type of security you can provide the most restrictive access over the database and objects it contains. When you use the user-level security, the Microsoft Jet Engine uses a workgroup information file named System.mdw to determine who can open a database and to secure its objects.

The workgroup information file holds group and user information, including passwords. The information contained in this file determines not only who can open the database but also the permissions users/groups have on the objects in the database. The workgroup information file contains built-in groups (Admins and Users) and a generic user account (Admin) with unlimited privileges on the database and the objects it contains. When an MDB file is open in Access 2007, the Access user interface provides commands that allow you to manually implement user-level security (see Figure 10-10).

Figure 10-10: Setting user-level security in Access 2007 for earlier versions of Access.

To open an MDB database that is secured at the user level, you must supply the:

- Full path to the workgroup information file (system database)
- User ID
- Password

◎ Hands-On 10-8: Opening a Database Secured at the User Level

1. Use Windows Explorer to create a copy of the **C:\Acc07_ByExample\ Northwind.mdb** database file and name it **NorthSecureUser.mdb**.

2. Open the **C:\Acc07_ByExample\NorthSecureUser.mdb** database and choose **Database Tools | Users and Permissions | User-Level Security Wizard** to begin creating a new workgroup information file.

3. Follow the steps of the Security Wizard. Do not change anything until you get to the screen asking for user name and password. Set up a user account named **Developer** with a password of **WebMaster**, and click the **Add This User to The List** button. Click the **Next** button, assign Developer to the **Admins** group, and press the **Finish** button. Access will display the One-Step Security Wizard Report. Print it out for your reference. Next, close the Microsoft Access application window with the NorthSecureUser database.

4. Return to the Visual Basic Editor window in the **Chap10.accdb** database and choose **Insert | Module**.

5. In the module's Code window, type the **Open_WithUserSecurity** procedure shown below, or copy the procedure code from **C:\Acc07_HandsOn\HandsOn10.txt**.

```
Sub Open_WithUserSecurity()
    Dim conn As ADODB.Connection
    Dim strDb As String
    Dim strSysDb As String

    On Error GoTo ErrorHandler
    strDb = CurrentProject.Path & "\NorthSecureUser.mdb"
    strSysDb = CurrentProject.Path & "\Security.mdw"
    Set conn = New ADODB.Connection
    With conn
        .Provider = "Microsoft.Jet.OLEDB.4.0;"
        .ConnectionString = "Data Source=" & strDb & ";" & _
```

```
        "Jet OLEDB:System Database=" & strSysDb
    .Open, "Developer", "WebMaster"
  End With
  MsgBox "Secured database was opened."
  conn.Close
  Set conn = Nothing
  MsgBox "Database was closed."
  Exit Sub
ErrorHandler:
  MsgBox Err.Number & ": " & Err.Description
End Sub
```

6. Position the insertion point anywhere within the procedure code and press **F5** or choose **Run | Run Sub/UserForm** to execute the procedure.

As mentioned earlier, ADO syntax is very flexible. You can use a variety of ways to specify property settings. The code snippet below demonstrates how to avoid formatting problems with long connection strings by using the ADO Connection object's Properties collection.

```
With conn
  .Provider = "Microsoft.Jet.OLEDB.4.0;"
  .Properties("Jet OLEDB:System Database") = strSysDb
  .Open strDb, "Developer", "WebMaster"
End With
```

Notice that before you can reference provider-specific properties from the Connection object's Properties collection, you must indicate which provider you are using.

 Note: The Security Wizard places a shortcut to the NorthSecureUser.mdb file on your desktop to make it easy for you to start the secured database using the new workgroup information file (Security.mdw). For more information on MDW files and implementing database security with ADOX and JRO, see Chapter 17.

Connecting to the Current Access Database

Microsoft Access provides a quick way to access the current DAO database by using the CurrentDb method. This method returns an object variable of type Database that represents the database currently open in the Microsoft Access window. In ADO, however, to access the currently open database, use the CurrentProject.Connection statement. The CurrentProject object refers to the project for the current Microsoft Access database. These statements work only in VBA procedures created in Microsoft Access. If you'd like to reuse your VBA procedures in other Microsoft Office or Visual Basic applications, you will be better off by creating a connection via an appropriate OLE DB provider.

The procedure in Hands-On 10-9 uses the CurrentProject.Connection statement to return a reference to the current database. Once the connection to the current database is established, the example procedure loops through the

Properties collection of the Connection object to retrieve its property names and settings. The results are written both to the Immediate window and to a text file named C:\Acc07_ByExample\Propfile.txt.

⊚ Hands-On 10-9: Establishing a Connection to the Current Access Database

1. In the Visual Basic Editor window, choose **Insert | Module**.

2. In the module's Code window, type the **Connect_ToCurrentDB** procedure shown below, or copy the procedure code from **C:\Acc07_HandsOn\ HandsOn10.txt**.

```
Sub Connect_ToCurrentDB()
    Dim conn As ADODB.Connection
    Dim fs As Object
    Dim txtfile As Object
    Dim i As Integer
    Dim strFileName As String

    strFileName = "C:\Acc07_ByExample\Propfile.txt"

    Set conn = CurrentProject.Connection
    Set fs = CreateObject("Scripting.FileSystemObject")
    Set txtfile = fs.CreateTextFile(strFileName, True)

    For i = 0 To conn.Properties.Count - 1
        Debug.Print conn.Properties(i).Name & "=" & _
            conn.Properties(i).Value
        txtfile.WriteLine (conn.Properties(i).Name & "=" & _
            conn.Properties(i).Value)
    Next i
    MsgBox "Please check results in the " & _
        "Immediate window." & vbCrLf _
        & "The results have also been written to the " _
        & strFileName & " file."

    txtfile.Close
    Set fs = Nothing
    conn.Close
    Set conn = Nothing
End Sub
```

3. Choose **Run | Run Sub/UserForm** to execute the procedure.

The Connect_ToCurrentDB procedure uses the CurrentProject.Connection statement to get a reference to the currently open database. To create a text file from a VBA procedure, the CreateObject function is used to access the Scripting.FileSystemObject. This function returns the FileSystemObject (fs). The CreateTextFile method of the FileSystemObject creates the TextStream object that represents a text file (txtfile). The WriteLine method writes each property and the corresponding setting to the newly created text file (C:\Propfile.txt). Finally, the Close method closes the text file.

Opening Other Databases, Spreadsheets, and Text Files from Access 2007

Microsoft Access Jet/ACE database engine can be used to access other databases, spreadsheets, and text files. The following subsections of this chapter demonstrate how to connect to SQL Server, Excel spreadsheets, and text files.

Connecting to an SQL Server Database

The ADO provides a number of ways of connecting to an SQL Server database. To access data residing on Microsoft SQL Server 6.5, 7.0, or 2000, use SQLOLEDB, which is the native Microsoft OLE DB Provider for SQL.

You can also connect to an SQL database using the MSDASQL provider. This provider allows you to access any existing ODBC data sources. You can open a connection to the SQL Server by using an ODBC DSN (Data Source Name) or ODBC DSN-less connection. Both of these connection types are discussed earlier in this chapter. For example, the code snippet below opens and then closes a connection with the SQL Server database based on a DSN named Pubs.

```
With conn
    .Open "Provider=MSDASQL; DSN=Pubs"
    .Close
End With
```

Recall that you can skip setting the Provider property because MSDASQL is the default provider for ODBC. All you really need to establish a connection in this case is a DSN.

Hands-On 10-10: Connecting to an SQL Server Database Using SQLOLEDB Provider

➔ Note: To try out this procedure, modify the connection information in the connection string to connect to the SQL Server database you have access to.

1. In the Visual Basic Editor window, choose **Insert | Module**.
2. In the module's Code window, type the **ConnectToSQL_SQLOLEDB** procedure shown below, or copy the procedure code from **C:\Acc07_HandsOn\HandsOn10.txt**.

```
Sub ConnectToSQL_SQLOLEDB()
    Dim conn As ADODB.Connection

    Set conn = New ADODB.Connection
    ' Modify the connection information
    With conn
        .Provider = "SQLOLEDB"
        .ConnectionString = "Data Source=Mozartv4;" & _
            "database=Musicians; UserId=sa; Password=;"
```

```
      .Open
    End With
    If conn.State = adStateOpen Then
      MsgBox "Connection was established."
    End If
    conn.Close
    Set conn = Nothing
  End Sub
```

3. Choose **Run | Run Sub/UserForm** to execute the procedure.

In the ConnectToSQL_SQLOLEDB procedure, the Connection object's Provider property is set to SQLOLEDB, and the ConnectionString property includes a server name, database name, user ID, and password information.

The following VBA procedure uses the ODBC DSN-less connection to an SQL Server database:

```
Sub Connect_ToSQLServer()
  Dim conn As ADODB.Connection

  Set conn = New ADODB.Connection
  With conn
    ' DSN-less connection using the ODBC driver
    ' (modify the data source information below)
    .Open "Driver={SQL Server};" & _
      "Server=11.22.17.153;" & _
      "UID=myId;" & _
      "PWD=myPassword;" & _
      "Database=SupportDb"
    .Close
  End With
  Set conn = Nothing
End Sub
```

Opening a Microsoft Excel Spreadsheet

You can open a Microsoft Excel spreadsheet from Access by writing procedures that use DAO or ADO objects.

To open a Microsoft Excel 2007 spreadsheet file with the new XLSX file format with DAO, use the OpenDatabase method like this:

```
Dim db As DAO.Database
Set db = OpenDatabase("C:\Acc07_ByExample\Report2007.xlsx", _
    False, True, "Excel 12.0; HDR=YES;")
```

In the first parameter, specify the path and filename to your spreadsheet. The second parameter of the OpenDatabase method (False) indicates that the file is to be opened in shared mode (this is the default). The third parameter is set to True, which means the spreadsheet file opens in read-only mode. The fourth parameter is the connection information. It specifies the version of the Excel sheet. For Excel 2007, set it to Excel 12.0, for Excel 2000/2002/2003, set it to Excel 8.0, and for Excel version 97, set it to Excel 5.0. The HDR=YES; indicates that the first row contains column names. To indicate that the spreadsheet does not contain column names, set it to NO.

To open a Microsoft Excel 2007 spreadsheet file with the new XLSX file format with ADO, use the Microsoft.ACE.OLEDB.12.0 Provider and use the Extended Properties of the ADO Connection object to pass the connection string like this:

```
Dim conn As ADO.Connection
Set conn = New ADO.Connection
conn.Open "Provider=Microsoft.ACE.OLEDB.12.0;" & _
          "Data Source=C:\Acc07_ByExample\Report2007.xlsx;" & _
          "Extended Properties=""Excel 12.0; HDR=YES"";"
```

To open spreadsheet files created in Excel 2000/2002/2003, use the Microsoft Jet 4.0 OLE DB Provider and Excel 8.0 in the Extended Properties:

```
Dim conn As ADO.Connection
conn.Open "Provider=Microsoft.Jet.OLEDB.4.0;" & _
          "Data Source=C:\Acc07_ByExample\Report.xls;" & _
          "Extended Properties=""Excel 8.0; HDR=YES"";"
```

You can also use ODBC to open an Excel spreadsheet. For example, the following code snippet establishes an ODBC DSN-less connection:

```
Dim conn As ADO.Connection
Set conn = New ADO.Connection

With conn
    .ConnectionString="Driver={Microsoft Excel Driver (*.xls, *.xlsx, & _
        *.xlsm, *.xlsb)};"DBQ=C:\Acc07_ByExample\Report2007.xlsx;"
    .Open
End With
```

Hands-On 10-11 demonstrates how to use DAO to open a Microsoft Excel spreadsheet created in version 2007 or earlier.

⊚ Hands-On 10-11: Opening an Excel Spreadsheet with DAO

1. In the Visual Basic Editor window, choose **Insert | Module**.

2. In the module's Code window, type the **Open_Excel_DAO** procedure shown below, or copy the procedure code from **C:\Acc07_HandsOn\ HandsOn10.txt**.

```
Sub Open_Excel_DAO(strFileName)
    Dim db As DAO.Database
    Dim rst As DAO.Recordset
    Dim strHeader As String
    Dim strValues As String

    strHeader = ""
    strValues = ""

    If Right(strFileName, 1) = "x" Then

        Set db = OpenDatabase(CurrentProject.Path & _
            "\Report2007.xlsx", _
            False, True, "Excel 12.0; HDR=YES;")
```

```
Else

    Set db = OpenDatabase(CurrentProject.Path & _
        "\Report.xls", _
        False, True, "Excel 8.0; HDR=YES;")

End If

Set rst = db.OpenRecordset("Sheet1$")

'get names of columns
For Each fld In rst.Fields
    strHeader = strHeader & fld.Name & vbTab
Next

Debug.Print strHeader

' get cell values
Do Until rst.EOF
    For Each f In rst.Fields
        strValues = strValues & f.Value & vbTab & vbTab
    Next
    Debug.Print strValues
    strValues = ""
    rst.MoveNext
Loop

rst.Close
Set rst = Nothing
db.Close
Set db = Nothing
End Sub
```

3. In the Visual Basic Editor window, press **Ctrl+G** to open the Immediate window or choose **View | Immediate Window**.

4. To run the Open_Excel_DAO procedure, type **Open_Excel_DAO "Report.xls"** in the Immediate window and press **Enter**.

To run the Open_Excel_DAO procedure you must provide the name of the spreadsheet file to open. If the last character in the file extension is "x" (this is determined with the VBA Right function), then the procedure uses the connection string designed for opening Excel 2007 files. After making a connection to Excel file, the procedure goes on to retrieve information stored in the desired worksheet. Using the DAO's OpenRecordset method we can access the data on the Sheet1 worksheet. Notice a dollar sign ($) appended to the sheet name. You must use the dollar sign syntax, Sheet1$, to refer to a sheet name. The procedure uses the For Each...Next loop to obtain the names of all worksheet columns. The heading string is then written to the Immediate window. Next, Do Until...Loop loops through the records until the end of file (EOF) is reached. Cell values from each worksheet row are written to the strValues variable and then to the Immediate window. Once the data retrieval is completed, the Recordset is closed and its variable is destroyed. The same is done with the Connection object.

Hands-On 10-12 demonstrates how to open an Excel spreadsheet with ADO and modify its data.

◎ Hands-On 10-12: Opening an Excel Spreadsheet with ADO

1. In the same module where you entered the procedure in Hands-On 10-11, type the **Open_Excel_ADO** procedure shown below, or copy the procedure code from **C:\Acc07_HandsOn\HandsOn10.txt**.

```
Sub Open_Excel_ADO(strFileName As String)
    Dim conn As ADODB.Connection
    Dim rst As ADODB.Recordset
    Dim strFindWhat As String

    Set conn = New ADODB.Connection

    If Right(strFileName, 1) = "x" Then

        With conn
            .Provider = "Microsoft.ACE.OLEDB.12.0;"
            .ConnectionString = "Data Source=" & _
                CurrentProject.Path & _
                "\" & strFileName & _
                "; Extended Properties=""Excel 12.0; HDR=Yes"";"
            .Open
        End With
    Else
        conn.Open "Provider=Microsoft.Jet.OLEDB.4.0;" & _
                "Data Source=" & CurrentProject.Path & _
                "\" & strFileName & _
                ";Extended Properties=""Excel 8.0; HDR=Yes;"";"

    End If

    Set rst = New ADODB.Recordset
    rst.Open "SELECT * FROM [Sheet1$]", conn, adOpenStatic, adLockOptimistic

    strFindWhat = "[Excel Version] = 'Excel 2000'"
    rst.Find strFindWhat
    rst(1).Value = "500"
    rst.Update
    rst.Close
    Set rst = Nothing
    MsgBox "Excel spreadsheet was opened and updated."

    conn.Close
    Set conn = Nothing
End Sub
```

2. In the Visual Basic Editor window, press **Ctrl+G** to open the Immediate window or choose **View | Immediate Window**.

3. To run the Open_Excel_ADO procedure, type **Open_Excel_ADO "Report2007.xlsx"** in the Immediate window and press **Enter**.

Notice how the Open_Excel_ADO procedures passed the connection string to the ADO Connection object's Open method. Depending on the version of Microsoft Excel used, the provider name is set to Microsoft Jet OLEDB 4.0 or Microsoft.ACE.OLEDB.12.0, and Extended Properties is set to use either Excel 8.0 or Excel 12.0. Once the connection to the spreadsheet file is open, an ADO Recordset is opened. We instruct the procedure to select all data from Sheet1 using the following SQL statement:

```
"SELECT * FROM [Sheet1$]"
```

Notice that in the SELECT statement, the sheet name must be enclosed in square brackets and have a dollar sign ($) appended to it. The Recordset is opened using the open connection (conn). The procedure uses the ADO constants adOpenStatic (Cursor Type parameter) and adLockOptimistic (Lock Type parameter) to ensure that the Recordset is updatable. See Chapter 13 for using various parameters when opening a Recordset. Before you can modify data in a worksheet, you must find it. The search criteria string is defined in the strFindWhat variable. To find the data, the procedure uses the Find method of the Recordset object. Once the searched data is located, we simply assign a new value to the Recordset field using the Value property:

```
rst(1).Value = "500"
```

The ADO Recordset fields are counted beginning with zero (0). Therefore, the above statement sets the value in the second column in the worksheet. To save the changes to the file, you need to call the Update method, like this:

```
rst.Update
```

The remaining code in this procedure performs the standard cleanup: closing the objects and releasing the memory used by the object variables (rst, conn).

Opening a Text File Using ADO

There are several ways to open text files programmatically. This section demonstrates how to gain access to a text file by using the Microsoft Text Driver. Notice that this is a DSN-less connection (as explained earlier in this chapter). Hands-On 10-13 demonstrates how to open a Recordset based on a comma-separated file format and write the file contents to the Immediate window.

Hands-On 10-13: Opening a Text File with ADO

1. Copy the **C:\Acc07_HandsOn\Employees.txt** file to your **C:\Acc07_ByExample\Employees.txt** folder, or prepare the text file from scratch by typing the following in Notepad and saving the file as **C:\Acc07_ByExample\Employees.txt**:

   "Last Name", "First Name", "Birthdate", "Years Worked"
   "Krawiec","Bogdan",#1963-01-02#,3

```
"Górecka","Jadwiga",#1948-05-12#,1
"Olszewski","Stefan",#1957-04-07#,0
```

2. In the Visual Basic Editor window, choose **Insert | Module**.

3. In the module's Code window, type the **Open_TextFile** procedure shown below, or copy the procedure code from **C:\Acc07_HandsOn\Hands-On10.txt**.

```
Sub Open_TextFile()
    Dim conn As ADODB.Connection
    Dim rst As ADODB.Recordset
    Dim fld As ADODB.Field

    Set conn = New ADODB.Connection
    Debug.Print conn.ConnectionString
    conn.Open "DRIVER={Microsoft Text Driver (*.txt; *.csv)};" & _
            "DBQ=" & CurrentProject.Path & "\"

    Set rst = New ADODB.Recordset
    rst.Open "SELECT * FROM [Employees.txt]", conn, adOpenStatic, _
        adLockReadOnly, adCmdText
    Do Until rst.EOF
        For Each fld In rst.Fields
            Debug.Print fld.Name & "=" & fld.Value
        Next fld
        rst.MoveNext
    Loop
    rst.Close
    Set rst = Nothing
    conn.Close
    Set conn = Nothing
    MsgBox "Open the Immediate window to view the data."
End Sub
```

4. Make sure that the C:\Acc07_ByExample\Employees.txt file is closed and choose **Run | Run Sub/UserForm** to execute the procedure.

If you worked through the previous exercises in this chapter you should have no problem following the code of the Open_TextFile procedure. Because you are only reading the records, you can open the Recordset using the adOpenStatic and adLockReadOnly ADO constants. Notice that ADO constant adCmdText is used as the last parameter of the Recordset's Open method (see Chapter 15 for SQL examples):

```
rst.Open "SELECT * FROM [Employees.txt]", conn, adOpenStatic, _
    adLockReadOnly, adCmdText
```

The last parameter in the above statement can be any valid option. You can indicate the type of source you are using with the adCmdText constant (for an SQL statement), adCmdTable (to retrieve all the rows in a table), or adCmdStoredProc (to get records via a stored procedure). If you do not specify the type of source, then adCmdUnknown is used as the default.

Creating a New Access Database

You can create a new Microsoft Access database programmatically by using DAO or ADO. This section explains how to use both methods.

Creating a Database with DAO

When you start Microsoft Access, the program automatically creates a default workspace named DBEngine.Workspaces(0). The Workspace object has several useful methods, and the most frequently used are CreateDatabase (for creating a new database) and OpenDatabase (for opening an existing database). The CreateDatabase method requires that you specify the name and path of your database as well as the built-in constant indicating a collating order for creating the database. Use the built-in constant dbLangGeneral for English, German, French, Portuguese, Italian, and Modern Spanish.

The procedure in Hands-On 10-14 creates a new Access 2007 database and displays the number of system tables that Access automatically creates for its own use.

⊚ Hands-On 10-14: Creating a New Database Using DAO

1. In the Visual Basic Editor window, choose **Insert | Module**.
2. In the module's Code window, type the **CreateNewDB_DAO** procedure shown below, or copy the procedure code from **C:\Acc07_HandsOn\ HandsOn10.txt**.

```
Sub CreateNewDB_DAO()
    Dim db As DAO.Database
    Dim dbName As String

    dbName = "C:\Acc07_ByExample\TestDAO.accdb"

    On Error GoTo ErrorHandler

    Set db = CreateDatabase(dbName, dbLangGeneral)

    MsgBox "The database contains " & _
            db.TableDefs.Count & " tables."
    db.Close
    Set db = Nothing
ErrorHandler:
    MsgBox Err.Description
End Sub
```

3. Choose **Run | Run Sub/UserForm** to execute the procedure.

To create a Database object in code, first declare an object variable of type Database. Once the Database object variable is defined, set the variable to the object returned by the CreateDatabase method:

```
Set db = CreateDatabase(dbName, dbLangGeneral)
```

The CreateDatabase method creates a new Database object and appends it to the Databases collection. The new database contains several system tables that Access creates for its own use. If the database already exists, an error occurs. You can check for the existence of the database by using an If statement in combination with the VBA Dir function and then use the VBA Kill statement to delete the database (see Hands-On 15).

Creating a Database with ADO

To create a new Access database using ADO you must use the ADOX Catalog object's Create method. The ADOX library is discussed in Chapter 17. The Create method creates and opens a new ADO connection to the data source. An error will occur if the provider does not support creating new catalogs.

The procedure in Hands-On 10-15 creates a new blank database named TestADO.mdb in your C:\Acc07_ByExample directory. The error trap ensures that the procedure works correctly even if the specified file already exists. The VBA Kill statement is used to delete the file from your hard disk when the error is encountered.

⊙ Hands-On 10-15: Creating a New Microsoft Access Database Using ADO

1. In the Visual Basic Editor window, choose **Tools | References**. In the References dialog box, select the **Microsoft ADO Ext. 2.8 for DDL and Security Object Library** and press **OK**.

2. In the same module where you entered the procedure in Hands-On 1-14, type the **CreateNewDB_ADO** procedure shown below, or copy the procedure code from **C:\Acc07_HandsOn\HandsOn10.txt**.

```
Sub CreateNewDB_ADO()

' you must make sure that a reference to
' Microsoft ADO Ext. 2.8 for DDL and Security
' Object Library is set in the References dialog box


    Dim cat As ADOX.Catalog
    Dim strDb As String

    Set cat = New ADOX.Catalog
    strDb = "C:\Acc07_ByExample\TestADO.mdb"

    On Error GoTo ErrorHandler
    cat.Create "Provider=Microsoft.Jet.OLEDB.4.0;" & _
        "Data Source=" & strDb
    MsgBox "The database was created (" & strDb & ")."
    Set cat = Nothing
    Exit Sub

ErrorHandler:
    If Err.Number = -2147217897 Then
        Kill strDb
```

```
        Resume 0
      Else
        MsgBox Err.Number & ": " & Err.Description
      End If
    End Sub
```

3. Choose **Run | Run Sub/UserForm** to execute the procedure.

While creating a database, you may specify that the database should be encrypted by setting the Jet OLEDB:Encrypt Database property to True. You can also include the database version information with the Jet OLEDB:Engine Type property. Simply include these properties in the connection string, as shown in the following example:

```
cat.Create "Provider=Microsoft.Jet.OLEDB.4.0;" & _
    "Data Source=" & strDb & _
    "Jet OLEDB:Encrypt Database=True;" & _
    "Jet OLEDB:Engine Type=1;"
```

To create a Microsoft Access database (ACCDB) in Access 2007, you must change the name of the provider used to Microsoft.ACE.OLEDB. 12.0.

This procedure uses the error handler to detect whether a database of the specified name already exists. When error -2147217897 occurs, the procedure deletes the database file using the VBA Kill statement and returns to the statement that caused the error.

Copying a Database

At times you may want to duplicate your database programmatically. This can be easily done in DAO with the DBEngine object's CompactDatabase method. ADO does not have a special method for copying files. However, you can set up a reference to the File Scripting object (the Microsoft Scripting Runtime Library) to gain access to your computer file system, or use the CreateObject function to access this library without setting up a reference.

Copying a Database with DAO

Before using the CompactDatabase method, make sure the source database is closed and there is enough disk space to create a duplicate copy. Creating a copy of your database in code requires that you define two string variables: one to hold the name of the source database and the other to specify the name for the duplicate version.

Hands-On 10-16 shows how to use the CompactDatabase method to copy a database.

⊚ Hands-On 10-16: Copying a Database with DAO

This hands-on exercise makes a copy of the TestDAO.accdb database created in Hands-On 10-14.

1. In the Visual Basic Editor window, choose **Insert | Module**.

2. In the module's Code window, type the **CopyDB_DAO** procedure shown
    below, or copy the procedure code from **C:\Acc07_HandsOn\Hands-
    On10.txt**.

```
Sub CopyDB_DAO()
    Dim dbName As String
    Dim dbNewName As String

    dbName = InputBox("Enter the name of the database you want " & _
            "to copy: " & Chr(13) & _
            "(example: C:\Acc07_ByExample\TestDAO.accdb)", "Create a copy of")

    If dbName = "" Then Exit Sub

    If Dir(dbName) = "" Then
        MsgBox dbName & " was not found. " & Chr(13) _
        & "Check the database name or path."
        Exit Sub
    End If

    dbNewName = InputBox("Enter the name of the duplicate " & _
    "database:" & Chr(13) _
    & "(example: C:\Acc07_ByExample\Copy of TestDAO.accdb)", "Save As")

    If dbNewName = "" Then Exit Sub

    If Dir(dbNewName) <> "" Then
        Kill dbNewName
    End If

    DBEngine.CompactDatabase dbName, dbNewName
End Sub
```

3. Choose **Run | Run Sub/UserForm** to execute the procedure. You will be
    prompted to specify the name of the database you want to copy and the
    name for the copy.

The above procedure uses the VBA Dir function to check for the existence of
the database with the specified name:

```
If Dir(dbNewName) <> "" Then
    Kill dbNewName
End If
```

Because the database cannot be deleted programmatically using DAO, the
VBA Kill statement is used to perform the deletion. The last statement in the
above procedure uses the CompactDatabase method of the DBEngine object to
create a copy of a database using the user-supplied arguments: a source database name (dbName) and a destination database (dbNewName).

Copying a Database with FileSystemObject

You can use the CopyFile method of the FileSystemObject from the Microsoft
Scripting Runtime Library to copy any file. This method allows you to copy
one or more files and requires that you specify the source and destination. The

source is the name of the file you want to copy or file specification. For example, to copy all your MDB databases located in a specific directory, you can include wildcard characters to specify the source like this: C:\Acc07_ByExample*.mdb. The destination is the string specifying where the file or files are to be copied. You cannot use wildcard characters in the destination string. The third argument of the CopyFile method is optional. It indicates if existing files in the destination are to be overwritten. If True, files are overwritten; if False, they are not. The default is True.

Hands-On 10-17 demonstrates how to copy a file from one directory to another.

◎ Hands-On 10-17: Copying a File

This hands-on exercise makes a copy of the TestADO.accdb database created in Hands-On 10-15.

1. In the Visual Basic Editor window, choose **Insert | Module**.

2. In the module's Code window, type the **Copy_AnyFile** procedure shown below, or copy the procedure code from **C:\Acc07_HandsOn\Hands-On10.txt**.

```
Sub Copy_AnyFile()
    Dim fso As Object
    Dim strDb As String

    On Error GoTo ErrorHandler

    Set fso = CreateObject("Scripting.FileSystemObject")

    strDb = "C:\Acc07_ByExample\TestADO.accdb"
        fso.CopyFile strDb, "C:\"

    Set fso = Nothing
    Exit Sub
ErrorHandler:
    MsgBox Err.Number & ":" & Err.Description
End Sub
```

3. Choose **Run | Run Sub/UserForm** to execute the procedure.

The above procedure uses the CreateObject method to return a reference to a FileSystemObject from the Microsoft Scripting Runtime Library. The CopyFile method of the FileSystemObject is then used to copy the specified database to the root directory of your computer.

Database Errors

So far in this book you've seen several procedures that incorporated simple error handling. An *error handler* is a block of code that is executed when a run-time error occurs. The procedure execution is transferred to error-handling code via the On Error GoTo <Label> statement. There are three types of On Error statements:

■ **On Error GoTo <Label>** — This statement tells VBA to jump to the specified label when an error occurs. A label is any unreserved word followed by a colon and is placed on a separate line in the same procedure as the On Error statement. The code between the line that caused the error and the line label is simply ignored. The execution of the procedure continues from the line following the line label. The error-handling code is placed at the very bottom of the procedure. To ensure that the error handler is not executed if there are no errors, place an Exit Sub or Exit Function statement just before the line label.

If the procedure with error-handling code calls another procedure that does not have its own error handler, an error that occurs in the called procedure causes the execution to be transferred back to the calling procedure where the error will be handled.

■ **On Error Resume Next** — This statement tells VBA to resume the procedure execution at the line following the statement that caused the error. Place this statement in your code anywhere you think the error might occur. The run-time error will be trapped and stored in the VBA Err object. You should check the error number of the Err object immediately after that statement to determine how to handle the error.

■ **On Error GoTo 0** — This statement disables the error handler in the current procedure. When an error occurs, VBA will display its standard run-time error message box in which you can click the End button to terminate the procedure or press Debug to enter the break mode for troubleshooting.

VBA has a built-in Err object that has several properties useful for determining the type of error that occurred. Use the Err object's Number property to determine the error number. The Description property of the Err object contains the text description of the error. You can also find out the source of an error by using the Err object's Source property.

When using ADO to access data, you can get information about the errors from both the VBA Err object and the ActiveX Data Objects (ADO) Error object. When an error occurs in an application that uses the ADO Object Model, an Error object is appended to the ADO Errors collection of the Connection object and you are advised about the error via a message box.

While the VBA Err object holds information only about the most recent error, the ADO Errors collection can contain several entries regarding the last ADO error. You can count the errors caused by an invalid operation by using the Count property of the Errors collection. By checking the contents of the Errors collection you can learn more information about the nature of the error. The Errors collection is available only from the Connection object. Errors that occur in ADO itself are reported to the VBA Err object. Errors that are provider-specific are appended to the Errors collection of the ADO Connection object. These errors are reported by the specific OLE DB provider when ADO objects are being used to access data.

The DBError2 procedure in Hands-On 10-18 attempts to open a nonexistent database to demonstrate the capability of the VBA Err object and the ADO Errors collection.

◎ Hands-On 10-18: Using the VBA Err Object and ADO Errors Collection

1. In the Visual Basic Editor window, choose **Insert | Module**.

2. In the module's Code window, type the **DBError2** procedure shown below, or copy the procedure code from **C:\Acc07_HandsOn\ HandsOn10.txt**.

```
Sub DBError2()
    Dim conn As New ADODB.Connection
    Dim errADO As ADODB.Error

    On Error GoTo CheckErrors
    conn.Open "Provider=Microsoft.ACE.OLEDB.12.0;" _
        & "Data Source=C:\my.accdb"
    Debug.Print CurrentProject.Path
CheckErrors:
    Debug.Print "VBA error number: " _
        & Err.Number & vbCrLf _
        & " (" & Err.Description & ")"
    Debug.Print "Listed below is information " _
        & "regarding this error " & vbCrLf _
        & "contained in the ADO Errors collection."
    For Each errADO In conn.Errors
        Debug.Print vbTab & "Error Number: " & errADO.Number
        Debug.Print vbTab & "Error Description: " & errADO.Description
        Debug.Print vbTab & "Jet Error Number: " & errADO.SQLState
        Debug.Print vbTab & "Native Error Number: " & errADO.NativeError
        Debug.Print vbTab & "Source: " & errADO.Source
        Debug.Print vbTab & "Help Context: " & errADO.HelpContext
        Debug.Print vbTab & "Help File: " & errADO.HelpFile
    Next
    MsgBox "Errors were written to the Immediate window."
End Sub
```

3. Choose **Run | Run Sub/UserForm** to execute the procedure.

In the above procedure, an error is encountered when VBA attempts to open a database file that does not exist in the specified directory. The On Error GoTo CheckErrors statement tells VBA to jump over to the line labeled CheckErrors. The line that prints the current project path is never executed. The CheckErrors handler reads the content of the VBA Err object and prints the error number and its description to the Immediate window. After that, we retrieve more information about the encountered errors by looping through the ADO Errors collection.

 Note: To trace errors in your VBA procedures, don't forget to use the Step commands in the Visual Basic Debug menu.

Compacting a Database

With frequent use over a period of time, the performance of your database may deteriorate. When objects are deleted from a database but the space isn't reclaimed, fragmentation may occur. To improve database performance and reduce the database file size, you can compact or repair Microsoft Office Access databases. To compact a database, use one of the following methods:

- **CompactDatabase** (Microsoft Jet and Replication Objects (JRO) Library) — To use the JRO library, choose Tools | References in the Visual Basic application window and select Microsoft Jet and Replication Objects 2.6 Library. We will use this method to compact a database in Hands-On 10-19.

- **CompactDatabase** (DBEngine object) — This method requires that you specify the full path and filename of the database you want to compact, and the full path and filename of the compacted database.

```
DBEngine.CompactDatabase "C:\Acc07_ByExample\Northwind
2007.accdb","C:\CompNorthwind.accdb"
```

- **CompactRepair** (Application object) — The Application object refers to the active Microsoft Access application. This method requires that you specify the full path and filename of the database you want to compact, and the full path and filename of the compacted database. You may also specify an optional argument to indicate whether a log file should be created. True means that if corruption is detected in the source file, the log file will be created in the destination directory. If you omit the third argument or set it to False, no log file is created.

```
Application.CompactRepair("C:\Acc07_ByExample\Northwind.mdb","C:/
NewNorthwind.mdb",true)
```

When compacting/repairing a database, keep in mind the following:

- You cannot compact/repair a database that is currently open.

- You cannot compact a database to the same filename. You must specify a new name for the compacted database. After the compact/repair process is complete, simply delete the original database file and rename the compacted database using the original name.

- You cannot compact a database if it is secured and you don't have appropriate permissions.

Hands-On 10-19 demonstrates how to compact the Northwind database using JRO.

◎ Hands-On 10-19: Compacting a Database

1. In the Visual Basic Editor window, choose **Insert** | **Module**.

2. In the module's Code window, type the **CompactDb** procedure shown below, or copy the procedure code from **C:\Acc07_HandsOn\Hands-On10.txt**.

```
' use the References dialog box to set up a reference to the
' Microsoft Jet and Replication Objects Library

Sub CompactDb()
    Dim jetEng As JRO.JetEngine
    Dim strCompactFrom As String
    Dim strCompactTo As String
    Dim strPath As String

    strPath = CurrentProject.Path & "\"
    strCompactFrom = "Northwind.mdb"
    strCompactTo = "NorthwindComp.mdb"

    ' Make sure there isn't already a file with the
    ' name of the compacted database.
    On Error GoTo HandleErr

    ' Compact the database
    Set jetEng = New JRO.JetEngine
    jetEng.CompactDatabase "Data Source=" & _
        strPath & strCompactFrom & ";", _
        "Data Source=" & _
        strPath & strCompactTo & ";"

    ' Delete the original database
    Kill strPath & strCompactFrom

    ' Rename the file back to the original name
    Name strPath & strCompactTo As strPath & strCompactFrom
ExitHere:
    Set jetEng = Nothing
    MsgBox "Compacting completed."
    Exit Sub
HandleErr:
    MsgBox Err.Number & ": " & Err.Description
    Resume ExitHere
End Sub
```

3. Choose **Run** | **Run Sub/UserForm** to execute the procedure.

Chapter Summary

In this chapter you were introduced to the two database engines that Office Access 2007 uses (JET and ACE) as well as several object libraries that provide objects, properties, and methods for your VBA procedures. You mastered the art of programmatically connecting to native Microsoft Access databases and external databases and files using various connection strings and connection methods (ODBC/OLEDB, DSN, and DSN-less connections, UDL files). You also learned how to write VBA code to create, open, copy, compact, and delete a Microsoft Office Access database. Finally, you learned about statements (On Error GoTo...) and objects (Err, Error) that are helpful in trapping/troubleshooting database errors.

In the next chapter, you will learn the DAO and ADO techniques for creating and linking tables, adding and modifying fields, and setting up keys, indexes, and relationships between tables. In other words, you will learn which DAO/ADO objects can give you access to the structure of the database.

Chapter 11

Creating and Accessing Database Tables and Fields

Now that you know how to create a Microsoft Office Access database programmatically, it's time to fill it with some useful objects. The first object you will need to create is a table with a couple of fields. Typical types of operations you may want to perform on database tables and fields are listed below:

- Creating a table and setting field properties
- Making a copy of a table
- Deleting a table
- Listing table properties
- Adding new fields to an existing table
- Changing field properties
- Deleting a field from a table
- Linking a table to a database
- Listing tables in a database
- Changing the AutoNumber
- Listing data types

In this chapter you will write VBA procedures that use both DAO and ADO objects to perform the above-mentioned database tasks.

Creating a Microsoft Access Table and Setting Field Properties (DAO Method)

Each saved table in an Access database is an object called a TableDef object. The TableDef object has a number of properties that characterize it, such as Name, RecordCount, DateCreated, and DateUpdated. The TableDef object also has methods that act on the object. For example, the CreateField method creates a new field for the TableDef object and the OpenRecordset method creates an object called Recordset that is used to manipulate the data in the table.

The procedure in Hands-On 11-1 illustrates how to create a table in the current database using DAO.

◎ Hands-On 11-1: Creating a Table (DAO)

1. Start Microsoft Office Access 2007 and create a new Microsoft Office Access 2007 database named **Chap11.accdb** in your **C:\Acc07_ ByExample** folder.

2. Press **Alt+F11** to switch to the Visual Basic Editor window and choose **Insert | Module**.

3. In the module's Code window, type the **CreateTableDAO** procedure as shown below, or copy the procedure code from the **C:\Acc07_HandsOn\ Chap11.txt** file.

```
Sub CreateTableDAO()
    Dim db As DAO.Database
    Dim tblNew As DAO.TableDef
    Dim fld As DAO.Field
    Dim prp As DAO.Property

    On Error GoTo ErrorHandler
    Set db = CurrentDb
    Set tblNew = db.CreateTableDef("Agents")

    Set fld = tblNew.CreateField("AgentID", dbText, 6)
    fld.ValidationRule = "Like 'A*'"
    fld.ValidationText = "Agent ID must begin with the letter 'A' " & _
    "and cannot contain more than 6 characters."
    tblNew.Fields.Append fld

    Set fld = tblNew.CreateField("Country", dbText)
    fld.DefaultValue = "USA"
    tblNew.Fields.Append fld

    Set fld = tblNew.CreateField("DateOfBirth", dbDate)
    fld.Required = True
    tblNew.Fields.Append fld
    db.TableDefs.Append tblNew

    ' Create Caption property and set its value
    ' add it to the collection of field properties
    Set prp = tblNew.Fields("DateOfBirth").CreateProperty("Caption")
    prp.Type = dbText
    prp.Value = "Date of Birth"
    fld.Properties.Append prp
    MsgBox fld.Properties("Caption").Value

    Set prp = tblNew.CreateProperty("Description")
    prp.Type = dbText
    prp.Value = "Sample table created with DAO code"
    tblNew.Properties.Append prp
    Exit Sub
ErrorHandler:
    MsgBox Err.Number & ": " & Err.Description
End Sub
```

4. Choose **Run | Run Sub/UserForm** to execute the CreateTableDAO procedure.

The CreateTableDAO procedure uses the CurrentDb method to define an object variable (db) to point to the database that is currently open in the Microsoft Access window. This method allows you to access the current database from Visual Basic without having to know the database name. Next, a table is created using the CreateTableDef method of a DAO Database object. This method requires that you specify a string or string variable to hold the name of the new TableDef object. For instance, the following line sets the object variable tblNew to point to a table named Agents:

```
Set tblNew = db.CreateTableDef("Agents")
```

Because a table must have at least one field, the next step in the table creation process is to use the CreateField method of the TableDef object to create fields. For instance, in the following statement:

```
Set fld = tblNew.CreateField("AgentID", dbText, 6)
```

- tblNew is a table definition variable

- "AgentID" is a string specifying the name for the new field object

- dbText is an integer constant that determines the data type of the new Field object (see Table 11-1 below)

- 6 is an integer indicating the maximum size in bytes for a text field. Text fields can hold from 1 to 255 bytes. This argument is ignored for other types of fields.

Table 11-1: Constants for the Type property in VBA (DataTypeEnum enumeration)

Data Type Name	Value	Description
dbAttachment	101	Attachment data
dbBigInt	16	Big integer data
dbBinary	9	Binary data
dbBoolean	1	Boolean (True/False) data
dbByte	2	Byte (8-bit) data
dbChar	18	Text data (fixed width)
dbComplexByte	102	Multi-value byte data
dbComplexDecimal	108	Multi-value decimal data
dbComplexDouble	106	Multi-value double-precision floating-point data
dbComplexGUID	107	Multi-value GUID data
dbComplexInteger	103	Multi-value integer data
dbComplexLong	104	Multi-value long integer data
dbComplexSingle	105	Multi-value single-precision floating-point data
dbComplexText	109	Multi-value text data (variable width)
dbCurrency	5	Currency data
dbDate	8	Date value data

Data Type Name	Value	Description
dbDecimal	20	Decimal data (ODBCDirect only)
dbDouble	7	Double-precision floating-point data
dbFloat	21	Floating-point data (ODBCDirect only)
dbGUID	15	GUID data
dbInteger	3	Integer data
dbLong	4	Long integer data
dbLongBinary	11	Binary data (bitmap)
dbMemo	12	Memo data (extended text)
dbNumeric	19	Numeric data (ODBCDirect only)
dbSingle	6	Single-precision floating-point data
dbText	10	Text data (variable width)
dbTime	22	Data in time format (ODBCDirect only)
dbTimeStamp	23	Data in time and date format (ODBCDirect only)
dbVarBinary	17	Variable binary data (ODBCDirect only)

 Note: ODBCDirect workspaces are not supported in Microsoft Office Access 2007. Use ADO if you want to access external data sources without using the Microsoft Access database engine.

Constants for complex data types and the dbAttachment data type work only in Access 2007.

When creating fields for your table you may want to set certain field properties such as Validation Rule, Validation Text, Default Value, and Required. To define validation rules for a field you need to set two properties. The Validation Rule property is a text string that describes the rule for validation. In the CreateTableDAO procedure, we require that each entry in the AgentID field begin with the letter "A".

The Validation Text property is a string that is displayed to the user when the validation fails; that is, when the user attempts to enter data that does not comply with the specific validation rule.

The Default Value property sets or returns the default value of a Field object. In the example procedure above we make the data entry easier for the user by specifying "USA" as the default value in the Country field. Each new record will automatically have an entry of USA in the Country field. Because certain fields should not be left blank, to ensure that the user enters data in a particular field, you should set the Required property of that field to True.

In addition to built-in properties of an object, there are two other types of properties:

- application-defined properties
- user-defined properties

The application-defined property is created only if you assign a value to that property. A classic example of such a property is the Description property of the TableDef object. To set the Description property of a table in the Access user interface, simply right-click on the table name and choose Table Properties, then type the text you want in the Description field. Access will create a Description property for the table and will append it automatically to the Properties collection for that TableDef object. If you do not type a description in the Description field, Access will not create a Description property. Therefore, if you use the Description property in your code, Access will display an error. For this reason, it is a good idea to check beforehand whether a referenced property exists. Users may create their own properties to hold additional information about an object.

The CreateTableDAO procedure demonstrates how to use the Create-Property method of the TableDef object to create application-defined or user-defined properties. To create a property you will need to supply the name for the property, the property type, and the property value. For example, here's how we use the CreateProperty method to create a Caption property for the DateOfBirth field in the newly created table Agents:

```
Set prp = tblNew.Fields("DateOfBirth").CreateProperty("Caption")
```

Next, the data type of the Property object is defined:

```
prp.Type = dbText
```

See Table 11-1 above for the names of the Type property constants in VBA. Finally, a value is assigned to our new property:

```
prp.Value = "Date of Birth"
```

Instead of writing three separate lines of code, you can create a new property of an object with the following line:

```
Set prp = tblNew.Fields("DateOfBirth").CreateProperty("Caption", dbText, "Date
of Birth")
```

A user-defined property must be appended to the Properties collection of the corresponding object. In the example procedure above, the Caption property is appended to the Properties collection of the Field object, and the Description property is appended to the Properties collection of the TableDef object:

```
fld.Properties.Append prp
tblNew.Properties.Append prp
```

After creating a field and setting its built-in, application-defined, or user-defined properties, you should use the Append method to add the field to the Fields collection, as in the following example:

```
tblNew.Fields.Append fld
```

Once all the fields have been created and appended to the Fields collection, you must remember to append the new table to the TableDefs collection, as in the following example:

```
db.TableDefs.Append tblNew
```

You can delete user-defined properties from the Properties collection, but you can't delete built-in properties. If you set a property in the user interface, you don't need to create and append the property in code because the property is automatically included in the Properties collection.

After running the procedure code, a new table named Agents appears in the Microsoft Access window. If you can't see the table, press Ctrl+F5 to refresh the window.

To check the value of the Description property for the Agents table that was set as a result of running the example procedure, right-click the Agents table in the database window, and choose Table Properties from the shortcut menu.

To check the properties that were set and defined in this procedure, activate the Agents table in Design view, click the field name for which you set or created a custom property in the code, and examine the corresponding field properties. Figure 11-1 shows the current settings of the Validation Rule and Validation Text properties for the AgentID field.

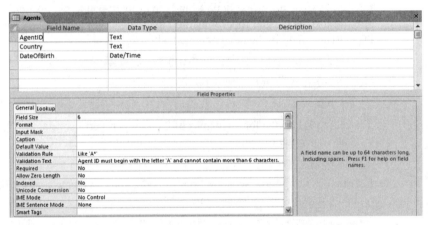

Figure 11-1: You can create a database table like this one using VBA code. You can also set appropriate field properties programmatically.

Creating a Microsoft Access Table and Setting Field Properties (ADO Method)

You can also get going with your database design by using Access objects contained in the ADOX library. The full name of this library is ActiveX Data Object Extensions for DDL and Security. To use ADOX in your VBA procedures, choose Tools | References from your Visual Basic Editor window and select Microsoft ADO Ext. 2.8 for DDL and Security. The ADOX Object Model is an extension of the ADODB library and is illustrated in Figure 11-2.

Figure 11-2: The ADOX Object Model.

When you take a look at Figure 11-2 you will notice the Catalog object at the very top of the ADOX Object Model. The Catalog object is extremely important, as it represents an entire database and contains database tables, columns, indexes, groups, users, procedures, and views. Use the ADOX Catalog object to create a table.

The following steps outline the process of creating a new Microsoft Access table:

1. Declare the variables representing the Connection, Catalog, and Table objects:

```
Dim conn As ADODB.Connection
Dim cat As ADOX.Catalog
Dim tbl As ADOX.Table
```

2. Open the connection to your database:

```
Set conn = New ADODB.Connection
conn.Open "Provider=Microsoft.Jet.OLEDB.4.0;" & _
    "Data Source=C:\NewAccessDb.mdb"
```

3. Supply the open connection to the ActiveConnection property of the ADOX Catalog object:

```
Set cat = New ADOX.Catalog
Set cat.ActiveConnection = conn
```

4. Create a new Table object:

```
Set tbl = New ADOX.Table
```

5. Provide the name for your table:

```
tbl.Name = "tblAssets"
```

The Table object is a member of the Tables collection, which in turn is a member of the Catalog object. Each Table object has a Name property and a Type property. The Type property specifies whether a Table object is a standard Microsoft Access table, a linked table, a system table, or a view. To see an example of using the Type property, refer to the section called "Listing Database Tables" later in this chapter.

6. Append the Table object to the Catalog object's Tables collection:

```
cat.Tables.Append tbl
```

At this point your table is empty.

7. Add new fields (columns) to your new table:

```
With tbl.Columns
    .Append "SiteID", adVarWChar, 10
    .Append "Category", adSmallInt
    .Append "InstallDate", adDate
End With
```

The code fragment above creates three fields named SiteID, Category, and InstallDate. You can create new fields in a table by passing the Column object's Name, Type, and DefinedSize properties as arguments of the Columns collection's Append method. Notice that ADOX uses different data types than those used in the Access user interface (see Table 11-2 for a comparison of the data types).

Note: The Table object contains the Columns collection that contains Column objects. To add a new field to a table, you could create a Column object and write the code like this:

```
Dim col As ADOX.Column
set col = New ADOX.Column
With col
    .Name = "SiteID"
    .DefinedSize = 10
End With
tbl.Columns.Append col
```

The last statement in the example above appends the new Column object (field) to the Columns collection of a table. The Name property specifies the name of the column. The DefinedSize property designates the maximum size of an entry in the column. To create another field, you would have to create a new Column object and set its properties. Creating fields in this manner takes longer and is less efficient than using the method demonstrated earlier.

The complete procedure is shown below:

```
' make sure to set up a reference to
' the Microsoft ActiveX Data Objects 2.8 Library
' and ADO Ext. 2.8 for DDL and Security
```

```
Sub CreateTableADO()
    Dim conn As ADODB.Connection
    Dim cat As ADOX.Catalog
    Dim tbl As ADOX.Table

    Set conn = New ADODB.Connection
    conn.Open "Provider=Microsoft.Jet.OLEDB.4.0;" & _
        "Data Source=C:\Acc07_ByExample\Chap11_Db2.mdb"

    Set cat = New ADOX.Catalog
    Set cat.ActiveConnection = conn

    Set tbl = New ADOX.Table
    tbl.Name = "tblAssets"

    cat.Tables.Append tbl

    With tbl.Columns
        .Append "SiteID", adVarWChar, 10
        .Append "Category", adSmallInt
        .Append "InstallDate", adDate
    End With

    Set cat = Nothing
    conn.Close
    Set conn = Nothing
End Sub
```

Table 11-2: ADO data types vs. Microsoft Access data types

ADO Data Type	Corresponding Data Type in Access
adBoolean	Yes/No
adUnsignedTinyInt	Number (FieldSize = Byte)
adSmallInt	Number (FieldSize = Integer)
adSingle	Number (FieldSize = Single)
adDouble	Number (FieldSize = Double)
adDecimal	Number (FieldSize = Decimal)
adInteger	Number (FieldSize = LongInteger) AutoNumber
adCurrency	Currency
adVarWChar	Text
adDate	Date/Time
adLongVarBinary	OLE object
adLongVarWChar	Memo
adLongVarWChar	Hyperlink

 Note: Only DAO supports the Access 2007 Attachment data type, multi-select lookup fields, and Append Only and Rich Text memo fields.

Copying a Table

The procedure in Hands-On 11-2 uses the SQL SELECT...INTO statement to select all records from the Customers table in the Northwind database into a new table called CustomersCopy. The SELECT...INTO statement is equivalent to a MakeTable query in the Microsoft Office Access user interface. This statement creates a new table and inserts data from other tables. To copy a table, the SQL statement is passed as the first argument of the Execute method of the ADO Connection object. Note that the copied table will not have the indexes that may exist in the original table.

⊚ Hands-On 11-2: Making a Copy of a Table (ADO)

1. In the Visual Basic Editor window, choose **Insert | Module**.

2. In the module's Code window, type the **Copy_Table** procedure shown below, or copy the procedure code from **C:\Acc07_HandsOn\Chap11.txt**.

```
' make sure to set up a reference to
' the Microsoft ActiveX Data Objects 2.8 Library

Sub Copy_Table()
    Dim conn As ADODB.Connection
    Dim strTable As String
    Dim strSQL As String

    On Error GoTo ErrorHandler

    strTable = "Customers"

    strSQL = "SELECT " & strTable & ".* INTO "
    strSQL = strSQL & strTable & "Copy "
    strSQL = strSQL & "FROM " & strTable

    Debug.Print strSQL

    Set conn = New ADODB.Connection
    conn.Open "Provider=Microsoft.Jet.OLEDB.4.0;" & _
        "Data Source=" & CurrentProject.Path & _
        "\Northwind.mdb"

    conn.Execute strSQL
    conn.Close
    Set conn = Nothing
    MsgBox "The " & strTable & " table was copied."
    Exit Sub

ErrorHandler:
    If Err.Number = -2147217900 Then
        conn.Execute "DROP Table " & strTable
        Resume
```

```
        Else
            MsgBox Err.Number & ": " & Err.Description
        End If
End Sub
```

3. Choose **Run | Run Sub/UserForm** to execute the procedure.

When you run this procedure, Access creates a copy of the Customers table named CustomersCopy.

Deleting a Database Table

You can use ADO to delete a table programmatically by opening the ADOX Catalog object, accessing its Tables collection, and calling the Delete method. The procedure in Hands-On 11-3 requires a parameter that specifies the name of the table you want to delete.

⊚ Hands-On 11-3: Deleting a Table from a Database (ADO)

1. In the Visual Basic Editor window, choose **Insert | Module**.

2. In the module's Code window, type the **Delete_Table** procedure shown below, or copy the procedure code from **C:\Acc07_HandsOn\Chap11.txt**.

```
Sub Delete_Table(strTblName As String)
    Dim conn As ADODB.Connection
    Dim cat As ADOX.Catalog

    On Error GoTo ErrorHandler

    Set conn = New ADODB.Connection
    conn.Open "Provider=Microsoft.Jet.OLEDB.4.0;" & _
        "Data Source=" & CurrentProject.Path & _
        "\Northwind.mdb"

    Set cat = New ADOX.Catalog

    cat.ActiveConnection = conn

    cat.Tables.Delete strTblName
    Set cat = Nothing
    conn.Close
    Set conn = Nothing

    Exit Sub

ErrorHandler:
    MsgBox "Table '" & strTblName & _
        "' cannot be deleted " & vbCrLf & _
        "because it does not exist."
    Resume Next
End Sub
```

3. To run the above procedure, type the following statement in the Immediate window and press **Enter**:

```
Delete_Table "CustomersCopy"
```

The CustomersCopy table was created by running the Copy_Table procedure in Hands-On 11-2. When you press Enter, Visual Basic will delete the specified table from the Northwind.mdb database. If the table does not exist, an appropriate message is displayed.

Adding New Fields to an Existing Table

At times you may want to programmatically add a new field to an existing table. The procedure below adds a new text field called MyNewField to a table located in the Northwind database.

Hands-On 11-4: Adding a New Field to a Table (ADO)

The procedure demonstrated in this hands-on exercise uses the CustomersCopy table in the Northwind database. Since we deleted this table in the previous exercise, you need to rerun the procedure in Hands-On 11-2 to recreate the table as instructed in step 3 below.

1. In the Visual Basic Editor window, choose **Insert | Module**.
2. In the module's Code window, type the **Add_NewFields** procedure shown below, or copy the procedure code from **C:\Acc07_HandsOn\Chap11.txt**.

```
Sub Add_NewFields()
    Dim conn As ADODB.Connection
    Dim cat As New ADOX.Catalog
    Dim myTbl As New ADOX.Table

    Set conn = New ADODB.Connection
    conn.Open "Provider=Microsoft.Jet.OLEDB.4.0;" & _
        "Data Source=" & CurrentProject.Path & _
        "\Northwind.mdb"

    Set cat = New ADOX.Catalog
    cat.ActiveConnection = conn
    cat.Tables("CustomersCopy").Columns.Append _
        "MyNewField", adWChar, 15

    Set cat = Nothing
    conn.Close
    Set conn = Nothing
End Sub
```

3. Run the **Copy_Table** procedure in Hands-On 11-2 to ensure that the CustomersCopy table exists in the Northwind database.
4. Choose **Run | Run Sub/UserForm** to run the Add_NewFields procedure.

In DAO, use the CreateField and Append methods to add new fields to the existing table.

Hands-On 11-5: Adding a New Field to a Table (DAO)

1. In the Visual Basic Editor window, choose **Insert | Module**.
2. In the module's Code window, type the **Add_NewFieldsDAO** procedure shown below, or copy the procedure code from **C:\Acc07_HandsOn\ Chap11.txt**.

```
Sub Add_NewFieldsDAO()
    Dim db As DAO.Database
    Dim tdf As DAO.TableDef
    Dim tblName As String

    tblName = "CustomersCopy"

    On Error GoTo ErrorHandler
    Set db = OpenDatabase("C:\Acc07_ByExample\Northwind.mdb")
    Set tdf = db.TableDefs(tblName)

    MsgBox "Number of fields in the table: " & _
        db.TableDefs(tblName).Fields.Count

    With tdf
        .Fields.Append .CreateField("NoOfMeetings", dbInteger)
        .Fields.Append .CreateField("Result", dbMemo)
    End With

    MsgBox "Number of fields in the table: " & _
        db.TableDefs(tblName).Fields.Count

    db.Close
    Exit Sub
ErrorHandler:
    MsgBox Err.Number & ": " & Err.Description
End Sub
```

3. Choose **Run | Run Sub/UserForm** to run the Add_NewFieldsDAO procedure.

The Add_NewFieldsDAO procedure shown above uses the following With...End With construct to quickly add two new fields to an existing table:

```
With tdf
    .Fields.Append .CreateField("NoOfMeetings", dbInteger)
    .Fields.Append .CreateField("Result", dbMemo)
End With
```

Each new field is appended to the Fields collection of the specified DAO TableDef object. In the above example, we create a new field on the fly while calling the Append method. Be sure to include a space between the Append method and the dot operator in front of the CreateField method. To add two new fields to an existing table without using the With...End With construct, you would use the following statements:

```
tdf.Fields.Append tdf.CreateField("NoOfMeetings", dbInteger)
tdf.Fields.Append tdf.CreateField("Result", dbMemo)
```

However, using the With...End With construct makes the code both clearer and faster to execute.

Removing a Field from a Table

You may remove any field from an existing table, whether or not this field contains data. However, you can't delete a field after you have created an index that references that field. You must first delete the index.

The procedure in Hands-On 11-6 illustrates how to access the ADOX Columns collection of a Table object and use the Columns collection's Delete method to remove a field from a table. This procedure will fail if the field you want to delete is part of an index.

◎ Hands-On 11-6: Removing a Field from a Table (ADO)

This hands-on exercise requires that you created the procedure in Hands-On 11-4.

1. In the Visual Basic Editor window, choose **Insert | Module**.

2. In the module's Code window, type the **Delete_Field** procedure shown below, or copy the procedure code from **C:\Acc07_HandsOn\Chap11.txt**.

```
Sub Delete_Field()
    Dim conn As ADODB.Connection
    Dim cat As New ADOX.Catalog

    Set conn = New ADODB.Connection
    conn.Open "Provider=Microsoft.Jet.OLEDB.4.0;" & _
        "Data Source=" & CurrentProject.Path & _
        "\Northwind.mdb"

    Set cat = New ADOX.Catalog
    cat.ActiveConnection = conn
    cat.Tables("CustomersCopy").Columns.Delete "MyNewField"

    Set cat = Nothing
    conn.Close
    Set conn = Nothing
End Sub
```

3. Choose **Run | Run Sub/UserForm** to execute the procedure.

In DAO, you use the Delete method to remove a field from an existing table.

◎ Hands-On 11-7: Removing a Field from a Table (DAO)

The following procedure removes from the CustomersCopy table two fields that were added by the procedure in Hands-On 11-5.

1. In the Visual Basic Editor window, choose **Insert | Module**.

2. In the module's Code window, type the **DeleteFields_DAO** procedure shown below, or copy the procedure code from **C:\Acc07_HandsOn\ Chap11.txt**.

```
Sub DeleteFields_DAO()
    Dim db As DAO.Database
    Dim tdf As DAO.TableDef
    On Error GoTo ErrorHandler

    Dim tblName As String

    tblName = "CustomersCopy"

    On Error GoTo ErrorHandler

    Set db = OpenDatabase("C:\Acc07_ByExample\Northwind.mdb")
    Set tdf = db.TableDefs(tblName)

    MsgBox "Number of fields in the table: " & _
           db.TableDefs(tblName).Fields.Count

    With tdf
        .Fields.Delete "NoOfMeetings"
        .Fields.Delete "Result"
    End With

    MsgBox "Number of fields in the table: " & _
           db.TableDefs(tblName).Fields.Count

    db.Close
    Exit Sub
ErrorHandler:
    MsgBox Err.Number & ": " & Err.Description
End Sub
```

3. Choose **Run | Run Sub/UserForm** to execute the procedure.

Retrieving Table Properties

Using the Properties collection of an ADOX Table object you can set or retrieve table properties. The Properties collection exposes standard ADO properties as well as properties specific to the data provider. You can iterate through all of the properties of an object using the For Each...Next programming structure.

The following procedure accesses the table called CustomersCopy and lists its properties and their values in the Immediate window.

◉ Hands-On 11-8: Listing Table Properties

1. In the Visual Basic Editor window, choose **Insert | Module**.

2. In the module's Code window, type the **List_TableProperties** procedure shown below, or copy the procedure code from **C:\Acc07_HandsOn\ Chap11.txt**.

```
Sub List_TableProperties()
    Dim conn As ADODB.Connection
    Dim cat As ADOX.Catalog
```

```
    Dim tbl As ADOX.Table
    Dim pr As ADOX.Property

    Set conn = New ADODB.Connection
    conn.Open "Provider=Microsoft.Jet.OLEDB.4.0;" & _
        "Data Source=" & CurrentProject.Path & _
        "\Northwind.mdb"

    Set cat = New ADOX.Catalog
    cat.ActiveConnection = conn

    Set tbl = cat.Tables("CustomersCopy")

    ' retrieve table properties
    For Each pr In tbl.Properties
        Debug.Print tbl.Name & ": " & _
            pr.Name & "= "; pr.Value
    Next
    Set cat = Nothing
    conn.Close
    Set conn = Nothing
End Sub
```

3. Choose **Run | Run Sub/UserForm** to execute the procedure.

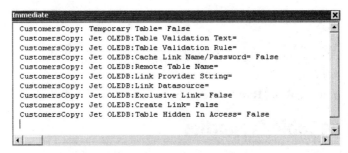

Figure 11-3: You can list the names of table properties and their values programmatically as shown in Hands-On 11-8.

The following procedure uses the Properties collection of the DAO TableDef object to list properties of the Agents table in the currently open Access Chap11.accdb database.

```
Sub List_TableProperties_DAO()
    Dim prp As DAO.Property
    Dim tdf As DAO.TableDef
    Dim db As DAO.Database

    Set db = CurrentDb
    Set tdf = db.TableDefs("Agents")

    For Each prp In tdf.Properties
        On Error Resume Next
        Debug.Print prp.Name & ": " & prp.Value
    Next
```

```
    MsgBox "Finished processing."
    End Sub
```

Retrieving Field Properties

The procedure in Hands-On 11-9 retrieves the field properties of the field named AgentID located in the Agents table in the current database.

⊙ Hands-On 11-9: Listing Field Properties

1. In the Visual Basic Editor window, choose **Insert | Module**.

2. In the module's Code window, type the **List_FieldProperties** procedure shown below, or copy the procedure code from **C:\Acc07_HandsOn\ Chap11.txt**.

```
Sub List_FieldProperties()
    Dim cat As ADOX.Catalog
    Dim col As ADOX.Column
    Dim pr As ADOX.Property

    Set cat = New ADOX.Catalog
    Set cat.ActiveConnection = CurrentProject.Connection
    Set col = New ADOX.Column
    Set col = cat.Tables("Agents").Columns("AgentID")

    Debug.Print "Properties of the AgentID field " & _
        "(" & col.Properties.Count & ")"
    ' retrieve Field properties
    For Each pr In col.Properties
        Debug.Print pr.Name & "="; pr.Value
    Next

    Set cat = Nothing
End Sub
```

3. Choose **Run | Run Sub/UserForm** to execute the procedure.

```
Immediate                                                                    x
Properties of the AgentID field (15)
Autoincrement=False
Default=
Description=
Nullable=True
Fixed Length=False
Seed= 1
Increment= 1
Jet OLEDB:Column Validation Text=Agent ID must begin with the letter 'A' and cannot contain more than 6 characte
Jet OLEDB:Column Validation Rule=Like 'A*'
Jet OLEDB:IISAM Not Last Column=False
Jet OLEDB:AutoGenerate=False
Jet OLEDB:One BLOB per Page=False
Jet OLEDB:Compressed UNICODE Strings=False
Jet OLEDB:Allow Zero Length=False
Jet OLEDB:Hyperlink=False
```

Figure 11-4: Running the procedure in Hands-On 11-9 generates a list of field properties and their values in the Immediate window.

Linking a Microsoft Access Table

In Microsoft Office Access 2007, you can create links to tables in Access databases as well as other data formats such as Excel, dBASE, Paradox, Exchange/Outlook, Lotus, text, and HTML.

To create a linked Access table, you must set the following table properties:

```
Jet OLEDB:LinkDatasource
Jet OLEDB:Remote Table Name
Jet OLEDB:CreateLink
```

The procedure in Hands-On 11-10 demonstrates how to establish a link to the Customers table located in the Northwind.mdb database.

Hands-On 11-10: Linking a Microsoft Jet Table

1. In the Visual Basic Editor window, choose **Insert | Module**.
2. In the module's Code window, type the **Link_JetTable** procedure shown below, or copy the procedure code from **C:\Acc07_HandsOn\Chap11.txt**.

```
Sub Link_JetTable()
    Dim cat As ADOX.Catalog
    Dim lnkTbl As ADOX.Table
    Dim strDb As String
    Dim strTable As String

    On Error GoTo ErrorHandler

    strDb = CurrentProject.Path & "\Northwind.mdb"
    strTable = "Customers"
    Set cat = New ADOX.Catalog
    cat.ActiveConnection = CurrentProject.Connection

    Set lnkTbl = New ADOX.Table
    With lnkTbl
        ' Name the new Table and set its ParentCatalog property to the
        ' open Catalog to allow access to the Properties collection.
        .Name = strTable
        Set .ParentCatalog = cat

        ' Set the properties to create the link
        .Properties("Jet OLEDB:Create Link") = True
        .Properties("Jet OLEDB:Link Datasource") = strDb
        .Properties("Jet OLEDB:Remote Table Name") = strTable
    End With

    ' Append the table to the Tables collection
    cat.Tables.Append lnkTbl

    Set cat = Nothing
    MsgBox "The current database contains a linked " & _
        "table named " & strTable
    Exit Sub
```

```
ErrorHandler:
    MsgBox Err.Number & ": " & Err.Description
End Sub
```

3. Choose **Run | Run Sub/UserForm** to execute the procedure.

   To access the linked Customers table after running this procedure, be sure to refresh the Access window by pressing **Ctrl+F5**.

Linking a dBASE Table

You can also link tables that reside in other programs or file formats such as Microsoft Excel, Microsoft FoxPro, dBASE, or Paradox. In DAO, to link a table to an Access database, use the CreateTableDef method to create a new table:

```
Set myTable = db.CreateTableDef("TableDBASE")
```

Next, specify the Connect property of the TableDef object. For example, the following statement specifies the connect string:

```
myTable.Connect = "dBase 5.0;Database=C:\AccO7_ByExample"
```

Next, specify the SourceTableName property of the TableDef object to indicate the actual name of the table in the source database:

```
myTable.SourceTableName = "Customer.dbf"
```

Finally, use the Append method to append the TableDef object to the TableDefs collection:

```
db.TableDefs.Append myTable
```

The following procedure demonstrates how to link a dBASE table to the current database:

```
Sub LinkDBaseTable_DAO()
    Dim db As DAO.Database
    Dim myTable As DAO.TableDef

    On Error GoTo err_LinkDbaseTable

    Set db = CurrentDb
    Set myTable = db.CreateTableDef("TableDBASE")

    myTable.Connect = "dBase 5.0;Database=C:\AccO7_ByExample"
    myTable.SourceTableName = "Customer.dbf"

    db.TableDefs.Append myTable
    db.TableDefs.Refresh

    MsgBox "dBase table has been successfully linked."
    Exit Sub
err_LinkDbaseTable:
    MsgBox Err.Number & ": " & Err.Description
End Sub
```

Linking a Microsoft Excel Spreadsheet

You can link an Excel spreadsheet to a Microsoft Access database by using the TransferSpreadsheet method of the DoCmd object, as shown in Hands-On 11-11. Note, however, that neither the DoCmd object nor its Transfer-Spreadsheet method are members of the ADO Object Model. The DoCmd object is built into the Microsoft Access library.

⊚ Hands-On 11-11: Linking an Excel Spreadsheet

This hands-on exercise uses the Regions.xls spreadsheet file provided in the book's downloadable files. This spreadsheet has been created with Excel 2007. You can revise the procedure code to use any spreadsheet file that you have available; however, you must match the constant name with the Excel version. The following table shows the constant names and values if you need a different spreadsheet format.

Table 11-3: Spreadsheet constants

Constant	Value	Description
acSpreadsheetTypeExcel3	0	Microsoft Excel 3.0 format
acSpreadsheetTypeExcel4	6	Microsoft Excel 4.0 format
acSpreadsheetTypeExcel5	5	Microsoft Excel 5.0 format
acSpreadsheetTypeExcel7	5	Microsoft Excel 95 format
acSpreadsheetTypeExcel8	8	Microsoft Excel 97 format
acSpreadsheetTypeExcel9	8	Microsoft Excel 2000-2003 format
acSpreadsheetTypeExcel12	9	Microsoft Excel 2007 format (XLS)
acSpreadsheetTypeExcel12Xml	10	Microsoft Excel 2007 format (XML)
acSpreadsheetTypeLotusWK1	2	Lotus 1-2-3 WK1 format
acSpreadsheetTypeLotusWK3	3	Lotus 1-2-3 WK3 format
acSpreadsheetTypeLotusWK4	7	Lotus 1-2-3 WK4 format

1. In the Visual Basic Editor window, choose **Insert | Module**.

2. In the module's Code window, type the **Link_ExcelSheet** procedure shown below, or copy the procedure code from **C:\Acc07_HandsOn\ Chap11.txt**.

```
Sub Link_ExcelSheet()
    Dim rst As ADODB.Recordset

    DoCmd.TransferSpreadsheet acLink, _
        acSpreadsheetTypeExcel12, _
        "mySheet", _
        CurrentProject.Path & "\Regions.xls", _
        -1, _
        "Regions!A1:B15"

    Set rst = New ADODB.Recordset
```

```
With rst
    .ActiveConnection = CurrentProject.Connection
    .CursorType = adOpenKeyset
    .LockType = adLockOptimistic
    .Open "mySheet", , , , adCmdTable
End With

Do Until rst.EOF
    Debug.Print rst.Fields(0).Value, rst.Fields(1).Value
    rst.MoveNext
Loop
rst.Close
Set rst = Nothing
End Sub
```

3. Choose **Run | Run Sub/UserForm** to execute the procedure.

The Link_ExcelSheet procedure begins by creating a linked table named mySheet from the specified range of cells (A1:B15), located in the Regions worksheet in the Regions.xls file. The first argument in the DoCmd statement indicates that the first row of the spreadsheet contains column headings. Next, the procedure uses the ADO Recordset object to retrieve the data from the mySheet table into the Immediate window. Notice that prior to opening the Recordset object, several properties of the Recordset object must be set.

■ The ActiveConnection property sets the reference to the current database.

■ The CursorType property specifies how the Recordset object should interact with the data source.

The adOpenKeyset setting tells Visual Basic that instead of retrieving all the records from the data source, only the keys are to be retrieved. The data for these keys is retrieved only as you scroll through the recordset. This guarantees better performance than retrieving big chunks of data at once.

■ The LockType property determines how to lock the data while it is being manipulated.

The adLockOptimistic setting locks the record only when you attempt to save it.

■ Opening the Recordset object also requires that you specify the data source. The data source in this procedure is the linked table named mySheet. The parameter passed depends on the source type used.

The adCmdTable setting indicates that all rows from the source table should be included.

You could also open the Recordset object by passing all the required parameters at once, as follows:

```
rst.Open "mySheet", _
CurrentProject.Connection, adOpenKeyset, _
adLockOptimistic, adCmdTable
```

Listing Database Tables

The procedure in Hands-On 11-12 generates a list of tables in the Northwind database. It uses the ADOX Catalog object to gain access to the database, then iterates through the Tables collection to retrieve the names of Access tables, system tables, and views. The ADOX Tables collection stores various types of Table objects, as shown in Table 11-3.

Table 11-4: Types of tables in the ADOX Tables collection

Name	Description
ACCESS TABLE	An Access system table
LINK	A linked table from a non-ODBC data source
PASS-THROUGH	A linked table from an ODBC data source
SYSTEM TABLE	A Microsoft Jet system table
TABLE	A Microsoft Access table
VIEW	A table from a row-returning, non-parameterized query

⊚ Hands-On 11-12: Creating a List of Database Tables

1. In the Visual Basic Editor window, choose **Insert | Module**.

2. In the module's Code window, type the **ListTbls** procedure shown below, or copy the procedure code from **C:\Acc07_HandsOn\Chap11.txt**.

```
Sub ListTbls()
    Dim cat As ADOX.Catalog
    Dim tbl As ADOX.Table

    Set cat = New ADOX.Catalog
    cat.ActiveConnection = "Provider=Microsoft.Jet.OLEDB.4.0;" & _
        "Data Source=" & CurrentProject.Path & _
        "\Northwind.mdb"

    For Each tbl In cat.Tables
        If tbl.Type <> "VIEW" And _
            tbl.Type <> "SYSTEM TABLE" And _
            tbl.Type <> "ACCESS TABLE" Then Debug.Print tbl.Name
    Next tbl
    Set cat = Nothing
    MsgBox "View the list of tables in the Immediate window."
End Sub
```

3. Choose **Run | Run Sub/UserForm** to execute the procedure.

To list tables in your database you can also use the OpenSchema method of the ADO Connection object (see the next section, "Listing Tables and Fields").

Listing Tables and Fields

Earlier in this chapter you learned how to enumerate tables in the Northwind database by accessing the Tables collection of the ADOX Catalog object. The procedures in Hands-On 11-13 and Hands-On 11-14 demonstrate how to use the OpenSchema method of the ADO Connection object to obtain more information about a database table and its fields.

⊚ Hands-On 11-13: Using the OpenSchema Method to List Database Tables

1. In the Visual Basic Editor window, choose **Insert | Module**.

2. In the module's Code window, type the **ListTbls2** procedure shown below, or copy the procedure code from **C:\Acc07_HandsOn\Chap11.txt**.

```
Sub ListTbls2()
    ' This procedure lists database tables using the OpenSchema method
    Dim rst As ADODB.Recordset
    Set rst = CurrentProject.Connection.OpenSchema(adSchemaTables)

    Do Until rst.EOF
        Debug.Print rst.Fields("TABLE_TYPE") & " ->" _
            & rst.Fields("TABLE_NAME")
        rst.MoveNext
    Loop
End Sub
```

3. Choose **Run | Run Sub/UserForm** to execute the procedure.

Obtaining the names of fields requires that you use adSchemaColumns as the parameter for the OpenSchema method. The ListTblsAndFields procedure in Hands-On 11-14 retrieves the names of fields in each table of the Northwind database.

⊚ Hands-On 11-14: Listing Tables and Their Fields Using the OpenSchema Method

1. In the Visual Basic Editor window, choose **Insert | Module**.

2. In the module's Code window, type the **ListTblsAndFields** procedure shown below, or copy the procedure code from **C:\Acc07_HandsOn\ Chap11.txt**.

```
Sub ListTblsAndFields()
    Dim conn As ADODB.Connection
    Dim rst As ADODB.Recordset
    Dim curTable As String
    Dim newTable As String
    Dim counter As Integer

    Set conn = New ADODB.Connection
    conn.Open "Provider=Microsoft.Jet.OLEDB.4.0;" _
```

```
          & "Data Source=" & CurrentProject.Path & _
          "\Northwind.mdb"

      Set rst = conn.OpenSchema(adSchemaColumns)
      curTable = ""
      newTable = ""
      counter = 1
      Do Until rst.EOF
          curTable = rst!table_Name
          If (curTable <> newTable) Then
              newTable = rst!table_Name
              Debug.Print "Table: " & rst!table_Name
              counter = 1
          End If
          Debug.Print "Field" & counter & ": " & rst!Column_Name
          counter = counter + 1
          rst.MoveNext
      Loop
      rst.Close
      conn.Close
      Set rst = Nothing
      Set conn = Nothing
  End Sub
```

3. Choose **Run | Run Sub/UserForm** to execute the procedure.

Listing Data Types

The ListDataTypes procedure in Hands-On 11-15 uses the adSchemaProvider-Types parameter of the ADO Connection object's OpenSchema method to list the data types supported by the Microsoft Jet OLE DB 4.0 provider.

◎ Hands-On 11-15: Listing Data Types

1. In the Visual Basic Editor window, choose **Insert | Module**.

2. In the module's Code window, type the **ListDataTypes** procedure shown below, or copy the procedure code from **C:\Acc07_HandsOn\Chap11.txt**.

```
Sub ListDataTypes()
    Dim conn As ADODB.Connection
    Dim rst As ADODB.Recordset

    Set conn=New ADODB.Connection
    conn.Open "Provider=Microsoft.Jet.OLEDB.4.0;" _
        & "Data Source=" & CurrentProject.Path & _
        "\Northwind.mdb"
    Set rst=conn.OpenSchema(adSchemaProviderTypes)
    Do Until rst.EOF
        Debug.Print rst!Type_Name & vbTab _
            & "Size: " & rst!Column_Size
        rst.MoveNext
    Loop
```

```
rst.Close
conn.Close
Set rst = Nothing
Set conn = Nothing
End Sub
```

3. Choose **Run | Run Sub/UserForm** to execute the procedure.

Changing the AutoNumber

When you create a table in a Microsoft Office Access 2007 database, you can assign an AutoNumber data type to a primary key field manually using the Access user interface. The AutoNumber is a unique sequential number (incremented by 1) or a random number assigned by Microsoft Access whenever a new record is added to a table. You can set the start and step value of auto-increment fields programmatically by using Jet 4.0 SQL statements (see Chapter 19 for more information).

The procedure in Hands-On 11-16 opens the ADO Recordset object based on the Shippers table located in the Northwind database, retrieves the last used AutoNumber value, and determines the current step (increment) value in effect.

◉ Hands-On 11-16: Changing the Value of an AutoNumber

1. In the Visual Basic Editor window, choose **Insert | Module**.

2. In the module's Code window, type the **ChangeAutoNumber** procedure shown below, or copy the procedure code from **C:\Acc07_HandsOn\ Chap11.txt**.

```
Sub ChangeAutoNumber()
    Dim conn As ADODB.Connection
    Dim rst As ADODB.Recordset
    Dim strSQL As String
    Dim beginNum As Integer
    Dim stepNum As Integer

    Set conn = New ADODB.Connection
    conn.Open "Provider = Microsoft.Jet.OLEDB.4.0;" & _
        "Data Source=" & CurrentProject.Path & _
        "\Northwind.mdb"

    Set rst = New ADODB.Recordset
    With rst
        .CursorType = adOpenKeyset
        .LockType = adLockReadOnly
        .Open "Shippers", conn
        .MoveLast
    End With
    beginNum = rst(0)
    rst.MovePrevious
    stepNum = beginNum - rst(0)
```

```
    MsgBox "Last Auto Number Value = " & beginNum & vbCr & _
        "Current Step Value = " & stepNum, vbInformation, _
        "AutoNumber"

    rst.Close
    conn.Close
    Set conn = Nothing
End Sub
```

3. Choose **Run | Run Sub/UserForm** to execute the procedure.

Chapter Summary

This chapter has shown you how to programmatically create Microsoft Access tables by using ADO and DAO objects. You learned how to add fields to your tables and define field data types. You found out how to list both tables and fields, and investigate their properties. In addition to creating new tables from scratch, you discovered how to work with linked tables. You also learned how to copy and delete tables.

The next chapter will demonstrate how to create indexes and set up table relationships from your VBA procedures.

Chapter 12

Setting Up Primary Keys, Indexes, and Table Relationships

After defining the fields for your tables, take the time to define primary keys, indexes, and relationships between tables. This chapter focuses on the DAO and ADOX objects that are designed to work with these features.

Creating a Primary Key Index

Indexes determine the order of records accessed from database tables and whether or not duplicate records are accepted. While indexes can speed up access to specific records in large tables, too many indexes can also slow down updates to the database. Each table in your database should include a field (or set of fields) that uniquely identifies each individual record in a table. Such a field or set of fields is called a *primary key*. A primary key is an index with its Unique and Primary properties set to True. There can be only one primary key per table.

In ADO, indexes are created using the Key object from the ADOX library. The Type property of the Key object allows you to determine whether the key is primary, foreign, or unique. For example, to create a primary key, set the Key object's Type property to adKeyPrimary.

The procedure in Hands-On 12-1 demonstrates how to add a primary key to the table called tblFilters.

⊚ Hands-On 12-1: Creating a Primary Key (ADO)

1. Start Microsoft Office Access 2007 and create a new Microsoft Office Access 2007 database named **Chap12.accdb** in your **C:\Acc07_ ByExample** folder.

2. In the Access window, press **Alt+F11** to switch to the Visual Basic Editor window.

3. In the Visual Basic Editor window, choose **Insert | Module**.

4. In the module's Code window, type the **Create_PrimaryKey** procedure shown below, or copy the procedure code from **C:\Acc07_HandsOn\ Chap12.txt**.

```vba
' make sure to set up a reference to
' the Microsoft ActiveX Data Objects 2.8 Library
' and ADO Ext. 2.8 for DDL and Security

Sub Create_PrimaryKey()
    Dim cat As ADOX.Catalog
    Dim tbl As ADOX.Table
    Dim pKey As ADOX.Key

    On Error GoTo ErrorHandler

    Set cat = New ADOX.Catalog
    cat.ActiveConnection = CurrentProject.Connection

    Set tbl = New ADOX.Table
    tbl.Name = "tblFilters"

    cat.Tables.Append tbl

    With tbl.Columns
        .Append "ID", adVarWChar, 10
        .Append "Description", adVarWChar, 255
        .Append "Type", adInteger
    End With

SetKey:
    Set pKey = New ADOX.Key
    With pKey
        .Name = "PrimaryKey"
        .Type = adKeyPrimary
    End With

    pKey.Columns.Append "ID"
    tbl.Keys.Append pKey

    Set cat = Nothing
    Exit Sub

ErrorHandler:
    If Err.Number = -2147217856 Then
        MsgBox "The " & tblName & " is open.", _
            vbCritical, "Please close the table"
    ElseIf Err.Number = -2147217857 Then
        MsgBox Err.Description
        Set tbl = cat.Tables(tbl.Name)
        Resume SetKey
    ElseIf Err.Number = -2147217767 Then
        tbl.Keys.Delete pKey.Name
        Resume
    Else
        MsgBox Err.Number & ": " & Err.Description
```

```
    End If
End Sub
```

5. Choose **Run | Run Sub/UserForm** to execute the procedure.

   The Create_PrimaryKey procedure begins by creating a table named tblFilters in the currently open database and proceeds to set the primary key index on the ID field. If the tblFilters table already exists, the error handler code displays the error message and sets an object variable (tbl) to point to this table. The Resume SetKey statement refers the procedure execution to the label SetKey. The code that follows that label defines the primary key using the Name and Type properties of the Key object. Next, the procedure appends the ID column to the Columns collection of the Key object and the Key object itself is appended to the Keys collection of the table. Because errors could occur if a table is open or it already contains the primary key, the error handler is included to ensure that the procedure runs as expected.

6. Run the above procedure again using step mode (press **F8**).

In DAO, indexes are created using the CreateIndex method for a TableDef object. The following statement creates an index named PrimaryKey:

```
Set idx = tdf.CreateIndex("PrimaryKey")
```

To ensure that the correct type of index is created, you need to set index properties. For example, the Primary property of an index indicates that the index fields constitute the primary key for the table:

```
idx.Primary = True
```

Use the Unique property to specify whether or not the values in an index must be unique:

```
idx.Unique = True
```

The Required property indicates whether the index can accept Null values. When you set this property to True, nulls will not be accepted:

```
idx.Required = True
```

Use the IgnoreNulls property to determine whether a record with a Null value in the index fields should be included in the index:

```
idx.IgnoreNulls = False
```

To actually index a table, you must use the CreateField method on the Index object to create a Field object for each field to be included in the index:

```
Set fld = idx.CreateField("AgentID", dbText)
```

Once the Field object is created, you need to append it to the Fields collection:

```
idx.Fields.Append fld
```

The last step in index creation is appending the Index object to the Indexes collection:

```
tdf.Indexes.Append idx
```

The procedure in Hands-On 12-2 uses DAO to create a primary key index in the Agents table.

Hands-On 12-2: Creating a Primary Key (DAO)

The procedure in this hands-on uses the Agents table in the Chap11.accdb database that you created in Chapter 11.

1. In the Visual Basic Editor window, choose **Insert | Module**.
2. In the module's Code window, type the **Create_PrimaryKeyDAO** procedure shown below, or copy the procedure code from **C:\Acc07_HandsOn\ Chap12.txt**.

```
Sub Create_PrimaryKeyDAO()
    Dim db As DAO.Database
    Dim tdf As DAO.TableDef
    Dim fld As DAO.Field
    Dim idx As DAO.Index

    Set db = OpenDatabase("C:\Acc07_ByExample\Chap11.accdb")
    Set tdf = db.TableDefs("Agents")

    ' create a Primary Key
    Set idx = tdf.CreateIndex("PrimaryKey")
    idx.Primary = True
    idx.Required = True
    idx.IgnoreNulls = False
    Set fld = idx.CreateField("AgentID", dbText)
    idx.Fields.Append fld

    ' add the index to the Indexes collection in the Agents table
    tdf.Indexes.Append idx
    db.Close
    Set db = Nothing
End Sub
```

3. Choose **Run | Run Sub/UserForm** to execute the procedure.

The result of running the Create_PrimaryKeyDAO procedure is shown in Figure 12-1.

Figure 12-1: Indexes window after running the procedure in Hands-On 12-2.

Creating a Single-Field Index

In ADO, you can add an index to a table by using the ADOX Index object. Before creating an index, make sure the table is not open and that it does not already contain an index with the same name.

To define an index, perform the following:

- Append one or more columns to the index by using the Append method.

- Set the Name property of the Index object and define other index properties, if necessary.

- Use the Append method to add the Index object to the table's Indexes collection.

You can use the Unique property of the Index object to specify whether the index keys must be unique. The default value of the Unique property is False. Another property, IndexNulls, lets you specify whether Null values are allowed in the index. This property can have one of the constants shown in Table 12-1.

Table 12-1: Intrinsic constants for the IndexNulls property of the ADOX Index object

Constant Name	Description
adIndexNullsAllow	You can create an index if there is a Null value in the index field (an error will not occur).
adIndexNullsDisallow (This is the default value)	You cannot create an index if there is a Null in the index for the column (an error will occur).
adIndexNullsIgnore	You can create an index if there is a Null in the index field (an error will not occur). The Ignore Nulls property in the Indexes window in the user interface will be set to Yes.
adIndexNullsIgnoreAny (This value is not supported by the Microsoft Jet Provider)	You can create an index if there is a Null value in the index field. The Ignore Nulls property in the Indexes window in the user interface will be set to No.

The Add_SingleFieldIndex procedure in Hands-On 12-3 demonstrates how to add a single-field index called idxDescription to the table tblFilters.

⊙ Hands-On 12-3: Adding a Single-Field Index to an Existing Table (ADO)

This procedure uses the tblFilters table created in Hands-On 12-1.

1. In the Visual Basic Editor window, choose **Insert | Module**.

2. In the module's Code window, type the **Add_SingleFieldIndex** procedure shown below, or copy the procedure code from **C:\Acc07_HandsOn\ Chap12.txt**.

```
Sub Add_SingleFieldIndex()
    Dim cat As New ADOX.Catalog
    Dim myTbl As New ADOX.Table
    Dim myIdx As New ADOX.Index

    On Error GoTo ErrorHandler
```

```
cat.ActiveConnection = CurrentProject.Connection
Set myTbl = cat.Tables("tblFilters")

With myIdx
    .Name = "idxDescription"
    .Unique = False
    .IndexNulls = adIndexNullsIgnore
    .Columns.Append "Description"
    .Columns(0).SortOrder = adSortAscending
End With
myTbl.Indexes.Append myIdx

Set cat = Nothing
Exit Sub

ErrorHandler:
    If Err.Number = -2147217856 Then
        MsgBox "The 'tblFilters' cannot be open.", vbCritical, _
            "Close the table"
    ElseIf Err.Number = -2147217868 Then
        myTbl.Indexes.Delete myIdx.Name
        Resume 0
    Else
        MsgBox Err.Number & ": " & Err.Description
    End If
End Sub
```

3. Choose **Run | Run Sub/UserForm** to execute the procedure.

After setting the index properties, the Description column is appended to the index, and the index sort order is set to the default (adSortAscending). To set the index field's sort order to descending, use the adSortDescending constant. Next, the index is appended to the Indexes collection of the Table object.

Adding a Multiple-Field Index to a Table

The procedure in Hands-On 12-3 demonstrated adding a single-field index to an existing table by using the ADOX Index object. The procedure in the next hands-on exercise shows how to use DAO to add a multiple-field index to the Employees table in the Northwind database.

⊚ Hands-On 12-4: Adding a Multiple-Field Index to an Existing Table (DAO)

1. In the Visual Basic Editor window, choose **Insert | Module**.

2. In the module's Code window, type the **Add_MultiFieldIndex** procedure shown below, or copy the procedure code from **C:\Acc07_HandsOn\ Chap12.txt**.

```
Sub Add_MultiFieldIndex()
    Dim db As DAO.Database
    Dim tdf As DAO.TableDef
    Dim fld As DAO.Field
```

Access VBA Programming with DAO and ADO

```
    Dim idx As DAO.Index

    Set db = OpenDatabase("C:\Acc07_ByExample\Northwind.mdb")
    Set tdf = db.TableDefs("Employees")

    Set idx = tdf.CreateIndex("Location")
    Set fld = idx.CreateField("City", dbText)
    idx.Fields.Append fld

    Set fld = idx.CreateField("Region", dbText)
    idx.Fields.Append fld
    tdf.Indexes.Append idx

    MsgBox "New index (Location) was created."
    db.Close
    Set db = Nothing
End Sub
```

3. Choose **Run | Run Sub/UserForm** to execute the procedure.

The Add_MultiFieldIndex procedure creates a two-field index in the Employees table. To create an index, use the CreateIndex method on a TableDef object. Next, use the CreateField method on the Index object to create the first field to be included in the index, and then append this field to the Fields collection. Repeat the same two steps for the second field you want to include in the index. It is important to remember that the order in which the fields are appended has an effect on the index order. If you open the Indexes window in the Employees table of the Northwind database after running the above procedure, you should see the Location index consisting of two fields, as depicted in Figure 12-2.

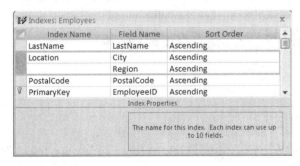

Figure 12-2: The Location index was created by running the procedure in Hands-On 12-4.

Listing Indexes in a Table

The ADO Indexes collection contains all Index objects of a table. You can retrieve all the index names from the Indexes collection. The procedure in the next hands-on exercise demonstrates how to list the names of indexes available in the Northwind database's Employees table in the Immediate window.

⊚ Hands-On 12-5: Listing Indexes in a Table (ADO)

1. In the Visual Basic Editor window, choose **Insert | Module**.

2. In the module's Code window, type the **List_Indexes** procedure shown below, or copy the procedure code from **C:\Acc07_HandsOn\Chap12.txt**.

```
Sub List_Indexes()
    Dim conn As New ADODB.Connection
    Dim cat As New ADOX.Catalog
    Dim tbl As New ADOX.Table
    Dim idx As New ADOX.Index

    With conn
        .Provider = "Microsoft.Jet.OLEDB.4.0"
        .Open "Data Source=" & CurrentProject.Path & _
            "\Northwind.mdb"
    End With
    cat.ActiveConnection = conn
    Set tbl = cat.Tables("Employees")

    For Each idx In tbl.Indexes
        Debug.Print idx.Name
    Next idx

    conn.Close
    Set conn = Nothing
    MsgBox "Indexes are listed in the Immediate window."
End Sub
```

3. Choose **Run | Run Sub/UserForm** to execute the procedure.

In DAO, you can use the For Each…Next VBA looping structure to retrieve the names of indexes from the Indexes collection of the TableDef object as illustrated in the following procedure:

```
Sub List_IndexesDAO()
    Dim db As DAO.Database
    Dim tdf As DAO.TableDef
    Dim idx As DAO.Index

    Set db = CurrentDb
    Set tdf = db.TableDefs("tblFilters")

    For Each idx In tdf.Indexes
        Debug.Print idx.Name
    Next
    ' show Immediate window
    SendKeys "^g"
    Set db = Nothing
End Sub
```

Deleting Table Indexes

Although you can delete unwanted or obsolete indexes from the Indexes window in the Microsoft Office Access 2007 user interface, it is much faster to remove them programmatically. The procedure in Hands-On 12-6 illustrates how to delete all but the primary key index from the Employees table located in the Northwind database.

⊚ Hands-On 12-6: Deleting Indexes from a Table (ADO)

The procedure in this hands-on exercise will delete all but the primary key index from the Employees table in the Northwind database. It is recommended that you prepare a backup copy of the original Northwind.mdb database prior to running this code.

1. In the Visual Basic Editor window, choose **Insert | Module**.

2. In the module's Code window, type the **Delete_Indexes** procedure shown below, or copy the procedure code from **C:\Acc07_HandsOn\Chap12.txt**.

```
Sub Delete_Indexes()
    ' This procedure deletes all but the primary key index
    ' from the Employees table in the Northwind database.
    ' Prior to running this procedure make a backup copy of
    ' the original Northwind.mdb database.

    Dim conn As New ADODB.Connection
    Dim cat As New ADOX.Catalog
    Dim tbl As New ADOX.Table
    Dim idx As New ADOX.Index
    Dim count As Integer

    With conn
        .Provider = "Microsoft.Jet.OLEDB.4.0"
        .Open "Data Source=" & CurrentProject.Path & _
            "\Northwind.mdb"
    End With

    cat.ActiveConnection = conn
Setup:
    Set tbl = cat.Tables("Employees")

    Debug.Print tbl.Indexes.count
    For Each idx In tbl.Indexes
        If idx.PrimaryKey <> True Then
            tbl.Indexes.Delete (idx.Name)
            GoTo Setup
        End If
    Next idx

    conn.Close
    Set conn = Nothing
    MsgBox "All Indexes but Primary Key were deleted."
End Sub
```

3. Choose **Run | Run Sub/UserForm** to execute the procedure.

Notice that each time you delete an index from the table's Indexes collection you must set the reference to the table because current settings are lost when an index is deleted. Hence, the GoTo Setup statement sends Visual Basic to the Setup label to get the new reference to the Table object.

Creating Table Relationships

In ADO, to establish a one-to-many relationship between tables, perform the following steps:

1. Use the ADOX Key object to create a foreign key and set the Type property of the Key object to adKeyForeign. A *foreign key* consists of one or more fields in a foreign table that uniquely identify all rows in a primary table.

2. Use the RelatedTable property to specify the name of the related table.

3. Use the Append method to add appropriate columns in the foreign table to the foreign key. A foreign table is usually located on the "many" side of a one-to-many relationship and provides a foreign key to another table in a database.

4. Set the RelatedColumn property to the name of the corresponding column in the primary table.

5. Use the Append method to add the foreign key to the Keys collection of the table containing the primary key.

The procedure in Hands-On 12-7 illustrates how to create a one-to-many relationship between two tables: Titles and Publishers.

Hands-On 12-7: Creating a One-to-Many Relationship

1. In the current database (Chap12.accdb), create the Titles and Publishers tables and add the fields as shown below:

Table Name	Field Name	Data Type	Size
Titles	TitleID	Text	8
Titles	PubID	Text	4
Titles	Title	Text	100
Titles	Price	Currency	
Publishers	PubID	Text	4
Publishers	PubName	Text	40
Publishers	City	Text	25
Publishers	Country	Text	25

2. Make **TitleID** the primary key for Titles and **PubID** the primary key for the Publishers table.

3. In the Visual Basic Editor window, choose **Insert | Module**.

4. In the module's Code window, type the **CreateTblRelation** procedure shown below, or copy the procedure code from **C:\Acc07_HandsOn\ Chap12.txt**.

```
Sub CreateTblRelation()
    Dim cat As New ADOX.Catalog
    Dim fKey As New ADOX.Key

    On Error GoTo ErrorHandle

    cat.ActiveConnection = CurrentProject.Connection

    With fKey
        .Name = "fkPubID"
        .Type = adKeyForeign
        .RelatedTable = "Publishers"
        .Columns.Append "PubID"
        .Columns("PubID").RelatedColumn = "PubID"
    End With
    cat.Tables("Titles").Keys.Append fKey
    MsgBox "Relationship was created."

    Set cat = Nothing
    Exit Sub

ErrorHandle:
    cat.Tables("Titles").Keys.Delete "fkPubID"
    Resume
End Sub
```

5. Choose **Run | Run Sub/UserForm** to execute the procedure.

You can view the relationship between the Publishers and Titles tables that was created by the above procedure in the Relationships window. To activate this window, switch to the Access window and choose Database Tools | Relationships. You should see the Publishers and Titles tables in the Relationships window linked together with a one-to-many relationship (see Figure 12-3).

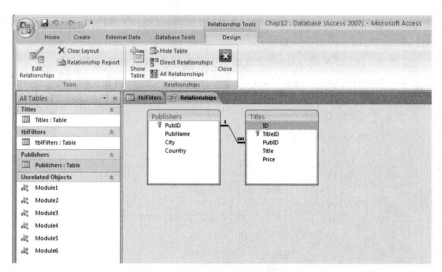

Figure 12-3: Table relationships can be created programmatically by accessing objects in the ADOX library (see the code in the CreateTblRelation procedure in Hands-On 12-7).

Chapter Summary

In this short chapter you acquired programming skills that enable you to create keys (primary keys and indexes) in Microsoft Access tables. You also learned how to establish a one-to-many relationship between tables.

In the next chapter, you will learn how to find and read database records.

Chapter 13

Finding and Reading Records

In order to work with data, you need to learn how to use the Recordset object. The *Recordset object* represents a set of records in a table, or a set of records returned by executing a stored query or an SQL statement. Each column of a Recordset represents a field, and each row represents a record. The Recordset is a temporary object and is not saved in the database. All Recordset objects cease to exist after the procedure ends. All open Recordset objects are contained in the Recordsets collection. Creating and using the Recordset objects depends on the type of the object library (DAO/ADO) that you've selected for your programming task. In this chapter, you will learn various methods of opening the Recordset object. You will also find out how to navigate in the Recordset, and how to find, filter, read, and count the records. Both DAO and ADO Recordsets will be covered.

Introduction to DAO Recordsets

In DAO there are five types of Recordset objects: Table-type, Dynaset-type, Snapshot-type, Forward-only-type, and Dynamic-type. Each of these recordsets offers a different functionality (see Table 13-1). You create a Recordset object using the OpenRecordset method. The type of the Recordset is specified by the *type* argument of the OpenRecordset method. If the Recordset's type is not specified, DAO will attempt to create a Table-type Recordset. If this type isn't available, attempts are made to create a Dynaset, Snapshot, or Forward-only-type Recordset object.

Table 13-1: Types of DAO Recordsets

Recordset Type	Description
Table-type	Used to access records in a table stored in a Microsoft Access database. You can retrieve, add, update, and delete records in a single table.
Dynaset-type	Used to retrieve, add, update, and delete records from one or more tables in a database as well as any table that is linked to the Access database.
Snapshot-type	Used to access records from a local table stored in a Microsoft Access database as well as any linked table or a query. Snapshot recordsets contain a copy of the records in RAM (random access memory) and provide no direct access to the underlying data. They are used for reading data only — you can't use them to add, update, or delete records.

Recordset Type	Description
Forward-only-type	This is a special type of a Snapshot recordset that only allows you to scroll forward through the records. It provides the fastest access when you want to make a single pass through the data.
Dynamic-type	This recordset is generated by a query based on one or more tables. It allows you to add, change, or delete records from a row-returning query. In addition, it includes the records that other users may have added, modified, or deleted.

In order to find and read database records, you must understand how to navigate through the recordset. When you open a Recordset object, the first record is the current record. All recordsets have a current record.

■ To move to subsequent records, use the MoveNext method.

■ To move to the previous record, use the MovePrevious method.

■ The MoveFirst and MoveLast methods move the cursor to the first and last records.

■ If you call the MoveNext method when the cursor is already pointing to the last record, the cursor will move off the last record to the area known as end of file (EOF), and the EOF property will be set to True.

■ If you call the MoveNext method when the EOF property is True, an error is generated because you cannot move past the end of the file. Similarly, by calling the MovePrevious method when the cursor is pointing to the first record, you will move the cursor to the area known as beginning of file (BOF). This will set the BOF property to True. When the BOF property is True and you call the MovePrevious method, an error will be generated.

When navigating through a recordset you may want to mark a specific record in order to return to it at a later time. You can use the Bookmark property to obtain a unique identification for a specific record.

The Recordset object has numerous properties and methods. We will discuss only those properties and methods that are required for performing a specific task, as demonstrated in the example procedures.

Opening Various Types of Recordsets

Use the OpenRecordset method to create or open a Recordset. For example, to open a Table-type recordset on a table named tblClients, use the following statement:

```
Set rst = CurrentDb.OpenRecordset("tblClients", dbOpenTable)
```

Notice that the second argument in the OpenRecordset method specifies the type of recordset. In this position, the RecordsetTypeEnum constants (see Table 13-2) can be used.

Table 13-2: Constants used in specifying the type of a DAO Recordset object

Type Constant	Value	Description
dbOpenTable	1	Opens a Table-type recordset
dbOpenDynaset	2	Opens a Dynaset-type recordset
dbOpenSnapshot	4	Opens a Snapshot-type recordset
dbOpenForwardOnly	8	Opens a Forward-only-type recordset
dbOpenDynamic	16	Opens a Dynamic-type recordset

In the above example, if you don't specify a recordset type, a Table-type recordset will be created based on tblClients. A Table-type recordset represents the records in a single table in a database.

The OpenRecordset method opens a new Recordset object for reading, adding, updating, or deleting records from a database. The OpenRecordset method can also be performed on a query. Note that a query can only be opened as a Dynaset or Snapshot Recordset object. For example, to open a Recordset based on a query, you could use the following statements:

```
Dim db As DAO.Database
Dim rst As DAO.Recordset
Set db = CurrentDb()
Set rst = db.OpenRecordset("qryMyQuery", dbOpenSnapshot)
```

The procedure in Hands-On 13-1 demonstrates how to open various types of DAO Recordsets on the Customers table in the Northwind 2007.accdb database and return the total number of records.

◎ Hands-On 13-1: Opening Table-, Dynaset-, and Snapshot-type Recordsets (DAO)

1. Start Microsoft Office Access 2007 and create a new Microsoft Office Access 2007 database named **Chap13.accdb** in your **C:\Acc07_By-Example** folder.

2. In the Access window, press **Alt+F11** to switch to the Visual Basic Editor window.

3. In the Visual Basic Editor window, choose **Insert | Module**.

4. In the module's Code window, type the **ThreeRecordsetsDAO** procedure shown below, or copy the procedure code from **C:\Acc07_HandsOn\ Chap13.txt**.

```
Sub ThreeRecordsetsDAO()
    Dim db As DAO.Database
    Dim tblRst As DAO.Recordset
    Dim dynaRst As DAO.Recordset
    Dim snapRst As DAO.Recordset

    Set db = OpenDatabase("C:\Acc07_ByExample\Northwind 2007.accdb")
```

```
Set tblRst = db.OpenRecordset("Customers", dbOpenTable)
Debug.Print "# of records in a table: " & tblRst.RecordCount

Set dynaRst = db.OpenRecordset("Customers", dbOpenDynaset)
Debug.Print "# of records in a Dynaset: " & dynaRst.RecordCount
dynaRst.MoveLast
Debug.Print "# of records in a Dynaset: " & dynaRst.RecordCount

Set snapRst = db.OpenRecordset("Customers", dbOpenSnapshot)
Debug.Print "# of records in a Snapshot: " & snapRst.RecordCount
snapRst.MoveLast
Debug.Print "# of records in a Snapshot: " & snapRst.RecordCount

tblRst.Close
dynaRst.Close
snapRst.Close
db.Close
Set db = Nothing

SendKeys "^g"
End Sub
```

5. Choose **Run | Run Sub/UserForm** to execute the procedure.

Notice that to get the correct count of records in Dynaset and Snapshot recordsets, you need to invoke the MoveLast method to access all the records. Counting records in covered in more detail in the next section.

The last statement in this procedure (SendKeys "^g") activates the Immediate window so that you can see the results for yourself.

Opening a Snapshot and Counting Records

When you want to search tables or queries, you will get the fastest results by opening a Snapshot-type recordset. A snapshot is simply a non-updatable set of records that contain fields from one or more tables or queries. Snapshot-type Recordset objects can be used only for retrieving data. Use the OpenRecordset method to create or open a recordset. For example, to open a Snapshot-type recordset on a table named Customers, use the following statement:

```
Set rst = CurrentDb.OpenRecordset("Customers", dbOpenSnapshot)
```

At times, you may need to know where you are in a recordset. There are two properties that can be used to determine your position in the recordset:

- The AbsolutePosition property allows you to position the current record pointer to a specific record based on its ordinal position in a Dynaset- or Snapshot-type Recordset object. This property allows determining the current record number. Zero (0) refers to the first record in the Recordset object. If there is no current record, the AbsolutePosition property returns −1. However, because the position of a record changes when preceding records are deleted, you should rely more on bookmarks to position the current record. The AbsolutePosition property can be used only with Dynasets and Snapshots. Because the AbsolutePosition property value is zero-based, 1 is added to the AbsolutePosition value to display current record information:

```
MsgBox "Current record: " & rst.AbsolutePosition + 1
```

■ The PercentPosition property shows the current position relative to the number of records that have been accessed. Both AbsolutePosition and PercentPosition are not accurate until you move to the last record.

The procedure in Hands-On 13-2 attempts to get the total number of records in the Snapshot-type recordset by using the RecordCount property.

◉ Hands-On 13-2: Opening a Snapshot-type Recordset and Retrieving the Number of Records (DAO)

1. In the Visual Basic Editor window, choose **Insert | Module**.
2. In the module's Code window, type the **OpenSnapshot** procedure shown below, or copy the procedure code from **C:\Acc07_HandsOn\Chap13.txt**.

```
Sub OpenSnapshot()
    Dim db As DAO.Database
    Dim rst As DAO.Recordset

    Set db = OpenDatabase("C:\Acc07_ByExample\Northwind 2007.accdb")
    Set rst = db.OpenRecordset("Customers", dbOpenSnapshot)

    MsgBox "Current record: " & rst.AbsolutePosition + 1
    MsgBox "Number of records: " & rst.RecordCount
    rst.MoveLast
    MsgBox "Current record: " & rst.AbsolutePosition + 1
    MsgBox "Number of records: " & rst.RecordCount
    rst.Close
    Set rst = Nothing
    db.Close
    Set db = Nothing
End Sub
```

3. Choose **Run | Run Sub/UserForm** to execute the procedure.

The RecordCount property of the Recordset object returns the number of records that have been accessed.

Zero (0) is returned if there are no records in the recordset, and 1 is returned if there are records in the recordset. If you open a Table-type recordset and check the RecordCount property, it will return the total number of records in a table. However, if you open a Dynaset- or Snapshot-type recordset, the RecordCount property will return 1, indicating that the recordset contains records. To find out the total number of records in a Dynaset or Snapshot, call the MoveLast method prior to retrieving the RecordCount property value. The record count becomes accurate after you've visited all the records in the recordset.

Retrieving the Contents of a Specific Field in a Table

To retrieve the contents of any field, start by creating a recordset based on the desired table or query, then loop through the recordset, printing the field's contents for each record to the Immediate window.

The procedure in Hands-On 13-3 generates a listing of all clients in the Customers table. Customer names are retrieved starting from the last record (see the MoveLast method). The BOF property of the Recordset object determines when the beginning of your recordset is reached.

⊙ Hands-On 13-3: Retrieving Field Values (DAO)

1. In the Visual Basic Editor window, choose **Insert | Module**.

2. In the module's Code window, type the **ReadFromEnd** procedure shown below, or copy procedure code from **C:\Acc07_HandsOn\Chap13.txt**.

```
Sub ReadFromEnd()
    Dim db As DAO.Database
    Dim rst As DAO.Recordset

    Set db = OpenDatabase("C:\Acc07_ByExample\Northwind 2007.accdb")
    Set rst = db.OpenRecordset("Customers", dbOpenTable)
    rst.MoveLast

    Do Until rst.BOF
        Debug.Print rst!Company
        rst.MovePrevious
    Loop

    SendKeys "^g"
    rst.Close
    Set rst = Nothing
    db.Close
    Set db = Nothing
End Sub
```

3. Choose **Run | Run Sub/UserForm** to execute the procedure.

Moving between Records in a Table

All recordsets have a current position and a current record. The current record is usually the record at the current position. However, the current position can be before the first record and after the last record. You can use one of the Move methods in Table 13-3 to change the current position. The procedure in Hands-On 13-4 demonstrates how to move between records in the Employees table using the Table-type or Dynaset-type recordset.

Table 13-3: Move methods used with DAO Recordsets

MoveFirst	Moves to the first record.
MoveLast	Moves to the last record.
MoveNext	Moves to the next record.
MovePrevious	Moves to the previous record.
Move n	Moves forward or backward n positions.

Hands-On 13-4: Moving between Records in a Table (DAO)

1. In the Visual Basic Editor window, choose **Insert | Module**.

2. In the module's Code window, type the **NavigateRecords** procedure shown below, or copy the procedure code from **C:\Acc07_HandsOn\ Chap13.txt**.

```
Sub NavigateRecords()
    Dim db As DAO.Database
    Dim tblRst As DAO.Recordset
    Dim dynaRst As DAO.Recordset

    Set db = OpenDatabase("C:\Acc07_ByExample\Northwind 2007.accdb")
    Set tblRst = db.OpenRecordset("Employees")
    tblRst.MoveFirst

    Do While Not tblRst.EOF
        Debug.Print "Employee: " & tblRst![Last Name]
        tblRst.MoveNext
    Loop

    Set dynaRst = db.OpenRecordset("Employees", dbOpenDynaset)
    dynaRst.MoveFirst

    Do While Not dynaRst.EOF
        Debug.Print "Hello " & dynaRst![Last Name]
        dynaRst.MoveNext
    Loop

    tblRst.Close
    dynaRst.Close

    Set tblRst = Nothing
    Set dynaRst = Nothing
    db.Close
    Set db = Nothing
    SendKeys "^g"
End Sub
```

3. Choose **Run | Run Sub/UserForm** to execute the procedure.

Finding Records in a Table-Type Recordset

While the Move methods are convenient for looping through records in a Recordset object, you should use Seek or Find methods to look for specific records. When you know exactly which record you want to find in a

Table-type recordset and the field you are searching is indexed, the quickest way to find that record is by using the Seek method. One thing to remember with the Seek method is that the table must contain an index. The Index property must be set before the Seek method can be used. If you try to use the Seek method on a Table-type recordset without first setting the current index, a run-time error will occur. The Seek method searches through the recordset and locates the first matching record. Once the record is found, it is made the current record and the NoMatch property is set to False. If the record is not found, the NoMatch property is set to True and the current record is undefined. Table 13-4 lists comparison operators that you can use with the Seek method.

Table 13-4: Comparison operators used with the Seek method

Operator	Description
"="	Finds the first record whose indexed field is equal to the specified value.
">="	Finds the first record whose indexed field is greater than or equal to the specified value.
">"	Finds the first record whose indexed field is greater than the specified value.
"<="	Finds the first record whose indexed field is less than or equal to the specified value.
"<"	Finds the first record whose indexed field is less than the specified value.

The comparison operator used with the Seek method must be enclosed in quotes. If there are several records that match your criteria, the Seek method returns the first record it finds. The Seek method cannot be used to search for records in a linked table. You must use the Find methods (see the next section) for locating specific records in linked tables, as well as Dynaset-type and Snapshot-type recordsets. The procedure in Hands-On 13-5 searches for an employee whose last name begins with the letter "K".

⊚ Hands-On 13-5: Finding Records in a Table-type Recordset (DAO)

1. In the Visual Basic Editor window, choose **Insert | Module**.

2. In the module's Code window, type the **FindRecordsInTable** procedure shown below, or copy the procedure code from **C:\Acc07_HandsOn\ Chap13.txt**.

```
Sub FindRecordsInTable()
    Dim db As DAO.Database
    Dim tblRst As DAO.Recordset

    Set db = OpenDatabase("C:\Acc07_ByExample\Northwind 2007.accdb")

    Set tblRst = db.OpenRecordset("Employees", dbOpenTable)
    ' find the first employee in the table whose name
    ' begins with the letter "K"

    tblRst.Index = "Last Name"
    tblRst.Seek ">=", "K"
```

```
        If Not tblRst.NoMatch Then
            MsgBox "Found the following employee: " & tblRst![Last Name]
        Else
            MsgBox "There is no employee with such a name."
        End If

        tblRst.Close
        Set tblRst = Nothing
        db.Close
        Set db = Nothing
    End Sub
```

3. Choose **Run | Run Sub/UserForm** to execute the procedure.

Finding Records in Dynasets or Snapshots

Use the Find methods to search for a record in Dynaset-type and Snapshot-type recordsets. The following table lists the available Find methods.

Table 13-5: Find methods in a DAO Recordset

FindFirst	Finds the first matching record in the recordset.
FindNext	Finds the next matching record, starting at the current record.
FindPrevious	Finds the previous matching record, starting at the current record.
FindLast	Finds the last matching record in the recordset.

If a record is not found for the given criteria, the NoMatch property of the Recordset object is set to True. Before searching for records, set a bookmark at the current record. If the search fails, you will be able to use the bookmark to return to the current record; otherwise, you will get the error "No current record." Each record in a Recordset object has a unique bookmark. You can use the bookmark to locate that record. To get the current record's bookmark, you need to move the cursor to that record and assign the value of the Bookmark property of the Recordset object to a Variant variable:

```
Dim mySpot As Variant
mySpot = dynaRst.Bookmark
```

In Hands-On 13-6 the bookmark is set on the first record of a Dynaset-type recordset. The procedure then searches for employees whose name ends with the string "er." The asterisk (*) in the search string is a wildcard character representing any number of letters (*er).

To return to the bookmarked record, set the Bookmark property to the value held by the Variant variable:

```
dynaRst.Bookmark = mySpot
```

While recordsets based on local Microsoft Access tables support bookmarks, non-Access databases may not support them. To determine whether a Recordset object supports bookmarks, you can check the Bookmarkable property. Bookmarks are supported if this property is True.

```
If dynaRst.Bookmarkable Then
  mySpot = dynaRst.Bookmark
End If
```

If the Recordset object does not support bookmarks, an error occurs. You can set as many bookmarks as you wish. Bookmarks can be created for a record other than the current record by moving to the desired record and assigning the value of the Bookmark property to a String variable that identifies that record.

Hands-On 13-6: Finding a Record in a Dynaset-type Recordset (DAO)

1. In the Visual Basic Editor window, choose **Insert | Module**.

2. In the module's Code window, type the **FindRecInDynaset** procedure shown below, or copy the procedure code from **C:\Acc07_HandsOn\ Chap13.txt**.

```
Sub FindRecInDynaset()
    Dim db As DAO.Database
    Dim dynaRst As DAO.Recordset
    Dim mySpot As Variant

    Set db = OpenDatabase("C:\Acc07_ByExample\Northwind 2007.accdb")
    Set dynaRst = db.OpenRecordset("Employees", dbOpenDynaset)

    MsgBox "Current employee: " & dynaRst![Last Name]
    mySpot = dynaRst.Bookmark

    ' find clients whose name contains the string "er"
    dynaRst.FindFirst "[Last Name] Like '*er'"

    Do While Not dynaRst.NoMatch
        Debug.Print dynaRst![Last Name]
        dynaRst.FindNext "[Last Name] Like '*er'"
    Loop

    dynaRst.Bookmark = mySpot
    MsgBox "Back to record: " & dynaRst![Last Name]
    dynaRst.Close

    Set dynaRst = Nothing
    db.Close
    Set db = Nothing
    SendKeys "^g"
End Sub
```

3. Choose **Run | Run Sub/UserForm** to execute the procedure.

The names of all employees that match the search criteria are printed to the Immediate window.

Finding the nth Record in a Snapshot

The procedure in Hands-On 13-7 demonstrates how to locate the nth record in a Snapshot-type recordset.

◉ Hands-On 13-7: Finding the nth Record in a Snapshot-type Recordset (DAO)

1. In the Visual Basic Editor window, choose **Insert | Module**.

2. In the module's Code window, type the **FindNthRecord** procedure shown below, or copy the procedure code from **C:\Acc07_HandsOn\Chap13.txt**.

```
Sub FindNthRecord()
    Dim rst As DAO.Recordset
    Dim fld As DAO.Field
    Dim totalRec As Integer
    Dim nth As String

    Set db = OpenDatabase("C:\Acc07_ByExample\Northwind 2007.accdb")
    Set rst = db.OpenRecordset("Employees", dbOpenSnapshot)
    rst.MoveLast

    totalRec = rst.RecordCount
    rst.MoveFirst
    nth = InputBox("Enter the number of positions to move forward:")

    On Error Resume Next
    If totalRec > nth Then
        rst.Move nth
        For Each fld In rst.Fields
            Debug.Print fld.Name & ": " & fld.Value
        Next fld
    Else
        MsgBox "You must enter a value that is less than " _
            & totalRec & "."
    End If

    rst.Close
    Set rst = Nothing
    db.Close
    Set db = Nothing
End Sub
```

3. Choose **Run | Run Sub/UserForm** to execute the procedure.

Notice that immediately after opening the recordset, the MoveLast method is used to ensure that all records have been visited. The total number of records is then retrieved with the RecordCount property of the Recordset object and stored in the totalRec variable. Next, the MoveFirst method is used to return to the first record and the InputBox method is used to prompt the user for the number of positions to move forward in the recordset. If the user-supplied value is less than the total number of records, the cursor moves to the specified record and the For...Each loop is used to print this record's field names and values to the Immediate window. An attempt to move beyond the end of the recordset will cause an error. Therefore, the procedure displays a message if the user-supplied position to move to is greater than the total number of records.

Introduction to ADO Recordsets

The Recordset object is one of the three most-used ADO objects (the other two are Connection and Command). What you can do with a recordset depends entirely on the built-in capabilities of its OLE DB provider. You can open an ADO Recordset by using the Recordset object's Open method. The information needed to open a recordset can be provided by first setting properties and then calling the Open method, or by using the Open method's parameters like this:

```
rst.Open [Source], [ActiveConnection], [CursorType], [LockType],
    [CursorLocation], [Options]
```

Notice that all the parameters are optional (they appear in square brackets). If you decide that you don't want to pass parameters, then you will need to use a different syntax to open a recordset. For example, examine the following code block:

```
With rst
    .Source = strSQL
    .ActiveConnection = strConnect
    .CursorType = adOpenStatic
    .LockType = adLockOptimistic
    .CursorLocation = adUseClient
    .Open Options := adCmdText
End with
```

The code segment above opens a recordset by first setting properties of the Recordset object, then calling its Open method. Notice that the names of the required Recordset properties are equivalent to the parameter names listed earlier. The values assigned to each property are discussed later. You will become familiar with both methods of opening a recordset as you work with the example procedures that follow.

Let's return to the syntax of the Recordset's Open method, which specifies the parameters. Needless to say, you need to know what each parameter is and how it is used. The Source parameter determines where you want your records to come from. The data source can be an SQL string, a table, a query, a stored procedure or view, a saved file, or a reference to a Command object. Later in this chapter you will learn how to open a recordset based on a table, a query, and an SQL statement.

The ActiveConnection parameter can be an SQL string that specifies the connection string or a reference to a Connection object. This parameter tells where to find the database as well as what security credentials to use.

Before we discuss the next three parameters, you need to know that the ADO Recordsets are controlled by a cursor. The *cursor* determines whether you are permitted to scroll through the recordset backward and forward or forward only, whether you can use it read-only or you can update the data, and whether changes made to the data are visible to other users.

The ADO cursors have three functions specified by the following parameters:

- CursorType
- LockType
- CursorLocation

Before you choose the cursor, you need to think of how your application will use the data. Some cursors yield better performance than others. It's important to determine where the cursor will reside and whether changes made while the cursor is open need to be visible immediately. The following subsection should assist you in choosing the correct cursor.

Cursor Types

The CursorType parameter specifies how the recordset interacts with the data source and what is allowed or not allowed when it comes to data changes or movement within the recordset. This parameter can take one of four constants: adOpenForwardOnly (0), adOpenKeyset (1), adOpenDynamic (2), and adOpenStatic (3).

You can find out what types of cursors are available by using the Object Browser. Before proceeding, make sure that the Chap13.accdb database file you created at the beginning of this chapter has a reference to the ActiveX Data Objects library. Set this reference by switching to the Visual Basic Editor window and choosing Tools | References. Find and select Microsoft ActiveX Data Objects 2.8 Library in the References dialog box and click OK. Next, activate the Object Browser window by pressing F2 or choose View | Object Browser. Select ADODB from the Project/Library drop-down list box and type CursorType in the Search text box, as shown in Figure 13-1.

Figure 13-1: The Object Browser lists four predefined constants you can use to specify the cursor type to be retrieved.

- When the cursor type is dynamic (adOpenDynamic = 2), users are allowed to view changes other users made to the database. The dynamic cursor is not supported by the Jet 4.0 engine in Microsoft Office Access. To use this cursor, you must use other OLE DB providers, such as MSDASQL or SQLOLEDB. Using the dynamic cursor you can move back and forth in the recordset.

- When the cursor type is forward-only (adOpenForwardOnly = 0), additions, changes, and/or deletions made by other users are not visible. This is the default and fastest cursor because it only allows you to scroll forward in the recordset.

- When the cursor type is keyset driven (adOpenKeyset = 1), you can scroll back and forth in the recordset; however, you cannot view records added or deleted by another user. Use the Recordset's Requery method to overcome this limitation.

- When the cursor type is static (adOpenStatic = 3), all the data is retrieved as it was at a point in time. This cursor is desirable when you need to find data or generate a report. You can scroll back and forth within a recordset, but additions, changes, or deletions by other users are not visible. Use this cursor to retrieve an accurate record count.

You must set the CursorType property before opening the recordset with the Open method. Otherwise, Access will create a Forward-only recordset. You may use a constant name or its value in your VBA procedures.

Lock Types

After you choose a cursor type, you need to specify how the ADO should lock the row when you make a change. The LockType parameter specifies whether the recordset is updatable. The default setting for LockType is read-only. The LockType predefined constants are listed in the Object Browser, as shown in Figure 13-2.

Figure 13-2: The Object Browser lists four predefined constants that you can use to specify what type of locking ADO should use when you make a change to the data.

- When the LockType property is batch optimistic (adLockBatchOptimistic = 4), batch updates made to the data are stored locally until the UpdateBatch method is called, during which all pending updates are committed all at once. Until the UpdateBatch method is called, no locks are placed on edited data. Batch optimistic locking eliminates network roundtrips that normally occur with optimistic locking (adLockOptimistic) when users make changes to one record and move to another. With batch optimistic locking, a user can make all the changes to all the records and then submit them as a single operation.

- When the LockType property is optimistic (adLockOptimistic = 3), no locks are placed on the data until you attempt to save a row. Records are locked only when you call the Update method, and the lock is released as soon as the Save operation is completed. Two users are allowed to update a record at the same time. Optimistic locking allows you to work with one row at a time. If you need to make multiple updates, it's better to save them all at once by using batch optimistic locking.

- When the LockType property is pessimistic (adLockPessimistic = 2), all the records are locked as soon as you begin editing a record. The record remains locked until the edit is committed or canceled. This type of lock guarantees that two users will not make changes to the same record. If you use pessimistic locking, ensure that your code does not require any input from the users. You certainly don't want a scenario where a user opens a record and makes a change, then leaves for lunch without saving the record. In that case, the record is locked until the user comes back and saves or discards the edit. In this situation, it is better to use optimistic locking.

- When the LockType property is read-only (adLockReadOnly =1), you will not be able to alter any data. This is the default setting.

Cursor Location

The CursorLocation parameter determines whether ADO or the SQL Server database engine manages the cursor. Cursors use temporary resources to hold the data. These resources can be memory, a disk paging file, temporary disk files, or even temporary storage in the database.

- When a cursor is created and managed by ADO, the recordset is said to be using a *client-side cursor* (adUseClient). With the client-side cursor, all the data is retrieved from the server in one operation and is placed on the client computer. Because all the requested data is available locally, the connection to the database can be closed and reopened only when another set of data is needed. Since the entire result set has been downloaded to the client computer, browsing through the rows is very fast.

- When a cursor is managed by a database engine, the recordset is said to be using a *server-side cursor* (adUseServer). With the server-side cursor, all the data is stored on the server and only the requested data is sent over the network to the user's computer. This type of cursor can provide better performance than the client-side cursor when excessive network traffic is an issue. However, it's important to point out that a server-side cursor consumes server resources for every active client and, because it provides only single-row access to the data, it can be quite slow.

It is recommended that you use the server-side cursor for working with local Access databases, and the client-side cursor when working with remote Access databases or SQL Server databases.

The CursorLocation predefined constants are listed in the Object Browser, as shown in Figure 13-3.

Figure 13-3: The CursorLocation parameter of the Recordset's Open method can be set by using the adUseClient or adUseServer constant.

The Options Parameter

The Options parameter specifies the data source type being used. Similar to the parameters related to cursors, the Options parameter can take one of many values, as shown in Figure 13-4.

Figure 13-4: The Options parameter of the Recordset's Open method is supplied by the constant values listed under the CommandType property of the Command object.

■ When the Options parameter is set to adCmdFile (256), it tells the ADO that the source of the recordset is a path or filename. ADO can open recordsets based on files in different formats.

- When the Options parameter is set to adCmdStoredProc (4), it tells the ADO that the source of the recordset is a stored procedure or parameterized query.

- When the Options parameter is set to adCmdTable (2), it tells the ADO that the source of the recordset is a table or view. The adCmdTable constant will cause the provider to generate an SQL query to return all rows from a table or view by prepending SELECT * FROM in front of the specified table or view name.

- When the Options parameter is set to adCmdTableDirect (512), it tells the ADO that the Source argument should be evaluated as a table name. How does this constant differ from adCmdTable? The adCmdTableDirect constant is used by OLE DB providers that support opening tables directly by name, using an interface called IOpenRowset, instead of an ADO Command object. Since the IOpenRowset method does not need to build and execute a Command object, it results in increased performance and functionality.

- When the Options parameter is set to adCmdText (1), it tells the ADO that you are using an SQL statement to open the recordset.

- When the Options parameter is set to adCmdUnknown (8), it tells the ADO that the command type in the Source argument is unknown. This is the default, which is used if you don't specify any other option. By using the adCmdUnknown constant, or not specifying any constant at all for the Options parameter, you force ADO to make an extra roundtrip to the server to determine the source type. As you would expect, this will decrease your VBA procedure's performance; therefore, you should use adCmdUknown only if you don't know what type of information the Source parameter will contain.

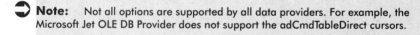

Note: Not all options are supported by all data providers. For example, the Microsoft Jet OLE DB Provider does not support the adCmdTableDirect cursors.

In addition to specifying the type of CommandType in the Options parameter (see Figure 13-4), you can pass additional information in the Options parameter. For example, you can tell ADO how to execute the command by specifying whether ADO should wait while all the records are being retrieved or should continue asynchronously.

Asynchronous Record Fetching

Asynchronous fetching is an ADO feature that allows some records to be downloaded to the client while the remaining records are still being fetched from the database. As soon as the user sees some records, he or she can begin paging through them. The user does not know that only a few records have been returned. As he or she pages through the rows backward and forward, a new connection is made to the server and more records are fetched and passed to the client. Once all records have been returned, paging is very quick because all records are on the client. Asynchronous fetching makes it seem to the user that the data retrieval is pretty fast. The downside is that records cannot be sorted until they have all been downloaded.

Additional Options parameters are listed and described below. Note that only the first three constants (adAsyncExecute, adAsyncFetch, and adAsyncFetchNonBlocking) can be used with the Recordset's Open method. Other constants are used with the Command or Connection object's Execute method.

- adAsyncExecute (16) — This tells ADO to execute the command asynchronously, meaning that all requested rows are retrieved as soon as they are available. Using adAsyncExecute enables the application to perform other tasks while waiting for the cursor to populate.

  Note that the adAsyncExecute constant cannot be used with adCmdTableDirect.

- adAsyncFetch (32) — Using this constant requires that you specify a value greater than 1 for the Recordset's CacheSize property. The CacheSize property is used to determine the number of records ADO will hold in local memory. For example, if the cache size is 100, the provider will retrieve the first 100 records after first opening the Recordset object. The adAsyncFetch constant tells ADO that the rows remaining after the initial quantity specified in the CacheSize property should be retrieved asynchronously.

- adAsyncFetchNonBlocking (64) — This option tells ADO that it should never wait for a row to be fetched. The application will continue execution while records are being continuously extracted from a very large data file. If the requested recordset row has not been retrieved yet, the current row automatically moves to the end of the file (causing the Recordset's EOF property to become True). In other words, the data retrieval process will not block other processes.

  Note that adAsynchFetchNonBlocking has no effect when the adCmdTableDirect option is used to open the recordset. Also, adAsyncFetchNonBlocking is not supported with a Server cursor (adUseServer) when you use the ODBC provider (MSDASQL).

▪ adExecuteNoRecords (128) — This option tells ADO not to expect any records when the command is executed. Use this option for commands that do not return records, such as INSERT, UPDATE, or DELETE. Use the adExecuteNoRecords constant with adCmdText to improve the performance of your application. When this option is specified, ADO does not create a Recordset object and does not set any cursor properties.

Note that adExecuteNoRecords can only be passed as an optional parameter to the Command or Connection object's Execute method and cannot be used when opening a recordset.

▪ adExecuteStream (256) — Indicates that the results of a Command execution should be returned as a stream. The adExecuteStream constant can only be passed as an optional parameter to the Command or Connection object's Execute method and it cannot be used when opening a recordset.

▪ adExecuteRecord (512) — Indicates that the value of the CommandText property is a command or stored procedure that returns a single row as a Record object (a Record object represents one row of data).

▪ adOptionUnspecified (–1) — Indicates that the command is unspecified. This is the default option.

Note that similar to adExecuteNoRecords, adExecuteStream, and adExecuteRecord, this constant can only be passed as an optional parameter to the Command or Connection object's Execute method and cannot be used when opening a recordset.

Opening a Recordset

ADO offers numerous ways of opening a Recordset object. To begin with, you can create ADO Recordsets from scratch without going through any other object. Suppose you want to retrieve all the records from the Employees table. The code you need to write is very simple. Let's try this out in Hands-On 13-8.

◉ Hands-On 13-8: Opening a Recordset (ADO)

1. In the Visual Basic Editor window, choose **Insert | Module**.

2. In the module's Code window, type the **OpenADORst** procedure shown below, or copy the procedure code from **C:\Acc07_HandsOn\Chap13.txt**.

```
' make sure to set up a reference to
' the Microsoft ActiveX Data Objects 2.8 Library

Sub OpenADORst()
    Dim conn As ADODB.Connection
    Dim rst As ADODB.Recordset

    Set conn = New ADODB.Connection
    With conn
        .Provider = "Microsoft.ACE.OLEDB.12.0"
```

```
    .Open "Data Source=" & CurrentProject.Path & _
        "\Northwind 2007.accdb"
End With

Set rst = New ADODB.Recordset
With rst
    .Source = "SELECT * FROM Employees"
    .ActiveConnection = conn
    .Open
    Debug.Print rst.Fields.Count
    .Close
End With

Set rst = Nothing
conn.Close
Set conn = Nothing
End Sub
```

3. Choose **Run | Run Sub/UserForm** to execute the procedure.

In the code example above, we first define and open a connection to the database. Next, we declare a Recordset object and create a new instance of it. The Recordset object's Source property specifies the data you want to retrieve. The source can be a table, query, stored procedure, view, saved file, or Command object. The SQL SELECT statement tells VBA to select all the data from the Employees table. Next, the ActiveConnection property specifies how to connect to the data. We set the ActiveConnection property to the object variable (conn) that holds the connection information. Finally, the Open method retrieves the specified records into the recordset. Before we close the recordset using the Recordset's Close method, we retrieve the number of fields in the open recordset by examining the Recordset's Fields collection, and write the result to the Immediate window.

Opening a Recordset Based on a Table or Query

A recordset can be based on a table, view, SQL statement, or command that returns rows. It can be opened via a Connection or Command object's Execute method or a Recordset's Open method (see the example procedures below).

■ Using the Execute method of the Connection object

```
Sub ConnectAndExec()
    Dim conn As ADODB.Connection
    Dim rst As ADODB.Recordset

    Set conn = New ADODB.Connection
    conn.Open "Provider=Microsoft.Jet.OLEDB.4.0;" & _
        "Data Source=" & CurrentProject.Path & _
        "\Northwind.mdb"
    Set rst = conn.Execute("SELECT * FROM Employees")
    Debug.Print rst.Source
    rst.Close
    Set rst = Nothing
    conn.Close
```

```
    Set conn = Nothing
End Sub
```

➜ **Note:** Once you open the recordset, you can perform the required operation on its data. In this example, we use the Recordset's Source property to write to the Immediate window the SQL command on which the recordset is based. To open the Northwind 2007.accdb database instead of the Northwind.mdb file, change the provider string to Microsoft.ACE.OLEDB.12.0 and the name of the database to Northwind 2007.accdb:

```
conn.Open "Provider=Microsoft.ACE.OLEDB.12.0;" & _
    "Data Source=" & CurrentProject.Path & _
    "\Northwind 2007.accdb"
```

▧ Using the Execute method of the Command object

```
Sub CommandAndExec()
    Dim conn As ADODB.Connection
    Dim cmd As ADODB.Command
    Dim rst As ADODB.Recordset

    Set conn = New ADODB.Connection
    With conn
        .ConnectionString = "Provider=Microsoft.Jet.OLEDB.4.0;" & _
            "Data Source=" & CurrentProject.Path & "\Northwind.mdb"
        .Open
    End With

    Set cmd = New ADODB.Command
    With cmd
        .ActiveConnection = conn
        .CommandText = "SELECT * FROM Customers"
    End With

    Set rst = cmd.Execute

    MsgBox rst.Fields(1).Value

    rst.Close
    Set rst = Nothing
    conn.Close
    Set conn = Nothing
End Sub
```

➜ **Note:** Once you open the recordset, you can perform the required operation on its data. In this example, we display a message with the name of the first customer.

▧ Using the Open method of the Recordset object

```
Sub RecSetOpen()
    Dim rst As ADODB.Recordset
    Dim strConnection As String
```

```
strConnection = "Provider=Microsoft.Jet.OLEDB.4.0;" & _
    "Data Source=" & CurrentProject.Path & _
    "\Northwind.mdb"

Set rst = New ADODB.Recordset
With rst
    .Open "SELECT * FROM Customers", _
        strConnection, adOpenForwardOnly
    .Save CurrentProject.Path & "\MyRst.dat"
    .Close
End With
Set rst = Nothing
End Sub
```

➡ **Note:**   Once you open the recordset, you can perform the required operation on its data. In this example, we save the entire recordset to a disk file named MyRst.data. In Chapter 16 you learn how to work with records that have been saved in a file.

The procedure in Hands-On 13-9 illustrates how to open a recordset based on a table or query.

◎ Hands-On 13-9: Opening a Recordset Based on a Table or Query (ADO)

1. In the Visual Basic Editor window, choose **Insert | Module**.

2. In the module's Code window, type the **OpenRst_TableOrQuery** procedure shown below, or copy the procedure code from **C:\Acc07_HandsOn\ Chap13.txt**.

```
Sub OpenRst_TableOrQuery()
    Dim conn As ADODB.Connection
    Dim rst As ADODB.Recordset

    Set conn = New ADODB.Connection
    With conn
        .Provider = "Microsoft.ACE.OLEDB.12.0"
        .Open "Data Source=" & CurrentProject.Path & _
            "\Northwind 2007.accdb"
    End With

    Set rst = New ADODB.Recordset

    rst.Open "Employees", conn

    Debug.Print "CursorType: " & rst.CursorType & vbCr _
        & "LockType: " & rst.LockType & vbCr _
        & "Cursor Location: " & rst.CursorLocation

    Do Until rst.EOF
        Debug.Print rst.Fields(2)
        rst.MoveNext
    Loop
```

```
            rst.Close
            Set rst = Nothing
            conn.Close
            Set conn = Nothing
        End Sub
```

3. Choose **Run | Run Sub/UserForm** to execute the procedure.

After opening the recordset, it's a good idea to check what type of recordset was created. Notice that the procedure above uses the CursorType, LockType, and CursorLocation properties to retrieve this information. After the procedure is run, the Immediate window displays the following:

```
            CursorType: 0
            LockType: 1
            Cursor Location: 2
```

Notice that because you did not specify any parameters in the Recordset's Open method, you obtained a default recordset. This recordset is forward-only (0), read-only (1), and server-side (2). (For more information, refer to the section titled "Introduction to ADO Recordsets" earlier in this chapter.)

To create a different type of recordset, pass the appropriate parameters to the Recordset's Open method. For example, if you open your recordset like this:

```
            rst.Open "Employees", conn, adUseClient, adLockReadOnly
```

you will get the static (3), read-only (1), and client-side (3) recordset. In this recordset, you can easily find out the number of records by using the Recordset's RecordCount property:

```
            Debug.Print rst.RecordCount
```

Next, the procedure above uses the MoveNext method to iterate through all the records in the recordset until the end of file (EOF) is reached. The Recordset's EOF property combined with a looping structure allows you to iterate through the recordset until the end of the file is reached.

Counting Records

Use the Recordset object's RecordCount property to determine the number of records in a recordset. If the number of records cannot be determined, this property will return –1. The RecordCount property setting depends on the cursor type and the capabilities of the provider. To get the actual count of records, open the recordset with the static (adOpenStatic) or dynamic (adOpenDynamic) cursor.

To quickly test the contents of the recordset, we write the employees' last names to the Immediate window. Since this recordset contains all the fields in the Employees table, you can add extra code to list the remaining field values.

Is This Recordset Empty?

A recordset may be empty. To check whether your recordset has any records in it, use the Recordset object's BOF and EOF properties. The BOF property stands for "beginning of file," and EOF indicates "end of file."

- If you open a Recordset object that contains no records, the BOF and EOF properties are both set to True.
- If you open a Recordset object that contains at least one record, the BOF and EOF properties are False and the first record is the current record.

You can use the following conditional statement to test whether there are any records:

```
If rst.BOF and rst.EOF Then
    MsgBox "This recordset contains no records"
End If
```

To open a recordset based on a saved query, replace the table name with your query name.

Opening a Recordset Based on an SQL Statement

The procedure in Hands-On 13-10 demonstrates how to use the Connection object's Execute method to open a recordset based on an SQL statement that selects all the employees from the Employees table in the sample Northwind 2007.accdb database. Only the name of the first employee is written to the Immediate window. As in the preceding example, the resulting recordset is forward-only and read-only.

◎ Hands-On 13-10: Opening a Recordset Based on an SQL Statement (ADO)

1. In the Visual Basic Editor window, choose **Insert | Module**.

2. In the module's Code window, type the **CreateRst_WithSQL** procedure shown below, or copy the procedure code from **C:\Acc07_HandsOn\ Chap13.txt**.

```
Sub CreateRst_WithSQL()
    Dim conn As ADODB.Connection
    Dim rst As ADODB.Recordset
    Dim strConn As String

    strConn = "Provider = Microsoft.ACE.OLEDB.12.0;" & _
        "Data Source=" & CurrentProject.Path & _
        "\Northwind 2007.accdb"

    Set conn = New ADODB.Connection
    conn.Open strConn

    Set rst = conn.Execute("SELECT * FROM Employees")
    Debug.Print rst("Last Name") & ", " & rst("First Name")

    rst.Close
    Set rst = Nothing
```

```
    conn.Close
    Set conn = Nothing
End Sub
```

3. Choose **Run | Run Sub/UserForm** to execute the procedure.

Opening a Recordset Based on Criteria

Instead of retrieving all the records from a specific table or query, you can use the SQL WHERE clause to get the records that meet certain conditions. The procedure in Hands-On 13-11 calls the Recordset's Open method to create a forward-only and read-only recordset populated with employees who perform the duties as a sales representative.

Hands-On 13-11: Opening a Recordset Based on Criteria (ADO)

1. In the Visual Basic Editor window, choose **Insert | Module**.

2. In the module's Code window, type the **OpenRst_WithCriteria** procedure shown below, or copy the procedure code from **C:\Acc07_HandsOn\ Chap13.txt**.

```
Sub OpenRst_WithCriteria()
    Dim conn As ADODB.Connection
    Dim rst As ADODB.Recordset
    Dim strConn As String

    strConn = "Provider=Microsoft.ACE.OLEDB.12.0;" & _
        "Data Source=" & CurrentProject.Path & _
        "\Northwind 2007.accdb"

    Set conn = New ADODB.Connection
    conn.Open strConn

    Set rst = New ADODB.Recordset
    rst.Open "SELECT * FROM Employees WHERE [Job Title] = " & _
        "'Sales Representative'", _
        conn, adOpenForwardOnly, adLockReadOnly

    Do While Not rst.EOF
        Debug.Print rst.Fields(2).Value
        rst.MoveNext
    Loop

    rst.Close
    Set rst = Nothing
    conn.Close
    Set conn = Nothing
End Sub
```

3. Choose **Run | Run Sub/UserForm** to execute the procedure.

Opening a Recordset Directly

If you are planning to open just one recordset from a specific data source, you can take a shortcut and open it directly without first opening a Connection object. This method requires you to specify the source and connection information prior to calling the Recordset object's Open method, as shown in Hands-On 13-12 below.

◎ Hands-On 13-12: Opening a Recordset Directly (ADO)

1. In the Visual Basic Editor window, choose **Insert | Module**.

2. In the module's Code window, type the **OpenRst_Directly** procedure shown below, or copy the procedure code from **C:\Acc07_HandsOn\ Chap13.txt**.

```
Sub OpenRst_Directly()
    Dim conn As ADODB.Connection
    Dim rst As ADODB.Recordset

    Set conn = New ADODB.Connection
    With conn
        .Provider = "Microsoft.ACE.OLEDB.12.0"
        .Open "Data Source=" & CurrentProject.Path & _
            "\Northwind 2007.accdb"
    End With

    Set rst = New ADODB.Recordset
    With rst
        .Source = "SELECT * FROM Employees"
        .ActiveConnection = conn
        .Open
    End With
    MsgBox rst.Fields(2)

    rst.Close
    Set rst = Nothing
    conn.Close
    Set conn = Nothing
End Sub
```

3. Choose **Run | Run Sub/UserForm** to execute the procedure.

Moving Around in a Recordset

You can navigate the ADO Recordset by using the following five methods: MoveFirst, MoveLast, MoveNext, MovePrevious, and Move. The procedure in Hands-On 13-13 demonstrates how to move around in a recordset and retrieve the names of fields and their contents for each record.

◎ Hands-On 13-13: Moving Around in a Recordset (ADO)

1. In the Visual Basic Editor window, choose **Insert | Module**.

2. In the module's Code window, type the **MoveAround** procedure shown below, or copy the procedure code from **C:\Acc07_HandsOn\Chap13.txt**.

```
Sub MoveAround()
    Dim conn As ADODB.Connection
    Dim rst As ADODB.Recordset
    Dim fld As ADODB.Field
    Dim strConn As String

    strConn = "Provider=Microsoft.Jet.OLEDB.4.0;" & _
        "Data Source=" & CurrentProject.Path & _
        "\Northwind.mdb"

    Set conn = New ADODB.Connection
    conn.Open strConn

    Set rst = New ADODB.Recordset
    rst.Open "SELECT * FROM Customers WHERE ContactTitle = 'Owner'", _
        conn, adOpenForwardOnly, adLockReadOnly
    Do While Not rst.EOF
        Debug.Print "New Record -------------"
        For Each fld In rst.Fields
            Debug.Print fld.Name & " = " & fld.Value
        Next
        rst.MoveNext
    Loop

    rst.Close
    Set rst = Nothing
    conn.Close
    Set conn = Nothing
End Sub
```

3. Choose **Run | Run Sub/UserForm** to execute the procedure.

Finding the Record Position

Use the AbosolutePosition property of the Recordset object to determine the current record number. This property specifies the relative position of a record in an ADO Recordset. The procedure in Hands-On 13-14 opens a recordset filled with employee records from the Employees table in the Northwind database and uses the AbsolutePosition property to return the record number three times during the procedure execution.

◎ Hands-On 13-14: Finding the Record Position (ADO)

1. In the Visual Basic Editor window, choose **Insert | Module**.

2. In the module's Code window, type the **FindRecordPosition** procedure shown below, or copy the procedure code from **C:\Acc07_HandsOn\ Chap13.txt**.

```
Sub FindRecordPosition()
    Dim conn As ADODB.Connection
    Dim rst As ADODB.Recordset
    Dim strConn As String

    strConn = "Provider=Microsoft.Jet.OLEDB.4.0;" & _
        "Data Source=" & CurrentProject.Path & _
        "\Northwind.mdb"

    Set conn = New ADODB.Connection
    conn.Open strConn

    Set rst = New ADODB.Recordset
    With rst
        .Open "SELECT * FROM Employees", conn, adOpenKeyset, _
            adLockOptimistic, adCmdText
    Debug.Print .AbsolutePosition
        .Move 3    ' move forward 3 records
        Debug.Print .AbsolutePosition
        .MoveLast ' move to the last record
        Debug.Print .AbsolutePosition
        Debug.Print .RecordCount
        .Close
    End With

    Set rst = Nothing
    conn.Close
    Set conn = Nothing
End Sub
```

3. Choose **Run | Run Sub/UserForm** to execute the procedure.

Notice that at the beginning of the recordset, the record number is 1. Next, the FindRecordPosition procedure uses the Move method to move the cursor three rows ahead, after which the AbsolutePosition property returns 4 (1 + 3) as the current record position. Finally, the MoveLast method is used to move the cursor to the end of the recordset. The AbsolutePosition property now determines that this is the ninth record (9). The RecordCount property of the Recordset object returns the total number of records (9).

Reading Data from a Field

Use the Fields collection of a Recordset object to retrieve the value of a specific field in an open recordset. The procedure in Hands-On 13-15 uses the Do...While loop to iterate through the recordset and prints the names of all the employees to the Immediate window.

Hands-On 13-15: Retrieving Field Values (ADO)

1. In the Visual Basic Editor window, choose **Insert | Module**.

2. In the module's Code window, type the **ReadField** procedure shown below, or copy the procedure code from **C:\Acc07_HandsOn\Chap13.txt**.

```
Sub ReadField()
    Dim conn As ADODB.Connection
    Dim rst As ADODB.Recordset

    Set conn = New ADODB.Connection
    With conn
        .Provider = "Microsoft.ACE.OLEDB.12.0"
        .Open "Data Source=" & CurrentProject.Path & _
            "\Northwind 2007.accdb"
    End With

    Set rst = New ADODB.Recordset
    rst.Open "SELECT * FROM Employees", conn, adOpenStatic

    Do While Not rst.EOF
        Debug.Print rst.Fields("Last Name").Value
        rst.MoveNext
    Loop

    rst.Close
    Set rst = Nothing
    conn.Close
    Set conn = Nothing
End Sub
```

3. Choose **Run | Run Sub/UserForm** to execute the procedure.

Returning a Recordset as a String

Instead of using a loop to read the values of fields in all rows of the open recordset, you can use the Recordset object's GetString method to get the desired data in one step. The GetString method returns a recordset as a string-valued Variant. This method has the following syntax:

```
Variant = Recordset.GetString(StringFormat, NumRows, _
    ColumnDelimiter, RowDelimiter, NullExpr)
```

▪ The first argument (StringFormat) determines the format for representing the recordset as a string. Use the adAddClipString constant as the value for this argument.

▪ The second argument (NumRows) specifies the number of recordset rows to return. If blank, GetString will return all the rows.

▪ The third argument (ColumnDelimiter) specifies the delimiter for the columns within the row (the default column delimiter is tab (vbTab)).

▪ The fourth argument (RowDelimiter) specifies a row delimiter (the default is carriage return (vbCrLf)).

▪ The fifth argument (NullExpr) specifies an expression to represent Null values (the default is an empty string ("")).

Hands-On 13-16: Converting the Recordset to a String (ADO)

1. In the Visual Basic Editor window, choose **Insert | Module**.

2. In the module's Code window, type the **GetRecords_AsString** procedure shown below, or copy the procedure code from **C:\Acc07_HandsOn\ Chap13.txt**.

```
Sub GetRecords_AsString()
    Dim conn As ADODB.Connection
    Dim rst As ADODB.Recordset
    Dim varRst As Variant
    Dim fso As Object
    Dim myFile As Object

    Set conn = New ADODB.Connection
    With conn
        .Provider = "Microsoft.JET.OLEDB.4.0"
        .Open "Data Source=" & CurrentProject.Path & _
            "\Northwind.mdb"
    End With

    Set rst = New ADODB.Recordset
    rst.Open "SELECT EmployeeId, " & _
        "LastName & "", "" & FirstName AS FullName " & _
        "FROM Employees", _
        conn, adOpenForwardOnly, adLockReadOnly, adCmdText

    If Not rst.EOF Then
        ' Return all rows as a formatted string with
        ' columns delimited by Tabs, and rows
        ' delimited by carriage returns

        varRst = rst.GetString(adClipString, , vbTab, vbCrLf)
        Debug.Print varRst
    End If

    ' save the recordset string to a text file
    Set fso = CreateObject("Scripting.FileSystemObject")
        Set myFile = fso.CreateTextFile(CurrentProject.Path & _
            "\RstString.txt", True)
    myFile.WriteLine varRst
    myFile.Close

    Set fso = Nothing
    rst.Close
    Set rst = Nothing
    conn.Close
    Set conn = Nothing
End Sub
```

3. Choose **Run | Run Sub/UserForm** to execute the procedure.

The GetRecords_AsString procedure demonstrates how you can transform a recordset into a tab-delimited list of values using the Recordset object's GetString method. You can use any characters you want to separate columns and rows. This procedure uses the following statement to convert a recordset to a string:

```
varRst = rst.GetString(adClipString, , vbTab, vbCrLf)
```

Notice that the second argument is omitted. This indicates that we want to obtain all the records. To convert only three records to a string, you could write the following line of code:

```
varRst = rst.GetString(adClipString, 3, vbTab, vbCrLf)
```

The vbTab and vbCrLf arguments are VBA constants that denote the Tab and carriage return characters.

Because adClipString, vbTab, and vbCrLf are default values for the GetString method's arguments, you can skip them altogether. Therefore, to put all of the records in this recordset into a string, you can simply use the GetString method without arguments, like this:

```
varRst = rst.GetString
```

Sometimes you may want to save your recordset string to a file. To gain access to a computer's file system, the procedure uses the CreateObject function to access the FileSystemObject from the Microsoft Scripting Runtime Library. Using the CreateTextFile method of this object, you can easily create a File object. Notice that the second argument of the CreateTextFile method (True) indicates that the file should be overwritten if it already exists. Once you have defined your file, you can use the WriteLine method of the File object to write the text to the file. In this example, your text is the variable holding the contents of a recordset converted to a string.

Finding Records Using the Find Method

The ADO Object Model provides you with two methods for locating records: Find and Seek. This section demonstrates how to use the ADO Find method to locate all the employee records based on a condition. ADO has a single Find method. The search always begins from the current record or an offset from it. The search direction and the offset from the current record are passed as parameters to the Find method. The SearchDirection parameter can have the following values: adSearchForward and adSearchBackward.

Hands-On 13-17: Finding Records Using the Find Method (ADO)

1. In the Visual Basic Editor window, choose **Insert | Module**.
2. In the module's Code window, type the **Find_WithFind** procedure shown below, or copy the procedure code from **C:\Acc07_HandsOn\Chap13.txt**.

```
Sub Find_WithFind()
    Dim conn As ADODB.Connection
    Dim rst As ADODB.Recordset

    Set conn = New ADODB.Connection
    conn.Open "Provider=Microsoft.Jet.OLEDB.4.0;" & _
```

```
                "Data Source=" & CurrentProject.Path & _
                "\Northwind.mdb"

    Set rst = New ADODB.Recordset
    rst.Open "Employees", conn, adOpenKeyset, adLockOptimistic

    ' find the first record matching the criteria
    rst.Find "TitleOfCourtesy ='Ms.'"
    Do Until rst.EOF
        Debug.Print rst.Fields("LastName").Value
        ' search forward starting from the next record
        rst.Find "TitleOfCourtesy ='Ms.'", SkipRecords:=1, _
            SearchDirection:=adSearchForward
    Loop

    rst.Close
    Set rst = Nothing
    conn.Close
    Set conn = Nothing
End Sub
```

3. Choose **Run | Run Sub/UserForm** to execute the procedure.

To find the last record, call the MoveLast method before using Find. If none of the records meets the criteria, the current record is positioned before the beginning of the recordset (if searching forward) or after the end of the recordset (if searching backward). You can use the EOF or BOF properties of the Recordset object to determine whether a matching record was found.

 Note: The ADO Find method does not support the Is operator. To locate the record that has a Null value, use the equal sign (=). For example:

```
' find records that do not have an entry in the ReportsTo field
rst.Find "ReportsTo = Null"

' find records that have data in the ReportsTo field
rst.Find " ReportsTo <> Null"
```

To find records based on more than one condition, use the Filter property of the Recordset object, as demonstrated in Hands-On 13-19 later in this chapter.

Finding Records Using the Seek Method

You can use the Recordset object's Seek method to locate a record based on an index. If you don't specify the index before searching, the primary key will be used. If the record is found, the current row position is changed to that row. The syntax of the Seek method looks like this:

```
recordset.Seek KeyValues, SeekOption
```

The first argument of the Seek method specifies the key values you want to find. The second argument specifies the type of comparison to be made between the columns of the index and the corresponding KeyValues.

The procedure in Hands-On 13-18 uses the Seek method to find the first company with an entry in the Region field equal to "SP":

```
rst.Seek "SP", adSeekFirstEQ
```

To find the last record that meets the same condition, use the following statement:

```
rst.Seek "SP", adSeekLastEQ
```

The type of Seek to execute is specified by the constants shown in Table 13-6.

Table 13-6: Seek method constants

Constant	Value	Description
adSeekFirstEQ	1	Seeks the first key equal to KeyValues.
adSeekLastEQ	2	Seeks the last key equal to KeyValues.
adSeekAfterEQ	4	Seeks either a key equal to KeyValues or just after where that match would have occurred.
adSeekAfter	8	Seeks a key just after where a match with KeyValues would have occurred.
adSeekBeforeEQ	16	Seeks either a key equal to KeyValues or just before where that match would have occurred.
adSeekBefore	32	Seeks a key just before where a match with KeyValues would have occurred.

The Seek method is recognized only by the Microsoft Jet 4.0/ACE 12.0 databases. To determine whether the Seek method can be used to locate a row in a recordset, use the Recordset object's Supports method. This method determines whether a specified Recordset object supports a particular type of feature. The Boolean value of True indicates that the feature is supported; False indicates that it is not.

```
' find out if the recordset supports the Seek method
MsgBox rst.Supports(adSeek)
```

⊚ Hands-On 13-18: Finding Records Using the Seek Method (ADO)

1. In the Visual Basic Editor window, choose **Insert | Module**.

2. In the module's Code window, type the **Find_WithSeek** procedure shown below, or copy the procedure code from **C:\Acc07_HandsOn\Chap13.txt**.

```
Sub Find_WithSeek()
    Dim conn As ADODB.Connection
    Dim rst As ADODB.Recordset

    Set conn = New ADODB.Connection
    conn.Open "Provider=Microsoft.Jet.OLEDB.4.0;" & _
        "Data Source=" & CurrentProject.Path & _
        "\Northwind.mdb"

    Set rst = New ADODB.Recordset
    With rst
        .Index = "Region"
```

```
    .Open "Customers", conn, adOpenKeyset, adLockOptimistic, _
        adCmdTableDirect

    ' find out if this recordset supports the Seek method
    MsgBox rst.Supports(adSeek)
    .Seek "SP", adSeekFirstEQ
    End With

    If Not rst.EOF Then
        Debug.Print rst.Fields("CompanyName").Value
    End If

    rst.Close
    Set rst = Nothing
    conn.Close
    Set conn = Nothing
End Sub
```

3. Choose **Run | Run Sub/UserForm** to execute the procedure.

If the Seek method is based on a multi-field index, use the VBA Array function to specify values for the KeyValues parameter. For example, the Order Details table in the Northwind.mdb database uses a multi-field index as the PrimaryKey. This index is a combination of the OrderID and ProductID fields. To find the order in which OrderID = 10295 and ProductID = 56, use the following statement:

```
    rst.Seek Array(10295, 56), adSeekFirstEQ
```

Finding a Record Based on Multiple Conditions

ADO's Find method does not allow you to find records based on more than one condition. The workaround is using the Recordset object's Filter property to create a view of the recordset that only contains records matching the specified criteria. The procedure in Hands-On 13-19 uses the Filter property to find the female employees who live in the United States.

⊚ Hands-On 13-19: Finding a Record Based on Multiple Criteria (ADO)

1. In the Visual Basic Editor window, choose **Insert | Module**.

2. In the module's Code window, type the **Find_WithFilter** procedure shown below, or copy the procedure code from **C:\Acc07_HandsOn\Chap13.txt**.

```
Sub Find_WithFilter()
    Dim conn As ADODB.Connection
    Dim rst As ADODB.Recordset

    Set conn = New ADODB.Connection
    conn.Open "Provider=Microsoft.Jet.OLEDB.4.0;" & _
        "Data Source=" & CurrentProject.Path & _
        "\Northwind.mdb"
```

```
Set rst = New ADODB.Recordset
rst.Open "Employees", conn, adOpenKeyset, adLockOptimistic
rst.Filter = "TitleOfCourtesy ='Ms.' and Country ='USA'"
Do Until rst.EOF
    Debug.Print rst.Fields("LastName").Value
    rst.MoveNext
Loop

rst.Close
Set rst = Nothing
conn.Close
Set conn = Nothing
End Sub
```

3. Choose **Run | Run Sub/UserForm** to execute the procedure.

Using Bookmarks

When you work with database records you have to keep in mind that the actual number of records in a recordset can change at any time as new records are added or others are deleted. Therefore, you cannot save a record number to return to it later. Because records change all the time, the record numbers cannot be trusted. However, programmers often need to save the position of a record after they've moved to it or found it based on certain criteria. Instead of scrolling through every record in a recordset comparing the values, you can move directly to a specific record by using a bookmark. A *bookmark* is a value that uniquely identifies a row in a recordset.

Use the Bookmark property of the Recordset object to mark the record so you can return to it later. The Bookmark property is read-write, which means that you can get a bookmark for a record or set the current record in a Recordset object to the record identified by a valid bookmark. The Recordset's Bookmark property always represents the current row. Therefore, if you need to mark more than one row for later retrieval, you may want to use an array to store multiple bookmarks (see Hands-On 13-20).

A single bookmark can be stored in a Variant variable. For example, when you get to a particular row in a recordset and decide that you'd like to save its location, store the recordset's bookmark in a variable, like this:

```
varMyBkmrk = rst.Bookmark
```

The varMyBkmrk is the name of a Variant variable declared with the following statement:

```
Dim varMyBkmrk As Variant
```

To retrieve the bookmark, move to another row, then use the saved bookmark to move back to the original row, like this:

```
rst.Bookmark = varMyBkmrk
```

Because not all ADO Recordsets support the Bookmark property, you should use the Supports method to determine if the recordset does. Here's how:

```
If rst.Supports(adBookmark) then
    MsgBox "Bookmarks are supported."
Else
    MsgBox "Sorry, can't use bookmarks!"
End If
```

Recordsets defined with a Static or Keyset cursor always support bookmarks. If you remove the adOpenKeyset intrinsic constant from the code used in the next procedure (Hands-On 13-20), the default cursor (adOpenForwardOnly) will be used, and you'll get an error because this cursor does not support bookmarks.

Another precaution to keep in mind is that there is no valid bookmark when the current row is positioned at the new row in a recordset. For example, if you add a new record with the following statement:

```
rst.AddNew
```

and then attempt to mark this record with a bookmark:

```
varMyBkmrk = rst.Book
```

you will get an error.

When you close the recordset, bookmarks you've saved become invalid. Also, bookmarks are unique to the recordset in which they were created. This means that you cannot use a bookmark created in one recordset to move to the same record in another recordset. However, if you clone a recordset (that is, you create a duplicate Recordset object), a Bookmark object from one Recordset object will refer to the same record in its clone. (See the section called "Cloning a Recordset" in Chapter 16.)

⊚ Hands-On 13-20: Marking Records with a Bookmark (ADO)

1. In the Visual Basic Editor window, choose **Insert | Module**.

2. In the module's Code window, type the **TestBookmark** procedure shown below, or copy the procedure code from **C:\Acc07_HandsOn\Chap13.txt**.

```
Sub TestBookmark()
    Dim conn As ADODB.Connection
    Dim rst As ADODB.Recordset
    Dim varMyBkmrk As Variant

    Set conn = New ADODB.Connection
    conn.Open "Provider=Microsoft.Jet.OLEDB.4.0;" & _
        "Data Source=" & CurrentProject.Path & _
        "\Northwind.mdb"

    Set rst = New ADODB.Recordset
    rst.Open "Employees", conn, adOpenKeyset

    If Not rst.Supports(adBookmark) Then
        MsgBox "This recordset does not support bookmarks!"
        Exit Sub
    End If
```

```
    varMyBkmrk = rst.Bookmark
    Debug.Print rst.Fields(1).Value

    ' Move to the 7th row
    rst.AbsolutePosition = 7
    Debug.Print rst.Fields(1).Value

    ' move back to the first row using bookmark
    rst.Bookmark = varMyBkmrk
    Debug.Print rst.Fields(1).Value
    rst.Close
    Set rst = Nothing
End Sub
```

3. Choose **Run | Run Sub/UserForm** to execute the procedure.

Notice that the procedure above uses the AbsolutePosition property of the Recordset object. The absolute position isn't the same as the record number. This property can change if a record with a lower number is deleted.

Using Bookmarks to Filter a Recordset

Bookmarks provide the fastest way of moving through rows. You can also use them to filter a recordset as shown in Hands-On 13-21.

Hands-On 13-21: Using Bookmarks to Filter Records (ADO)

1. In the Visual Basic Editor window, choose **Insert | Module**.

2. In the module's Code window, type the **Filter_WithBookmark** procedure shown below, or copy the procedure code from **C:\Acc07_HandsOn\ Chap13.txt**.

```
Sub Filter_WithBookmark()
    Dim rst As ADODB.Recordset
    Dim varMyBkmrk() As Variant
    Dim strConn As String
    Dim i As Integer
    Dim strCountry As String
    Dim strCity As String

    i = 0
    strCountry = "France"
    strCity = "Paris"

    strConn = "Provider=Microsoft.Jet.OLEDB.4.0;" & _
        "Data Source=" & CurrentProject.Path & _
        "\Northwind.mdb"

    Set rst = New ADODB.Recordset
    rst.Open "Customers", strConn, adOpenKeyset

    If Not rst.Supports(adBookmark) Then
        MsgBox "This recordset does not support bookmarks!"
        Exit Sub
```

```
    End If

    Do While Not rst.EOF
        If rst.Fields("Country") = strCountry And _
            rst.Fields("City") = strCity Then
            ReDim Preserve varMyBkmrk(i)
            varMyBkmrk(i) = rst.Bookmark
            i = i + 1
        End If
        rst.MoveNext

    Loop

    rst.Filter = varMyBkmrk()

    rst.MoveFirst
    Do While Not rst.EOF
        Debug.Print rst("CustomerId") & _
            " - " & rst("CompanyName")
        rst.MoveNext
    Loop
    rst.Close
    Set rst = Nothing
End Sub
```

3. Choose **Run | Run Sub/UserForm** to execute the procedure.

Using the GetRows Method to Fill the Recordset

To retrieve multiple rows from a recordset, use the GetRows method, which returns a two-dimensional array. To find out how many rows were retrieved, use VBA's UBound function, as illustrated in Hands-On 13-22 below. Because arrays are zero-based by default, you must add one (1) to the result of the UBound function to get the correct record count.

Hands-On 13-22: Counting the Number of Returned Records (ADO)

1. In the Visual Basic Editor window, choose **Insert | Module**.

2. In the module's Code window, type the **CountRecords** procedure shown below, or copy the procedure code from **C:\Acc07_HandsOn\Chap13.txt**.

```
Sub CountRecords()
    Dim conn As ADODB.Connection
    Dim rst As ADODB.Recordset
    Dim myarray As Variant
    Dim returnedRows As Integer
    Dim r As Integer 'record counter
    Dim f As Integer 'field counter

    Set conn = New ADODB.Connection
    conn.Open "Provider=Microsoft.Jet.OLEDB.4.0;" & _
        "Data Source=" & CurrentProject.Path & _
        "\Northwind.mdb"
```

```
Set rst = New ADODB.Recordset
rst.Open "SELECT * FROM Employees", _
    conn, adOpenForwardOnly, adLockReadOnly, adCmdText

' Return all rows into array
myarray = rst.GetRows()
returnedRows = UBound(myarray, 2) + 1

MsgBox "Total number of records: " & returnedRows

' Find upper bound of second dimension
For r = 0 To UBound(myarray, 2)
    Debug.Print "Record " & r + 1
    ' Find upper bound of first dimension
    For f = 0 To UBound(myarray, 1)
        ' Print data from each row in array
        Debug.Print Tab; _
            rst.Fields(f).Name & " = " & myarray(f, r)
    Next f
Next r

rst.Close
Set rst = Nothing
conn.Close
Set conn = Nothing
End Sub
```

3. Choose **Run | Run Sub/UserForm** to execute the procedure.

Notice how the CountRecords procedure prints the contents of the array to the Immediate window by using a nested loop.

Chapter Summary

In this chapter you familiarized yourself with various methods of opening DAO and ADO Recordsets, moving around in a recordset, finding and filtering, and bookmarking required records as well as reading the contents of a recordset. You have also learned how to use the Recordset object's properties such as EOF, BOF, and RecordCount. In addition, you found out how to fill the ADO Recordset with the GetString and GetRows methods.

In the next chapter, you will gain experience performing such important data manipulation tasks as adding, modifying, copying, deleting, and sorting records.

Chapter 14

Working with Records

Now that you've familiarized yourself with various methods of opening, moving around in, and finding records, and reading the contents of a recordset, let's look at DAO and ADO techniques for adding, modifying, copying, deleting, and sorting records.

Adding a New Record with DAO

In the Microsoft Access user interface, before you can add a new record to a table you must first open the appropriate table. In code, you simply open the Recordset object by calling the OpenRecordset method. For example, the following statements declare and open the Recordset object based on the Employees table:

```
Dim tblRst As DAO.Recordset
Set tblRst = db.OpenRecordset("Employees")
```

Once the Recordset object is open, use the AddNew method to create a blank record. For example:

```
tblRst.AddNew
```

Next, you may set values for all or some of the fields in the new record. You must set the field's value if the Required property of a field is set to True. In the Microsoft Access user interface in Table Design view, there will be a Yes entry next to the Required property if the entry in the selected field is required. Here are some examples of setting field values in code:

```
tblRst.Fields("Last Name").Value = "Smith"
tblRst.Fields("Job Title").Value = "Marketing Director"
```

Note that because Value is the default property of a Field object, the use of this keyword is optional and it was omitted in the code of the example procedure in Hands-On 14-1.

After filling in field values, you need to use the Update method on the Recordset object to ensure that the newly added record is saved:

```
tblRst.Update
```

Hands-On 14-1 demonstrates how to add a new record to the Employees table and populate some of its fields with values.

⊚ Hands-On 14-1: Adding a New Record to a Table (DAO)

1. Start Microsoft Office Access 2007 and create a new Microsoft Office Access 2007 database named **Chap14.accdb** in your **C:\Acc07_By-Example** folder.

2. In the Access window, press **Alt+F11** to switch to the Visual Basic Editor window.

3. In the Visual Basic Editor window, choose **Insert | Module**.

4. In the module's Code window, type the **AddNewRec_DAO** procedure shown below, or copy the procedure code from **C:\Acc07_HandsOn\ Chap14.txt**.

```
Sub AddNewRec_DAO()
    Dim db As DAO.Database
    Dim tblRst As DAO.Recordset

    Set db = OpenDatabase("C:\Acc07_ByExample\Northwind 2007.accdb")
    Set tblRst = db.OpenRecordset("Employees")

    With tblRst
        .AddNew
        .Fields("Company") = "Northwind Traders"
        .Fields("Last Name") = "Smith"
        .Fields("First Name") = "Regina"
        .Fields("Job Title") = "Marketing Director"
        .Fields("E-mail Address") = "regina@northwindtraders.com"
        .Update
    End With

    tblRst.Close
    Set tblRst = Nothing
    db.Close
    Set db = Nothing
End Sub
```

5. Choose **Run | Run Sub/UserForm** to execute the procedure.

In a Table-type recordset, the new record is placed in the order identified by the table's index. In a Dynaset-type recordset, the new record is added at the end of the recordset. When you add a new record to a table, the new record does not become the current record. The record that was current prior to adding the new record remains current. In other words, while a new record is being added to the end of the table, the cursor remains in the record that was selected prior to adding a new record. You can, however, make the newly added record current by using a Bookmark and the LastModified property, like this:

```
tblRst.Bookmark = tblRst.LastModified
```

Adding a New Record with ADO

To add a new record, use the ADO Recordset's AddNew method. Use the Update method if you are not going to add any more records. In ADO, it is not necessary to call the Update method if you are moving to the next record. Calling the Move method implicitly calls the Update method before moving to the new record. For example, look at the following statements:

```
rst![Last Name] = "Roberts"
rst.MoveNext
```

In the code fragment above, the Update method is automatically called when you move to the next record.

The procedure in Hands-On 14-2 demonstrates how to add a new record to the Employees table.

◎ Hands-On 14-2: Adding a New Record to a Table (ADO)

1. In the Visual Basic Editor window, choose **Insert | Module**.

2. In the module's Code window, type the **AddNewRec_ADO** procedure shown below, or copy the procedure code from **C:\Acc07_HandsOn\ Chap14.txt**.

```
' Use the References dialog box
' to set up a reference to
' the Microsoft ActiveX Data 2.8 Object Library

Sub AddNewRec_ADO()
    Dim conn As ADODB.Connection
    Dim rst As ADODB.Recordset
    Dim strConn As String

    strConn = "Provider=Microsoft.ACE.OLEDB.12.0;" & _
        "Data Source=" & CurrentProject.Path & _
        "\Northwind 2007.accdb"

    Set rst = New ADODB.Recordset
    With rst
        .Open "SELECT * FROM Employees", _
        strConn, adOpenKeyset, adLockOptimistic

        ' Add a record and specify some field values
        .AddNew
        ![Company] = "Northwind Traders"
        ![Last Name] = "Roberts"
        ![First Name] = "Paul"
        ![Job Title] = "Sales Representative"
        ![E-mail Address] = "paul@northwindtraders.com"

        ' Retrieve the Employee ID for the current record
        Debug.Print !ID.Value

        ' Move to the first record
```

```
        .MoveFirst
        Debug.Print !ID.Value
        .Close
    End With

    Set rst = Nothing
    Set conn = Nothing
End Sub
```

3. Choose **Run | Run Sub/UserForm** to execute the procedure.

When adding or modifying records, you can set the record's field values in one of the following ways:

```
rst.Fields("First Name").value = "Paul"
```

or

```
rst![First Name] = "Paul"
```

As mentioned earlier, when you use the AddNew method to add a new record and then use the Move method, the newly added record is automatically saved without explicitly having to call the Update method. In the example procedure above we used the MoveFirst method to move to the first record; however, you can call any of the other move methods (Move, MoveNext, MovePrevious) to have ADO implicitly call the Update method. After calling the AddNew method, the new record becomes the current record.

Modifying a Record with DAO

To edit an existing record, use the OpenRecordset method to open the Recordset object. Next, locate the record you want to modify. In a Table-type recordset, you can use the Seek method and a table index to find a record that meets your criteria. In Dynaset-type and Snapshot-type recordsets, you can use any of the Find methods (FindFirst, FindNext, FindPrevious, FindLast) to locate the appropriate record. However, recall that you can edit data only in Table-type or Dynaset-type recordsets (Snapshots are used for retrieving data only). Once you've located the record, use the Edit method of the Recordset object and proceed to change field values. When you are done with the record modification, invoke the Update method for the Recordset object.

The procedure in Hands-On 14-3 demonstrates how to modify a record in the Employees table.

◎ Hands-On 14-3: Modifying a Record in a Table (DAO)

This hands-on exercise requires the completion of Hands-On 14-1.

1. In the Visual Basic Editor window, choose **Insert | Module**.

2. In the module's Code window, type the **ModifyRecord_DAO** procedure shown below, or copy the procedure code from **C:\Acc07_HandsOn\ Chap14.txt**.

```
Sub ModifyRecord_DAO()
    Dim db As DAO.Database
    Dim rst As DAO.Recordset
    Dim strFind As String
    Dim intResult As Integer

    Set db = OpenDatabase("C:\Acc07_ByExample\Northwind 2007.accdb")
    Set rst = db.OpenRecordset("Employees", dbOpenTable)

    rst.MoveFirst
    ' change the Zip/Postal Code of all employees from 99999 to 99998

    Do While Not rst.EOF
        With rst
            .Edit
            .Fields("Zip/Postal Code") = "99998"
            .Update
            .MoveNext
        End With
    Loop

    ' find the record for Regina Smith - enter data in Country/Region field
    strFind = "Smith"
    rst.MoveFirst
    rst.Index = "Last Name"

    rst.Seek "=", strFind
    MsgBox rst![Last Name]
    Debug.Print rst.EditMode
    rst.Edit

    rst![Country/Region] = "USA"
    If rst.EditMode = dbEditInProgress Then
        intResult = MsgBox("Do you want to save the changes " & _
            "to this record?", vbYesNo, _
            "Save or Cancel Changes?")
    End If
    If intResult = 6 Then 'Save changes
        rst.Update
    ElseIf intResult = 7 Then 'Cancel changes
        rst.CancelUpdate
    End If

    'rst.Update
    rst.Close

    Set rst = Nothing
    db.Close
    Set db = Nothing
End Sub
```

3. Choose **Run | Run Sub/UserForm** to execute the procedure.

The procedure in Hands-On 14-3 opens a Table-type recordset based on the Employees table and changes the Zip/Postal Code of all employees. Next, the procedure locates a specific employee record. Note that the Index property must be set before using the Seek method for searching the Table-type recordset. If you set the Index property to an index that doesn't exist, a run-time error will occur. Once the desired record is located, the procedure displays the employee name in a message box. The exclamation point (!) is used to separate an object's name from the name of the collection of which it is a member. Because the default collection of the Recordset object is the Fields collection, you can omit the default collection name. Next, the procedure places the found employee record into Edit mode and modifies the value of the Country/Region field. The EditMode property of the Recordset object is used to determine if the Edit operation is in progress. The EditModeEnum constants, which are shown in Table 14-1, indicate the state of editing for the current record. Before committing the changes to the data, the user is asked to verify if changes should be saved or canceled. If the Yes button is selected in the message box, the Recordset's Update method is called; otherwise, the CancelUpdate method of the Recordset object will discard the changes to the current record.

Table 14-1: EditModeEnum constants used in the EditMode property of the DAO Recordset object

EditModeEnum Constant Name	Value	Description
dbEditNone	0	Edit method not invoked.
dbEditInProgress	1	Edit method invoked.
dbEditAdd	2	AddNew method invoked.

Note: At times when working with records you will need to leave the record and discard the changes. To cancel any pending updates to the data, call the CancelUpdate method of the DAO Recordset object. This method aborts any changes you've made to the current row. You can use the CancelUpdate method to cancel any changes made after the Edit or AddNew method was invoked. You can check if there is a pending operation that can be canceled by using the EditMode property of the Recordset object.

Modifying a Record with ADO

To modify data in a specific field, find the record and set the value property of the required field to a new value. Always call the Update method if you are not planning to edit any more records. If you modify a row and then try to close the recordset without calling the Update method first, ADO will trigger a run-time error.

The procedure in Hands-On 14-4 modifies an employee record.

 Hands-On 14-4: Modifying a Record (ADO)

This hands-on exercise requires the completion of Hands-On 14-2.

1. In the Visual Basic Editor window, choose **Insert | Module**.

2. In the module's Code window, type the **ModifyRecord_ADO** procedure shown below, or copy the procedure code from **C:\Acc07_HandsOn\ Chap14.txt**.

```
Sub ModifyRecord_ADO()
    Dim conn As ADODB.Connection
    Dim rst As ADODB.Recordset
    Dim strConn As String

    strConn = "Provider=Microsoft.ACE.OLEDB.12.0;" & _
        "Data Source=" & CurrentProject.Path & _
        "\Northwind 2007.accdb"

    Set rst = New ADODB.Recordset

    With rst
        .Open "SELECT * FROM Employees WHERE [Last Name] = 'Roberts'", _
            strConn, adOpenKeyset, adLockOptimistic
        .Fields("City").Value = "Redmond"
        .Fields("State/Province") = "WA"
        .Fields("Country/Region").Value = "USA"
        .Update
        .Close
    End With

    Set rst = Nothing
    Set conn = Nothing
End Sub
```

3. Choose **Run | Run Sub/UserForm** to execute the procedure.

The procedure above modifies a table record by first accessing the desired fields. You can modify several fields in a specific record by calling the Update method and passing it two arrays. The first array should specify the field names, the second one should list the new values to be entered. For example, the following statement updates the data in the City, State/Province, and Country/Region fields with the corresponding values:

```
rst.Update Array("City", "State/Province", "Country/Region"), Array("Redmond",
"WA", "USA")
```

You can use the same technique with the AddNew method.

 Note: At times when working with records you will need to leave the record and discard the changes. To prevent ADO from automatically committing that row of data, call the CancelUpdate method of the ADO Recordset object. This method aborts any changes you've made to the current row.

Editing Multiple Records with ADO

ADO has the ability to perform batch updates. This means that you can edit multiple records and send them to the OLE DB provider in a single operation. To take advantage of batch updates, you must use the Keyset or Static cursor (see Chapter 13).

The procedure in Hands-On 14-5 finds all records in the Employees table where Title is "Sales Representative" and changes them to "Sales Rep." The changes are then committed to the database in a single Update operation.

⊚ Hands-On 14-5: Performing Batch Updates (ADO)

1. In the Visual Basic Editor window, choose **Insert | Module**.
2. In the module's Code window, type the **BatchUpdate_Records_ADO** procedure shown below, or copy the procedure code from **C:\Acc07_ HandsOn\Chap14.txt**.

```
Sub BatchUpdate_Records_ADO()
    Dim conn As ADODB.Connection
    Dim rst As ADODB.Recordset
    Dim strConn As String
    Dim strCriteria As String

    strConn = "Provider=Microsoft.ACE.OLEDB.12.0;" & _
        "Data Source=" & CurrentProject.Path & _
        "\Northwind 2007.accdb"

    strCriteria = "[Job Title] = 'Sales Representative'"

    Set conn = New ADODB.Connection
    conn.Open strConn

    Set rst = New ADODB.Recordset

    With rst
        Set .ActiveConnection = conn
        .Source = "Employees"
        .CursorLocation = adUseClient
        .LockType = adLockBatchOptimistic
        .CursorType = adOpenKeyset
        .Open
        .Find strCriteria
        Do While Not .EOF
            .Fields("Job Title") = "Sales Rep"
            .Find strCriteria, 1
        Loop
        .UpdateBatch
    End With

    rst.Close
    Set rst = Nothing
    conn.Close
    Set conn = Nothing
End Sub
```

3. Choose **Run | Run Sub/UserForm** to execute the procedure.

The BatchUpdate_Records_ADO procedure uses the ADO Find method to locate all the records that need to be modified. Once the first record is located, it is changed in memory and the Find operation goes on to search for the next record and so on until the end of the recordset is reached. Notice that the following statement is issued to search past the current record:

```
.Find strCriteria, 1
```

Once all the records have been located and changed, the changes are all committed to the database in a single operation by issuing the UpdateBatch statement.

Updating Data: Differences between ADO and DAO

ADO differs from DAO in the way update and delete operations are performed. In DAO, you are required to use the Edit method of the Recordset object prior to making any changes to your data. ADO does not require you to do this; consequently, there is no Edit method in ADO. Also, in ADO, if you modify a record, your changes are automatically saved. In DAO, leaving a row without first calling the Update method of the Recordset object will automatically discard your changes.

Deleting a Record with DAO

To delete an existing record, open the Recordset object by calling the OpenRecordset method, then locate the record you want to delete. In a Table-type recordset, you can use the Seek method and a table index to find a record that meets your criteria. In a Dynaset-type recordset, you can use any of the Find methods (FindFirst, FindNext, FindPrevious, FindLast) to locate the appropriate record. Next, use the Delete method on the Recordset object to perform the deletion. Before using the Delete method, it is a good idea to write code to ask the user to confirm or cancel the deletion. Immediately after a record is deleted, there is no current record. Use the MoveNext method to move the record pointer to an existing record.

The example procedure in Hands-On 14-6 deletes those employees who have an ID greater than 9.

◎ Hands-On 14-6: Deleting a Record (DAO)

1. In the Visual Basic Editor window, choose **Insert | Module**.

2. In the module's Code window, type the **DeleteRecord_DAO** procedure shown below, or copy the procedure code from **C:\Acc07_HandsOn\ Chap14.txt**.

```
Sub DeleteRecord_DAO()
    Dim db As DAO.Database
    Dim tblRst As DAO.Recordset
    Dim counter As Integer

    Set db = OpenDatabase("C:\Acc07_ByExample\Northwind 2007.accdb")

    ' delete all the employees with ID greater than 9
    Set tblRst = db.OpenRecordset("Employees")
    tblRst.MoveFirst
    Do While Not tblRst.EOF
        Debug.Print tblRst!ID
        If tblRst![ID] > 9 Then
            tblRst.Delete
```

```
        counter = counter + 1
      End If
      tblRst.MoveNext
    Loop

    MsgBox "Number of deleted records: " & counter
    tblRst.Close
    Set tblRst = Nothing
    db.Close
    Set db = Nothing
  End Sub
```

3. Choose **Run | Run Sub/UserForm** to execute the procedure.

The statement Do While Not tblRst.EOF tells Visual Basic to execute the statements inside the loop until the end of file (EOF) is reached. The conditional statement inside the loop checks the value of the ID field, and deletes the current record only if the specified condition is True. Every time a record is deleted, the counter variable's value is increased by 1. The counter variable stores the total number of deleted records. After the record is deleted, the MoveNext method is called to move the record pointer to the next existing record as long as the end of file has not yet been reached. Even though you can use the Delete method and the While loop to remove the required records as shown in Hands-On 14-6, it is more efficient to delete records with a Delete query.

Deleting a Record with ADO

To delete a record, find the record you want to delete and call the Delete method. After you delete a record, it's still the current record. You must use the MoveNext method to move to the next row if you are planning to perform additional operations with your records. An attempt to do anything with the row that has just been deleted will generate a run-time error. The procedure in Hands-On 14-7 deletes a record from the Employees table.

Hands-On 14-7: Deleting a Record (ADO)

This hands-on requires the completion of Hands-On 14-2.

1. In the Visual Basic Editor window, choose **Insert | Module**.

2. In the module's Code window, type the **Delete_Record_ADO** procedure shown below, or copy the procedure code from **C:\Acc07_HandsOn\ Chap14.txt**.

```
Sub Delete_Record_ADO()
  Dim conn As ADODB.Connection
  Dim rst As ADODB.Recordset
  Dim strConn As String
  Dim strCriteria As String

  'call procedure from Hands-On 14-2 to ensure
  'that we have a record to delete
```

```
AddNewRec_ADO

strConn = "Provider=Microsoft.ACE.OLEDB.12.0;" & _
    "Data Source=" & CurrentProject.Path & _
    "\Northwind 2007.accdb"

Set conn = New ADODB.Connection
Set rst = New ADODB.Recordset

With rst
    .Open "SELECT * FROM Employees WHERE [Last Name] ='Roberts'", _
        strConn, adOpenKeyset, adLockOptimistic
    .Delete
    .Close
End With
Set rst = Nothing
Set conn = Nothing
End Sub
```

3. Choose **Run | Run Sub/UserForm** to execute the procedure.

Because we don't want to delete any original rows in the Employees table, to ensure that we have a custom row to delete, the procedure makes a call to the AddNewRec_ADO procedure that we created in Hands-On 14-2.

Copying Records to an Excel Spreadsheet

You can copy the contents of a DAO or ADO Recordset object directly to an Excel worksheet or a worksheet range by using the Workbook Range object's CopyFromRecordset method.

■ To copy all the records in the Recordset object to a worksheet range starting at cell A1, use the following statement:

```
Set rng = objSheet.Cells(2, 1)
rng.CopyFromRecordset rst
```

The rst following the name of the method is an object variable representing a Recordset object.

■ To copy five records to a worksheet range, use the following statement:

```
Set rng = objSheet.Cells(2, 1)
rng.CopyFromRecordset rst, 5
```

■ To copy five records and four fields to a worksheet range, use the following statement:

```
Set rng = objSheet.Cells(2, 1)
rng.CopyFromRecordset rst, 5, 4
```

You can also specify the number of records (rows) and fields to be copied using variables:

```
Set rng = objSheet.Cells(2, 1)
rng.CopyFromRecordset rst, myRows, myColumns
```

The procedure in Hands-On 14-8 uses the CopyFromRecordset method to copy data from the Employees table to an Excel worksheet.

◎ Hands-On 14-8: Copying Records to an Excel Worksheet (DAO)

1. In the Visual Basic Editor window, choose **Insert | Module**.
2. In the module's Code window, type the **ExportToExcel_DAO** procedure shown below, or copy the procedure code from **C:\Acc07_HandsOn\ Chap14.txt**.

```
Sub ExportToExcel_DAO()
    Dim db As DAO.Database
    Dim rst As DAO.Recordset
    Dim xlApp As Object
    Dim wkb As Object
    Dim rng As Object
    Dim strExcelFile As String
    Dim strDB As String
    Dim strTable As String
    Dim count As Integer
    Dim iCol As Integer
    Dim rowsToReturn As Integer

    strDB = "C:\Acc07_ByExample\Northwind 2007.accdb"
    strTable = "Employees"
    strExcelFile = CurrentProject.Path & "\ExcelFromAccess.xls"

    'If Excel file already exists delete it
    If Dir(strExcelFile) <> "" Then Kill strExcelFile

    Set db = OpenDatabase(strDB)
    Set rst = db.OpenRecordset(strTable)

    'get the number of records from the recordset
    count = rst.RecordCount

    rowsToReturn = CInt(InputBox("How many records to copy?"))
    If rowsToReturn <= count Then

        'set the reference to Excel and make Excel visible
        Set xlApp = CreateObject("Excel.Application")
        xlApp.Application.Visible = True

        'set references to the Excel workbook and worksheet
        Set wkb = xlApp.Workbooks.Add
        Set objSheet = xlApp.ActiveWorkbook.sheets(1)
        objSheet.Activate

        'write column names to the first worksheet row
        For iCol = 0 To rst.Fields.count - 1
            objSheet.Cells(1, iCol + 1).Value = rst.Fields(iCol).Name
        Next

        'specify the cell range that will receive the data
```

```
Set rng = objSheet.Cells(2, 1)

'copy the specified number of records to the worksheet
rng.CopyFromRecordset rst, rowsToReturn

'autofit the columns to make the data fit
objSheet.columns.AutoFit

'close the workbook
'and save it in Excel 97-2003 file format
wkb.SaveAs FileName:=strExcelFile, FileFormat:=56
wkb.Close

'quit Excel and release object variables
Set objSheet = Nothing
Set wkb = Nothing
xlApp.Quit
Set xlApp = Nothing
Else
MsgBox "Please specify a number less than " & count + 1 & "."
End If

db.Close
Set db = Nothing
End Sub
```

3. Position the insertion point anywhere within the procedure code and choose **Debug | Step Into** to execute the procedure one line at a time. (Press **F8** to execute each statement.)

The above procedure creates a recordset based on the Employees table and stores the total number of records in the count variable. The user is asked to specify the number of records to copy to Excel. If the specified number is less than or equal to the total number of records in the recordset, the code proceeds to copy the records to Excel using the CopyFromRecordset method. Notice that the above procedure uses the As Object clause to declare object variables that will contain references to Excel objects when the procedure is run. When you define an object variable as object, the variable is late bound. This means that VBA does not know what type of object the variable references until the program is run. To set a reference to Microsoft Excel it is necessary to use the CreateObject function. Once the object is created (Excel.Application), it is referenced with the object variable (xlApp). The CreateObject function will create a new instance of the Excel application. If Excel is already running, to use the current instance, or to start Excel and load a specific file, use the GetObject function. To view what's going on while the procedure is running, set the Visible property of the Microsoft Excel application to True. Then, if you run the above procedure in step mode, you will be able to check the contents of the Excel window as you execute each statement.

Before you can copy Access data to the Excel worksheet, you also need to set the references to the workbook, worksheet, and range objects. Once these references are defined, the procedure uses the Add method to add a new Excel workbook and then activates the first worksheet. The Recordset fields' names are written as column names to the first worksheet row. Next, the reference is set to the range object that will receive the data from the recordset. The CopyFromRecordset method is used to copy the specified number of records to the worksheet. Once data is placed in the worksheet it is fit into the columns with the AutoFit property. The Excel spreadsheet is then saved in the file format compatible with Excel 97-2003. The Workbook's SaveAs method requires the FileFormat parameter that specifies the file format for the workbook. The following file formats are used in Excel 2007:

- 50 (xlExcel12) — Excel binary workbook in 2007 with or without macros (XLSB)

- 52 (xlOpenXMLWorkbookMacroEnabled) — XML file format 2007 with or without macros (XLSM)

- 51 (xlOpenXMLWorkbook) — XML file format 2007 without macros (XLSX)

- 56 (xlExcel8) — 97-2003 format (XLS)

After saving the workbook, the procedure uses the Workbook Close method to close the Excel file. The Excel application object's Quit method is used to close the Excel application.

Copying Records to a Word Document

There are several techniques for placing Microsoft Access data in a Microsoft Word document. The procedure in Hands-On 14-9 demonstrates how to use the Recordset's GetString method to insert data from the Invoice Data table into a newly created Word document. Hands-On 14-10 shows how to insert data from the Shippers table and format the output using Word's Table object.

Hands-On 14-9: Copying Records to a Word Document (Example 1)

1. In the Visual Basic Editor window, choose **Insert | Module**.

2. Choose **Tools | References** in the Visual Basic Editor window. Scroll down to locate the Microsoft Word 12 Object Library, click the check box next to it, and then click **OK** to exit.

3. In the module's Code window, type the **SendToWord_ADO** procedure shown below, or copy the procedure code from **C:\Acc07_HandsOn\ Chap14.txt**.

```
Option Compare Database
Option Explicit
' be sure to select Microsoft Word 12 Object Library
' in the References dialog box

Public myWord As Word.Application

Sub SendToWord_ADO()
    Dim conn As ADODB.Connection
```

```
Dim rst As ADODB.Recordset
Dim doc As Word.Document
Dim strSQL As String
Dim varRst As Variant
Dim f As Variant
Dim strHead As String

Set conn = New ADODB.Connection
Set rst = New ADODB.Recordset

conn.Provider = "Microsoft.ACE.OLEDB.12.0;" & _
    "Data Source=" & CurrentProject.Path & _
    "\Northwind 2007.accdb"

strSQL = "SELECT [Order ID] AS OrderID,"
strSQL = strSQL & "[Ship Name], "
strSQL = strSQL & "[Ship City] FROM [Invoice Data]"

conn.Open
rst.Open strSQL, conn, adOpenForwardOnly, _
    adLockReadOnly, adCmdText

' retrieve data and table headings into variables
If Not rst.EOF Then
    varRst = rst.GetString(adClipString, , vbTab, vbCrLf)
    For Each f In rst.Fields
        strHead = strHead & f.Name & vbTab
    Next
End If

' notice that Word application is declared
' at the top of the module
Set myWord = New Word.Application

' create a new Word document
Set doc = myWord.Documents.Add
myWord.Visible = True

' paste contents of variables into
' Word document
doc.Paragraphs(1).Range.Text = strHead & vbCrLf
doc.Paragraphs(2).Range.Text = varRst

On Error GoTo ErrorHandler
    doc.Close SaveChanges:=wdPromptToSaveChanges
EndProc:
    myWord.Quit
    Set myWord = Nothing
    Exit Sub
ErrorHandler:
    If Err = 4198 Then MsgBox "You refused to save this document."
    Resume EndProc
End Sub
```

4. Choose **Run | Run Sub/UserForm** to execute the procedure.

The above procedure uses the Recordset object's GetString method to return recordset data as a string-valued Variant (see "Returning a Recordset as a String" in Chapter 13). Prior to running this procedure you must set a reference to the Microsoft Word 12 Object Library. This reference allows the procedure to access the Word application objects, properties, and methods via its own library. The top of the module contains the declaration of the myWord object variable that will point to the Word application. Notice that this variable is declared with the Public scope; therefore it can be accessed by other procedures in the current VBA project. (The next hands-on exercise also uses this variable.) To launch Word and create a new document, we set the Application object to a new instance of Word.Application using the New keyword:

```
Set myWord = New Word.Application
```

To work with a Word document, the Add method of the Word Documents collection is used to create a blank document. We store the reference to this document in the doc object variable. To enable the user to see what's going on while the procedure is running, the Visible property of the Word application is set to True. Next, the contents of the Recordset and the field names that we previously saved in the string variables are written to the Word document using the Document object's Paragraphs property. The procedure ends by prompting the user to save changes to the Word document. If the user does not opt to save the document, error 4198 is triggered.

◎ Hands-On 14-10: Copying Records to a Word Document (Example 2)

This procedure uses the myWord object variable that was declared in Hands-On 14-9 at the top of the module.

1. In the Visual Basic Editor window, choose **Insert | Module**.
2. In the module's Code window, type the **SendToWord2** procedure shown below, or copy the procedure code from **C:\Acc07_HandsOn\Chap14.txt**.

```
Sub SendToWord2()
    Dim db As DAO.Database
    Dim doc As Word.Document
    Dim WordTbl As Word.Table
    Dim f As Variant
    Dim numRows As Integer
    Dim numFields As Integer
    Dim r As Integer          ' row counter
    Dim c As Integer          ' column counter

    Set db = OpenDatabase("C:\Acc07_ByExample\Northwind.mdb")
    Set rst = db.OpenRecordset("Shippers")

    numRows = rst.RecordCount
    numFields = rst.Fields.count

    ' notice that the Word application is declared
    ' in the module where you entered the procedure
```

```
' from Hands-On 14-9

Set myWord = New Word.Application

' create a new Word document
Set doc = myWord.Documents.Add

' insert table
Set WordTbl = doc.Tables.Add _
    (doc.Range, numRows + 1, numFields)

c = 1
If numRows > 0 Then
    ' Create the column headings in table cells
    For Each f In rst.Fields
        With WordTbl
            .Cell(1, c).Range.Text = f.Name
            c = c + 1
        End With
    Next f
End If

r = 2
Do While Not rst.EOF
    For c = 1 To numFields
        WordTbl.Cell(r, c).Range.Text = rst.Fields(c - 1).Value
    Next c
    r = r + 1
    rst.MoveNext
Loop

myWord.Visible = True

rst.Close
Set rst = Nothing
Set myWord = Nothing
db.Close
Set db = Nothing
End Sub
```

3. Choose **Run | Run Sub/UserForm** to execute the procedure.

4. Close the Word document and exit the Word application after you've looked at the resulting document.

Copying Records to a Text File

To write records to a text file, save them as a string by using the Recordset object's GetString method. Next, create a text file with the CreateTextFile method of the FileSystemObject from the Microsoft Scripting Runtime Library.

The procedure in Hands-On 14-11 demonstrates how to write the records from the Order Details table in the Northwind.mdb database to a text file named TestFile. Figures 14-1 and 14-2 show the generated text file after it has been opened in Notepad and in Microsoft Excel.

⊚ Hands-On 14-11: Copy Records to a Text File (ADO)

1. In the Visual Basic Editor window, choose **Insert | Module**.

2. In the module's Code window, type the **WriteToFile** procedure shown below, or copy the procedure code from **C:\Acc07_HandsOn\Chap14.txt**.

```
Sub WriteToFile()
    Dim conn As ADODB.Connection
    Dim rst As ADODB.Recordset
    Dim f As ADODB.Field
    Dim fso As Object
    Dim txtfile As Object
    Dim strFileName As String

    Set conn = New ADODB.Connection
    conn.Open "Provider=Microsoft.Jet.OLEDB.4.0;" & _
        "Data Source=" & CurrentProject.Path & _
        "\Northwind.mdb"

    strFileName = CurrentProject.Path & "\TestFile.txt"

    Set fso = CreateObject("Scripting.FileSystemObject")
    Set txtfile = fso.CreateTextFile(strFileName, True)

    Set rst = New ADODB.Recordset
    rst.Open "[Order Details]", conn
    With rst
        For Each f In .Fields
            ' Write field name to the text file
            txtfile.Write (f.Name)
            txtfile.Write Chr(9)
        Next
        ' move to a new line
        txtfile.WriteLine
        ' write out all the records to the text file
        txtfile.Write rst.GetString(adClipString)
        .Close
    End With

    txtfile.Close
    Set rst = Nothing
    conn.Close
    Set conn = Nothing
End Sub
```

3. Choose **Run | Run Sub/UserForm** to execute the procedure.

The above procedure uses the CreateObject function to access the FileSystemObject. The File object is created using the FileSystemObject's CreateTextFile method. The first argument of this method specifies the name of the file to create, and the second argument (True) indicates that the file should be overwritten if it already exists. Next, the procedure iterates through the recordset based on the Order Details table and writes field names to the text file using the Write method of the File object. The data from the recordset is converted into a string using the GetString method of the Recordset object and then written to the text file using the File object's Write method.

The text file is then closed with the Close method.

Figure 14-1: After running the WriteToFile procedure in Hands-On 14-11, the records from the Order Details table are placed in a text file.

Figure 14-2: The Access-generated text file in Hands-On 14-11 opened in Excel 2007.

Filtering Records Using the SQL WHERE Clause

When you want to work only with a certain subset of records, you can filter out those records you don't want to see by using the SQL WHERE clause or the Filter property. You can apply a filter to a Dynaset-type or Snapshot-type Recordset object. The fastest way to filter records is to open a new Recordset object by using an SQL statement that includes a WHERE clause. Hands-On 14-12 provides an example of using the SQL WHERE clause to retrieve product orders with an order quantity greater than 100.

◎ Hands-On 14-12: Filtering Records with the SQL WHERE Clause (DAO)

1. In the Visual Basic Editor window, choose **Insert | Module**.

2. In the module's Code window, type the **FilterWithSQLWhere_DAO** procedure shown below, or copy the procedure code from **C:\Acc07_HandsOn\Chap14.txt**.

```
Sub FilterWithSQLWhere_DAO()
    Dim db As DAO.Database
    Dim rst As DAO.Recordset
    Dim qdf As DAO.QueryDef
    Dim qryName As String
    Dim mySQL As String

    Set db = OpenDatabase("C:\Acc07_ByExample\Northwind 2007.accdb")

    qryName = "qryOrdersOver100"
    mySQL = "SELECT * FROM " _
        & "[Product Orders] WHERE Quantity > 100;"
    Set qdf = db.CreateQueryDef(qryName)
    qdf.SQL = mySQL
    Set rst = db.OpenRecordset(qryName)
    Debug.Print "There are " & rst.RecordCount & _
        " orders with the order quantity greater than 100."

    rst.Close
    Set rst = Nothing
    Set qdf = Nothing
    db.Close
    Set db = Nothing
End Sub
```

3. Choose **Run | Run Sub/UserForm** to execute the procedure.

The above procedure creates a simple Select query in the Northwind 2007.accdb database based on the Product Orders table. The SQL WHERE clause in the SQL statement specifies that only orders with a quantity greater than 100 should be returned. If the expression contained in the WHERE clause is True, then the record is selected; otherwise, the record is excluded from the opened set of records.

The procedure in Hands-On 14-13 opens a recordset that contains only records having the value of Null in the Region field or an entry of "Mrs." in the TitleOfCourtesy field.

◉ Hands-On 14-13: Filtering Records with the SQL WHERE Clause (ADO)

1. In the Visual Basic Editor window, choose **Insert | Module**.

2. In the module's Code window, type the **FilterWithSQLWhere_ADO** procedure shown below, or copy the procedure code from **C:\Acc07_HandsOn\Chap14.txt**.

```
Sub FilterWithSQLWhere_ADO()
    Dim conn As ADODB.Connection
    Dim rst As ADODB.Recordset
    Dim strSQL As String

    strSQL = "SELECT * FROM Employees WHERE IsNull(Region)" & _
        " or TitleOfCourtesy = 'Mrs.' "

    Set conn = New ADODB.Connection
    conn.Open "Provider=Microsoft.Jet.OLEDB.4.0;" & _
```

```
                    "Data Source=" & CurrentProject.Path & _
                    "\Northwind.mdb"

                Set rst = New ADODB.Recordset
                rst.Open strSQL, conn, adOpenKeyset, adLockOptimistic
                MsgBox "Selected " & rst.RecordCount & " records."

                rst.Close
                Set rst = Nothing
                conn.Close
                Set conn = Nothing
            End Sub
```

3. Choose **Run | Run Sub/UserForm** to execute the procedure.

Filtering Records Using the Filter Property

You can use the DAO or ADO Filter property to obtain a set of records that meet specific criteria.

Hands-On 14-14 uses the Filter property with the DAO Recordset to restrict the subset of records to those in which the employee's city begins with the letter "R".

Hands-On 14-14: Filtering Records Using the Filter Property (DAO)

1. In the Visual Basic Editor window, choose **Insert | Module**.

2. In the module's Code window, type the **FilterRecords_DAO** procedure shown below, or copy the procedure code from **C:\Acc07_HandsOn\ Chap14.txt**.

```
Sub FilterRecords_DAO()
    Dim db As DAO.Database
    Dim rst As DAO.Recordset
    Dim FilterRst As DAO.Recordset

    Set db = OpenDatabase("C:\Acc07_ByExample\Northwind 2007.accdb")
    Set rst = db.OpenRecordset("Employees", dbOpenDynaset)
    rst.Filter = "City like 'R*'"
    Set FilterRst = rst.OpenRecordset()

    Do Until FilterRst.EOF
        Debug.Print FilterRst.Fields("Last Name").Value
        FilterRst.MoveNext
    Loop

    FilterRst.Close
    Set FilterRst = Nothing
    rst.Close
    Set rst = Nothing
    db.Close
    Set db = Nothing
End Sub
```

3. Choose **Run | Run Sub/UserForm** to execute the procedure.

The above procedure begins by opening a Dynaset-type Recordset object based on the Empoyees table and setting the Filter property on this recordset:

```
rst.Filter = "City like 'R*'"
```

For the filter to take effect after you set it, you must open a new recordset based on the Recordset object to which the filter was applied:

```
Set FilterRst = rst.OpenRecordset()
```

Next, the procedure writes to the Immediate window the value of the Last Name field for all of the records in the filtered recordset.

The procedure in Hands-On 14-15 creates a filtered view of customers listed in the Northwind database who are located in Madrid, Spain.

◉ Hands-On 14-15: Filtering Records Using the Filter Property (ADO)

1. In the Visual Basic Editor window, choose **Insert | Module**.

2. In the module's Code window, type the **FilterRecords_ADO** procedure shown below, or copy the procedure code from **C:\Acc07_HandsOn\ Chap14.txt**.

```
Sub FilterRecords_ADO()
    Dim conn As ADODB.Connection
    Dim rst As ADODB.Recordset

    Set conn = New ADODB.Connection
    conn.Open "Provider=Microsoft.Jet.OLEDB.4.0;" & _
        "Data Source=" & CurrentProject.Path & _
        "\Northwind.mdb"

    Set rst = New ADODB.Recordset
    With rst
        .Open "Customers", conn, adOpenKeyset, adLockOptimistic
        .Filter = "City='Madrid' and Country='Spain'"
        MsgBox .RecordCount & " records meet the criteria.", _
            vbInformation, "Customers in Madrid (Spain)"
    End With

    Do Until rst.EOF
        Debug.Print rst.Fields(1).Value
        rst.MoveNext
    Loop

    rst.Filter = adFilterNone
    MsgBox "Filter was removed. " & vbCr _
        & "The table contains " & rst.RecordCount & " records."

    rst.Close
    Set rst = Nothing
    conn.Close
    Set conn = Nothing
End Sub
```

3. Choose **Run | Run Sub/UserForm** to execute the procedure.

The above procedure defines the filter on the Customers table and displays the filtered records. Then the filter is removed by setting the Filter property to adFilterNone.

Use the Filter property as a workaround to the ADO Find method whenever you need to find records that meet more than one condition. If the specific set of records you want to obtain is located on the SQL Server, you should use stored procedures instead of the Filter property.

Sorting Records

You can use the Recordset object's Sort property to change the order in which records are displayed. The Sort property does not physically rearrange the records; it merely displays the records in the order specified by the index. If you are sorting on non-indexed fields, a temporary index is created for each field specified in the index. This index is removed automatically when you set the Sort property to an empty string. In ADO you can only use Sort on client-side cursors. If you use the server-side cursor, you will receive this error: "The operation requested by the application is not supported by the provider."

The default sort order is ascending. To order a recordset by country in ascending order, then by city in descending order, you would use the following statement:

```
rst.Sort = "Country ASC, City DESC"
```

Although you can use the Sort property to sort your data, you will most likely get better performance by specifying an SQL ORDER BY clause in the SQL statement or query used to open the recordset. The procedure in Hands-On 14-16 displays customer records from the Northwind database in ascending order by country.

Hands-On 14-16: Sorting Records (ADO)

1. In the Visual Basic Editor window, choose **Insert | Module**.
2. In the module's Code window, type the **SortRecords_ADO** procedure shown below, or copy the procedure code from **C:\Acc07_HandsOn\ Chap14.txt**.

```
Sub SortRecords_ADO()
    Dim conn As ADODB.Connection
    Dim rst As ADODB.Recordset

    Set conn = New ADODB.Connection
    conn.Open "Provider=Microsoft.Jet.OLEDB.4.0;" & _
        "Data Source=" & CurrentProject.Path & _
        "\Northwind.mdb"

    Set rst = New ADODB.Recordset

    ' sort on non-indexed field
    With rst
```

```
.CursorLocation = adUseClient
.Open "Customers", conn, adOpenKeyset, adLockOptimistic
.Sort = "Country"
Do Until rst.EOF
    Debug.Print rst.Fields("CompanyName").Value & ": " & _
        rst.Fields("Country").Value
    .MoveNext
Loop
Debug.Print "-----------original sort"
.Sort = ""
Do Until .EOF
    Debug.Print rst.Fields("CompanyName").Value & ": " & _
        rst.Fields("Country").Value
    .MoveNext
Loop
.Close
End With

    Set rst = Nothing
    conn.Close
    Set conn = Nothing
End Sub
```

3. Choose **Run | Run Sub/UserForm** to execute the procedure.

In the procedure above, after sorting records in the specified order the Sort property is set to an empty string and records are displayed in the order in which they physically appear in the table.

Chapter Summary

This chapter demonstrated several methods of the DAO and ADO Recordset object you can use for working with records. You learned about the AddNew, Update, and Delete methods for performing such common database tasks as adding, modifying, and deleting records. These methods are suitable for handling a small number of records. Better performance can be achieved by using the SQL INSERT, UPDATE, and DELETE statements, as you will see in Chapters 15 and 23.

This chapter also showed you how to render your database records into three popular formats: an Excel spreadsheet, a Word document, and a text file. Because working with large quantities of records can be difficult unless data is properly organized, this chapter also covered methods for filtering and sorting your records.

In the next chapter you will learn how to create and run Access queries from your VBA procedures.

Chapter 15

Creating and Running Queries with DAO/ADO

Having worked with Microsoft Access for a while, you already know that to retrieve relevant information from your database and perform data-oriented tasks you need to write queries. Queries are SQL statements that are saved in the database and can be run at any time. Microsoft Office Access 2007 supports several types of queries.

The simplest queries allow you to select a set of records from a table. However, when you need to extract information from more than one table at a time, you must write a more complex query by using an SQL JOIN statement. Other queries perform specific actions on existing data, such as making a new table, appending rows to a table, updating the values in a table, or deleting rows from a table. Although Microsoft Office Access provides a friendly interface — the Query Design view — for creating queries manually, this chapter teaches you how to create and execute the same queries by using DAO and ADO objects as well as SQL Data Manipulation Language (DML) statements in VBA code.

Creating a Select Query Manually

Select queries retrieve a set of records from a database table. These queries are easily recognized by the SELECT and FROM keywords in their syntax. Let's take a look at a couple of examples:

`SELECT LastName FROM Employees`	Selects the LastName field from the Employees table. If there is a space in the field name, enclose the field name in square brackets: [Last Name].
`SELECT FirstName, LastName, PhoneNo FROM Employees`	Selects the FirstName, LastName, and PhoneNo fields from the Employees table.
`SELECT * FROM Employees`	Selects all fields for all records from the Employees table. The asterisk (*) is used to represent all fields.

Often the WHERE clause is used with Select queries to specify criteria that determine which records the query will affect. Some examples of using the WHERE clause to restrict records are shown below:

`SELECT * FROM Employees`
`WHERE City IN ('Redmond',`
`'London')`
	Selects from the Employees table all fields for all records that have the value Redmond or London in the City field.

`SELECT * FROM Employees`
`WHERE City IN ('Redmond',`
`'London') AND`
`ReportsTo LIKE 'Buchanan, Steven'`
	Selects from the Employees table all fields for all records that have the value Redmond or London in the City field and have a value Buchanan, Steven in the ReportsTo field.

`SELECT * FROM Employees`
`WHERE ((Year([HireDate])<1993) OR`
`(City='Redmond'))`
	Selects from the Employees table all fields for all records that have a value less than 1993 in the HireDate field or have the value Redmond in the City field.

`SELECT * FROM Products` `WHERE UnitPrice BETWEEN 10 AND 25`	Selects from the Products table all fields for all records that have an amount in the UnitPrice field between $10 and $25.
`SELECT * FROM Employees` `WHERE ReportsTo IS NULL`	Selects from the Employees table all fields for all records that do not have a value in the ReportsTo field.

You can use expressions in WHERE clauses to qualify SQL statements. An SQL expression is a string that is used in SQL statements. Expressions can contain literal values, constants, field names, operators, and functions. Several operators that are often used in expressions are shown in Table 15-1.

Table 15-1: Operators commonly used in expressions

Operator Name	Description/Usage

IN	The IN operator is used to determine whether the value of an expression is equal to any of several values in a specified list. If the expression is found in the list of values, the IN operator returns True; otherwise, it returns False. You can include the NOT logical operator to determine whether the expression is not in the list of values.
	
	For example, you can use NOT IN to determine which employees don't live in Redmond or London:
	`SELECT * FROM Employees`
	`WHERE City NOT IN ('Redmond', 'London')`

LIKE	The LIKE operator compares a string expression to a pattern in an SQL expression. For a pattern, you specify the complete value (for example, LIKE 'Buchanan, Steven'), or you can use wildcard characters to find a range of values (for example, LIKE 'B*'). You can use a number of wildcard characters in the LIKE operator pattern (see Table 15-2).

Operator Name	Description/Usage

BETWEEN...AND	The BETWEEN...AND operator is used to determine whether the value of an expression falls within a specified range of values. If the value of the expression is between value1 and value2 (inclusive), the BETWEEN...AND operator returns True; otherwise, it returns False. You can include the NOT logical operator to evaluate the opposite condition, that is, whether the expression falls outside the range defined by value1 and value2.
	
	For example, you can select all products with the amount in the UnitPrice field less than $10 and greater than $25:
	
	`SELECT * FROM Products`
	`WHERE UnitPrice NOT BETWEEN 10 AND 25`

IS NULL	The IS NULL operator is used to determine whether the expression value is equal to the Null value. A Null value indicates missing or unknown data. You can include the NOT logical operator to return only records that have values in the specified field.
	
	For example, you can extract only the employee records that have a value in the ReportsTo field. Records where the ReportsTo field is blank will not be included:
	
	`SELECT * FROM Employees`
	`WHERE ReportsTo IS NOT NULL`

Table 15-2: Wildcard characters used in the LIKE operator patterns

Wildcard	Description
* (asterisk)	Matches any number of characters.
? (question mark)	Matches any single character.
% (percent sign)	Matches any number of characters (used only with the ADO and Jet OLE DB Provider; not in the Access user interface).
_ (underscore)	Matches any single character (used only with the ADO and Jet OLE DB Provider; not in the Access user interface).
# (number sign)	Matches any single digit.
[] (square brackets)	Matches any single character within the list of characters enclosed in brackets.
! (exclamation point)	Matches any single character that is not found in the list enclosed in the square brackets.
- (hyphen)	Matches any one of the range of characters enclosed in the square brackets.

In addition to the WHERE clause, you can use predicates to further restrict the set of records to be retrieved. A *predicate* is an SQL statement that qualifies the SELECT statement, similar to the WHERE clause; however, the predicate must be placed before the column list. Several popular predicates are shown in Table 15-3.

Table 15-3: Commonly used predicates in SQL SELECT statements

Predicate Name	Description/Usage

ALL	The ALL keyword is the default keyword and is used when no predicate is declared in the SQL statement.
	
	The following two examples are equivalent and return all records from the Employees table:
	
	`SELECT ALL *`
	`FROM Employees`
	`ORDER BY EmployeeID;`
	
	`SELECT *`
	`FROM Employees`
	`ORDER BY EmployeeID`

DISTINCT	The DISTINCT keyword eliminates duplicate values from the returned set of records. The values for each field listed in the SELECT statement must be unique.
	
	For example, to return a list of non-duplicate (unique) cities from the Employees table, you can write the following SELECT statement:
	
	`SELECT DISTINCT City`
	`FROM Employees`
	
	Note: The output of a query that uses DISTINCT isn't updatable (it's read-only).

DISTINCTROW	While the DISTINCT keyword is based on duplicate fields, the DISTINCTROW keyword is based on entire rows. It is used only with multiple tables.
	
	For example, if you join the Customers and Orders tables on the CustomerID field, you can find customers that have at least one order. The Customers table contains no duplicate CustomerID fields, but the Orders table does because each customer can have many orders.
	
	`SELECT DISTINCTROW CompanyName`
	`FROM Customers, Orders`
	`WHERE Customers.CustomerID =`
	`Orders.CustomerID`
	`ORDER BY CompanyName;`
	
	Note: If you omit DISTINCTROW, this SELECT statement will produce multiple rows for each company that has more than one order. DISTINCTROW has an effect only when you select fields from some, but not all, of the tables used in the query. DISTINCTROW is ignored if your query includes only one table or if you output fields from all tables.

Predicate Name	Description/Usage
TOP or PERCENT	The TOP keyword returns a certain number of records that fall at the top or bottom of a range specified by an ORDER BY clause.
	For example, suppose you want to select the five most expensive products:
	`SELECT TOP 5 * FROM Products` `ORDER BY UnitPrice DESC`
	The TOP predicate doesn't choose between equal values. If there are equal values present, the TOP keyword will return all rows that have the equal value.
	You can also use the PERCENT keyword to return a percentage of records that fall at the top or the bottom of a range specified by an ORDER BY clause.
	For example, to return the lowest 10 percent priced products, you can write the following statement:

	`SELECT TOP 10 PERCENT *`
	`FROM Products`
	`ORDER BY UnitPrice ASC;`

	Note: If you don't include the ORDER BY clause, the SELECT TOP statement will return a random set of rows.

If you'd like to sort records returned by the SELECT statement, use the ORDER BY clause with the ASC (ascending sort) or DESC (descending sort) keywords, as shown in the following example:

`SELECT * FROM Employees` `ORDER BY Country DESC`	Select all records from the Employees table and arrange them in descending order based on the Country field. If no order is specified, the order is ascending (ASC) by default.

By default, records are sorted in ascending order. The fields you want to sort by do not need to be enumerated in the SELECT statement's field list. Instead of sorting by field name, you can sort by field position. For example, the statement:

```
SELECT * FROM EMPLOYEES
ORDER BY 2
```

will sort the records in ascending order by the second field.

Creating a Select Query with DAO

Select queries retrieve a set of records from a database table. These queries are easily recognized by the SELECT and FROM keywords in their syntax. In DAO, the QueryDef object represents a saved query in a database. All QueryDef objects are contained in the QueryDefs collection. You can read and set the SQL definition of a Query object using the SQL property. To create a query in code, use the CreateQueryDef method. For example, to create a Select query named myQuery, the following statement is used:

```
Set qdf = db.CreateQueryDef("myQuery", strSQL)
```

When you specify the name for your query, the new QueryDef object is automatically appended to the QueryDefs collection when it is created. The second argument of the CreateQueryDef method is a string variable that holds a valid Access SQL statement. Prior to using this variable, you must assign to it a string expression:

```
strSQL = "SELECT * FROM Employees WHERE TitleOfCourtesy = 'Ms.'"
```

The WHERE clause is used with Select queries to specify criteria that determine which records the query will affect. (See "Creating a Select Query Manually" at the beginning of this chapter).

The procedure in Hands-On 15-1 selects from the Employees table all records that have a value of "Ms." in the TitleOfCourtesy field. The keyword LIKE can be substituted for the equal sign (=), as in the following:

```
strSQL = "SELECT * FROM Employees WHERE TitleOfCourtesy LIKE 'Ms.'"
```

When creating queries in code, be sure to include an error handler. After all, the query you are trying to create may already exist, or an unexpected error could occur.

◎ Hands-On 15-1: Creating a Select Query with DAO

1. Create a new Microsoft Office Access database named **Chap15.accdb** and save it in your **C:\Acc07_ByExample** folder.

2. In the database window, press **Alt+F11** to switch to the Visual Basic Editor window.

3. In the Visual Basic Editor window, choose **Insert | Module**.

4. In the module's Code window, type the **Create_SelectQuery_DAO** procedure shown below, or copy the procedure code from **C:\Acc07_HandsOn\ Chap15.txt**.

```
Sub Create_SelectQuery_DAO()
    Dim db As DAO.Database
    Dim qdf As DAO.QueryDef
    Dim strSQL As String

    On Error GoTo Err_SelectQuery

    strSQL = "SELECT * FROM Employees "
    strSQL = strSQL & "WHERE TitleOfCourtesy = 'Ms.'"
    Set db = OpenDatabase("C:\Acc07_ByExample\Northwind.mdb")
    Set qdf = db.CreateQueryDef("myQuery", strSQL)
ExitHere:
    Set qdf = Nothing
    db.Close
    Set db = Nothing
    Exit Sub
Err_SelectQuery:
    If Err.Number = 3012 Then
        MsgBox "Query with this name already exists."
    Else
```

```
            MsgBox Err.Description
        End If
        Resume ExitHere
    End Sub
```

5. Choose **Run | Run Sub/UserForm** to execute the procedure.

If you run the Create_SelectQuery_DAO procedure in Hands-On 15-1, the next time you open the Northwind.mdb database you should see the query named myQuery in the list of stored queries in the Access window.

 Note: Instead of a query that is saved in the database for future use, it is possible to create a temporary query by setting the QueryDefName property to a zero-length string (""), as in the following example:

```
    Set qdf = db.CreateQueryDef("", strSQL)
```

The advantage of temporary queries is that they don't clutter the Access window.

Creating a Select Query with ADO

In ADO, queries, SQL statements, views, and stored procedures are represented by the Command object. This object is part of the ADOX Object Model (see Chapter 11, Figure 11-2). The Command object has many properties and methods that will allow you to return records or execute changes to your data (inserts, updates, and deletes). In this chapter you will get to know the properties of the Command object, including ActiveConnection, CommandText, and CommandType. These properties will be discussed as they appear in the example procedure code. You will also learn how to use the Command object's Execute method to run your queries.

The procedure in Hands-On 15-2 demonstrates how to create and save a Select query using ActiveX Data Objects (ADO).

⊙ Hands-On 15-2: Creating a Select Query with ADO

1. In the Visual Basic Editor window of the Chap15.accdb database, choose **Insert | Module**.

2. Choose **Tools | References** and select the following object libraries: **Microsoft ADO Ext. 2.8 for DDL and Security Object Library** and **Microsoft ActiveX Data Objects 2.8 Object Library**.

3. In the module's Code window, type the **Create_SelectQuery_ADO** procedure shown below, or copy the procedure code from **C:\Acc07_HandsOn\Chap15.txt**.

```
Sub Create_SelectQuery_ADO()
    Dim cat As ADOX.Catalog
    Dim cmd As ADODB.Command
    Dim strPath As String
    Dim strSQL As String
    Dim strQryName As String
```

```
On Error GoTo ErrorHandler

' assign values to string variables
strPath = CurrentProject.Path & "\Northwind 2007.accdb"
strSQL = "SELECT Employees.* FROM Employees WHERE " _
    & "Employees.City='Redmond';"

strQryName = "Redmond Employees"

' open the Catalog
Set cat = New ADOX.Catalog
cat.ActiveConnection = _
    "Provider=Microsoft.ACE.OLEDB.12.0;" & _
    "Data Source=" & strPath

' create a query based on the specified
' SELECT statement
Set cmd = New ADODB.Command
cmd.CommandText = strSQL

' add the new query to the database
cat.Views.Append strQryName, cmd

MsgBox "The procedure completed successfully.", _
    vbInformation, "Create Select Query"
ExitHere:
    Set cmd = Nothing
    Set cat = Nothing
    Exit Sub

ErrorHandler:
    If InStr(Err.Description, "already exists") Then
        cat.Views.Delete strQryName
        Resume
    Else
        MsgBox Err.Number & ": " & Err.Description
        Resume ExitHere
    End If
End Sub
```

4. Choose **Run | Run Sub/UserForm** to execute the procedure.

The Create_SelectQuery_ADO procedure opens the Catalog object and sets its ActiveConnection property to the Northwind 2007.accdb database:

```
Set cat = New ADOX.Catalog
cat.ActiveConnection="Provider=Microsoft.ACE.OLEDB.12.0;" & _
    "Data Source=" & strPath
```

As you may recall from Chapter 11, the Catalog object represents an entire database. It contains objects that represent all the elements of the database: tables, stored procedures, views, columns of tables, and indexes. The ActiveConnection property of the Catalog object indicates the ADO Connection object the Catalog belongs to. The value of this property can be a reference to the Connection object or a connection string containing the definition for a connection. Next, the procedure defines a Command object and uses its CommandText property to set the SQL statement for the query:

```
Set cmd = New ADODB.Command
cmd.CommandText = strSQL
```

The CommandText property contains the text of a command you want to issue against a provider. In this procedure, we assigned the string variable's value (strSQL) to the CommandText property.

The ADO Command object always creates a temporary query. So, to create a stored (saved) query in a database, the procedure must append the Command object to the ADOX Views collection, like this:

```
cat.Views.Append strQryName, cmd
```

If you open the sample Northwind 2007.accdb database after running the above procedure, you will find the Redmond Employees query in the Access window.

Row-returning, Non-parameterized Queries

Queries that return records, such as Select queries, are known as row-returning, non-parameterized queries.

In ADO, use the View object to work with queries that return records and do not take parameters. All View objects are contained in the Views collection of the ADOX Catalog object. To save these queries in a database, append the ADO Command object to the ADOX Views collection as shown in Hands-On 15-2.

Executing an Existing Select Query with ADO

There's more than one way of executing a row-returning query with ADO. This section demonstrates two procedures that run the Products by Category query located in the Northwind.mdb database.

The procedure in Hands-On 15-3 uses the Command and Recordset objects to perform this task.

⊚ Hands-On 15-3: Executing a Select Query

1. In the Visual Basic Editor window, choose **Insert | Module**.

2. In the module's Code window, type the **Execute_SelectQuery_ADO** procedure shown below, or copy the procedure code from **C:\Acc07_HandsOn\Chap15.txt**.

```
Sub Execute_SelectQuery_ADO()
    Dim cmd As ADODB.Command
    Dim rst As ADODB.Recordset
    Dim strPath As String

    strPath = CurrentProject.Path & "\Northwind.mdb"

    Set cmd = New ADODB.Command
```

```
With cmd
    .ActiveConnection = "Provider=Microsoft.Jet.OLEDB.4.0;" & _
        "Data Source=" & strPath
    .CommandText = "[Products by Category]"
    .CommandType = adCmdTable
End With

Set rst = New ADODB.Recordset
Set rst = cmd.Execute

Debug.Print rst.GetString

rst.Close
Set rst = Nothing
Set cmd = Nothing
MsgBox "View results in the Immediate window."
End Sub
```

3. Choose **Run | Run Sub/UserForm** to execute the procedure.

In the Execute_Select Query_ADO procedure above, the connection to the database is opened by setting the ActiveConnection property of the Command object. Next, the Command object's CommandText property specifies the name of the query you want to run. Notice that you need to place square brackets around the query's name when it contains spaces. The query type is determined by setting the CommandType property of the Command object. Use the adCmdTable or adCmdStoredProc constants if the query string in the CommandText property is a query name. Finally, the Execute method of the Command object executes the query. Notice that the resulting recordset is passed to the Recordset object variable so that you can access the records retrieved by the query. Instead of looping through the records to read the returned records, the procedure uses the Recordset object's GetString method to print all the recordset rows to the Immediate window. The GetString method returns the recordset as a string (for more information, please see Chapter 13).

Figure 15-1: This is a sample result of records that were generated by executing a Select query (see Hands-On 15-3).

The next example procedure (Hands-On 15-4) demonstrates another method of running a row-returning query with ADO. Notice that in addition to the ADO Command and Recordset objects, this procedure uses the ADOX Catalog object. The connection to the database is established by setting the ActiveConnection property of the Catalog object, and not the Command object, as was the case in Hands-On 15-3.

⊚ Hands-On 15-4: Executing a Select Query with an ADO Catalog Object

1. In the Visual Basic Editor window, choose **Insert | Module**.

2. In the module's Code window, type the **Execute_SelectQuery2_ADO** procedure shown below, or copy the procedure code from **C:\Acc07_ HandsOn\Chap15.txt**.

```
Sub Execute_SelectQuery2_ADO()
    Dim cat As ADOX.Catalog
    Dim cmd As ADODB.Command
    Dim rst As ADODB.Recordset
    Dim strPath As String

    strPath = CurrentProject.Path & "\Northwind.mdb"

    Set cat = New ADOX.Catalog
    cat.ActiveConnection = "Provider=Microsoft.Jet.OLEDB.4.0;" & _
        "Data Source=" & strPath

    Set cmd = New ADODB.Command
    Set cmd = cat.Views("Products by Category").Command

    Set rst = New ADODB.Recordset
    rst.Open cmd, , adOpenStatic, adLockReadOnly, adCmdTable

    Debug.Print rst.GetString
    MsgBox "The query returned " & rst.RecordCount & vbCr & _
        " records to the Immediate window."
    rst.Close
    Set rst = Nothing
    Set cmd = Nothing
    Set cat = Nothing
End Sub
```

3. Choose **Run | Run Sub/UserForm** to execute the procedure.

In the above procedure, the following line of code is used to indicate the name of the query to be executed:

```
Set cmd = cat.Views("Products by Category").Command
```

This statement sets the cmd object variable to the desired query stored in the Views collection of the ADOX Catalog object. Next, the Open method of the Recordset object is used to open the recordset based on the specified query:

```
rst.Open cmd, , adOpenStatic, adLockReadOnly, adCmdTable
```

Notice that several optional arguments of the Open method are used to specify the data source: cmd, ActiveConnection (a comma appears in this spot because the existing connection is being used), CursorType (adOpenStatic), LockType (adLockReadOnly), and Options (adCmdTable). Refer to Chapter 13 for information about using these ADO constants. Next, the procedure dumps the contents of the records into the Immediate window (just as the procedure in Hands-On 15-3 did) by using the Recordset's GetString method. The MsgBox function contains a string that includes the information about the number of records retrieved. The RecordCount property of the Recordset object is used to get the record count. To get the correct record count you must set the CursorType argument of the Recordset's Open method to adOpenStatic. If you set this argument to adOpenDynamic or adOpenForwardOnly, the Record-Count property will return –1. To learn more about these constants, refer to the sections on working with Recordset objects in ADO in Chapter 13.

Modifying an Existing Query with ADO

If you'd like to modify an existing query, follow these steps:

1. Retrieve the query from the Views or Procedures collection of the Catalog object.

2. Set the CommandText property of the Command object to the new SQL statement.

3. Save the changes by setting the Procedure or View object's Command property to the modified Command object.

Earlier in this chapter you learned how to create a Select query named Redmond Employees by using ADO (see Hands-On 15-2). The following hands-on exercise modifies this query so that employee records are ordered by last name.

◎ Hands-On 15-5: Modifying a Select Query with ADO

1. In the Visual Basic Editor window, choose **Insert** | **Module**.

2. In the module's Code window, type the **Modify_Query_ADO** procedure shown below, or copy the procedure code from **C:\Acc07_HandsOn\ Chap15.txt**.

```
Sub Modify_Query_ADO()
    Dim cat As ADOX.Catalog
    Dim cmd As ADODB.Command
    Dim strPath As String
    Dim newStrSQL As String
    Dim oldStrSQL As String
    Dim strQryName As String

    strPath = CurrentProject.Path & "\Northwind 2007.accdb"

    newStrSQL = "SELECT Employees.* FROM Employees" & _
        " WHERE Employees.City='Redmond'" & _
        " ORDER BY [Last Name];"

    strQryName = "Redmond Employees"

    Set cat = New ADOX.Catalog
    cat.ActiveConnection = _
        "Provider=Microsoft.ACE.OLEDB.12.0;" & _
        "Data Source=" & strPath
```

```
Set cmd = New ADODB.Command
Set cmd = cat.Views(strQryName).Command

' get the existing SQL statement for this query
oldStrSQL = cmd.CommandText

MsgBox oldStrSQL, vbInformation, _
    "Current SQL Statement"

' now update the query's SQL statement
cmd.CommandText = newStrSQL
MsgBox newStrSQL, vbInformation, _
    "New SQL Statement"

' save the modified query
Set cat.Views(strQryName).Command = cmd

Set cmd = Nothing
Set cat = Nothing
End Sub
```

3. Choose **Run | Run Sub/UserForm** to execute the procedure.

When you run the above procedure the "Redmond Employees" query created in Hands-On 15-2 is modified from the following SQL statement:

```
SELECT Employees.*
FROM Employees
WHERE Employees.City='Redmond';
```

to:

```
SELECT Employees.*
FROM Employees
WHERE Employees.City='Redmond' ORDER BY [Last Name];
```

Creating and Running a Parameter Query with DAO

A special type of a Select query is known as a Parameter query. Instead of retrieving the same records each time a query is run, a user can enter the search criteria in a special dialog box at run time. In DAO, the parameters of a Parameter query are represented by Parameter objects. The QueryDef object contains a Parameters collection. Parameter objects represent existing parameters.

To create a Parameter query, create a query string that includes the PARAMETERS keyword:

```
strSQL = "PARAMETERS [Enter Country] Text;"&_
    "SELECT * FROM CUSTOMERS WHERE Country = [Enter Country];"
```

Before executing an existing Parameter query, assign a value to the parameter, as shown in Hands-On 15-6. Once the parameter value is specified, you need to open a recordset based on the query.

The procedure in Hands-On 15-6 demonstrates how to create and run a Parameter query to retrieve the names of the companies in the user-specified country.

◎ Hands-On 15-6: Creating a Parameter Query with DAO

1. In the Visual Basic Editor window, choose **Insert | Module**.
2. In the module's Code window, type the **CreateRun_ParameterQuery_ DAO** procedure shown below, or copy the procedure code from **C:\Acc07_HandsOn\Chap15.txt**.

```
Sub CreateRun_ParameterQuery_DAO()
    Dim db As DAO.Database
    Dim qdf As DAO.QueryDef
    Dim rst As DAO.Recordset
    Dim strQryName As String
    Dim strSQL As String

    On Error GoTo Err_Handler

    strQryName = "myParamQuery"
    strSQL = "PARAMETERS [Enter Country] Text; " & _
        "SELECT * FROM Customers WHERE Country = [Enter Country];"

    Set db = OpenDatabase("C:\Acc07_ByExample\Northwind.mdb")
    Set qdf = db.CreateQueryDef(strQryName, strSQL)

RunQuery:
    'specify the parameter
    qdf.Parameters("Enter Country") = _
        InputBox("Enter the country name:", _
        "Which Country?", "Germany")

    If IsNull(qdf.Parameters("Enter Country").Value) _
        Then GoTo ExitHere

    'open a recordset based on the specified query
    Set rst = qdf.OpenRecordset(dbOpenDynaset)
    rst.MoveLast
    MsgBox "Number of records: " & rst.RecordCount

    'write the contents of the second field
    'to the Immediate window
    rst.MoveFirst
    Do Until rst.EOF
        Debug.Print rst(1)
        rst.MoveNext
    Loop

ExitHere:
    If Not rst Is Nothing Then
        rst.Close
        Set rst = Nothing
    End If
    Set qdf = Nothing
    db.Close
    Set db = Nothing
    Exit Sub
```

```
Err_Handler:
    If Err.Number = 3012 Then
        MsgBox "This query already exists."
        Set qdf = db.QueryDefs(strQryName)
        Resume RunQuery
    Else
        MsgBox Err.Description
    End If
    Resume ExitHere
End Sub
```

3. Choose **Run | Run Sub/UserForm** to execute the procedure.

The procedure in Hands-On 15-6 defines a Parameter query that contains one parameter named Enter Country. Prior to running this query, the procedure retrieves the name of the country from the user via the VBA InputBox method. While the suggested default country name is Germany, the user can supply the name of another country. The supplied value is then used as the value of the Enter Country parameter. Next, the recordset is opened based on the specified query and the number of records for the specified country is retrieved via the RecordCount property of the Recordset object. In order to get the correct record count we must move to the end of the recordset, using the MoveLast method, to access all records. The procedure ends by retrieving to the Immediate window the names of all the companies in the specified country. The procedure contains several labels such as RunQuery, ExitHere, and Err_Handler, which are used in error trapping and ensuring that certain code lines are run only when required. For example, when you execute this procedure again, the statement that attempts to create a query will fail and VBA will generate error 3012. At this point, we want to run the existing query, so we must set the qdf object variable with the following statement:

```
Set qdf = db.QueryDefs(strQryName)
```

And then we can safely resume running the code from the label RunQuery.

Creating and Running a Parameter Query with ADO

In ADO, to create a row-returning, parameterized query, simply add the parameters to the query's SQL string. The parameters must be defined by using the PARAMETERS keyword, as in the following:

```
strSQL = "PARAMETERS [Country Name] Text;" & _
    "SELECT Customers.* FROM Customers WHERE " _
    & "Customers.Country=[Type Country Name];"
```

The above SQL statement begins by defining one parameter called Country Name. This parameter will be able to accept text entries. The second part of the SQL statement selects all the records from the Customers table that have an entry in the Country field equal to the provided parameter value. The complete procedure is shown in Hands-On 15-7.

◎ Hands-On 15-7: Creating a Parameter Query with ADO

1. In the Visual Basic Editor window, choose **Insert | Module**.

2. In the module's Code window, type the **Create_ParameterQuery_ADO** procedure shown below, or copy the procedure code from **C:\Acc07_ HandsOn\Chap15.txt**.

```
Sub Create_ParameterQuery_ADO()
    Dim cat As ADOX.Catalog
    Dim cmd As ADODB.Command
    Dim strPath As String
    Dim strSQL As String
    Dim strQryName As String

    On Error GoTo ErrorHandler

    strPath = CurrentProject.Path & "\Northwind.mdb"

    strSQL = "PARAMETERS [Country Name] Text;" & _
        "SELECT Customers.* FROM Customers WHERE " _
        & "Customers.Country=[Country Name];"

    strQryName = "Customers by Country"

    Set cat = New ADOX.Catalog
    cat.ActiveConnection = _
        "Provider=Microsoft.Jet.OLEDB.4.0;" & _
        "Data Source=" & strPath

    Set cmd = New ADODB.Command
    cmd.CommandText = strSQL

    cat.Procedures.Append strQryName, cmd
    Set cmd = Nothing
    Set cat = Nothing

    MsgBox "The procedure completed successfully.", _
            vbInformation, "Create Parameter Query"
    Exit Sub

ErrorHandler:
    If InStr(Err.Description, "already exists") Then
        cat.Procedures.Delete strQryName
        Resume
    Else
        MsgBox Err.Number & ": " & Err.Description
    End If
End Sub
```

3. Choose **Run | Run Sub/UserForm** to execute the procedure.

The above procedure creates a simple Parameter query with one parameter. Because the ADO Command object always creates a temporary query, you must append the Command object to the ADOX Procedures collection in order to save a parameterized query in a database.

Row-returning, Parameterized Queries

Queries that return records and take parameters are known as row-returning, parameterized queries.

In ADO, to work with queries that return records and take parameters, use the ADOX Procedure object. All Procedure objects are contained in the Procedures collection of the ADOX Catalog object. To save these queries in a database, append the ADO Command object to the ADOX Procedures collection.

To execute a Parameter query you must specify the parameter value using the Parameters collection of the Command object, like this:

```
cmd.Parameters("Country Name") = "France"
```

The procedure in Hands-On 15-8 shows how to run the Parameter query created by the procedure in Hands-On 15-7.

Hands-On 15-8: Executing a Parameter Query with ADO

1. In the Visual Basic Editor window, choose **Insert | Module**.
2. In the module's Code window, type the **Execute_ParamQuery_ADO** procedure shown below, or copy the procedure code from **C:\Acc07_HandsOn\Chap15.txt**.

```
Sub Execute_ParamQuery_ADO(strCountry As String)
    Dim cat As ADOX.Catalog
    Dim cmd As ADODB.Command
    Dim rst As ADODB.Recordset
    Dim strQryName As String
    Dim strPath As String

    strQryName = "Customers by Country"
    strPath = CurrentProject.Path & "\Northwind.mdb"

    Set cat = New ADOX.Catalog
    cat.ActiveConnection = _
        "Provider=Microsoft.Jet.OLEDB.4.0;" & _
        "Data Source=" & strPath

    Set cmd = New ADODB.Command
    Set cmd = cat.Procedures(strQryName).Command

    ' specify a parameter value
    cmd.Parameters("[Country Name]") = strCountry

    ' use the Execute method of the Command
    ' object to open the recordset
    Set rst = cmd.Execute

    ' return company names to the Immediate window
    Do Until rst.EOF
        Debug.Print rst(1)
        rst.MoveNext
```

```
        Loop

        rst.Close
        Set rst = Nothing
        Set cmd = Nothing
        Set cat = Nothing
    End Sub
```

3. Execute the above procedure from the Immediate window by typing the following statement and pressing **Enter**:

```
Execute_ParamQuery_ADO "Argentina"
```

The Execute_ParamQuery_ADO procedure shown above establishes the connection to the Northwind database. Next, the name of the query is supplied in the following statement:

```
Set cmd = cat.Procedures(strQryName).Command
```

Because this is a Parameter query, the parameter value is specified by using the Parameters collection of the Command object, like this:

```
cmd.Parameters("[Country Name]") = strCountry
```

Then, the Recordset object is opened by using the Execute method of the Command object:

```
Set rst = cmd.Execute
```

Finally, the procedure loops through the recordset to retrieve the company names and print them to the Immediate window. After running this procedure, the following lines are returned to the Immediate window for the specified country:

```
Cactus Comidas para llevar
Océano Atlántico Ltda.
Rancho grande
```

➲ **Note:** Instead of specifying the parameter values before the recordset is open, you can use the Parameters argument of the Command object's Execute method to pass the parameter value, as shown below:

```
Set rst = cmd.Execute(Parameters:=strCountry)
```

Creating and Running a Make-Table Query with DAO

A Make-Table query creates a new table out of records from one or more tables or queries. Make-Table queries are often used to preserve data as it existed at a particular time or to create a backup copy of a table without backing up the entire database. Use the SELECT INTO statement to create a Make-Table query. This statement consists of the following parts:

SELECT fieldName	Field name (use * for all fields)
INTO newTableName	Name of the new table
FROM table/queryName	Name of a table or query from which data is taken
WHERE condition	Criteria/limit operation to desired rows (Optional)
ORDER BY fieldName	Order of the records in the new table (Optional)

The procedure in Hands-On 15-9 creates a table of the Brazilian customers.

◎ Hands-On 15-9: Creating and Running a Make-Table Query with DAO

1. In the Visual Basic Editor window, choose **Insert | Module**.

2. In the module's Code window, type the **MakeATableQuery_DAO** proce-dure shown below, or copy the procedure code from **C:\Acc07_HandsOn\ Chap15.txt**.

```
Sub MakeATableQuery_DAO()
    Dim db As DAO.Database
    Dim qdf As DAO.QueryDef
    Dim strSQL As String

    On Error GoTo Err_Handler

    strSQL = "SELECT * INTO SouthAmericanClients " & _
            "FROM Customers WHERE Country='Brazil';"
    Set db = OpenDatabase("C:\Acc07_ByExample\Northwind.mdb")
    Set qdf = db.CreateQueryDef("", strSQL)
    qdf.Execute
ExitHere:
    Set qdf = Nothing
    db.Close
    Set db = Nothing
    Exit Sub
Err_Handler:
    MsgBox Err.Description
    Resume ExitHere
End Sub
```

3. Choose **Run | Run Sub/UserForm** to execute the procedure.

The SELECT INTO statement in the MakeATableQuery_DAO procedure shown above is used to make a new table named SouthAmericanClients with the names of all Brazilian customers from the Customers table in the Northwind.mdb database. Notice that by not assigning a name to the query, we create a Make-Table query that is temporary (not stored in the Access window):

```
Set qdf = db.CreateQueryDef("", strSQL)
```

Creating and Running an Update Query with DAO

An Update query is a type of Action query. Update queries are very convenient to use when you want to change fields for a single record or for multiple records in a table. The UPDATE statement consists of the following three parts:

UPDATE	TableName or QueryName
SET	Expression/operation to perform
WHERE	Criteria/limit operation to desired rows

For example, to mark product 10 as discontinued, you would use the following UPDATE statement:

```
UPDATE Products SET Discontinued = True WHERE ProductID = 10
```

The criteria in the WHERE clause is used to determine which rows will be updated. The Update query does not produce a result table. To avoid updating the wrong records, always determine which rows you want to be updated by creating and running a Select query first.

The Execute method of a QueryDef object is used to run any type of Action query. The procedure in Hands-On 15-10 demonstrates how to create and run an Update query with DAO.

⊚ Hands-On 15-10: Creating and Running an Update Query with DAO

1. In the Visual Basic Editor window, choose **Insert | Module**.

2. In the module's Code window, type the **CreateRunUpdateQuery_DAO** procedure shown below, or copy the procedure code from **C:\Acc07_ HandsOn\Chap15.txt**.

```
Sub CreateRunUpdateQuery_DAO()
    Dim db As DAO.Database
    Dim qdf As DAO.QueryDef
    Dim strSQL As String

    On Error GoTo Err_Handler

    strSQL = "UPDATE Suppliers INNER JOIN Products ON " & _
        "Suppliers.SupplierID = Products.SupplierID " & _
        "SET Products.UnitPrice = [UnitPrice]+2 " & _
        "WHERE (((Suppliers.CompanyName)='Tokyo Traders'));"
    Set db = OpenDatabase("C:\Acc07_ByExample\Northwind.mdb")

    Set qdf = db.CreateQueryDef("PriceIncrease", strSQL)
    qdf.Execute
ExitHere:
    Set db = Nothing
    Exit Sub
Err_Handler:
    If Err.Number = 3012 Then
```

```
        MsgBox "Query with this name already exists."
    Else
        MsgBox Err.Description
    End If
    Resume ExitHere
End Sub
```

To perform the required update, the above procedure needs to join two tables. The Products table is joined with the Suppliers table on the SupplierID field that exists in both tables. Use the INNER JOIN statement to combine column values from one row of a table with column values from another row of another (or the same) table to obtain a single row of data. The join condition is specified after the ON keyword and determines how the two tables are to be compared to each other to produce the join result. Because the update must occur only for a specific supplier, we also specify the supplier's company name in the WHERE clause.

3. Choose **Run | Run Sub/UserForm** to execute the procedure.

After running the above procedure, the prices for all products supplied by Tokyo Traders are increased by $2.00.

The following procedure demonstrates how to use the Execute method of the DAO Database object to run an existing (previously saved) Update query.

```
Sub UpdateRun_DAO()
    Dim db As DAO.Database
    Set db = OpenDatabase("C:\Acc07_ByExample\Northwind.mdb")
    db.Execute "PriceIncrease"
    db.Close
    Set db = Nothing
End Sub
```

Executing an Update Query with ADO

Executing bulk queries that update data is quite easy with ADO. You can use the Execute method of the Connection or Command object. The procedure in Hands-On 15-11 uses the Connection object's Execute method to update records in the Products table of the Northwind.mdb database where CategoryId is equal to 8. The UnitPrice of the records that match this condition will be increased by one dollar. Note that the number of updated records is returned by the Execute method in the NumOfRec variable.

Hands-On 15-11: Executing an Update Query

1. In the Visual Basic Editor window, choose **Insert | Module**.

2. In the module's Code window, type the **Execute_UpdateQuery_ADO** procedure as shown below, or copy the procedure code from **C:\Acc07_HandsOn\Chap15.txt**.

```
Sub Execute_UpdateQuery_ADO()
    Dim conn As ADODB.Connection
    Dim NumOfRec As Integer
```

```
Dim strPath As String

strPath = CurrentProject.Path & "\Northwind.mdb"

Set conn = New ADODB.Connection

conn.Open "Provider=Microsoft.Jet.OLEDB.4.0;" & _
    "Data Source=" & strPath

conn.Execute "UPDATE Products " & _
    "SET UnitPrice = UnitPrice + 1" & _
    " WHERE CategoryId = 8", _
    NumOfRec, adExecuteNoRecords

MsgBox NumOfRec & " records were updated."
conn.Close
Set conn = Nothing
End Sub
```

3. Choose **Run | Run Sub/UserForm** to execute the procedure.

The above procedure uses the Data Manipulation Language (DML) UPDATE statement to make a change in the UnitPrice field of the Products table. The Execute method of the Connection object allows the provider to return the number of records that were affected via the RecordsAffected parameter. This parameter applies only to Action queries or stored procedures. To get the number of records returned by a result-returning query or stored procedure, you must use the RecordCount property. In the procedure shown above, we store the number of records affected in the string variable NumOfRec. Note that when a command does not return a recordset, you should include the constant adExecuteNoRecords. The adExecuteNoRecords constant can only be passed as an optional parameter to the Command or Connection object's Execute method.

The procedure in Hands-On 15-12 demonstrates how to execute an Update query by using the ADO Command object instead of the Connection object used in the preceding example. By running the following example, the UnitPrice of all the records in the Products table will be increased by 10 percent.

⊚ Hands-On 15-12: Executing an Update Query Using the Command Object

1. In the Visual Basic Editor window, choose **Insert | Module**.

2. In the module's Code window, type the **Execute_UpdateQuery2_ADO** procedure shown below, or copy the procedure code from **C:\Acc07_HandsOn\Chap15.txt**.

```
Sub Execute_UpdateQuery2_ADO()
    Dim cmd As ADODB.Command
    Dim NumOfRec As Integer
    Dim strPath As String
```

```
strPath = CurrentProject.Path & "\Northwind.mdb"

Set cmd = New ADODB.Command
With cmd
    .ActiveConnection = _
        "Provider=Microsoft.Jet.OLEDB.4.0;" & _
        "Data Source=" & strPath
    .CommandText = "Update Products " & _
        "Set UnitPrice = UnitPrice *1.1"
    .Execute NumOfRec, adExecuteNoRecords
End With
MsgBox NumOfRec
Set cmd = Nothing
End Sub
```

3. Choose **Run | Run Sub/UserForm** to execute the procedure.

Non-row-returning Queries

Queries that do not return records, such as Action queries or Data Definition Language (DDL) queries, are known as non-row-returning queries.

- Action queries are Data Manipulation Language (DML) queries that perform bulk operations on a set of records. They allow you to add, update, or delete records.

- The DDL queries are used for creating database objects and altering the structure of a database.

- Use the ADOX Procedure object to work with queries that don't return records. All Procedure objects are contained in the Procedures collection of the ADOX Catalog object. To save these types of queries in a database, append the ADO Command object to the ADOX Procedures collection.

Running an Append Query with DAO/ADO

Append queries are used for adding records from one or more tables to other tables. You can append records to a table in a current database or another Access or non-Access database. An Append query is an Action query that adds new records to the end of an existing table or query. Append queries don't return records. They are useful for archiving records. Before you can archive the records, you need to create a new table structure to hold the records. To add a record or multiple records to a table, use the INSERT INTO statement. This statement has the following parts:

INSERT INTO target [(Field1, Field2)]	The name of the table or query to which records are appended. You may indicate the names of the fields to which data is appended.
SELECT fieldName(s)	The names of fields from which data is obtained.
FROM tableName or expression	The name of the table or tables from which records are inserted, the name of a saved query, or a SELECT statement.
WHERE condition	Criteria/limit operation to desired rows.

The procedure in Hands-On 15-13 demonstrates how to execute an Append query using the Execute method of the DAO Database object.

◎ Hands-On 15-13: Running an Append Query with DAO

1. In the Visual Basic Editor window, choose **Insert | Module**.
2. In the module's Code window, type the **RunAppendQry_DAO** procedure shown below, or copy the procedure code from **C:\Acc07_HandsOn\ Chap15.txt.**

```
Sub RunAppendQry_DAO()
    Dim db As DAO.Database
    Dim rst As DAO.Recordset
    Dim strSQL As String

    strSQL = "SELECT * FROM SouthAmericanClients " & _
             "WHERE Country = 'Argentina'"
    Set db = OpenDatabase("C:\Acc07_ByExample\Northwind.mdb")
    Set rst = db.OpenRecordset(strSQL, dbOpenSnapshot)

    If rst.EOF Or rst.BOF Then
        ' Argentina clients not found in destination
        ' table - proceed with insert
        db.Execute "INSERT INTO SouthAmericanClients " & _
                   "SELECT * FROM Customers " & _
                   "WHERE Country = 'Argentina'"

        MsgBox "Argentina clients have been appended."
    Else
        MsgBox "Clients from Argentina already exist " & _
               "in the destination table."
    End If

    rst.Close
    Set rst = Nothing
    db.Close
    Set db = Nothing
End Sub
```

3. Choose **Run | Run Sub/UserForm** to execute the procedure.

The above procedure begins by opening the Northwind database and creating a Snapshot-type recordset based on the supplied SQL query string. Prior to executing the Append query that inserts customers from Argentina into the SouthAmericanClients table, we check the EOF and BOF properties of the DAO Recordset object to determine if the recordset contains any records. If "rst.EOF Or rst.BOF" is True, then there is no current record (the recordset is empty), so we go ahead and use the Execute method of the database object to add Argentina customers to the destination table.

The following procedure demonstrates how to execute an Append query using the Execute method of the ADO Connection object.

```
Sub RunAppendQry_ADO()
    Dim conn As ADODB.Connection
    Dim strSQL As String
    Dim recAffected As Long

    On Error Resume Next
    Set conn = New ADODB.Connection

    conn.Provider = "Microsoft.Jet.OLEDB.4.0"
    conn.Open "C:\Acc07_ByExample\Northwind.mdb"
    strSQL = "INSERT INTO SouthAmericanClients " & _
            "SELECT * FROM Customers " & _
            "WHERE Country = 'Venezuela'"

    conn.Execute strSQL, recAffected
    If Err <> 0 Then
        Debug.Print "Error Number: " & Err.Number
        Debug.Print "Error Description: " & Err.Description
    Else
        Debug.Print recAffected & " records were inserted."
    End If
    conn.Close
    Set conn = Nothing
End Sub
```

The above procedure opens a connection to the Northwind.mdb database. Once the database is open, the Execute method of the ADO Connection object is used to execute the specified SQL INSERT INTO statement. You can use an optional RecordsAffected parameter (see the recAffected variable in the above procedure) with the Execute method to determine the number of records that the Execute method affected. This parameter must be a variable of the Long data type. If the Insert operation was successful, the VBA Err object will return zero (0). The default property of the Err object is Number. Therefore, the statement:

```
If Err <> 0
```

is equivalent to:

```
If Err.Number <> 0
```

If a run-time error occurs, for example, the destination table does not exist, the procedure will print to the Immediate window the error number and its description text. If there were no errors, the Immediate window will contain the number of records that were affected by the Insert operation.

Running a Delete Query with DAO

With a Delete query you can delete a single record or multiple records from a database. The DELETE statement used to delete rows from a table consists of the following three parts:

DELETE	
FROM	Table name
WHERE	Criteria/limit operation to desired rows

For example, to delete discontinued products from the Products table you would use the following DELETE statement:

```
DELETE FROM Products WHERE Discontinued = True
```

And, to delete all the rows from the Products table, the following statement can be executed:

```
DELETE FROM Products
```

You cannot reverse the operation performed by the DELETE statement. Always make a backup copy of your table prior to running a Delete query. It is a good idea to create and run a Select query before using DELETE to see which rows will be affected by the Delete operation.

The Execute method is used to run Action queries or execute an SQL statement. This method can take optional arguments. For example, in the statement:

```
qdf.Execute dbFailOnError
```

the constant dbFailOnError will generate a run-time error and will roll back updates or deletes if an error occurs. Use the RecordsAffected property of the QueryDef object to determine the number of records affected by the most recent Execute method. For example, the following statement displays the number of records that were deleted:

```
MsgBox qdf.RecordsAffected & " records were deleted."
```

The procedure in Hands-On 15-14 creates a Delete query and then executes it if the user responds positively to the message shown in Figure 15-2.

Figure 15-2: You can display an SQL statement underlying a query in a message box.

⊚ Hands-On 15-14: Running a Delete Query with DAO

1. In the Visual Basic Editor window, choose **Insert | Module**.

2. In the module's Code window, type the **CreateRunDeleteQuery_DAO** procedure shown below, or copy the procedure code from **C:\Acc07_ HandsOn\Chap15.txt**.

```
Sub CreateRunDeleteQuery_DAO()
    Dim db As DAO.Database
    Dim qdf As DAO.QueryDef
    Dim strQryName As String
```

```
Dim strSQL As String

On Error GoTo ErrorHandler

strQryName = "DeletePolishOrders"
strSQL = "DELETE * FROM Orders WHERE [ShipCountry] = 'Poland'"

Set db = OpenDatabase("C:\Acc07_ByExample\Northwind.mdb")
Set qdf = db.CreateQueryDef(strQryName, strSQL)

' Chr(13) & Chr(13) is a double carriage return
If (MsgBox("Do you want to perform the following: " & _
    Chr(13) & Chr(13) _
    & qdf.SQL, vbYesNo + vbDefaultButton2, _
    "SQL Expression")) = vbYes Then

    qdf.Execute dbFailOnError
    MsgBox qdf.RecordsAffected & _
            " records were deleted."
End If
ExitHere:
    Set qdf = Nothing
    db.Close
    Set db = Nothing
    Exit Sub
ErrorHandler:
    If Err.Number = 3012 Then
        Set qdf = db.QueryDefs(strQryName)
        Resume Next
    Else
        MsgBox Err.Number & ":" & Err.Description
        Resume ExitHere
    End If
End Sub
```

3. Choose **Run | Run Sub/UserForm** to execute the procedure.

The above procedure creates a Delete query named DeletePolishOrders in the Northwind database and then runs this query if the user clicked OK to the message. If the specified Delete query already exists in the database, the qdf object variable is set to the existing query name and the user is prompted to make a decision about whether the records should be deleted.

Creating and Running a Pass-Through Query with DAO

A Pass-Through query works directly with an external ODBC (Open Database Connectivity) data source. Instead of linking to a table that resides on a server, you can send commands directly to the server to retrieve data.

To create a Pass-Through query manually in the Access window, choose Create | Query Design. Close the Show Table dialog box and click Design | Pass-Through. This will bring up a window where you can type a query statement. The SQL statement must be in the format understood by the external data source from which you are retrieving data. Pass-Through queries can also be used in lieu of Action queries when you need to bulk append, update, or delete data in remote databases.

Pass-Through queries can be created and executed programmatically from your VBA procedures. In DAO, to execute an SQL Pass-Through query, use the Connect property. If you do not specify a connection string in the Connect property, Access will ask you for the connection information every time you run the Pass-Through query (and this can be very annoying).

The following procedure uses the MaxRecords property to return 15 records from the dbo.entity table located on an SQL server. Notice that the ReturnsRecords property is set to True. If your query does not need to return records, set the ReturnsRecords property to False.

```
Sub PassThruQry_DAO()
    Dim db As DAO.Database
    Dim qdfPass As DAO.QueryDef

    On Error GoTo err_PassThru

    Set db = CurrentDb
    Set qdfPass = db.CreateQueryDef("GetRecords")

    ' enter your own connect string
    ' supply the server database name you
    ' want to connect to, your User ID,
    ' password, and the Data Source name

    qdfPass.Connect = "ODBC;Database=myDbName; " & _
        "UID=MILL;PWD=year00;DSN=myDataS"
    qdfPass.SQL = "SELECT * FROM dbo.entity"
    qdfPass.ReturnsRecords = True
    qdfPass.MaxRecords = 15

    DoCmd.OpenQuery "GetRecords"
    Exit Sub
err_PassThru:
    If Err.Number = 3151 Then
        MsgBox Err.Description
        Exit Sub
    End If
    db.QueryDefs.Delete "GetRecords"
    Resume 0
    Exit Sub
End Sub
```

Instead of displaying a datasheet with the records retrieved from the SQL database, the following procedure reads the records to a temporary query and proceeds to open a recordset based on that query. Next, the contents of two fields are printed to the Immediate window.

```
Sub PassThru2()
    Dim db As DAO.Database
    Dim qdfPass As DAO.QueryDef
    Dim rstTemp As DAO.Recordset
```

```
On Error GoTo err_PassThru

Set db = CurrentDb
Set qdfPass = db.CreateQueryDef("")

' enter your own connect string
' supply the server database name you
' want to connect to, your User ID,
' password, and the Data Source name

qdfPass.Connect = "ODBC;Database=myDbName;UID=MILL;" & _
    "PWD=year00;DSN=myDataS"
qdfPass.SQL = "SELECT * FROM dbo.entity"
qdfPass.ReturnsRecords = True
qdfPass.MaxRecords = 15
Set rstTemp = qdfPass.OpenRecordset()
' print data from two fields to the Immediate window
With rstTemp
    Do While Not .EOF
        Debug.Print .Fields("entity_id"), .Fields("entity_name")
            .Fields("entity_name")
        .MoveNext
    Loop
    .Close
End With
SendKeys "^g"
ExitHere:
    Set db = Nothing
    Exit Sub
err_PassThru:
    MsgBox Err.Number & ":" & Err.Description
    Resume ExitHere
End Sub
```

Creating and Executing a Pass-Through Query with ADO

As mentioned earlier, SQL Pass-Through queries are SQL statements that are sent directly to the database server for processing. In earlier versions of Microsoft Access, Pass-Through queries were used with Data Access Objects (DAO) to increase performance when accessing external ODBC data sources. In ADO, you can use the Microsoft OLE DB Provider for SQL Server to directly access the SQL Server. For this reason, you do not need to create Pass-Through queries. However, since it is possible to create a Pass-Through query using ADOX and Microsoft Jet Provider, the next hands-on demonstrates how to do this.

⊚ Hands-On 15-15: Creating a Pass-Through Query with ADO

This hands-on exercise requires that you have access to an SQL Server Northwind database.

1. In the Visual Basic Editor window, choose **Insert | Module**.

2. In the module's Code window, type the **Create_PassThroughQuery** procedure shown below, or copy the procedure code from **C:\Acc07_ HandsOn\Chap15.txt.**

```
Sub Create_PassThroughQuery()
    Dim cat As ADOX.Catalog
    Dim cmd As ADODB.Command
    Dim rst As ADODB.Recordset
    Dim strPath As String
    Dim strSQL As String
    Dim strQryName As String
    Dim strODBCConnect As String

    On Error GoTo ErrorHandler

    strSQL = "SELECT Customers.* FROM Customers WHERE " _
        & "Customers.Country='France';"

    strQryName = "French Customers"

    ' modify the following string to connect
    ' to your SQL Server
    strODBCConnect = "ODBC;Driver=SQL Server;" & _
        "Server=JULITTA733\JKDESKTOP1;" & _
        "Database=Northwind;" & _
        "UID=;" & _
        "PWD="

    ' strODBCConnect = "ODBC;DSN=ODBCNorth;UID=sa;PWD=;"

    Set cat = New ADOX.Catalog
    cat.ActiveConnection = CurrentProject.Connection

    Set cmd = New ADODB.Command
    With cmd
        .ActiveConnection = cat.ActiveConnection
        .CommandText = strSQL
        .Properties("Jet OLEDB:ODBC Pass-Through Statement") = True
        .Properties("Jet OLEDB:Pass-Through Query Connect String") = _
            strODBCConnect
    End With

    cat.Procedures.Append strQryName, cmd

    Set cmd = Nothing
    Set cat = Nothing
    MsgBox "The procedure completed successfully.", _
        vbInformation, "Create Pass-Through Query"
    Exit Sub

ErrorHandler:
    If InStr(Err.Description, "already exists") Then
        cat.Procedures.Delete strQryName
        Resume
    Else
```

```
        MsgBox Err.Number & ": " & Err.Description
    End If
End Sub
```

3. Choose **Run | Run Sub/UserForm** to execute the procedure.

The above procedure creates a Pass-Through query named French Customers in the current database. Notice that to connect to the SQL Server database, the following string is built and later assigned to the Jet OLEDB:Pass-Through Query Connect String property of the Command object:

```
strODBCConnect = "ODBC;Driver=SQL Server;" & _
    "Server=JULITTA733\JKDESKTOP1;" & _
    "Database=Northwind;" & _
    "UID=;" & _
    "PWD="
```

Needless to say, if you want to try this procedure, you must have access to a remote data source (such as an SQL Server database) and you'll need to modify the above string to point to your server. The above string allows you to connect via the DSN-less connection. If you prefer, you may build your connection string to the remote data source using the Data Source Name (DSN) that you define in the Control Panel via Administrative Tools (ODBC). Your connection string could then look like this:

```
strODBCConnect = "ODBC;DSN=myDSN;UID=sa;PWD=;"
```

To create a Pass-Through query you must also set two provider-specific properties of the Command object: Jet OLEDB:ODBC Pass-Through Statement and Jet OLEDB:Pass-Through Query Connect String.

To permanently store the Pass-Through query in your database, you need to append it to the Catalog object's Procedures collection, like this:

```
cat.Procedures.Append strQryName, cmd
```

After you run the Create_PassThroughQuery procedure, the query can be viewed and accessed from the navigation pane in the Microsoft Access window.

In Hands-On 15-15, you learned how to create a Pass-Through query in VBA with ADO. This query retrieved the list of French customers from the Northwind database located on the SQL Server. The Pass-Through query was named French Customers and was saved permanently in the Chap15.accdb database. Let's see how you can execute this query from a VBA procedure.

Hands-On 15-16: Executing a Pass-Through Query Saved in Access (ADO)

1. In the Visual Basic Editor window, choose **Insert | Module**.

2. In the module's Code window, type the **Execute_PassThroughQuery_ADO** procedure shown below, or copy the procedure code from **C:\Acc07_HandsOn\Chap15.txt**.

```
Sub Execute_PassThroughQuery_ADO()
    Dim cat As ADOX.Catalog
    Dim cmd As ADODB.Command
```

```
Dim rst As ADODB.Recordset
Dim strConnect As String

' modify the connection string to connect
' to your SQL Server Northwind database
strConnect = "Provider=SQLOLEDB;" & _
    "Data Source=Julitta733\JKDesktop1;" & _
    "Initial Catalog=Northwind;" & _
    "User Id=sa;" & _
    "Password="

Set cat = New ADOX.Catalog
cat.ActiveConnection = CurrentProject.Connection

Set cmd = New ADODB.Command
Set cmd = cat.Procedures("French Customers").Command
Set rst = cmd.Execute

Debug.Print "--French Customers Only--" & vbCrLf _
    & rst.GetString

Set rst = Nothing
Set cmd = Nothing
Set cat = Nothing
End Sub
```

3. Choose **Run | Run Sub/UserForm** to execute the procedure.

The procedure begins by building a connection string to the SQL Server database. This is a standard connection that uses the native OLE DB SQL Server Provider (SQLOLEDB). This connection requires that you also provide the name of the SQL Server (Data Source), the name of the database from which to retrieve records (Initial Catalog), and the security context with which to log in (User Id, Password). If you connect to your SQL Server database using the NT integrated security, your connection string will look like this:

```
strConnect = "Provider=SQLOLEDB;" & _
    "Data Source=yourServerName;" & _
    "Integrated Security=SSPI;" & _
    "Initial Catalog=Northwind"
```

Because the Pass-Through query you want to execute has been saved in the Access database, you need to open the ADOX Catalog object to access its Procedures collection. The following line of code specifies the name of the query you want to execute and assigns it to the Command object:

```
Set cmd = cat.Procedures("French Customers").Command
```

To execute a Pass-Through query that returns records, you need to use the Recordset object in addition to the Command object. The following statement executes the Pass-Through query:

```
Set rst = cmd.Execute
```

The Pass-Through query executes on the server. To quickly view data on the
client machine, we retrieve the contents of the recordset by using the GetString
method:

```
Debug.Print "--French Customers Only--" & vbCrLf _
    & rst.GetString
```

Performing Other Operations with Queries

Now that you know how to programmatically create and run various queries
using DAO and ADO objects, you may be interested to find out how to use
Visual Basic to perform other operations related to queries, such as retrieving a
list of queries and their properties, deleting a query, and determining if a query
is updatable.

Retrieving Query Properties with DAO

Just like tables and other database objects, queries have properties. To generate
a list of properties for a specific query, use the For Each…Next looping structure to iterate through the Properties collection of the DAO QueryDef object.
The procedure in Hands-On 15-17 demonstrates this.

◎ Hands-On 15-17: Listing Query Properties with DAO

1. In the Visual Basic Editor window, choose **Insert | Module**.

2. In the module's Code window, type the **List_QryProperties_DAO**
   procedure shown below, or copy the procedure code from **C:\Acc07_
   HandsOn\Chap15.txt**.

```
Sub List_QryProperties_DAO()
    Dim db As DAO.Database
    Dim prp As DAO.Property
    Dim strDBName As String

    On Error Resume Next

    strDBName = "C:\Acc07_ByExample\Northwind 2007.accdb"
    Set db = OpenDatabase(strDBName)
    For Each prp In db.QueryDefs("Invoice Data").Properties
        Debug.Print prp.Name & "= " & prp.Value
    Next prp
    Set db = Nothing
End Sub
```

3. Choose **Run | Run Sub/UserForm** to execute the procedure.

Below are some of the properties printed to the Immediate window by running
the code in the List_QryProperties_DAO procedure shown above.

```
Name= Invoice Data
DateCreated= 12/28/2006 5:30:24 PM
LastUpdated= 6/10/2007 6:03:43 PM
Type= 0
```

```
SQL= SELECT Orders.[Order ID], Orders.[Ship Name], Orders.[Ship Address],
Orders.[Ship City], Orders.[Ship State/Province], Orders.[Ship ZIP/Postal
Code], Orders.[Ship Country/Region], Orders.[Customer ID], Customers.Company AS
[Customer Name], Customers.Address, Customers.City, Customers.[State/Province],
Customers.[ZIP/Postal Code], Customers.[Country/Region], [Employees
Extended].[Employee Name] AS Salesperson, Orders.[Order Date], Orders.[Shipped
Date], Shippers.Company AS [Shipper Name], [Order Details].[Product ID],
Products.ID AS [Product ID], [Order Details].[Unit Price], [Order
Details].Quantity, [Order Details].Discount, CCur(Nz([Unit
Price]*[Quantity]*(1-[Discount]),0)/100)*100 AS ExtendedPrice, Orders.[Shipping
Fee], Products.[Product Name]
FROM (Shippers RIGHT JOIN (Customers RIGHT JOIN (Orders LEFT JOIN [Employees
Extended] ON Orders.[Employee ID]=[Employees Extended].ID) ON
Customers.ID=Orders.[Customer ID]) ON Shippers.ID=Orders.[Shipper ID]) LEFT
JOIN ([Order Details] LEFT JOIN Products ON [Order Details].[Product
ID]=Products.ID) ON Orders.[Order ID]=[Order Details].[Order ID];

Updatable= True
Connect=
ReturnsRecords= True
ODBCTimeout= 60
RecordsAffected= 0
MaxRecords= 0
RecordsetType= 0
Description= (Criteria) Record source for Invoice report. Based on six tables.
Includes expressions that concatenate first and last employee name and that use
the CCur function to calculate extended price.
OrderByOn= False
Orientation= 0
DefaultView= 2
FilterOnLoad= False
OrderByOnLoad= True
TotalsRow= False
```

Listing All Queries in a Database with DAO/ADO

You can obtain the listing of all queries in a database by using the For...Each loop to enumerate the QueryDefs collection of the DAO QueryDef object. The following procedure writes to the Immediate window the names of all queries in the Northwind 2007.accdb database.

```
Sub List_AllQueries_DAO()
    Dim db As DAO.Database
    Dim qdf As DAO.QueryDef

    Set db = OpenDatabase("C:\Acc07_ByExample\Northwind 2007.accdb")
    For Each qdf In db.QueryDefs
        Debug.Print qdf.Name
    Next qdf

    Set qdf = Nothing
    db.Close
    Set db = Nothing
End Sub
```

The procedure in Hands-On 15-18 retrieves the names of all saved queries in the Northwind.mdb database by iterating through the View objects stored in the ADOX Catalog object's Views collection.

Hands-On 15-18: Listing Queries in a Database with ADO

1. In the Visual Basic Editor window, choose **Insert | Module**.

2. In the module's Code window, type the **List_AllQueries_ADO** procedure shown below, or copy the procedure code from **C:\Acc07_HandsOn\ Chap15.txt**.

```
Sub List_AllQueries_ADO()
    Dim cat As New ADOX.Catalog
    Dim v As ADOX.View
    Dim strPath As String

    strPath = CurrentProject.Path & "\Northwind.mdb"
    cat.ActiveConnection = _
        "Provider=Microsoft.Jet.OLEDB.4.0;" & _
        "Data Source= " & strPath

    For Each v In cat.Views
        Debug.Print v.Name
    Next

    Set cat = Nothing
End Sub
```

3. Choose **Run | Run Sub/UserForm** to execute the procedure.

4. After running the above procedure, open the Immediate window to view the list of all saved queries in the Northwind.mdb database.

Deleting a Query from a Database with DAO/ADO

To remove a DAO QueryDef object from a QueryDefs collection, use the Delete method as shown in Hands-On 15-19. The DeleteAQuery_DAO procedure deletes the query that was created in Hands-On 15-1.

Hands-On 15-19: Deleting a Query from a Database (DAO)

1. In the Visual Basic Editor window, choose **Insert | Module**.

2. In the module's Code window, type the **DeleteAQuery_DAO** procedure shown below, or copy the procedure code from **C:\Acc07_HandsOn\ Chap15.txt**.

```
Sub DeleteAQuery_DAO()
    Dim db As DAO.Database
    Dim qdf As DAO.QueryDef

    On Error GoTo ErrorHandler
```

```
    Set db = OpenDatabase("C:\Acc07_ByExample\Northwind.mdb")
    db.QueryDefs.Delete "myQuery"
ExitHere:
    db.Close
    Set db = Nothing
    Exit Sub
ErrorHandler:
    MsgBox Err.Number & ": " & Err.Description
    Resume ExitHere
End Sub
```

3. Choose **Run | Run Sub/UserForm** to execute the procedure.

After running the procedure in Hands-On 15-19, the query named myQuery is removed from the Northwind.mdb database.

To delete a query in ADO, use the Procedures or Views collection's Delete method. By running the procedure in Hands-On 15-20, you can quickly delete the Redmond Employees query created in Hands-On 15-2.

◎ Hands-On 15-20: Deleting a Query from a Database (ADO)

1. In the Visual Basic Editor window, choose **Insert | Module**.

2. In the module's Code window, type the **DeleteAQuery_ADO** procedure shown below, or copy the procedure code from **C:\Acc07_HandsOn\ Chap15.txt**.

```
Sub DeleteAQuery_ADO()
    Dim cat As New ADOX.Catalog
    Dim strPath As String

    On Error GoTo ErrorHandler

    strPath = CurrentProject.Path & "\Northwind 2007.accdb"
    cat.ActiveConnection = _
        "Provider=Microsoft.ACE.OLEDB.12.0;" & _
        "Data Source= " & strPath

    cat.Views.Delete "Redmond Employees"

ExitHere:
    Set cat = Nothing
    Exit Sub
ErrorHandler:
    If Err.Number = 3265 Then
        MsgBox "Query does not exist."
    Else
        MsgBox Err.Number & ": " & Err.Description
    End If
    Resume ExitHere
End Sub
```

3. Choose **Run | Run Sub/UserForm** to execute the procedure.

After running the procedure in Hands-On 15-20, the query named Redmond Employees is removed from the Northwind 2007.accdb database.

Determining if a Query Is Updatable

When a query is updatable you may edit the values in the result set of records and your changes are automatically reflected in the underlying tables. Microsoft Access's online help lists situations when query results can or cannot be updated (see Figure 15-3). The DAO QueryDef object has an Updatable property that you can use in your VBA code to find out if the query definition can be updated. However, to determine whether the resulting recordset can be updated, you must use the Updatable property of the DAO Recordset object as demonstrated in Hands-On 15-21. If the Recordset object cannot be edited, the value of the Updatable property is False.

Note: The Updatable property of the DAO Snapshot and Forward-only-type Recordset objects is always False. The same is true if the Recordset object contains read-only fields. However, when one or more fields are updatable, the property's value is True. Because a recordset can contain fields that can't be updated, you may want to check the DataUpdatable property of each field in the Fields collection of the Recordset object before attempting to edit a record.

Figure 15-3: Records returned by a query may or may not be updatable. For more information, search Access help by entering "Edit data in a query."

The procedure in Hands-On 15-21 checks whether records returned by two queries in the Northwind.mdb database can be edited.

◎ Hands-On 15-21: Determining if Records Returned by a Query Can Be Edited (DAO)

1. In the Visual Basic Editor window, choose **Insert | Module**.
2. In the module's Code window, type the **IsQryUpdatable_DAO** procedure shown below, or copy the procedure code from **C:\Acc07_HandsOn\ Chap15.txt**.

```
Sub IsQryUpdatable_DAO()
    Dim db As DAO.Database
    Dim rst As DAO.Recordset
    Dim fld As DAO.Field
    Dim strQryName1 As String
    Dim strQryName2 As String

    strQryName1 = "Order Subtotals"
    strQryName2 = "Invoices"

    Set db = OpenDatabase("C:\Acc07_ByExample\Northwind.mdb")

    Set rst = db.OpenRecordset(strQryName1)
    Debug.Print strQryName1 & _
        ": Updatable=" & rst.Updatable
    Set rst = db.OpenRecordset(strQryName2)
    Debug.Print strQryName2 & _
        ": Updatable=" & rst.Updatable
    For Each fld In rst.Fields
        If Not fld.DataUpdatable Then
            Debug.Print fld.Name & _
            " cannot be edited."
        End If
    Next

    rst.Close
    Set rst = Nothing
    db.Close
    Set db = Nothing
End Sub
```

3. Choose **Run | Run Sub/UserForm** to execute the procedure.

When you run the above procedure, the Updatable property returns True for the Invoices query, and False for the Order Subtotals query. The Open-Recordset method is used to open each of these queries. The Order Subtotals query is not updatable because its SQL statement contains a GROUP BY clause. While the Invoices query is updatable, not all fields in the resulting recordset can be edited (see Figure 15-4).

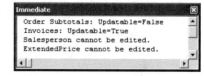

Figure 15-4: An updatable query can contain one or more fields that cannot be edited (see Hands-On 15-21).

Chapter Summary

Creating and executing queries are the most frequently performed database operations. This chapter has shown you how to create, run, and modify various types of queries using the DAO and ADO code.

In the next chapter, you will get to know more of the advanced features of the ADO/DAO Object Model.

Chapter 16

Using Advanced ADO/DAO Features

So far you should feel pretty comfortable using ADO in most of your Microsoft Office Access programming endeavors. What's more, using the knowledge acquired during the last few chapters, you can switch to any other Office application (Excel, Word, PowerPoint, or Outlook) and start programming. Because you already know the ADO methods of accessing databases and manipulating records, all you need to learn is the object model that the specific application is using. Learning a new type library is not very hard. Recall that VBA offers the Object Browser that lists all the application's objects, properties, methods, and intrinsic constants that you may need for writing code. However, if you'd like to accomplish more with ADO, this chapter will introduce you to a couple of more advanced ADO features that will set you apart from beginning programmers. You will learn about fabricating, persisting, disconnecting, cloning, and shaping recordsets. You will also learn how to process data modifications and additions by using ADO and DAO transactions.

Fabricating a Recordset

In previous chapters, you worked with recordsets that were created from data that came from a Microsoft Access database, a text or dBASE file, an Excel spreadsheet, or a Word document. You may have also practiced working with a recordset generated from an SQL Server database. In each of these circumstances, to get the necessary data you needed to establish a connection to the appropriate data source. In other words, you worked with recordsets that had a live connection to the data source. These connected recordsets obtained their structure and data from a query to a data source to which they were connected. But what if you need to create a recordset with data that does not come from a data source? As you may recall from Chapter 10, the ADO Object Model allows you to work with both relational and non-relational data stores.

To store non-relational data in an ADO Recordset, you can create your recordset from scratch. This recordset will be defined programmatically in memory and will not be connected to any data source. For example, you can easily fabricate a custom recordset that holds non-relational data, such as the information about the files located in one of your hard drive's directories.

Part II

When you create your own recordset from scratch, you define the types of fields in the recordset and then populate the recordset with the information you want. The fields are defined using the Fields collection's Append method. You must specify the field name, the data type, and the size. The syntax for the Append method looks like this:

```
Fields.Append Name, DataType[, FieldSize], [Attribute]
```

Arguments in square brackets are optional. FieldSize specifies the size in characters or bytes. Attribute specifies characteristics such as whether the field enables Null values or whether it is a primary key or an identity column.

Once you have defined the structure of your recordset, simply open it and populate it with the desired data. You can add data to your custom recordset in the same way you add data to a connected recordset: by using the Recordset object's AddNew method.

The procedure in Hands-On 16-1 demonstrates how to create an empty recordset containing three fields (Name, Size, and Modified) and then populate it with files located in a user-specified file folder.

◎ Hands-On 16-1: Creating a Custom Recordset (ADO)

1. Start Microsoft Office Access 2007 and create a new Microsoft Office Access 2007 database named **Chap16.accdb** in your **C:\Acc07_ ByExample** folder.

2. In the database window, press **Alt+F11** to switch to the Visual Basic Editor window.

3. In the Visual Basic Editor window, choose **Tools | References**. In the References dialog box, locate and select **Microsoft ActiveX Data Objects 2.8 Library** and then click **OK** to close this dialog box.

4. In the Visual Basic Editor window, choose **Insert | Module**.

5. In the module's Code window, type the **Custom_Recordset** procedure shown below, or copy the procedure code from **C:\Acc07_HandsOn\ Chap16.txt**.

```
Sub Custom_Recordset()
    Dim rst As ADODB.Recordset
    Dim strFile As String
    Dim strPath As String
    Dim strFolder As String

    strPath = InputBox("Enter pathname, e.g., C:\My Folder")
    If Right(strPath, 1) <> "\" Then strPath = strPath & "\"

        strFolder = strPath
        strFile = Dir(strPath & "*.*")
        If strFile = "" Then
            MsgBox "This folder does not contain files."
            Exit Sub
        End If
```

```
Set rst = New ADODB.Recordset
  ' Create an empty recordset with 3 fields
  With rst
    Set .ActiveConnection = Nothing
    .CursorLocation = adUseClient
    With .Fields
      .Append "Name", adVarChar, 255
      .Append "Size", adDouble
      .Append "Modified", adDBTimeStamp
    End With
    .Open
    Do While strFile <> ""
      If strFile = "" Then Exit Do
        ' Add a new record to the recordset
        .AddNew Array("Name", "Size", "Modified"), _
          Array(strFile, FileLen(strFolder & strFile), _
          FileDateTime(strFolder & strFile))
        strFile = Dir
    Loop
    .MoveFirst
    ' Print the contents of the recordset to the Immediate window
    Do Until .EOF
      Debug.Print !Name & vbTab & !Size & vbTab & !Modified
      .MoveNext
    Loop
    .Close
  End With
  Set rst = Nothing
End Sub
```

6. Choose **Run | Run Sub/UserForm** to execute the procedure.

In the Custom_Recordset procedure shown above, we start by creating a Recordset object variable. To tell ADO that your recordset is not connected to any database, we set the ActiveConnection property of the Recordset object to Nothing. We also set the CursorLocation property to adUseClient to indicate that the processing will occur on the client machine as opposed to the database server. Next, we determine what columns the recordset should contain and add these columns to the Recordset's Fields collection by using the Append method. Once the structure of your recordset is defined, you can call the Open method to actually open your custom recordset. Now you can populate the recordset with the data you want. We obtain the data by looping through the folder the user specified in the input box and reading the information about each file. The VBA FileLen function is used to retrieve the size of a file in bytes. Another VBA function, FileDateTime, is used to retrieve the date and time a file was last modified. To retrieve the date and time separately, use the FileDateTime function as an argument of the DateValue or TimeValue functions.

Check the following statements in the Immediate window while stepping through the Custom_Recordset procedure:

```
? DateValue(FileDateTime(myFolder & myFile))
? TimeValue(FileDateTime(myFolder & myFile))
```

Now that the recordset is fabricated and populated with the required data, you can display its contents in the Immediate window or send the output to another application. You can also save the recordset to a disk file as explained later in this chapter.

Disconnected Recordsets

In the previous section, you learned how to create a recordset from scratch. This recordset had a structure custom-defined by you and was populated with data that did not come from a database. In other words, it was a disconnected recordset that was defined on the fly. A *disconnected recordset* is a recordset that is not connected to a data source. A disconnected recordset can be defined programmatically (as you saw in Hands-On 16-1) or it can get its information from the data source (as shown in Hands-On 16-2).

Using disconnected recordsets allows you to connect to a database, retrieve some records, return the records to the client, and then disconnect from the database. By keeping your connection to a database open just long enough to obtain the required data, you can help conserve valuable server resources. You can work with the disconnected recordset offline and then connect to the database again to add your changes.

To get started using disconnected recordsets, perform Hands-On 16-2. The example procedure retrieves some data from the Orders table in the Northwind database, then disconnects from the database. While disconnected from the database, you can manipulate and examine the content of the retrieved recordset.

Hands-On 16-2: Creating a Disconnected Recordset (ADO)

1. In the Visual Basic Editor window, choose **Insert | Module**.
2. In the module's Code window, type the **Rst_Disconnected** procedure shown below, or copy the procedure code from **C:\Acc07_HandsOn\ Chap16.txt**.

```
Sub Rst_Disconnected()
    Dim conn As ADODB.Connection
    Dim rst As ADODB.Recordset
    Dim strConn As String
    Dim strSQL As String
    Dim strRst As String

    strSQL = "SELECT * FROM Orders WHERE CustomerID = 'VINET'"

    strConn = "Provider=Microsoft.Jet.OLEDB.4.0;"
    strConn = strConn & "Data Source = C:\Acc07_ByExample\Northwind.mdb"

    Set conn = New ADODB.Connection
    conn.ConnectionString = strConn
    conn.Open

    Set rst = New ADODB.Recordset
```

```
Set rst.ActiveConnection = conn

' retrieve the data
rst.CursorLocation = adUseClient
rst.LockType = adLockBatchOptimistic
rst.CursorType = adOpenStatic
rst.Open strSQL, , , , adCmdText

' disconnect the recordset
Set rst.ActiveConnection = Nothing

' change the CustomerID in the first record to 'OCEAN'
rst.MoveFirst
Debug.Print rst.Fields(0) & " was " & rst.Fields(1) & " before."
rst.Fields("CustomerID").Value = "OCEAN"
rst.Update

' stream out the recordset as a comma-delimited string
strRst = rst.GetString(adClipString, , ",")
Debug.Print strRst
End Sub
```

3. Choose **Run | Run Sub/UserForm** to execute the procedure.

Notice that to create a disconnected recordset that gets its data from a data source, you need to set the CursorLocation, LockType, and CursorType properties of the Recordset object. CursorLocation should be set to adUseClient. This setting indicates that the cursor will reside on the client computer that is creating the recordset. Set LockType to adLockBatchOptimistic to enable multiple records to be updated. Finally, set CursorType to adOpenStatic to retrieve the snapshot of the data.

To disconnect a recordset, you must set the Recordset object's ActiveConnection property to Nothing after you've called the Recordset's Open method.

When the recordset is disconnected from the database, you can freely manipulate its data or pass it to another application or process. In the example procedure above, we manipulate our recordset by changing the value of the CustomerID field in the first retrieved record from VINET to OCEAN. Then we create a comma-delimited string using the Recordset object's GetString method. The content of the disconnected recordset is then printed out to the Immediate window, as shown here:

```
10274 was VINET before.
10274,OCEAN,6,8/6/1996,9/3/1996,8/16/1996,1,6.01,Vins et alcools Chevalier,59
rue de l'Abbaye,Reims,,51100,France
10295,VINET,2,9/2/1996,9/30/1996,9/10/1996,2,1.15,Vins et alcools Chevalier,59
rue de l'Abbaye,Reims,,51100,France
10737,VINET,2,11/11/1997,12/9/1997,11/18/1997,2,7.79,Vins et alcools
Chevalier,59 rue de l'Abbaye,Reims,,51100,France
10739,VINET,3,11/12/1997,12/10/1997,11/17/1997,3,11.08,Vins et alcools
Chevalier,59 rue de l'Abbaye,Reims,,51100,France
```

Saving a Recordset to Disk

The ADO has a Save method that allows you to save a recordset to disk and work with it from your VBA application. This method takes two parameters. You must specify a filename and one of the following two data formats:

- adPersistADTG — Advanced Data TableGram
- adPersistXML — Extensible Markup Language

A *saved* (or *persisted*) *recordset* is a recordset that is saved to a file. This file can later be reopened without an active connection.

In this section, you will persist a recordset into a file using the adPersistADTG format. You will work with the adPersistXML format in Part V of this book.

To save a recordset in a file, you must first open it. When you have applied a filter to a recordset and then decide to save this recordset, only the filtered records will be saved. Using the Save method does not close the recordset. You can continue to work with the recordset after it has been saved. However, always remember to close the recordset when you are done working with it.

The procedure in Hands-On 16-3 opens the recordset based on the Customers table. Once the recordset is open, the Save method is called to persist the customer records into a file.

◎ Hands-On 16-3: Saving Records to a Disk File (ADO)

1. In the Visual Basic Editor window, choose **Insert | Module**.

2. In the module's Code window, type the **SaveRecordsToDisk** procedure shown below, or copy the procedure code from **C:\Acc07_HandsOn\ Chap16.txt**.

```
Sub SaveRecordsToDisk()
    Dim conn As ADODB.Connection
    Dim rst As ADODB.Recordset
    Dim strFileName As String
    Dim strNorthPath As String

    strFileName = CurrentProject.Path & "\Companies.rst"
    strNorthPath = CurrentProject.Path & "\Northwind.mdb"

    On Error GoTo ErrorHandler

    Set conn = New ADODB.Connection

    With conn
        .Provider = "Microsoft.Jet.OLEDB.4.0"
        .ConnectionString = "Data Source = " & strNorthPath
        .Mode = adModeReadWrite
        .Open
    End With

    Set rst = New ADODB.Recordset
```

```
        With rst
          .CursorLocation = adUseClient
          ' Retrieve the data
          .Open "Customers", conn, _
            adOpenKeyset, adLockBatchOptimistic, adCmdTable

          ' Disconnect the recordset
          .ActiveConnection = Nothing

          ' Save the recordset to disk
          .Save strFileName, adPersistADTG
          .Close
        End With

        MsgBox "Records were saved in " & strFileName & "."

ExitHere:
    ' Cleanup
    Set rst = Nothing
    Exit Sub
ErrorHandler:
    If Not IsEmpty(Dir(strFileName)) Then
        Kill strFileName
        Resume
    Else
        MsgBox Err.Number & ": " & Err.Description
        Resume ExitHere
    End If
End Sub
```

3. Choose **Run | Run Sub/UserForm** to execute the procedure.

The above procedure saves all the data located in the Customers table to a file with an .rst extension. We named this file Companies.rst, but you are free to choose any filename and extension while saving your recordset.

Persisted recordsets are very useful for populating combo boxes or list boxes, especially when the data is located on a server and does not change too often. You can update your data as needed by running a procedure that creates a new dump of the required records and deletes the old disk file. This way, your Access application can display the most recent data in its combo or list boxes without having to connect to a database. Let's look at how you can fill a combo box with a saved recordset by working with Custom Project 16-1.

◎ Custom Project 16-1: Filling a Combo Box with a Disconnected Recordset (ADO)

This custom project requires that you complete Hands-On 16-2.

1. Create an Access form as shown in Figure 16-1. Place a combo box control in the form. Change the Name property of this control to **cboCompany**. Set the Caption property of the label control to **Company:**.

Figure 16-1: This custom form is used to demonstrate how you can fill the combo box control with a disconnected recordset.

2. Set the form's Caption property to **Disconnected combo**.

3. Save the form as **frmFillCombo**.

4. In the form's property sheet, activate the **Event** tab and click the button next to the **On Load** event name. In the Choose Builder dialog box, select **Code Builder** and click **OK**.

5. Complete the **Form_Load** procedure as shown below, or copy the procedure code from **C:\Acc07_HandsOn\Chap16.txt**.

```
Private Sub Form_Load()
    Dim rst As ADODB.Recordset
    Dim strRowSource As String
    Dim strName As String

    strName = CurrentProject.Path & "\Companies.rst"

    Set rst = New ADODB.Recordset
        With rst
            .CursorLocation = adUseClient
            .Open strName, , , , adCmdFile
            Do Until .EOF
                strRowSource = strRowSource & rst!CompanyName & ";"
                .MoveNext
            Loop
            With Me.cboCompany
                .RowSourceType = "Value List"
                .RowSource = strRowSource
            End With

            .Close
        End With
    Set rst = Nothing
End Sub
```

6. Open the **frmFillCombo** form in Form view.

To populate a combo box with values, the code in the Form_Load procedure changes the RowSourceType property of the combo box control to Value List and sets the RowSource property to the string obtained by iterating though the recordset. When the form opens, its caption is changed to Disconnected combo.

Figure 16-2: After opening the form prepared in Custom Project 16-1, the combo box is filled with the names of companies obtained via a persisted recordset.

7. Close the Disconnected combo (frmFillCombo) form.

Persisted recordsets are especially handy when you need to support disconnected users or when you want to take data on the road with you. You can save the required set of records to a disk file, send it to your users in remote locations, or take it with you. While disconnected from the database, you or your users can view or modify the records. The next time you connect to the database you can update the original data with your changes using the BatchUpdate method. Custom Project 16-2 demonstrates this scenario.

⊚ Custom Project 16-2: Taking Persisted Data on the Road

This custom project requires that you complete Hands-On 16-2.

Part 1: Saving a Recordset to Disk

Before you can take a recordset on the road with you, you must save the records to a disk file. To create the data for this project, prepare and run the procedure in Hands-On 16-2. You should have the Companies.rst file available in your C:\Acc07_ByExample folder before you proceed to Part 2.

Part 2: Creating an Unbound Access Form to View and Modify Data

Once you've saved the recordset to a disk file, the recordset becomes portable. You can take the file with you on the road or send it to someone else. But, before either one of you can view the data and modify it, you need some sort of a user interface. In this part, you will create an unbound Access form that will enable you to work with the file that contains the saved recordset.

1. Create a form as shown in Figure 16-3. Notice that this form contains only a couple of fields from the Customers table. This form serves only as an example. You can use as many fields as you have saved in the disk file.

Figure 16-3: This custom form is used to demonstrate how you can use the saved recordset in an unbound form.

2. Set the following properties for the form's controls:

Object	Property	Setting
Label1	Caption	Company Name:
Text box next to the Company Name label	Name	txtCompany
Label2	Caption	City:
Text box next to the City label	Name Back Color	txtCity Select any color you like
Label3	Caption	Country:
Text box next to the Country label	Name	txtCountry
Label4	Caption Name	90 lbRecordNo
Command button 1	Caption Name	First cmdFirst
Command button 2	Caption Name	Previous cmdPrevious
Command button 3	Caption Name	Next cmdNext
Command button 4	Caption Name	Last cmdLast

Note: We have set the Back Color property of the txtCity text box in the example application to visually indicate that the user can update only this field's data.

3. To visually match the form in Figure 16-3, draw a rectangle control over the command buttons and set its **Back Color** property to any color you like. Select the rectangle and choose **Arrange | Send to Back** to move the rectangle behind the command buttons.

4. In the property sheet, select **Form** from the drop-down list and activate the **Format** tab. Set the following properties for the form:

Property Name	Setting
Scroll Bars	Neither
Record Selectors	No
Navigation Buttons	No

5. Save the form as **frmCompanyInfo**.

Part 3: Writing Procedures to Control the Form and Its Data

Now that you've designed the form for your data, you need to write a couple of VBA procedures. The first procedure you'll write is an event procedure for the Form_Load event. This procedure will load the form with data from the persisted file. You will start by declaring a module-level Recordset object variable called rst and a module-level Integer variable called counter. You will also write Click procedures for all the command buttons and a procedure to fill the text boxes with the data from the current record in the recordset. Let's get started!

1. In the form's property sheet, activate the **Event** tab and click the **Build** button next to the **On Load** event name. In the Choose Builder dialog box, select **Code Builder** and click **OK**.

2. Enter the code for the **Form_Load** event procedure as shown below, starting with the declaration of module-level variables:

```
Option Compare Database
Dim rst As ADODB.Recordset
Dim counter As Integer

Private Sub Form_Load()
    Dim strFileName As String

    strFileName = CurrentProject.Path & "\Companies.rst"
    On Error GoTo ErrorHandler

    Set rst = New ADODB.Recordset
    With rst
        .CursorLocation = adUseClient
        .Open strFileName, , adOpenKeyset, adLockBatchOptimistic, adCmdFile
    End With

    counter = 1
    Call FillTxtBoxes(rst, Me)

    Me.txtCompany.SetFocus
    Me.cmdFirst.Enabled = False
    Me.cmdPrevious.Enabled = False
    Me.lbRecordNo.Caption = counter
ExitHere:
    Exit Sub
```

```
ErrorHandler:
    MsgBox Err.Number & ": " & Err.Description
    Resume ExitHere
End Sub
```

The Form_Load event procedure loads Companies.rst from a disk file. To fill the text boxes with the data from the current record in the recordset, you need to write the following code:

```
Me.txtCompany = rst!CompanyName
Me.txtCity = rst!City
Me.txtCountry = rst!Country
```

Because the above code will need to be entered in several procedures in this application, you can save yourself a great deal of typing by placing this code in a subroutine and calling it like this:

```
Call FillTxtBoxes(rst, Me)
```

The above statement calls the subroutine named FillTxtBoxes and passes it two arguments: the Recordset object variable and the reference to the current form. The FillTxtBoxes procedure (see step 3 below) is entered in a standard module and contains the code shown in the next step.

The counter variable, which was declared at the module level, is initialized to the value of 1. We will use this variable to control the display of command buttons on the form. The Form_Load event procedure ends by setting the focus to the first text box (txtCompanyName) and disabling the first two command buttons. These buttons will not be required when the form first opens on the first record.

3. In the Visual Basic Editor Code window, choose **Insert | Module** and type the code of the **FillTxtBoxes** procedure as shown below:

```
Sub FillTxtBoxes(ByVal rst As ADODB.Recordset, frm As Form)
    With frm
        .txtCompany = rst!CompanyName
        .txtCity = rst!City
        .txtCountry = rst!Country
    End With
End Sub
```

The procedure above fills the three text boxes placed on the form with the data from the current record in the recordset. This procedure is called from the Form_Load event procedure and the Click event procedures for each command button.

4. Write the following **Click** event procedure for the First command button:

```
Private Sub cmdFirst_Click()
    On Error GoTo Err_cmdFirst_Click

    rst.Update "City", Me.txtCity
    rst.MoveFirst

    Call FillTxtBoxes(rst, Me)
```

```
Me.txtCompany.SetFocus
Me.cmdFirst.Enabled = False
Me.cmdLast.Enabled = True
Me.cmdPrevious.Enabled = False
Me.cmdNext.Enabled = True

counter = 1
Me.lbRecordNo.Caption = counter

Exit_cmdFirst_Click:
   Exit Sub
Err_cmdFirst_Click:
   MsgBox Err.Description
   Resume Exit_cmdFirst_Click
End Sub
```

5. Write the following **Click** event procedure for the Next command button:

```
Private Sub cmdNext_Click()
   On Error GoTo Err_cmdNext_Click

   rst.Update "City", Me.txtCity
   rst.MoveNext
   counter = counter + 1

   Me.cmdFirst.Enabled = True

   Call FillTxtBoxes(rst, Me)

   Me.cmdPrevious.Enabled = True
   Me.lbRecordNo.Caption = counter
   Me.txtCompany.SetFocus
   If counter = rst.RecordCount Then
      Me.cmdNext.Enabled = False
      Me.cmdLast.Enabled = False
   End If

Exit_cmdNext_Click:
   Exit Sub
Err_cmdNext_Click:
   MsgBox Err.Description
   Resume Exit_cmdNext_Click
End Sub
```

6. Write the following **Click** event procedure for the Previous command button:

```
Private Sub cmdPrevious_Click()
   On Error GoTo Err_cmdPrevious_Click

   rst.Update "City", Me.txtCity
   rst.MovePrevious
   counter = counter - 1
```

```
Call FillTxtBoxes(rst, Me)

Me.txtCompany.SetFocus
Me.cmdLast.Enabled = True
Me.cmdNext.Enabled = True
Me.lbRecordNo.Caption = counter
If counter = 1 Then
   Me.cmdFirst.Enabled = False
   Me.cmdPrevious.Enabled = False
End If

Exit_cmdPrevious_Click:
   Exit Sub
Err_cmdPrevious_Click:
   MsgBox Err.Description
   Resume Exit_cmdPrevious_Click
End Sub
```

7. Write the following **Click** event procedure for the Last command button:

```
Private Sub cmdLast_Click()
   On Error GoTo Err_cmdLast_Click

   rst.Update "City", Me.txtCity
   rst.MoveLast

   Call FillTxtBoxes(rst, Me)

   Me.txtCompany.SetFocus
   Me.cmdFirst.Enabled = True
   Me.cmdPrevious.Enabled = True
   Me.cmdLast.Enabled = False
   Me.cmdNext.Enabled = False

   counter = rst.RecordCount
   Me.lbRecordNo.Caption = counter

Exit_cmdLast_Click:
   Exit Sub
Err_cmdLast_Click:
   MsgBox Err.Description
   Resume Exit_cmdLast_Click
End Sub
```

Notice that all the Click event procedures you prepared in steps 4-7 above contain the following line of code:

```
rst.Update "City", Me.txtCity
```

This statement updates the value of the City field in the recordset with the current value found in the txtCity text box on the form as you move through the records. Although the user can enter data in other text boxes, all modifications are ignored as there is no code in the Click event procedures that will allow changes to fields other than City. Of course, you can easily change this behavior by adding the necessary lines of code. Depending on which button was clicked, certain command buttons are disabled and others are enabled. This gives the user a visual clue of what actions are allowed at a particular moment.

To make the form work, we need to write one more event procedure. Before closing the form, we must make sure that the changes to the City field in the current record are saved and all changes in the City field we made while working with the form data are written back to the disk file. In other words, we must replace the Companies.rst disk file with a new file. This is done in the Form_Unload event procedure as shown in step 8.

8. Write the code of the **Form_Unload** event procedure as shown below:

```
Private Sub Form_Unload(Cancel As Integer)
    If rst.Fields("City").OriginalValue <> Me.txtCity Then
        rst.Update "City", Me.txtCity
    End If
    Kill (CurrentProject.Path & "\Companies.rst")
    rst.Save CurrentProject.Path & "\Companies.rst", _
        adPersistADTG
End Sub
```

The ADO Recordsets have a special property called OriginalValue, which is used for storing original values that were retrieved from a database. These original values are left unchanged while you edit the recordset offline. Any changes to the data made locally are recorded using the Value property of the Recordset object. The OriginalValue property is updated with the values changed locally when you reconnect to the database and perform an UpdateBatch operation (see Part 5 in this custom project).

The Form_Unload event occurs when you attempt to close a form but before the form is actually removed from the screen. This is a good place to perform those operations that must be executed before the form is closed. In the Form_Unload procedure above, we use the Recordset's OriginalValue property to check whether changes were made to the content of the City field in the current record. If OriginalValue is different from the value found in the current record's txtCity text box, we want to save the record by using the Update method of the recordset. Next, we delete the file containing the original recordset and save the current recordset to a file with the same name.

Part 4: Viewing and Editing Data Offline

Now that you've written all the procedures for the custom application, let's begin using the form to view and edit the data.

1. Open the **frmCompanyInfo** form in Form view.

2. In the first record, replace Berlin with **Drezden**.

3. Click the **Last** button, and replace Warszawa with **Opole**.

4. Click the **First** button and notice that the value of City is Drezden, just as you changed it in step 2.

5. Use the **Next** button to move to the fourth record and replace London with **Dover**.

6. Close the form and then reopen it. Check the values in the City text box in the first, fourth, and last records. You should see Drezden, Dover, and Opole.

7. Close the frmCompanyInfo form.

Part 5: Connecting to a Database to Update the Original Data

After you've made changes to the data by using the custom form, you can send the file with the modified recordset to your database administrator so that he or she can update the underlying database with your changes. Let's write a procedure that will take care of this task.

 Note: The procedure that you are about to write will modify the Customers table in the Northwind database. I recommend that you take a few minutes now and create a copy of this database so that you can restore the original data later if necessary.

1. In the Visual Basic Editor window, choose **Insert | Module**.

2. In the module's Code window, type the **UpdateDb** procedure as shown below, or copy the procedure code from **C:\Acc07_HandsOn\Chap16.txt**.

```
Sub UpdateDb()
    Dim conn As ADODB.Connection
    Dim rst As ADODB.Recordset
    Dim strNorthPath As String
    Dim strRecStat As String

    On Error GoTo ErrorHandler
    strNorthPath = CurrentProject.Path & "\Northwind.mdb"

    ' Open the connection to the database
    Set conn = New ADODB.Connection
    With conn
        .Provider = "Microsoft.Jet.OLEDB.4.0"
        .ConnectionString = "Data Source = " & strNorthPath
        .Mode = adModeReadWrite
        .Open
    End With

    ' Open the recordset from the local file
    ' that was persisted to the hard drive
    ' and update the data source with the changes
    Set rst = New ADODB.Recordset
    With rst
        .CursorLocation = adUseClient
        .Open CurrentProject.Path & "\Companies.rst", conn, _
            adOpenKeyset, adLockBatchOptimistic, adCmdFile
        .UpdateBatch adAffectAll

        ' Check if there were records with conflicts
        ' during the update
        .Filter = adFilterAffectedRecords
```

```
                Do Until .EOF
                    strRecStat = strRecStat & rst!City & ":" & rst.Status
                    .MoveNext
                Loop
                .Close
                Debug.Print strRecStat
            End With

    ExitHere:
        Set rst = Nothing
        Set conn = Nothing
        Exit Sub
    ErrorHandler:
        MsgBox Err.Number & ": " & Err.Description
        Resume ExitHere
    End Sub
```

3. Choose **Run | Run Sub/UserForm** to execute the procedure.

In the UpdateDb procedure shown above, we used the UpdateBatch method of the ADO Recordset object to update the underlying database with the changes we made to the data while working with it offline. The UpdateBatch method takes an optional parameter that determines how many records will be affected by the update. This parameter can be one of the constants shown in Table 16-1.

Table 16-1: Enumerated constants used with the UpdateBatch method

Constant	Value	Description
adAffectCurrent	1	Pending changes will be written only for the current record.
adAffectGroup	2	Pending changes will be written for the records that satisfy the current filter.
adAffectAll	3	Pending changes will be written for all the records in the recordset. This is the default.

When you update the data, your changes are compared with values that are currently in the database. The update will fail if the record was deleted or updated in the underlying database since the recordset was saved to disk. Therefore, after calling the UpdateBatch method, you should check the status of the records to locate records with conflicts. To do this, we must filter the recordset to see only the affected records:

```
rst.Filter = adFilterAffectedRecords
```

Next, we loop through the recordset and check the Status property of each record. This property can return different values, as shown in Table 16-2. You can locate these values in the Object Browser by typing RecordStatus-Enum in the Search box.

Table 16-2: RecordStatusEnum constants returned by the Status property

Constant	Value	Description
adRecCanceled	0x100	The record was not saved because the operation was canceled.
adRecCantRelease	0x400	The new record was not saved because the existing record was locked.
adRecConcurrencyViolation	0x800	The record was not saved because optimistic concurrency was in use.
adRecDBDeleted	0x40000	The record has already been deleted from the data source.
adRecDeleted	0x4	The record was deleted.
adRecIntegrityViolation	0x1000	The record was not saved because the user violated integrity constraints.
adRecInvalid	0x10	The record was not saved because its bookmark is invalid.
adRecMaxChangesExceeded	0x2000	The record was not saved because there were too many pending changes.
adRecModified	0x2	The record was modified.
adRecMultipleChanges	0x40	The record was not saved because it would have affected multiple records.
adRecNew	0x1	The record is new.
adRecObjectOpen	0x4000	The record was not saved because of a conflict with an open storage object.
adRecOK	0	The record was successfully updated.
adRecOutOfMemory	0x8000	The record was not saved because the computer has run out of memory.
adRecPendingChanges	0x80	The record was not saved because it refers to a pending insert.
adRecPermissionDenied	0x10000	The record was not saved because the user has insufficient permissions.
adRecSchemaViolation	0x20000	The record was not saved because it violates the structure of the underlying database.
adRecUnmodified	0x8	The record was not modified.

If the updates occurred without any conflict, the Status property will return the value of 8 (adRecUnmodified). While iterating through the recordset you can add additional code to resolve any encountered conflicts or check, for example, the original value and the updated value of the fields in updated records. As mentioned earlier, the OriginalValue property returns the field value that existed prior to any changes (since the last Update method was called). You can cancel all pending updates by using the CancelBatch method.

When you execute the UpdateDb procedure, your changes are written to the database.

4. Open the Northwind database and review the content of the City field in the Customers table. You should see Drezden, Dover, and Opole in the first, fourth, and last records.

5. Close the Northwind database and the Access window in which it was displayed. Do not close the Chap16.accdb database.

This completes Custom Project 16-2 in which you learned how to:

■ Save the recordset to disk with the Save method

■ Create a custom form to view and edit the recordset data in the disk file

■ Open the recordset from disk with the Open method

■ Work with the recordset offline (view and edit data)

■ Reopen the connection to the original database and write your changes with the UpdateBatch method

➜ **Note:** Refer to Part V of this book to find out how you can save a recordset in XML format using the adPersistXML format.

Cloning a Recordset

Sometimes you may want to manipulate a recordset without losing the current position in the recordset. You can do this by *cloning* your original recordset. Use the ADO Clone method to create a recordset that is a copy of another recordset. You can create a recordset clone like this:

```
Dim rstOrg As ADODB.Recordset       ' your original recordset
Dim rstClone As ADODB.Recordset     ' cloned recordset

Set rstClone = rstOrg.Clone
```

As you can see from the assignment statement above, the rstClone object variable contains a reference to the original recordset. After you've used the Clone method, you end up with two copies of the recordset that contain the same records but can be filtered and manipulated separately. You can create more than one clone of the original recordset.

Use the Clone method when you want to perform an operation on a recordset that requires multiple current records. The Clone object and the original Recordset object each have their own current records; therefore, the record pointers in the original and cloned recordsets can move independently of one another. And, because the clone points to the same set of data as the original, any changes made using either the original recordset or any of its clones will be visible in the original and its clones. However, the original recordset and its clones can get out of sync if you requery the original recordset against the database. When you close the original recordset, the clones remain open until you close them. Closing any of the clones does not close the original recordset.

Because the Clone method does not create another copy of the data (it only points to the data), cloning a recordset is faster and more efficient than opening a second recordset based on the same criteria. A recordset created by a method other than cloning will have a different set of bookmarks than the original recordset, even when it is based on the same SQL statement.

You can make a clone read-only by using an optional parameter like this:

```
Set rstClone = rstOrg.Clone(adLockReadOnly)
```

It's worth mentioning that you can only clone bookmarkable recordsets. Use the Recordset object's Supports method to find out if the recordset supports bookmarks (see the section called "Using Bookmarks" in Chapter 13). If you try to clone a non-bookmarkable recordset, you will receive a run-time error. The clone and the original recordset have the same bookmarks, which you can share. A bookmark reference from one Recordset object refers to the same record in any of its clones.

Custom Project 16-3 demonstrates how the Clone method can be used to create a single form for displaying the current and previous records side by side (see Figure 16-4).

◎ Custom Project 16-3: Displaying the Contents of the Current and Previous Record by Using the Clone Method

1. In the Microsoft Access window of the Chap16.accdb database, choose **External Data | Access**. In the File name box of the Get External Data dialog box, enter **C:\Acc07_ByExample\Northwind.mdb**, and then click **OK**. In the Import Objects window, select the **Customers** table and click **OK**. Click **Close** to exit the Get External Data dialog box.

2. Choose **Create | Form Design** and create a form like the one depicted in Figure 16-4. Follow the steps below to set up the form and its control properties.

Figure 16-4: This custom form is used to demonstrate how you can use recordset cloning to read the contents of the previous record.

3. In the Controls area of the Design tab, click the **Combo Box** control and click inside the form area to position it in the location shown in Figure 16-4. In the Combo Box Wizard's first screen, choose the option button labeled **I want the combo box to look up the values in a table or query**. Click **Next**. Make sure the **Customers** table is selected and click **Next**. The fields available in the Customers table should appear. Move **CustomerID** and **CompanyName** from the Available Fields box to the Selected Fields box, and then click **Next**. Specify **CompanyName** as the Ascending sort order for your combo box, and then click **Next**. In the next Wizard dialog, adjust the width of the combo box column to fit the longest company name and click **Finish**. Now you should see the combo box placed on your form.

4. Now place the remaining controls on the form and set their properties as shown below (properties of controls that are not listed do not need to be set for this example to work):

Object	Property	Setting
Label1 (in front of the combo box)	Caption Tag	Select Company Name cbo
Combo0 (created by the Combo Box Wizard)	Name Tag	CboCompany cbo
Label2	Caption Tag	Previous Record PrevRec
Label3	Caption	Current Record
Rectangle: Box1	Tag	PrevRec
Label4 (in front of Text box 1)	Caption Tag	Customer ID: PrevRec
Text box 1	Name Tag Control Source	CustIdPrev PrevRec should be blank
Label5 (in front of Text box 2)	Caption Tag	Company Name: PrevRec
Text box 2	Name Tag Control Source	CompanyPrev PrevRec should be blank
Label6 (in front of Text box 3)	Caption Tag	Contact Name: PrevRec
Text box 3	Name Tag Control Source	ContactPrev PrevRec should be blank
Label7 (in front of Text box 4)	Caption Tag	Contact Title: PrevRec
Text box 4	Name Tag Control Source	TitlePrev PrevRec should be blank
Label8 (in front of Text box 5)	Caption	Customer ID:
Text box 5	Name Control Source	CustomerID CustomerID
Label9 (in front of Text box 6)	Caption	Company Name:

Object	Property	Setting
Text box 6	Name Control Source	CompanyName CompanyName
Label10 (in front of Text box 7)	Caption	Contact Name:
Text box 7	Name Control Source	ContactName ContactName
Label11 (in front of Text box 8)	Caption	Contact Title:
Text box 8	Name Control Source	ContactTitle ContactTitle

5. In the property sheet, select **Form** from the drop-down box and set the following form properties:

Property Name	Setting
Caption	Record Comparison
Scroll Bars	Neither
Record Selectors	No
Navigation Buttons	No

6. Save the form as **frmCompare**.

7. Click the Combo Box control on the form to select it. Activate the **Event** tab in the property sheet and click to the right of the **AfterUpdate** event name. Select **[Event Procedure]** from the drop-down box, and then click the **Build** button (...) to activate the Code window. Complete the **cboCompany_AfterUpdate** procedure as shown below, or copy the procedure code from **C:\Acc07_HandsOn\Chap16.txt**.

```
Private Sub cboCompany_AfterUpdate()
' Find the record that matches the control.
    Dim rs As Object
    Dim c As Control

    On Error GoTo ErrHandle

    Set rs = Me.Recordset.Clone
    rs.FindFirst "[CustomerID] = '" & Me![cboCompany] & "'"
    If Not rs.EOF Then Me.Bookmark = rs.Bookmark
    ' Move to the previous record in the clone
    ' so that we can load the previous records'
    ' data in the form's text boxes
    rs.MovePrevious
    If Not rs.BOF Then
        For Each c In Me.Controls
            c.Visible = True
        Next
        Me.CustIdPrev = rs.Fields(0).Value
        Me.CompanyPrev = rs.Fields(1)
        Me.ContactPrev = rs.Fields(2)
        Me.TitlePrev = rs.Fields(3)
    Else
```

```
        For Each c In Me.Controls
            If c.Tag = "PrevRec" Then
                c.Visible = False
            End If
        Next
    End If
ExitHere:
    Exit Sub
ErrHandle:
    MsgBox Err.Number & ":" & Err.Description
    Resume ExitHere
End Sub
```

Notice that the above event procedure begins by creating a clone of the form's recordset. Next, the FindFirst method is used to locate the customer record based on the entry selected in the combo box. To ensure that the form's record is in sync with the entry selected in the combo box, the following line of code moves the form's bookmark to the same location as the recordset clone's bookmark as long as we are not at the end of file (EOF):

```
If Not rs.EOF Then Me.Bookmark = rs.Bookmark
```

Next, the procedure ensures that the controls used to display the contents of the previous record are visible whenever the selected record is not the first record. The control's Tag property is used to allow easy selection of controls that need to be hidden or made visible.

8. Press **Ctrl+S** to save the current changes.

9. Test your form by opening it in Form view. Selecting a company name from the combo box should fill the text boxes placed under the Current Record label with the selected company's data. The boxes under the Previous Record label should pull company data from the previous record.

   Before we start working with this custom project, let's write a Form_Load event procedure to ensure that only the combo box and its label are visible when the form is opened.

10. In the Code window where you have written the cboCompany_AfterUpdate event procedure, select **Form** from the object drop-down box in the top-left corner. Select **Load** from the procedure drop-down box on the right. Complete the code for the **Form_Load** event procedure as shown below, or copy the procedure code from the **C:\Acc07_HandsOn\ Chap16.txt**.

```
Private Sub Form_Load()
    Dim c As Control

    For Each c In Me.Controls
        If c.Tag <> "cbo" Then
            c.Visible = False
        End If
    Next
End Sub
```

11. Make sure there are no errors in your code by choosing **Debug | Compile Chap16**.

12. Save and close your form.

13. Open the **frmCompare** form in the Form view and test it by choosing various company names from the combo box.

14. Close the form.

Think of other ways to improve this form. For example, add a set of controls and write additional code to display the next record.

Introduction to Data Shaping

Designing database applications often requires that you pull information from multiple tables. For instance, to obtain a listing of customers and their orders, you must link the required tables with SQL JOIN statements as demonstrated below:

```
SELECT Customers.CustomerID AS [Cust Id],
    Customers.CompanyName,
    Orders.OrderDate,
    [Order Details].OrderID,
    Products.ProductName,
    [Order Details].UnitPrice,
    [Order Details].Discount,
    CCur([Order Details].[UnitPrice]*[Quantity]*(1-[Discount])/100)*100 AS
        [Extended Price]
FROM Products
    INNER JOIN ((Customers
    INNER JOIN Orders ON Customers.CustomerID = Orders.CustomerID)
    INNER JOIN [Order Details] ON Orders.OrderID = [Order Details].OrderID)
    ON Products.ProductID = [Order Details].ProductID
ORDER BY Customers.CustomerID, Orders.OrderDate DESC;
```

When you execute the above SQL statement, your output will match Figure 16-5.

Customer ID	Company Name	Order Date	Order ID	Product Name	Unit Price	Discount	Extended Price
ALFKI	Alfreds Futterkiste	09-Apr-1998	11011	Fløtemysost	$21.50	0%	$430.00
ALFKI	Alfreds Futterkiste	09-Apr-1998	11011	Escargots de Bourgogne	$13.25	5%	$503.50
ALFKI	Alfreds Futterkiste	16-Mar-1998	10952	Grandma's Boysenberry Spread	$25.00	5%	$380.00
ALFKI	Alfreds Futterkiste	16-Mar-1998	10952	Rössle Sauerkraut	$45.60	0%	$91.20
ALFKI	Alfreds Futterkiste	15-Jan-1998	10835	Original Frankfurter grüne Soße	$13.00	20%	$20.80
ALFKI	Alfreds Futterkiste	15-Jan-1998	10835	Raclette Courdavault	$55.00	0%	$825.00
ALFKI	Alfreds Futterkiste	13-Oct-1997	10702	Lakkalikööri	$18.00	0%	$270.00
ALFKI	Alfreds Futterkiste	13-Oct-1997	10702	Aniseed Syrup	$10.00	0%	$60.00
ALFKI	Alfreds Futterkiste	03-Oct-1997	10692	Vegie-spread	$43.90	0%	$878.00
ALFKI	Alfreds Futterkiste	25-Aug-1997	10643	Chartreuse verte	$18.00	25%	$283.50
ALFKI	Alfreds Futterkiste	25-Aug-1997	10643	Spegesild	$12.00	25%	$18.00
ALFKI	Alfreds Futterkiste	25-Aug-1997	10643	Rössle Sauerkraut	$45.60	25%	$513.00
ANATR	Ana Trujillo Emparedados y helados	04-Mar-1998	10926	Teatime Chocolate Biscuits	$9.20	0%	$64.40
ANATR	Ana Trujillo Emparedados y helados	04-Mar-1998	10926	Mozzarella di Giovanni	$34.80	0%	$348.00
ANATR	Ana Trujillo Emparedados y helados	04-Mar-1998	10926	Queso Cabrales	$21.00	0%	$42.00
ANATR	Ana Trujillo Emparedados y helados	04-Mar-1998	10926	Konbu	$6.00	0%	$60.00
ANATR	Ana Trujillo Emparedados y helados	28-Nov-1997	10759	Mascarpone Fabioli	$32.00	0%	$320.00
ANATR	Ana Trujillo Emparedados y helados	08-Aug-1997	10625	Camembert Pierrot	$34.00	0%	$340.00
ANATR	Ana Trujillo Emparedados y helados	08-Aug-1997	10625	Singaporean Hokkien Fried Mee	$14.00	0%	$70.00
ANATR	Ana Trujillo Emparedados y helados	08-Aug-1997	10625	Tofu	$23.25	0%	$69.75

Figure 16-5: When you use SQL JOIN statements you get a flat recordset with a lot of duplicate information.

When you output your data in a standard way by using the SQL JOIN syntax, you get a lot of duplicate information. You can eliminate this redundant information by using an advanced feature of ADO known as a shaped (or hierarchical) recordset.

Data shaping allows you to create recordsets within recordsets with a single ADO object. This sort of hierarchical data arrangement is often seen as a *parent-child relationship*. The parent recordset contains the child recordset. A child recordset can contain another child recordset, a grandchild of the original recordset. A parent-child relationship can be placed in an easy-to-read tree structure. You will produce such a structure in Custom Project 16-4 later in this chapter. For now, let's focus on learning a couple of new concepts that will enable you to present your data in a format that's easy to view and navigate.

Writing a Simple SHAPE Statement

You can easily create a hierarchy of data by using a data shaping language. All you need to know is how to use the following three commands: SHAPE, APPEND, and RELATE. The basic syntax looks like this:

```
SHAPE {parent-command}
APPEND ({child-command} [[AS] table-alias])
RELATE (parent-column TO child-column)
```

The parent-command and child-command are often SQL SELECT statements that pull the data from the required tables. Let's look at the following example that uses the above syntax:

```
SHAPE {SELECT CustomerID AS [Cust Id], CompanyName AS [Company] FROM
Customers}
APPEND ({SELECT CustomerId, OrderDate, OrderId, Freight FROM Orders} AS
custOrders
RELATE (CustomerID TO CustomerID)
```

The statement above is a shaped recordset. This statement selects two fields from the Customers table and four fields from the Orders table. By using this SHAPE statement, you can list all orders for each of the customers in the Customers table without returning any redundant information.

Notice that there are two SELECT statements in this recordset:

■ The first SELECT statement is the parent recordset. This recordset retrieves the data from the Customers table. Notice this SELECT statement is surrounded by curly braces and preceded by the SHAPE command, which defines a recordset.

■ The second SELECT statement is the child recordset. It gets the data from the Orders table. Notice that this SELECT statement is also surrounded by curly braces; however, it is preceded by the APPEND clause and an opening parenthesis. The APPEND clause will add the child recordset to the parent.

Note: When you append a child recordset to the parent recordset, a new field (column) is created in a parent recordset. This field is called a chapter column and has a data type called adChapter. You can use the AS clause to assign a name to the chapter column. If the appended column has no chapter-alias, a name will be generated for it automatically. In our example, the chapter column is called custOrders. Always specify an alias for your child recordset if you are planning to refer to it later in your code.

After specifying the SELECT statement for the child recordset, you must also indicate how you want the two recordsets to be linked. You do this with the RELATE clause. The column (CustomerID) from the parent recordset is related to the column (CustomerID) of the child recordset. Notice that you don't have to specify table names in the RELATE clause. Always specify the name of the parent column first.

 Note: The fields you use to relate parent and child recordsets must be in both recordsets. For example, you could not relate both recordsets if you did not select CustomerID from the Orders table.

Finally, remember to place a closing parenthesis at the end of the statement.

Working with Data Shaping

To work with data shaping in your VBA procedure, you need two providers: one for the data shaping functionality and the other one for the data itself. Therefore, before you can create shaped (hierarchical) recordsets in your programs, you will need to specify:

- **The name of a service provider**

  The data shaping functionality is provided by the data shaping service for OLE DB. The name of this service provider is MSDataShape and it is specified as the value of the Connection object's Provider property like this:

  ```
  conn.Provider = "MSDataShape"
  ```

  or it can be a connection string like this:

  ```
  "Provider=MSDataShape"
  ```

- **The name of a data provider**

  Because a shaped recordset needs to be populated with rows of data, you must specify the name of a data provider as the value of the DataProvider property of the Connection object:

  ```
  conn.DataProvider = "Microsoft.Jet.OLEDB.4.0;"
  ```

  or in the connection string like this:

  ```
  "Data Provider=Microsoft.Jet.OLEDB.4.0;"
  ```

The following is a code fragment from the procedure in Hands-On 16-4 that demonstrates how to specify the names of the data and service providers:

```
' define database connection string
' using the OLE DB provider
' and Northwind database as Data Source
strConn = "Data Provider=Microsoft.Jet.OLEDB.4.0;"
strConn = strConn & "Data Source = " & _
    "C:\Acc07_ByExample\Northwind.mdb"

' specify Data Shaping provider
' and open connection to the database
Set conn = New ADODB.Connection
With conn
    .ConnectionString = strConn
    .Provider = "MSDataShape"
    .Open
End With
```

Data Shaping with Other Databases

The data shaping service creates a shaped (hierarchical) recordset from any data supplied by a data provider. In order to provide shaped data from a database other than Microsoft Access, let's say, an SQL Server database, a connection string might look like this:

```
Dim conn As ADODB.Connection
Set conn = New ADODB.Connection
conn.Open = "Provider = MSDataShape;" & _
    "Data Provider = SQLOLEDB;" & _
    "Server=myServerName;" & _
    "Initial Catalog = Northwind;" & _
    "User ID = myId; Password="
```

or like this:

```
Dim conn As ADODB.Connection
Set conn = New ADODB.Connection
conn.Provider = "MSDataShape"
conn.Open "Data Provider=SQLOLEDB; Integrated Security=SSPI;
Database=Northwind"
```

In Hands-On 16-4 you learn how to create a shaped recordset in a VBA procedure and display hierarchical data in the Immediate window.

◉ Hands-On 16-4: Creating a Shaped Recordset (ADO)

1. In the Visual Basic Editor window of the Chap16 database, choose **Insert | Module**.

2. In the module's Code window, enter the **ShapeDemo** procedure as shown below, or copy the procedure code from **C:\Acc07_HandsOn\Chap16.txt**.

```
Sub ShapeDemo()
    Dim conn As ADODB.Connection
```

```
Dim rst As ADODB.Recordset
Dim rstChapter As Variant
Dim strConn As String
Dim shpCmd As String

' define database connection string
' using the OLE DB provider
' and Northwind database as Data Source
strConn = "Data Provider=Microsoft.Jet.OLEDB.4.0;"
strConn = strConn & "Data Source = " & _
   "C:\Acc07_ByExample\Northwind.mdb"

' specify Data Shaping provider
' and open connection to the database
Set conn = New ADODB.Connection
With conn
   .ConnectionString = strConn
   .Provider = "MSDataShape"
   .Open
End With

' define the SHAPE command for the shaped recordset
shpCmd = "SHAPE {SELECT CustomerID AS [Cust Id], " & _
   " CompanyName AS Company FROM Customers}" & _
   " APPEND ({SELECT CustomerID, OrderDate," & _
   " OrderID, Freight FROM Orders} AS custOrders" & _
   " RELATE [Cust Id] TO CustomerID)"

' create and open the parent recordset
' using the open connection
Set rst = New ADODB.Recordset
rst.Open shpCmd, conn

' output data from the parent recordset
Do While Not rst.EOF
   Debug.Print rst("Cust Id"); _
       Tab; rst("Company")
     rstChapter = rst("custOrders")
     ' write out column headings
     ' for the child recordset
     Debug.Print Tab; _
       "OrderDate", "Order #", "Freight"
     ' output data from the child recordset
     Do While Not rstChapter.EOF
       Debug.Print Tab; _
         rstChapter("OrderDate"), _
         rstChapter("OrderID"), _
         Format(rstChapter("Freight"), "$ #.##")
       rstChapter.MoveNext
     Loop
   rst.MoveNext
Loop

' Cleanup
rst.Close
Set rst = Nothing
```

```
    Set conn = Nothing
End Sub
```

3. Choose **Run | Run Sub/UserForm** to execute the procedure.

The above procedure begins by specifying the data provider and data source name in the strConn variable. Next, we define a new ADO Connection object and set the ConnectionString property of this object to the strConn variable. Now that we have the data provider name and also know which database we need to pull the data from, we go on to specify the data shaping service provider. This is done by using the Provider property of the Connection object. We set this property to MSDataShape, which is the name of the service provider for the hierarchical recordsets. Now we are ready to actually open a connection to the database. Before we can pull the required data from the database, we define the shaped recordset statement and store it in the shpCmd String variable. Next, we create a new Recordset object and open it using the open database connection. Then, we populate it with the content of the shpCmd variable like this:

```
    Set rst = New ADODB.Recordset
    rst.Open shpCmd, conn
```

Now that we have filled the hierarchical recordset, we begin to loop through the parent recordset. The first statement in the loop:

```
    Debug.Print rst("Cust Id"); Tab; rst("Company")
```

will write out the customer ID (Cust Id) and the company name (Company) to the Immediate window.

In the second statement in the loop:

```
    rstChapter = rst("custOrders")
```

we create a Recordset object variable based on the value of the custOrders field. As you recall from an earlier discussion, custOrders is an alias for the child recordset. The object variable (rstChapter) can be any name you like as long as it's not a VBA keyword.

Note: Because a child recordset is simply a field in a parent recordset, when you retrieve the value of that field you will get the entire recordset filtered to include only the related records.

Before iterating through the child recordset, the column headings are output to the Immediate window for the fields we want to display. This way it is much easier to understand the meaning of the data in the child recordset. The next block of code loops through the child recordset and dumps the data to the Immediate window under the appropriate column heading. Once the data is retrieved for each parent record, we can close the recordset and release the memory.

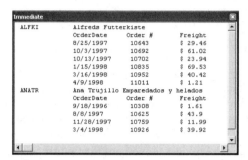

Figure 16-6: After running the ShapeDemo procedure in Hands-On 16-4, you can see the contents of the hierarchical recordset in the Immediate window.

How to Determine If a Recordset Contains a Field Pointing to Another Recordset

To find out if a certain recordset contains another recordset, you can use the following conditional statement:

```
Dim rst as New ADODB.Recordset

If rst.Fields("custOrders").Type = adChapter then
    Debug.Print "This is a child recordset"
End If
```

 Note: custOrders is the chapter column alias you created with the AS clause while appending a child recordset to the parent.

Writing a Complex SHAPE Statement

In the previous section, you worked with a simple SHAPE statement that displayed order information for each customer in the Northwind.mdb database in the Immediate window. You learned how to nest a child recordset within a parent recordset and access the fields in both. In the following sections, you will learn how to write more complex SHAPE statements that include multiple child and grandchild recordsets.

Shaped Recordsets with Multiple Children

Data shaping does not limit you to having just one child recordset within a parent recordset. You can specify as many children as you want. For example, to display a parent with two children, use the following syntax:

```
SHAPE {SELECT * FROM Parent}
APPEND ({SELECT * FROM Child1}
            RELATE parent-column TO child1-column) AS child1-alias,
        ({SELECT * FROM Child2}
            RELATE parent-column TO child2-column) AS child2-alias
```

Notice that additional children (siblings) are added to the end of the APPEND clause.

Suppose you want to display both the orders and products for a customer in the Northwind database. Using the syntax provided earlier, you can shape your hierarchical recordset as demonstrated in the ShapeMultiChildren procedure shown in Hands-On 16-5.

⊙ Hands-On 16-5: Creating a Shaped Recordset with Multiple Children (ADO)

1. In the Visual Basic Editor window of the Chap16 database, choose **Insert |
Module.**
2. In the module's Code window, enter the **ShapeMultiChildren** procedure as shown below, or copy the procedure code from **C:\Acc07_HandsOn\ Chap16.txt.**

```
Sub ShapeMultiChildren()
    Dim conn As ADODB.Connection
    Dim rst As ADODB.Recordset
    Dim rstChapter1 As Variant
    Dim rstChapter2 As Variant
    Dim strConn As String
    Dim shpCmd As String
    Dim strParent As String
    Dim strChild1 As String
    Dim strChild2 As String
    Dim strLink As String
    Dim str1stChildName As String
    Dim str2ndChildName As String

    ' define database connection string
    ' using the OLE DB provider
    ' and Northwind database as Data Source
    strConn = "Data Provider=Microsoft.Jet.OLEDB.4.0;"
    strConn = strConn & "Data Source = " & _
        "C:\Acc07_ByExample\Northwind.mdb"

    ' specify Data Shaping provider
    ' and open connection to the database
    Set conn = New ADODB.Connection
    With conn
        .ConnectionString = strConn
        .Provider = "MSDataShape"
        .Open
    End With

    ' define the SHAPE command for the shaped recordset

    strParent = "SELECT CustomerID AS [Cust Id], " & _
        "CompanyName AS Company FROM Customers"

    strChild1 = "SELECT CustomerID, OrderDate," & _
        "OrderID, Freight FROM Orders"

    strChild2 = "SELECT Customers.CustomerID," & _
        "Products.ProductName FROM Products " & _
        "INNER JOIN ((Customers INNER JOIN Orders ON " & _
```

```
          "Customers.CustomerID = Orders.CustomerID) " & _
          "INNER JOIN [Order Details] ON " & _
          "Orders.OrderID = [Order Details].OrderID) ON " & _
          "Products.ProductID = [Order Details].ProductID " & _
          "Order By Products.ProductName"

   str1stChildName = "custOrders"
   str2ndChildName = "custProducts"

   strLink = "RELATE [Cust Id] TO CustomerID"

   shpCmd = "SHAPE {"
   shpCmd = shpCmd & strParent
   shpCmd = shpCmd & "}"
   shpCmd = shpCmd & " APPEND ({"
   shpCmd = shpCmd & strChild1
   shpCmd = shpCmd & "}"
   shpCmd = shpCmd & strLink
   shpCmd = shpCmd & ")"
   shpCmd = shpCmd & " AS " & str1stChildName
   shpCmd = shpCmd & ", ({"
   shpCmd = shpCmd & strChild2
   shpCmd = shpCmd & "} "
   shpCmd = shpCmd & strLink
   shpCmd = shpCmd & ")"
   shpCmd = shpCmd & " AS " & str2ndChildName

   ' create and open the parent recordset
   ' using the open connection
   Set rst = New ADODB.Recordset
   rst.Open shpCmd, conn

   ' output data from the parent recordset
   Do While Not rst.EOF

      Debug.Print rst("Cust Id"); Tab; rst("Company")
         rstChapter1 = rst("custOrders")

         ' write out column headings
         ' for the 1st child recordset
         Debug.Print Tab(4); " (" & rst("Cust Id") & " Orders)"
         Debug.Print Tab; "OrderDate", "Order #", "Freight"

         ' output data from the 1st child recordset
         Do While Not rstChapter1.EOF
            Debug.Print Tab; _
               rstChapter1("OrderDate"), _
               rstChapter1("OrderID"), _
               Format(rstChapter1("Freight"), "$ #,#0.00")
            rstChapter1.MoveNext
         Loop

         rstChapter2 = rst("custProducts")
         ' write out column headings
         ' for the 2nd child recordset
```

```
              Debug.Print Tab(4); " (" & rst("Cust Id") & " Products)"

              ' output data from the 2nd child recordset
              Do While Not rstChapter2.EOF
                  Debug.Print Tab; _
                      rstChapter2("ProductName")
                  rstChapter2.MoveNext
              Loop
          rst.MoveNext
      Loop

      ' Cleanup
      rst.Close
      Set rst = Nothing
      Set conn = Nothing
  End Sub
```

3. Choose **Run | Run Sub/UserForm** to execute the procedure.

The SHAPE statement in the above procedure has been specially formatted so that you can easily create any shaped recordset containing multiple children by replacing SELECT statements with your own. This procedure produces the output in the Immediate window as shown in Figure 16-7. Notice that each customer has two child records: Orders and Products.

```
ALFKI          Alfreds Futterkiste
(ALFKI Orders)
      OrderDate      Order #         Freight
      8/25/1997      10643          $ 29.46
      10/3/1997      10692          $ 61.02
      10/13/1997     10702          $ 23.94
      1/15/1998      10835          $ 69.53
      3/16/1998      10952          $ 40.42
      4/9/1998       11011          $ 1.21
(ALFKI Products)
      Aniseed Syrup
      Chartreuse verte
      Escargots de Bourgogne
      Flotemysost
      Grandma's Boysenberry Spread
      Lakkalikööri
      Original Frankfurter grüne Soße
      Raclette Courdavault
      Rössle Sauerkraut
      Rössle Sauerkraut
      Spegesild
      Vegie-spread
ANATR          Ana Trujillo Emparedados y helados
(ANATR Orders)
      OrderDate      Order #         Freight
      9/18/1996      10308          $ 1.61
      8/8/1997       10625          $ 43.90
      11/28/1997     10759          $ 11.99
      3/4/1998       10926          $ 39.92
(ANATR Products)
      Camembert Pierrot
      Gudbrandsdalsost
```

Figure 16-7: After running the ShapeMultiChildren procedure in Hands-On 16-5, you can see the output of the hierarchical recordset with multiple children in the Immediate window.

Shaped Recordsets with Grandchildren

In addition to the parent recordset having multiple children, the child recordset can contain a child of its own. Simply put, your hierarchical recordset can contain grandchildren. Creating such a hierarchy is a bit harder, but it can be tackled in no time if you take a step-by-step approach. The SHAPE syntax that includes grandchildren looks like this:

```
SHAPE {SELECT * FROM Parent}
APPEND ((SHAPE {SELECT * FROM Child}
```

```
APPEND ({SELECT * FROM Grandchild}
  RELATE child-column TO grandchild-column) AS grandchild-alias)
  RELATE parent-column TO child-column) as child-alias
```

Notice that when grandchildren are present, the child recordset is appended with another SHAPE command.

Although you can have as many children or grandchildren as you want, it will be more difficult to write a SHAPE statement that uses more than three or four levels.

Quickly Generate SHAPE Commands

If you happen to have a copy of Visual Basic 6.0, you can use the Data Environment Designer to visually create SHAPE commands. Using this tool can save you time, especially when you need to create complex shapes containing grandchildren and aggregations. You can also use the hierarchical FlexGrid ActiveX control to quickly display your shaped recordset.

In Custom Project 16-4 you create a shaped recordset that contains both children and grandchildren. Next, you display this recordset on the Access form in the ActiveX TreeView control (see Figure 16-11 for the final output). This project will also introduce you to using aggregate functions within your shaped recordsets.

⊚ Custom Project 16-4: Using Hierarchical Recordsets

Part 1: Creating a Form with a TreeView Control

1. In the Access window of the Chap16.accdb database, choose **Create | Form Design**. The Form design window opens.

2. In the Controls area of the Design tab, click the **Insert ActiveX Control** button.

3. In the Insert ActiveX Control window, choose **Microsoft TreeView Control, version 6.0** as shown in Figure 16-8, and click **OK** to place a TreeView control on the form.

Figure 16-8: The Microsoft TreeView control provides an excellent way to display shaped recordsets in an Access form.

4. Resize the TreeView control and the form to match Figure 16-9.

5. Click the TreeView control to select it. In the property sheet, change the Name property of the TreeView control from TreeView0 to **myTreeCtrl**.

Figure 16-9: A TreeView control after being placed and resized on the Access form.

6. Right-click the TreeView control in Design view and choose **TreeCtr_Object | Properties**. Adjust the custom properties of the TreeView control as listed on the General tab in Figure 16-10.

   In addition to the properties listed in the property sheet, the ActiveX TreeView control exposes a number of custom properties that can be adjusted via the TreeCtrl Properties dialog box, as shown in Figure 16-10.

Figure 16-10: You can set custom properties of the TreeView control in the TreeCtrl Properties dialog box.

7. Save the form as **frmOrders**.

Part 2: Writing an Event Procedure for the Form Load Event

1. In the property sheet, select **Form** from the drop-down box and click the **Event** tab for the selected form.

2. Click next to the **On Load** event property.

3. Click the **Build** button (...) next to the OnLoad property to display the Choose Builder dialog box.

4. In the Choose Builder dialog box, select **Code Builder** and click **OK**. The form module window appears with the following Form_Load event procedure stub:

```
Private Sub Form_Load()

End Sub
```

5. Write the code for the **Form_Load** event procedure as shown below, or copy the procedure code from **C:\Acc07_HandsOn\Chap16.txt**.

```
Private Sub Form_Load()
    Dim conn As ADODB.Connection
    Dim rstCustomers As ADODB.Recordset
    Dim rstOrders As ADODB.Recordset
    Dim rstOrderDetails As ADODB.Recordset
    Dim fld As Field
    Dim objNode1 As Node
    Dim objNode2 As Node
    Dim strConn As String
    Dim strSQL As String

    Dim strSQLCustomers As String
    Dim strSQLOrders As String
    Dim strSQLOrderDetails As String
    Dim strSQLRelParentToChild As String
    Dim strSQLRelGParentToParent As String

    ' Create the ADO Connection object
    Set conn = New ADODB.Connection

    ' Specify a valid connection string
    strConn = "Data Provider=Microsoft.Jet.OLEDB.4.0;"
    strConn = strConn & "Data Source = " & _
        "C:\Acc07_ByExample\Northwind.mdb"
    conn.ConnectionString = strConn

    ' Specify the Data Shaping provider
    conn.Provider = "MSDataShape"

    ' Open the connection
    conn.Open

    ' Specify SELECT statement for the Grandparent
    strSQLCustomers = "SELECT CustomerID AS [Cust #]," & _
        "CompanyName AS [Customer] " & _
        "FROM Customers"
```

```
' Specify SELECT statement for the Parent
strSQLOrders = "SELECT OrderID AS [Order #]," & _
    "OrderDate AS [Order Date]," & _
    "Orders.CustomerID AS [Cust #] " & _
    "FROM Orders ORDER BY OrderDate DESC"

' Specify SELECT statement for the Child
strSQLOrderDetails = "SELECT od.OrderID AS [Order #]," & _
    "p.CategoryId AS [Category]," & _
    "p.ProductName AS [Product]," & _
    "od.Quantity," & _
    "od.ProductId," & _
    "od.UnitPrice AS [Unit Price]," & _
    "(od.UnitPrice * od.Quantity) " & _
    "AS [Extended Price] " & _
    "FROM [Order Details] od " & _
    "INNER JOIN Products p " & _
    "ON od.ProductID = p.ProductID " & _
    "ORDER BY p.CategoryId, p.ProductName"

' Specify RELATE clause to link Parent to Child
strSQLRelParentToChild = "RELATE [Order #] TO [Order #]"

' Specify RELATE clause to link Grandparent to Parent
strSQLRelGParentToParent = "RELATE [Cust #] TO [Cust #]"

' Build complete SQL statement for the shaped recordset
' adding aggregate functions for the Grandparent and Parent
strSQL = "SHAPE(SHAPE{" & strSQLCustomers & "}"
strSQL = strSQL & "APPEND((SHAPE{" & strSQLOrders & "} "
strSQL = strSQL & "APPEND({" & strSQLOrderDetails & "} "
strSQL = strSQL & strSQLRelParentToChild & ") AS rstOrderDetails,"
strSQL = strSQL & "COUNT(rstOrderDetails.Product) "
strSQL = strSQL & "        AS [Items On Order],"
strSQL = strSQL & "SUM(rstOrderDetails.[Extended Price]) "
strSQL = strSQL & "        AS [Order Total])"
strSQL = strSQL & strSQLRelGParentToParent & ") AS [rstOrders],"
strSQL = strSQL & "SUM(rstOrders.[Order Total]) "
strSQL = strSQL & "        AS [Cust Grand Total]"
strSQL = strSQL & ") AS rstCustomers"

' Create and open the Grandparent recordset
Set rstCustomers = New ADODB.Recordset
rstCustomers.Open strSQL, conn

' Fill the TreeView control
Do While Not rstCustomers.EOF
    Set objNode1 = myTreeCtrl.Nodes.Add _
        (Text:=rstCustomers.Fields(0) & _
        "   " & rstCustomers.Fields(1) & _
        "   ($ " & rstCustomers.Fields(3) & ")")
    Set rstOrders = rstCustomers.Fields("rstOrders").Value
        Do While Not rstOrders.EOF
            Set objNode2 = myTreeCtrl.Nodes.Add _
                (relative:=objNode1.Index, _
                relationship:=tvwChild, _
```

```
                    Text:=rstOrders.Fields(0) & _
                    "  " & rstOrders.Fields(1) & _
                    "  " & rstOrders.Fields(4) & " (items)" & _
                    "    $" & rstOrders.Fields(5) & _
                    " (Order Total)")
                Set rstOrderDetails = _
                    rstOrders.Fields("rstOrderDetails").Value
                        Do While Not rstOrderDetails.EOF
                            myTreeCtrl.Nodes.Add _
                                relative:=objNode2.Index, _
                                relationship:=tvwChild, _
                                Text:=rstOrderDetails.Fields(3) & _
                                "  " & rstOrderDetails.Fields(2) & _
                                " $" & rstOrderDetails.Fields(6) & _
                                " (" & rstOrderDetails.Fields(3) & _
                                " x $" & rstOrderDetails.Fields(5) & ")"
                            rstOrderDetails.MoveNext
                        Loop
            rstOrders.MoveNext
        Loop
        rstCustomers.MoveNext
    Loop

    ' Cleanup
        rstCustomers.Close
        Set rstCustomers = Nothing
        Set conn = Nothing
End Sub
```

6. In the Access window, open **frmOrders** in Form view.

When you open the frmOrders form, the Form_Load procedure populates the TreeView control with the data from the Northwind.mdb database. As you can see from Figure 16-11, the results are quite impressive. Clicking on the nodes in the TreeView control expands and collapses the details underneath the node.

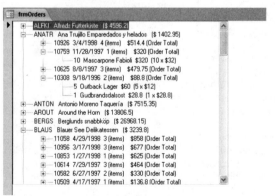

Figure 16-11: The TreeView control is filled with the data from the Northwind database when the user opens the form.

Prior to populating the TreeView control with the data, we connect to the database and enlist the services of the Data Shaping provider:

```
conn.Provider = "MSDataShape"
```

Because a TreeView control displays data as a hierarchy, we need to build a complex SQL statement using the SHAPE syntax we learned in preceding sections. To make things easier for ourselves, we start by defining SQL statements with fields we want to display for parent, child, and grandchild recordsets. Notice that we renamed some fields using the AS clause. We also defined separate statements to allow us to link grandparent to parent and parent to child. The structure we need to create can be illustrated like this:

```
Grandparent
      Parent
            Child
```

Now that we've defined the relationship and the fields for our data hierarchy, we use the SHAPE commands to build the complete SHAPE statement:

```
strSQL = "SHAPE(SHAPE{" & strSQLCustomers & "}"
strSQL = strSQL & "APPEND((SHAPE{" & strSQLOrders & "} "
strSQL = strSQL & "APPEND({" & strSQLOrderDetails & "} "
strSQL = strSQL & strSQLRelParentToChild & ") AS rstOrderDetails,"
strSQL = strSQL & "COUNT(rstOrderDetails.Product) "
strSQL = strSQL & "          AS [Items On Order]) "
strSQL = strSQL & "SUM(rstOrderDetails.[Extended Price]) "
strSQL = strSQL & "          AS [Order Total])"
strSQL = strSQL & strSQLRelGParentToParent & ") AS [rstOrders],"
strSQL = strSQL & "SUM(rstOrders.[Order Total]) "
strSQL = strSQL & "          AS [Cust Grand Total]"
strSQL = strSQL & ") AS rstCustomers"
```

While creating the SHAPE statement, we added additional calculated fields using the aggregate functions. For instance, in the parent recordset (rstOrders) we calculated the number of items ordered using the COUNT function:

```
COUNT(rstOrderDetails.Product) AS [Items On Order]
```

And used the SUM function to obtain the total amount of the order:

```
SUM(rstOrderDetails.[Extended Price]) AS [Order Total]
```

In the grandparent recordset (rstCustomers), we used the SUM function to calculate the total amount owed by a customer.

When expanded, the complete SHAPE statement will look as follows:

```
strSQL = "SHAPE(SHAPE{"
strSQL = strSQL & "SELECT CustomerID AS [Cust #],"
strSQL = strSQL & "CompanyName AS [Customer]"
strSQL = strSQL & "FROM Customers"
strSQL = strSQL & "}"
strSQL = strSQL & "APPEND((SHAPE{"
strSQL = strSQL & "SELECT OrderID AS [Order #],"
strSQL = strSQL & "OrderDate AS [Order Date],"
strSQL = strSQL & "Orders.CustomerID AS [Cust #]"
strSQL = strSQL & "FROM Orders "
strSQL = strSQL & "ORDER BY OrderDate DESC"
strSQL = strSQL & "}"
strSQL = strSQL & "APPEND({"
strSQL = strSQL & "SELECT od.OrderID AS [Order #],"
strSQL = strSQL & "p.CategoryId AS [Category],"
```

```
strSQL = strSQL & "p.ProductName AS [Product],"
strSQL = strSQL & "od.Quantity,"
strSQL = strSQL & "od.ProductId,"
strSQL = strSQL & "od.UnitPrice AS [Unit Price],"
strSQL = strSQL & "(od.UnitPrice * od.Quantity) "
strSQL = strSQL & "AS [Extended Price] "
strSQL = strSQL & "FROM [Order Details] od INNER JOIN Products p "
strSQL = strSQL & "ON od.ProductID = p.ProductID "
strSQL = strSQL & "ORDER BY p.CategoryId, p.ProductName"
strSQL = strSQL & "}"
strSQL = strSQL & "RELATE [Order #] TO [Order #]"
strSQL = strSQL & ")"
strSQL = strSQL & "AS rstOrderDetails,"
strSQL = strSQL & "COUNT(rstOrderDetails.Product) "
strSQL = strSQL & "AS [Items On Order],"
strSQL = strSQL & "SUM(rstOrderDetails.[Extended Price]) "
strSQL = strSQL & "AS [Order Total])"
strSQL = strSQL & "RELATE [Cust #] TO [Cust #]"
strSQL = strSQL & ") "
strSQL = strSQL & "AS [rstOrders],"
strSQL = strSQL & "SUM(rstOrders.[Order Total]) "
strSQL = strSQL & "AS [Cust Grand Total]) AS rstCustomers"
```

Notice that the SHAPE statement we built contains standard fields pulled from the database tables and child recordsets (rstOrders, rstOrderDetails), as well as calculated columns. The rstOrders recordset is a field in the rstCustomers recordset. This field contains order information for a customer. rstOrderDetails is a field within the rstOrders recordset. This field contains the order details information for a customer's order.

Now that we've completed the SHAPE statement, we can open the grand-parent recordset and begin populating the TreeView control with our data.

A TreeView control consists of Node objects, which you can expand or collapse to display or hide child nodes. Nodes that have child nodes are referred to as *parent* nodes. The nodes located at the top of the tree control are referred to as *root* nodes. Root nodes can have *sibling* nodes that are located on the same level. For example, customer ALFKI (see Figure 16-11) is a root node, and so is the customer ANATR, ANTON, and so on. They are also siblings of one another.

To populate a TreeView control, we use the Add method of the Nodes collection like this:

```
Set objNode1 = myTreeCtrl.Nodes.Add
```

The objNode1 above is an object variable representing the Node object. The first node added to a TreeView is a root node. The Add method of the Nodes collection uses the following syntax:

```
object.Add([relative,] [relationship,] [key], text[, image,] [selectedimage])
```

In the syntax above, the only required arguments are object and text. The object is the object variable (myTreeCtrl) representing the TreeView control. The text is a string that appears in the node. Now, looking at the complete statement:

```
Set objNode1 = myTreeCtrl.Nodes.Add _
    (Text:=rstCustomers.Fields(0) & _
    "    " & rstCustomers.Fields(1) & _
    "    ($ " & rstCustomers.Fields(3) & ")")
```

we have created a root node to display the following information:

```
Cust # (rstCustomers.Fields(0))
Customer (rstCustomers.Fields(1))
Cust Grand Total (rstCustomers.Fields(3))
```

Because the above statement appears inside a looping structure, the TreeView control will display all the customers at their root level.

Now that we've taken care of the root node, we go on to add children and grandchildren. A child node has a relationship to a parent node that has already been added. To define a child node, in addition to the required text argument, we will use two optional arguments of the Add method as described below:

- relative — This is the index number or key of a pre-existing Node object. In our example, we used the index of the parent node that we just created (relative:=objNode1.Index).

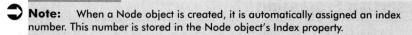

Note: When a Node object is created, it is automatically assigned an index number. This number is stored in the Node object's Index property.

- relationship — Specifies the type of relationship you are creating. Use the tvwChild setting to create a child node of the node named in the relative argument (see above). The statement that creates a child node looks like this:

```
Set objNode2 = myTreeCtrl.Nodes.Add _
    (relative:=objNode1.Index, _
    relationship:=tvwChild, _
    Text:=rstOrders.Fields(0) & _
    "    " & rstOrders.Fields(1) & _
    "    " & rstOrders.Fields(4) & " (items)" & _
    "     $" & rstOrders.Fields(5) & _
    " (Order Total)")
```

The above statement displays order information for a customer. The child node text argument is set to display:

```
Order # (rstOrders.Fields(0))
Order Date (rstOrders.Fields(1))
Items On Order (rstOrders.Fields(4))
Order Total (rstOrders.Fields(5))
```

Because the statement above appears inside a looping structure, the TreeView control will display the order information for each customer. Finally, we add grandchildren using the following statement:

```
myTreeCtrl.Nodes.Add _
    relative:=objNode2.Index, _
    relationship:=tvwChild, _
    Text:=rstOrderDetails.Fields(3) & _
```

```
"   " & rstOrderDetails.Fields(2) & _
"  $" & rstOrderDetails.Fields(6) & _
"  (" & rstOrderDetails.Fields(3) & _
"  x $" & rstOrderDetails.Fields(5) & ")"
```

The above statement displays order details for a customer's order. Notice that this Node object references the index number of the child object that has just been added (relative:=objNode2.Index).

The grandchild node text argument is set to display:

```
Quantity (rstOrderDetails.Fields(3))
Product (rstOrderDetails.Fields(2))
Extended Price (rstOrderDetails.Fields(6))
Quantity x Unit Price (rstOrderDetails.Fields(3) & "x $" &
rstOrderDetails.Fields(5))
```

The looping structure ensures that the order details above are listed for all customers' orders.

Now that you are done with this custom project, you should be able to provide your own hierarchical data in a pretty neat user interface.

Transaction Processing

To improve your application's performance and to ensure that database activities can be recovered in case an unexpected hardware or software error occurs, consider grouping sets of database activities into a transaction. A *transaction* is a set of operations that are performed together as as a single unit. If you use an automatic teller machine (ATM), you are already familiar with transaction processing. When you go to the bank to get cash, your account must be debited. In other words, the cash withdrawal must be deducted from your savings or checking account. A transaction is a two-sided operation. If anything goes wrong during the transaction, the entire transaction is canceled. If both operations succeed, that is, you get the cash and the bank debits your account, the transaction's work is saved (or committed).

Database transactions often involve modifications and additions of one or more records in a single table or in several tables. When a transaction has to be undone or canceled, the transaction is rolled back. Often, when you perform batch updates to database tables and an error occurs, updates to all tables must be canceled or the database could be left in an inconsistent state.

Transactions are extremely important for maintaining data integrity and consistency. If you don't use transactions for operations that should be performed together, the database could be left in an inconsistent state, resulting not only in loss of important information but also in a number of other headaches.

In ADO, the Connection object offers three methods (BeginTrans, CommitTrans, and RollbackTrans) for managing transaction processing. You should use these methods to save or cancel a series of changes made to the data as a single unit.

■ BeginTrans — Begins a new transaction

- CommitTrans — Saves any changes and ends the current transaction
- RollbackTrans — Cancels any changes made during the current transaction and ends the transaction

Please note that in ADO a transaction is limited to one database because the Connection object can only point to one database.

To work with transaction processing in DAO, use the transaction methods of the Workspace or DBEngine object: BeginTrans, CommitTrans, and Rollback. Within a Workspace transaction you can perform operations on more than one connection or database.

Creating a Transaction with ADO

Use the BeginTrans method to specify the beginning of a transaction. Use the CommitTrans method to save the changes. BeginTrans and CommitTrans are used in pairs. The data-modifying instructions you place between these keywords are stored in memory until Visual Basic encounters the CommitTrans statement. After reaching CommitTrans, Access writes the changes that have occurred since the BeginTrans statement to the disk; therefore, any changes you've made in the tables become permanent.

If an error is generated during the transaction process, the RollbackTrans statement placed further down in your procedure will undo all changes made since the BeginTrans statement. The rollback ensures that the data is returned to the state it was in before you started the transaction.

Using transaction processing helps improve database performance since the operations carried out during a transaction are run in memory. If the transaction succeeds, the results are written to the disk in a single operation. If any operation included in a transaction fails, the transaction is simply aborted and no changes are written to the database. If you don't use transactions, the results of each operation must be written to the disk separately — a process that consumes more database resources.

The procedure in Hands-On 16-6 assumes that you want to enter an order for a new customer. Because this customer does not exist in the database, you will use a transaction to ensure that the new order is entered only after the customer record has been created in the Customers table.

⊚ Hands-On 16-6: Using a Database Transaction to Insert Records (ADO)

1. In the Visual Basic Editor window of the Chap16 database, choose **Insert | Module**.

2. In the module's Code window, enter the **Create_Transaction_ADO** procedure as shown below, or copy the procedure code from **C:\Acc07_ HandsOn\Chap16.txt**.

```
Sub Create_Transaction_ADO()
    Dim conn As ADODB.Connection
```

```
On Error GoTo ErrorHandler

Set conn = New ADODB.Connection

With conn
    .Provider = "Microsoft.Jet.OLEDB.4.0"
    .ConnectionString = "Data Source = " & _
        "C:\Acc07_ByExample\Northwind.mdb"
    .Open
    .BeginTrans

    ' insert a new customer record
    .Execute "INSERT INTO Customers " & _
        "Values ('GWIPO','Gwiazda Polarna'," & _
        "'Marcin Garnia', 'Sales Manager', 'ul.Majewskiego 10'," & _
        "'Warszawa', Null, '02-106', 'Poland', '0114822230445', Null)"

        ' insert the order for that customer
        .Execute "INSERT INTO Orders " & _
            " (CustomerId, EmployeeId, OrderDate, RequiredDate) " & _
            " Values ('GWIPO', 1, Date(), Date()+5)"
    .CommitTrans
    .Close
    MsgBox "Both inserts completed."
End With

ExitHere:
    Set conn = Nothing
    Exit Sub
ErrorHandler:
    If Err.Number = -2147467259 Then
        MsgBox Err.Description
        Resume ExitHere
    Else
        MsgBox Err.Description
        With conn
            .RollbackTrans
            .Close
        End With
        Resume ExitHere
    End If
End Sub
```

3. Choose **Run | Run Sub/UserForm** to execute the procedure.

The first SQL INSERT INTO statement inserts the customer data into the Customers table in the Northwind.mdb database. Before the customer can actually order specific products, a record must be added to the Orders table. The second SQL INSERT INTO statement takes care of this task. Because both inserts must occur prior to filling in order details, they are treated as a single transaction. If an error occurs anywhere (for example, the Orders table is open in Design view), the entire transaction is rolled back. Notice how the INSERT INTO statement is used in this procedure. If you do not specify the field names, you will need to include values for each field in the table.

Figure 16-12: After running the procedure in Hands-On 16-6, a record for a new customer, "GWIPO," is added to the Customers and Orders tables.

Creating a Transaction with DAO

The DAO Object Model supports transactions through the BeginTrans, CommitTrans, and Rollback methods of Workspace and DBEngine objects. When you use these methods with the DBEngine object, the transaction is applied to the default workspace — DBEngine.Workspaces(0). If you need to manage transactions or connections to multiple databases, use the Workspace object. A Workspace object represents a user's session. A transaction on a workspace will affect all data modifications made within the workspace. You can manage transactions independently across Database objects by creating additional Workspace objects.

As in ADO, use the BeginTrans method to specify the beginning of a transaction, the CommitTrans method to save the changes, and Rollback to cancel the transaction. BeginTrans and CommitTrans are used in pairs. The data-modifying instructions you place between these keywords are stored in memory until Visual Basic encounters the CommitTrans statement. After reaching CommitTrans, Access writes the changes that have occurred since the BeginTrans statement to the disk; therefore, any changes you've done in the tables become permanent.

If an error is generated during the transaction process, the Rollback statement placed further down in your procedure will undo all changes made since the BeginTrans statement, which ensures that the data is returned to the state it was in before you started the transaction.

Transaction processing should be used for archiving historical data. For instance, the procedure in Hands-On 16-7 selects all orders placed in 1996 and appends them to an archive table in another database (Chap11.accdb). Then, the records are deleted from the source table.

Hands-On 16-7: Using a Database Transaction to Archive Records (DAO)

1. In the Microsoft Access window of the Chap16.accdb database, choose **External Data** | **Access**. In the File name box of the Get External Data dialog box, enter **C:\Acc07_ByExample\Northwind.mdb**, and then click

OK. In the Import Objects window, select the **Orders** table and click **OK**. Click **Close** to exit the Get External Data dialog box.

2. In the Visual Basic Editor window of the Chap16 database, choose **Insert | Module**.

3. In the module's Code window, enter the **OrdersArchive1996_DAO** procedure as shown below, or copy the procedure code from **C:\Acc07_ HandsOn\Chap16.txt**.

```
Sub OrdersArchive1996_DAO()
    Dim db As DAO.Database
    Dim blnTrans As Boolean
    Dim strSQL As String

    On Error GoTo ErrorHandler

    'begin transaction
    DBEngine.BeginTrans
    blnTrans = True

    Set db = CurrentDb()

    ' create an archive table on the fly
    ' and fill it with records
    strSQL = "SELECT * INTO OrdersArchive1996 IN " & _
            """C:\Acc07_ByExample\Chap11.accdb""" & _
            " FROM Orders WHERE Orders.OrderDate " & _
            "BETWEEN #1/1/1996# AND #12/31/1996#;"

    db.Execute strSQL, dbFailOnError

    ' delete records from the source table
    If db.RecordsAffected <> 0 Then
        strSQL = "DELETE FROM Orders " & _
                "WHERE Orders.OrderDate " & _
                "BETWEEN #1/1/1996# AND #12/31/1996#;"

        db.Execute strSQL, dbFailOnError

    ' ask user if OK to commit changes
        If MsgBox("Click OK if you want to archive " _
            & db.RecordsAffected & " records.", vbOKCancel + _
            vbQuestion + vbDefaultButton2, "Procceed?") = vbOK Then

            DBEngine.CommitTrans
        Else
            If blnTrans Then DBEngine.Rollback
        End If
    Else
        DBEngine.Rollback
        MsgBox "There are no records to archive " & _
                "with the specified criteria.", vbInformation + vbOKOnly, _
                "Records not found"
    End If
Cleanup:
```

```
        Set db = Nothing
        Exit Sub
ErrorHandler:
    If Err.Number = 3010 Then
        strSQL = "INSERT INTO OrdersArchive1996 IN " & _
                 """C:\Acc07_ByExample\Chap11.accdb""" & _
                 " SELECT * FROM Orders WHERE Orders.OrderDate " & _
                 "BETWEEN #1/1/1996# AND #12/31/1996#;"

        Resume 0
    Else
        If blnTrans Then DBEngine.Rollback
        MsgBox Err.Description
        Resume Cleanup
    End If
End Sub
```

4. Choose **Run | Run Sub/UserForm** to execute the procedure.

   In the above procedure we start a transaction with the DBEngine object's BeginTrans method and set the transaction flag to True (blnTrans) to indicate that the transaction is active. We also initiate the Database object variable to point to the current database. The first data operation in this transaction requires that we create a table in another Access database to store the selected records from the Orders table in the current database. In the Access user interface we would simply create a Make-Table query; in VBA programming we can use the SQL SELECT…INTO statement. The first part of this statement specifies the fields we want to select; in this case we use a wildcard (*) to denote that all fields should be copied into the new table. This is followed by the INTO clause and the name of the table to be created.

   If the table already exists, then the SELECT…INTO statement will fail and VBA will respond with an error 3010. We must set an error trap (see the ErrorHandler code). To add the data to the existing table, we must use the SQL INSERT INTO statement. The name of the table in the SELECT …INTO statement is followed by the IN clause and the name of the external database into which data is to be inserted. You need to specify the full path to the database file.

➥ **Note:** It is possible to specify in the SELECT…INTO statement the name of an external non-Microsoft database; see the online help for the details.

The name of the external database is followed by the FROM clause and the name of the existing table from which records are selected. You may select data from more than one table. You may also specify selection criteria following the WHERE clause. After creating the SQL statement, we execute it using the Execute method of the Database object.

Notice the use of the dbFailOnError option with the Execute method. If the statement fails, dbFailOnError will generate an error message we can trap. Without it, you are not notified of any errors, and the entire procedure may not produce the intended results. You can see how the error trap works by running the procedure more than once. If the Execute statement succeeds, we proceed to delete records from the source table. However, we don't want to execute the delete code if the SELECT statement returned no records. After the Execute command is run, we use the RecordsAffected property of the Database object to obtain the number of records affected by the most recent Execute command.

If we have more than one record, we specify the records to delete using the SQL DELETE statement, and then carry out the delete operation by calling the Execute method of the Database object. If dbFailOnError did not notify us of any errors, we assume that the Execute statement succeeded and we can commit the transaction. Before carrying out this operation, we ask the user to confirm or cancel the transaction. If the user chooses not to go ahead with the changes, we roll back the transaction. We also withdraw changes to the records if there were no records to archive.

It is important to keep in mind that in case of an error you must roll back the transaction. Always check if the transaction is still active by using a flag. Rolling back the transaction will ensure that the transaction doesn't stay active after your VBA procedure has ended.

5. Run the procedure once again in step mode (using **F8**) to walk through the error code.

Chapter Summary

This chapter covered quite a bit of advanced ADO and DAO material you will find useful in developing professional applications in Microsoft Access. You started by creating your own recordset from scratch and using it for storing non-relational data. Next, you learned how to disconnect a recordset from a database and work with it offline. You also learned that a recordset can be saved to a disk file and later reopened without an active connection to the database. Next, you discovered how you can use the Clone method of the Recordset object to create a recordset that is a copy of another recordset. Finally, you familiarized yourself with the concepts of data shaping and learned statements that make it possible to create impressive, hierarchical views of your data. You also learned how transactions are used to ensure that certain database operations are always performed as a single unit.

In the next chapter, you will learn how to write VBA procedures that handle database security.

Chapter 17

Implementing Database Security

The new Access 2007 ACCDB file format does not support user-level security. This means that you cannot create user and group accounts or assign object permissions in Access ACCDB databases. This chapter focuses on implementing database security in Access databases created in the MDB file format.

In the course of this chapter, you will learn how to:

- Use the Users and Groups collections of the ADOX Catalog object to create and manage security user accounts.

- Use the GetPermissions and SetPermissions methods of the ADOX User and Group objects to retrieve and set permissions on database objects.

- Use the ChangePassword method of the ADOX User object to change the user's password.

- Use the CompactDatabase method of the JRO JetEngine object to set a database password.

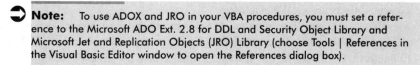

Note: To use ADOX and JRO in your VBA procedures, you must set a reference to the Microsoft ADO Ext. 2.8 for DDL and Security Object Library and Microsoft Jet and Replication Objects (JRO) Library (choose Tools | References in the Visual Basic Editor window to open the References dialog box).

Two Types of Security in Microsoft Access

Depending on your requirements, Microsoft Office Access allows you to implement share-level or user-level security to protect and secure your Access database. User-level security can only be implemented in Access databases created in the MDB file format.

Share-Level Security (in Access ACCDB and MDB File Formats)

Using passwords to secure the database or objects in the database is known as *share-level security*. When you set a password on the database, users are required to enter a password in order to gain access to the data and database objects. Anyone with the password has unrestricted access to all Access data and database objects.

To manually change the database password:

■ For an Access database in the ACCDB file format, choose Database Tools | Encrypt with Password.

■ For an Access database in the MDB file format, choose Database Tools | Set Database Password.

 Note: Refer to the sections titled "Setting a Database Password Using the CompactDatabase Method" and "Setting a Database Password Using the NewPassword Method" later in this chapter to set a database password from within a VBA procedure for Access databases.

User-Level Security

User-level security is a relatively complex process that secures the code and objects in your database so that users can't accidentally modify or change them. With this type of security you can provide the most restrictive access over the database and the objects it contains. When you use user-level security, a *workgroup information file* is used to determine who can open a database and what objects are available to them.

The workgroup information file holds group and user information, including passwords. The information contained in this file determines not only who can open the database, but also the permissions users/groups have on the objects in the database. The workgroup information file contains built-in groups (Admins and Users) and a generic user account (Admin) with unlimited privileges on the database and the objects it contains.

When an Access MDB database file is open in Access 2007, you can manually implement user-level security by choosing Database Tools | Users and Permissions. You can also define user and group accounts and their passwords from your VBA procedures by using ADO code, as demonstrated later in this chapter.

Understanding Workgroup Information Files

To successfully run the procedures demonstrated in this chapter, you need to know the location of the workgroup information file on your computer. This file, also known as system database (System.mdw), is created automatically on your computer (see Table 17-1).

Please note that the Application Data folder (used for storing System.mdw file for an Access 2002-2003 database) is a hidden folder. To browse this folder, switch to Microsoft Windows Explorer and choose Tools | Folder Options. In the Folder Options window, click the View tab, click the option button next to Show hidden files and folders, and click OK. Now you should be able to access the path, where <user name> is the name of your user profile. Take a few minutes right now to locate the System.mdw file on your machine.

Table 17-1: The workgroup information file in different versions of Access

Access Version	Default Workgroup Information Filename	Workgroup Information File Location
2.0	System.mda	C:\Access
95	System.mdw	C:\MSOffice\Access
97	System.mdw	C:\Windows\System
2000	System.mdw	C:\Program Files\Common Files\System
2002/2003	System.mdw	C:\Documents and Settings\<user name>\Application Data\Microsoft\Access

You can also find the location and name of the workgroup information file by starting Microsoft Access 2007 and opening any MDB database. Switch to the Visual Basic Editor window and activate the Immediate window. Type the following statement beginning with a question mark and press Enter to execute:

```
? CurrentProject.Connection.Properties("Jet OLEDB:System Database").Value
```

When you press Enter, Access displays the full path of the workgroup information file that the currently open database uses for its security information. Jet OLEDB:System Database is a provider-specific property of the Microsoft OLE DB Provider for Jet in the ADO Properties collection of the Connection object.

Access uses the workgroup information file to store the following information:

■ The name of each user and group

■ The list of users who belong to each group

■ The encrypted logon password for each workgroup user

■ The Security Identifier (SID) of each user and group in a binary format

Once you add user and group accounts to your database, the workgroup information file will contain vital security information. YOU DON'T WANT TO LOSE THIS INFORMATION. Always take time to make a backup copy of the System.mdw file and store it in a safe location. This way, if the original file gets corrupted, you'll be able to quickly restore your backup file and avoid having to recreate user and group accounts.

The workgroup information file is like any other Access database except that it contains hidden system tables with information regarding user and group accounts and their actual permissions. However, you cannot change the security information by opening this file directly. All the security data stored in hidden system tables is encrypted and protected. Changes to the workgroup information file are done automatically by the Jet Engine when you use the built-in Access commands to manage security or execute ADO/JRO code in your VBA procedures.

You can use the same workgroup information file for more than one database or you can create a separate workgroup information file for each database you are securing. You can also give this file a name other than the default System.mdw. I find it best to use the same name as the database file. For example, if my secured database file is named Assets.mdb, I would create a workgroup information file called Assets.mdw and put it in the same folder as the database file. This way I know right away that these two files are associated with one another even after many weeks or months have passed since I created them. Keeping track of which workgroup information file goes with which database can be quite challenging, especially if you are managing more than a couple of secured Access databases.

 Note: If you try to open a secured database while another workgroup information file is active, Access displays the following message:

> *You do not have the necessary permissions to use the <name> object. Have your system administrator or the person who created this object establish the appropriate permissions for you.*

If you receive the above message while opening an Access database in the MDB file format, you should look for the accompanying workgroup information file and perform one of the following:

Set Up a Shortcut

Set up a shortcut to the database file that uses the /WRKGRP command-line switch to load the specified workgroup information file when the database is opened (see Part 3 in Custom Project 17-1).

Use the Workgroup Administrator Tool in Microsoft Office Access 2007

1. Start Access and open any Access database.
2. Press **Alt+F11** to switch to the Visual Basic Editor window.
3. Choose **View | Immediate Window**.
4. In the Immediate window, type the following statement and press **Enter** to execute:

    DoCmd.RunCommand acCmdWorkgroupAdministrator

5. In the Workgroup Administrator dialog box, click **Join**, then click **Browse**.
6. Locate the workgroup information file and then click **Open**. See Table 17-1 for the .mdw filenames used with various versions of Access.
7. In the Workgroup Administrator dialog box, click **OK**, then click **Exit**.

Creating and Joining Workgroup Information Files

When you open a database, Microsoft Access reads the workgroup information file to find out who is allowed to access the database. If security was put into place, you will be prompted for the user ID and password. Custom Project 17-1 walks you through the steps required to create and join a new workgroup information file. Once you join the workgroup, you create a new Access database and set up a password for the Admin user. This information is saved in the workgroup information file that you just joined. The workgroup information file is created using the User-Level Security Wizard. This option is available by choosing Database Tools | Users and Permissions.

Securing a database boils down to creating a new workgroup information file, adding a new member to the Admins group, and removing the default Admin user from that group. You also need to remove permissions from the Admin user and from the Users group, and assign permissions to your own groups that you create. Don't be discouraged if you need to go over the security steps more than once. Access security is complex and can be approached from many different angles. Books of several hundred pages have been written to explain its inner workings. The approach presented here simply provides us with a secured Access database file we use to perform the programming exercises in this chapter. Although you could learn how to use the ADOX commands for managing security using the currently open unsecured Access database, I think this particular approach gives you a better set of skills to begin with. So let's begin.

◎ Custom Project 17-1: Securing a Microsoft Access MDB Database

You must complete this custom project in order to work with the hands-on exercises in this chapter.

Part 1: Creating a New Access Database in the MDB File Format

1. Start Microsoft Office Access 2007 and create a new blank database called **SpecialDb.mdb** in your C:\Acc07_ByExample folder. Keep this database open and proceed to Part 2 below.

Part 2: Establishing User-Level Security

We use the built-in User-Level Security Wizard to secure the blank Access database (SpecialDb.mdb) we created in Part 1.

1. Choose **Database Tools | User and Group Permissions | User-Level Security Wizard**.

2. Click **Yes** in response to the message that the database should be opened in the shared mode to run the Security Wizard. Microsoft Access closes the database and reopens it in the shared mode.

3. Microsoft Access then automatically activates the Security Wizard (see Figure 17-1). Click **Next** to continue.

Figure 17-1: Security Wizard (screen 1)

4. Another Security Wizard window appears (see Figure 17-2). Do not make any changes in this screen. Click **Next** to continue.

Figure 17-2: Security Wizard (screen 2) The workgroup information file named Security1.mdb stores user and group account information for the SpecialDb database.

5. The Security Wizard window now shows an empty tabbed screen that normally displays database objects (Figure 17-3). Because our database does not contain any tables, queries, reports, etc., there's nothing you can do in this screen. Click **Next** to continue.

Figure 17-3: Security
Wizard (screen 3)

6. The Security Wizard window now goes on to display a list of optional
   security accounts that you could include in your new workgroup information file (Figure 17-4). Because we will define our accounts in
   programming code later in this chapter, do not make any selections in this
   screen. Click **Next** to continue.

Figure 17-4: Security
Wizard (screen 4)

7. Now the Security Wizard asks you whether you want to grant permissions
   to the Users group. Do not make any changes in this screen. The Users
   group will have no permissions. We will work with permissions in our
   VBA procedures later. Click **Next** to continue.

445 | Chapter 17

Figure 17-5: Security
Wizard (screen 5)

8. Now the Security Wizard shows a screen (Figure 17-6) where we finally can do a little bit of work. We need to define a new user in our database. This user will function as a new Admin. We'll call our new user a **Developer** and allow him to log into the database using **chapter17** as a password. Fill in the User name and the Password boxes as shown in Figure 17-6 and click the **Add This User to the List** button. The Developer should now appear in the users list. Do not leave this screen yet.

Figure 17-6: Security
Wizard (screen 5 —
filling in data)

9. Now we remove the user account with which we logged into Access. In the list of users, select the user name you logged in with (I selected Julitta) and click the **Delete User from the List** button. Now Developer is the only user in our database, as shown in Figure 17-7. Click **Next** to continue.

Figure 17-7: Security Wizard (screen 5 — with new data added)

10. The Security Wizard shows the screen where you can assign users to groups in the workgroup information file (Figure 17-8). Notice that the Developer user you created in step 9 is a member of the Admins group. Click **Next** to continue.

Figure 17-8: Security Wizard (screen 6)

11. The Security Wizard has now collected all the required information. As a final step, it suggests the name for the backup copy of the unsecured database (Figure 17-9). The unsecured database is, in this case, the blank database we started with. When we are done with this final step, our database will still be blank; however, it will be secured. Do not make any changes in this screen. Click **Finish**.

Figure 17-9: Security Wizard (screen 7)

12. Access performs its final tasks of securing your database and displays the Security Wizard report (Figure 17-10). If you are connected to the printer, it's a good idea to take a minute now to print this report. You can also magnify the report to read it on screen. When you are done, close the Security Wizard report window.

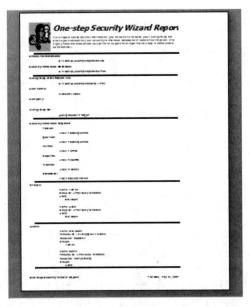

Figure 17-10: Security Wizard report

13. Upon closing the window, the Security Wizard displays a warning message that asks whether you would like to save the report as a Snapshot (.snp) file that you can view later. For this exercise, click **No** in response to this question. You should see the confirmation message that the Security Wizard has encoded your database and to reopen the database you must use the new

workgroup file you created by closing Access and reopening it. We'll do as suggested in Part 3. Click **OK** to this message.

14. Close the Microsoft Access window.

Part 3: Opening a Secured MDB Database

After completing the previous two parts of this custom project, the following files have been added to your C:\Acc07_ByExample folder:

- A database file named SpecialDb.mdb

- A workgroup information file named Security1.mdb that stores user and group account information for the SpecialDb database

- A backup copy of the SpecialDb database named SpecialDb.bak

Also, there is a shortcut on your desktop (created by the Security Wizard) that allows you to quickly start the SpecialDb database using the new workgroup information file (Security1.mdb). If you right-click that desktop shortcut and choose Properties, you will see in the Target box the following path:

```
"C:\Program Files\Microsoft Office\OFFICE12\MSACCESS.EXE "
    "C:\Acc07_ByExample\SpecialDb.mdb" /WRKGRP
    "C:\Acc07_ByExample\Security1.mdw"
```

Because this path is very long it's shown on three lines. Notice that the first part of this path is the location of the Microsoft Access executable program on your disk surrounded by quotation marks. The path to the MSAccess.exe is then followed by a space and the full path of the database file (also in quotation marks). Because this database file is secured, we must also include a space and a command-line switch, /WRKGRP, followed by a space and the name of the accompanying workgroup information file (also in quotation marks).

The /WRKGRP command-line switch tells Access that you want to start a database with a specific workgroup. If you know what user account you want to log on with, you can use the /User and /Pwd command-line switches to avoid being prompted by Access for the user name and password:

```
"C:\Program Files\Microsoft Office\OFFICE12\MSACCESS.EXE "
    "C:\Acc07_ByExample\SpecialDb.mdb" /WRKGRP
    "C:\Acc07_ByExample\Security1.mdw "
        /User "Developer"  /Pwd "chapter17"
```

The information about the user name and password follows the name of the workgroup information file and a single space.

Now that you know how the path to a secured database is built, you can create similar shortcuts to other secured databases if they use different workgroup information files.

1. On your desktop, double-click the shortcut to **SpecialDb.mdb** to open this database. Because this database is protected, a logon box appears. Enter **Developer** in the Name box and **chapter17** in the Password box and click **OK**.

2. Now that your secured database file is open, we will take a look at the changes the Security Wizard has made in the Users and Groups accounts.

Choose **Database Tools | Users and Permissions | User and Group Accounts**. Notice that the Admin user is a member of the Users group (see Figure 17-11). The Security Wizard removed the Admin account from the Admins group. If you open the Name drop-down list in the User area of this screen and select Developer, you will see that Developer is a member of two groups: Admins and Users. Click **Cancel** to exit the User and Group Accounts window.

Figure 17-11: In Custom Project 17-1, we removed the default Admin user from the Admins group while running the built-in User-Level Security Wizard.

3. Having checked the Users and Groups accounts, you can also examine the changes made by the Security Wizard in the group permissions. Choose **Database Tools | Users and Permissions | User and Group Permissions**. The Developer and Admin users don't have permissions on any new objects (see Figure 17-12). To view group permissions, click the **Groups** option button. The Admins group has all the necessary permissions to administer the database while the Users group has no permissions at all. We will learn how to grant and revoke permissions to database objects in the example procedures in this chapter. Now click **Cancel** to exit the User and Group Permissions window.

Figure 17-12: Use the User and Group Permissions window to check current permissions for the Admin and Developer users after running the User-Level Security Wizard in Custom Project 17-1.

4. Now let's import a couple of objects into this database. Later in this chapter when we learn to handle permissions to database objects we will need them for our tests. In the Access window, choose **External Data | Access**. In the Get External Data dialog box, enter **C:\Acc07_ByExample\ Northwind.mdb** in the File name box and click **OK**.

5. In the Import Objects window, click **Select All** to select all the tables. Click the **Queries** tab, and then choose **Select All** to select all the queries. Finally, click **OK** to begin importing. When the import operation is completed, click the **Close** button.

6. The objects you selected in step 5 have now been added to your database. Close the SpecialDb database and close the Access application. This step concludes the special project of creating a secured Access database. Now, let's proceed to the programming part.

Creating and Managing Group and User Accounts

To create a new group account from a VBA procedure using ADO, open the ADOX Catalog object by specifying the connection to the appropriate database and use the Append method of the Catalog object's Groups collection to add a new group account.

To create a new user account, pass the name and password to the Append method of the Users collection. Specifying a password at this time is optional. You can assign a password later with the ChangePassword method for the User object.

The procedure in Hands-On 17-1 illustrates how to create two group accounts and a user account in the secured database (SpecialDb.mdb) that you created in Custom Project 17-1.

Hands-On 17-1: Creating User and Group Accounts (ADO)

This hands-on exercise requires that you have completed Custom Project 17-1.

1. Start Microsoft Office Access 2007 and create a new database named **Chap17.mdb** in your **C:\Acc07_ByExample** folder. Make sure you type .mdb as the file extension.

2. Press **Alt+F11** to switch to the Visual Basic Editor window and choose **Insert | Module**.

3. Choose **Tools | References** and click the check box next to the following three object libraries: **Microsoft ActiveX Data Objects 2.8 Library**, **Microsoft ADO Ext. 2.8 for DDL and Security Object Library**, and **Microsoft Jet and Replication Objects 2.6 Library**. After making these selections, click **OK** to exit the References dialog box.

4. Activate the Immediate window by choosing **View | Immediate Window**. Type the following statement in the Immediate window and press **Enter**:

```
DoCmd.RunCommand acCmdWorkgroupAdministrator
```

When you press Enter, Access loads the Workgroup Administrator tool, which lets you check the path to the workgroup information file that is currently used. Note: In Access 2007 there is no command in the user interface to access this tool. You must use the above code to use the Workgroup Administrator tool.

Perform one of the following steps:

a. If System.mdw appears in the Workgroup path, click **OK** to exit the Workgroup Administrator dialog box and proceed with step 5 below.

b. If the Workgroup path includes the Security1.mdw file that was created in Custom Project 17-1, click the **Join** button to join another workgroup. Use the **Browse** button in the Workgroup Information File dialog box to select and open **System.mdw**. Refer to the beginning of this chapter for information on the default location of this file. Once you select the correct file, the dialog box should display its full path. Click **OK** to exit this dialog box. Access will display a message box saying you successfully joined the workgroup defined by the selected information file. Click **OK** to the message and click **OK** in the Workgroup Administrator dialog box to exit. Proceed to step 5.

5. In the module's Code window, enter the **Create_UserAndGroup_ADO** procedure as shown below, or copy the procedure code from **C:\Acc07_ HandsOn\Chap17.txt**.

```
Sub Create_UserAndGroup_ADO()
    Dim cat As ADOX.Catalog
    Dim conn As ADODB.Connection
    Dim strDB As String
    Dim strSysDB As String
    Dim strGrpName1 As String
    Dim strGrpName2 As String
    Dim strUsrName As String

    On Error GoTo ErrorHandler

    strDB = "C:\Acc07_ByExample\SpecialDb.mdb"
    strSysDB = "C:\Acc07_ByExample\Security1.mdw"
    strGrpName1 = "Masters"
    strGrpName2 = "Elite"
    strUsrName = "PowerUser"
    ' open connection to the database
    ' using the specified system database
    Set conn = New ADODB.Connection
        With conn
            .Provider = "Microsoft.Jet.OLEDB.4.0"
            .Properties("Jet OLEDB:System Database") = strSysDB
            .Properties("User ID") = "Developer"
            .Properties("Password") = "chapter17"
            .Open strDB
        End With

    ' Open the catalog
```

```
Set cat = New ADOX.Catalog
With cat
    .ActiveConnection = conn
    'create group accounts
    .Groups.Append strGrpName1
    .Groups.Append strGrpName2
    Debug.Print "Successfully created group accounts."
    'create a user account
    .Users.Append strUsrName, "star"
    Debug.Print "Successfully created user account."
    'Add user to the group
    .Users(strUsrName).Groups.Append strGrpName2
    Debug.Print strUsrName & " is a member of the " & _
        strGrpName2 & " group account."
End With

ExitHere:
    Set cat = Nothing
    conn.Close
    Set conn = Nothing
    Exit Sub
ErrorHandler:
    MsgBox Err.Description
    Resume ExitHere
End Sub
```

6. Choose **Run | Run Sub/UserForm** to execute the Create_UserAndGroup_ ADO procedure.

Upon executing the above procedure, two new group accounts named Masters and Elite are established in the secured SpecialDb database that you created in Custom Project 17-1. A new user account named PowerUser is added and made a member of the Elite group account. Notice that before opening the database we need to set the Jet OLEDB:System Database property in the Properties collection of the ADO Connection object to specify the path and name of the workgroup information file that should be active when the database is opened. We also set the User ID and Password properties to log onto the database. After opening the database, we open the Catalog object and use the Append method of the Catalog's Groups collection to add new group accounts. The Groups collection contains all groups in the specified workgroup information file. The Append method of the Catalog's Users collection is used to create a new user account. This user account is then appended to the Groups collection and made a member of a particular group (Elite). You can verify that the accounts were indeed created by opening the SpecialDb.mdb file.

7. If you'd like to take a moment now, open the SpecialDb database using the shortcut on your desktop. Once the database is open, choose **Database Tools | Users and Permissions | User and Group Accounts**. Notice that the database now contains the Masters and Elite groups in addition to the default Admins and Users groups (see Figure 17-13).

Figure 17-13: The Elite and Masters group accounts are created by running the procedure in Hands-On 17-1.

8. Close the SpecialDb database and the Access window in which it was displayed. Be careful not to close the Chap17.mdb database you are working with.

Deleting User and Group Accounts

Use the Delete method of the Catalog object's Users collection to delete a user account. Use the Delete method of the Catalog object's Groups collection to delete a group account.

The procedure in Hands-On 17-2 deletes the user account named PowerUser and the group account named Masters created in Hands-On 17-1.

Hands-On 17-2: Deleting User and Group Accounts (ADO)

This hands-on exercise requires the prior completion of Custom Project 17-1 and Hands-On 17-1.

1. In the Visual Basic Editor window of Chap17.mdb, choose **Insert | Module**.

2. In the module's Code window, enter the **Delete_UserAndGroup** procedure as shown below, or copy the procedure code from **C:\Acc07_ HandsOn\Chap17.txt**.

```
Sub Delete_UserAndGroup(UserName As String, _
                        GroupName As String)
    Dim cat As ADOX.Catalog
    Dim conn As ADODB.Connection
    Dim strDB As String
    Dim strSysDB As String

    On Error GoTo ErrorHandler

    strDB = "C:\Acc07_ByExample\SpecialDb.mdb"
    strSysDB = "C:\Acc07_ByExample\Security1.mdw"

    ' Open connection to the database using
    ' the specified system database
```

```
    Set conn = New ADODB.Connection
    With conn
        .Provider = "Microsoft.Jet.OLEDB.4.0"
        .Properties("Jet OLEDB:System Database") = strSysDB
        .Properties("User ID") = "Developer"
        .Properties("Password") = "chapter17"
        .Open strDB
    End With


    ' Open the catalog
    Set cat = New ADOX.Catalog
    With cat
        .ActiveConnection = conn
        ' Delete user
        .Users.Delete UserName
        ' Delete group
        .Groups.Delete GroupName
    End With

ExitHere:
    Set cat = Nothing
    conn.Close
    Set conn = Nothing
    Exit Sub
ErrorHandler:
    MsgBox Err.Description
    Resume ExitHere
End Sub
```

3. To run the **Delete_UserAndGroup** procedure shown above, enter the following statement in the Immediate window and press **Enter** to execute it:

```
Delete_UserAndGroup "PowerUser", "Masters"
```

After running the procedure in Hands-On 17-2, the Masters group account and the PowerUser user account are removed from the SpecialDb database.

Listing User and Group Accounts

The procedure in Hands-On 17-3 demonstrates how to retrieve the names of all defined group and user accounts from the Groups and Users collections of the Catalog object.

Hands-On 17-3: Listing Group and User Accounts (ADO)

1. In the Visual Basic Editor window of Chap17.mdb, choose **Insert | Module**.

2. In the module's Code window, enter the **List_GroupsAndUsers_ADO** procedure as shown below, or copy the procedure code from **C:\Acc07_HandsOn\Chap17.txt.**

```
Sub List_GroupsAndUsers_ADO()
    Dim conn As ADODB.Connection
    Dim cat As ADOX.Catalog
```

```
Dim grp As New ADOX.Group
Dim usr As New ADOX.User
Dim strDB As String
Dim strSysDB As String

strDB = "C:\Acc07_ByExample\SpecialDb.mdb"
strSysDB = "C:\Acc07_ByExample\Security1.mdw"

' Open connection to the database using
' the specified system database
Set conn = New ADODB.Connection
    With conn
        .Provider = "Microsoft.Jet.OLEDB.4.0"
        .Properties("Jet OLEDB:System Database") = strSysDB
        .Properties("User ID") = "Developer"
        .Properties("Password") = "chapter17"
        .Open strDB
    End With

' Open the catalog
Set cat = New ADOX.Catalog
cat.ActiveConnection = conn
'list group and user accounts
For Each grp In cat.Groups
    Debug.Print "Group: " & grp.Name
Next

For Each usr In cat.Users
    Debug.Print "User: " & usr.Name
Next

Set cat = Nothing
conn.Close
Set conn = Nothing

MsgBox "Groups and users are listed in the Immediate window."
End Sub
```

3. Choose **Run | Run Sub/UserForm** to execute the procedure.

Figure 17-14: The names of existing security group and user accounts are written to the Immediate window by the procedure in Hands-On 17-3.

Notice that in addition to the user accounts that you have defined, Access reveals the names of its two built-in users: Creator and Engine. To keep these built-in users from showing up in your users listing, use the following conditional statement:

```
If usr.Name <>"Creator" And usr.Name <> "Engine" Then
    Debug.Print "User:" & usr.Name
End If
```

Listing Users in Groups

Sometimes you will need to know what users belong to what groups. The procedure in Hands-On 17-4 demonstrates how to obtain such a list.

◉ Hands-On 17-4: Listing Users in Groups (ADO)

1. In the Visual Basic Editor window of Chap17.mdb, choose **Insert | Module**.

2. In the module's Code window, enter the **List_UsersInGroups** procedure as shown below, or copy the procedure code from **C:\Acc07_HandsOn\ Chap17.txt.**

```
Sub List_UsersInGroups()
    Dim conn As ADODB.Connection
    Dim cat As ADOX.Catalog
    Dim grp As New ADOX.Group
    Dim usr As New ADOX.User
    Dim strDB As String
    Dim strSysDB As String

    strDB = "C:\Acc07_ByExample\SpecialDb.mdb"
    strSysDB = "C:\Acc07_ByExample\Security1.mdw"

    ' Open connection to the database using
    ' the specified system database
    Set conn = New ADODB.Connection
        With conn
            .Provider = "Microsoft.Jet.OLEDB.4.0"
            .Properties("Jet OLEDB:System Database") = strSysDB
            .Properties("User ID") = "Developer"
            .Properties("Password") = "chapter17"
            .Open strDB
        End With

    ' Open the catalog
    Set cat = New ADOX.Catalog
    cat.ActiveConnection = conn
    For Each grp In cat.Groups
        Debug.Print "Group: " & grp.Name
        If cat.Groups(grp.Name).Users.Count = 0 Then
            Debug.Print vbTab & "There are no users in the " & _
                grp & " group."
        End If
        For Each usr In cat.Groups(grp.Name).Users
            Debug.Print vbTab & "User: " & usr.Name
        Next usr
    Next grp
```

```
      Set cat = Nothing
      conn.Close
      Set conn = Nothing
      MsgBox "Groups and Users are listed in the Immediate window."
   End Sub
```

3. Choose **Run | Run Sub/UserForm** to execute the procedure.

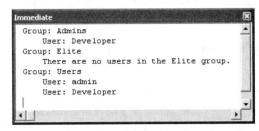

Figure 17-15: After running the procedure in Hands-On 17-4, security group account names and the corresponding user accounts are listed in the Immediate window.

Setting and Retrieving User and Group Permissions

Users and groups of users can be granted specific permissions to database objects. For example, a user or an entire group of users can be authorized to only read an object's contents, while other users or groups can have less restrictive access to a database, allowing them to modify or delete objects.

It is important to understand that when you set permissions for a group, every user in that group automatically inherits those permissions. Also, keep in mind that while the user and group accounts are stored in the workgroup information file, the permissions that those users/groups have to specific objects are stored in system tables in your database.

The following sections of this chapter will familiarize you with using ADOX to retrieve, list, and set permissions for various database objects.

Determining the Object Owner

The database, and every object in the database, has an owner. The owner is the user that created that particular object. The object owner has special privileges. He or she can always assign or revoke permissions for that object. To retrieve the name of the object owner, use the GetObjectOwner method of a Catalog object. This method takes two parameters: the object's name and type. For example, to determine the owner of a table, use the following syntax:

```
cat.GetObjectOwner(myObjName, adPermObjTable)
```

where cat is an object variable representing the ADOX Catalog object, myObjName is the name of a database table, and adPermObjTable is a built-in ADOX constant specifying the type of object. The constants for the Type parameter can be looked up in the Object Browser, as shown in Figure 17-16.

Access VBA Programming with DAO and ADO

Figure 17-16: The Object Browser displays the required constants for the Type parameter of the GetObjectOwner method.

Hands-On 17-5: Retrieving the Name of the Object Owner (ADO)

1. In the Visual Basic Editor window of Chap17.mdb, choose **Insert** | **Module**.

2. In the module's Code window, enter the **Get_ObjectOwner** procedure as shown below, or copy the procedure code from **C:\Acc07_HandsOn\ Chap17.txt**.

```
Sub Get_ObjectOwner()
    Dim conn As ADODB.Connection
    Dim cat As ADOX.Catalog
    Dim strObjName As Variant
    Dim strDB As String
    Dim strSysDB As String

    strDB = "C:\Acc07_ByExample\SpecialDb.mdb"
    strSysDB = "C:\Acc07_ByExample\Security1.mdw"
    strObjName = "Customers"

    ' Open connection to the database using
    ' the specified system database
    Set conn = New ADODB.Connection
        With conn
            .Provider = "Microsoft.Jet.OLEDB.4.0"
            .Properties("Jet OLEDB:System Database") = strSysDB
            .Properties("User ID") = "Developer"
            .Properties("Password") = "chapter17"
            .Open strDB
        End With

    ' Open the catalog
    Set cat = New ADOX.Catalog
    cat.ActiveConnection = conn
```

```
' Display the name of the table owner
MsgBox "The owner of the " & strObjName & _
       " table is " & vbCr _
    & cat.GetObjectOwner(strObjName, adPermObjTable) & "."

    Set cat = Nothing
    conn.Close
    Set conn = Nothing
End Sub
```

3. Choose **Run | Run Sub/UserForm** to execute the procedure.

To set the ownership of an object by using ADOX, use the SetObjectOwner method of the Catalog object like this:

```
cat.SetObjectOwner("Customers", adPermObjTable, "PowerUser")
```

The above statement says that the ownership of the Customers table is to be transferred to the user named PowerUser. Note that currently there is no such user in the SpecialDb database. We created the PowerUser user account in Hands-On 17-1 and deleted it in Hands-On 17-2. If you want to experiment with changing object ownership, you need to make appropriate changes in the example procedure using the information you have already learned.

Setting User Permissions for an Object

With ADOX, you set permissions on an object by using the SetPermissions method. User-level security can be easier to manage if you set permissions only for groups, and then assign users to the appropriate groups. Recall that permissions set for the group are automatically inherited by all users in that group. The SetPermissions method, which can be used for setting both user and group permissions, has the following syntax:

```
GroupOrUser.SetPermissions(Name, ObjectType, Action, Rights[, Inherit]
[,ObjectTypeId])
```

- Name — The name of the object to set permissions on.
- ObjectType — The type of object the permissions are set for. (See Figure 17-16 for the names of the ADOX built-in constants that can be used to specify the Type parameter.)
- Action — The type of action to perform when setting permissions. Use the adAccessSet constant for Microsoft Access databases to specify that the group of users will have exactly the requested permissions.
- Rights —A Long value containing a bitmask indicating the permissions to set. The Rights argument can consist of a single permissions constant or several constants combined by using the OR operator. See Figure 17-17 for the names of the ADOX built-in constants that can be used in the Rights argument to specify the type of permissions to set.

> **Note:** A *bitmask* is a numeric value intended for a bit-by-bit value compari-
> son with other numeric values, usually to flag options in parameters or return
> values. In Visual Basic, this comparison is done with bitwise logical operators,
> such as AND and OR. The ADOX GetPermissions and SetPermissions methods
> use the bitwise logical operator OR to retrieve the bitmask for the existing per-
> missions and to add new permissions to the bitmask.

The last two arguments (those in square brackets) are optional:

- Inherit — A Long value that specifies how objects will inherit these permissions. The default value is adInheritNone.

- ObjectTypeId — A Variant value that specifies the GUID (global unique
  identifier) for a provider object type not defined by OLE DB. This parameter is required if ObjectType is set to adPermObjProviderSpecific (which is
  used for setting permissions for forms, reports, and macros); otherwise, it
  is not used.

Table 17-2: GUIDs for provider objects

Object	GUID
Form	{c49c842e-9dcb-11d1-9f0a-00c04fc2c2e0}
Report	{c49c8430-9dcb-11d1-9f0a-00c04fc2c2e0}
Macro	{c49c842f-9dcb-11d1-9f0a-00c04fc2c2e0}

Figure 17-17: In ADOX,
you can use a great many
security constants for setting permissions to data-
base objects.

The example procedure in Hands-On 17-6 grants a user the permission to read
(adRightRead), insert (adRightInsert), update (adRightUpdate), and delete
(adRightDelete) records.

Hands-On 17-6: Setting User Permissions for an Object (ADO)

1. In the Visual Basic Editor window of Chap17.mdb, choose **Insert | Module**.

2. In the module's Code window, enter the **Set_UserObjectPermissions** procedure as shown below, or copy the procedure code from **C:\Acc07_HandsOn\Chap17.txt**.

```
Sub Set_UserObjectPermissions()
    Dim conn As ADODB.Connection
    Dim cat As ADOX.Catalog
    Dim strDB As String
    Dim strSysDB As String

    On Error GoTo ErrorHandler

    strDB = "C:\Acc07_ByExample\SpecialDb.mdb"
    strSysDB = "C:\Acc07_ByExample\Security1.mdw"

    ' Open connection to the database using
    ' the specified system database
    Set conn = New ADODB.Connection


        With conn
            .Provider = "Microsoft.Jet.OLEDB.4.0"
            .Properties("Jet OLEDB:System Database") = strSysDB
            .Properties("User ID") = "Developer"
            .Properties("Password") = "chapter17"
            .Open strDB
        End With


    ' Open the catalog
    Set cat = New ADOX.Catalog
    cat.ActiveConnection = conn
    ' add a user account
    cat.Users.Append "PowerUser", "star"

    ' Set permissions for PowerUser on the Customers table
    cat.Users("PowerUser").SetPermissions "Customers", _
        adPermObjTable, _
        adAccessSet, _
        adRightRead Or _
        adRightInsert Or _
        adRightUpdate Or _
        adRightDelete
    MsgBox "Read, Insert, Update and Delete permissions " & _
        vbCrLf & " were set on Customers table " & _
        "for PowerUser."
ExitHere:
    Set cat = Nothing
    conn.Close
    Set conn = Nothing
    Exit Sub
ErrorHandler:
```

```
    If Err.Number = -2147467259 Then
        MsgBox "PowerUser user already exists."
        Resume Next
    Else
        MsgBox Err.Description
        Resume ExitHere
    End If
End Sub
```

3. Choose **Run | Run Sub/UserForm** to execute the procedure.

Setting User Permissions for a Database

To specify permissions for the database, specify an empty string ("") as the name of the database:

```
cat.Users("PowerUser").SetPermissions "", _
    adPermObjDatabase, _
    adAccessSet, adRightExclusive
```

The above statement gives the user named PowerUser the right to open the database exclusively.

Hands-On 17-7: Setting User Permissions for a Database (ADO)

1. In the Visual Basic Editor window of Chap17.mdb, choose **Insert | Module**.

2. In the module's Code window, enter the **Set_UserDbPermissions_ADO** procedure as shown below, or copy the procedure code from **C:\Acc07_ HandsOn\Chap17.txt**.

```
Sub Set_UserDbPermissions_ADO()
    Dim conn As ADODB.Connection
    Dim cat As ADOX.Catalog
    Dim strDB As String
    Dim strSysDB As String

    On Error GoTo ErrorHandler

    strDB = "C:\Acc07_ByExample\SpecialDb.mdb"
    strSysDB = "C:\Acc07_ByExample\Security1.mdw"

    ' Open connection to the database using
    ' the specified system database
    Set conn = New ADODB.Connection
        With conn
            .Provider = "Microsoft.Jet.OLEDB.4.0"
            .Properties("Jet OLEDB:System Database") = strSysDB
            .Properties("User ID") = "Developer"
            .Properties("Password") = "chapter17"
            .Open strDB
        End With

    ' Open the catalog
    Set cat = New ADOX.Catalog
```

```
    cat.ActiveConnection = conn

    ' add a user account
    cat.Users.Append "PowerUser", "star"

    ' Set permissions for PowerUser
    cat.Users("PowerUser").SetPermissions "", adPermObjDatabase, _
        adAccessSet, adRightExclusive
    MsgBox "PowerUser has been granted permission to " & vbCrLf & _
            "open the database exclusively."
ExitHere:
    Set cat = Nothing
    conn.Close
    Set conn = Nothing
    Exit Sub
ErrorHandler:
    If Err.Number = -2147467259 Then
        ' because PowerUser user already exists
        ' we ignore this statement
        Resume Next
    Else
        MsgBox Err.Description
        Resume ExitHere
    End If
End Sub
```

3. Choose **Run | Run Sub/UserForm** to execute the procedure.

Figure 17-18: The following settings are found in the User and Group Permissions window for the SpecialDb database after running the Set_UserDbPermissions_ADO procedure in Hands-On 17-7.

Setting User Permissions for Containers

Now that you've learned how to grant permissions to a user for a specific object such as a table or query, you may want to know how to specify permissions for a whole set of objects such as tables, queries, forms, reports, and macros.

Each Database object has a Containers collection consisting of built-in Container objects. A Container object groups together similar types of Document objects. You can use the Containers collection to set security for all Document objects of a given type. You can set the permissions that users and groups will receive by default on all newly created objects in a database by passing in Null for the object name argument of the ADOX SetPermissions method, as shown in the example procedure in Hands-On 17-8.

⊚ Hands-On 17-8: Setting User Permissions for Containers (ADO)

1. In the Visual Basic Editor window of Chap17.mdb, choose **Insert | Module**.

2. In the module's Code window, enter the **Set_UserContainerPermissions_ ADO** procedure as shown below, or copy the procedure code from **C:\Acc07_HandsOn\Chap17.txt**.

```
Sub Set_UserContainerPermissions_ADO()
    Dim conn As ADODB.Connection
    Dim cat As ADOX.Catalog
    Dim strDB As String
    Dim strSysDB As String

    On Error GoTo ErrorHandler

    strDB = "C:\Acc07_ByExample\SpecialDb.mdb"
    strSysDB = "C:\Acc07_ByExample\Security1.mdw"

    ' Open connection to the database using
    ' the specified system database
    Set conn = New ADODB.Connection
        With conn
            .Provider = "Microsoft.Jet.OLEDB.4.0"
            .Properties("Jet OLEDB:System Database") = strSysDB
            .Properties("User ID") = "Developer"
            .Properties("Password") = "chapter17"
            .Open strDB
        End With

    ' Open the catalog
    Set cat = New ADOX.Catalog
    cat.ActiveConnection = conn

    ' add a user account
    cat.Users.Append "PowerUser", "star"

    ' Set permissions for PowerUser on the Tables Container
    cat.Users("PowerUser").SetPermissions Null, _
        adPermObjTable, _
        adAccessSet, _
        adRightRead Or _
        adRightInsert Or _
        adRightUpdate Or _
        adRightDelete, adInheritNone
    MsgBox "You have successfully granted permissions " & vbCrLf & _
            "to PowerUser on the Tables Container."
ExitHere:
    Set cat = Nothing
```

```
        conn.Close
        Set conn = Nothing
        Exit Sub
    ErrorHandler:
        If Err.Number = -2147467259 Then
            ' because PowerUser user already exists
            ' we ignore this statement
            Resume Next
        Else
            MsgBox Err.Description
            Resume ExitHere
        End If
    End Sub
```

3. Choose **Run | Run Sub/UserForm** to execute the procedure.

The above procedure gives the PowerUser account the permission to design, read, update, insert, and delete data for all newly created tables and queries. Notice that Null is passed as the first argument of the SetPermissions method to indicate that permissions are to be set only on new objects of the type specified by the second argument of this method.

After executing the procedure above, the user account PowerUser has the permissions listed in Figure 17-19 on all newly created Table and Query objects.

Figure 17-19: The following settings are found in the User and Group Permissions window after running the Set_UserContainerPermissions_ADO procedure in Hands-On 17-8.

Checking Permissions for Objects

You can retrieve the permissions for a particular user or group on a particular object with the ADOX GetPermissions method. Because this method returns a numeric permission value for the specified object, if you want to display the names of constants representing permissions, you must write more code to decipher the returned value. The procedure in Hands-On 17-9 demonstrates how to retrieve the permissions set for PowerUser on the Customers table in a sample database.

⊙ Hands-On 17-9: Checking Permissions for a Specific Object (ADO)

1. In the Visual Basic Editor window of Chap17.mdb, choose **Insert |**
   Module.

2. In the module's Code window, enter the **GetObjectPermissions_ADO**
   procedure as shown below, or copy the procedure code from **C:\Acc07_**
   HandsOn\Chap17.txt.

```
Sub GetObjectPermissions_ADO(strUserName As String, _
                    varObjName As Variant, _
                    lngObjType As ADOX.ObjectTypeEnum)

    Dim conn As ADODB.Connection
    Dim cat As ADOX.Catalog
    Dim strDB As String
    Dim strSysDB As String
    Dim listPerms As Long
    Dim strPermsTypes As String

    On Error GoTo ErrorHandler

    strDB = "C:\Acc07_ByExample\SpecialDb.mdb"
    strSysDB = "C:\Acc07_ByExample\Security1.mdw"

    ' Open connection to the database using
    ' the specified system database
    Set conn = New ADODB.Connection
        With conn
            .Provider = "Microsoft.Jet.OLEDB.4.0"
            .Properties("Jet OLEDB:System Database") = strSysDB
            .Properties("User ID") = "Developer"
            .Properties("Password") = "chapter17"
            .Open strDB
        End With

    ' Open the catalog
    Set cat = New ADOX.Catalog
    cat.ActiveConnection = conn
    ' add a user account
    cat.Users.Append "PowerUser", "star"

    listPerms = cat.Users(strUserName) _
        .GetPermissions(varObjName, lngObjType)
    Debug.Print listPerms

    If (listPerms And ADOX.RightsEnum.adRightCreate) = adRightCreate Then
        strPermsTypes = strPermsTypes & "adRightCreate" & vbCr
    End If
    If (listPerms And RightsEnum.adRightRead) = adRightRead Then
        strPermsTypes = strPermsTypes & "adRightRead" & vbCr
    End If
    If (listPerms And RightsEnum.adRightUpdate) = adRightUpdate Then
        strPermsTypes = strPermsTypes & "adRightUpdate" & vbCr
    End If
    If (listPerms And RightsEnum.adRightDelete) = adRightDelete Then
```

```
            strPermsTypes = strPermsTypes & "adRightDelete" & vbCr
    End If
    If (listPerms And RightsEnum.adRightInsert) = adRightInsert Then
            strPermsTypes = strPermsTypes & "adRightInsert" & vbCr
    End If
    If (listPerms And RightsEnum.adRightReadDesign) = adRightReadDesign Then
            strPermsTypes = strPermsTypes & "adRightReadDesign" & vbCr
    End If

    Debug.Print strPermsTypes
    MsgBox "Permissions are listed in the Immediate Window."
ExitHere:
    Set cat = Nothing
    conn.Close
    Set conn = Nothing
    Exit Sub
ErrorHandler:
    If Err.Number = -2147467259 Then
        ' because PowerUser user already exists
        ' we ignore this statement
        Resume Next
    Else
        MsgBox Err.Description
        Resume ExitHere
    End If
End Sub
```

3. To run the **GetObjectPermissions_ADO** procedure shown above, type the following statement in the Immediate window and press **Enter** to execute it:

```
GetObjectPermissions_ADO "PowerUser", "Customers", adPermObjTable
```

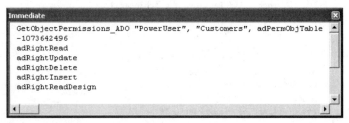

Figure 17-20: The procedure in Hands-On 17-9 writes the permissions found for PowerUser in the Customers table to the Immediate window.

Setting a Database Password Using the CompactDatabase Method

You can implement share-level security by setting a database password. When you set a database password, the password dialog box will appear when you open the database. Only users with a valid password can open the database.

To set a database password you cannot use ADOX objects. Instead, you have to use the objects from the Microsoft Jet and Replication Objects (JRO)

Library. Use the CompactDatabase method of the JRO JetEngine object and specify the Password parameter. Remember that passwords are case sensitive.

The procedure in Hands-On 17-10 sets the sample database password to "welcome." Prior to running the procedure in Hands-On 17-10, you must set a reference to the Microsoft Jet and Replication Objects Library. To do this, choose Tools | References in the Visual Basic Editor window and select the required library in the list of Available References.

◉ Hands-On 17-10: Setting a Database Password (JRO)

1. Create a new Access database named **PasswordTest.mdb** in your **C:\Acc07_ByExample** folder. Close this database before proceeding to step 2.

2. In the Visual Basic Editor window of Chap17.mdb, choose **Insert | Module**.

3. In the module's Code window, enter the **Change_DBPassword** procedure as shown below, or copy the procedure code from **C:\Acc07_HandsOn\ Chap17.txt**.

```
Sub Change_DBPassword()
    Dim jetEng As JRO.JetEngine
    Dim strCompactFrom As String
    Dim strCompactTo As String
    Dim strPath As String

    On Error GoTo ErrHandler
    strPath = CurrentProject.Path & "\"

    strCompactFrom = "PasswordTest.mdb"
    strCompactTo = "PasswordTest_Compact.mdb"

    Set jetEng = New JRO.JetEngine
    ' Compact the database specifying the new database password
    jetEng.CompactDatabase "Data Source=" & strPath & strCompactFrom & ";", _
        "Data Source=" & strPath & strCompactTo & ";" & _
        "Jet OLEDB:Database Password=welcome"

ExitHere:
    Set jetEng = Nothing
    Exit Sub
ErrHandler:
    If Err.Number = -2147217897 Then
        Kill strPath & strCompactTo
        Resume
    Else
        MsgBox Err.Number & ": " & Err.Description
        Resume ExitHere
    End If
End Sub
```

4. Choose **Run | Run Sub/UserForm** to execute the procedure.

5. After you run the procedure in Hands-On 17-10, open the **PasswordTest_ Compact.mdb** database file. You should be prompted for the password. Type **welcome** to log in.

6. Close the **PasswordTest_Compact.mdb** file.

Setting a Database Password Using the NewPassword Method

The DAO Object Model in Access 2007 has a NewPassword method of the Database object that you can use to change the password of an existing Microsoft Access database in ACCDB or MDB file format. The NewPassword method requires two parameters. The first one specifies the old password, and the second one provides the new password. Both passwords can be up to 20 characters long and can include any characters except the ASCII character 0 (Null). Use a zero-length string ("") for the old password if the database does not have a password. Use a zero-length string ("") for the new password parameter to clear the password. Password operations require that the database is open in exclusive mode. Remember that passwords are case sensitive.

The procedure in Hands-On 17-11 sets the password for the Chap01.accdb database that you created at the beginning of this book.

⊙ Hands-On 17-11: Setting a Database Password (DAO)

1. In the Visual Basic Editor window of Chap17.mdb, choose **Insert | Module**.

2. In the module's Code window, enter the **Set_DBPassword_DAO** procedure as shown below, or copy the procedure code from **C:\Acc07_ HandsOn\Chap17.txt**.

```
Sub Set_DBPassword_DAO()
    Dim db As DAO.Database
    Dim strDB As String

    strDB = CurrentProject.Path & "\Chap01.accdb"

    Set db = OpenDatabase(strDB, True)

    db.NewPassword "", "chapter1"
    db.Close
    Set db = Nothing

End Sub
```

3. Choose **Run | Run Sub/UserForm** to execute the procedure.

   The second parameter (True) in the OpenDatabase method tells VBA to open the database in exclusive mode.

4. Open the **Chap01.accdb** database and notice that you are now prompted to enter a password. Type **chapter1** for the password and click **OK**. When the

database opens, close it and close the Access window in which it was opened. Do not close the Chap17.mdb file.

You can unset the password on the Chap01.accdb database by running the following procedure:

```
Sub Unset_DBPassword_DAO()
    Dim db As DAO.Database
    Dim strDB As String

    strDB = CurrentProject.Path & "\Chap01.accdb"
    Set db = OpenDatabase(strDB, True, False, ";pwd=chapter1")

    db.NewPassword "chapter1", ""
    db.Close
    Set db = Nothing
End Sub
```

Notice the parameters of the OpenDatabase method. True specifies that the database is to be opened in exclusive mode. False indicates that the database should be opened in read/write mode. Because the Chap01.accdb database has been protected with a password by the Set_DBPassword_DAO procedure in Hands-On 17-11, we also had to specify the password in the connect parameter. After you run the above procedure, you will not be prompted for a password on opening the Chap01.accdb database.

Changing a User Password

User passwords are stored in the workgroup information file. To change a user's password from your VBA code, use the ADOX User object's ChangePassword method. This method takes as parameters the user's current password and the new password. If a user does not yet have a password, use an empty string ("") for the user's current password.

The procedure in Hands-On 17-12 demonstrates how to change a password for the Admin user. Recall that Admin is the default user account that has a blank password. In an unsecured Access database, all users are automatically logged on using the Admin account. When establishing user-level security you should start by changing the password for the Admin user. Changing an Admin password activates the Logon dialog box the next time you start Microsoft Access. Only users with a valid user name and password will be able to log onto the database. Although users are permitted to change their own passwords, only a user that belongs to the Admins account can clear a password that another user has forgotten.

⊚ Hands-On 17-12: Changing a User Password (ADO)

1. Create a new Access database named **AdminPwd.mdb** in your **C:\Acc07_ ByExample** folder. Close this database before proceeding to step 2.

2. In the Visual Basic Editor window of Chap17.mdb, choose **Insert | Module**.

3. In the module's Code window, enter the **Change_UserPassword_ADO** procedure as shown below, or copy the procedure code from **C:\Acc07_ HandsOn\Chap17.txt**.

```
Sub Change_UserPassword_ADO()
    Dim cat As ADOX.Catalog
    Dim strDB As String
    Dim strSysDB As String

    On Error GoTo ErrorHandler

    strDB = CurrentProject.Path & "\AdminPwd.mdb"
    ' change the path to use the default workgroup information file
    ' on your computer
    strSysDB = "C:\Documents and Settings\Julitta\" & _
               "Application Data\Microsoft\Access\System.mdw"

    'strSysDB = "C:\Acc07_ByExample\Security1.mdw"

    ' Open the catalog, specifying the system database to use
    Set cat = New ADOX.Catalog
    With cat
        .ActiveConnection = "Provider='Microsoft.Jet.OLEDB.4.0';" & _
            "Data Source='" & strDB & "';" & _
            "Jet OLEDB:System Database='" & strSysDB & "';" & _
            "User Id=Admin;Password=;"

        ' Change the password for the Admin user
        .Users("Admin").ChangePassword "", "secret"
    End With

ExitHere:
    Set cat = Nothing
    Exit Sub
ErrorHandler:
    MsgBox Err.Description
    GoTo ExitHere
End Sub
```

4. Choose **Run | Run Sub/UserForm** to execute the procedure.

Figure 17-21: When you open the AdminPwd.mdb database after running the procedure in Hands-On 17-12, a Logon dialog will appear. Enter Admin in the Name text box and secret for the Admin password.

5. Remove the Admin password by choosing **Database Tools | Users and Permissions | User and Group Accounts**. Click the **Change Logon Password** tab and type the old password (**secret**). Click the **Apply** button, and click **OK** to exit the User and Group Accounts window (Figure 17-22).

Figure 17-22: You can remove the Admin password manually via the Change Logon Password tab in the User and Group Accounts window, or by modifying the VBA code shown in Hands-On 17-12.

6. After removing the Admin password, reopen the **AdminPwd.mdb** file. The database should now open without prompting you to enter a password.

7. Close the AdminPwd.mdb database and exit the Access window in which the file was opened.

Encrypting a Secured MDB Database

To achieve a higher level of security and protect your database from unauthorized access, you can encrypt it. Prior to encrypting, secure your database by setting user and group permissions on database objects. To encrypt a database you must be the owner or the creator of the database, or a member of the Admins group in the workgroup information file (System.mdw) that was in use when the database was created.

Use the CompactDatabase method of the Microsoft Jet and Replication Objects (JRO) JetEngine object to encrypt or decrypt a database. To use the JRO JetEngine object, you must set a reference to the Microsoft Jet and Replication Objects Library. To encrypt the database, set the Jet OLEDB:Encrypt Database property to True in the connection string destination argument of the CompactDatabase method.

After a database has been encrypted, it cannot be read or written to directly by using any utility program or word processor. The procedure in Hands-On 17-13 creates an encrypted version of the SpecialDb.mdb database that you created in Custom Project 17-1.

◉ Hands-On 17-13: Encrypting a Database (JRO)

The procedure in this hands-on should be run after you have initially secured your database by creating the necessary user and group accounts and assigned user and group permissions on database objects.

1. In the Visual Basic Editor window of Chap17.mdb, choose **Insert | Module**.

2. In the module's Code window, enter the **EncryptDb** procedure as shown below, or copy the procedure code from **C:\Acc07_HandsOn\Chap17.txt**.

```
Sub EncryptDb()
    Dim jetEng As JRO.JetEngine
    Dim strCompactFrom As String
    Dim strCompactTo As String
    Dim strSource As String
    Dim strDest As String
    Dim strSysDB As String

    strCompactFrom = CurrentProject.Path & "\SpecialDb.mdb"
    strCompactTo = CurrentProject.Path & "\SpecialDb_Enc.mdb"
    strSysDB = CurrentProject.Path & "\Security1.mdw"

    On Error GoTo HandleErr

    ' Use the CompactDatabase method to create
    ' a new, encrypted version of the database
    Set jetEng = New JRO.JetEngine

    strSource = "Data Source=" & strCompactFrom & ";" & _
                "Jet OLEDB:System Database=" & strSysDB & ";" & _
                "User ID=Developer" & ";" & _
                "Password=chapter17"

    strDest = "Data Source=" & strCompactTo & ";" & _
              "Jet OLEDB:Engine Type=5;" & _
              "Jet OLEDB:Encrypt Database=True"

    jetEng.CompactDatabase strSource, strDest

ExitHere:
    Set jetEng = Nothing
    Exit Sub
HandleErr:
    MsgBox Err.Number & ": " & Err.Description
    Resume ExitHere
End Sub
```

3. Choose **Run | Run Sub/UserForm** to execute the procedure.

Figure 17-23: After running the procedure in Hands-On 17-13, your C:\Acc07_ByExample folder will contain an encrypted database named SpecialDb_Enc.mdb. You cannot open this database by simply double-clicking the filename in Windows Explorer. If you do so, Access will display this message.

To open the secured SpecialDb_Enc database file, you must provide the name of the workgroup information file as shown below:

```
"C:\Program Files\Microsoft Office\Office12\MSACCESS.EXE"
"C:\Acc07_ByExample\SpecialDb_Enc.mdb" /WRKGRP
"C:\Acc07_ByExample\Security1.mdw"
```

Use the above command to set up a shortcut on your desktop similar to the one that was set up by the Access Security Wizard when you completed Custom Project 17-1.

Chapter Summary

In this chapter, you worked with VBA procedures that implemented share-level and user-level security in Microsoft Access databases. You found out that in Access 2007 user-level security can only be used in Access databases created in the MDB file format. You practiced creating and modifying user and group accounts, and setting user permissions to a database and its objects. You also learned how to set a database password on Access databases in the MDB and ACCDB file formats, and wrote a procedure that encrypts a secured MDB file.

In the next chapter, you discover how you can make a database in the MDB file format available to users in remote locations via database replication.

Chapter 18

Database Replication

To make your database available to users in various geographical locations, you can provide them with a full or partial copy of the database. Mobile or remote users can maintain a local copy of a database, make changes to data offline, and synchronize with the main database on a regular basis. All this can be achieved via the technology known as *database replication*. When you replicate a database you simply create multiple copies (replicas) of your application and distribute them to users in remote locations so that they can easily share the changes they are making to a database. Database replication also offers other advantages, such as:

- Convenient distribution of updates to existing applications — Changes made to queries, forms, reports, and other application components can be automatically updated in remote copies of the database during the next synchronization.

- Reduction of network traffic — Database replicas can be placed on different servers serving different groups of users, thus reducing the network load.

- Data backup — There is no need to make a separate backup copy of your database as each member of the replica set can serve as a backup. If the Design Master is corrupted, you can always make another member of the replica set the Design Master. You learn about creating the Design Master and replicas later in this chapter.

Although you can create a replica of your database via the Microsoft Office Access 2007 user interface (see the Database Tools | Replication Options), in the following sections of this chapter, you will learn how to perform the replication tasks from your VBA procedures.

➦ **Note:** The information presented in this chapter can only be used with Access MDB database files. The replication functionality is not supported in the Access 2007 default file format (ACCDB). Before beginning your experiments with database replication by writing code, it is necessary to set a reference to the Microsoft Jet and Replication Objects 2.6 Library by choosing Tools | References in the Microsoft Visual Basic Editor window.

Figure 18-1: After setting the reference to the Microsoft Jet and Replication Objects (JRO) Library you can use the Object Browser to view available objects, properties, and methods.

The Replica object has methods for determining if an object is replicable (GetObjectReplicability method), creating a replica (CreateReplica method), converting a database to a Design Master (MakeReplicable method), populating a partial replica (PopulatePartial method), setting an object's replicability (SetObjectReplicability method), and synchronizing replicas (Synchronize method). In addition to methods, there are quite a few Replica properties that allow you to set or retrieve various characteristics such as DesignMasterId, ReplicaId, Visibility, RetentionPeriod, and ConflictTables. The VBA procedures in this chapter will give you a head start in database replication.

 Note: This chapter requires that you complete all hands-on exercises in order.

Creating a Design Master

A *replica* is a copy of a database. There are three types of replicas: Design Master, full replica, and partial replica. To work with replication, start by creating a backup copy of your database. You will need it in case there is a problem with the replicated database. Next, create a replica of your database by using the Replica object's MakeReplicable method. This method requires that you provide a full path to your database and indicate whether you want column-level tracking. With column-level tracking, changing different columns in the same row of a table in two replicas doesn't cause a conflict. The MakeReplicable method converts a normal Access database into a Design Master. This is a master replica from which you can create additional replicas with the CreateReplica method.

The Design Master is the first member of a replica set. When you create a Design Master, new system tables are added to a database and new fields are added to the existing tables. Only the Design Master can accept changes to the database structure. If the Design Master is damaged, you can promote one of the replicas to become the Design Master.

Hands-On 18-1 demonstrates how to make a backup copy of the original database and create a Design Master.

◎ Hands-On 18-1: Creating a Design Master

1. Start Microsoft Office Access 2007 and create a new database named **Chap18.mdb** in your **C:\Acc07_ByExample** folder. Make sure you type .mdb as the file extension.

2. Press **Alt+F11** to switch to the Visual Basic Editor window and choose **Insert | Module**.

3. Choose **Tools | References** and add the following two libraries: **Microsoft Jet and Replication Objects 2.6 Library** and **Microsoft Scripting Runtime Library**. Click **OK** to exit the References dialog box.

4. In the module's Code window, enter the **Create_DesignMaster** procedure as shown below, or copy the procedure code from **C:\Acc07_HandsOn\ Chap18.txt**.

```
Sub Create_DesignMaster(dbName As String, strPath As String)
    Dim repDesignMaster As New JRO.Replica
    Dim fso As Scripting.FileSystemObject
    Dim strDb As String

    ' create a new instance of the FileSystemObject
    Set fso = New FileSystemObject

    ' store a file name for the Design Master in a variable
    strDb = strPath & "DM_" & dbName

    ' create a copy of the sample Northwind database
    If Not fso.FileExists(strDb) Then
        fso.CopyFile strPath & dbName, strDb
    Else
        MsgBox "The " & strDb & " database file already exists."
        Exit Sub
    End If

    ' make the database replicable
    repDesignMaster.MakeReplicable strDb, True
    MsgBox "Your Design Master was successfully created." _
            , , "DM_Northwind"

    Set repDesignMaster = Nothing
    Set fso = Nothing
End Sub
```

5. To execute the Create_DesignMaster procedure, type the following statement in the Immediate window and press **Enter**:

```
Create_DesignMaster "Northwind.mdb", CurrentProject.Path & "\"
```

For the above statement to work you must ensure that the Northwind.mdb file is located in the same folder as the Chap18.mdb file (C:\Acc07_ByExample).

To access your computer's file system, the above procedure uses the FileSystemObject from the Microsoft Scripting Runtime Library. The FileSystemObject gives you access to numerous methods and properties for working with drives, folders, and files. Notice how the procedure uses the FileExists method of FileSystemObject to find out if a file named DM_Northwind.mdb already exists in the specified folder. If the file does not exist, another method (CopyFile) of the FileSystemObject is used to create a copy of the Northwind database and name it DM_Northwind.mdb. Next, the MakeReplicable method of the JRO Replica object is used to create a master replica (Design Master). After running the Create_DesignMaster procedure, the current folder should contain a database file named DM_Northwind.mdb, which is a Design Master. This file is necessary for working with this chapter's hands-on exercises.

Creating a Full Replica

After you've created your Design Master, you can create additional replicas from it by using the CreateReplica method. This method takes two required arguments. The first argument is replicaName, which specifies the name and path of the full or partial replica to be created. The second argument is description, a string value describing the replica to be created. The CreateReplica method can also take several optional arguments that let you specify the type of replica and its visibility, priority, and updatability. By omitting additional arguments, a full replica is created. This replica will have global visibility and be fully updatable.

Hands-On 18-2 demonstrates how to create a full replica without optional arguments.

Hands-On 18-2: Creating a Full Replica

1. Switch to the Visual Basic Editor window and choose **Insert | Module**.

2. In the module's Code window, enter the **Make_FullReplica** procedure as shown below, or copy the procedure code from **C:\Acc07_HandsOn\ Chap18.txt**.

```
Sub Make_FullReplica(DesignMasterName As String, _
                NewRepName As String)
    Dim repDesignMaster As New JRO.Replica

    On Error GoTo ErrorHandler

    With repDesignMaster
        .ActiveConnection = DesignMasterName
        .CreateReplica CurrentProject.Path & "\" & NewRepName, _
            "Replica of " & DesignMasterName
    End With

    MsgBox "Full replica named " & NewRepName & " was created."
```

```
ExitHere:
    Set repDesignMaster = Nothing
    Exit Sub
ErrorHandler:
    If Err.Number = -2147217897 Then
        Kill CurrentProject.Path & "\" & NewRepName
        Resume
    Else
        MsgBox Err.Number & ": " & Err.Description
        Resume ExitHere
    End If
End Sub
```

3. Execute the Make_FullReplica procedure by typing the following statement in the Immediate window and pressing **Enter**:

   ```
   Make_FullReplica CurrentProject.Path & "\DM_Northwind.mdb", "Replica_North.mdb"
   ```

   When you run the Make_FullReplica procedure, a new file named
   Replica_North.mdb is created. This file is a full replica of the
   DM_Northwind.mdb database.

 Note: You can create as many replicas of the original database (Design
Master) as you want. All replicas created from the same Design Master belong
to the same replica set, and only replicas from the same set can synchronize
and exchange data with each other.

Creating a Partial Replica

A *partial replica* is a replica that does not contain all the data of the original
object. This type of replica is useful for those who only need to see or work
with certain data. A partial replica is created by setting an expression-based or
relationship-based filter on tables or queries. A partial replica contains all the
tables that exist in the full replica; however, the user only sees the data as
allowed by the specified filter. Therefore, some of the tables in a partial replica
are empty. Because partial replicas have fewer records, they can synchronize
quicker than full replicas.

You can create a partial replica by using the CreateReplica method and
specifying two required arguments (the partial replica's name and description)
and an enumeration constant of jrRepTypePartial for the optional argument.
For instance, in Hands-On 18-3 you use the following statement to create a
partial replica to display records for only Spanish customers:

```
repDesignMaster.CreateReplica repPartialName, _
    "Partial Replica (Spanish Customers)", _
    jrRepTypePartial
```

The above statement creates a partial replica. Next, you must specify which
records the partial replica will contain by defining filters. Each replica can
have one or more filters.

There are two types of filters in JRO:

- An *expression-based filter* is a criterion that a record in the partial replica table must satisfy in order to be replicated from the full replica. This criterion is like the SQL WHERE clause without the WHERE keyword. For example, the procedure that follows uses a criterion to allow access only to customer records from the specified country:

```
"[Country] ='Spain'"
```

- The second type of filter, a *relationship-based filter*, restricts the records based on relationships between tables. In Hands-On 18-3 below, only information related to Spanish customers will be accessible to the user.

After setting the filters, use the PopulatePartial method to add records to a partial replica based on the specified filter. For instance:

```
repPartial.PopulatePartial repMasterName
```

In the statement above, repPartial is an object variable that points to the partial replica. repMasterName is a string variable that denotes the path and filename for the full replica set.

The PopulatePartial method will first clear all records in the partial replica, and then repopulate the replica based on the specified filters. This type of operation requires that the partial replica be opened with exclusive access.

⊚ Hands-On 18-3: Creating a Partial Replica

1. Switch to the Visual Basic Editor window and choose **Insert | Module**.
2. In the module's Code window, enter the **Make_PartialReplica** procedure as shown below, or copy the procedure code from **C:\Acc07_HandsOn\ Chap18.txt**.

```
Sub Make_PartialReplica(FilterOption As Integer)
    Dim repDesignMaster As New JRO.Replica
    Dim repPartial As New JRO.Replica
    Dim flt As JRO.Filter
    Dim repMasterName As String
    Dim repPartialName As String
    Dim strFilterType As String

    On Error GoTo ErrorHandle

    repMasterName = CurrentProject.Path & "\DM_Northwind.mdb"
    repPartialName = CurrentProject.Path & "\Spanish.mdb"

    ' Create partial replica
    repDesignMaster.ActiveConnection = repMasterName
    repDesignMaster.CreateReplica repPartialName, _
        "Partial Replica (Spanish Customers)", _
        jrRepTypePartial

    Set repDesignMaster = Nothing
```

```
' open an exclusive connection to the partial replica
repPartial.ActiveConnection = "Provider=Microsoft.Jet.OLEDB.4.0;" & _
    "Data Source= " & repPartialName & ";Mode=Share Exclusive"

If FilterOption = 1 Then
    ' Create an expression-based filter in the partial replica
    repPartial.Filters.Append "Customers", jrFilterTypeTable, _
    "[Country] ='Spain'"

ElseIf FilterOption = 2 Then
    ' Create a relationship-based filter in the partial replica
    repPartial.Filters.Append "Customers", jrFilterTypeTable, _
    "[Country] ='Spain'"

    repPartial.Filters.Append "Orders", jrFilterTypeRelationship, _
        "CustomersOrders"
End If

' Populate the partial replica based on the specified filter
repPartial.PopulatePartial repMasterName

MsgBox "Partial replica named " & repPartialName & vbCrLf _
    & "was created based on the selected filter type." & vbCrLf _
    & "Please view filter information in the Immediate window."

' Print filter information to the Immediate window
For Each flt In repPartial.Filters
    If flt.FilterType = jrFilterTypeTable Then
        strFilterType = "Table Filter"
    Else
        strFilterType = "Relationship Filter"
    End If
    Debug.Print "Table Name: " & flt.TableName & vbCr _
        ; vbTab & "Filter Type: " & strFilterType & vbCr _
        ; vbTab & "Filter Criteria: " & flt.FilterCriteria
Next

ExitHere:
    Set repPartial = Nothing
    Exit Sub
ErrorHandle:
    If Err.Number = -2147217897 Then
        Kill repPartialName
        Resume
    Else
        MsgBox Err.Number & ": " & Err.Description
        Resume ExitHere
    End If
End Sub
```

3. Execute the Make_PartialReplica procedure by typing the following statement in the Immediate window and pressing **Enter**:

```
Make_PartialReplica 1
```

The above statement specifies that the Make_PartialReplica procedure should use the expression-based filter (1) when repopulating the partial replica. The filter information is printed to the Immediate window:

```
Table Name: MSysCmdbars
    Filter Type: Table Filter
    Filter Criteria: TRUE
Table Name: MSysIMEXColumns
    Filter Type: Table Filter
    Filter Criteria: TRUE
Table Name: MSysIMEXSpecs
    Filter Type: Table Filter
    Filter Criteria: TRUE
Table Name: MSysAccessObjects
    Filter Type: Table Filter
    Filter Criteria: TRUE
Table Name: Customers
    Filter Type: Table Filter
    Filter Criteria: [Country] ='Spain'
```

4. Execute the Make_PartialReplica procedure again by typing the following statement in the Immediate window and pressing **Enter**:

```
Make_PartialReplica 2
```

The above statement specifies that the Make_PartialReplica procedure should use the relationship-based filter (2) when repopulating the partial replica.

Replicating Objects

When you create additional replicas from your Design Master you may choose to replicate all objects or keep some objects local and prevent them from being replicated. You can set object replicability with the SetObjectReplicability method. This method requires three arguments: a string indicating the name of a table or query, the string "Tables," and a Boolean value of True if the object is to be replicable, or False otherwise.

⊚ Hands-On 18-4: Checking If an Object Is Replicable

1. Open the Design Master file named **DM_Northwind.mdb** located in the **C:\Acc07_ByExample** folder. Recall that this Design Master file was created by running the procedure in Hands-On 18-1.

2. In the DM_Northwind Design Master database, create a new query named **SampleQuery** based on any available tables. For example, you can use the following SQL statement to create the sample for this hands-on exercise:

```
SELECT Employees.LastName,
       Employees.FirstName,
       Orders.OrderDate,
       Orders.ShipCity,
       Orders.ShipCountry
FROM Employees
       INNER JOIN Orders ON Employees.EmployeeID = Orders.EmployeeID;
```

3. Upon creation, the SampleQuery object is local to your database. To confirm this, right-click the query name in the Access window and choose **Object Properties** from the shortcut menu. Notice that the Replicable check box is not checked.

Figure 18-2: When you open the Design Master file you will notice different icons in front of object names that are replicable. The local query you created in step 2 is highlighted in this screen shot.

Figure 18-3: You can determine whether a certain database object is replicable or not by looking at the object's properties. The Replicable check box is not checked for local objects.

If at this time you create an additional replica from the Design Master or try to synchronize with an existing replica, this new Query object will not be replicated. To ensure the new object is replicated, you can check the Replicable property in the Properties box (see Figure 18-3) or set the object's replicability in VBA code by using the SetObjectReplicability method. We will set the replicability of the SampleQuery object in the procedure code in Hands-On 18-5.

4. Close the **SampleQuery Properties** dialog box without making any changes in this window.

5. Close the DM_Northwind.mdb database file.

⊚ Hands-On 18-5: Making an Object Replicable

1. Switch to the Visual Basic Editor window and choose **Insert | Module**.
2. In the module's Code window, enter the **MakeObject_Replicable** procedure as shown below.

```
Sub MakeObject_Replicable(repName As String, objName As String)
    Dim repDesignMaster As New JRO.Replica
    With repDesignMaster
        .ActiveConnection = repName
        .SetObjectReplicability objName, "Tables", True
    End With
    Set repDesignMaster = Nothing
    MsgBox objName & " is now replicable."
End Sub
```

3. Run the MakeObject_Replicable procedure from the Immediate window of the Chap18.mdb file by typing the following statement and pressing **Enter**:

```
MakeObject_Replicable CurrentProject.Path & "\DM_Northwind.mdb", "SampleQuery"
```

The procedure in Hands-On 18-5 takes two arguments: the full path of your Design Master and the object name you want to make replicable.

4. Open the Design Master **DM_Northwind.mdb** file and switch to the Queries pane. Notice that SampleQuery is now replicable.
5. Close the DM_Northwind.mdb database file.

Keeping Objects Local

When your database contains confidential information that most users do not need to see, you may want to prevent specific objects (like a payroll table) from being replicated by setting the object's replicability to False. A newly created object in a Design Master is local by default. If you want this object to be seen by another replica, you must set the object's Replicable property to True (see the preceding section). If you want to make a previously replicated object local, be sure to synchronize first to avoid losing any changes that could have been made to this object in another replica. When you make a replicated object local in the Design Master and then synchronize, the object will be deleted from the replica.

The next hands-on exercise prevents a previously replicated object from being replicated by setting its Replicable property to False using the SetObjectReplicability method that was introduced in the preceding section.

⊚ Hands-On 18-6: Preventing an Object from Being Replicated

1. Switch to the Visual Basic Editor window and choose **Insert | Module**.
2. In the module's Code window, enter the **MakeObjectLocal_InDesignMaster** procedure as shown below, or copy the procedure code from **C:\Acc07_HandsOn\Chap18.txt**.

```
Sub MakeObjectLocal_InDesignMaster(myDb As String, _
    objName As String, _
    objType As String)
Dim repDesignMaster As New JRO.Replica

With repDesignMaster
  .ActiveConnection = myDb
  .SetObjectReplicability objName, objType, False
End With

Set repDesignMaster = Nothing

MsgBox "The object named " & objName & _
    " in the collection of " & _
    objType & vbCr & "will not be replicated. " & _
    "It has been set as local.", vbInformation, _
    "Operation Completed"
End Sub
```

3. Run the MakeObjectLocal_InDesignMaster procedure from the Immediate window by typing the following statement and pressing **Enter**:

```
MakeObjectLocal_InDesignMaster CurrentProject.Path & "\DM_Northwind.mdb",
    "Current Product List", "Tables"
```

 Note: You must type the above statement on one line in the Immediate window.

Notice that the above procedure takes three arguments: the full path of your Design Master, the object name, and the object type.

After running the above procedure, the Current Product List table will no longer be replicable. You can confirm this by opening your Design Master (DM_Northwind.mdb).

Synchronizing Replicas

Synchronization allows reconciliation of all changes between replicas. This means that any changes, additions, or deletions can be exchanged between replicas, thus keeping all the copies current and up to date. In JRO, there are three types of synchronization, as shown in Table 18-1.

Table 18-1: Replica synchronization types

Synchronization Type	Constant	Description
Bidirectional, import/export	jrSyncTypeImpExp	Updates are mutual; they flow from the target replica to the source replica and from the source replica to the target replica.
Import only	jrSyncTypeImport	Updates will flow only from the target replica to the source replica.
Export only	jrSyncTypeExport	Updates will flow only from the source replica to the target replica.

In addition to the type of synchronization, you can specify the synchronization mode, as shown in Table 18-2.

Table 18-2: Replica synchronization modes

Synchronization Mode	Constant	Description
Direct (default setting)	jrSyncModeDirect	Both replicas must reside on computers connected to a common local area network (LAN) or wide area network (WAN).
Indirect	jrSyncModeIndirect	When a replica resides on a computer disconnected from a network, updates are placed in a dropbox folder and are automatically synchronized when the user connects to the network. This process requires synchronizers to be installed both on the network and on the disconnected computer.
Internet	jrSyncModeInternet	Used for synchronizing with a database connected to a web server.

To synchronize one replica with another, both database files must belong to the same replica set. Each replica set is identified by a unique replica set ID. For two replicas to belong to the same replica set, they must be created from the same Design Master. It is not sufficient to create replicas from the same nonreplicable original database. If you created two replicas that belong to different replica sets and want to bring data from one replica set to another, you can copy and paste or import the data. You cannot use synchronization to reconcile the changes between two replicas from different replica sets.

Hands-On 18-7 demonstrates how to use direct, bidirectional (two-way) synchronization.

◎ Hands-On 18-7: Synchronizing Replicas

1. Switch to the Visual Basic Editor window and choose **Insert | Module**.

2. In the module's Code window, enter the **Sync_Replicas** procedure as shown below, or copy the procedure code from **C:\Acc07_HandsOn\ Chap18.txt.**

```
Sub Sync_Replicas(strRep As String, strReplica As String, _
            Optional sncType As SyncTypeEnum, _
            Optional sncMode As SyncModeEnum)
    Dim repDesignMaster As New JRO.Replica

    repDesignMaster.ActiveConnection = strRep

    ' exchange data and design changes between replicas
    repDesignMaster.Synchronize strReplica, sncType, sncMode
    Set repDesignMaster = Nothing
    MsgBox strRep & vbCrLf & _
        "and " & vbCrLf & _
        strReplica & vbCrLf & _
        "were synchronized."
End Sub
```

3. Run the Sync_Replicas procedure from the Immediate window by typing the following statement and pressing **Enter**:

```
Sync_Replicas CurrentProject.Path & "\DM_Northwind.mdb",
    CurrentProject.Path & "\Replica_North.mdb",
    jrSyncTypeImpExp, jrSyncModeDirect
```

 Note: The above statement must be entered on one line in the Immediate window.

Notice that the Sync_Replicas procedure takes two required and two optional arguments.

When you execute the procedure, the full replica named Replica_North.mdb (see Hands-On 18-2) will be synchronized with the Design Master named DM_Northwind.mdb (see Hands-On 18-1).

Retrieving Replica Properties

The procedure in Hands-On 18-8 examines Microsoft Office Access database files in the specified path and lists their replication properties to the Immediate window.

Table 18-3: List of replica properties checked in Hands-On 18-8

Property	Description
ReplicaType	Specifies the type of replica — full, partial, Design Master, or database is not replicable. Use the following enumerators: jrReplicaTypeFull jrReplicaTypePartial jrRepTypeDesignMaster jrRepTypeNotReplicable
DesignMasterID	Unique ID for the Design Master in a replica set.
RetentionPeriod	Number of days that the replica set retains details of deleted records, schema changes, and other information. The default RetentionPeriod is 60 days.
Priority	Determines who wins and who loses in case of a synchronization conflict. The priority values range from 0 to 100. The Design Master has a default priority of 90. The maximum value for priority of any replica is 90 percent of its parent.
Visibility	Ability to synchronize with other replicas.
ReplicaID	Unique ID for each replica in the replica set.

◎ Hands-On 18-8: Retrieving Replica Properties

1. Switch to the Visual Basic Editor window and choose **Insert | Module**.

2. In the module's Code window, enter the **Get_ReplicaProperties** procedure as shown below, or copy the procedure code from **C:\Acc07_HandsOn\ Chap18.txt**.

```
Sub Get_ReplicaProperties(strPath As String)
    Dim fso As Object
    Dim mdbFile As Object
    Dim myFolder As Object
    Dim typeNum As Integer
    Dim repName As String
    Dim repMaster As New JRO.Replica

    On Error Resume Next

    Set fso = CreateObject("Scripting.FileSystemObject")
    Set myFolder = fso.GetFolder(strPath)
        For Each mdbFile In myFolder.Files
            If InStr(mdbFile.Name, ".mdb") Then
                repName = strPath & mdbFile.Name
                repMaster.ActiveConnection = repName

                Select Case repMaster.ReplicaType
                    Case jrRepTypeNotReplicable
                        Debug.Print repName & " is not replicable."
                    Case jrRepTypeDesignMaster
                        Debug.Print repName & " is a Design Master."
                        Debug.Print "Design Master Id: " & _
                            repMaster.DesignMasterID
                        Debug.Print "Retention Period: " & _
                            repMaster.RetentionPeriod
                        Debug.Print "Priority: " & repMaster.Priority
                        Debug.Print "Visibility: " & repMaster.Visibility
                    Case jrRepTypeFull
                        Debug.Print repName & " is a Full Replica."
                        Debug.Print "Replica Id: " & repMaster.ReplicaID
                        Debug.Print "Retention Period: " & _
                            repMaster.RetentionPeriod
                        Debug.Print "Priority: " & repMaster.Priority
                        Debug.Print "Visibility: " & repMaster.Visibility
                    Case jrRepTypePartial
                        Debug.Print repName & " is a Partial Replica."
                        Debug.Print "Retention Period: " & _
                            repMaster.RetentionPeriod
                        Debug.Print "Priority: " & repMaster.Priority
                        Debug.Print "Visibility: " & repMaster.Visibility
                End Select
            End If
        Next mdbFile
    MsgBox "View Replica Properties in the Immediate window."
End Sub
```

3. Run the Get_ReplicaProperties procedure from the Immediate window by typing the following statement and pressing **Enter**:

```
Get_ReplicaProperties currentProject.Path & "\"
```

To retrieve replica properties, the above procedure must be able to access your computer's file system. This is done by using the FileSystemObject from the Microsoft Scripting Runtime Library (see Hands-On 18-1). We use the GetFolder method of the FileSystemObject object to return a Folder object corresponding to the folder in a specified path. Then we look at all the MDB files in this folder and, if the file is replicable, we check the properties listed in Table 18-3.

Synchronization Conflicts

During the synchronization of replicas errors may occur. An error may be caused when the same record is updated in two members of the replica set and Microsoft Jet attempts to synchronize the two versions.

The following custom project illustrates how you can use the Database Tools | Replication Options in the Access window to create and synchronize replicas. To learn about conflicts during the synchronization of replicas, we will create two replicas, Replica_England.mdb and Replica_France.mdb, and enter some conflicting data into the same record in both of these replicas.

⊚ Custom Project 18-1: Replication via Microsoft Access User Interface

Part 1: Creating a Replica Named Replica_England.mdb

1. Open the Design Master **DM_Northwind.mdb** file that you created in Hands-On 18-1.

2. Choose **Database Tools | Replication Options | Create Replica**. In the Filename text box, enter **Replica_England.mdb** as the name of the new replica and click **OK**.

3. Microsoft Access displays a Creating Replica message box. When the process of creating a new replica is finished, you are asked whether you want to close and reopen the database. Click **Yes** in response to this message. Access reloads the Design Master DM_Northwind database.

Part 2: Creating a Replica Named Replica_France.mdb

1. In the Design Master **DM_Northwind.mdb** file, choose **Tools | Replication Options | Create Replica**. In the Filename text box, enter **Replica_France.mdb** as the name of the new replica and click **OK**.

2. Microsoft Access displays a Creating Replica message box. When the process of creating a new replica is finished, you are asked whether you want to close and reopen the database. Click **Yes** in response to this message. Access reloads the Design Master DM_Northwind database.

3. Close the Design Master DM_Northwind.mdb database file.

Part 3: Making Changes in the Replica_England Database

1. Open Windows Explorer. Locate the **Replica_England.mdb** database file that you created in step 2 of Part 1 above. Double-click this file to open it.

2. In the **Customers** table, locate the customer record **Around the Horn**. Type **98051** in the Postal Code field for this record. Click on any other record to ensure that the data you entered is saved.

3. Close the **Customers** table.

4. Close the Replica_England.mdb database file.

Part 4: Making Changes in the Replica_France Database

1. Switch to Windows Explorer. Locate the **Replica_France.mdb** database file that you created in step 1 of Part 2 above. Double-click this file to open it.

2. In the **Customers** table, locate the customer record **Around the Horn**. Type **98053** in the Postal Code field for this record. Click on any other record to ensure that the data you entered is saved.

3. Close the **Customers** table.

4. Close the Replica_France.mdb database file.

Part 5: Synchronizing Replicas

1. Open the Design Master **DM_Northwind.mdb** database.

2. Choose **Database Tools | Replication Options | Synchronize Now**.

3. When the Synchronize Database dialog box appears (see Figure 18-4), select the **Replica_England.mdb** file and click **OK**.

Figure 18-4: To synchronize the Design Master directly with the replica, use the Browse button to find the Replica_England.mdb file on your computer.

4. Click **Yes** in response to the message that the database must be closed prior to synchronization. Access reloads the Design Master **DM_Northwind.mdb** database.

5. Click **OK** to confirm the completion of the synchronization process.

6. In the Design Master DM_Northwind.mdb database, choose **Database Tools | Replication Options | Synchronize Now**.

7. When the Synchronize Database dialog box appears (see Figure 18-5), select the **Replica_France.mdb** file and click **OK**.

Figure 18-5: To synchronize the Design Master directly with the second replica that you created in this custom project, use the Browse button to find the Replica_France.mdb file on your computer.

8. Click **Yes** in response to the message that the database must be closed prior to synchronization. Access reloads the Design Master DM_Northwind.mdb database.

9. Click **OK** to confirm the completion of the synchronization process.

10. Microsoft Access displays a message indicating that synchronization finished. This is followed by another message regarding a synchronization problem (see Figure 18-6).

Figure 18-6: This message appears when Access finds out that a member of the replica set has a conflict with another member of the same replica set.

11. Click **Yes** in response to the above message to indicate that you want to resolve the conflicts now. The Microsoft Replication Conflict Viewer window appears (see Figure 18-7).

Figure 18-7: When you click Yes in response to the message shown in Figure 18-6, Access displays the Microsoft Replication Conflict Viewer, which lists tables with conflicts.

12. In the Microsoft Replication Conflict Viewer window, click the **View** button. Microsoft Access now displays a window specifying the reason for conflict (see Figure 18-8) and allows you to resolve the conflict.

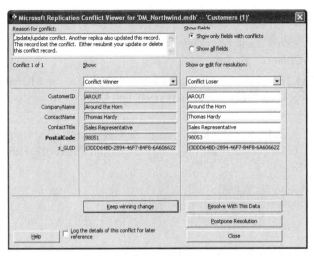

Figure 18-8: This window with conflict details appears when you click the View button in the Microsoft Replication Conflict Viewer window (see Figure 18-7).

13. For this example, click **Close** to exit the Microsoft Replication Conflict Viewer for DM_Northwind.mdb -- Customers (1) window without making any changes. Click **Close** again to close the Microsoft Replication Conflict Viewer (shown in Figure 18-7).

14. Close the Design Master DM_Northwind.mdb database file.

The steps you've just completed demonstrate how to create and synchronize replicas using the Microsoft Access user interface. By entering conflicting data in the same field of the same record you were able to see how Access can locate the problem area during the synchronization process and how you can resolve the data conflict using the Microsoft Replication Conflict Viewer window.

Hands-On 18-9 illustrates how you can use the ConflictTables property to find out whether any conflicts occurred during the synchronization of replicas. This property returns the name of the conflict table that contains the database records that conflicted during synchronization.

The conflict table has two columns. The first column contains the names of the tables where conflicts occurred and the second one lists the associated conflict table names. If there is no conflict table (or the database is nonreplicable), the ConflictTables property returns a zero-length string (""). If you find out that the conflict occurred during synchronization, you should write a custom conflict-resolution procedure to handle the conflicts depending on your needs.

◎ Hands-On 18-9: Retrieving the Name of the Conflict Table

1. In the Visual Basic Editor window of the Chap18.mdb database file, choose **Insert | Module**.

2. Choose **Tools | References** and add the reference to the **Microsoft ActiveX Data Objects 2.8 Library**. Click **OK** to exit the References dialog box.

3. In the module's Code window, enter the **Get_ConflictTables** procedure as shown below, or copy the procedure code from **C:\Acc07_HandsOn\ Chap18.txt**.

```
Sub Get_ConflictTables()
    Dim repDesignMaster As New JRO.Replica
    Dim rst As ADODB.Recordset
    Dim strPath As String

    strPath = CurrentProject.Path & "\DM_Northwind.mdb"
    repDesignMaster.ActiveConnection = strPath
    Set rst = repDesignMaster.ConflictTables
    With rst
        If .EOF Then
            Debug.Print "There are no conflicts."
        Else
            Do Until .EOF
                Debug.Print "Table: " & rst.Fields(0) & vbCr _
                    ; "Conflict Table: " & .Fields(1) & vbCrLf
                .MoveNext
            Loop
            .Close
        End If
    End With
    Set repDesignMaster = Nothing
    Set rst = Nothing
End Sub
```

4. Run the **Get_ConflictTables** procedure to find out the name of the conflict table.

The above procedure uses the ConflictTables property of the Replica object to determine which tables had conflicts. This property returns an ADO Recordset object that contains one row for each table containing conflicts.

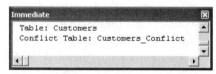

Figure 18-9: The procedure in Hands-On 18-9 prints the location of the synchronization conflict table and the name of the table in which conflict has occurred.

Figure 18-10: The conflict table is hidden in the Access window of the Design Master. To unhide it, choose the Office button and click Access Options. Choose Current Database | Navigation | Navigation Options. In the Display Options area of the dialog box, click the check box next to Show Hidden Objects.

Figure 18-11: The conflict table lists the conflicting record.

Chapter Summary

This chapter introduced you to numerous objects, properties, and methods available in the Microsoft Jet and Replication Objects (JRO) Library for programmatic control and management of database replication tasks. You learned how to convert a normal Access database file in the MDB file format into a Design Master. You used the new Design Master to create both full and partial replicas. You learned how to ensure that a Database object is replicable as well as how to avoid replicating some of the objects by keeping them local. You also tried out basic replication tasks such as synchronization and conflict resolution.

This chapter concludes Part II of this book in which you learned how to perform important database tasks using DAO and ADO.

Programming with the Jet Data Definition Language

The Data Definition Language (DDL) is a component of the Structured Query Language (SQL), which is used for defining database objects (tables, views, stored procedures, primary keys, indexes, and constraints) and managing database security.

In this part of the book, you learn how to use the DDL language with Jet databases, ADO, and the Jet 4.0/ACE OLE DB Provider.

Chapter 19

Creating, Modifying, and Deleting Tables and Fields

In Part II of this book you tried out different methods that are available in Microsoft Office Access 2007 for creating and manipulating databases via VBA programming code using the DAO and ADO object models. In particular, you learned how to create new databases from scratch, add tables and indexes, set up relationships between tables, secure a database with a password, define user and group security accounts, and handle object permissions. In addition to using DAO and ADO, you can perform many of the mentioned database tasks by using the Data Definition Language (DDL), which is a component of the Structured Query Language (SQL).

SQL is a widely used language for data retrieval and manipulation in databases. The SQL specification (known as ANSI SQL-89) was first published in 1989 by the American National Standards Institute (ANSI). The ANSI SQL standard was revised in 1992 and this version is referred to as ANSI SQL-92 or SQL-2. This revised specification is supported by the major database vendors, many of whom have created their own extensions of the SQL language. Microsoft Office Access 2007 supports both SQL specifications and refers to them as *ANSI SQL query modes*.

While the ANSI-89 SQL query mode (also called Microsoft Jet SQL and ANSI SQL) uses the traditional Jet SQL syntax, the ANSI-92 SQL mode uses syntax that is more compliant with SQL-92 and Microsoft SQL Server. For example, ANSI-92 uses the percent sign (%) and the underscore character (_) for its wildcards instead of the asterisk (*) and the question mark (?), which are commonly used in VBA. Microsoft Access Jet Engine does not implement the complete ANSI SQL-92 standard and provides its own Jet 4.0 ANSI SQL-92 extensions to support new features of Access. For more information about syntax differences, see the topic "Comparison of Microsoft Access SQL and ANSI SQL" in the Microsoft Office Access help files.

You can use the ANSI-92 syntax in your VBA procedures with the Microsoft OLE DB Provider for Jet or with the Data Definition Language, which we cover in this part of the book. ANSI-89 is the default setting for a new Microsoft Access database in Access 2002-2003 and 2000 file format. Because the two ANSI SQL query modes are not compatible, you must decide which query mode you are going to use for the current database. This can easily be done in the Microsoft Access user interface as outlined in Hands-On 19-1.

◎ Hands-On 19-1: Setting the ANSI SQL Query Mode

1. Start Microsoft Office Access 2007 and create a new Microsoft Office Access 2007 database named **Chap19.accdb** in your **C:\Acc07_ ByExample** folder.

2. Click the **Microsoft Office** button and select the **Access Options** button.

3. In the left pane of the Access Options window, select **Object Designers**.

4. In the right pane, in the Query design section look for the SQL Server Compatible Syntax (ANSI 92) area (see Figure 19-1). Set the query mode to ANSI-92 SQL by clicking the **This database** check box. (You can set the query mode to ANSI-89 SQL by clearing the **This database** check box.)

5. Click **OK** to exit the Access Options window. Microsoft Access displays a message as shown in Figure 19-2.

6. Click the **Help** button to read more information about the ANSI SQL query mode.

7. Return to the message and click **OK**. The Microsoft Access database will close and reopen with the new settings in effect.

Figure 19-1: Use the Access Options window to set the ANSI SQL query mode for the current database or all new databases.

Figure 19-2: When you change the query mode to ANSI-92, Microsoft Access displays an informational message alerting you to possible problems.

There are two areas of Microsoft Access SQL:

- Data Definition Language (DDL) offers a number of SQL statements to manage database security and to create and alter database components (such as tables, indexes, relationships, views, and stored procedures). These statements are: CREATE TABLE, DROP TABLE, ALTER TABLE, CREATE INDEX, DROP INDEX, CHECK CONSTRAINT, CREATE VIEW, DROP VIEW, CREATE PROCEDURE, DROP PROCEDURE, EXECUTE, ALTER DATABASE, ADD USER, ALTER USER, CREATE USER, CREATE GROUP, DROP GROUP, DROP USER, GRANT, and REVOKE.

- Data Manipulation Language (DML) offers SQL statements that allow you to retrieve and manipulate data contained in the database tables as well as perform transactions. These statements are: SELECT, UNION, UPDATE, DELETE, INSERT INTO, SELECT INTO, INNER JOIN, LEFT JOIN, RIGHT JOIN, TRANSFORM, PARAMETERS, BEGIN TRANSACTION, COMMIT, and ROLLBACK.

This chapter and the remaining chapters of Part III focus on using the DDL language for creating and changing the underlying structure of a database. To get the most out of these chapters, you should be familiar with using DAO and ADO, which was discussed in Part II.

Creating Tables

Using the Microsoft Access SQL CREATE TABLE statement and the DAO Database object's Execute method or the ADO Connection object's Execute method, you can define a new table, its fields, and field constraints. The CREATE TABLE statement can only be used with Microsoft Jet and Microsoft Access engine databases. The two examples that follow illustrate how to create a table named tblSchools in the currently open database and in a new database using ADO.

Hands-On 19-2: Creating a Table in the Current Database (DDL with ADO)

1. In the **Chap19.accdb** database that you created in Hands-On 19-1, switch to the Visual Basic Editor window and choose **Tools | References**. In the References dialog box, scroll down to locate the **Microsoft ActiveX 2.8 Data Objects Library**. Click the check box to the left of this library name to set a reference to it and click **OK** to exit the dialog box.

2. Choose **Insert | Module** to add a new module to the current VBA project.

3. In the module's Code window, type the **CreateTable** procedure shown below, or copy the procedure code from **C:\Acc07_HandsOn\Chap19.txt**.

```
Sub CreateTable()
    ' you must set up a reference to
    ' the Microsoft ActiveX Data Objects Library
    ' in the References dialog box
    Dim conn As ADODB.Connection
    Dim strTable As String

    On Error GoTo ErrorHandler

    Set conn = CurrentProject.Connection

    strTable = "tblSchools"
    conn.Execute "CREATE TABLE " & strTable & _
        "(SchoolID AUTOINCREMENT(100, 5), " & _
        "SchoolName CHAR," & _
        "City CHAR (25), District CHAR (35), " & _
        "YearEstablished DATE);"

    Application.RefreshDatabaseWindow
ExitHere:
    conn.Close
    Set conn = Nothing
    Exit Sub
ErrorHandler:
    MsgBox Err.Number & ":" & Err.Description
    Resume ExitHere
End Sub
```

4. Position the insertion point anywhere within the code of the CreateTable procedure and press **F5** or choose **Run | Run Sub/UserForm** to execute the procedure.

The above procedure uses ADO to establish a connection to the current database (Chap19.accdb). The ADO Connection object's Execute method is used to execute the Data Definition Language CREATE TABLE statement that defines a new table and its fields. The first field is named SchoolID and its data type is defined as AutoNumber.

The seed and increment values of AutoNumber columns are specified using the following syntax:

```
Column_name AUTOINCREMENT (seed, increment)
```

The table, tblSchools, has an AutoNumber column with a seed of 100 and an increment of 5:

```
SchoolID AUTOINCREMENT(100, 5)
```

When you switch to the database window and open this table in Datasheet view, the SchoolID for the first record will be 100, the second will be 105, the third 110, and so on.

Three fields are defined as Text fields and one field as a Date/Time field. The Text fields are defined using the CHAR data type (see Table 19-1). To specify the size of the Text field, put the appropriate value between parentheses. If the size of the Text field is not specified, it is assumed to be 255 characters long.

When you examine the code of the CreateTable procedure and compare the resultant table in Figure 19-3, you will notice that Access SQL uses different data types than those available in the Table Design window. Table 19-1 shows the equivalent SQL data types.

Figure 19-3: The tblSchools table was generated by the CreateTable procedure in Hands-On 19-2 using the Microsoft Access SQL statement CREATE TABLE.

Table 19-1: Table design data types and their Access SQL equivalents

Table Design Data Types	Access SQL Data Types
Text	TEXT, ALPHANUMERIC, CHAR, CHARACTER, STRING, or VARCHAR
Memo	LONGTEXT, MEMO, LONGCHAR, or NOTE
Number (Field Size = Byte)	BYTE or INTEGER1
Number (Field Size = Integer)	SHORT, INTEGER2, or SMALLINT
Number (Field Size = Long Integer)	COUNTER, INTEGER, INT, or AUTOINCREMENT
Number (Field Size = Single)	SINGLE, FLOAT4, or REAL

Table Design Data Types	Access SQL Data Types
Number (Field Size = Double)	DOUBLE, FLOAT, or NUMBER
Date/Time	DATETIME, DATE, TIME, or TIMESTAMP
Currency	CURRENCY or MONEY
AutoNumber (Field Size = Long Integer)	AUTOINCREMENT or COUNTER
AutoNumber (Field Size = Replication Id)	GUID
Yes/No	BOOLEAN, BIT, LOGICAL, LOGICAL1, or YESNO
OLE Object	LONGBINARY, OLEOBJECT, or GENERAL

The RefreshDatabaseWindow method of the Application object ensures that the database window is updated after the creation of the new table object. The error-handling code will alert you if an error is encountered. Try to run this procedure again in step mode (F8) to see what happens. Notice that the procedure uses two labels to mark appropriate sections in the procedure. The On Error GoTo ErrorHandler statement will transfer the procedure execution to the line labeled ErrorHandler when an error is triggered. Statements following this label will be executed until the Resume statement is encountered. This statement will direct the code execution to the line labeled ExitHere. The Exit Sub statement in the ExitHere block of code will allow us to exit the procedure when an error is encountered and when there are no errors.

The following procedure uses the DAO Database object's Execute method to create the same type of table as the one created in Hands-On 19-2.

```
Sub CreateTable2()
    Dim db As DAO.Database
    Dim strTable As String

    On Error GoTo ErrorHandler

    Set db = CurrentDb()

    strTable = "tblSchools2"

    db.Execute "CREATE TABLE " & strTable & _
        "(SchoolID AUTOINCREMENT(100, 5), " & _
        "SchoolName CHAR," & _
        "City CHAR (25), District CHAR (35), " & _
        "YearEstablished DATE);"

    Application.RefreshDatabaseWindow
ExitHere:
    Set db = Nothing
    Exit Sub
ErrorHandler:
    MsgBox Err.Number & ":" & Err.Description
    Resume ExitHere
End Sub
```

Sometimes you may be required to create a new database and a new table in one procedure. Hands-On 19-3 demonstrates how to create a table in a brand-new database.

Programming with the Jet Data Definition Language

◎ Hands-On 19-3: Creating a Table in a New Database (DDL with ADO/ADOX)

1. In the Visual Basic Editor window, choose **Tools** | **References**. In the References dialog box, scroll down to locate the **Microsoft ADO Ext. 2.8 for DDL and Security Object Library**. Click the check box to the left of the library name to set a reference to it and click **OK** to exit the dialog box.

2. In the module's Code window, enter the **CreateTableInNewDB** procedure as shown below, or copy the procedure code from **C:\Acc07_HandsOn\ Chap19.txt**.

```
Sub CreateTableInNewDB()
    ' use the References dialog box to set up a reference to
    ' Microsoft ADO Ext. for DDL and Security Object Library
    ' and Microsoft ActiveX Data Objects Library
    Dim cat As ADOX.Catalog
    Dim conn As ADODB.Connection
    Dim strDB As String
    Dim strTable As String
    Dim strConnect As String

    On Error GoTo ErrorHandler

    Set cat = New ADOX.Catalog
    strDB = CurrentProject.Path & "\Sites.mdb"
    strConnect = "Provider=Microsoft.Jet.OLEDB.4.0;" & _
        "Data Source=" & strDB

    ' create a new database file
    cat.Create strConnect
    MsgBox "The database was created (" & strDB & ")."

    ' set connection to currently open catalog
    Set conn = cat.ActiveConnection

    strTable = "tblSchools"
    conn.Execute "CREATE TABLE " & strTable & _
        "(SchoolID AUTOINCREMENT(100, 5), " & _
        "SchoolName CHAR," & _
        "City CHAR (25), District CHAR (35), " & _
        "YearEstablished DATE);"
ExitHere:
    Set cat = Nothing
    Set conn = Nothing
    Exit Sub
ErrorHandler:
    If Err.Number = -2147217897 Then
        ' delete the database file if it exists
        Kill strDB
        ' start from statement that caused this error
        Resume 0
    Else
        MsgBox Err.Number & ": " & Err.Description
```

```
        GoTo ExitHere
    End If
End Sub
```

3. Position the insertion point anywhere within the code of the CreateTableInNewDB procedure and press **F5** or choose **Run | Run Sub/UserForm** to execute the procedure.

The CreateTableInNewDB procedure shown above creates a new database named Sites.mdb in the current folder. As you may recall from Chapter 10, you can create a new Microsoft Access database by using the Create method of the ADOX Catalog object. Before creating a table in the new database, set the conn object variable to the currently open Catalog, like this:

```
Set conn = cat.ActiveConnection
```

Use the Connection object's Execute method to create a new table named tblSchools in the Sites.mdb file. Like other procedure examples in this section, this table contains an AutoNumber field with a sequence starting at 100 that will be incremented by 5 as new columns are added. Notice that the error-handling code demonstrated in this procedure is slightly different from previous examples. If you know the type of error that is most likely to occur, you can check for the error number in the error handler and execute the appropriate statement when the condition is met. If the database already exists it will be deleted using the VBA Kill statement (don't do this in the production environment unless you are absolutely certain this is what you want to do). The statement Resume 0 in the error-handling code will return the code execution to the line that caused the error. If other errors are encountered, error information will appear in a message box and the code execution will continue from the line following the ExitHere label.

Deleting Tables

It's time to remove some of our test data by using the DROP TABLE statement to delete an existing table from a database. Note that a table must be closed before it can be deleted. The procedure in Hands-On 19-4 will delete the tblSchool table that was created in Hands-On 19-2.

Hands-On 19-4: Deleting a Table

This hands-on exercise requires the prior completion of Hands-On 19-2.

1. In the Visual Basic Editor window, choose **Insert | Module**.

2. In the module's Code window, enter the **DeleteTable** procedure as shown below, or copy the procedure code from **C:\Acc07_HandsOn\Chap19.txt**.

```
Sub DeleteTable()
    Dim conn As ADODB.Connection
    Dim strTable As String

    On Error GoTo ErrorHandler
```

Programming with the Jet Data Definition Language

```
    Set conn = CurrentProject.Connection

    strTable = "tblSchools"
    conn.Execute "DROP TABLE " & strTable
    Application.RefreshDatabaseWindow
ExitHere:
    conn.Close
    Set conn = Nothing
    Exit Sub
ErrorHandler:
    If Err.Number = -2147217900 Then
        DoCmd.Close acTable, strTable, acSavePrompt
        Resume 0
    Else
        MsgBox Err.Number & ":" & Err.Description
        Resume ExitHere
    End If
End Sub
```

3. Position the insertion point anywhere within the code of the DeleteTable procedure and press **F5** or choose **Run | Run Sub/UserForm** to execute the procedure.

You can also execute the DROP TABLE statement directly in the Microsoft Office Access user interface's Data Definition Query window by following these steps:

1. Choose **Create | QueryDesign**.

2. Click the **Close** button in the Show Table dialog box.

3. Choose **Design | SQL | Data Definition**.

4. Enter the following statement in the Query window:

```
Drop Table tblSchools2;
```

5. Choose **Design | Run**.

Modifying Tables with DDL

You can modify a table definition by altering, adding, or dropping columns and constraints. *Constraints* allow you to enforce integrity by creating rules for a table. The procedures in the following sections illustrate how to use Microsoft Access SQL DDL statements to:

■ Add new columns to a table

■ Change the column's data type

■ Change the size of a Text column

■ Delete a field from a table

■ Add a primary key to an existing table

■ Add a unique, multiple-field index to an existing table

■ Delete an index

- Delete an indexed column
- Set a default value for a column in a table
- Change the seed and increment value of AutoNumber columns

Adding New Fields to a Table

Use the ALTER TABLE statement followed by a table name to modify the design of a table after it has been created with the CREATE TABLE statement. Prior to modifying the structure of an existing table, it's recommended that you make a backup copy of the table.

The ALTER TABLE statement can be used with the ADD COLUMN clause to add a new field to the table. For example, the procedure in Hands-On 19-5 adds a Currency field called Budget2008 to the tblSchools table using the following statement:

```
ALTER TABLE tblSchools ADD COLUMN Budget2008 MONEY
```

When you add a new field to a table you should specify the name of the field, its data type and, for Text and Binary fields, the size of the data type.

Hands-On 19-5: Adding a New Field to an Existing Table

1. Run the procedure in Hands-On 19-2 to create the **tblSchools** table in the current database if you deleted the table in Hands-On 19-4.
2. In the Visual Basic Editor window, choose **Insert | Module**.
3. In the module's Code window, enter the **AddNewField** procedure as shown below, or copy the procedure code from **C:\Acc07_HandsOn\ Chap19.txt**.

```
Sub AddNewField()
    Dim conn As ADODB.Connection
    Dim strTable As String
    Dim strCol As String

    On Error GoTo ErrorHandler
    Set conn = CurrentProject.Connection

    strTable = "tblSchools"
    strCol = "Budget2008"

    conn.Execute "ALTER TABLE " & strTable & _
        " ADD COLUMN " & strCol & " MONEY;"
ExitHere:
    conn.Close
    Set conn = Nothing
    Exit Sub
ErrorHandler:
    MsgBox Err.Number & ":" & Err.Description
    Resume ExitHere
End Sub
```

4. Position the insertion point anywhere within the code of the AddNewField procedure and press **F5** or choose **Run | Run Sub/UserForm** to execute the procedure.

Changing the Data Type of a Table Column

You can use the ALTER COLUMN clause in the ALTER TABLE statement to change the data type of a table column. You must specify the name of the field, the desired data type, and the size of the data type, if required.

The procedure in Hands-On 19-6 changes the data type of the SchoolID field in the tblSchools table from AutoNumber to a 15-character Text field.

⊚ Hands-On 19-6: Changing the Field Data Type

This hands-on exercise uses the tblSchools table created in Hands-On 19-2 and recreated in Hands-On 19-5.

1. In the same module where you entered the procedure in Hands-On 19-5, enter the **ChangeFieldType** procedure as shown below, or copy the procedure code from **C:\Acc07_HandsOn\Chap19.txt**.

```
Sub ChangeFieldType()
    Dim conn As ADODB.Connection
    Dim strTable As String
    Dim strCol As String

    On Error GoTo ErrorHandler
    Set conn = CurrentProject.Connection

    strTable = "tblSchools"
    strCol = "SchoolID"
    conn.Execute "ALTER TABLE " & strTable & _
        " ALTER COLUMN " & strCol & " CHAR(15);"
ExitHere:
    conn.Close
    Set conn = Nothing
    Exit Sub
ErrorHandler:
    MsgBox Err.Number & ":" & Err.Description
    Resume ExitHere
End Sub
```

2. Position the insertion point anywhere within the code of the ChangeFieldType procedure and press **F5** or choose **Run | Run Sub/UserForm** to execute the procedure.

The above procedure modifies the SchoolID data type to store text data. You can double-check the procedure changes by switching to the Microsoft Office Access window and opening the tblSchools table in Design view.

When done, make sure you close the tblSchools table.

Changing the Size of a Text Column

It's easy to increase or decrease the size of a Text column. Simply use the ALTER TABLE statement followed by the name of the table, and the ALTER COLUMN clause followed by the name of the column whose size you want to modify. Next, specify the data type of the column and the new column size.

Hands-On 19-7 modifies the size of the SchoolName field from the default 255 characters to 40.

⊚ Hands-On 19-7: Changing the Size of a Field

This hands-on exercise uses the tblSchools table created in Hands-On 19-2.

1. In the same module where you entered previous hands-on exercises, enter the **ChangeFieldSize** procedure as shown below, or copy the procedure code from **C:\Acc07_HandsOn\Chap19.txt**.

```
Sub ChangeFieldSize()
    Dim conn As ADODB.Connection
    Dim strTable As String
    Dim strCol As String

    On Error GoTo ErrorHandler
    Set conn = CurrentProject.Connection

    strTable = "tblSchools"
    strCol = "SchoolName"

conn.Execute "ALTER TABLE " & strTable & _
    " ALTER COLUMN " & strCol & " CHAR(40);"
ExitHere:
    conn.Close
    Set conn = Nothing
    Exit Sub
ErrorHandler:
    MsgBox Err.Number & ":" & Err.Description
    Resume ExitHere
End Sub
```

2. Position the insertion point anywhere within the code of the ChangeField-Size procedure and press **F5** or choose **Run | Run Sub/UserForm** to execute the procedure.

The above procedure sets the size of the SchoolName field to 40 characters. You can double-check the procedure changes by switching to the Microsoft Office Access window and opening the tblSchools table in Design view.

When done, be sure to close the tblSchools table.

Deleting a Column from a Table

Use the DROP COLUMN clause in the ALTER TABLE statement to delete a column from a table. You only need to specify the name of the field you want to remove.

The example procedure in Hands-On 19-8 deletes the Budget2008 column from the tblSchools table.

⊚ Hands-On 19-8: Deleting a Field from a Table

This hands-on exercise uses the tblSchools table created in Hands-On 19-2. Make sure this table contains the Budget2008 column, which was added in Hands-On 19-5.

1. In the same module where you entered previous hands-on exercises, enter the **DeleteField** procedure as shown below, or copy the procedure code from **C:\Acc07_HandsOn\Chap19.txt**.

```
Sub DeleteField()
    Dim conn As ADODB.Connection
    Dim strTable As String
    Dim strCol As String

    On Error GoTo ErrorHandler
    Set conn = CurrentProject.Connection

    strTable = "tblSchools"
    strCol = "Budget2008"

    conn.Execute "ALTER TABLE " & strTable & _
        " DROP COLUMN " & strCol & ";"
ExitHere:
    conn.Close
    Set conn = Nothing
    Exit Sub
ErrorHandler:
    MsgBox Err.Number & ":" & Err.Description
    Resume ExitHere
End Sub
```

2. Position the insertion point anywhere within the code of the DeleteField procedure and press **F5** or choose **Run | Run Sub/UserForm** to execute the procedure.

The above procedure removes the Budget2008 field from the tblSchools table.

Adding a Primary Key to a Table

You can use the ADD CONSTRAINT clause in the ALTER TABLE statement to define one or more columns as a primary key. The primary key is defined using the PRIMARY KEY keywords.

Hands-On 19-9 defines a primary key for the tblSchools table created in Hands-On 19-2.

◎ Hands-On 19-9: Adding a Primary Key to a Table

This hands-on exercise uses the tblSchools table created in Hands-On 19-2.

1. In the same module where you entered previous hands-on exercises, enter the **AddPrimaryKey** procedure as shown below, or copy the procedure code from **C:\Acc07_HandsOn\Chap19.txt**.

```
Sub AddPrimaryKey()
    Dim conn As ADODB.Connection
    Dim strTable As String
    Dim strCol As String

    On Error GoTo ErrorHandler
    Set conn = CurrentProject.Connection

    strTable = "tblSchools"
    strCol = "SchoolID"

conn.Execute "ALTER TABLE " & strTable & _
    " ADD CONSTRAINT pKey PRIMARY KEY " & _
    "(" & strCol & ");"
ExitHere:
    conn.Close
    Set conn = Nothing
    Exit Sub
ErrorHandler:
    MsgBox Err.Number & ":" & Err.Description
    Resume ExitHere
End Sub
```

2. Position the insertion point anywhere within the code of the AddPrimary-Key procedure and press **F5** or choose **Run | Run Sub/UserForm** to execute the procedure.

Adding a Multiple-Field Index to a Table

Use the ADD CONSTRAINT clause and the UNIQUE keyword in the ALTER TABLE statement to add a multiple-field index. The UNIQUE keyword prevents duplicate values in the index.

◎ Hands-On 19-10: Adding a Unique Index Based on Two Fields to an Existing Table

This hands-on exercise uses the tblSchools table created in Hands-On 19-2.

1. In the same module where you entered previous hands-on exercises, enter the **AddMulti_UniqueIndex** procedure as shown below, or copy the procedure code from **C:\Acc07_HandsOn\Chap19.txt**.

```
Sub AddMulti_UniqueIndex()
    Dim conn As ADODB.Connection
    Dim strTable As String
    Dim strCol As String
```

```
    On Error GoTo ErrorHandler
    Set conn = CurrentProject.Connection

    strTable = "tblSchools"
    strCol = "SchoolID, District"

    conn.Execute "ALTER TABLE " & strTable & _
        " ADD CONSTRAINT multiIdx UNIQUE " & _
        "(" & strCol & ");"
ExitHere:
    conn.Close
    Set conn = Nothing
    Exit Sub
ErrorHandler:
    MsgBox Err.Number & ":" & Err.Description
    Resume ExitHere
End Sub
```

2. Position the insertion point anywhere within the code of the AddMulti_
   UniqueIndex procedure and press **F5** or choose **Run | Run Sub/UserForm**
   to execute the procedure.

Figure 19-4: After running the procedures in Hands-On 19-9 and
19-10, the tblSchools table contains a primary key and a unique
index based on two fields.

Deleting an Indexed Column

Deleting an index field is a two-step process:

■ Use the DROP CONSTRAINT clause to delete an index. You must specify
the index name.

■ Use the DROP COLUMN clause to delete the desired column. You must
specify the column name.

Both clauses must be used in the ALTER TABLE statement.

The procedure in Hands-On 19-11 deletes the District column from the
tblSchools table. Recall that the procedure in Hands-On 19-10 added a multiple-field index based on the SchoolID and District columns.

Hands-On 19-11: Deleting a Field that Is a Part of an Index

This hands-on exercise uses the tblSchools table created in Hands-On 19-2. You must perform Hands-On 19-10 prior to running this procedure.

1. In the same module where you entered previous hands-on exercises, enter the **DeleteIdxField** procedure as shown below, or copy the procedure code from **C:\Acc07_HandsOn\Chap19.txt**.

```
Sub DeleteIdxField()
    Dim conn As ADODB.Connection
    Dim strTable As String
    Dim strCol As String
    Dim strIdx As String

    On Error GoTo ErrorHandler
    Set conn = CurrentProject.Connection

    strTable = "tblSchools"
    strCol = "District"
    strIdx = "multiIdx"

    conn.Execute "ALTER TABLE " & strTable & _
        " DROP CONSTRAINT " & strIdx  & ";"

    conn.Execute "ALTER TABLE " & strTable & _
        " DROP COLUMN " & strCol & ";"

ExitHere:
    conn.Close
    Set conn = Nothing
    Exit Sub
ErrorHandler:
    MsgBox Err.Number & ":" & Err.Description
    Resume ExitHere
End Sub
```

2. Position the insertion point anywhere within the code of the DeleteIdxField procedure and press **F5** or choose **Run | Run Sub/UserForm** to execute the procedure.

Deleting an Index

Use the DROP CONSTRAINT clause to delete an index. You must specify the index name.

The procedure in Hands-On 19-12 deletes a primary key index from the tblSchools table.

Hands-On 19-12: Deleting an Index

This hands-on exercise uses the tblSchools table created in Hands-On 19-2. You must perform Hands-On 19-10 prior to running this procedure.

1. In the same module where you entered previous hands-on exercises, enter the **RemovePrimaryKeyIndex** procedure as shown below, or copy the procedure code from **C:\Acc07_HandsOn\Chap19.txt**.

```
Sub RemovePrimaryKeyIndex()
    Dim conn As ADODB.Connection
    Dim strTable As String
    Dim strIdx As String

    On Error GoTo ErrorHandler
    Set conn = CurrentProject.Connection

    strTable = "tblSchools"
    strIdx = "pKey"

    conn.Execute "ALTER TABLE " & strTable & _
        " DROP CONSTRAINT " & strIdx & ";"

ExitHere:
    conn.Close
    Set conn = Nothing
    Exit Sub
ErrorHandler:
    MsgBox Err.Number & ":" & Err.Description
    Resume ExitHere
End Sub
```

2. Position the insertion point anywhere within the code of the Remove-PrimaryKeyIndex procedure and press **F5** or choose **Run | Run Sub/UserForm** to execute the procedure.

After running the procedures in Hands-On 19-11 and 19-12, the Indexes window (see Figure 19-4 earlier) should be empty.

Setting a Default Value for a Table Column

Specifying a default value for a field automatically enters that value in the field each time a new record is added to a table unless the user provides a value for the field. Using DDL, you can add a default value for an existing column with the SET DEFAULT clause. The required syntax is as follows:

```
ALTER TABLE table_name ALTER [COLUMN] column_name SET DEFAULT default-value;
```

The [COLUMN] in the above syntax is optional.

⊚ Hands-On 19-13: Setting a Default Value for a Field

This hands-on exercise uses the tblSchools table created in Hands-On 19-2.

1. In the same module where you entered previous hands-on exercises, enter the **SetDefaultFieldValue** procedure as shown below, or copy the procedure code from **C:\Acc07_HandsOn\Chap19.txt**.

```
Sub SetDefaultFieldValue()
    Dim conn As ADODB.Connection
```

```
Dim strTable As String
Dim strCol As String
Dim strDefVal As String
Dim strSQL As String

On Error GoTo ErrorHandler
Set conn = CurrentProject.Connection

strTable = "tblSchools"
strCol = "City"
strDefVal = "Boston"
strSQL = "ALTER TABLE " & strTable & _
    " ALTER " & strCol & " SET DEFAULT " & strDefVal

conn.Execute strSQL

ExitHere:
    conn.Close
    Set conn = Nothing
    Exit Sub
ErrorHandler:
    MsgBox Err.Number & ":" & Err.Description
    Resume ExitHere
End Sub
```

2. Position the insertion point anywhere within the code of the SetDefault-FieldValue procedure and press **F5** or choose **Run | Run Sub/UserForm** to execute the procedure.

Figure 19-5: After running the procedure in Hands-On 19-13, the Default Value property of the City field is set to Boston.

Changing the Seed and Increment Value of AutoNumber Columns

When a table contains a field with an AutoNumber data type, you can set a seed value and an increment value. The seed value is the initial value for the column, and the increment value is the number added to the seed value to obtain a new counter value for the next record. If not specified, both seed and increment values default to 1. You can use the DDL to change the seed and increment values of AutoNumber columns by using one of the following three statements:

```
ALTER TABLE Table_name ALTER COLUMN Column_name AUTOINCREMENT (seed, increment)

ALTER TABLE Table_name ALTER COLUMN Column_name COUNTER (seed, increment)

ALTER TABLE Table_name ALTER COLUMN Column_name IDENTITY (seed, increment)
```

The example procedure in Hands-On 19-15 modifies the seed value of the existing AutoNumber column in the SchoolID column to start at 1000. Because we changed the SchoolID column's data type to the Text data type in one of the earlier hands-on exercises, you will modify the SchoolID column in the Sites.mdb file you created in Hands-On 19-3 at the beginning of this chapter.

⊚ Hands-On 19-14: Changing the Start (Seed) Value of the AutoNumber Field

This hands-on exercise uses the Sites.mdb database file and tblSchools table created in Hands-On 19-3.

1. In the same module where you entered previous hands-on exercises, enter the **ChangeAutoNumber** procedure as shown below, or copy the procedure code from **C:\Acc07_HandsOn\Chap19.txt**.

```
Sub ChangeAutoNumber()
    Dim conn As ADODB.Connection
    Dim strDb As String
    Dim strConnect As String
    Dim strTable As String
    Dim strCol As String
    Dim intSeed As Integer

    On Error GoTo ErrorHandler

    strDb = CurrentProject.Path & "\" & "Sites.mdb"
    strConnect = "Provider=Microsoft.Jet.OLEDB.4.0;" & _
        "Data Source=" & strDb

    strTable = "tblSchools"
    strCol = "SchoolID"
    intSeed = 1000
```

```
        Set conn = New ADODB.Connection
        conn.Open strConnect
        conn.Execute "ALTER TABLE " & strTable & _
            " ALTER COLUMN " & strCol & _
            " COUNTER (" & intSeed & ");"
    ExitHere:
        conn.Close
        Set conn = Nothing
        Exit Sub
    ErrorHandler:
        If Err.Number = -2147467259 Then
            MsgBox "The database file cannot be located.", _
                    vbCritical, strDb
            Exit Sub
        Else
            MsgBox Err.Number & ":" & Err.Description
            Resume ExitHere
        End If
    End Sub
```

2. Position the insertion point anywhere within the code of the ChangeAuto-Number procedure and press **F5** or choose **Run | Run Sub/UserForm** to execute the procedure.

3. Launch Microsoft Office Access with the **Sites.mdb** database and open the **tblSchools** table.

4. Enter a couple of new records in this table. In the YearEstablished field, enter the date in the format mm/dd/yyyy. Note that the first new record is numbered 1000, the second 1001, the third 1002, and so on.

5. Close the Sites.mdb database file.

Chapter Summary

In this chapter, you learned various Data Definition Language (DDL) commands for creating a new Access database, as well as creating, modifying, and deleting tables. You also learned how to add, modify, and delete fields and indexes, how to change the seed and increment values for AutoNumber fields, and how to change a field's data type. You also practiced assigning default values to table fields.

In the next chapter, you will get to know several DDL commands used for establishing relationships between tables and controlling referential integrity.

Chapter 20

Enforcing Data Integrity and Relationships between Tables

When creating tables in a database, you often need to define rules regarding the values allowed in columns (fields). As mentioned in Chapter 19, constraints allow you to enforce integrity by creating rules for a table. The five types of constraints are listed below.

Table 20-1: Table constraints

Constraint Name	Usage
PRIMARY KEY	Identifies the column or set of columns whose values uniquely identify a row in a table.
FOREIGN KEY	Defines the relationship between tables and maintains data integrity when records are being added, changed, or deleted in a table.
UNIQUE	Ensures that no duplicate values are entered in a specific column or combination of columns that is not a table's primary key.
NOT NULL	Specifies that a column cannot contain a Null value. Primary key columns are automatically defined as NOT NULL.
	Note: A Null value is not the same as zero (0), blank, or a zero-length character string (""). A Null value indicates that no entry has been made. You can determine if a field contains a Null value by using the IsNull function.
CHECK	Enforces integrity by limiting the values that can be placed in a column.

When constraints are added, all existing data is verified for constraint violations.

Using CHECK Constraints

Tables and columns can contain multiple CHECK constraints. A *CHECK constraint* can validate a column value against a logical expression or another column in the same or another table. What you can't do with the CHECK constraint is to specify the custom validation message, as is possible to do in the Access user interface.

The procedure in Hands-On 20-1 uses a PRIMARY KEY constraint explicitly named PrimaryKey to identify the ID column as a primary key. The CHECK constraint used in this procedure ensures that only numbers within the specified range are entered in the YearsWorked table column. You can apply CHECK constraints to a single column or to multiple columns. When a table is deleted, CHECK constraints are also dropped.

⊚ Hands-On 20-1: Using a CHECK Constraint to Specify a Condition for All Values Entered for the Column

1. Start Microsoft Office Access 2007 and create a new Microsoft Office Access 2007 database named **Chap20.accdb** in your **C:\Acc07_ByExample** folder.

2. Switch to the Visual Basic Editor window and choose **Tools | References**. In the References dialog box, scroll down to locate the **Microsoft ActiveX 2.8 Data Objects Library**. Click the check box to the left of this library name to set a reference to it and click **OK** to exit the dialog box.

3. Choose **Insert | Module** to add a new module to the current VBA project.

4. In the module's Code window, type the **CheckColumnValue** procedure shown below, or copy the procedure code from **C:\Acc07_HandsOn\ Chap20.txt**.

```
Sub CheckColumnValue()
    ' you must set up a reference to
    ' the Microsoft ActiveX Data Objects Library
    ' in the References dialog box

    Dim conn As ADODB.Connection
    Dim strTable As String

    On Error GoTo ErrorHandler

    Set conn = CurrentProject.Connection
    strTable = "tblAwards"
    conn.Execute "CREATE TABLE " & strTable & _
        "(ID AUTOINCREMENT CONSTRAINT PrimaryKey PRIMARY KEY," & _
        "YearsWorked INT, CONSTRAINT FromTo " & _
        "CHECK (YearsWorked BETWEEN 1 AND 30));"

ExitHere:
    conn.Close
    Set conn = Nothing
    Exit Sub
ErrorHandler:
    MsgBox Err.Number & ":" & Err.Description
    Resume ExitHere
End Sub
```

5. Position the insertion point anywhere within the code of the Check-ColumnValue procedure and press **F5** or choose **Run | Run Sub/ UserForm** to execute the procedure.

Programming with the Jet Data Definition Language

The CheckColumnValue procedure creates the tblAwards table with the CHECK constraint.

6. Open the **tblAwards** table and enter a value that does not fall between 1 and 30 in the YearsWorked column. You should receive the message shown in Figure 20-1.

Figure 20-1: This message appears when you attempt to enter a value in the YearsWorked column that is not within the range of values specified by the FromTo constraint.

Hands-On 20-2 demonstrates how to create a CHECK constraint to ensure that the value of the Items column in the tblBookOrders table is less than the value of the MaxUnits column in the tblSupplies table for the specified ISBN number. This hands-on exercise also illustrates using the SQL Data Manipulation Language (DML) statements INSERT INTO, BEGIN TRANSACTION, COMMIT TRANSACTION, and ROLLBACK TRANSACTION.

◉ Hands-On 20-2: Creating a Table with a Validation Rule Referencing a Column in Another Table

1. In the same module where you entered the procedure in Hands-On 20-1, enter the **ValidateAgainstCol_InAnotherTbl** procedure as shown below, or copy the procedure code from **C:\Acc07_HandsOn\Chap20.txt**.

```
Sub ValidateAgainstCol_InAnotherTbl()
    Dim conn As ADODB.Connection
    Dim strTable1 As String
    Dim strTable2 As String
    Dim InTrans As Boolean

    On Error GoTo ErrorHandler

    Set conn = CurrentProject.Connection
    strTable1 = "tblSupplies"
    strTable2 = "tblBookOrders"

    conn.Execute "BEGIN TRANSACTION"
    InTrans = True
    conn.Execute "CREATE TABLE " & strTable1 & _
        "(ISBN CHAR CONSTRAINT " & _
        "PrimaryKey PRIMARY KEY, " & _
        "MaxUnits LONG);", adExecuteNoRecords

    conn.Execute "INSERT INTO " & strTable1 & _
        " (ISBN, MaxUnits) " & _
        " Values ('158-76609-09', 5);", _
```

```
        adExecuteNoRecords

    conn.Execute "INSERT INTO " & strTable1 & _
        " (ISBN, MaxUnits) " & _
        " Values ('167-23455-69', 7);", _
        adExecuteNoRecords

    conn.Execute "CREATE TABLE " & strTable2 & _
        "(OrderNo AUTOINCREMENT CONSTRAINT " & _
        "PrimaryKey PRIMARY KEY, " & _
        "ISBN CHAR, Items LONG, " & _
        "CONSTRAINT OnHandConstr CHECK " & _
        "(Items <(SELECT MaxUnits FROM " & strTable1 & _
        " WHERE ISBN = " & strTable2 & ".ISBN)));", _
        adExecuteNoRecords
    conn.Execute "COMMIT TRANSACTION"
    InTrans = False
    Application.RefreshDatabaseWindow
ExitHere:
    conn.Close
    Set conn = Nothing
    Exit Sub
ErrorHandler:
    If InTrans Then
        conn.Execute "ROLLBACK TRANSACTION"
        Resume ExitHere
    Else
        MsgBox Err.Number & ":" & Err.Description
        Exit Sub
    End If
End Sub
```

2. Position the insertion point anywhere within the code of the Validate-AgainstCol_InAnotherTbl procedure and press **F5** or choose **Run | Run Sub/UserForm** to execute the procedure.

The above procedure creates two tables. Because the Items column in the tblBookOrders table needs to be validated against the contents of the MaxUnits column in the tblSupplies table, we wrapped the process of creating these tables and entering data in the tblSupplies table into a transaction. To trap errors that could occur during the procedure execution, we declared a Boolean variable named InTrans to help us determine whether an error occurred during the transaction. Therefore, if the value of the InTrans variable is True, we will cancel the transaction. Notice that in Access SQL syntax we use the BEGIN TRANSACTION statement to start the transaction, the COMMIT TRANSACTION statement to save the results of the transaction, and the ROLLBACK TRANSACTION statement to cancel any changes. These transaction statements can only be used through the Jet OLE DB Provider and ADO. They will cause an error when used with the Access user interface or DAO (Data Access Objects).

   In this example procedure we used the adExecuteNoRecords option to specify that no rows should be returned. You can use this setting with the Connection or Command object's Execute method to improve performance when no rows are returned or when you don't plan to access the returned rows in your procedure code. If you omit this setting, your ADO code will still execute successfully, but the ADO will unnecessarily create a Recordset object as the return value for the Execute method. Using the adExecuteNoRecords setting is one of several techniques of optimizing data access using ADO.

3. Open the **tblBookOrders** table and enter the record shown at the top of Figure 20-2.

   When you try to save this record or move to the next data row, Access will display a message informing you that the value you are trying to enter is prohibited.

4. Enter the value of **4** in the Items column. This time Access approves of the entry and no error message is displayed.

5. Close the tblBookOrders table.

Figure 20-2: When you attempt to enter a value that does not meet the validation rule, Microsoft Office Access displays an error message.

6. Click **OK** to dismiss the message box and then press **Esc** to cancel the data entry.

7. Right-click the **tblBookOrders** tab and choose **Close** from the shortcut menu.

8. In the object Navigation pane on the left side of the database window, right-click the **tblBookOrders** table and choose **Delete**. Click **Yes** to confirm the deletion. Access will respond with the error message shown in Figure 20-3.

Figure 20-3: If you try to manually delete a table referenced by the CHECK constraint, Microsoft Office Access will display an error message.

Now, let's see how you can use the Access user interface to issue commands that delete tables and CHECK constraints.

◎ Hands-On 20-3: Deleting Tables and Constraints Using the Access User Interface

This hands-on exercise requires that you have created the tblBookOrders and tblAwards tables from Hands-On 20-1 and 20-2.

1. In the database window, choose **Create | Query Design**.
2. In the Show Table dialog box, click the **Close** button.
3. Choose **Design | Data Definition**.
4. In the Data Definition Query window, enter the statement shown in Figure 20-4.

```
Query1                                              ×
Drop table tblBookOrders;
```

Figure 20-4: To delete a table that contains a CHECK constraint, type the DROP TABLE statement in the Data Definition Query window and click Run.

5. To run the Data Definition Query, click the **Run** button in the Ribbon.

   Note that a table must be closed before it can be deleted. If you don't want to delete the table but need to remove the constraint from a table, use the following syntax:

   ```
   ALTER TABLE table_name DROP CONSTRAINT constraint_name
   ```

   To remove a constraint, you must know its name.

6. To delete the constraint from the tblAwards table, type the statement shown in Figure 20-5 in the Data Definition Query window.

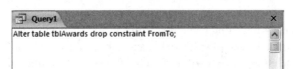

```
Query1                                              ×
Alter table tblAwards drop constraint FromTo;
```

Figure 20-5: To remove a table constraint, use the DROP CONSTRAINT statement with ALTER TABLE.

 Note: Before using ALTER TABLE, it is a good idea to make a backup copy of the table.

7. Click the **Run** button on the Ribbon to execute the statement to delete the constraint.
8. On your own, delete the tblSupplies table using the Data Definition Query window.

Establishing Relationships between Tables

To establish a link between the data in two tables, you add one or more columns that hold one table's primary key values to the other table. This column becomes a *foreign key* in the second table. In SQL DDL, you can use a FOREIGN KEY constraint to reference another table. Foreign keys can be single- or multi-column.

A *FOREIGN KEY constraint* enforces referential integrity by ensuring that changes made to data in the primary key table do not break the link to data in the foreign key table. For example, you cannot delete a record in a primary key table or change a primary key value if the deleted or changed primary key value corresponds to a value in the FOREIGN KEY constraint of another table. The REFERENCES clause identifies the parent table of the relation.

To create a brand-new table and relate it to an existing table, the following steps are required:

1. Use the CREATE TABLE statement followed by a table name.

   ```
   CREATE TABLE tblOrder_Details
   ```

2. Follow the table name with one or more column definitions. A *column definition* consists of ColumnName followed by the data type and column size (if required).

   ```
   InvoiceID CHAR, ProductId CHAR, Units LONG, Price MONEY
   ```

3. To designate a primary key, use the CONSTRAINT clause followed by the constraint name, the PRIMARY KEY clause, and the name of the column or columns to be designated as the primary key.

   ```
   CONSTRAINT PrimaryKey PRIMARY KEY (InvoiceId, ProductId)
   ```

4. To designate a foreign key, use the CONSTRAINT clause followed by the constraint name, the FOREIGN KEY clause, and the name of the column to be designated as the foreign key.

   ```
   CONSTRAINT fkInvoiceId FOREIGN KEY (InvoiceId)
   ```

5. Use the REFERENCES clause to specify the parent table to which a relationship is established.

   ```
   REFERENCES tblProduct_Orders
   ```

6. If required, specify ON UPDATE CASCADE and/or ON DELETE CASCADE to enable referential integrity rules with cascading updates or deletes.

   ```
   ON UPDATE CASCADE ON DELETE CASCADE
   ```

➥ **Note:** You may choose not to enforce referential integrity rules by specifying ON UPDATE NO ACTION or ON DELETE NO ACTION, or skipping the ON UPDATE or ON DELETE keywords. If you choose this path, you will not be able to change the value of a primary key if matching records exist in the foreign table.

Refer to the procedure in Hands-On 20-4 to find out how to correctly combine the above example statements into a single SQL statement.

◎ Hands-On 20-4: Relating Two Tables and Setting up Cascading Referential Integrity Rules

1. In the Visual Basic Editor window, choose **Insert | Module**.

2. In the module's Code window, enter the **RelateTables** procedure as shown below, or copy the procedure code from **C:\Acc07_HandsOn\Chap20.txt**.

```
Sub RelateTables()
    Dim conn As ADODB.Connection
    Dim strPrimaryTbl As String
    Dim strForeignTbl As String

    On Error GoTo ErrorHandler

    Set conn = CurrentProject.Connection
    strPrimaryTbl = "tblProduct_Orders"
    strForeignTbl = "tblOrder_Details"

    conn.Execute "CREATE TABLE " & strPrimaryTbl & _
        "(InvoiceID CHAR(15), PaymentType CHAR(20), " & _
        " PaymentTerms CHAR(25), Discount LONG, " & _
        " CONSTRAINT PrimaryKey PRIMARY KEY (InvoiceID));", _
        adExecuteNoRecords

    conn.Execute "CREATE TABLE " & strForeignTbl & _
        "(InvoiceID CHAR(15), ProductID CHAR(15), " & _
        " Units LONG, Price MONEY, " & _
        "CONSTRAINT PrimaryKey PRIMARY KEY (InvoiceID, ProductID), " & _
        "CONSTRAINT fkInvoiceID FOREIGN KEY (InvoiceID) " & _
        "REFERENCES " & strPrimaryTbl & _
        " ON UPDATE CASCADE ON DELETE CASCADE);", _
        adExecuteNoRecords

    Application.RefreshDatabaseWindow
ExitHere:
    conn.Close
    Set conn = Nothing
    Exit Sub
ErrorHandler:
    MsgBox Err.Number & ":" & Err.Description
    Resume ExitHere
End Sub
```

3. Position the insertion point anywhere within the code of the RelateTables procedure and press **F5** or choose **Run | Run Sub/UserForm** to execute the procedure.

The RelateTables procedure creates and joins two tables. A primary key table named tblProduct _Orders is created with a primary key on the InvoiceID field. The foreign key table named tblOrder_Details is created with a multi-field primary key index based on the ProductID and InvoiceID fields. The

REFERENCES clause specifies the tblProduct_Orders table as the parent table. The created relationship has the referential integrity rules enforced via the ON UPDATE CASCADE and ON DELETE CASCADE statements.

The outcome of the RelateTables procedure is illustrated in the following figures. Figure 20-6 displays the one-to-many relationship between tblProduct_Orders and tblOrder_Details. Figure 20-7 presents the Edit Relationships window in which both cascading updates and deletes are selected.

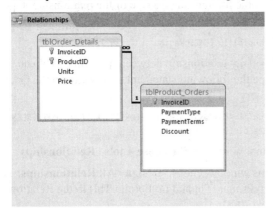

Figure 20-6: To access the Relationships window, choose Database Tools | Relationships.

Figure 20-7: To access the Edit Relationships window, choose Design | Edit Relationship.

Using the Data Definition Query Window

To enhance your understanding about creating tables and relationships with the Data Definition Language, perform Hands-On 20-5 using the Data Definition Query window.

◎ Hands-On 20-5: Running Data Definition Statements in the Microsoft Access User Interface

Each of the statements in this hands-on exercise can be executed by choosing Design | Run.

1. In the database window, choose **Create** | **Query Design**.

2. In the Show Table dialog box, click the **Close** button.

3. Choose **Design** | **Data Definition**.

4. In the Data Definition Query window that appears, enter the statement shown in Figure 20-4 and run the query.

5. To create a table on the primary (one) side of the relationship, type the following statement on one line in the Query window and run the query:

```
CREATE TABLE myPrimaryTbl(ID COUNTER CONSTRAINT pKey PRIMARY KEY, COUNTRY
    TEXT(15));
```

6. To create a table on the foreign (many) side of the relationship, type the following statement and run the query:

```
CREATE TABLE myForeignTbl(ID LONG, Region TEXT (15));
```

7. To create a one-to-many relationship between myPrimaryTbl and myForeignTbl, type the following statement on one line in the Query window and run the query:

```
ALTER TABLE myForeignTbl ADD CONSTRAINT Rel FOREIGN KEY(ID) REFERENCES
    myPrimaryTbl (ID);
```

8. In the database window, choose **Database Tools | Relationships**.

9. In the Relationships window, choose **Design | All Relationships**. This will add both tables (myPrimaryTbl and myForeignTbl) to the Relationships window (see Figure 20-8).

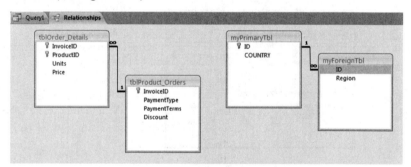

Figure 20-8: Notice that the tables you created by running the DDL statements in steps 5 and 6 above are joined on the ID column (see step 7).

10. Double-click the joining line between the two tables (myPrimaryTbl and myForeignTbl) and choose **Edit Relationship**.

Programming with the Jet Data Definition Language

Figure 20-9: You can edit relationships between tables via the Edit Relationships window.

11. To delete the relationship between the tables, type the following statement and run the query:

```
ALTER TABLE myForeignTbl DROP CONSTRAINT Rel;
```

12. To delete the table on the one side (myPrimaryTbl), type the following statement and run the query:

```
DROP TABLE myPrimaryTbl;
```

13. To delete the table on the many side (myForeignTbl), type the following statement and run the query:

```
DROP TABLE myForeignTbl;
```

Chapter Summary

In this chapter, you learned how to enforce data integrity by creating rules for tables with constraints. You learned how to validate data against another column in the same table or a column located in another table. You also learned how to use the Access Data Definition Query window to delete tables that have constraints and remove constraints from a table. Finally, you saw how you can establish relationships between tables using the DDL commands inside your VBA procedures. In addition, one of the procedures in this chapter introduced you to a couple of advanced Data Manipulation Language (DML) statements used for inserting data into tables and executing transactions.

The next chapter focuses on ways to use DDL for defining and removing indexes and primary keys.

Chapter 21

Defining Indexes and Primary Keys

Indexes speed the processes of finding and sorting records. You should create indexes for fields that are frequently used in searches and in sorting. You can create an index on a new or existing table. An index can be made of one or more fields. This chapter presents a number of procedures that use Data Definition Language statements to define indexes and primary keys.

Creating Tables with Indexes

You can create an index while creating a table by using the CONSTRAINT clause with the CREATE TABLE statement. The procedure in Hands-On 21-1 creates a new table called Supplier1 with a unique index called idxSupplier-Name based on the SupplierName field.

◎ Hands-On 21-1: Creating a Table with a Single-Field Index

1. Start Microsoft Office Access 2007 and create a new Microsoft Office Access 2007 database named **Chap21.accdb** in your **C:\Acc07_ByExample** folder.

2. Switch to the Visual Basic Editor window and choose **Tools | References**. In the References dialog box, scroll down to locate the **Microsoft ActiveX 2.8 Data Objects Library**. Click the check box to the left of this library name to set a reference to it and click **OK** to exit the dialog box.

3. Choose **Insert | Module** to add a new module to the current VBA project.

4. In the module's Code window, type the **SingleField_Index** procedure shown below, or copy the procedure code from **C:\Acc07_HandsOn\ Chap21.txt**.

```
Sub SingleField_Index()
    Dim conn As ADODB.Connection
    Dim strTable As String

    On Error GoTo ErrorHandler

    Set conn = CurrentProject.Connection
```

```
strTable = "Supplier1"

conn.Execute "CREATE TABLE " & strTable _
    & "(SupplierID INTEGER, " _
    & "SupplierName CHAR (30), " _
    & "SupplierPhone CHAR (12), " _
    & "SupplierCity CHAR (19), " _
    & "CONSTRAINT idxSupplierName UNIQUE " _
    & "(SupplierName));"
Application.RefreshDatabaseWindow
ExitHere:
    conn.Close
    Set conn = Nothing
    Exit Sub
ErrorHandler:
    MsgBox Err.Number & ":" & Err.Description
    Resume ExitHere
End Sub
```

5. Position the insertion point anywhere within the code of the SingleField_ Index procedure and press **F5** or choose **Run | Run Sub/UserForm** to execute the procedure.

When you run this procedure and then switch to the Access database window, you will notice a table named Supplier1. This table contains four fields. There is a unique index on the SupplierName field as shown in Figure 21-1.

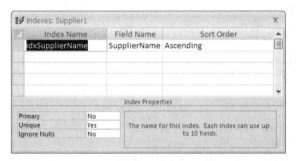

Figure 21-1: The idxSupplierName index was created by running the procedure in Hands-On 21-1.

Adding an Index to an Existing Table

To add an index to an existing table, use the CREATE INDEX statement. You can add an index based on one or more fields. The procedure in Hands-On 21-2 demonstrates how to add an index to the Supplier1 table that you created in Hands-On 21-1.

⊚ Hands-On 21-2: Adding a Single-Field Index to an Existing Table

1. In the same module where you entered the procedure in Hands-On 21-1, enter the **SingleField_Index2** procedure as shown below, or copy the procedure code from **C:\Acc07_HandsOn\Chap21.txt**.

```
Sub SingleField_Index2()
    Dim conn As ADODB.Connection
    Dim strTable As String

    On Error GoTo ErrorHandler

    Set conn = CurrentProject.Connection
        strTable = "Supplier1"

    conn.Execute "CREATE INDEX idxCity ON " & strTable & _
        "(SupplierCity) ;"
ExitHere:
    conn.Close
    Set conn = Nothing
    Exit Sub
ErrorHandler:
    MsgBox Err.Number & ":" & Err.Description
    Resume ExitHere
End Sub
```

2. Position the insertion point anywhere within the code of the SingleField_ Index2 procedure and press **F5** or choose **Run | Run Sub/UserForm** to execute the procedure.

The above procedure adds a single-field index named idxCity to the Supplier1 table. The following procedure will add a multiple-field index named idxSupplierNameCity to the Supplier2 table.

```
Sub MultiField_Index()
    Dim conn As ADODB.Connection
    Dim strTable As String

    On Error GoTo ErrorHandler
    Set conn = CurrentProject.Connection

    strTable = "Supplier2"

    conn.Execute "CREATE TABLE " & strTable _
        & "(SupplierID INTEGER, " _
        & "SupplierName CHAR (30), " _
        & "SupplierPhone CHAR (12), " _
        & "SupplierCity CHAR (19), " _
        & "CONSTRAINT idxSupplierNameCity UNIQUE " _
        & "(SupplierName, SupplierCity));"

    Application.RefreshDatabaseWindow
ExitHere:
    conn.Close
    Set conn = Nothing
    Exit Sub
ErrorHandler:
    MsgBox Err.Number & ":" & Err.Description
    Resume ExitHere
End Sub
```

Creating a Table with a Primary Key

When you create a database table you should define a primary key to uniquely identify rows within the table. A *primary key* allows you to relate a particular table with other tables in the database (for procedure examples, refer to the previous chapter). A table can have only one primary key; however, a primary key can consist of more than one column.

To create a table with a primary key, use the CONSTRAINT clause with the CREATE TABLE statement. The procedure in Hands-On 21-3 uses the following CONSTRAINT clause to create a single-field primary key based on the SupplierID field:

```
CONSTRAINT idxPrimary PRIMARY KEY(SupplierID)
```

To create a table with a primary key based on two or more columns, specify column names in parentheses following the PRIMARY KEY keywords. For example, the following CONSTRAINT clause will create a primary key based on the SupplierID and SupplierName columns:

```
CONSTRAINT idxPrimary PRIMARY KEY (SupplierID, SupplierName)
```

Hands-On 21-3: Creating a Single-Field Primary Key

1. Switch to the Visual Basic Editor window and insert a new module.

2. In the module's Code window, enter the **SingleField_PKey** procedure as shown below, or copy the procedure code from **C:\Acc07_HandsOn\ Chap21.txt**.

```
Sub SingleField_PKey()
    Dim conn As ADODB.Connection
    Dim strTable As String

    On Error GoTo ErrorHandler

    Set conn = CurrentProject.Connection
    strTable = "Supplier3"

    conn.Execute "CREATE TABLE " & strTable _
        & "(SupplierID INTEGER, " _
        & "SupplierName CHAR (30), " _
        & "SupplierPhone CHAR (12), " _
        & "SupplierCity CHAR (19), " _
        & "CONSTRAINT idxPrimary PRIMARY KEY " _
        & "(SupplierID));"
    Application.RefreshDatabaseWindow
ExitHere:
        conn.Close
        Set conn = Nothing
        Exit Sub
ErrorHandler:
        MsgBox Err.Number & ":" & Err.Description
        Resume ExitHere
End Sub
```

3. Position the insertion point anywhere within the code of the SingleField_
PKey procedure and press **F5** or choose **Run | Run Sub/UserForm** to exe-
cute the procedure.

Figure 21-2: The result
of running the
SingleField_PKey pro-
cedure in Hands-On
21-3 is a primary key
index named
idxPrimary based on
the SupplierID column.

Creating Indexes with Restrictions

You can use the CREATE INDEX statement to add an index to an existing
table. The CREATE INDEX statement can be used with the following options:

- PRIMARY option — Creates a primary key index that does not allow
  duplicate values in the key.

- DISALLOW NULL option — Creates an index that does not allow adding
  records with Null values in the indexed field.

- IGNORE NULL option — Creates an index that does not include records
  with Null values in the key.

Use the WITH keyword to declare the above index options.

The procedure in Hands-On 21-4 designates the SupplierID field as the primary key by using the PRIMARY option.

◎ Hands-On 21-4: Creating a Primary Key Index with Restrictions

1. Switch to the Visual Basic Editor window and insert a new module.

2. In the module's Code window, enter the **Index_WithPrimaryOption**
   procedure as shown below, or copy the procedure code from **C:\Acc07_
   HandsOn\Chap21.txt**.

```
Sub Index_WithPrimaryOption()
    Dim conn As ADODB.Connection
    Dim strTable As String

    On Error GoTo ErrorHandler

    Set conn = CurrentProject.Connection
    strTable = "Supplier1"

    conn.Execute "CREATE INDEX idxPrimary1 ON " & strTable _
        & "(SupplierID) WITH PRIMARY ;"
ExitHere:
    conn.Close
```

```
Set conn = Nothing
Exit Sub
ErrorHandler:
MsgBox Err.Number & ":" & Err.Description
Resume ExitHere
End Sub
```

3. Position the insertion point anywhere within the code of the Index_With-PrimaryOption procedure and press **F5** or choose **Run | Run Sub/ UserForm** to execute the procedure.

Figure 21-3: The index created by the procedure in Hands-On 21-4 has the Primary and Unique properties set to Yes, which means that this index is a primary key and every value in this index must be unique.

Note: Primary key indexes are automatically created as unique indexes.

You can prohibit the entry of Null values in the indexed fields by using the DISALLOW NULL option as shown in the example procedure in Hands-On 21-5.

Hands-On 21-5: Creating an Index that Disallows Null Values in the Key

1. Switch to the Visual Basic Editor window and insert a new module.

2. In the module's Code window, enter the **Index_WithDisallowNullOption** procedure as shown below, or copy the procedure code from **C:\Acc07_ HandsOn\Chap21.txt**.

```
Sub Index_WithDisallowNullOption()
Dim conn As ADODB.Connection
Dim strTable As String

On Error GoTo ErrorHandler
Set conn = CurrentProject.Connection

strTable = "Supplier3"
conn.Execute "CREATE INDEX idxSupplierCity ON " & strTable _
& "(SupplierCity) WITH DISALLOW NULL ;"
ExitHere:
conn.Close
Set conn = Nothing
Exit Sub
ErrorHandler:
```

```
    MsgBox Err.Number & ":" & Err.Description
    Resume ExitHere
End Sub
```

3. Position the insertion point anywhere within the code of the Index_With-DisallowNullOption procedure and press **F5** or choose **Run | Run Sub/UserForm** to execute the procedure.

Figure 21-4: The result of running the procedure in Hands-On 21-5 is an index called idxSupplierCity that does not allow Null values.

You can prevent records with Null values in the indexed fields from being included in the index by using the IGNORE NULL option, as illustrated in Hands-On 21-6.

⊚ Hands-On 21-6: Creating an Index with the Ignore Null Option

1. Switch to the Visual Basic Editor window and insert a new module.

2. In the module's Code window, enter the **Index_WithIgnoreNullOption** procedure as shown below, or copy the procedure code from **C:\Acc07_HandsOn\Chap21.txt**.

```
Sub Index_WithIgnoreNullOption()
    Dim conn As ADODB.Connection
    Dim strTable As String

    On Error GoTo ErrorHandler

    Set conn = CurrentProject.Connection

    strTable = "Supplier3"

    conn.Execute "CREATE INDEX idxSupplierPhone ON " & strTable _
        & "(SupplierPhone) WITH IGNORE NULL ;"
ExitHere:
    conn.Close
    Set conn = Nothing
    Exit Sub
ErrorHandler:
    MsgBox Err.Number & ":" & Err.Description
    Resume ExitHere
End Sub
```

3. Position the insertion point anywhere within the code of the Index_With-IgnoreNullOption procedure and press **F5** or choose **Run | Run Sub/UserForm** to execute the procedure.

Figure 21-5: The result of running the procedure in Hands-On 21-6 is an index called idxSupplierPhone that allows Null values in the key. However, records containing Null values will be excluded from any searches that use that index.

Deleting Indexes

Use the DROP INDEX statement to remove an index. Anytime you want to delete a column that is part of an index, you must first remove the index using the DROP CONSTRAINT or DROP INDEX statement. Before removing the index, make sure that the table containing the index is closed. The procedure in Hands-On 21-7 deletes the index named idxSupplierName from the Supplier1 table.

⊚ Hands-On 21-7: Deleting an Index

1. Switch to the Visual Basic Editor window and insert a new module.
2. In the module's Code window, enter the **DeleteIndex** procedure as shown below, or copy the procedure code from **C:\Acc07_HandsOn\Chap21.txt**.

```
Sub DeleteIndex()
    Dim conn As ADODB.Connection
    Dim strTable As String

    On Error GoTo ErrorHandler

    Set conn = CurrentProject.Connection
    strTable = "Supplier1"

    conn.Execute "DROP INDEX idxSupplierName ON " & strTable & ";"
ExitHere:
    conn.Close
    Set conn = Nothing
    Exit Sub
ErrorHandler:
    MsgBox Err.Number & ":" & Err.Description
    Resume ExitHere
End Sub
```

3. Position the insertion point anywhere within the code of the DeleteIndex procedure and press **F5** or choose **Run | Run Sub/UserForm** to execute the procedure.

4. On your own, write a procedure to remove other indexes created in this chapter's procedures.

Chapter Summary

This chapter introduced you to using DDL statements for creating indexes. Columns that are frequently used in database queries should be indexed to allow for faster access to the information. However, if you frequently add, delete, and update rows, you might want to limit the number of indexes, as they take up disk space and slow data operations. You also learned that a primary key is a special type of index that allows you to uniquely identify rows in a table as well as create a relationship between two tables, as demonstrated in the previous chapter.

The next chapter introduces you to the DDL statements that are used to manage database security.

Chapter 22

Database Security

The procedures in this chapter demonstrate how to use simple Data Definition Language statements to easily manage database and user passwords, create or delete user and group accounts, and grant or delete permissions for database objects.

Setting the Database Password

Database security can be handled at share level or user level. Share-level security is the easiest to implement, as it only requires that you set a password on the database. As mentioned earlier in this book, user-level security can only be used with Access databases created in the MDB file format.

To set a new database password or change an existing password, use the ALTER DATABASE PASSWORD statement in the following format:

```
ALTER DATABASE PASSWORD newPassword oldPassword
```

When setting the password for the first time, use Null for the old password (see the example procedure in Hands-On 22-1). The Access database must be opened in exclusive mode to perform password operations. Therefore, when using ADO, set the ADO Connection object's Mode property to adModeShareExclusive before opening a database.

⊚ Hands-On 22-1: Setting a Database Password

This hands-on exercise sets a database password on the Chap21.accdb database file.

1. Start Microsoft Office Access 2007 and create a new Microsoft Office Access 2007 database named **Chap22.accdb** in your **C:\Acc07_ByExample** folder.

2. Switch to the Visual Basic Editor window and choose **Tools | References**. In the References dialog box, scroll down to locate the **Microsoft ActiveX 2.8 Data Objects Library**. Click the check box to the left of this library name to set a reference to it and click **OK** to exit the dialog box.

3. Choose **Insert | Module** to add a new module to the current VBA project.

4. In the module's Code window, type the **SetDBPassword** function shown below, or copy the procedure code from **C:\Acc07_HandsOn\Chap22.txt**.

```
Function SetDBPassword(strFullFilePath)
    Dim conn As ADODB.Connection
    On Error GoTo ErrorHandler
    Set conn = New ADODB.Connection
    With conn
        .Mode = adModeShareExclusive
        .Open "Provider = Microsoft.ACE.OLEDB.12.0;" & _
            "Data Source=" & strFullFilePath & ";"
        .Execute "ALTER DATABASE PASSWORD secret null  "
    End With
ExitHere:
    If Not conn Is Nothing Then
        If conn.State = adStateOpen Then conn.Close
    End If
    Set conn = Nothing
    Exit Function
ErrorHandler:
    MsgBox Err.Number & ":" & Err.Description
    Resume ExitHere
End Function
```

5. Execute the SetDBPassword function from the Immediate window by typing the following statement and pressing **Enter**:

```
SetDBPassword "C:\Acc07_ByExample\Chap21.accdb"
```

While you may supply the name of a different Access database to the SetDBPassword function, the database must be in the new ACCDB file format because the function opens a connection to the database file using the ACE OLE DB Provider.

After opening a database in exclusive mode, the above function procedure changes the database password from Null to "secret." Notice that the new password is listed first, followed by the old password. Notice also how the above function uses the State property of the ADO Connection object to determine whether the connection to the database is open. State returns adStateOpen if the Connection object is open and adStateClosed if it is not.

Removing the Database Password

To remove a database password, replace the existing password with Null. The password can be removed by using the ALTER DATABASE PASSWORD statement, as illustrated in the preceding section. When the database is secured with a password, you will need to use the Jet/ACE OLEDB:Database Password property to specify the password to open the database. This is a Microsoft Jet 4.0/ACE OLE DB provider-specific property of the Connection object. The following procedure shows how to remove the password "secret" from the Chap21.accdb database that was set by the SetDBPassword function in Hands-On 22-1.

Programming with the Jet Data Definition Language

◎ Hands-On 22-2: Deleting a Database Password

This procedure requires prior completion of Hands-On 22-1.

1. In the same module where you entered the SetDBPassword function (Hands-On 22-1), enter the **ResetDBPassword** function as shown below, or copy the procedure code from **C:\Acc07_HandsOn\Chap22.txt.**

```
Function ResetDBPassword(strFullFilePath, _
                    strNewPwd, strOldPwd)
    Dim conn As ADODB.Connection
    On Error GoTo ErrorHandler
    Set conn = New ADODB.Connection

    With conn
        .Mode = adModeShareExclusive
        .Open "Provider = Microsoft.ACE.OLEDB.12.0;" & _
            "Data Source=" & strFullFilePath & _
            "; Jet OLEDB:Database Password=" & strOldPwd & ";"
        .Execute "ALTER DATABASE PASSWORD " & strNewPwd & " " & _
            strOldPwd
    End With
ExitHere:
    If Not conn Is Nothing Then
        If conn.State = adStateOpen Then conn.Close
    End If
    Set conn = Nothing
    Exit Function
ErrorHandler:
    MsgBox Err.Number & ":" & Err.Description
    Resume ExitHere
End Function
```

2. Execute the ResetDBPassword function from the Immediate window by typing the following statement and pressing **Enter**:

```
ResetDBPassword "C:\Acc07_ByExample\Chap21.accdb", "null", "secret"
```

3. Close the Chap22.accdb database file.

Creating a User Account

Establishing database security at a user level is more involved than setting a database password. It requires that you create group and user accounts and assign permissions to groups and users to perform operations on various database objects. Use the CREATE USER statement to create a new user account. Specify the user name to log in to the account followed by the required password and a personal identifier (PID) to make the account unique. The syntax of creating a user account looks like this:

```
CREATE USER userLoginName password PID
```

You can create more than one user account at a time by separating the user names with a comma.

The procedure in Hands-On 22-3 sets up a new user account for GeorgeM with "fisherman" as the login password and "0302" as the PID. While this example procedure uses a simple PID number, in the production environment, the PID number you choose should be from 4 to 20 characters long (preferably a combination of numbers and uppercase and lowercase characters that are difficult for someone to guess).

◎ Hands-On 22-3: Creating a User Account

1. Create a new Microsoft Office Access 2007 database named **Chap22.mdb** in your **C:\Acc07_ByExample** folder. Use the .mdb extension in the filename to ensure that Access creates a database using the 2002-2003 file format.

2. Switch to the Visual Basic Editor window and choose **Tools | References**. In the References dialog box, scroll down to locate the **Microsoft ActiveX 2.8 Data Objects Library**. Click the check box to the left of this library name to set a reference to it and click **OK** to exit the dialog box.

3. Choose **Insert | Module** to add a new module to the current VBA project.

4. In the module's Code window, enter the **CreateUserAccount** procedure as shown below, or copy the procedure code from **C:\Acc07_HandsOn\ Chap22.txt**.

```
Sub CreateUserAccount()
    Dim conn As ADODB.Connection

    On Error GoTo ErrorHandler

    Set conn = CurrentProject.Connection

    conn.Execute "CREATE USER GeorgeM fisherman 0302"
ExitHere:
    If Not conn Is Nothing Then
        If conn.State = adStateOpen Then conn.Close
    End If
    Set conn = Nothing
    Exit Sub
ErrorHandler:
    MsgBox Err.Number & ":" & Err.Description
    Resume ExitHere
End Sub
```

5. Run the CreateUserAccount procedure.

6. Press **Alt+F11** to switch to the Microsoft Access application window. Choose **Database Tools | Users and Permissions | User and Group Accounts**.

After running the CreateUserAccount procedure in Hands-On 22-3, you will see a listing for the GeorgeM user account in the User and Group Accounts window.

Figure 22-1: The User and Group Accounts window.

7. Click **Cancel** to close the User and Group Accounts window.

Changing a User Password

A user account password can be changed by using the ALTER USER statement in the following form:

```
ALTER USER userAccountName PASSWORD newPassword oldPassword
```

The procedure in Hands-On 22-4 changes the GeorgeM account's user password from "fisherman" to "primate."

◉ Hands-On 22-4: Changing a User Password

This hands-on exercise requires prior completion of Hands-On 22-3.

1. In the same module where you entered the CreateUserAccount procedure in Hands-On 22-3, enter the **ChangeUserPassword** procedure as shown below, or copy the procedure code from **C:\Acc07_HandsOn\Chap22.txt**.

```
Sub ChangeUserPassword()
    Dim conn As ADODB.Connection

    On Error GoTo ErrorHandler

    Set conn = CurrentProject.Connection

    conn.Execute "ALTER USER GeorgeM PASSWORD primate fisherman"
ExitHere:
    If Not conn Is Nothing Then
        If conn.State = adStateOpen Then conn.Close
    End If
    Set conn = Nothing
    Exit Sub
ErrorHandler:
    MsgBox Err.Number & ":" & Err.Description
    Resume ExitHere
End Sub
```

2. Run the ChangeUserPassword procedure.

Creating a Group Account

Use the CREATE GROUP statement to create a new group account. You must specify the group name followed by a unique PID (personal identifier):

```
CREATE GROUP groupName PID
```

You can create more than one group at a time by separating the group names with a comma. The procedure in Hands-On 22-5 creates a new group account called Mozart with "2007Best" as the PID.

◎ Hands-On 22-5: Creating a Group Account

1. In the same module where you entered the ChangeUserPassword procedure in Hands-On 22-4, enter the **CreateGroupAccount** procedure as shown below, or copy the procedure code from **C:\Acc07_HandsOn\Chap22.txt**.

```
Sub CreateGroupAccount()
    Dim conn As ADODB.Connection

    On Error GoTo ErrorHandler

    Set conn = CurrentProject.Connection

    conn.Execute "CREATE GROUP Mozart 2007Best"
ExitHere:
    If Not conn Is Nothing Then
        If conn.State = adStateOpen Then conn.Close
    End If
    Set conn = Nothing
    Exit Sub
ErrorHandler:
    MsgBox Err.Number & ":" & Err.Description
    Resume ExitHere
End Sub
```

2. Run the CreateGroupAccount procedure.

The Groups tab in the User and Group Accounts window (see Figure 22-1) will now list the name of the newly created Mozart user group.

Adding Users to Groups

Use the ADD USER statement to make a user account a member of a group. Specify the user account name followed by the TO keyword and a group name:

```
ADD USER userAccountName TO groupName
```

◎ Hands-On 22-6: Making a User Account a Member of a Group

This hands-on exercise requires prior completion of Hands-On 22-3 and 22-5.

1. In the same module where you entered the procedure in Hands-On 22-5, enter the **AddUserToGroup** procedure as shown below, or copy the procedure code from **C:\Acc07_HandsOn\Chap22.txt**.

```
Sub AddUserToGroup()
    Dim conn As ADODB.Connection

    On Error GoTo ErrorHandler

    Set conn = CurrentProject.Connection

    conn.Execute "ADD USER GeorgeM TO Mozart"
ExitHere:
    If Not conn Is Nothing Then
        If conn.State = adStateOpen Then conn.Close
    End If
    Set conn = Nothing
    Exit Sub
ErrorHandler:
    MsgBox Err.Number & ":" & Err.Description
    Resume ExitHere
End Sub
```

2. Run the AddUserToGroup procedure.

The user account GeorgeM is now a member of the Mozart group account. This can be easily verified by opening the User and Group Accounts window in the Access application window (see step 6 in Hands-On 22-3) and selecting GeorgeM from the Name drop-down.

Removing a User from a Group

To delete a user from a group, use the DROP USER statement followed by the username, the FROM keyword, and the group name. For example, to delete the GeorgeM account from the Mozart group, use the following statement:

```
DROP USER GeorgeM FROM Mozart
```

◉ Hands-On 22-7: Removing a User Account from a Group

This hands-on exercise requires prior completion of Hands-On 22-5 and 22-6.

1. In the same module where you entered the procedure in Hands-On 22-6, enter the **RemoveUserFromGroup** procedure as shown below, or copy the procedure code from **C:\Acc07_HandsOn\Chap22.txt**.

```
Sub RemoveUserFromGroup()
    Dim conn As ADODB.Connection

    On Error GoTo ErrorHandler

    Set conn = CurrentProject.Connection

    conn.Execute "DROP USER GeorgeM FROM Mozart"
```

```
ExitHere:
    If Not conn Is Nothing Then
        If conn.State = adStateOpen Then conn.Close
    End If
    Set conn = Nothing
    Exit Sub
ErrorHandler:
    MsgBox Err.Number & ":" & Err.Description
    Resume ExitHere
End Sub
```

2. Run the RemoveUserFromGroup procedure to remove the GeorgeM user account from the Mozart group.

Deleting a User Account

To delete a user account, use the DROP USER statement followed by the user account name, as demonstrated by the DeleteUserAccount procedure in Hands-On 22-8.

Hands-On 22-8: Deleting a User Account

This procedure requires prior completion of Hands-On 22-3.

1. In the same module where you entered the procedures in the previous hands-on exercises, enter the **DeleteUserAccount** procedure as shown below, or copy the procedure code from **C:\Acc07_HandsOn\Chap22.txt**.

```
Sub DeleteUserAccount()
    Dim conn As ADODB.Connection

    On Error GoTo ErrorHandler

    Set conn = CurrentProject.Connection

    conn.Execute "DROP USER GeorgeM"
ExitHere:
    If Not conn Is Nothing Then
        If conn.State = adStateOpen Then conn.Close
    End If
    Set conn = Nothing
    Exit Sub
ErrorHandler:
    MsgBox Err.Number & ":" & Err.Description
    Resume ExitHere
End Sub
```

2. Run the DeleteUserAccount procedure to delete the user account named GeorgeM.

Granting Permissions for an Object

Use the GRANT statement to assign security permissions for an object in a database to an existing user or group account. The procedure in Hands-On 22-9 grants the SELECT, DELETE, INSERT, and UPDATE permissions on all tables to the Mozart group.

The GRANT statement requires the following:

- A list of privileges to be granted
- The keyword ON followed by the name of a table, a non-table object, or an object container (e.g., Tables, Forms, Reports, Modules, Scripts)
- The keyword TO followed by the user or group name

```
GRANT listOfPermissions ON tableName | objectName | containerName TO
accountName
```

Please note that in addition to tables, the Tables container contains queries, views, and procedures, and the Scripts container includes macros.

⊚ Hands-On 22-9: Granting Permissions for Tables to an Existing Group

This hands-on exercise requires prior completion of Hands-On 22-5.

1. In the same module where you entered the procedure in Hands-On 22-8, enter the **SetTblPermissions** procedure as shown below, or copy the procedure code from **C:\Acc07_HandsOn\Chap22.txt**.

```
Sub SetTblPermissions()
    Dim conn As ADODB.Connection

    On Error GoTo ErrorHandler

    Set conn = CurrentProject.Connection

    conn.Execute "GRANT SELECT, DELETE, INSERT, " _
        & "UPDATE ON CONTAINER TABLES TO Mozart"
ExitHere:
    If Not conn Is Nothing Then
        If conn.State = adStateOpen Then conn.Close
    End If
    Set conn = Nothing
    Exit Sub
ErrorHandler:
    MsgBox Err.Number & ":" & Err.Description
    Resume ExitHere
End Sub
```

2. Run the SetTblPermissions procedure.

After running the SetTblPermissions procedure, you can open the User and Group Permissions window (choose Database Tools | Users and Permissions | User and Group Permissions) to check out the privileges granted to the members of the Mozart group.

Figure 22-2: Verifying the group permissions to database objects.

Revoking Security Permissions

Use the REVOKE statement to revoke security permissions for an object from an existing user or group account. This statement has the following form:

```
REVOKE listOfPermissions ON tableName | objectName | containerName FROM
accountName
```

The procedure in Hands-On 22-10 removes the privilege of deleting tables from the members of the Mozart group.

Hands-On 22-10: Revoking Security Permissions

This hands-on exercise requires prior completion of Hands-On 22-5 and 22-9.

1. In the same module where you entered the procedure in Hands-On 22-9, enter the **RevokePermission** procedure as shown below, or copy the procedure code from **C:\Acc07_HandsOn\Chap22.txt**.

```
Sub RevokePermission()
    Dim conn As ADODB.Connection

    On Error GoTo ErrorHandler

    Set conn = CurrentProject.Connection

    conn.Execute "REVOKE DELETE ON CONTAINER TABLES FROM Mozart"
ExitHere:
    If Not conn Is Nothing Then
        If conn.State = adStateOpen Then conn.Close
    End If
    Set conn = Nothing
    Exit Sub
ErrorHandler:
    MsgBox Err.Number & ":" & Err.Description
    Resume ExitHere
End Sub
```

2. Run the RevokePermission procedure.

Figure 22-3: After running the procedure in Hands-On 22-10, the Delete Data permission on new tables and queries for the members of the Mozart group is turned off.

Deleting a Group Account

Use the DROP GROUP statement to delete a group account. You only need to specify the name of the group account you want to delete. If you'd like to delete more than one account, separate each group name with a comma.

◎ Hands-On 22-11: Deleting a Group Account

This hands-on exercise requires prior completion of Hands-On 22-5.

1. In the same module where you entered the procedure in Hands-On 22-9, enter the **DeleteGroupAccount** procedure as shown below, or copy the procedure code from **C:\Acc07_HandsOn\Chap22.txt**.

```
Sub DeleteGroupAccount()
    Dim conn As ADODB.Connection

    On Error GoTo ErrorHandler

    Set conn = CurrentProject.Connection

    conn.Execute "DROP GROUP Mozart"
ExitHere:
    If Not conn Is Nothing Then
        If conn.State = adStateOpen Then conn.Close
    End If
    Set conn = Nothing
    Exit Sub
ErrorHandler:
    MsgBox Err.Number & ":" & Err.Description
    Resume ExitHere
End Sub
```

2. Run the DeleteGroupAccount procedure to delete the Mozart group account.

Chapter Summary

This chapter demonstrated the use of the Data Definition Language (DDL) statements in VBA procedures for managing security in a Microsoft Access database. You used the ALTER DATABASE statement to create, modify, and remove the database password. You managed the user-level accounts with the CREATE, ADD, ALTER, and DROP statements. You learned how to use the GRANT and REVOKE statements to establish and remove permissions on database objects for user and group accounts in an Access MDB database created in the 2002-2003 file format.

In the next chapter, you learn how to organize your data using structures known as views, and how to use stored procedures in lieu of Access Action and Parameter queries.

Chapter 23

Views and Stored Procedures

In this chapter, we will work with advanced Data Definition Language statements that are used for creating, altering, and deleting two special database objects known as views and stored procedures. These objects are used to perform various query operations. *Views* are like Access Select queries; however, you can't use the ORDER BY clause to sort your data or use parameters to filter records. *Stored procedures* perform the same operations as Access Action and Parameter queries. They can also be used for creating sorted Select queries. Stored procedures are saved precompiled so that at run time the procedure executes much faster than a standard SQL statement. Learning how to create and use views and stored procedures will give you more control over your database.

Creating a View

If you want users to view and update data in a table or set of tables, but you do not want them to open the underlying tables directly, you can create a view. An SQL *view* is like a virtual table. Similar to an Access Select query, a view can display data from one or more tables. Instead of providing all the available data in your tables, you decide exactly what fields you'd like to include for viewing.

To create a view, use a SELECT statement to select the columns you want to include in a view and the FROM keyword to specify the table. Next, associate the SELECT statement with a CREATE VIEW statement. The syntax looks like this:

```
CREATE VIEW viewName [(columnNames)]
AS
    SELECT (columnNames)
    FROM tableName;
```

Views must have unique names in the database. The name of the view cannot be the same as the name of an existing table. Specifying the names of columns following the name of the view is optional (note the square brackets in the syntax above). Column names must be specified in the SELECT statement. Use the asterisk (*) to select all columns.

Let's put more meaning into the above syntax. The example statement below creates a view that lists only orders with a Freight amount less than $20.

```
CREATE VIEW cheapFreight
AS
        SELECT Orders.OrderID,
               Orders.Freight,
               Orders.ShipCountry
        FROM Orders
        WHERE Orders.Freight < 20;
```

The SELECT statement that defines the view cannot contain any parameters and cannot be typed directly in the SQL pane of the Query window. It must be used through the ADO Connection object's Execute method after establishing the connection to a database, as illustrated below:

```
Sub Create_View_CheapFreight()
    Dim conn As ADODB.Connection
    Set conn = CurrentProject.Connection
    conn.Execute "CREATE VIEW CheapFreight AS " & _
        "SELECT Orders.[Order ID], Orders.[Shipping Fee], " & _
        "Orders.[Ship Country/Region] " & _
        "FROM Orders WHERE Orders.[Shipping Fee] < 20;"
    Application.RefreshDatabaseWindow
    conn.Close
    Set conn = Nothing
End Sub
```

The Application.RefreshDatabaseWindow statement ensures that after the view is created it is immediately listed in the Navigation pane in the Access application window. If you omit this statement, you will need to refresh the Navigation pane manually by selecting any object in it and pressing Shift+F5.

To return data from the CheapFreight view, simply double-click its name in the Navigation pane.

A view can be used as if it were a table. The following statement can be used to return all records from the CheapFreight view:

```
SELECT * FROM CheapFreight;
```

Remember that a view never stores any data; it simply returns the data as stated in the SELECT statement used in the view definition. Because a view is like a Select query, you can use the OpenQuery method of the Access DoCmd object to open it from your VBA code:

```
Sub OpenView()
    DoCmd.OpenQuery "CheapFreight", acViewNormal
End Sub
```

The OpenQuery method is used to carry out the OpenQuery action in Visual Basic.

To get working experience with the views, let's proceed to the hands-on section. We will start by creating a view called vw_Employees. This view is based on the Employees and Orders tables, and contains four columns (Employee ID, Full Name, Job Title, and Order ID).

◎ Hands-On 23-1: Creating a View Based on a Table

1. Start Microsoft Office Access 2007 and create a new Microsoft Office Access 2007 database named **Chap23.accdb** in your **C:\Acc07_ByExample** folder.

2. Choose **External Data | Access**.

3. In the File name box of the Get External Data dialog box, enter C:**Acc07_ByExample\Northwind 2007.accdb** and click **OK**.

4. In the Import Objects dialog box, select the **Employees** and **Orders** tables and click **OK**.

5. Click **Close** to exit the Get External Data dialog box.

   The Employees and Orders tables are now listed in the Navigation pane.

6. Switch to the Visual Basic Editor window and choose **Tools | References**. In the References dialog box, scroll down to locate the **Microsoft ActiveX 2.8 Data Objects Library**. Click the check box to the left of this library name to set a reference to it and click **OK** to exit the dialog box.

7. Choose **Insert | Module** to add a new module to the current VBA project.

8. In the module's Code window, type the **Create_View** procedure shown below, or copy the procedure code from **C:\Acc07_HandsOn\Chap23.txt**.

```
' Don't forget to set up a reference to the
' Microsoft ActiveX Data Objects Library
' in the References dialog box

Sub Create_View()
    Dim conn As ADODB.Connection

    Set conn = CurrentProject.Connection

    On Error GoTo ErrorHandler

    conn.Execute "CREATE VIEW vw_Employees AS " & _
        "SELECT Employees.ID AS [Employee ID], " & _
        "[First Name] & chr(32) & [Last Name] AS [Full Name], " & _
        "[Job Title], Orders.[Order ID] AS [Order ID] " & _
        "FROM Employees " & _
        "INNER JOIN Orders ON " & _
        "Orders.[Employee ID] = Employees.ID;"
    Application.RefreshDatabaseWindow
ExitHere:
    If Not conn Is Nothing Then
        If conn.State = adStateOpen Then conn.Close
    End If
    Set conn = Nothing
    Exit Sub
ErrorHandler:
    If Err.Number = -2147217900 Then
        conn.Execute "DROP VIEW vw_Employees"
        Resume
```

```
    Else
        MsgBox Err.Number & ":" & Err.Description
        Resume ExitHere
    End If
End Sub
```

9. Run the Create_View procedure.

The procedure above creates a view named vw_Employees. If the view already exists, it will be deleted using the DROP VIEW statement. The chr(32) statement will insert a space between the first and last name.

Notice that views don't differ much from saved queries. When you open the view created by the Create_View procedure in Design view, you will notice that this view is simply a Select query. Because the query defined by the SELECT statement is updatable, the vw_Employees view is also updatable. If the query was not updatable, the view would be read-only.

Views cannot contain the ORDER BY clause. To return the records in a specific order, you might want to use the view in a stored procedure, as discussed later in this chapter.

Enumerating Views

You can find out the names of the views by iterating through the Views collection of the ADOX Catalog object, as illustrated in Hands-On 23-2.

Hands-On 23-2: Generating a List of Saved Views

1. In the Visual Basic Editor window, choose **Tools | References**. In the References dialog box, scroll down to locate the **Microsoft ADO Ext. 2.8 for DDL and Security Object Library**. Click the check box to the left of this library name to set a reference to it and click **OK** to exit the dialog box.

2. Choose **Insert | Module** to add a new module to the current VBA project.

3. In the module's Code window, enter the **List_Views** procedure as shown below, or copy the procedure code from **C:\Acc07_HandsOn\Chap23.txt**.

```
' Don't forget to set up a reference to the
' Microsoft ADO Ext. 2.8 for DDL and Security

Sub List_Views()
    Dim cat As New ADOX.Catalog
    Dim myView As ADOX.View

    cat.ActiveConnection = CurrentProject.Connection

    For Each myView In cat.Views
        Debug.Print myView.Name
    Next myView
End Sub
```

4. Run the List_Views procedure.

The List_Views procedure illustrated above writes the names of the existing views to the Immediate window.

Deleting a View

Use the DROP VIEW statement to delete a particular view from the database. You must specify the name of the view you want to delete. The example procedure below deletes a view named vw_Employees created by the procedure in Hands-On 23-1.

Note that both the CREATE VIEW and DROP VIEW statements can only be executed using the Execute method of the ADO Connection object.

⊚ Hands-On 23-3: Deleting a View

1. In the same module where you entered the procedure in Hands-On 23-2, enter the **Delete_View** procedure as shown below, or copy the procedure code from **C:\Acc07_HandsOn\Chap23.txt**.

```
Sub Delete_View()
    Dim conn As ADODB.Connection

    Set conn = CurrentProject.Connection

    On Error GoTo ErrorHandler
    conn.Execute "DROP VIEW vw_Employees"
ExitHere:
    If Not conn Is Nothing Then
        If conn.State = adStateOpen Then conn.Close
    End If
    Set conn = Nothing
    Exit Sub
ErrorHandler:
    If Err.Number = -2147217865 Then
        MsgBox "The view was already deleted."
    Exit Sub
    Else
        MsgBox Err.Number & ":" & Err.Description
        Resume ExitHere
    End If
End Sub
```

2. Run the Delete_View procedure.

3. Run the List_Views procedure from Hands-On 23-2 to ensure that the vw_Employees view was deleted.

Creating a Stored Procedure

Stored procedures allow you to perform bulk operations that delete, update, or append records. Unlike views, stored procedures allow the ORDER BY clause and parameters. Use the CREATE PROCEDURE (or CREATE PROC) statement to create a stored procedure. You must specify the name of the stored procedure and the AS keyword followed by the desired SQL statement that performs the required database operation. The syntax is as follows:

```
CREATE PROC[EDURE] procName
[(param1 datatype1 [, param2 datatype2 [, ...] ])]
AS
sqlStatement;
```

The name of the stored procedure must be different from the name of an existing table. To pass values to a stored procedure, include parameters after the procedure name. Parameter names are followed by a data type and are separated by commas. The parameters are listed in parentheses (see Hands-On 23-4 in the next section). Up to 255 parameters can be specified in the parameter list. If the stored procedure does not require parameters, the AS keyword immediately follows the name of the stored procedure.

The SQL statement for the stored procedure can be prepared in the Access Query Design and then copied to the VBA procedure from the SQL view and appropriately formatted.

To return the employee records from the vw_Employees view (see Hands-On 23-1) ordered by Full Name, the following stored procedure can be written:

```
CREATE PROCEDURE usp_EmpByFullName
AS
SELECT * FROM vw_Employees
ORDER BY [Full Name];
```

The stored procedure above selects all columns that exist in the vw_Employees view and orders the returned data by the Full Name field. Notice that this procedure does not require any parameters. You might want to precede the stored procedure name with a prefix indicating the type of stored procedure. The "usp" prefix is often used to indicate a user-defined stored procedure.

Like views, stored procedures are created via the ADO Connection object's Execute method after establishing a connection to the database. Therefore, you can use the following VBA code to create the usp_EmpByFullName stored procedure:

```
Sub Create_StoredProc()
    Dim conn As ADODB.Connection

    Set conn = CurrentProject.Connection
    conn.Execute "CREATE PROCEDURE usp_EmpByFullName AS " & _
        "SELECT * FROM vw_Employees " & _
        "ORDER BY [Full Name];"
    Application.RefreshDatabaseWindow
    conn.Close
    Set conn = Nothing
End Sub
```

Once created, stored procedures can be executed in the Access user interface by double-clicking the stored procedure name in the Navigation pane, or from VBA code by calling the EXECUTE statement with the ADO Connection object's Execute method (see Hands-On 23-5).

Creating a Parameterized Stored Procedure

Most advanced stored procedures require one or more parameters. The parameters are then used as part of the SQL statement, usually the WHERE clause. When creating a parameterized stored procedure, Access allows you to specify up to 255 parameters in the parameters list. The stored procedure parameters must be separated by commas and enclosed in parentheses.

The procedure in Hands-On 23-4 creates a stored procedure that allows you to insert a new record into the Shippers table on the fly by supplying the required parameter values. Note that the SQL Data Manipulation Language (DML) INSERT INTO statement is used for adding new records to a table.

⊚ Hands-On 23-4: Creating a Stored Procedure that Accepts Parameters

1. Import the **Shippers** table from the **C:\Acc07_ByExample\Northwind 2007.accdb** database.

2. Switch to the Visual Basic Editor window and insert a new module.

3. In the module's Code window, enter the **Create_SpWithParam** procedure as shown below, or copy the procedure code from **C:\Acc07_HandsOn\ Chap23.txt**.

```
Sub Create_SpWithParam()
    Dim conn As ADODB.Connection

    On Error GoTo ErrorHandler

    Set conn = CurrentProject.Connection

    conn.Execute "CREATE PROCEDURE usp_procEnterData " & _
        "(@Company TEXT (50), " & _
        "@Tel TEXT (25)) AS " & _
        "INSERT INTO Shippers (Company, [Business Phone]) " & _
        "VALUES (@Company, @Tel);"
    Application.RefreshDatabaseWindow
ExitHere:
    If Not conn Is Nothing Then
        If conn.State = adStateOpen Then conn.Close
    End If
    Set conn = Nothing
    Exit Sub
ErrorHandler:
    If InStr(1, Err.Description, "procEnterData") Then
        conn.Execute "DROP PROC procEnterData"
        Resume
    Else
        MsgBox Err.Number & ":" & Err.Description
        Resume ExitHere
    End If
End Sub
```

4. Run the Create_SpWithParam procedure.

The stored procedure above will require two values to be entered at run time. The first value is passed by the @Company parameter and the second one by the parameter named @Tel. In this example, the names of the parameters have been preceded with the @ sign for easy migration of the stored procedure into the SQL Server environment. If you omit the @ sign, the procedure will still execute correctly in Microsoft Access. If the procedure already exists, it will be dropped using the DROP PROC statement.

Similar to views, stored procedures appear in the Navigation pane in the Access application window. Because we used the SQL INSERT INTO statement, Microsoft Office Access is treating this stored procedure as a parameterized Append query.

5. Run the stored procedure named **usp_procEnterData** by double-clicking its name in the Navigation pane of the Access application window. Figures 23-1 through 23-6 outline the process of running this stored procedure.

Figure 23-1: When you double-click a stored procedure name in the Navigation pane of the Access database window, Access displays this message when the stored procedure expects parameters and its SQL statement attempts to insert data into a table.

Figure 23-2: Since the stored procedure expects some input, you are being prompted for the first parameter value.

Figure 23-3: Here you are being prompted to enter the phone number for the second stored procedure parameter.

Figure 23-4: Once all input has been gathered via the parameters, Access informs you about the action that is to be performed. Click Yes to execute the stored procedure or No to cancel.

ID	▾	Company	▾	Last Name	▾	First Name	▾	E-mail Address	▾	Job Title	▾	Business Phone	▾	Hom
1		Shipping Company A												
2		Shipping Company B												
3		Shipping Company C												
4		Orient Express										800-234-0747		
* (New)														

Figure 23-5: Once you click Yes, Access runs the Append query. To view the result of this operation, double-click the Shippers table in the Navigation pane. Notice that a new record (Orient Express) was added to the Shippers table.

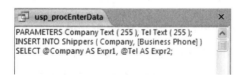

Figure 23-6: You can examine the contents of the stored procedure by right-clicking on the usp_procEnterData procedure in the Navigation pane and choosing Design View. This example displays the Design view of the Append query. Other stored procedures that you create may be presented as different Action queries.

```
usp_procEnterData                              ×

PARAMETERS Company Text ( 255 ), Tel Text ( 255 );
INSERT INTO Shippers ( Company, [Business Phone] )
SELECT @Company AS Expr1, @Tel AS Expr2;
```

Figure 23-7: You can examine the SQL statements used by Access to execute your stored procedure by switching to the SQL view (click Design | View and select SQL View).

Executing a Parameterized Stored Procedure

In the preceding section, you learned how to run a parameterized stored procedure from the Access user interface. To execute an existing stored procedure from VBA code, use the Execute method of the ADO Connection or Command object. Here's how:

■ With the Execute method of the Connection object:

```
conn.Execute "usp_procEnterData"
```

■ With the Execute method of the Command object:

```
cmd.CommandText = "usp_procEnterData"
cmd.CommandType = adCmdStoredProc
```

```
cmd.Execute
rst. Open cmd
```

If the stored procedure requires parameters, parameter values follow the procedure name as a comma-separated list. Here's an example procedure that
executes the usp_procEnterData stored procedure and contains the values for
its two parameters:

```
Sub RunProc_WithParam()
    Dim conn As ADODB.Connection

    Set conn = CurrentProject.Connection
    conn.Execute "usp_procEnterData ""My Company2"", ""(234) 334-3344"""
    conn.Close
    Set conn = Nothing
End Sub
```

Instead of surrounding parameters with sets of double quotes, you can use
single quotes like this:

```
conn.Execute "procEnterData 'My Company2', '(234) 334-3344'"
```

The procedure in Hands-On 23-5 runs the stored procedure named
usp_procEnterData created in Hands-On 23-4. Notice how this procedure uses
the InputBox function to obtain the parameter values from the user instead of
hard-coding them in the Execute method of the Connection object (as shown
above). Still another way of providing parameter values to a stored procedure
would be via an Access form. I will leave this idea for you to try on your own.

Hands-On 23-5: Executing a Parameterized Stored Procedure

1. Switch to the Visual Basic Editor window and insert a new module.
2. In the module's Code window, enter the **Execute_StoredProcWithParam**
   procedure as shown below, or copy the procedure code from **C:\Acc07_
   HandsOn\Chap23.txt**.

```
Sub Execute_StoredProcWithParam()
    Dim conn As ADODB.Connection
    Dim strCompany As String
    Dim strPhone As String

    On Error GoTo ErrorHandler

    Set conn = CurrentProject.Connection

    strCompany = InputBox("Please enter company name:", "Input Company")

    strPhone = InputBox("Please enter the phone number:", "Input Phone")

    If strCompany <> "" And strPhone <> "" Then
        conn.Execute "usp_procEnterData " & strCompany & ", " & strPhone
    End If
```

```
ExitHere:
    If Not conn Is Nothing Then
        If conn.State = adStateOpen Then conn.Close
    End If
    Set conn = Nothing
    Exit Sub
ErrorHandler:
    MsgBox Err.Number & ":" & Err.Description
    Resume ExitHere
End Sub
```

3. Run the Execute_StoredProcWithParam procedure.

When you run the parameterized stored procedure in Hands-On 23-5, Access displays an input box for each parameter. After you have supplied values for both required parameters, a new record is entered into the Shippers table.

Deleting a Stored Procedure

Use the DROP PROCEDURE (or DROP PROC) statement to delete a stored procedure. The syntax looks like this:

```
DROP PROCEDURE procedureName
```

The example procedure below deletes the stored procedure named usp_procEnterData from the current database.

◎ Hands-On 23-6: Deleting a Stored Procedure

1. Switch to the Visual Basic Editor window and insert a new module.

2. In the module's Code window, enter the **Delete_StoredProc** procedure as shown below, or copy the procedure code from **C:\Acc07_HandsOn\ Chap23.txt**.

```
Sub Delete_StoredProc()
    Dim conn As ADODB.Connection

    On Error GoTo ErrorHandler

    Set conn = CurrentProject.Connection

    conn.Execute "DROP PROCEDURE usp_procEnterData; "
ExitHere:
    If Not conn Is Nothing Then
        If conn.State = adStateOpen Then conn.Close
    End If
    Set conn = Nothing
    Exit Sub
ErrorHandler:
    If InStr(1, Err.Description, "cannot find") Then
        MsgBox "The procedure you want to delete " & _
            "does not exist.", _
            vbDefaultButton1 + vbInformation, "Request failed"
```

```
        Else
            MsgBox Err.Number & ":" & Err.Description
        End If
        Resume ExitHere
    End Sub
```

3. Run the Delete_StoredProc to remove the usp_procEnterData procedure from the database.

Changing Database Records with Stored Procedures

Stored procedures can perform various actions similar to what Access Action queries and Select queries with parameters can do. For example, here's how you would write a statement to create a stored procedure that, when executed, deletes a record from the Shippers table:

```
conn.Execute "CREATE PROCEDURE usp_DeleteRec " & _
             "(ID Integer) " & _
             "AS " & _
             "DELETE * FROM Shippers WHERE ID = ID;"
```

To update a phone number in a specified record in the Shippers table, you may want to create a stored procedure that performs the specified record update with the following statement:

```
conn.Execute "CREATE PROCEDURE usp_UpdatePhone " & _
             "(ID Integer, tel text (25)) " & _
             "AS " & _
             "UPDATE Shippers SET [Business Phone] = tel " & _
             "WHERE ID = ID;"
```

Chapter Summary

This chapter introduced you to two powerful database objects you can use in Access: views and stored procedures. You learned how views are used as virtual tables to make specific rows and columns from one or more tables available to your Access users. Remember that views are similar to SELECT statements, except they cannot contain the ORDER BY clause to sort the data and they do not allow parameters. Views can be used in queries to hide from users the complexity of joins between the tables. Converting your Access queries into views and stored procedures will help with migration of your Access applications to the SQL Server environment in the future.

This chapter concludes Part III of this book, which presented numerous examples of using SQL DDL statements inside VBA procedures. In particular, you learned how DDL statements are used to create tables, views, stored procedures, primary keys, indexes, and constraints that define the database. You also learned a couple of advanced Data Manipulation Language (DML) statements. Although there is more to Access SQL than this part has covered, the information presented in this section should be quite sufficient to get you started using SQL in your own Access database applications.

PART IV

Event Programming in Forms and Reports

The behavior of Microsoft Access objects such as forms, reports, and controls can be modified by writing programming code known as an event procedure or an event handler.

In this part of the book, you learn how you can make your forms, reports, and controls do useful things by writing event procedures in class modules.

Chapter 24

Using Form Events

In Chapter 1, you got a quick introduction to events, event properties, and event procedures. I walked you through an event procedure that changed the background color of a text box control placed on a form. Now is a good time to go back to the beginning of this book and review these topics. Here's a run-down of the terms you need to be familiar with:

- **Event** — Events are things that happen to an object. Events occur when you move a mouse, press a key, make changes to data, open a form, or add, modify, or delete a record, etc. An event can be triggered by the user or by the operating system.

- **Event property** — Forms, reports, and controls have various event properties you can use to trigger desired actions. When an event occurs, Microsoft Access runs a procedure assigned to an event property. Event properties are listed in the Event tab of the object's property sheet. The name of the event property begins with the word On followed by the event's name. Therefore, the On Click event property corresponds to the Click event, and the On Got Focus event property is used for responding to the GotFocus event.

- **Event procedure** — This is a programming code you write to specify how a form, report, or control should respond to a particular event. By writing event procedures you can modify the application's built-in response to an event.

- **Event trapping** — When you assign a program to an event property, you set an event trap. When you trap an event you interrupt the default processing that Access would normally carry out in response to the user's key press or mouse click.

- **Sequence of events** — Events occur in a predefined order. For example, the Click event occurs before the DoubleClick event. When you perform an action, several events occur, one after the other. For instance, the following form and control events occur when you open a form:

  Open - Load - Resize - Activate - Current - Enter (control) - GotFocus (control)

  Closing the form triggers the following control and form events:

  Exit (control) - LostFocus (control) - Unload - Deactivate - Close

To find out whether a particular event is triggered in response to a user action, you may want to place the MsgBox statement inside the event procedure for the event you want to test. Microsoft Access forms, reports, and controls recognize various events.

Events can be organized by object (form, report, control) or by cause (what caused the event to happen). This chapter is filled with numerous examples of event procedures you can write to make your forms and reports dynamic. You can also experiment with various events in the data entry/lookup application located in the downloadable AssetsDataEntry.mdb file. You will find several examples from this application discussed in Chapter 26.

Microsoft Access forms can respond to a variety of events. These events allow you to manage entire records and respond to changes in the data. You can determine what happens when records are added, changed, or deleted, or when a different record becomes current. You can decide how the form appears to the user when it is first displayed on the screen and what happens when the form is closed. You can also manage problems that occur when the data is unavailable. As you design your custom forms, you will find that some form events are used more frequently than others. The following sections show hands-on examples of event procedures you can write for Access forms.

Data Events

Data events occur when you change the data in a control or record placed on a form, or when you move the focus from one record to another.

Current

The Current event occurs when the form is opened or requeried and when the focus moves to a different record. Use the Current event to synchronize data among forms or move focus to a specific control.

The event procedure in Hands-On 24-1 sets the BackColor property of the form's header (Section 1) to red (255) for each discontinued product. The Form_Current event will occur each time you move to a new record if the specified condition is true.

◎ Hands-On 24-1: Writing the Form_Current Event Procedure

1. Start Microsoft Office Access 2007 and create a new Microsoft Office Access 2007 database named **Chap24.accdb** in your **C:\Acc07_ByExample** folder.

2. Import all the tables, queries, forms, reports, macros, and modules from the Northwind.mdb sample database to your Chap24.accdb database. To do this, in the Access window, choose **External Data | Access**. In the File name box, type **C:\Acc07_ByExample\Northwind.mdb** and click **OK**. In the Import Objects window, select the **Tables** tab and click the **Select All** button. This will highlight all the tables. Select the **Queries** tab and click the **Select All** button. Select the **Forms** tab and click the **Select All** button.

Select the **Reports** tab and click the **Select All** button. Do the same for macros and modules. After selecting all the objects on the specified tabs, click **OK** to begin importing. Click the **Close** button when done.

3. In the Access window of the Chap24.accdb database, right-click on the **Products** form and choose **Design View**. Make sure the form's property sheet is visible. To activate the property sheet, choose **Property Sheet** in the Tools section of the Design tab.

4. In the form's property sheet, click the **Event** tab. Click next to the **On Current** event property and choose **[Event Procedure]** from the drop-down box. Click the **Build** button (...).

   Access opens the Visual Basic Editor window and writes the stub of the Form_Current event procedure.

5. Complete the code of the **Form_Current** event procedure as shown below, or copy and paste the code from **C:\Acc07_HandsOn\Chap24.txt**.

```
Private Sub Form_Current()
    If Discontinued = True Then
        Me.Section(1).BackColor = 255
        Me.Picture = ""
    Else
        Me.Picture = "C:\Program Files\" & _
            "Microsoft Office\Office12\" & _
            "Bitmaps\Styles\Stone.bmp"
    End If
End Sub
```

6. To test the above event procedure, activate the **Products** form that is currently open in Design view. You can quickly switch to the selected form from Visual Basic by clicking the View Object button in the Project Explorer window. Next, in the Access window, click the **View** button on the Ribbon to display the form in Form view. Use the record selectors to move to record 5. Because this record is marked as Discontinued, the code in the Form_Current event will change the form header section's color to red.

7. Close the Products form and save all the changes when prompted.

BeforeInsert

This event occurs when the first character is typed in a new record but before the new record is created. Use the BeforeInsert event to verify that the data is valid or to display information about data being added. This event is quite useful for placing default values in the fields at run time. The BeforeInsert event can be canceled if the data being added does not meet specific criteria. The event procedure in Hands-On 24-2 demonstrates how to enter a default value in the Country field when a user begins to enter data in the form.

⊚ Hands-On 24-2: Writing the Form_BeforeInsert Event Procedure

For this hands-on exercise we will create a new form based on the Customers table.

1. Highlight the **Customers** table in the left pane of the Access window. Choose **Create | More Forms | Form Wizard**.

2. Select the following fields: **CustomerID**, **CompanyName**, **Address**, **City**, **Region**, **PostalCode**, and **Country**. Step through the Form Wizard screens, pressing the **Next** button until you get to the screen where you are asked for the form's title. Type **New Customers** for the form's title, select the **Modify the form's design** option button, and click **Finish**.

   Access opens the New Customers form in Design View.

3. In the property sheet, select **Form** from the drop-down box, and click the **Data** tab. Set the Data Entry property to **Yes**.

4. In the form's property sheet, click the **Event** tab. Click next to the **Before Insert** event property and choose **[Event Procedure]** from the drop-down box. Click the **Build** button (…).

   Access opens the Visual Basic Editor window and writes the stub of the Form_BeforeInsert event procedure.

5. Complete the code of the **Form_BeforeInsert** event procedure as shown below, or copy and paste the code from **C:\Acc07_HandsOn\Chap24.txt**.

```
Private Sub Form_BeforeInsert(Cancel As Integer)
    Me.Country = "USA"
End Sub
```

6. To test this event procedure, activate the **New Customers** form that is currently open in the Design view. You can quickly switch to the selected form from Visual Basic by clicking the View Object button in the Project Explorer window. In the Access window, click the **View** button on the Ribbon to display the New Customers form in Form view.

7. Type **JANIT** in the CustomerID field. Notice that as soon as you start filling in the form's text boxes, the text "USA" appears in the Country field.

8. Click the **Esc** key twice to undo the changes to the form.

9. Close the New Customers form and save all the changes when prompted.

AfterInsert

The AfterInsert event occurs when a new record has been inserted. Use this event to requery the recordset when a new record is added or to display other information. The event procedure in Hands-On 24-3 retrieves the total number of records in the Customers table after a new record has been inserted.

◎ Hands-On 24-3: Writing the Form_AfterInsert Event Procedure

This hands-on exercise uses the New Customers form created in Hands-On 24-2.

1. In the Visual Basic Editor's Project Explorer window, double-click **Form_New Customers**.

2. In the Code window, you will see the Form_BeforeInsert event procedure prepared in Hands-On 24-2. Below this procedure code, enter the **Form_AfterInsert** event procedure as shown below, or copy and paste the code from **C:\Acc07_HandsOn\Chap24.txt**.

```
Private Sub Form_AfterInsert()
    Dim db As DAO.Database
    Dim rst As DAO.Recordset

    Set db = CurrentDb()
    Set rst = db.OpenRecordset("Customers")

    MsgBox "Added " & rst.RecordCount & _
        "th customer."

    rst.Close
    Set rst = Nothing
    Set db = Nothing
End Sub
```

3. To test the above event procedure, open the **New Customers** form in Form view. Type **TRYIT** in the Customer ID text box. Type **Test Events** in the Company Name text box. Now use the record selector to move to the next record. Access executes the code in the Form_AfterInsert event procedure and displays the total number of records.

4. Close the New Customers form and save all the changes when prompted.

BeforeUpdate

This event occurs after a record has been edited but before it is written to the table. This event is triggered by moving to another record or attempting to save the current record. The BeforeUpdate event takes place after the BeforeInsert event. Use this event to validate the entire record and display a message to confirm the change. The BeforeUpdate event can be canceled if the record cannot be accepted. The event procedure in Hands-On 24-4 will supply the value for the EmployeeID field before the newly entered record is saved.

◎ Hands-On 24-4: Writing the Form_BeforeUpdate Event Procedure

This hands-on exercise uses the New Customers form created in Hands-On 24-2.

1. In the Visual Basic Editor's Project Explorer window, double-click **Form_New Customers**.

2. In the Code window, other event procedures prepared in Hands-On 24-2 and 24-3 will be listed. Enter the following **Form_BeforeUpdate** event procedure below the last procedure code, or copy and paste the code from **C:\Acc07_HandsOn\Chap24.txt**.

```
Private Sub Form_BeforeUpdate(Cancel As Integer)
    If Not IsNull(Me.CompanyName) Then
        Me.CustomerID = Left(CompanyName, 3) & _
            Right(CompanyName, 2)
        MsgBox "You just added Customer ID: " & _
            Me.CustomerID
    Else
        MsgBox "Please enter Company Name.", _
            vbOKOnly, "Missing Data"
        Me.CompanyName.SetFocus
        Cancel = True
    End If
End Sub
```

3. To test the above event procedure, open the **New Customers** form in Form view. Type **Event Enterprises** in the Company Name box. Click the record selector to move to the next record. The BeforeUpdate event procedure code will run at this point and you will see a message box with the custom-generated Customer ID. Click **OK** to the message. Another message will appear with the number of total records. This message box is generated by the AfterInsert event procedure that was prepared in Hands-On 24-3. Click **OK** to this message.

4. Close the New Customers form and save changes to the form when prompted.

AfterUpdate

This event occurs after the record changes have been saved in the database. It is also invoked when a control loses focus and after the data in the control has changed. Use the AfterUpdate event to update data in other controls on the form or to move the focus to a different record or a control. The event procedure in Hands-On 24-5 creates an audit trail for all newly added records, as illustrated in Figure 24-1.

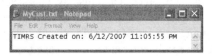

Figure 24-1: The Form_AfterUpdate event procedure is used here to store information about newly added records in a text file.

Hands-On 24-5: Writing the Form_AfterUpdate Event Procedure

This hands-on requires the New Customers form that was created in Hands-On 24-2.

1. In the Visual Basic Editor window, choose **Tools | References**. Locate and select **Microsoft Scripting Runtime** in the Available References list and click **OK**.

2. In the Project Explorer window, double-click **Form_New Customers**.

3. Other procedures that were prepared in Hands-On 24-2, 24-3, and 24-4 will be listed in the Code window. Enter the following **Form_AfterUpdate** event procedure below the last procedure code, or copy and paste the code from **C:\Acc07_HandsOn\Chap24.txt**.

```
Private Sub Form_AfterUpdate()
    Dim fso As FileSystemObject
    Dim objFile As Object
    Dim strFileName As String

    On Error Resume Next

    strFileName = "C:\ACC07_ByExample\MyCust.txt"
    Set fso = New FileSystemObject
    Set objFile = fso.GetFile(strFileName)

    If Err.Number = 0 Then
        ' open text file
        Set objFile = fso.OpenTextFile(strFileName, 8)
    Else
        ' create a text file
        Set objFile = fso.CreateTextFile(strFileName)
    End If

    objFile.writeLine UCase(Me.CustomerID) & _
        " Created on: " & Date & " " & Time
    objFile.Close
    Set fso = Nothing
    MsgBox "This record was logged in:" & strFileName
End Sub
```

The above event procedure first checks whether the specified text file exists on your computer. If the file is found, then the Err.Number statement returns zero. At this point you want to open the file. The "8" represents the open mode for appending. Use "2" if you want to replace the contents of a file with the new data.

4. To test the above event procedure, open the **New Customers** form in Form view. Type **Time Organizers** in the Company Name box. Click the record selector to move to the next record. The BeforeUpdate event procedure code you prepared in Hands-On 24-4 will run at this point and you should see a message box that displays the custom-generated Customer ID. Click **OK** to the message. The next message box notifies you about the location of the audit trail (the result of the AfterUpdate event procedure prepared in this hands-on exercise). Click **OK** to the message. Another message will appear with the number of total records. This message box is generated by

the AfterInsert event procedure that was prepared in Hands-On 24-3. Click **OK** to this message.

As you enter more customer records using the New Customers form, events are executed in the following order:

BeforeInsert (Hands-On 24-2)
BeforeUpdate (Hands-On 24-4)
AfterUpdate (Hands-On 24-5)
AfterInsert (Hands-On 24-3)

5. Close the New Customers form and save changes to the form when prompted.

Dirty

The Dirty event occurs when the contents of a form or the text portion of a combo box changes. This event will be triggered by an attempt to enter a character directly in the form's text box or combo box. Use this event to determine if the record can be changed. The event procedure in Hands-On 24-6 disallows changes to form data when the CategoryID is less than or equal to 4.

◎ Hands-On 24-6: Writing the Form_Dirty Event Procedure

1. Highlight the **Categories** table in the left pane of the Access window. Choose **Create | More Forms | Form Wizard**.

2. Add all the fields as listed in the Categories table. Step through the Form Wizard screens, clicking the **Next** button until you get to the screen where you are asked for the form's title. Type **Product Categories** for the form's title, select the **Modify the form's design** option button, and click **Finish**.

   Access opens the Product Categories form in Design view.

3. In the property sheet, select **Form** from the drop-down box, and click the **Event** tab. Click next to the **On Dirty** event property and choose **[Event Procedure]** from the drop-down box. Click the **Build** button (...).

   Access opens the Visual Basic Editor window and writes the stub of the Form_Dirty event procedure.

4. Complete the code of the **Form_Dirty** event procedure as shown below, or copy and paste the code from **C:\Acc07_HandsOn\Chap24.txt**.

```
Private Sub Form_Dirty(Cancel As Integer)
    If CategoryID <= 4 Then
        MsgBox "You cannot make changes in this record."
        Cancel = True
    End If
End Sub
```

5. To test the above event procedure, open the **Product Categories** form in Form view. Try to make any changes to the original records. You will not

be able to make changes to the data if the product's CategoryID is less than or equal to 4.

6. Close the Product Categories form and save changes to the form when prompted.

OnUndo

The OnUndo event occurs when the user undoes a change to a combo box control, form, or text box control. By setting the Cancel argument to True, you can cancel the undo operation and leave the control or form in its edited state. The Undo event for forms is triggered when the user clicks the Undo button, presses the Esc key, or calls the Undo method.

Delete

The Delete event occurs when you select one or more records for deletion and before the records are actually removed from the table. Use this event to place restrictions on the data that can be deleted. When deleting multiple records, the Delete event occurs for each record. This enables you to confirm or cancel each deletion in your event procedure code. You can cancel the deletion in the Delete or BeforeDelConfirm events by setting the Cancel argument to True. After the record is deleted, the focus moves to the next record and the current event for that record occurs.

The event procedure in Hands-On 24-7 demonstrates how to disallow deletion of records when CategoryID is less than or equal to 8 and ask the user to confirm the deletion for other records.

Hands-On 24-7: Writing the Form_Delete Event Procedure

This hands-on exercise uses the Product Categories form created in Hands-On 24-6.

1. In the Visual Basic Editor's Project Explorer window, double-click **Form_Product Categories**, which was created in Hands-On 24-6.

2. In the Code window, you will see the Form_Dirty event procedure that was prepared in Hands-On 24-6. Below this procedure code, enter the **Form_Delete** event procedure as shown below, or copy and paste the code from **C:\Acc07_HandsOn\Chap24.txt**.

```
Private Sub Form_Delete(Cancel As Integer)
    If CategoryID <= 8 Then
        MsgBox "You can't delete the original categories."
        Cancel = True
    Else
        If MsgBox("Do you really want to delete " & _
            "this record?", vbOKCancel, _
            "Delete Verification") = vbCancel Then
                Cancel = True
        End If
```

```
    End If
End Sub
```

3. To test the above event procedure, open the **Product Categories** form in Form view. Click on the record selector to the left of the first record and press the **Delete** key. You can also click the Delete button on the Ribbon. At this point Access will execute the code of the Form_Delete event procedure. You should see the message that you cannot delete original product categories.

4. Click the **New** button on the Ribbon to add a new record to the form. Enter a new category named **Organic Food** and save the record. Now press the **Delete** button on the Ribbon to delete this record. If there is no code in the Form_BeforeDelConfirm event procedure (see Hands-On 24-8), you will be prompted twice to confirm the deletion. Go ahead with the deletion; click **OK** to the first message and **Yes** to the second.

5. Close the Product Categories form and save changes to the form when prompted.

BeforeDelConfirm

This event occurs after the Delete event, before the Delete Confirm message box is displayed. If you don't write your own BeforeDelConfirm event, Access will display a standard delete confirmation message as described in Hands-On 24-7. You can use this event to write a custom deletion confirmation message. The event procedure in Hands-On 24-8 demonstrates how to eliminate the default delete confirmation message.

◉ Hands-On 24-8: Writing the Form_BeforeDelConfirm Event Procedure

This hands-on exercise uses the Product Categories form created in Hands-On 24-6.

1. In the Visual Basic Editor's Project Explorer window, double-click **Form_Product Categories**, which was created in Hands-On 24-6 and modified in Hands-On 24-7.

2. In the Code window, two event procedures are shown that were prepared in Hands-On 24-6 and 24-7. Enter the following **Form_BeforeDelConfirm** event procedure below the last procedure code, or copy and paste the code from **C:\Acc07_HandsOn\Chap24.txt**.

```
Private Sub Form_BeforeDelConfirm(Cancel _
    As Integer, Response As Integer)
  Response = acDataErrContinue
End Sub
```

In the procedure code above, the statement Response = acDataErrContinue will suppress the default message box that Microsoft Access normally displays when you attempt to delete a record.

3. To test the above event procedure, open the **Product Categories** form in Form view. Click the **New** button on the Ribbon to add a new record, save it, and then delete it. The Form_Delete event procedure prepared in Hands-On 24-7 will be executed at this point, and you will see a dialog with your custom prompt to confirm the deletion. Click **Yes**. Notice that Access does not display its default message asking you to confirm the deletion of the specified number of records.

4. Close the Product Categories form and save changes to the form when prompted.

➲ **Note:** Instead of writing your custom confirmation message in the Form_Delete event procedure, you can place it in the Form_BeforeDelConfirm event procedure as shown below:

```
Private Sub Form_BeforeDelConfirm(Cancel As Integer, _
                    Response As Integer)
    ' remove the default Access message box that prompts to confirm deletion
    Response = acDataErrContinue
    If MsgBox("Do you really want to delete this record?", _
        vbOKCancel) = vbCancel Then
        Cancel = True
    End If
End Sub
```

AfterDelConfirm

This event occurs after the record is actually deleted or after deletion is canceled in the BeforeDelConfirm event procedure. Use the AfterDelConfirm event to move to another record or to display a message indicating whether the deletion was successful. The Status argument allows you to check whether deletion progressed normally or was canceled by the user or Visual Basic. The following constants can be used for the Status argument in the AfterDelConfirm event procedure: acDelete(6), acDeleteCancel(1), acDeleteOK(0), or acDeleteUserCancel(2).

The event procedure in Hands-On 24-9 displays a message when a record is successfully deleted.

⊚ **Hands-On 24-9: Writing the Form_AfterDelConfirm Event Procedure**

This hands-on exercise uses the Product Categories form created in Hands-On 24-6.

1. In the Visual Basic Editor's Project Explorer window, double-click **Form_Product Categories**.

2. The Code window appears with several event procedures that were prepared in previous hands-on exercises. Enter the following **Form_After-DelConfirm** event procedure below the last procedure code, or copy and paste the code from **C:\Acc07_HandsOn\Chap24.txt**.

```
Private Sub Form_AfterDelConfirm(Status As Integer)
    MsgBox "The selected record was deleted."
    Debug.Print "Status = " & Status
End Sub
```

3. To test the above event procedure, open the **Product Categories** form in Form view. Add a new record, save it, and delete it. Access will execute the code in the Form_Delete event procedure (Hands-On 24-7) that displays a message box asking you whether you want to delete the record. Click **Yes**. Access will then check the code in Form_BeforeDelConfirm (Hands-On 24-8). The statement Response = acDataErrContinue will cause Access to suppress its default Delete Confirm message box and you will not be prompted again to reconfirm the deletion. Finally, Form_AfterDel-Confirm will run and you will see a message about the successful deletion.

4. Close the Product Categories form and save changes to the form when prompted.

Focus Events

Focus events occur when a form becomes active or inactive and when a form or form control loses or gains the focus.

Activate

The Activate event occurs whenever the form gains the focus and becomes the active window. This situation occurs when the form is first opened, and when the user activates the form again by clicking on the form or one of its controls. Use this event to display or hide supporting forms.

The event procedure in Hands-On 24-10 will hide the tab labeled Personal Information when the Employees form is displayed. Notice that the tabs are numbered beginning with 0, hence the second tab in the tab control placed on the form has an index value of 1.

◎ Hands-On 24-10: Writing the Form_Activate Event Procedure

1. In the Visual Basic Editor's Project Explorer window, double-click **Form_Employees**.

2. In the Code window there are a number of event procedures and functions already written for this form. Enter the following **Form_Activate** event procedure below the last procedure code, or copy and paste the code from **C:\Acc07_HandsOn\Chap24.txt**.

```
Private Sub Form_Activate()
    Me.TabCtl0.Pages(1).Visible = False
End Sub
```

3. To test the above event procedure, open the **Employees** form in Form view. Notice that only the tab labeled Company Info is shown.

4. Close the Employees form and save changes to the form when prompted.

Deactivate

The Deactivate event occurs when the user switches to another form or closes the form. Use this event to display or hide supporting forms. The event procedure in Hands-On 24-11 will display a message when the focus moves to a different form.

⊚ Hands-On 24-11: Writing the Form_Deactivate Event Procedure

1. In the Visual Basic Editor's Project Explorer window, double-click **Form_Employees**.

2. In the Code window there are a number of event procedures and functions already written for this form. Enter the following **Form_Deactivate** event procedure below the last procedure code, or copy and paste the code from **C:\Acc07_HandsOn\Chap24.txt**.

```
Private Sub Form_Deactivate()
    MsgBox "You are leaving the " & Me.Name & _
        " form."
    If Me.Dirty Then
        DoCmd.Save acForm, Me.Name
        MsgBox "Your changes have been saved."
    End If
End Sub
```

3. To test the above event procedure, open the **Products** form in Form view. Next, activate the **Employees** form in Form view and change the phone extension in the first employee record. Now go back to the Products form. You should get two messages as programmed in the Form_Deactivate event procedure. Click **OK** to each message.

4. Close the Employees and the Products forms.

GotFocus

This event happens when a form receives the focus, provided that there are no visible or enabled controls on the form. The GotFocus event is frequently used for controls placed on the form and hardly ever used for the form itself.

LostFocus

The LostFocus event happens when a form loses focus, provided there are no visible or enabled controls on the form. This event is frequently used for controls placed on the form and rarely used for a form itself.

Mouse Events

Mouse events occur when you move a mouse or click any of the available mouse buttons.

Click

The Click event occurs when you click a mouse button on a blank area of a form, a form's record selector, or a control placed on the form.

The event procedure in Hands-On 24-12 will cause a text box control to move one inch to the right when you click the record selector.

◉ Hands-On 24-12: Writing the Form_Click Event Procedure

1. Create a new form with two text boxes. Position both text boxes starting at 1 inch on the horizontal ruler. Save the form as **Mouse Test**.

2. In the form's property sheet, make sure **Form** is selected and click the **Event** tab. Click next to the **On Click** event property and choose **[Event Procedure]** from the drop-down box. Click the **Build** button (…).

   Access opens the Visual Basic Editor window and writes the stub of the Form_Click event procedure.

3. Complete the code of the **Form_Click** event procedure as shown below, or copy and paste the code from **C:\Acc07_HandsOn\Chap24.txt**.

```
Private Sub Form_Click()
    MsgBox "Form Click Event Occurred."
    Me.Text0.Left = Text0.Left + 1440
End Sub
```

   The first text box control placed on the form is automatically named Text0. The Left property is used to specify an object's location on a form or report. The above procedure moves a text box control one inch to the right. Screen measurements are expressed in units called twips and there are 1440 twips per inch. Thus, to calculate the new position of the text box, you must add 1440 to the current position.

4. To test the above event procedure, open the **Mouse Test** form in Form view. Click on the record selector (a bar to the left of a record). This will cause the Form_Click event procedure code to execute and you will see a message box. After clicking **OK** in response to the message, the first text box control will move one inch to the right.

5. Close the Mouse Test form and save changes to the form when prompted.

DblClick

The DblClick event occurs when you double-click on a blank area of the form, the form's record selector, or a control placed on the form.

MouseDown

The MouseDown event occurs when you click and hold on a blank area of the form, the form's record selector, or a control placed on the form. This event occurs before the Click event. The MouseDown event has four arguments:

- **Button** — Identifies the state of the mouse buttons. Use acLeftButton to check for the left mouse button, acRightButton to check for the right mouse button, and acMiddleButton to check for the middle mouse button.

- **Shift** — Specifies the state of the Shift, Ctrl, and Alt keys when the button specified by the Button argument was pressed or released. Use acShiftMask(1) to test for the Shift key, acCtrlMask(2) to test for the Ctrl key, and acAltMask(4) to test for the Alt key. You can test for any combination of buttons. For example, to specify that Ctrl and Alt were pressed, use the value of 6 (2+4) as the Shift argument.

- **X** — Specifies the horizontal (x) position from the left edge of the form or control.

- **Y** — Specifies the vertical (y) position from the top edge of the form or control.

The event procedure in Hands-On 24-13 displays two messages when the form's MouseDown event is fired. The first message tells whether you pressed the Alt, Ctrl, or Shift key, and the second one announces which mouse button was used.

◎ Hands-On 24-13: Writing the Form_MouseDown Event Procedure

1. Create a new form based on the Products table. Add all the available fields to the form. Save this form as **Products Test**.

2. In the form's property sheet, make sure **Form** is selected and click the **Event** tab. Click next to the **On Mouse Down** event property and choose **[Event Procedure]** from the drop-down box. Click the **Build** button (…).

3. Enter the code shown below in the **Form_MouseDown** event, or copy and paste the code from **C:\Acc07_HandsOn\Chap24.txt**.

```
Private Sub Form_MouseDown(Button As Integer, _
                           Shift As Integer, _
                           X As Single, _
                           Y As Single)
    Debug.Print "Mouse Down"

    Select Case Shift
        Case 0
            MsgBox "You did not press a key."
        Case 1 ' or acShiftMask
            MsgBox "You pressed SHIFT."
        Case 2 ' or acCtrlMask
            MsgBox "You pressed CTRL."
        Case 3
            MsgBox "You pressed CTRL and SHIFT."
```

```
Case 4 ' or acAltMask
    MsgBox "You pressed ALT."
Case 5
    MsgBox "You pressed ALT and SHIFT."
Case 6
    MsgBox "You pressed CTRL and ALT."
Case 7
    MsgBox "You pressed CTRL, ALT, and SHIFT."
End Select

If Button = 1 Then ' acLeftButton
    MsgBox "You pressed the left button."
ElseIf Button = 2 Then 'acRightButton
    MsgBox "You pressed the right button."
ElseIf Button = 4 Then 'acMiddleButton
    MsgBox "You pressed the middle button."
End If
End Sub
```

4. To test the above event procedure, switch to the **Products Test** form and open it in Form view. Click on the record selector while holding down any mouse button and pressing the Shift, Ctrl, or Alt keys or their combinations.

5. Close the Products Test form and save changes to the form when prompted.

MouseMove

The MouseMove event occurs when you move the mouse over the blank area of the form, the form's record selector, or a control placed on the form. The MouseMove event occurs before the Click event and has the same arguments as the MouseDown event.

MouseUp

The MouseUp event occurs when you release the mouse button. It occurs before the Click event and uses the same arguments as the MouseDown and MouseMove events.

MouseWheel

The MouseWheel event occurs in Form view, Datasheet view, PivotChart view, or PivotTable view when the user rotates the mouse wheel on a mouse device that has a wheel. This event takes the following two arguments:

■ **Page** — Returns True if the page was changed.

■ **Count** — Specifies the number of lines that were scrolled with the mouse wheel.

 Note: Because there is no Cancel argument, you cannot use the MouseWheel event to prevent users from using the mouse wheel to scroll through records on a form.

Keyboard Events

Keyboard events occur when you hold down, press, or release a key on the keyboard or send a keystroke by using the SendKeys statement in Visual Basic or the SendKeys action in a macro.

The keyboard events occur in the following sequence:

KeyDown → KeyPress → KeyUp

If the form's KeyPreview property is set to Yes, all keyboard events occur first for the form, and then for the control that has the focus. When you press and hold down the key, the KeyDown and KeyPress events occur repeatedly. When you release the key, the KeyUp event occurs.

KeyDown

The KeyDown event occurs when you press a key while a form or control has the focus. This event is also triggered by using the SendKeys statement in Visual Basic or the SendKeys action in a macro. If the form's KeyPreview property is set to Yes, all keyboard events occur first for the form, and then for the control that has the focus.

The KeyDown event takes the following two arguments:

- **KeyCode** — Determines which key was pressed. To specify key codes, use members of the KeyCodeConstants class in the VBA Object Library in the Object Browser. To prevent an object from receiving the keystroke, set KeyCode to zero (0).

- **Shift** — Determines if the Shift, Ctrl, or Alt key was pressed. Use acShiftMask(1) to test for the Shift key, acCtrlMask(2) to test for the Ctrl key, and acAltMask(4) to test for the Alt key. You can test for any combination of buttons. For example, to specify that Ctrl and Alt were pressed, use the value of 6 (2+4) as the Shift argument.

The event procedure in Hands-On 24-14 displays a message when you press one of the following keys: F1, Home, Tab, Shift, Ctrl, Alt, or Delete.

⊚ Hands-On 24-14: Writing the Form_KeyDown Event Procedure

1. Open the **Products** form in Design view. In the form's property sheet, make sure **Form** is selected and click the **Event** tab. Set the Key Preview property to **Yes**.

2. Save the **Products** form.

3. Click next to the **On Key Down** event property and choose **[Event Procedure]** from the drop-down box. Click the **Build** button (...).

   In the Code window there are a couple of event procedures already written for this form.

4. Enter the following **Form_KeyDown** event procedure below the last procedure code, or copy and paste the code from **C:\Acc07_HandsOn\
Chap24.txt.**

```
Private Sub Form_KeyDown _
        (KeyCode As Integer, Shift As Integer)
    Select Case KeyCode
        Case vbKeyF1
            MsgBox "You pressed the F1 key."
        Case vbKeyHome
            MsgBox "You pressed the Home key."
        Case vbKeyTab
            MsgBox "You pressed the Tab key."
    End Select
    Select Case Shift
        Case acShiftMask
            MsgBox "You pressed the SHIFT key."
        Case acCtrlMask
            MsgBox "You pressed the CTRL key."
        Case acAltMask
            MsgBox "You pressed the ALT key."
    End Select
    If KeyCode = vbKeyDelete Then
        MsgBox "Delete Key is not allowed."
        KeyCode = 0
    End If
End Sub
```

5. To test the above event procedure, open the **Products** form in Form view.
Press one of the following keys: **F1**, **Home**, **Tab**, **Shift**, **Ctrl**, **Alt**, or
Delete. Click **OK** to the message.

6. Close the Products form and save changes to the form when prompted.

KeyPress

The KeyPress event occurs when you press and release a key or a key combination. This event is also triggered by using the SendKeys statement in Visual
Basic or the SendKeys action in a macro. If the form's KeyPreview property is
set to Yes, all keyboard events occur first for the form, and then for the control
that has the focus.

The KeyPress event responds only to the ANSI characters generated by the
keyboard, the Ctrl key combined with a character from the standard alphabet
or a special character, and the Enter or Backspace key. Other keystrokes are
handled by the KeyDown and KeyUp event procedures. KeyAscii is a read/
write argument that specifies which ANSI key was pressed. To cancel the keystroke in the KeyPress event, set the KeyAscii argument to 0. The KeyPress
event treats uppercase and lowercase letters as separate characters.

The event procedure in Hands-On 24-15 prints the ASCII code and the
value of the pressed key to the Immediate window. Upon pressing the Escape

key (KeyAscii=27), the user is prompted to save changes. Clicking Yes to the message will cause the form to be closed. All other keystrokes are ignored.

⊚ Hands-On 24-15: Writing the Form_KeyPress Event Procedure

1. Open the **Suppliers** form in Design view. In the property sheet, make sure that **Form** is selected and click the **Event** tab. Set the Key Preview property to **Yes**. Click next to the **On Key Press** event property and choose **[Event Procedure]** from the drop-down box. Click the **Build** button (...).

   In the Code window there are a couple of event procedures already written for this form.

2. Enter the following **Form_KeyPress** event procedure below the last procedure code, or copy and paste the code from **C:\Acc07_HandsOn\ Chap24.txt**.

```
Private Sub Form_KeyPress(KeyAscii As Integer)
    Debug.Print "Key Press: KeyAscii = " & KeyAscii & _
        Space(1) & "= " & Chr(KeyAscii)
    If KeyAscii = 27 Then
        If MsgBox("Save changes to this form?", _
            vbYesNo) = vbYes Then
            DoCmd.Close acForm, Me.Name, acSaveYes
        Else
            KeyAscii = 0
        End If
    Else
        KeyAscii = 0
    End If
End Sub
```

   The statement KeyAscii = 0 will disable any input to all the controls on the form. Recall that a form's Key Preview property determines whether form keyboard events are invoked before control keyboard events. To prevent keystrokes from going to the form's controls, the KeyPreview property must be set to Yes.

   Note that the KeyPress event is not triggered by the Delete key. You can delete any data on this form as long as there is no custom VBA code written in the KeyDown or KeyUp event procedure that blocks the use of this key.

3. To test the above event procedure, open the **Suppliers** form in Form view. Try to edit a field by typing some text. Because the input to all the controls on the form has been disabled by the Form_KeyPress event procedure, you cannot see any input. However, when you switch to the Immediate window, you will see the complete listing of keys that you pressed. Switch back to the Suppliers form and press the **Escape** key. If you agree to save changes to this form, the form will be closed.

KeyUp

The KeyUp event occurs when you release a key while a form or control has the focus. This event is also triggered by using the SendKeys statement in Visual Basic or the SendKeys action in a macro. If the form's KeyPreview property is set to Yes, all keyboard events occur first for the form, and then for the control that has the focus.

The KeyUp event takes the following two arguments:

- **KeyCode** — Determines which key was pressed. To specify key codes, use members of the KeyCodeConstants class in the VBA Object Library in the Object Browser. To prevent an object from receiving the keystroke, set KeyCode to zero (0).

- **Shift** — Determines if the Shift, Ctrl, or Alt key was pressed. Use acShiftMask(1) to test for the Shift key, acCtrlMask(2) to test for the Ctrl key, and acAltMask(4) to test for the Alt key. You can test for any combination of buttons. For example, to specify that Ctrl and Alt were pressed, use the value of 6 (2+4) as the Shift argument.

The event procedure in Hands-On 24-16 will print to the Immediate window the code and the value of the key that was released. Also, the information about KeyCode and the state of the Shift key will be shown in the form's caption.

◎ Hands-On 24-16: Writing the Form_KeyUp Event Procedure

1. Open the **Suppliers** form in Design view. In the form's property sheet, make sure **Form** is selected and click the **Event** tab. Make sure the Key Preview property is set to **Yes**.

2. Click next to the **On Key Up** event property and choose **[Event Procedure]** from the drop-down box. Click the **Build** button (…).

   In the Code window there are a couple of event procedures already written for this form.

3. Enter the following **Form_KeyUp** event procedure below the last procedure code, or copy and paste the code from **C:\Acc07_HandsOn\ Chap24.txt**.

```
Private Sub Form_KeyUp(KeyCode As Integer, _
                    Shift As Integer)
    Debug.Print "Key up : " & Chr(KeyCode) & _
            "(" & KeyCode & ") " & _
            Shift
    Me.Caption = Me.Name
    Me.Caption = Me.Caption & ": KeyCode=" & _
        KeyCode & " " & "Shift=" & Shift
End Sub
```

4. To test the above event procedure, open the **Suppliers** form in Form view. Press various keys on the keyboard and notice the key information in the form's caption.

5. Switch to the Visual Basic Editor window and activate the Immediate window.

   You should see a listing of the keys that were pressed and released while performing step 4 above.

6. Close the Suppliers form and save changes to the form when prompted.

Error Events

The Error event is triggered by run-time errors generated either in the Microsoft Access interface or by the Microsoft Jet/ACE database engine. The Error event does not trap VBA errors.

Error

The Error event occurs when there is a problem accessing data for the form. Use this event to suppress the standard error messages and display a custom error message instead.

The Error event takes the following two arguments:

- **DataErr** — Contains the number of the Microsoft Access error that occurred.

- **Response** — Determines whether or not error messages should be displayed. It may be one of the following constants:

  - *acDataErrContinue* — Ignore the error and continue without displaying the default Microsoft Access error message.

  - *acDataErrDisplay* — Display the default Microsoft Access error message. This is the default.

The event procedure in Hands-On 24-17 displays a custom message when an attempt is made to add a new record with a customer ID that already exists. The standard Microsoft Access error message is not displayed.

Hands-On 24-17: Writing the Form_Error Event Procedure

1. Create a new form based on the Customers table. Add all the fields from the Customers table and save the new form as **Customers Data Entry**.

2. Activate the **Customers Data Entry** form in Design view. In the property sheet, make sure **Form** is selected and click the **Data** tab. Set the form's DataEntry property to **Yes**.

3. Click the **Event** tab, set the On Error property to **[Event Procedure]**, and press the **Build** button (…).

   Access will create the event procedure stub.

4. Enter the following **Form_Error** event procedure, or copy and paste the code from **C:\Acc07_HandsOn\Chap24.txt**.

```
Private Sub Form_Error(DataErr As Integer, _
                       Response As Integer)

    Dim strMsg As String
    Dim custId As String

    Const conDuplicateKey = 3022
    custId = Me.CustomerID

    If DataErr = conDuplicateKey Then
        ' Don't show built-in error messages
        Response = acDataErrContinue
        strMsg = "Customer " & custId & " already exists."
        ' Show a custom error message
        MsgBox strMsg, vbCritical, "Duplicate Value"
    End If
End Sub
```

5. Open the **Customers Data Entry** form in Form view. Enter **ALFKI** in the CustomerID field and **Alfred Fiki** in the Company Name field. Click the **Save** button. When you try to save this record, the Form_Error event procedure code will cause a message box to appear, saying that the customer already exists. Click **OK** to the message. Press **Esc** to cancel the changes to this record.

6. Close the Customers Data Entry form and save the changes to the form.

Filter Events

Filter events are triggered by opening or closing a filter window or when you are applying or removing a filter.

Filter

The Filter event occurs when you design a filter to limit the form's records to those matching specified criteria. This event takes place when you select the Filter by Form or Advanced Filter/Sort options. Use this event to remove the filter that was previously set, to enter initial settings for the filter, or to call your own custom filter dialog box. To cancel the filtering command, set the Cancel argument for the event procedure to True.

The event procedure in Hands-On 24-18 allows the user to use the Filter by Form option but disallows the use of the Advanced Filter/Sort option.

Hands-On 24-18: Writing the Form_Filter Event Procedure

This hands-on exercise uses the Product Categories form created in Hands-On 24-6.

1. In the Visual Basic Editor's Project Explorer window, double-click **Form_Product Categories**.

2. The Code window shows other event procedures already written for this form. Enter the following **Form_Filter** event procedure below the last procedure code, or copy and paste the code from **C:\Acc07_HandsOn\ Chap24.txt**.

```
Private Sub Form_Filter(Cancel As Integer, _
                FilterType As Integer)
    Select Case FilterType
        Case acFilterByForm
            MsgBox "You selected to filter records " & _
                "by form.", vbOKOnly + vbInformation, _
                "Filter By Form"
            Me.CategoryName.SetFocus
            Me.CategoryID.Enabled = False
        Case acFilterAdvanced
            MsgBox "You are not authorized to use " & _
                " Advanced Filter/Sort.", _
                vbOKOnly + vbInformation, _
                "Advanced Filter By Form"
            Cancel = True
    End Select
End Sub
```

3. To test the above event procedure, open the **Product Categories** form in Form view.

4. In the Sort & Filter area of the Ribbon, choose **Advanced | Filter by Form**. The code in the Form_Filter event procedure runs and you will see a message box. Click **OK**. The Filter by Form dialog box appears with the Category ID text box disabled. You can disable certain controls on the form if you don't want the user to filter by them.

5. Filter the form to display only records for **Seafood and Meat/Poultry**. Be sure to click **Toggle Filter** in the Sort & Filter area of the Ribbon after setting up filter criteria.

6. Now, remove the filter by clicking **Toggle Filter** again.

7. Choose **Advanced | Advanced Filter/Sort**. You will not be able to use the advanced filter for this form because the form's Filter event has disabled this action.

8. Close the Product Categories form and save changes to the form when prompted.

ApplyFilter

The ApplyFilter event occurs when you apply the filter to restrict the records. This event takes place when you select the Apply Filter/Sort, Filter by Selection, or Remove Filter/Sort options. Use this event to change the form display before the filter is applied or undo any changes made when the Filter event occurred.

The ApplyType argument can be one of the predefined constants shown in Table 24-1.

Table 24-1: ApplyType argument constants

Constant Name	Constant Value
acShowAllRecords	0
acApplyFilter	1
acCloseFilterWindow	2
acApplyServerFilter	3
acCloseServerFilterWindow	4

The event procedure in Hands-On 24-19 displays a different message depending on whether or not the user has made a selection in the Filter by Form dialog box.

Hands-On 24-19: Writing the Form_ApplyFilter Event Procedure

This hands-on exercise uses the Product Categories form created in Hands-On 24-6.

1. In the Visual Basic Editor's Project Explorer window, double-click **Form_Product Categories**.

2. The Code window shows other event procedures already written for this form. Enter the following **Form_ApplyFilter** event procedure below the last procedure code, or copy and paste the code from **C:\Acc07_HandsOn\ Chap24.txt**.

```
Private Sub Form_ApplyFilter(Cancel As Integer, _
                ApplyType As Integer)
    Dim Response As Integer
    If ApplyType = acApplyFilter Then
        If Me.Filter = "" Then
            MsgBox "You did not select any criteria.", _
                vbOKOnly + vbCritical, "No Selection"
            GoTo ExitHere
        End If
        Response = MsgBox("The selected criteria " & _
            "is as follows:" & vbCrLf & _
            Me.Filter, vbOKCancel + vbQuestion, _
            "Filter Criteria")
    End If
    If Response = vbCancel Then
        Cancel = True
    End If
    If ApplyType = acShowAllRecords Then
        Me.Filter = ""
        MsgBox "Filter was removed."
    End If
    If ApplyType = acCloseFilterWindow Then
```

```
        Response = MsgBox("Are you sure you " & _
            "want to close the Filter window?", vbYesNo)
        If Response = vbNo Then
            Cancel = True
        End If
    End If
ExitHere:
    With Me.CategoryID
        .Enabled = True
        .SetFocus
    End With
End Sub
```

3. To test the above event procedure, open the **Product Categories** form in Form view.

4. From the Sort & Filter area of the Ribbon, choose **Advanced | Filter by Form**. The Form_Filter event will be triggered (see Hands-On 24-18). Click **OK** to the message box.

5. Select a category from the **Category Name** combo box and click **Toggle Filter** on the Ribbon. This action will trigger the Form_ApplyFilter event procedure. Experiment with the form filter, testing other situations such as clicking Toggle Filter when the filtering criteria were not specified or closing the Filter by Form dialog box.

6. To test the condition that removes the filter, choose the filtering criteria and press **OK** to limit the records. Next, click **Toggle Filter**. Notice that the name of this button changes to Remove Filter or Apply Filter depending on the situation.

7. Close the Product Categories form and save changes to the form when prompted.

Timing Events

Timing events occur in response to a specified amount of time passing.

Timer

The Timer event occurs when the form is opened. The duration of this event is determined by the value (milliseconds) entered in the TimerInterval property located on the Event tab of the form's property sheet. Use this event to display a splash screen when the database is opened. The Timer event is helpful in limiting the time the record remains locked in multi-user applications.

The event procedure in Hands-On 24-20 will flash the button's text, "Preview Product List" (or the entire button if you use the commented code instead). For the code to work you must start the timer by changing the TimerInterval property from 0 (stopped) to the desired interval. A timer interval of 1,000 will invoke a timer event every second. The form's Load event procedure sets the form's TimerInterval property to 250, so the button text (or the entire button) is toggled once every quarter second. You may change the timer interval manually by typing the value next to the form's TimerInterval property in the property sheet or by placing the following statement in the Form_Load event:

```
Me.TimerInterval = 250
```

⊚ Hands-On 24-20: Writing the Form_Timer Event Procedure

1. In the Visual Basic Editor's Project Explorer window, double-click the **Products** form.

2. The Code window shows other event procedures already written for this form. Enter the following **Form_Timer** event procedure below the last procedure code, or copy and paste the code from **C:\Acc07_HandsOn\ Chap24.txt**.

```
Private Sub Form_Timer()
    Static OnOff As Integer
    If OnOff Then
        Me.PreviewReport.Caption = "Preview Product List"
        ' Me.PreviewReport.Visible = True
    Else
        Me.PreviewReport.Caption = ""
        ' Me.PreviewReport.Visible = False
    End If
    OnOff = Not OnOff
End Sub
```

3. Activate the **Products** form in Design view. In the property sheet, make sure **Form** is selected and click the **Event** tab. Enter **250** for the TimerInterval property.

4. Switch the form to Form view. Notice the flashing effect of the Preview Product List button's text.

5. Close the Products form and save changes to the form when prompted.

 Note: To make the entire button flash, uncomment the commented lines of code and comment the original lines. Next, open the Products form in Form view and notice that the entire button is now flashing.

PivotTable/PivotChart Events

Beginning with Access 2002, table and query data can be presented in an Access form in a PivotTable or PivotChart view, allowing users to perform interactive data analysis. PivotTable and PivotChart views can be built programmatically in a Microsoft Access form by using the Office Web Components Object Model. To give programmers enhanced control over PivotTable and PivotChart views, Access forms offer a number of events that are available when the form is displayed in one of these views. These events are organized in five categories, as shown in Table 24-2.

Event Programming in Forms and Reports

Table 24-2: PivotTable/PivotChart events

Category Name	Event Name	PivotTable Event	PivotChart Event
Data Source Events	OnConnect	Yes	No
	OnDisconnect	Yes	No
	BeforeQuery	Yes	No
	Query	Yes	No
Display Events	BeforeScreenTip	Yes	Yes
	AfterLayout	No	Yes
	BeforeRender	No	Yes
	AfterRender	No	Yes
	AfterFinalRender	No	Yes
Change Events	DataChange	Yes	No
	DataSetChange	No	Yes
	PivotTableChange	Yes	No
	SelectionChange	Yes	Yes
	ViewChange	Yes	Yes
Command Events	CommandEnabled	Yes	Yes
	CommandChecked	Yes	Yes
	CommandBeforeExecute	Yes	Yes
	CommandExecute	Yes	Yes
Keyboard and Mouse Events	KeyDown	Yes	Yes
	KeyPress	Yes	Yes
	KeyUp	Yes	Yes
	MouseDown	Yes	Yes
	MouseMove	Yes	Yes
	MouseUp	Yes	Yes
	MouseWheel	Yes	Yes
	Click	Yes	Yes
	DblClick	Yes	Yes

Note: Microsoft Office Web Components (OWC) is a set of ActiveX controls that provide four components: Spreadsheet, Chart, PivotTable, and Data Source Control (DSC). While OWC was provided with the last three releases of Microsoft Office (Office 2003, Office XP, and Office 2000) and was considered a useful tool by many developers, Microsoft is discontinuing this technology with the release of Microsoft Office 2007. Although discontinued, you can still develop solutions using previous versions of OWC, which you can download from the Microsoft Download Center, but keep in mind that Microsoft is not going to add any new features. If you have access to the previous installations of Microsoft Office 2003, you can find detailed documentation about using and programming these components in the help files (OWCVBA11.CHM, OWCDCH11.CHM, OWCDPL11.CHM) installed on your computer's system drive in the following folder: \Program Files\Common Files\Microsoft Shared\Web Components\11\1033.

Referencing the Microsoft Office Web Components Object Library

The next several sections of this chapter demonstrate event procedures for PivotTable and PivotChart views. To successfully work with these events, download the Microsoft Office Web Components from the Microsoft Download Center. Once they are installed on your computer, follow the steps below to add a reference to the Microsoft Office Web Components 11 Object Library:

1. In the Microsoft Access database window, choose **Tools | Macro | Visual Basic Editor.**

2. In the Visual Basic Editor window, choose **Tools | References.**

3. Click the **Browse** button and locate the following file:

   C:\Program Files\Common Files\Microsoft Shared\WebComponents\
   11\1033\OWCI11.DLL

4. Click the **OWCI11.DLL** file, and then click **Open.** A reference to Microsoft Office Web Components 11.0 should appear in the Available References list.

5. Click **OK** to close the References dialog box.

After you add a reference to the Microsoft Office Web Components Object Library, you can use the Object Browser to view the properties, methods, events, and constants for each class of a web component. To see the available classes of a web component, select OWC11 in the Project/Library box in the Object Browser.

Data Source Events

Data source events occur when the PivotTable connects to or disconnects from its data source or when the data source is queried.

OnConnect

The OnConnect event occurs when the PivotTable report connects to its data source. Use this event to perform the required operations once the PivotTable has connected to the data source.

The procedure in Hands-On 24-21 notifies the user that the connection to the data source has been established and displays the SELECT statement that provides the dataset for the PivotTable view.

◎ Hands-On 24-21: Writing the Form_OnConnect Event Procedure

1. In the Chap24.accdb database, create a query as shown in Figure 24-2.

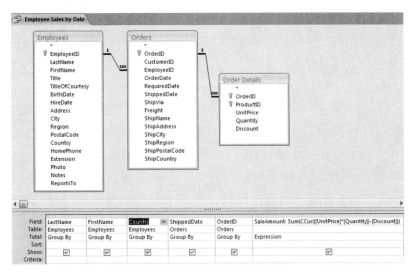

Figure 24-2: Creating the Employee Sales by Date query.

2. Save this query as **Employee Sales by Date**.

The query's SQL statement is shown below:

```
SELECT Employees.LastName, Employees.FirstName, Employees.Country,
Orders.ShippedDate, Orders.OrderID,
Sum(CCur(([UnitPrice]*[Quantity])-[Discount])) AS SaleAmount
FROM Employees INNER JOIN (Orders INNER JOIN [Order Details] ON
Orders.OrderID=[Order Details].OrderID) ON
Employees.EmployeeID=Orders.EmployeeID
GROUP BY Employees.LastName, Employees.FirstName, Employees.Country,
Orders.ShippedDate, Orders.OrderID;
```

3. In the Navigation pane, highlight the **Employee Sales by Date** query and choose **Create | More Forms | PivotTable**.

Access displays the PivotTable view as shown in Figure 24-3.

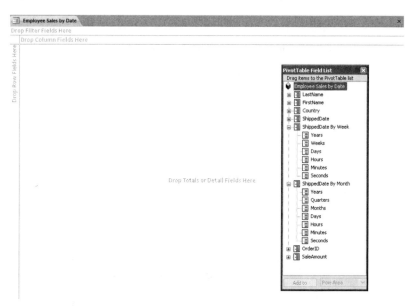

Figure 24-3: PivotTable view in Microsoft Access 2007.

4. Click in the white area of the PivotTable view to display the PivotTable
   Field List window. Drag the **Country** field from the PivotTable Field List
   to the Filter Fields area at the left-top corner of the form. Drag and drop the
   Years and **Quarters** fields into the Drop Row Fields area. Drag and drop
   Last Name field to the Drop Column Fields area. Finally, drag and drop
   the **Sale Amount** to the Drop Totals or Detail Fields area. The completed
   PivotTable is shown in Figure 24-4.

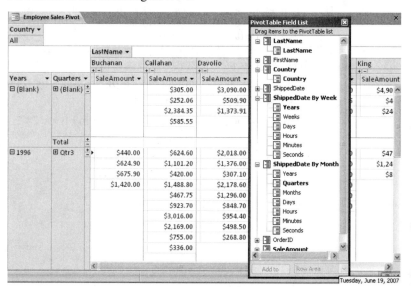

Figure 24-4: Creating a PivotTable form (PivotTable view).

5. Save the form as **Employee Sales Pivot**.

6. Switch the **Employee Sales Pivot** form from PivotTable view to Design view.

7. In the property sheet, ensure that **Form** is selected and click the **Event** tab. Set the On Connect property to **[Event Procedure]**, and press the **Build** button (...).

8. Access will create the event procedure stub. Enter the following **Form_OnConnect** event procedure, or copy and paste the code from **C:\Acc07_HandsOn\Chap24.txt**.

```
Private Sub Form_OnConnect()
    MsgBox "You have connected to the data source." & vbCrLf _
        & "This PivotTable is based on: " & Me.RecordSource
End Sub
```

9. Switch to the Employee Sales Pivot form and close it. Click **Yes** when asked to save the design changes.

10. In the Navigation pane, double-click the **Employee Sales Pivot** form. The Form_OnConnect event procedure will run and you should see the message as coded in step 8 above. Click **OK** to the message to open the form.

11. Close **the Employee Sales Pivot** form.

OnDisconnect

The OnDisconnect event occurs when the PivotTable report disconnects from its data source or the connection to the data source is changed. Use this event to notify the user that the connection to the data source has been lost. This event does not occur when you close the form.

BeforeQuery

The BeforeQuery event occurs before the PivotTable queries its data source. Actions such as adding new fields to the PivotTable report, moving fields, and sorting and filtering data will trigger this event. Because running a complex query could take longer than expected, you may want to let the user know that a query is in progress by changing the mouse pointer to an hourglass and turning it off during the Query event (see Hands-On 24-22). There is no way to determine what type of query is going to be performed.

Query

The Query event occurs after a PivotTable view sends a query to its data source. Actions such as adding new fields to the PivotTable report, moving fields, and sorting and filtering data will trigger this event. There is no way to determine what type of query has been performed.

The procedure in Hands-On 24-22 demonstrates how to change the mouse pointer to an hourglass before the query is sent to the data source and how to turn off the hourglass pointer after the query has run. Prior to sending the query, we also ask the user to specify the background color of the detail rows.

⊚ Hands-On 24-22: Writing the Form_BeforeQuery and Form_Query Event Procedures

1. In the Visual Basic Editor's Project Explorer window, double-click **Form_Employee Sales Pivot**.

2. The Code window shows the Form_OnConnect event procedure you prepared in Hands-On 24-21. Enter the following **Form_BeforeQuery** and **Form_Query** event procedures below the last procedure code, or copy and paste the code from **C:\Acc07_HandsOn\Chap24.txt**.

```
Private Sub Form_BeforeQuery()
    Dim strColor As String
    strColor = InputBox("Type 1 for Red, 2 for Yellow, " & _
                        "or 3 for Green", "Specify Background Color for " & _
                        "Detail Rows")

    Select Case strColor
        Case 1
            strColor = "Red"
        Case 2
            strColor = "Yellow"
        Case 3
            strColor = "Green"
        Case Else
            strColor = "White"
    End Select

    DoCmd.Hourglass True
    Me.PivotTable.ActiveView.DataAxis.FieldSets(0). _
        Fields(0).DetailBackColor = strColor
    Debug.Print "Executing the BeforeQuery event"
    Debug.Print "(Changed detail color to: " & strColor & ")"
End Sub

Private Sub Form_Query()
    Debug.Print "Executing the Query event"
    DoCmd.Hourglass False
    Debug.Print "(Turned off the hourglass mouse pointer)"
End Sub
```

Let's look at the two event procedures that you wrote in this hands-on exercise. Notice that to display the hourglass pointer, we used the statement DoCmd.Hourglass True in the Form_BeforeQuery event procedure. To turn off the hourglass, we put the statement DoCmd.Hourglass False in the Form_Query event procedure.

Also, notice the following statement that sets the background color for the PivotTable detail rows in the Form_BeforeQuery event procedure:

```
Me.PivotTable.ActiveView.DataAxis.FieldSets(0).Fields(0).DetailBackColor
    = strColor
```

In the above statement, the PivotTable property is used to access the PivotTable object exposed by a form. The ActiveView property represents the layout of the PivotTable report. The DataAxis property refers to one of the four areas of the PivotTable where you can drop fields of data. The DataAxis property contains the Totals and Details fields, which are displayed at the intersection of each row and column. Other areas of a PivotTable are used to display row fields (RowAxis), column fields (ColumnAxis), and filter fields (FilterAxis).

In addition to axes, a PivotTable contains a field list that shows which fields are available for use in the PivotTable report based on the form's RecordSource. The field list displays expandable nodes listing fields available on the form (see Figure 24-4 earlier).

To manipulate a particular PivotField object in the PivotTable report via VBA code, you need to access the Fieldset object in the Fieldsets collection of the ActiveView object. Each Fieldset object (a top-level node in the field list) contains a Fields collection, which contains PivotField objects. If you look at the expanded nodes in Figure 24-4 you will notice the Country Fieldset with one PivotField (Country), the Last Name Fieldset with a LastName PivotField, and the Shipped Date By Week Fieldset with six PivotField objects representing different time intervals (Years, Weeks, Days, Hours, Minutes, and Seconds).

3. To test the above event procedures, switch to the Access application window and double-click the **Employee Sales Pivot** form in the Navigation pane.

4. You should first see the message as coded in the Form_OnConnect event procedure (see Hands-On 24-21). Click **OK** to the message to open the form. You should then be prompted for the color of the detail rows as coded in the Form_BeforeQuery event procedure. Type your selection and click **OK**. The hourglass should disappear when the form loading process is completed.

5. Open the Visual Basic Editor window and check out the results in the Immediate window.

6. Close the Employee Sales Pivot form and save the changes to the form when prompted.

Display Events

Display events are used to draw custom lines, text, and drawings in a PivotChart view before or after a PivotChart has been rendered.

BeforeScreenTip

The BeforeScreenTip event occurs before a ScreenTip is displayed for an element in a PivotChart view or PivotTable view. This event takes the following two arguments:

▪ **TipText** — Specifies the default text of the ScreenTip. By setting this argument to an empty string (TipText = "") you can hide the ScreenTip. Set this argument to any other text to display the required text in the ScreenTip.

▪ **SourceObject** — Specifies the object that generates the ScreenTip.

AfterLayout

The AfterLayout event occurs after the chart in the PivotChart view has been laid out but before the chart elements have been drawn on screen. Use this event to draw custom lines, text, and various drawings on the chart.

The drawObject parameter in the AfterLayout event represents a chChartDraw object. The DrawEllipse, DrawLine, DrawPolyLine, and DrawPolygon methods of the chChartDraw object can be used to add drawing objects to a chart. The DrawText method can be used to add text to a chart. The Border, Font, Interior, and Line properties can be used to format each drawing object before it is added to the chart.

The AfterLayout event can also be used to reposition the chTitle, chLegend, chChart, and chAxis objects of each PivotChart view by changing their Left and Top properties. You can reposition the chPlotArea object by changing its Left, Top, Right, and Bottom properties.

The event procedure in Hands-On 24-23 changes the chart legend and Last Name Drop Zone button position on the screen.

◎ Hands-On 24-23: Writing the Form_AfterLayout Event Procedure

This hands-on exercise requires completion of Hands-On 24-21 and 24-22.

1. In the Navigation pane of Chap24.accdb, open the **Employee Sales Pivot** form in Design view.

2. In the property sheet, make sure that **Form** is selected and click the **All** tab. Set Allow PivotChart View to **Yes**.

3. Choose **Home | View | PivotChart View**.

   Access displays the PivotChart layout as shown in Figure 24-5.

Figure 24-5: PivotChart layout.

4. Drag the **SaleAmount** from the Chart Field List to the Drop Data Fields area. Click the **Axis Title** and choose **Design | Property Sheet**. In the property sheet, click the **Format** tab and type **Year - Quarters** in the Caption box. Click the **General** tab and select **Value Axis 1 Title** from the drop-down box. Click the **Format** tab and type **Total Sales** in the Caption box. Close the property sheet.

5. Choose **Design | Legend** to add a legend to the chart. Do not worry about the legend position over the Last Name button. We will make an adjustment programmatically in the event procedure. The resulting chart is shown in Figure 24-6.

Figure 24-6: Adding a legend and data fields to the PivotChart.

6. Press **Ctrl+S** to save the changes to the PivotChart form.

7. Activate the Design view of the PivotChart, and in the property sheet make sure that **Form** is selected. Click the **Event** tab. Set the After Layout property to **[Event Procedure]** and press the **Build** button (...).

8. The Code window shows event procedures you prepared earlier. Enter the following **Form_AfterLayout** event procedure in the place where Access has created the event procedure stub, or copy and paste the code from **C:\Acc07_HandsOn\Chap24.txt**.

```
Private Sub Form_AfterLayout(ByVal drawObject As Object)
    Dim oSeriesDropZ As Object

    Me.ChartSpace.ChartSpaceLegend.Top = 50
    Set oSeriesDropZ = Me.ChartSpace.DropZones(chDropZoneSeries)
    oSeriesDropZ.Top = 30
End Sub
```

In the procedure above, the ChartSpace object represents the chart workspace. The ChartSpaceLegend property of the ChartSpace object returns a chLegend object that represents the chart workspace legend. To reposition the chart legend on the screen, its Top property was set to 50 pixels. Along with the chart legend, the procedure repositions the Last Name Drop Zone button in the series drop zone by using the DropZones method of the ChartSpace object. This method takes one required argument, ChartDropZonesEnum, which represents the drop zone you want to format. ChartDropZonesEnum can be one of the following constants:

chDropZoneCategories = 2
chDropZoneCharts = 4
chDropZoneData = 3
chDropZoneFilter = 0
chDropZoneSeries = 1

9. Open the **Employee Sales Pivot** form in the PivotChart view or choose **Design | Refresh Pivot**. You should see the chart legend repositioned below the Last Name Drop Zone button and the Last Name Drop Zone button positioned in the top left-hand corner of the PivotChart view.

10. Close the Employee Sales Pivot form and save the changes to the form when prompted.

BeforeRender

The BeforeRender event occurs before elements of a PivotChart view are drawn on the screen. Use this event to draw lines, text, and drawings on the chart before a specific chart element is drawn or to change the position and properties of the chart element before it is drawn on the screen. You can use the TypeName function to determine what type of object is about to be rendered. The procedure in Hands-On 24-24 draws a red ellipse around each legend entry and cancels drawing of the grid lines.

◎ Hands-On 24-24: Writing the Form_BeforeRender Event Procedure

1. In the Visual Basic Editor's Project Explorer window, double-click **Form_Employee Sales Pivot**.

2. The Code window shows the Form_AfterLayout event procedure you prepared in Hands-On 24-23. Enter the following **Form_BeforeRender** event procedure below the last procedure code, or copy and paste the code from **C:\Acc07_HandsOn\Chap24.txt**.

```
Private Sub Form_BeforeRender(ByVal drawObject As Object, _
                    ByVal chartObject As Object, _
                    ByVal Cancel As Object)

    If TypeName(chartObject) = " ChLegendEntry " Then
        drawObject.Border.Color = "red"
        drawObject.DrawEllipse chartObject.Left, _
                        chartObject.Bottom, _
                        chartObject.Right, _
                        chartObject.Top
    End If

    If TypeName(chartObject) = "ChGridlines" Then
        Cancel.Value = True
    End If
End Sub
```

3. Open the **Employee Sales Pivot** form in PivotChart view or choose **Design | Refresh Pivot**. You should see the PivotChart formatted as shown in Figure 24-7.

Figure 24-7: This PivotChart view has been altered in the BeforeRender event (see Hands-On 24-24).

4. Save and close the Employee Sales Pivot form.

AfterRender

The AfterRender event occurs after elements of a PivotChart view have been drawn on the screen. Use this event to draw custom lines, text, and various shapes/drawings on the chart after a specific chart element is drawn. You can use the TypeName function to determine what type of object has just been rendered. The procedure in Hands-On 24-25 adds text in the chart's plot area after the chart legend (chLegend) object has been rendered on the screen.

◎ Hands-On 24-25: Writing the Form_AfterRender Event Procedure

1. In the Visual Basic Editor's Project Explorer window, double-click **Form_Employee Sales Pivot**.

2. The Code window shows the procedures created in the previous hands-on exercises for this chapter. Enter the following **Form_AfterRender** event procedure below the last procedure code, or copy and paste the code from **C:\Acc07_HandsOn\Chap24.txt**.

```
Private Sub Form_AfterRender(ByVal drawObject As Object, _
                             ByVal chartObject As Object)

    Dim oChart As Object
    Set oChart = Me.ChartSpace.Charts.Item(0)

    If TypeName(chartObject) = "ChLegend" Then

        drawObject.DrawText "Chart legend has been rendered", _
                oChart.PlotArea.Left + 15, _
                oChart.PlotArea.Top

    End If
End Sub
```

The DrawText method is used to draw a text string on a chart. This method uses the following syntax:

```
expression.DrawText(bstrText, Left, Top)
```

The expression returns a chChartDraw object. All arguments are required. The bstrText argument is a string specifying the text to draw on the chart. Left is a pixel coordinate of the left edge of the text. Top is a pixel coordinate of the top edge of the text.

3. Open the **Employee Sales Pivot** form in PivotChart view or choose **Design | Refresh Pivot**. You should see the text "Chart legend has been rendered" in the chart's plot area.

4. Save and close the form.

AfterFinalRender

The AfterFinalRender event occurs after all elements of a PivotChart view have been drawn on the screen. Use this event to draw custom lines, text, and drawings on the topmost layer of the chart after all the chart elements have been drawn. The procedure in Hands-On 24-26 adds a text message to the chart space, specifying the total number of data points used in the chart.

◎ Hands-On 24-26: Writing the Form_AfterFinalRender Event Procedure

1. In the Visual Basic Editor's Project Explorer window, double-click **Form_Employee Sales Pivot**.

2. The Code window shows the procedures created in the previous hands-on exercises for this chapter. Enter the following **Form_AfterFinalRender** event procedure below the last procedure code, or copy and paste the code from **C:\Acc07_HandsOn\Chap24.txt**.

```
Private Sub Form_AfterFinalRender(ByVal drawObject As Object)
    Dim oChart As Object
    Dim s As Object
    Dim p As Object
    Dim strText As String
    Dim num As Integer

    Set oChart = Me.ChartSpace.Charts(0)

    For Each s In oChart.SeriesCollection
        For Each p In s.Points
            num = num + 1
            Debug.Print num
        Next
    Next

    strText = "This chart contains " & num & " data points."

    With drawObject.Font
        .Size = 9
        .Color = "blue"
        .Italic = True
    End With
    drawObject.DrawText strText, 200, 20
End Sub
```

3. Open the **Employee Sales Pivot** form in the PivotChart view or choose **Design | Refresh Pivot**. You should see the PivotChart formatted as shown in Figure 24-8.

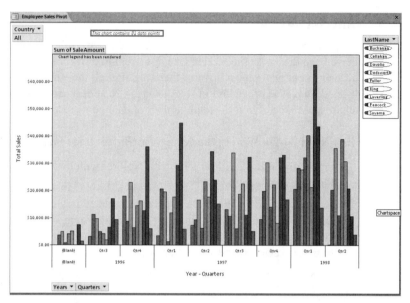

Figure 24-8: After all the elements of the PivotChart have been drawn on the screen, the procedure in Hands-On 24-26 calculates the total number of data points in the chart and places this information in the text message in the PivotChart view.

4. Save and close the form.

Change Events

When the user views and manipulates the data in the PivotTable and PivotChart views, various events are bound to happen. For example, data underlying a PivotChart view may have changed, or the user may have selected, added, removed, or filtered data in the PivotTable or PivotChart view. You can determine specific changes that occurred and take appropriate action by using one of the events discussed below.

DataChange

The DataChange event occurs when certain properties of the PivotTable view are changed or when certain methods are executed from a PivotTable view. You can find out what sort of change occurred by evaluating the Reason argument. This argument contains a value from the PivotDataReasonEnum enumeration. For example, you can use Reason to determine if the user added or removed columns from the PivotTable view.

The event procedure in Hands-On 24-27 evaluates whether a change occurred in the PivotTable Last Name drop-down list. For all other changes in the PivotTable view, the procedure writes the Reason code to the Immediate window. To find out the meaning of the returned Reason codes, search for the PivotDataReasonEnum constant in the Object Browser.

◎ Hands-On 24-27: Writing the Form_DataChange Event Procedure

1. In the Visual Basic Editor's Project Explorer window, double-click **Form_Employee Sales Pivot**.

2. The Code window shows the procedures created in the previous hands-on exercises for this chapter. Enter the following **Form_Data Change** event procedure below the last procedure code, or copy and paste the code from **C:\Acc07_HandsOn\Chap24.txt.**

```
Private Sub Form_DataChange(ByVal Reason As Long)
    Select Case Reason
        Case OWC11.plDataReasonAllIncludeExcludeChange
            Debug.Print "Change in the included/excluded members."
        Case OWC11.plDataReasonIncludedMembersChange
            Debug.Print "Included Members Change"
        Case OWC11.plDataReasonExcludedMembersChange
            Debug.Print "Excluded Members Change"
        Case Else
            Debug.Print "Reason code: " & Reason
    End Select
End Sub
```

3. To test the above event procedure, open the **Employee Sales Pivot** form in PivotTable view. Because you've already created several event procedures for this form, various events will be triggered as the form is being loaded. Respond to all the prompts and, once the form opens, click the drop-down arrow next to the Last Name button and choose to add or remove an employee. Then switch to the Immediate window in the Visual Basic screen to see the captured Reason codes and changes in the included/excluded members.

4. Save and close the form.

DataSetChange

The DataSetChange event occurs whenever the dataset for a PivotChart view changes. This happens when a query supplying the underlying data for the PivotChart has changed or the data displayed in the current PivotChart view has been changed by the addition or removal of a data series. You cannot use this event to find out the reason for a change to the dataset. You must use the display events introduced earlier to trap for specific changes to the PivotChart view.

PivotTableChange

The PivotTableChange event occurs when you add or delete a field, fieldset, or total from the PivotTable field list. Use the Reason argument to determine which operation type has occurred. This argument contains a value from the PivotDataReasonEnum enumeration. The event procedure in Hands-On 24-28 evaluates the Reason argument to determine if the Total was added in the Totals area in the field list.

◎ Hands-On 24-28: Writing the Form_PivotTableChange Event Procedure

1. In the Visual Basic Editor's Project Explorer window, double-click **Form_Employee Sales Pivot**.

2. The Code window shows the procedures created in the previous hands-on exercises for this chapter. Enter the following **Form_PivotTableChange** event procedure below the last procedure code, or copy and paste the code from **C:\Acc07_HandsOn\Chap24.txt**.

```
Private Sub Form_PivotTableChange(ByVal Reason As Long)
    If Reason = OWC11.plPivotTableReasonTotalAdded Then
    MsgBox "Just added a Total."
    End If
End Sub
```

3. To test the above event procedure, open the **Employee Sales Pivot** form in PivotTable view. Because you've already created several event procedures for this form, various events will be triggered. Respond appropriately to the prompts. During the course of events, you should see the message informing you that a Total field has just been added.

4. Save and close the form.

SelectionChange

The SelectionChange event occurs whenever the user makes a new selection within the PivotTable or PivotChart object. Use the SelectionType property to determine the object type of the current selection. The event procedure in Hands-On 24-29 prints the name of the selected object to the Immediate window.

◎ Hands-On 24-29: Writing the Form_SelectionChange Event Procedure

1. In the Visual Basic Editor's Project Explorer window, double-click **Form_Employee Sales Pivot**.

2. The Code window shows the procedures created in the previous hands-on exercises for this chapter. Enter the following **Form_SelectionChange** event procedure below the last procedure code, or copy and paste the code from **C:\Acc07_HandsOn\Chap24.txt**.

```
Private Sub Form_SelectionChange()
    Debug.Print "Selection Type: " & Me.PivotTable.SelectionType
End Sub
```

3. To test the above event procedure, open the **Employee Sales Pivot** form in PivotTable view. Because you've already created several event procedures for this form, various events will be triggered. Respond appropriately to the prompts. Once the form opens in the PivotTable view, click on various areas of the PivotTable and open the Immediate window to see the names of the selected objects. Notice that the SelectionType values are always returned in plural:

```
Selection Type: PivotFields
Selection Type: PivotDetailRange
Selection Type: PivotColumnMembers
Selection Type: PivotRowMembers
Selection Type: PivotAggregates
```

4. Save and close the form.

ViewChange

The ViewChange event occurs whenever the PivotTable or PivotChart objects are redrawn. This event may occur multiple times for a single operation. For PivotTable views, you can use the Reason argument to determine how the view was changed. This argument contains a value from the PivotDataReasonEnum enumeration. Do not use the Reason argument with a PivotChart. The event procedure in Hands-On 24-30 displays a message when the user clicks the Show/Hide Details button in PivotTable view.

⊚ Hands-On 24-30: Writing the Form_ViewChange Event Procedure

1. In the Visual Basic Editor's Project Explorer window, double-click **Form_Employee Sales Pivot**.

2. The Code window shows the procedures created in the previous hands-on exercises for this chapter. Enter the following **Form_ViewChange** event procedure below the last procedure code, or copy and paste the code from **C:\Acc07_HandsOn\Chap24.txt**.

```
Private Sub Form_ViewChange(ByVal Reason As Long)
    Select Case Reason
        Case OWC11.plViewReasonHideDetails
            MsgBox "You selected to hide the details."
        Case OWC11.plViewReasonShowDetails
            MsgBox "You selected to show the details."
    End Select
End Sub
```

3. To test the above event procedure, open the **Employee Sales Pivot** form in PivotTable view. Because you've already created several event procedures for this form, various events will be triggered. Respond appropriately to the prompts. Once the form opens in the PivotTable view, click the **Show/Hide Details** (+ /–) button below any employee name.

4. Save and close the form.

Command Events

CommandEnabled

The CommandEnabled event occurs whenever the enabled state of a menu bar or toolbar command changes. This event takes two arguments:

- **Command** — Returns a PivotCommandId constant and allows you to determine which command has been enabled or disabled. You can use the Object Browser to view the list of available commands for this constant.

- **Enabled** — An object whose Value property indicates whether the command is enabled or disabled.

The event procedure in Hands-On 24-31 checks whether the Copy command (plCommandCopy) is enabled or disabled.

◎ Hands-On 24-31: Writing the Form_CommandEnabled Event Procedure

1. In the Visual Basic Editor's Project Explorer window, double-click **Form_Employee Sales Pivot**.

2. The Code window shows the procedures created in the previous hands-on exercises for this chapter. Enter the following **Form_CommandEnabled** event procedure below the last procedure code, or copy and paste the code from **C:\Acc07_HandsOn\Chap24.txt**.

```
Private Sub Form_CommandEnabled(ByVal Command As Variant, _
                    ByVal Enabled As Object)

    If Command = OWC11.plCommandCopy Then
        If Enabled.Value = True Then
            Debug.Print "Copy command enabled."
        Else
            Debug.Print "Copy command disabled."
        End If
    End If
End Sub
```

3. To test the above event procedure, open the **Employee Sales Pivot** in PivotTable view. Because you've already created several event procedures for this form, various events will be triggered. Respond appropriately to the prompts. Once the form opens, switch to the Immediate window and examine the results of the events that were executed.

4. Save and close the form.

CommandChecked

The CommandChecked event occurs whenever a menu bar command becomes checked or unchecked or a toolbar command's state changes from pressed to not pressed and vice versa. The CommandChecked event takes the following two arguments:

- **Command** — Returns a PivotCommandId constant and allows you to determine which command has been checked or unchecked. You can use the Object Browser to view the list of available commands for this constant.

- **Checked** — An object whose Value property indicates whether the command is checked or unchecked. For example, the Sort Ascending command is available on the menu bar, toolbar, and shortcut menu of the form. Whenever the Sort Ascending command becomes checked or unchecked, the CommandChecked event will fire at least three times.

The event procedure in Hands-On 24-32 checks whether the Sort Ascending command has been checked or unchecked.

⊚ Hands-On 24-32: Writing the Form_CommandChecked Event Procedure

1. In the Visual Basic Editor's Project Explorer window, double-click **Form_Employee Sales Pivot**.

2. The Code window shows the procedures created in the previous hands-on exercises for this chapter. Enter the following **Form_CommandChecked** event procedure below the last procedure code, or copy and paste the code from **C:\Acc07_HandsOn\Chap24.txt**.

```
Private Sub Form_CommandChecked(ByVal Command As Variant, _
                    ByVal Checked As Object)

    If Command = OWC11.plCommandSortAsc Then
        If Checked.Value = True Then
            Debug.Print "Sort Ascending command is checked."
        Else
            Debug.Print "Sort Ascending command unchecked."
        End If
    End If
End Sub
```

3. To test the above event procedure, clear the Immediate window by pressing **Ctrl+A** to select all the text and pressing **Delete** to clear the window. Next, open the **Employee Sales Pivot** form in PivotTable view. Because you've already created several event procedures for this form, various events will be triggered. Respond appropriately to the prompts. Once the form opens, choose **Home | Sort Descending**. Switch to the Immediate window to see the results of the events that were executed.

4. Close the Employee Sales Pivot form and save changes to the form when prompted.

CommandBeforeExecute

The CommandBeforeExecute event occurs when a user selects a command from the menu bar or toolbar but before the action associated with the command takes place. You can use this event to cancel the command selected or to impose certain restrictions before a command is executed. This event takes the following two arguments:

- **Command** — Returns a PivotCommandId constant and allows you to determine which command the user wishes to execute. You can use the Object Browser to view the list of commands for this constant.

- **Cancel** — Returns an object. By setting the Value property of this argument to True, the specified command will not be executed.

CommandExecute

The CommandExecute event occurs after a user selects a command from the menu bar or toolbar. You can use this event when you want to execute a set of commands after a particular command is executed. This event takes the Command argument that returns a PivotCommandId constant, which allows you to determine which command the user executed. You can use the Object Browser to view the list of commands for this constant.

The event procedure in Hands-On 24-33 checks whether the user used the Copy command. If the Copy command was executed, the procedure displays a message.

⊚ Hands-On 24-33: Writing the Form_CommandExecute Event Procedure

1. In the Visual Basic Editor's Project Explorer window, double-click **Form_Employee Sales Pivot.**

2. The Code window shows the procedures created in the previous hands-on exercises for this chapter. Enter the following **Form_CommandExecute** event procedure below the last procedure code, or copy and paste the code from **C:\Acc07_HandsOn\Chap24.txt.**

```
Private Sub Form_CommandExecute(ByVal Command As Variant)
    If Command = OWC11.plCommandCopy Then
        MsgBox "You just copied some data to the clipboard."
    End If
End Sub
```

3. To test the above event procedure, open the **Employee Sales Pivot** form in PivotTable view. Because you've already created several event procedures for this form, various events will be triggered. Respond appropriately to the prompts. Once the form is opened, right-click any amount in the detail rows in the PivotTable and choose **Copy** from the shortcut menu. After choosing the Copy command you should see the message informing you that the text was copied to the clipboard.

4. Close the Employee Sales Pivot form and save changes to the form when prompted.

Keyboard and Mouse Events

PivotTable and PivotChart views in Access can also respond to the following events: KeyDown, KeyPress, KeyUp, MouseDown, MouseMove, MouseUp, MouseWheel, Click, and DblClick. These events are the same as the form's keyboard and mouse events discussed earlier in this chapter.

Events Recognized by Form Sections

In addition to trapping events for the entire form, you can write event procedures for the following form sections: Detail, FormHeader, FormFooter, PageHeader, and PageFooter. Form sections respond to the following events: Click, DblClick, MouseDown, MouseUp, and MouseMove.

DblClick (Form Section Event)

The DblClick event occurs when you double-click inside the form's header or footer section.

The example procedure in Hands-On 24-34 demonstrates how to randomly change the background color for each of the form's sections every time you double-click anywhere within the form's Detail section.

⊚ Hands-On 24-34: Writing the Detail_DblClick Event Procedure

1. In the Navigation pane of the Chap24.accdb database, open the **Product Categories** form in Design view. Recall that you created this form in Hands-On 24-6.

2. Increase the size of the header and footer so that they are visible when you run the form.

3. In the property sheet, choose **Details** from the drop-down box. Click the **Event** tab and select **[Event Procedure]** next to the DblClick property name. Click the **Build** button (...).

4. In the Code window, you should have the stub of the Detail_DblClick event procedure already written for you. Complete this procedure as shown below, or copy and paste the code from **C:\Acc07_HandsOn\Chap24.txt**.

```
Private Sub Detail_DblClick(Cancel As Integer)
    With Me
        .Section(acHeader).BackColor = _
            RGB(Rnd * 128, _
            Rnd * 256, _
            Rnd * 255)
        .Section(acDetail).BackColor = _
            RGB(Rnd * 128, _
            Rnd * 256, _
            Rnd * 255)
        .Section(acFooter).BackColor = _
            RGB(Rnd * 128, _
            Rnd * 256, _
            Rnd * 255)
    End With
End Sub
```

5. To test the above event procedure, open the **Product Categories** form in Form view. Double-click anywhere in the **Detail** section of the form and see the colors of the Detail, Header, and Footer sections change.

Chapter Summary

In this chapter, you learned that numerous events can occur on a Microsoft Access form and that you can react to a specific form event by writing an event procedure. If you don't write your own code to handle a particular form event, Access will handle this event in its default way.

After trying out the 34 hands-on exercises presented in this chapter, you should have a good understanding of how to write event procedures for an Access form. You should also be able to recognize the importance of form events in an Access application. You will find more examples of using form events in a custom application introduced in Chapter 26.

For more hands-on experience with event programming, proceed to the next chapter, which discusses the events recognized by an Access report and its sections.

Chapter 25

Using Report Events

When an Access report is run, a number of events can occur. The following examples demonstrate how to control what happens not only when the report is opened, activated, deactivated, or closed, but also when there are no records for the report to display or the report record source simply does not exist.

Open

The Open event for a report occurs when the report is opened. Use this event to display support forms or custom buttons, or to change the record source for the report. The event procedure in Hands-On 25-1 demonstrates how to change a report's record source on the fly.

◎ Hands-On 25-1: Writing the Report_Open Event Procedure

1. Start Microsoft Office Access 2007 and create a new Microsoft Office Access 2007 database named **Chap25.accdb** in your **C:\Acc07_ByExample** folder.

2. Import all the tables, queries, forms, reports, macros, and modules from the Northwind.mdb sample database to your Chap25.accdb database. To do this, in the Access window, choose **External Data | Access**. In the File name box, type **C:\Acc07_ByExample\Northwind.mdb** and click **OK**. In the Import Objects window, select the **Tables** tab and click the **Select All** button. This will highlight all the tables. Select the **Queries** tab and click the **Select All** button. Select the **Forms** tab and click the **Select All** button. Select the **Reports** tab and click the **Select All** button. Do the same for macros and modules. After selecting all the objects on the specified tabs, click **OK** to begin importing. Click the **Close** button when done.

3. In the Access window's Navigation pane, select the **Customers** table and choose **Create | Report Wizard**. Select all the fields for the report and click the **Next** button. Continue clicking **Next** until you get to the Report Wizard screen where you can specify the title for your report. Type **rptCustomers** for the title and click **Finish**.

4. Choose **Home | View | Design View** to switch to the Design view of the rptCustomers report.

5. In the Report Header area, click the report title (label control) to select it. In the property sheet for the selected label control, click the **All** tab and type **lblCustomers** as the Name property and enter **Customers** as the Caption property.

6. In the property sheet, select **Report** from the drop-down box and click the **Event** tab. Click next to the **On Open** event property and choose **[Event Procedure]** from the drop-down box. Click the **Build** button (…).

7. Access opens the Visual Basic Editor window and writes the stub of the Report_Open event procedure. Complete the code of the **Report_Open** event procedure as shown below, or copy and paste the code from **C:\Acc07_HandsOn\Chap25.txt.**

```
Private Sub Report_Open(Cancel As Integer)
    Dim strCustName As String
    Dim strSQL As String
    Dim strWHERE As String

    On Error GoTo ErrHandler
    strSQL = "SELECT * FROM Customers"

    strCustName = InputBox("Type the first letter of " & _
        " the Company Name or type an asterisk (*) to view" & _
        " all companies.", "Show All /Or Filter")

    If strCustName = "" Then
        Cancel = True
    ElseIf strCustName = "*" Then
        Me.RecordSource = strSQL
        Me.lblCustomers.Caption = "All Customers"
    Else
        strCustName = "'" & Trim(strCustName) & "*" & "'"
        strWHERE = " WHERE CompanyName Like " _
            & strCustName & ""
        Debug.Print strSQL
        Debug.Print strWHERE
        Me.RecordSource = strSQL & strWHERE
        Me.lblCustomers.Caption = "Selected Customers" & _
            " (" & UCase(strCustName) & ")"
    End If
    Exit Sub
ErrHandler:
    MsgBox Err.Description
End Sub
```

8. Switch to the rptCustomers report's Design view and choose **Home | View | Print Preview**. A message box will appear where you can enter an asterisk (*) to view all customers or the first letter of a company name if you'd like to limit your records. To cancel the report, click **Cancel** or press the **Esc** key.

Close

The Close event occurs when you close the report. Use this event to close supporting forms or to perform other cleanup operations. You cannot cancel the Close event. Figure 25-1 shows the Report_Close event procedure for the Sales by Year report in the Northwind.mdb database. This report opens via the Sales by Year Dialog form where the user can specify the report beginning and ending dates. This form remains open while the report is open and is closed during the Report_Close event.

```
Private Sub Report_Close()
' Close the Sales by Year Dialog form.

    Dim strDocName As String

    strDocName = "Sales by Year Dialog"

    DoCmd.Close acForm, strDocName

End Sub
```

Figure 25-1: The Report_Close event procedure is often used to close supporting forms.

Activate

The Activate event occurs when the report is opened right after the Open event but before the event for the first section of the report. The procedure in Hands-On 25-2 displays a message when the report is open in Print Preview and returns the name of the default printer to the Immediate window.

◎ Hands-On 25-2: Writing the Report_Activate Event Procedure

This hands-on exercise uses the rptCustomers report created in Hands-On 25-1.

1. In the Visual Basic Editor's Project Explorer window, double-click the **rptCustomers** report. In the Code window, enter the following Report_Activate event procedure, or copy and paste the code from **C:\Acc07_HandsOn\Chap25.txt.**

```
Private Sub Report_Activate()
    If Me.CurrentView = acCurViewPreview Then
        MsgBox "Activating Print Preview of " _
        & Me.Name & " report."
        Debug.Print "Default Printer: " & _
        Application.Printer.DeviceName
    End If
End Sub
```

Notice how the CurrentView property is used to determine the current view of an object. The following table lists the CurrentView property constants.

Table 25-1: CurrentView property names and values

CurrentView Property Name	Value	Description
acCurViewDesign	0	The object is in Design view.
acCurViewFormBrowse	1	The object is in Form view.
acCurViewDatasheet	2	The object is in Datasheet view.
acCurViewPivotTable	3	The object is in PivotTable view.
acCurViewPivotChart	4	The object is in PivotChart view.
acCurViewPreview	5	The object is in Print Preview.
acCurViewReportBrowse	6	The object is in Report view.
acCurViewLayout	7	The object is in Layout view.

2. In the Navigation pane of the Access window, right-click the **rptCustomers** report and choose **Print Preview**. Enter your report criteria when prompted. Upon activation of the report, the Report_Activate event will fire and you should see a message. Click **OK** to the message, then switch to the Immediate window to check out the name of the default printer.

3. Close the rptCustomers report and save changes to the report when prompted.

Deactivate

The Deactivate event occurs when a report loses the focus to a table, query, form, report, macro, module, or database window. This event occurs before the Close event for the report.

NoData

The NoData event occurs when the record source for the report contains no records. This event allows you to cancel the report when no records are available. The event procedure in Hands-On 25-3 displays a message when the user enters criteria that are not met.

◉ Hands-On 25-3: Writing the Report_NoData Event Procedure

This hands-on exercise uses the rptCustomers report created in Hands-On 25-1.

1. In the Visual Basic Editor's Project Explorer window, double-click the **Report_ rptCustomers** report. In the Code window, enter the following **Report_NoData** event procedure, or copy and paste the code from **C:\Acc07_HandsOn\Chap25.txt**.

```
Private Sub Report_NoData(Cancel As Integer)
    MsgBox "There is no data for the criteria " & _
        "you entered."
    Cancel = True
End Sub
```

2. Switch to the Access window and open the **rptCustomers** report. Request to see customers with a company name starting with the letter "X." Because there aren't any company names beginning with "X," a message box will be displayed, saying that there is no data for the criteria entered, and the report will be canceled.

Page

The Page event occurs after a page is formatted but before it is printed. Use the Page event to customize the appearance of your printed reports by adding lines, circles, and graphics. The event procedure in Hands-On 25-4 will draw a red border around the report pages.

⊚ Hands-On 25-4: Writing the Report_Page Event Procedure

This hands-on exercise uses the rptCustomers report created in Hands-On 25-1.

1. In the Visual Basic Editor's Project Explorer window, double-click the **rptCustomers** report. In the Code window, enter the following Report_ Page event procedure, or copy and paste the code from **C:\Acc07_ HandsOn\Chap25.txt**.

```
Private Sub Report_Page()
    Me.DrawWidth = 15 ' pixels
    Me.Line (0, 0)-(Me.ScaleWidth, _
        Me.ScaleHeight), vbRed, B
End Sub
```

Notice that the DrawWidth method specifies the thickness of the line and the Line method draws a line with an upper-left corner at (0, 0) and the lower-right corner at (Me.ScaleWidth, MeScaleHeight). The ScaleWidth and ScaleHeight properties specify the width and height of the report.

2. Switch to the Access window and open the **rptCustomers** report in the Print Preview. Notice that when the report appears on the screen, a red border surrounds the pages (see Figure 25-2).

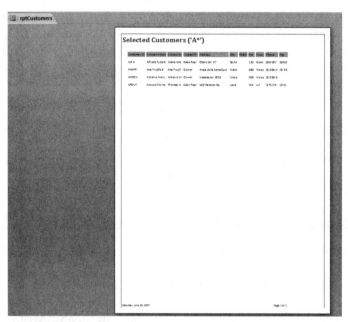

Figure 25-2: You can frame your Access report pages with a red line by implementing the Report_Page event procedure as shown in Hands-On 25-4.

Error

The Error event is triggered by errors in accessing the data for the report. Use this event to replace the default error message with your custom message. The Error event takes the following two arguments:

- **DataErr** — Contains the number of the Microsoft Access error that occurred.

- **Response** — Determines whether or not error messages should be displayed. It may be one of the following constants:

    - *acDataErrContinue* — Ignore the error and continue without displaying the default Microsoft Access error message.

    - *AcDataErrDisplay* — Display the default Microsoft Access error message. This is the default.

The Report_Error event procedure in Hands-On 25-5 illustrates how to use the value of the DataErr argument together with the AccessError method to determine the error number and its descriptive string.

The statement:

```
Response = acDataErrContinue
```

will prevent the standard Microsoft Access error message from appearing. The Error event for reports works the same as the Error event for forms — but only the Microsoft Access ACE or the Jet Engine errors can be trapped here.

To trap errors in your VBA code, use the On Error GoTo statement to direct the procedure flow to the location of the error-handling statements within your procedure.

⊚ Hands-On 25-5: Writing the Report_Error Event Procedure

1. In the Navigation pane, rename the Customers table to **Customers2**.

2. In the Visual Basic Editor's Project Explorer window, double-click the **rptCustomers** report. In the Code window, enter the following **Report_Error** event procedure, or copy and paste the code from **C:\Acc07_HandsOn\Chap25.txt**.

```
Private Sub Report_Error(DataErr As Integer, _
            Response As Integer)
    ' obtain information about the error
    ' MsgBox Application.AccessError(DataErr), _
        vbOKOnly, "Error Number: " & DataErr
    If DataErr = 3078 Then
    Response = acDataErrContinue
        MsgBox "Your custom error message goes here."
    End If
End Sub
```

3. Switch to the Access window and open the **rptCustomers** report. When the input box appears prompting you for the criteria, type any letter and press **OK**. At this point the Report_Error event will fire because the underlying data for the rptCustomers report does not exist. Because you renamed the Customers table that this report uses for its data source, Microsoft Access cannot locate the data, which generates the error.

4. In the Navigation pane, change the Customers2 table's name back to **Customers** and open the **rptCustomers** report to ensure that it does not produce unexpected errors.

5. Close the report when finished and save the changes when prompted.

Events Recognized by Report Sections

A Microsoft Access report can contain various sections such as Report Header/Footer, Page Header/Footer, the Detail section, and Group Headers/Footers. All report sections can respond to the Format and Print events. These events occur when you print or preview a report. In addition, the Report Header/Footer and the Detail section recognize the Retreat event that occurs when Access returns to a previous section during report formatting.

Format (Report Section Event)

A Format event occurs for each section in a report before Microsoft Access formats the section for previewing or printing. This event takes the following two arguments:

- **Cancel** — Determines if the formatting of the section occurs. To cancel the section formatting, set this argument to True.

- **FormatCount** — An integer that specifies whether the Format event has occurred more than once for a section. If a section does not fit on one page and the rest of the section needs to be moved to the next page of the report, the FormatCount argument is set to 2.

Use the Format event in the appropriate report section for changes that affect page layout. For changes that don't affect page layout, use the Print event for the report section.

Table 25-2: Effect of Format event on report sections

Report Sections	Description of Format Event
Detail	The Format event occurs for each record in the section just before Microsoft Access formats the data in the record. You can access the data in the current record using the event procedure.
Group Headers	The Format event occurs for each new group. You can access the data in the Group Header and the data in the first record in the Detail section using the event procedure.
Group Footers	The Format event occurs for each new group. You can access the data in the Group Footer and the data in the last record in the Detail section via an event procedure.

The event procedure in Hands-On 25-6 demonstrates how to make reports easier to read by shading alternate rows.

◎ Hands-On 25-6: Writing the Detail_Format Event Procedure

1. In the Visual Basic Editor's Project Explorer window, double-click the **rptCustomers** report. In the Code window, enter the following **Detail_Format** event procedure, or copy and paste the code from **C:\Acc07_HandsOn\Chap25.txt**. Do not type the Option Compare Database and Option Explicit statements if they are already at the top of the Code window.

```
Option Compare Database
Option Explicit

Dim shaded As Boolean

Private Sub Detail_Format(Cancel As Integer, _
        FormatCount As Integer)
    If shaded Then
        Me.Detail.BackColor = vbYellow
    Else
        Me.Detail.BackColor = vbWhite
```

```
      End If
          shaded = Not shaded
      End Sub
```

Notice that at the top of the module sheet (in the module's Declarations area) we have placed the following statement:

```
Dim shaded As Boolean
```

The above statement declares the global variable of the Boolean type to keep track of the alternate rows.

When you run the report, upon printing the Detail section, Access will check the value of the shaded variable. If the value is True, it will change the background of the formatted row to yellow (which produces a light gray background when printed on a laser printer). The shaded value will then be set to False for the next row by using the following statement:

```
shaded = Not shaded
```

The above statement works as a toggle. If shaded was True, it will be False now, and so on.

2. Switch to the Access window and open the **rptCustomers** report in Print Preview. When the input box prompts you for the criteria, type an asterisk (*) and press **OK**.

Figure 25-3: The formatting result after implementing the Detail_Format event in Hands-On 25-6 is illustrated here.

The next hands-on exercise demonstrates how to suppress the Page Footer on the first page of your report by placing code in the PageFooterSection_Format event procedure.

Hands-On 25-7: Writing the PageFooterSection_Format Event Procedure

1. Using the Report Wizard, create a report called **rptProducts** based on the **Products** table. Choose the following fields for this report: **ProductID**, **ProductName**, **UnitPrice**, and **UnitsInStock**.

2. In the Design view of the rptProducts report, select **PageFooterSection** in the property sheet. Click the **Event** tab. Click next to the **On Format** property and select **[Event Procedure]** from the drop-down list. Click the **Build** button (…) to activate the Code window.

3. In the Code window for rptProducts, enter the following **PageFooterSection_Format** event procedure, or copy and paste the code from **C:\Acc07_HandsOn\Chap25.txt**.

```
Private Sub PageFooterSection_Format(Cancel As Integer, _
    FormatCount As Integer)
    Dim ctrl As Control

    For Each ctrl In Me.PageFooterSection.Controls
        If Me.Page = 1 Then
            ctrl.Visible = False
        Else
            ctrl.Visible = True
        End If
    Next ctrl
End Sub
```

4. Switch to the Access window and open the rptProducts report in Print Preview. Notice that the Footer section does not appear on the first page of the report.

5. Close the rptProducts report and save changes to the report when prompted.

Print (Report Section Event)

The Print event occurs after the data in a report section has been formatted but before the data is printed. The Print event occurs only for sections that are actually printed. To access data from sections that are not printed, use the Format event.

You can use the PrintCount argument to check whether the Print event has occurred more than once for a record. If part of a record is printed on one page and the rest is printed on the next page, the Print event will occur twice, and the PrintCount argument will be set to 2. You can use the Cancel argument to cancel the printing of a section.

Table 25-3: Effect of Print event on report sections

Report Section	Description of Event
Detail	The Print event occurs for each record in the Detail section just before Microsoft Access prints the data in the record.
Group Headers	The Print event occurs for each new group.
Group Footers	The Print event occurs for each new group.

The event procedure in Hands-On 25-8 demonstrates how to print a record range indicator in the report's Footer. This indicator will display the range of records printed on each page. You can easily modify this example procedure to print the first and last customer ID on the page (see the discussion before Figure 25-5).

◎ Hands-On 25-8: Writing the Detail_Print Event Procedure

This hands-on exercise uses the rptCustomers report you created in Hands-On 25-1.

1. Open the **rptCustomers** report in the Design view and place two unbound text boxes in the report's Page Footer section.

2. Change the Name property of the first box to **txtPage** and set its Visible property to **No**. Delete the label control in front of this text box.

3. Name the second text box **txtRange** and set the Caption property of its label control to **Records:**.

4. In the property sheet, select **Detail** from the drop-down box and click the **Event** tab. Set the On Print property of the Detail section to **[Event Procedure]** and write the code for the **Detail_Print** event as shown below, or copy and paste the code from **C:\Acc07_HandsOn\Chap25.txt**.

```
Private Sub Detail_Print(Cancel As Integer, _
            PrintCount As Integer)
    Static rCount As Integer
    Static start As Integer
    Static firstId As String
    Static lastId As String

    If Me.Page <> Me.txtPage Then
        start = Me.CurrentRecord
        firstId = CustomerID
        Me.txtPage = Me.Page
        rCount = 0
    End If
        rCount = rCount + 1
        lastId = CustomerID
    If start <= rCount Then
        Me.txtRange = start & "-" & rCount
        ' Me.txtRange = UCase(firstId) & "-" & UCase(lastId)
    Else
        rCount = Me.CurrentRecord
        lastId = CustomerID
```

```
        End If
      End Sub
```

The Detail_Print event procedure occurs for each record. It uses the start and rCount variables to keep track of the first and last item on the page.

5. In the Code window, enter the **PageHeaderSection_Print** event procedure as shown below.

```
Private Sub PageHeaderSection_Print(Cancel As Integer, _
                        PrintCount As Integer)
    Me.txtPage = 0
End Sub
```

6. To test the above event procedure, switch to the Access window and open the **rptCustomers** report in Print Preview. Notice the record range indicator at the bottom of the report page.

The PageHeaderSection_Print event procedure will set the value of the unbound txtPage text box to zero (0) whenever the Print event occurs for a new page.

Figure 25-4: This report displays the record range indicator at the bottom of the page (see Hands-On 25-8).

You can modify the event procedure in Hands-On 25-8 to print the first and last customer ID on the page as shown in Figure 25-5. Simply replace the following statement in the Detail_Print event procedure:

```
Me.txtRange = start & "-" & rCount
```

with the following line of code:

```
Me.txtRange = UCase(firstId) & "-" & UCase(lastId)
```

CACTU	Cactus Comida	Patricio Si	Sales Agen	Cerrito 333		Buen	101	Argen (1) 135-5 (1) 13
CENTC	Centro comerc	Francisco	Marketing	Sierras de Granada 99		Mèxic	050	Mèxic (5) 555-3 (5) 55
CHOPS	Chop-suey Chi	Yang Wan	Owner	Hauptstr. 29		Bern	301	Switz 0452-07
COMMI	Comércio Min	Pedro Afo	Sales Asso	Av. dos Lusíadas, 23	São P SP		054	Brazil (11) 555-
CONSH	Consolidated	Elizabeth	Sales Repr	Berkeley Gardens		Lond	WX UK	(171) 55 (171)
DRACD	Drachenblut D	Sven Ottlie	Order Ad	Walserweg 21		Aach	520	Germ 0241-03 0241-
DUMON	Du monde enti	Janine Lab	Owner	67, rue des Cinquante		Nant	440	Franc 40.67.88 40.67
EASTC	Eastern Conne	Ann Devo	Sales Agen	35 King George		Lond	WX UK	(171) 55 (171)
ERNSH	Ernst Handel	Roland Me	Sales Man	Kirchgasse 6		Graz	801	Austri 7675-34 7675-
FAMIA	Família Arquib	Aria Cruz	Marketing	Rua Orós, 92	São P SP		054	Brazil (11) 555-
FISSA	FISSA Fabrica l	Diego Roel	Accountin	C/ Moralzarzal, 86		Madri	280	Spain (91) 555 (91) 5
FOLIG	Folies gourma	Martine R	Assistant S	184, chaussée de Tour		Lille	590	Franc 20.16.10 20.16
FOLKO	Folk och fä HB	Maria Lars	Owner	Åkergatan 24		Bräck	S-84	Swed 0695-34
FRANK	Frankenversan	Peter Fran	Marketing	Berliner Platz 43		Münc	808	Germ 089-087 089-0
FRANR	France restaur	Carine Sch	Marketing	54, rue Royale		Nant	440	Franc 40.32.21 40.32
FRANS	Franchi S.p.A.	Paolo Acc	Sales Repr	Via Monte Bianco 34		Torin	101	Italy 011-498 011-4
FURIB	Furia Bacalhau	Lino Rodri	Sales Man	Jardim das rosas n. 32		Lisbo	167	Portu (1) 354-2 (1) 35
GALED	Galería del gas	Eduardo S	Marketing	Rambla de Cataluña, 2		Barce	080	Spain (93) 203 (93) 2
GODOS	Godos Cocina	José Pedro	Sales Man	C/ Romero, 33		Sevill	411	Spain (95) 555
GOURL	Gourmet Lanc	André Fon	Sales Asso	Av. Brasil, 442		Camp SP	048	Brazil (11) 555-
GREAL	Great Lakes Fo	Howard Sn	Marketing	2732 Baker Blvd.		Euge OR	974	USA (503) 55

Records: ALFKI-GREAL

Saturday, June 23, 2007 · Page 1 of 3

Figure 25-5: This report displays the first and last Customer ID for a specific page at the bottom of each printed page.

Retreat

The Retreat event occurs when Microsoft Access returns to previous sections of the report during report formatting. For example, after formatting a report section, if Access discovers that the data will not fit on the page, it will go back to the necessary location in the report to ensure that the section can properly begin on the next page.

The Retreat event occurs after the Format event but before the Print event. This event applies to all report sections except Page Headers and Footers. The Retreat event occurs for Group Headers and Footers whose KeepTogether property has been set to Whole Group or With First Detail. This event is also triggered in subreports whose CanGrow or CanShrink properies have been set to True.

The Retreat event makes it possible to undo any changes made during the Format event for the section.

The Retreat event is demonstrated in the sample Northwind.mdb database's Sales by Year report, as shown in Figure 25-6.

```
Private Sub GroupFooter1_Retreat()
' If ShowDetails check box on Sales by Year Dialog form is checked,
' set value of Show text box to True so that page header will print on
' next page.

    If Forms![Sales by Year Dialog]!ShowDetails Then Me!Show.Value = True

End Sub
```

Figure 25-6: The Sales by Year report in the Northwind.mdb database uses the GroupFooter1_Retreat event procedure to control printing of a page header.

Chapter Summary

In this chapter you learned about several events that fire when the Access report is run. By writing your own event procedures you can specify what happens when the report is opened, activated/deactivated, or closed. You can also display a custom message when an error occurs or the report does not contain any data; or you can make last-minute changes to the report layout before it is printed or previewed.

In the next chapter, you will learn about events recognized by various form controls while working with a custom application.

Chapter 26

Events Recognized by Controls

In addition to the events for forms and reports introduced in Chapters 24 and 25, you can control a great many events that occur for labels, text boxes, combo and list boxes, option buttons, check boxes, and other controls installed by default with an Access application. These events make it possible to manage what happens on a field level.

The best way to learn about events that a form, report, and/or control can respond to is to develop an application that addresses specific needs. For example, the AssetsDataEntry.mdb database keeps track of computer assets in various companies. We will use this database to further experiment with event programming. The main data entry form is divided into four easy-to-maintain sections as illustrated in Figure 26-1.

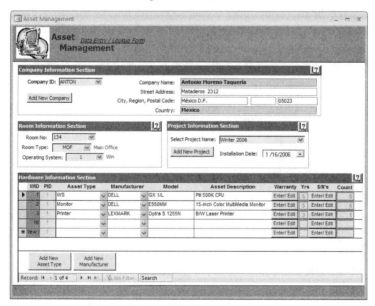

Figure 26-1: Custom data entry form.

625

◎ Hands-On 26-1: Launching the Custom Access Application

1. Copy the **AssetsDataEntry.mdb** file from the **C:\Acc07_HandsOn** folder to your **C:\Acc07_ByExample** folder.

2. To gain access to the database source code, double-click the **C:\Acc07_ByExample\AssetsDataEntry.mdb** file while holding down the **Shift** key.

3. When Access loads the database, locate in the Navigation pane the **frmDataEntryMain** form and open it in Design view.

Now that the main data entry form is open, we will proceed to examine the events that this form's controls respond to.

Enter (Control)

The Enter event occurs before a control actually receives the focus from another control on the same form. The Enter event applies to text boxes, combo and list boxes, option buttons, check boxes, option groups, command buttons, toggle buttons, bound and unbound object frames, and subform and subreport controls. You can use the Enter event to display a message directing the user to first fill in another control on the form.

For example, when a user attempts to make a selection from the combo box controls located in the Room Information and Project Information sections of the Asset Management form (Figure 26-1) without first specifying the Company ID, the following Enter event procedures may be triggered: cboRooms_Enter, cboRoomType_Enter, cboOS_Enter, and cboProject_Enter.

◎ Hands-On 26-2: Using the Enter Event Procedure for the Combo Box Control

1. Open the **frmDataEntryMain** form in Form view.

2. Click inside the combo box control located to the right of the **Room No:** label. This action will fire the following Enter event procedure:

```
Private Sub cboRooms_Enter()
   If Me.cboCompanyID = "" Or IsNull(Me.cboCompanyID) Then
      MsgBox "Please select Company ID.", _
         vbInformation + vbOKOnly, _
         "Missing Company ID"
      Me.cboCompanyID.SetFocus
      Exit Sub
   End If
End Sub
```

3. Click **OK** to the information message generated by the cboRooms_Enter event procedure and notice that the cursor has been positioned inside the combo box control containing Company IDs. Don't make any selections from the Company ID combo box at this time.

4. Click on the combo box control next to the **Room Type** label. This action will fire the following Enter event procedure:

```
Private Sub cboRoomType_Enter()
    If Me.cboCompanyID = "" Or IsNull(Me.cboCompanyID) Then
        MsgBox "Please select Company ID.", _
            vbInformation + vbOKOnly, "Missing Company ID"
        Me.cboCompanyID.SetFocus
        Exit Sub
    End If
    If Me.cboRooms = "" Or IsNull(Me.cboRooms) Then
        MsgBox "Please specify or select Room number.", _
            vbInformation + vbOKOnly, "Missing Room Number"
        Me.cboRooms.SetFocus
        Exit Sub
    End If
End Sub
```

When you click the cboRoomType combo box control, the Enter event checks whether the cboCompanyID combo box control or cboRooms combo box control is empty. If no selection has been made in these controls, a message box is displayed and the focus is moved to the appropriate combo box control.

5. Click **OK** to the information message generated by the cboRoomType_Enter event procedure and notice that the cursor has again been positioned inside the Company ID combo box control.

BeforeUpdate (Control)

The BeforeUpdate event occurs when you attempt to save the record or leave the control after making changes. This event applies to text boxes, combo and list boxes, option buttons, check boxes, and bound object frames. Use this event to validate the entry.

For example, the combo box control in the Company Information section of the Asset Management form causes Microsoft Access to display a custom message if the value of the cboCompanyID combo box control is Null. To cancel the Update event, the Cancel argument has been set to True.

⊚ Hands-On 26-3: Using the BeforeUpdate Event Procedure for the Combo Box Control

1. Make sure that the **frmDataEntryMain** form is open in Design view.

2. Right-click the combo box control to the right of the **Company ID** label and choose **Build Event** from the shortcut menu.

3. The Microsoft Visual Basic Editor window will appear with the cursor positioned inside the following event procedure:

```
Private Sub cboCompanyID_BeforeUpdate(Cancel As Integer)
    Dim strMsg As String, strTitle As String
    Dim intStyle As Integer

    If IsNull(Me!cboCompanyID) Or Me!cboCompanyID = "" Then
        strMsg = "You must pick a value from the Company ID list."
```

```
      strTitle = "Company ID Required"
      intStyle = vbOKOnly
      MsgBox strMsg, intStyle, strTitle
      Cancel = True
   End If
End Sub
```

4. Position the cursor inside the If statement, then press **F9** or choose **Debug |**
   Toggle Breakpoint.

5. Activate the **frmDataEntryMain** form in Form view and make a selection
   from the Company ID combo box.

   When you make your selection, the BeforeUpdate event procedure is fired
   and the Code window appears in break mode. Press **F8** to step through the
   code line by line. Because you have not set up more breakpoints, you cannot see that two other events (cboCompanyID_AfterUpdate and
   cboRooms_Enter) were triggered when you made a selection from the
   Company ID combo box.

6. When the procedure finishes executing, activate the **frmDataEntryMain**
   form. You should see the text boxes filled with a company name and
   address and the cursor positioned inside the Room No combo box and
   ready for the next selection or data entry.

AfterUpdate (Control)

The AfterUpdate event occurs after the data in the control has been modified.
It applies to text boxes, combo and list boxes, option buttons, check boxes, and
bound object frames. Unlike the BeforeUpdate event, the AfterUpdate event
cannot be canceled. Use this event to fill in other controls on the form based on
the newly entered or selected value.

For example, after updating the cboCompanyID combo box in the Company
Information section of the Asset Management form, the following event procedure is executed:

```
Private Sub cboCompanyID_AfterUpdate()
   With Me
      .txtCompanyName = Me.[cboCompanyID].Column(1)
      .txtAddress = Me.cboCompanyID.Column(2)
      .txtCity = Me.cboCompanyID.Column(3)
      .txtRegion = Me.cboCompanyID.Column(4)
      .txtPostalCode = Me.cboCompanyID.Column(5)
      .txtCountry = Me.cboCompanyID.Column(6)
      .cboRooms.Value = vbNullString
      .cboRooms.Requery
      .txtRoomDescription = vbNullString
      .cboRoomType = vbNullString
      .cboOS = vbNullString
      .txtOperatingSystem = vbNullString
      .cboProject = vbNullString
      .txtPID = vbNullString
   End With
```

```
If Me.cboRooms.ListCount = 0 Then
    'do not display column headings
    Me.cboRooms.ColumnHeads = False
Else
    Me.cboRooms.ColumnHeads = True
End If
Me.cboRooms.SetFocus
End Sub
```

In the procedure shown above, the company address information is filled in based on the contents of the cboCompanyID columns. For example, to fill in the street address, you can read the value of the Columns() property of the cboCompanyID control, even though this column is not visible when you view the combo box:

```
Me.txtStreet = Me.cboCompanyID.Column(2)
```

Note that because the combo box column numbering begins with zero (0), the above statement actually reads the contents of the third column. Next, the combo box labeled "Room No" is requeried and a number of other controls on the form are cleared.

Also, note how the intrinsic constant named vbNullString is used here instead of an empty string ("") to clear text boxes or combo boxes on a form. The final code segment above contains the If…Then…Else statement that sets the ColumnHeads property of the cboRooms control to False if there are no rooms associated with the selected Company ID.

The last line of the code:

```
Me.cboRooms.SetFocus
```

moves the focus to the combo box control with the room numbers. When this code is executed, the cboRooms_Enter event procedure will be triggered.

◉ Hands-On 26-4: Using the AfterUpdate Event Procedure for the Combo Box Control

1. Make sure that the **frmDataEntryMain** form is open in Design view.

2. Right-click the list box control to the right of the **Company ID** label and choose **Build Event** from the shortcut menu.

3. In the Code window, choose the **AfterUpdate** event from the Procedure drop-down box and set a breakpoint on the first line of this procedure.

4. Switch to Form view of the frmDataEntryMain form and make another selection from the **Company ID** combo box. When the Code window appears in break mode, step through the code line by line by pressing **F8**. Notice that the following three event procedures are run:

```
cboCompanyID_BeforeUpdate
cboCompanyID_AfterUpdate
cboRooms_Enter
```

5. When the procedure finishes executing, activate the **frmDataEntryMain** form.

NotInList (Control)

The NotInList event is triggered if the user enters a value that is not in the list when the LimitToList property of a combo box control is set to True. The NotInList event procedure can take the following two arguments:

- **NewData** — A string that Access uses for passing to the event procedure the text that the user entered.

- **Response** — An integer specifying what Access should do after the procedure executes. This argument can be set to one of the following constants:

    - *acDataErrAdded* — Set the Response argument to acDataErrAdded if the event procedure enters a new value in the combo box. This constant tells Access to requery the combo box, adding the new value to the list.

    - *acDataErrDisplay* — Set the Response argument to acDataErrDisplay if you want Access to display the default error message when a user attempts to add a new value to the combo box. The default Access message requires the user to enter a valid value from the list.

    - *acDataErrContinue* — Set the Response argument to acDataErr-Continue if you display your own message in the event procedure. Access will forgo displaying its default error message.

The NotInList event applies only to combo boxes. Use this event to display a custom warning message or trigger a custom function that allows the user to add a new item to the list. For example, after attempting to enter a nonexisting value in the combo box labeled Room Type in the Room Information section of the Asset Management form, the following event procedure is executed:

```
Private Sub cboRoomType_NotInList(NewData As String, _
                        Response As Integer)
    MsgBox "Please select a value from the list.", _
            vbInformation + vbOKOnly, "Invalid entry"
    ' Continue without displaying default error message.
    Response = acDataErrContinue
End Sub
```

The code above displays a custom message if a user attempts to type an invalid entry in the cboRoomType combo box control on the form.

Hands-On 26-5: Using the NotInList Event Procedure for the Combo Box Control

1. Open the **frmDataEntryMain** form in Form vew.

2. Select a company ID from the Company ID combo box.

3. Select a room number from the Room No combo box, or type a value in this box.

4. Type any value in the **Room Type** combo box and click on the **Operating System** combo box. This will trigger the cboRoomType_NotInList event procedure code to run. Your custom error message should appear. Click

OK to the message box. Notice that Access does not display its own default message because we set the Response argument to acDataErrContinue.

5. Select a value from the Room Type combo box.

Click (Control)

The Click event occurs when the user clicks a control with the left mouse button or presses an Enter key when a command button placed on a form has its Default property set to Yes. The Click event applies only to forms, form sections, and controls on a form. The Asset Management data entry form contains several command buttons that allow the user to add new values to appropriate combo box selections. For example, when the user clicks the button labeled "Add New Company," the following Click event procedure is triggered:

```
Private Sub cmdNewCompany_Click()
    On Error GoTo Err_cmdNewCompany_Click

    Dim stDocName As String
    Dim stLinkCriteria As String

    stDocName = "frmAddCompany"
    DoCmd.OpenForm stDocName, , , stLinkCriteria

Exit_cmdNewCompany_Click:
    Exit Sub
Err_cmdNewCompany_Click:
    MsgBox Err.Description
    Resume Exit_cmdNewCompany_Click
End Sub
```

The above event procedure opens a window titled New Company Data Entry Screen (Figure 26-2), where the user can enter new company information.

Figure 26-2: This data entry form is used for adding new companies to the database.

When the user clicks the Save button on the New Company Data Entry Screen window, the Click event procedure attached to this button ensures that:

- All text boxes have been filled in

- The Company ID does not contain more than five characters

- The Zip Code text box contains a five-digit zip code for the United States
- The Company ID does not already exist in the table

Notice that the New Company Data Entry form is unbound (it isn't connected to a record source such as a table, query, or SQL statement). After successful data validation, the procedure uses the AddNew method of the ADO Recordset object to create a new record. This record is added to the tblCompanies table that provides the record source for the Company ID combo box control on the Asset Management data entry form. Next, the cboCompanyID combo box control on the Asset Management form is requeried so that the new Company ID can be accessed from the drop-down list when the user returns to the form.

```
Private Sub cmdSaveCompanyInfo_Click()
    Dim conn As ADODB.Connection
    Dim rst As New ADODB.Recordset
    Dim ctrl As Control
    Dim count As Integer

    On Error GoTo Err_cmdSaveCompanyInfo_Click

    'validate data prior to save

    For Each ctrl In Me.Controls
        If ctrl.ControlType = acTextBox And IsNull(ctrl) _
                    Or IsEmpty(ctrl) Then
            count = count + 1
            If count > 0 Then
                MsgBox "All text fields must be filled in.", _
                    vbInformation + vbOKOnly, _
                    "Missing Data"
                ctrl.SetFocus
                Exit Sub
            End If
        End If
    Next

    If Len(Me.txtAddCompanyID) <> 5 Then
        MsgBox "There must be 5 characters in the Company ID field."
        Me.txtAddCompanyID.SetFocus
        Exit Sub
    End If

    'check the zipcode field
    If Len(Me.txtAddPostalCode) <> 5 And _
        UCase(Me.txtAddCountry) = "USA" Then
            MsgBox "Please enter a five-digit zip code " & _
                "for the United States.", _
                vbInformation + vbOKOnly, "Invalid Zip Code"
            Me.txtAddPostalCode.SetFocus
        Exit Sub
    End If
```

```
    'are any alphabetic characters in zip code?
    If Not IsNumeric(Me.txtAddPostalCode) And _
      UCase(Me.txtAddCountry) = "USA" Then
        MsgBox "You can't have letters in Zip Code.", _
        vbInformation + vbOKOnly, "Invalid Zip Code"
      Me.txtAddPostalCode.SetFocus
      Exit Sub
    End If
    'save the data
    Set conn = CurrentProject.Connection
      With rst
        .Open "SELECT * FROM tblCompanies", _
        conn, adOpenKeyset, adLockOptimistic
        'check if the CompanyID is not a duplicate
        .Find "CompanyID='" & Me.txtAddCompanyID & "'"
        'if Company already exists then get out
      If Not rst.EOF Then
        MsgBox "This Company is already in the list : " _
        & rst("CompanyID"), _
        vbInformation + vbOKOnly, "Duplicate Company ID"
        Me.txtAddCompanyID.SetFocus
      Exit Sub
      End If
        .AddNew
          !CompanyID = Me.txtAddCompanyID
          !CompanyName = Me.txtAddCompanyName
          !Address = Me.txtAddAddress
          !City = Me.txtAddCity
          !Region = Me.txtAddRegion
          !PostalCode = Me.txtAddPostalCode
          !Country = Me.txtAddCountry
        .Update
        .Close
      End With
    Set rst = Nothing
    conn.Close
    Set conn = Nothing

    'requery the combo box on the main form
    Forms!frmDataEntryMain.cboCompanyID.Requery
    'close the form
    DoCmd.Close

Exit_cmdSaveCompanyInfo_Click:
    Exit Sub
Err_cmdSaveCompanyInfo_Click:
    MsgBox Err.Description
    Resume Exit_cmdSaveCompanyInfo_Click
End Sub
```

⊚ Hands-On 26-6: Using the Click Event Procedure for the Command Button Control

1. Open the **frmDataEntryMain** form in Form view.
2. Click the **Add New Company** command button.
3. When the New Company Data Entry Screen window appears, enter the information shown in Figure 26-3.

Figure 26-3: After saving the new company information, the Company ID will appear in the Company ID combo box on the main form.

4. Click the **Save** button to save the company information. Access will run the cmdSaveCompanyInfo_Click event procedure, as shown earlier. If you have not entered data according to the criteria listed inside this event procedure, Access will not allow you to save data until you correct the problem.
5. Back on the main form, select the newly added company (**GOSPO**) from the Company ID combo box.

The Asset Management data entry form also displays a number of icons with a question mark. Each icon is actually a command button with a Click event attached to it. When you click on the question mark button, you will get a simple form with help information pertaining to the form's section or the data entry screen.

For example, the following Click event procedure is executed upon clicking the question mark button in the Room Information section on the Asset Management data entry form:

```
Private Sub cmdRoomInfoSec_Click()
    Dim stDocName As String
    Dim stLinkCriteria As String

    On Error GoTo Err_cmdRoomInfoSec_Click

    stDocName = "frmHelpMe"
    stLinkCriteria = "HelpId = 2"
    DoCmd.OpenForm stDocName, , , stLinkCriteria

Exit_cmdRoomInfoSec_Click:
    Exit Sub
```

```
Err_cmdRoomInfoSec_Click:
    MsgBox Err.Description
    Resume Exit_cmdRoomInfoSec_Click
End Sub
```

The above procedure loads the appropriate help topic into the text box control, as illustrated in Figure 26-4.

Figure 26-4: By clicking the question mark button in each section of the data entry form, users can get detailed guidelines on how to work with the section.

DblClick (Control)

The DblClick event occurs when the user double-clicks the form or control. This event applies only to forms, form sections, and controls on a form, not controls on a report.

For example, Hands-On 26-7 demonstrates how the user of the Asset Management application can delete an asset by double-clicking on its name.

⊚ Hands-On 26-7: Using the DblClick Event Procedure for the List Box Control

1. Open the **frmDataEntryMain** form in Form view.

2. Make appropriate selections on the Asset Management data entry form.

3. Click the **Add New Asset Type** button in the Hardware Information section. If this button cannot be clicked, you have not made all the necessary selections in the upper part of the form.

   The Add New Asset Type Data Entry Screen window will appear, as shown in Figure 26-5.

Figure 26-5: This form allows the user to add a new entry to the Asset Type column in the Hardware Information section of the Asset Management form or delete the Asset entry by double-clicking on the entry in the Available Assets list box.

4. In the Add New Asset Type Data Entry Screen window, enter **Zip Drive** in the Asset Type text box and click the **Save** button.

5. In the main form, open the combo box in the **Asset Type** column and scroll down to view the newly added asset type — Zip Drive. Do not make any selection in this combo box.

6. Click the **Add New Asset Type** button in the Hardware Information section to return to the Add New Asset Type Data Entry Screen window.

The left-hand side of the data entry screen (see Figure 26-5) displays a list box with the currently available assets. The user can double-click any item in the list and the DblClick event procedure shown below will determine whether or not the item can be deleted.

```
Private Sub lboxCategories_DblClick(Cancel As Integer)
    Dim conn As ADODB.Connection
    Dim myAsset As String
    Dim myAssetDesc As String
    Dim Response As String
    Dim strSQL As String

    myAsset = Me.lboxCategories.Value
    myAssetDesc = Me.lboxCategories.Column(1)

        If myAsset >= 1 And myAsset <= 11 Then
          MsgBox "Cannot Delete - This item is being used.", _
              vbOKOnly + vbCritical, "Asset Type: " & myAsset
          Exit Sub
        End If

        If (Not IsNull(DLookup("[AssetType]", "tblProjectDetails", _
          "[AssetType] = " & myAsset))) Or _
          Not IsNull(DLookup("[EquipCategoryID]", "tblEquipInventory", _
          "[EquipCategoryID] = " & myAsset)) Then

        MsgBox "This item cannot be deleted.", _
            vbOKOnly + vbCritical, "Asset Type: " & myAsset
        Else
            Response = MsgBox("Do you want to delete this Asset?", _
            vbYesNo, "Delete - " & myAssetDesc & " ?")
        If Response = 6 Then
            Set conn = CurrentProject.Connection
            strSQL = "DELETE * FROM tblEquipCategories Where EquipCategoryID = "
            conn.Execute (strSQL & myAsset)
            conn.Close
            Set conn = Nothing
            Me.lboxCategories.Requery
        End If
      End If
    DoCmd.Close

    ' requery the combo box on the subform
    Forms!frmDataEntryMain.frmSubProjectDetails.Form.EquipCatId.Requery
End Sub
```

7. Double-click on **Zip Drive** in the Available Assets list box. The DblClick event procedure attached to the list box will ask you whether you want to delete this asset. Click **Yes** to the message.

Notice that the Zip Drive entry disappears from the Available Assets list box.

8. Click the **Cancel** button to exit the Add New Asset Type Data Entry Screen window.

Chapter Summary

In this chapter you worked with a custom Microsoft Access application and examined event procedures for various controls placed on an Access form. There are a number of other event procedures not discussed here that control how the Asset Management form and its controls respond to the user's actions. As you explore this application on your own you will start noticing the areas where writing additional event handlers would prove beneficial to the application's users. So get to it. Tear this sample application apart. Rebuild it. Add new features. Change the user interface if you want. Learn how to handle whatever event may come your way. And be prepared, because events happen frequently in an Access application, and sooner or later you'll need to respond to them.

In the next chapter you learn how to handle an object's events from classes other than the form classes, as well as how to program and raise your own events.

Chapter 27

More about Event Programming

So far in this book you've worked with event procedures that executed from the form or report class module when a certain event occurred for a form, report, or a control. You probably noticed that event programming, as you've seen it implemented in the form and report class modules, requires that you copy and paste your existing event code into new form or report events in order to obtain exactly the same functionality. For instance, say you added certain features to a text box on one form and now you'd like to have a text box on other forms behave in the same way. You could react to the text box's events in the same way on all your forms by entering the same event procedure code in a form class module for each form, or you could save keystrokes by learning how to centralize and reuse your event code.

You can avoid typing the same event procedure code again and again by using classes. Recall that we've already used classes in this book — in Chapter 8 you learned how you can design your own objects in VBA by writing code in a standalone class module. You worked with property procedures that allowed data to be read or written to the object. You also learned how to create functions in a class module that worked as object methods. In this chapter you learn how to react to an object's events from a standalone class module.

The following new VBA terms will be introduced:

- **Event sink** — A class that implements an event. Only classes can sink events.

- **Event source** — An object that raises events. An event source can have multiple event sinks. Note: Source and sink terminology is derived from electronics. A device that outputs current when active is said to be sourcing current. A device that draws current into it when active is said to be sinking current.

- **WithEvents** — A keyword that allows you to handle an object's events inside classes other than form or report classes. The variable that you declare for the WithEvents keyword is used to handle an object's events.

- **Event** — A statement used to declare a user-defined event. The Event declaration must appear in a class module.

■ **RaiseEvent** — A statement used to call a custom event. The custom event must first be declared using the Event statement.

Sinking Events in Standalone Class Modules

Instead of writing your event procedures in the form and report class modules, you can make the maintenance of your Microsoft Access applications much simpler by writing the event code in standalone class modules.

Recall that a *standalone class module* is a special type of a class module that is not associated with any particular form or report. This class module can be inserted in the Visual Basic Editor window by choosing Insert | Class Module. In addition to creating custom objects (see examples in Chapter 8), standalone class modules can implement object events.

The process of listening to an object's events is called *sinking the event*. To sink (handle) events in a standalone class module you must use the WithEvents keyword. This keyword will tell the class that you want to sink some or all of the object's events in the class module. You determine which events you want to sink by writing appropriate event code (see Custom Project 27-1). Only classes can sink events. Therefore, the WithEvents keyword can only be used in classes. You can use the WithEvents keyword to declare as many individual variables as you need; however, you cannot create arrays using WithEvents.

An object that generates events is called an *event source*. The process of broadcasting an event is called *sourcing the event*. To handle events raised by an event source you must declare an object variable using the WithEvents keyword. For example, to react to form events in a standalone class module, you would need to enter the following module-level variable declaration in the class module:

```
Private WithEvents m_frm As Access.Form
```

In the above statement, m_frm is the name of the object variable that references the Form object. While you can use any variable name you want, this variable cannot be a generic object. That means you cannot declare it as Object. If the variable were declared as Object, Visual Basic wouldn't know what type library should be used. Therefore, it would not be able to provide you with the names of events that you can write code for.

Now, let's walk through these new concepts step by step. Custom Project 27-1 demonstrates how to create a record logger class that handles a form's AfterUpdate event. Each time the AfterUpdate event occurs, this class will enter information about the newly created record into a text file. With minor modifications, this class will use the same event code that was introduced in Hands-On 24-5 (see Chapter 24).

⊚ Custom Project 27-1: Sinking Events in a Standalone Class Module

Part 1: File Preparation

1. Start Microsoft Office Access 2007 and create a new Microsoft Office Access 2007 database named **Chap27.accdb** in your **C:\Acc07_ByExample** folder.

2. Import the Customers, Products, Suppliers, and Categories tables from the sample Northwind.mdb database. To do this, in the Access window, choose **External Data | Access**. In the File name box, type **C:\Acc07_ByExample\Northwind.mdb** and click **OK**. In the Import Objects window, on the **Tables** tab, select the **Customers, Products, Suppliers**, and **Categories** tables and click **OK** to begin importing. Click the **Close** button when done.

3. Switch to the Navigation pane of the Access window and choose **Create | More Forms | Forms Wizard** to create a new form based on the Customers table. Select all the fields from the **Customers** table and specify **Columnar** layout, **Module** style, and **frmCustomers** as the form's title. After you click **Finish**, the newly designed frmCustomers form will appear in the Form view as shown in Figure 27-1.

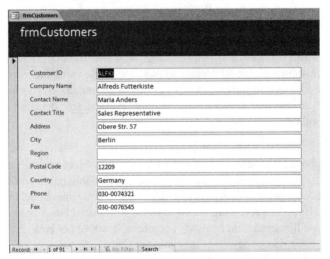

Figure 27-1: The frmCustomers form is used in Custom Project 27-1 to demonstrate how an object's event can be handled outside of the form class module.

4. Close the frmCustomers form created in step 2 above.

Part 2: Creating the cRecordLogger Class

1. Press **Alt+F11** to activate the Visual Basic Editor window.

2. In the Project Explorer window, select **Chap27(Chap27)** and choose **Insert | Class Module**. A new class called Class1 will appear in the Project Explorer window. Use the Name property in the Properties window to change the name of the class to **cRecordLogger** (see Figure 27-2) or press Ctrl+S to assign the name to the class module during the save operation.

Figure 27-2: Use the Name property in the Properties window to change the name of the class module.

3. In the cRecordLogger class module's Code window, enter the following module-level variable declaration just below the Option Compare Database and Option Explicit statements:

```
Private WithEvents m_frm As Access.Form
```

After declaring the object variable using WithEvents, the variable name m_frm appears in the Object box in your class module (see Figure 27-3). When you select this variable from the drop-down list, the valid events for that object will appear in the Procedure box (see Figure 27-4). By choosing an event from the Procedure drop-down list, an empty procedure stub will be added to the class module where you can write your code for handling the selected event. By default, Access adds the Load event procedure stub after selecting an object from the Object drop-down list.

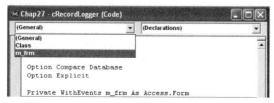

Figure 27-3: The Object drop-down list in the cRecordLogger's Code window lists the m_frm object variable that was declared using the WithEvents keyword.

Figure 27-4: The Procedure drop-down list in the cRecordLogger's Code window lists the valid events for the object declared with the WithEvents keyword.

4. In the cRecordLogger class module's Code window, enter the following Property procedure just below the variable declaration, or copy and paste the procedure code from **C:\Acc07_HandsOn\Chap27.txt**.

```
Public Property Set Form(cur_frm As Form)
    Set m_frm = cur_frm
    m_frm.AfterUpdate = "[Event Procedure]"
End Property
```

In order to sink events in the class module, you must tell the class which specific form's events the class should be responding to. You do this by writing the Property Set procedure. Recall from Chapter 8 that Property Set procedures are used to assign a reference to an object. Therefore, the statement:

```
Set m_frm = cur_frm
```

will assign the current form (passed in the cur_frm variable) to the m_frm object variable declared in step 3 above. Pointing the object variable (m_frm) at the object (cur_frm) isn't enough. Access will not raise the event unless the object's Event property is set to [Event Procedure]. Therefore, the second statement in the procedure above:

```
m_frm.AfterUpdate = "[Event Procedure]"
```

will ensure that Access knows that it must raise the form's AfterUpdate event.

5. Choose **Tools | References** and add the **Microsoft Scripting Runtime Library** to the class module. You will need this library to gain access to the FileSystemObject in the next step.

6. In the cRecordLogger class module's Code window, enter the following **m_frm_AfterUpdate** event procedure, or copy and paste the procedure code from **C:\Acc07_HandsOn\Chap27.txt**.

```
Private Sub m_frm_AfterUpdate()
    Dim fso As FileSystemObject
    Dim myFile As Object
    Dim strFileN As String
    Dim ctrl As Control

    On Error Resume Next

    Set fso = New FileSystemObject
    strFileN = "C:\Acc07_ByExample\MyCust.txt"
    Set myFile = fso.GetFile(strFileN)

    If Err.Number = 0 Then
        Set myFile = fso.OpenTextFile(strFileN, 8) ' open text file
    Else
        Set myFile = fso.CreateTextFile(strFileN) ' create a text file
    End If

    For Each ctrl In m_frm.Controls
        If ctrl.ControlType = acTextBox And _
            InStr(1, ctrl.Name, "ID") Then
            myFile.WriteLine "ID:" & ctrl.Value & _
                " Created on: " & Date & " " & Time & _
                " (Form: " & m_frm.Name & ")"
            MsgBox "See the audit trail in " & strFileN & "."
            Exit For
        End If
    Next
    myFile.Close
    Set fso = Nothing
End Sub
```

The code inside the m_frm_AfterUpdate event procedure will be executed after Access finds that the form's AfterUpdate property is set to [Event Procedure]. This code tells Access to open or create a text file named C:\Acc07_ByExample\MyCust.txt and write a line consisting of the value of the ID control on the form, the date and time the record was inserted or modified, and the name of the form. Notice how the InStr function is used to locate the control whose name contains the "ID" string. The first argument of the InStr function determines the character position where the search should begin, the second argument is the string being searched, and the third argument is the string expression being sought within the string specified in the second argument.

Figure 27-5: A custom cRecordLogger class is used to handle a form's AfterUpdate event.

7. Save the code that you wrote in the class module by clicking the **Save** button on the toolbar or choosing **File | Save**. When the Save As dialog box appears with cRecordLogger in the text box, click **OK**.

For the events to actually fire now that you've written the code to handle the event in the standalone class module, you need to instantiate the class and pass it the object whose events you want to track. This requires that you write a couple of lines of code in your form's class module.

Part 3: Creating an Instance of the Custom Class in the Form's Class Module

1. Switch to the Access window by pressing **Alt+F11**. In the Navigation pane, right-click the **frmCustomers** form you created in step 2 of Part 1. Select **Design View** from the shortcut menu.

2. In the property sheet, make sure **Form** is selected in the drop-down list, and activate the **Event** tab. Click next to the **On Open** property and select **[Event Procedure]**. Click the **Build** button. Access activates the Code window and writes the procedure stub for the Form_Open event. Complete the code of this event procedure as shown below or copy and paste the code from **C:\Acc07_HandsOn\Chap27.txt**.

```
Private clsRecordLogger As cRecordLogger

Private Sub Form_Open(Cancel As Integer)
    Set clsRecordLogger = New cRecordLogger
    Set clsRecordLogger.Form = Me
End Sub

Private Sub Form_Close()
    Set clsRecordLogger = Nothing
End Sub
```

To instantiate a custom class module, we begin by declaring a module-level object variable, clsRecordLogger, as the name of our custom class, cRecordLogger. You can choose any name you wish for your variable name.

Next, we instantiate the class in the Form_Open event procedure by using the following Set statement:

```
Set clsRecordLogger = New cRecordLogger
```

Notice that you must use the New keyword to create a new object of a particular class. By setting the reference to an actual instance of the object when the form first opens, we ensure that the object refers to an actual object by the time the event is first fired. The second statement in the Form_Open event procedure:

```
Set clsRecordLogger.Form = Me
```

sets the Form property defined by the Property procedure in the class module (see step 4 of Part 2) to the Form object whose events we want to sink. The Me keyword represents the current instance of the Form class. When you are done pointing the object variable to the instance of the custom class, it is a good idea to release the variable reference. We've done this by setting the object variable clsRecordLogger to Nothing in the Form_Close event procedure. The complete code entered in the frmCustomers form class module is shown in Figure 27-6.

Figure 27-6: To sink form events in a custom class module, you must enter some code in the form class module.

3. Save the code you entered in step 2 above by pressing **Ctrl+S** or clicking the **Save** button on the toolbar.
4. Close the frmCustomers form.

Now that all the code has been written in the standalone class module and in the form class module, it's time to test our project.

Part 4: Testing the cRecordLogger Custom Class

1. Switch to the Access window and open the **frmCustomers** form in Form view.

2. Choose **Home | New**.

3. Enter **MARSK** in the Customer ID text box and **Marski Enterprises** in the Company Name text box (see Figure 27-7). Press the record selector on the left side of the form to save the record.

Figure 27-7: The frmCustomers form in the Data Entry mode is used for testing out the custom cRecordLogger class.

When you save the newly entered record, a message box appears with the text "See the audit trail in C:\Acc07_ByExample\MyCust.txt." Recall that this message was programmed inside the m_frm_AfterUpdate() event procedure in the cRecordLogger class module. It looks like our custom class has successfully sunk the AfterUpdate event. The form's AfterUpdate event was propagated to the custom class module.

4. Click **OK** to close the message box.

5. Activate Windows Explorer and open the **C:\Acc07_ByExample\ MyCust.txt** file.

   The MyCust.txt file (see Figure 27-8) displays the record log. You may want to revise the m_frm_AfterUpdate() event procedure so that you can track whether a record was created or modified.

Figure 27-8: The MyCust.txt file is used by the cRecordLogger custom class for tracking record additions.

6. Close the C:\Acc07_ByExample\MyCust.txt file.

7. Add a few more records to the frmCustomers form and check out the
   C:\Acc07_ByExample\MyCust.txt file.

8. Close the frmCustomers form.

Now that you know how to sink the form's AfterUpdate event outside the form
class module, you can use the same idea to sink other form events in a class
module and make your code easier to implement and maintenance free. Just
remember that if you want to sink events in a standalone class module, you
must write code in two places: in your class module and in your form or report
class module. The class module must contain a module-level WithEvents variable declaration and you must set the reference to an actual instance of the
object in the form or report module.

Part 5: Using the cRecordLogger Custom Class with another Form

The code you've written so far in this project is ready for reuse in another
Microsoft Access form. In the remaining steps, we will hook it up to the
frmProducts form. Let's begin by creating this form.

1. In the Navigation pane of the Access window, select the **Products** table
   and choose **Create | Form**. Access creates a form and displays it in the
   Form Layout view.

2. Press **Ctrl+S** or click the **Save** button on the toolbar to save the form. In
   the Save As dialog box, type **frmProducts** for the form name and click
   OK.

3. Activate the **frmProducts** form in Design view. In the property sheet,
   make sure **Form** is selected from the drop-down box and click the **Other**
   tab. Set the Has Module property of the form to **Yes**. Save the changes to
   the form by pressing **Ctrl+S**.

4. Switch to the Visual Basic Editor window, and double-click the **Form_
   frmProducts** object in the Project Explorer window. Access opens the
   Code module for the form.

5. Copy the code from the frmCustomers Code window to the **frmProducts**
   Code window. The code in the frmProducts Code window should match
   Figure 27-6 shown earlier.

6. In the frmProducts Code window, replace all the references to the object
   variable clsRecordLogger with **clsRecordLogger2**.

Note: To quickly perform this operation, position the cursor inside the first clsRecordLogger variable name and choose Edit | Replace. The Find What text box should automatically display the name of the variable you want to replace. Type clsRecordLogger2 in the Replace With text box and click the Replace All button. Click OK to confirm the replacement of four variable names. Click Cancel to exit the Replace dialog box.

7. Save and close the frmProducts form.

8. Open the **frmProducts** form in Form view and choose **Home | New**.

9. Enter **Delicious Raisins** in the Product Name text box and press the record selector on the left side of the form to save the record.

    At this point you should receive the custom message about the audit trail that you defined in the AfterUpdate event procedure within the custom cRecordLogger class module. This indicates that the AfterUpdate event that was raised by the form when you saved the newly entered record was successfully propagated to the custom class module.

10. Click **OK** to close the message box.

11. Close the frmProducts form.

12. Open the **C:\Acc07_ByExample\MyCust.txt** file to view the record log. Close this file when you are finished.

You may want to choose a more generic name for your record log text file if it will be used for tracking various types of information.

Writing Event Procedure Code in Two Places

If you write event procedure code for the same event both in the form module and the class module, the code defined in the form class module will run first, followed by the code in the custom class module. You can easily test this by entering the following Form_AfterUpdate event procedure code in the form class module of the frmCustomers or frmProducts forms prepared in Custom Project 27-1:

```
Private Sub Form_AfterUpdate()
    MsgBox "Transferring control to the custom class."
    ' when you click OK to this message, the code
    ' inside the AfterUpdate procedure in the custom
    ' class module will run
End Sub
```

When you open the form and add and save a new record, the Form_After-Update event will fire and you will see the message about transferring control to the custom class. Next, the AfterUpdate event procedure will run in the custom class, and you will see a message informing you that you can view the audit trail in the specified text file.

Responding to Control Events in a Class

Everyone designing Microsoft Access forms sooner or later realizes that it takes a long time to customize some of the controls placed on the form. It's no wonder then that once the control is working correctly, there is a tendency toward copying the control and its event procedures to a new form that requires a control with the same functionality. If you followed this chapter carefully, you already know a better (and a neater) solution. By using the WithEvents keyword you can create an object variable that points to the control raising the events. Instead of responding to control events in the form module, you will react to these events in a different location: a standalone class module. This lets you write centralized code that is easy to implement in other form controls of the same type.

Suppose you need a text box that converts lowercase letters to uppercase and disallows numbers. Hands-On 27-1 demonstrates how to create a text box with these features and hook it up with any Microsoft Access form.

⊚ Hands-On 27-1: Responding to Control Events in a Class

This hands-on exercise requires prior completion of Custom Project 27-1.

1. Activate the Visual Basic Editor window and choose **Insert | Class Module**. A new class named Class1 will appear in the Project Explorer window.

2. In the Properties window, click the **(Name)** property and type **UCaseBox** as the new name of Class1. Click again on the **(Name)** property to save the new name. You should see the UCaseBox entry under the Class Modules folder in the Project Explorer.

3. In the UCaseBox class module's Code window, enter the following code:

```
Private WithEvents txtBox As Access.TextBox

Public Function InitializeMe(myTxt As TextBox)
    Set txtBox = myTxt
    txtBox.OnKeyPress = "[Event Procedure]"
End Function

Private Sub txtBox_KeyPress(KeyAscii As Integer)
    Select Case KeyAscii
        Case 48 To 57
            MsgBox "Numbers are not allowed!"
            KeyAscii = 0
        Case Else
        ' convert to uppercase
            KeyAscii = Asc(UCase(Chr(KeyAscii)))
    End Select

    txtBox.FontBold = True
    txtBox.FontItalic = True
    txtBox.BackColor = vbYellow
End Sub
```

Notice that to respond to a control's events in a class module you start by declaring a module-level object variable using the WithEvents keyword. In our text box example, we declared the object variable txtBox as an Access text box control.

Because the form can contain more than one text box control, we should tell the class which text box it needs to respond to. We do this by creating a Property Set procedure (similar to the one created in Custom Project 27-1) or a function procedure like the one shown above. We called this function InitializeMe, but you can use any name you wish. Recall from Chapter 8 that a function entered in a class module serves as an object's method. We will call the InitializeMe method later from a form class module and pass it the actual control we want it to respond to (see step 7). The InitializeMe method will assign the passed control to the WithEvents object variable like this:

```
Set txtBox = myTxt
```

Next, we set the text box KeyPress property to [Event Procedure] to tell the class that we are interested in tracking this particular event.

Finally, we write the event procedure code for the text box control's KeyPress event. This code begins by checking the value of the key that was pressed by the user. If a number was entered, the user is advised that numbers aren't allowed and the digit is removed from the text box by setting the value of KeyAscii to zero (0). Otherwise, if the user typed a lowercase letter, the character is converted to uppercase using the following statement:

```
KeyAscii = Asc(UCase(Chr(KeyAscii)))
```

KeyAscii is an integer that returns a numerical ANSI key code. To convert the KeyAscii argument into a character, we use the Chr function:

```
Chr(KeyAscii)
```

Once we've converted a key into a character, we use the UCase function to convert it to uppercase:

```
UCase(Chr(KeyAscii))
```

Finally, we translate the character back to an ANSI number by using the Asc function:

```
Asc(UCase(Chr(KeyAscii)))
```

The txtBox_KeyPress event procedure ends by adding some visual enhancements to the text box. The text entered in it will appear in italics and bold type on a yellow background.

4. Save the code you entered in the UCaseBox class module's Code window by pressing the **Save** button on the toolbar.

5. In the Project Explorer window, double-click the **Form_frmProducts**. The Form_frmProducts class module's Code window should already contain code you entered while working with Part 3 of Custom Project 27-1 earlier in this chapter. To connect the UCaseBox class module with the actual text box on any Access form, you would need to enter the code as shown below in a form's class module (do not enter it yet):

```
' module-level variable declaration
Private clsTextBox1 As UCaseBox

Private Sub Form_Open(Cancel As Integer)
    Set clsTextBox1 = New UCaseBox
    clsTextBox1.InitializeMe Me.Controls("ProductName")
End Sub

Private Sub Form_Close()
    Set clsTextBox1 = Nothing
End Sub
```

Since the frmProducts form already contains a call to the cRecordLogger class created earlier, all of the procedures we need are already in place; therefore, we will simply add the appropriate lines of code to the existing procedures. So let's proceed.

6. In the Form_frmProducts Code window, enter the following module-level variable declaration just above the Form_Open event procedure (see Figure 27-9):

```
Private clsTextBox1 As UCaseBox
```

The above statement declares the clsTextBox1 class variable. This variable is used in instantiating the UCaseBox object and connecting it with the actual text box control on the form (see step 7 below).

7. Enter the following lines of code before the End Sub statement of the Form_Open event procedure (see Figure 27-9):

```
Set clsTextBox1 = New UCaseBox
clsTextBox1.InitializeMe Me.Controls("ProductName")
```

Before our UCaseBox class can respond to a text box's events you need these two lines of code; the first one sets the class variable clsTxtBox1 to a new instance of the UCaseBox class, and the second one calls the class InitializeMe method and supplies it with the name of the text box control.

8. Enter the following line of code before the End Sub statement of the Form_Close event procedure (see Figure 27-9):

```
Set clsTextBox1 = Nothing
```

When we are done with the object variable, we set it to Nothing to release the resources that have been assigned to it.

Figure 27-9: The form class module shows code that instantiates and hooks up objects created in the cRecordLogger and UCaseBox class modules with the form and text box control.

9. Save the changes made in the Code window by clicking the **Save** button on the toolbar.

10. Open the **frmProducts** form in Form view and choose **Home | New**.

11. Enter **prune butter** in the Product Name text box. Notice that as you type, the characters you enter are converted to uppercase. They are also made bold and italic, and appear on a yellow background. If you happen to press a number key, which is disallowed by your custom KeyPress event, you receive an error message. Click on the record selector to save the record. Because this form also responds to the AfterUpdate event that we programmed in Custom Project 27-1, you should see two message boxes when you save this form.

12. Close the frmProducts form.

Declaring and Raising Events

Standalone class modules automatically support two events: Initialize and Terminate. Use the Initialize event to give the variables in your classes initial values. The Initialize event is called when you make a new instance of a class. The Terminate event is called when you set the instance to Nothing. In addition to these default events, you can define custom events for your class module.

To create a custom event, use the Event statement in the declaration section of a class module. For example, the following statement declares an event named SendFlowers that requires two arguments:

```
Public Event SendFlowers(ByVal strName As String, cancel As Boolean)
```

The Event statement declares a user-defined event. This statement is followed by the name of the event and any arguments that will be passed to the event procedure. Arguments are separated by commas. An event can have ByVal and ByRef arguments. Recall that when passing the variable ByRef, you are actually passing the memory location of the variable. If you pass a variable ByVal, you are sending the copy of the variable.

When declaring events with arguments, bear in mind that events cannot have named arguments, optional arguments, or ParamArray arguments. The Public keyword is optional as events are public by default.

Use the RaiseEvent statement to fire the event. This is usually done by creating a method in a class module. For example, here's how you could trigger the SendFlowers event:

```
Public Sub Dispatch(ByVal toWhom As String, cancel As Boolean)
    RaiseEvent SendFlowers(toWhom, True)
End Sub
```

Events can only be raised in the module in which they are declared using the Event statement. After declaring the event and writing the method that will be used for raising the event, you need to switch to the form class module and perform the following tasks:

- Declare a module-level variable of the class type using the WithEvents keyword

- Assign an instance of the class containing the event to the object defined using the WithEvents statement

- Write a procedure that calls the class method

- Write the event handler code

The next hands-on exercise demonstrates how a user-defined event can be used in a class. We will learn how to raise the SendFlowers event from a Microsoft Access form.

Hands-On 27-2: Declaring and Raising Events

1. Activate the Visual Basic Editor window and choose **Insert | Class Module**. A new class named Class1 will appear in the Project Explorer window.

2. In the Properties window, click the **(Name)** property and type **cDispatch** as the new name of Class1. Click again on the **(Name)** property to save the new name. You should see the cDispatch entry under the Class Modules folder in the Project Explorer.

3. In the cDispatch class module's Code window, enter the following code:

```
Public Event SendFlowers(ByVal strName As String, _
                cancel As Boolean)

Sub Dispatch(ByVal ToWhom As String, cancel As Boolean)
    If ToWhom = "Julitta" Then
        cancel = True
        MsgBox "Dispatch to " & ToWhom & " was cancelled.", _
            vbInformation + vbOKOnly, "Reason Unknown"
    Else
        RaiseEvent SendFlowers(ToWhom, True)
```

```
      End If
    End Sub
```

The first statement in the code above declares a custom event called SendFlowers. This event will accept two arguments: the name of the person to whom flowers should be sent and a Boolean value of True or False that will allow you to cancel the event if necessary.

Next, the Dispatch procedure is used as a class method. The code states that the flowers should be sent to the person whose name is passed in the ToWhom argument as long as the person's name is not "Julitta." The RaiseEvent statement will call the event handler that we will write in a form module in a later step.

4. Create a new form as shown in Figure 27-10. This form isn't bound to any data source. Use the property sheet to set the Name property of the text box control to **Recipient** and the Caption property of the accompanying label control to **Recipient Name:**. Set the Name property of the command button to **cmdFlowers** and its Caption property to **Send Flowers**. Save this form as **frmFlowers**.

Figure 27-10: The frmFlowers form is used in Hands-On 27-2 to demonstrate the process of raising and handling custom events.

5. While the frmFlowers form is in Design view, click the **View Code** button in the Tools area of the Design tab.

6. Enter the following code in the **Form_frmFlowers** Code window, or copy and paste the procedure code from **C:\Acc07_HandsOn\Chap27.txt**.

```
Private WithEvents clsDispatch As cDispatch

Private Sub Form_Load()
    Set clsDispatch = New cDispatch
End Sub

Private Sub Form_Close()
    Set clsDispatch = Nothing
End Sub
```

Our form class can only respond to events from an object if it has a reference to that object. Therefore, at the top of the form class module we declare the object variable clsDispatch by using the WithEvents keyword.

This means that from now on the instance of the cDispatch class is associated with events.

The next step involves setting the object variable to an object. In the Form_Load event procedure we create a class object with the Set statement and the New keyword. When the object variable is no longer needed, we release the reference to the object by setting the object variable to Nothing (see the Form_Close event procedure above).

Now that we are done with declaring, setting, and resetting the object variable, let's proceed to write some code that will allow us to raise the SendFlowers event when we click on the Send Flowers button.

7. In the Form_frmFlowers Code window, enter the following **Click** event procedure for the cmdFlowers command button that you placed on the frmFlowers form:

```
Private Sub cmdFlowers_Click()
    If Len(Me.Recipient) > 0 Then
        clsDispatch.Dispatch Me.Recipient, False
    Else
        MsgBox "Please specify the recipient name."
        Me.Recipient.SetFocus
        Exit Sub
    End If
End Sub
```

Notice that the above event procedure begins by checking whether the user has entered data in the Recipient text box. If the data exists, the Dispatch method is called; otherwise, the user is asked to enter data in the text box. When calling the Dispatch method we must provide two arguments that this method expects: the name of the recipient and the value for the Boolean variable Cancel. Recall that the Dispatch method has the necessary code that raises the SendFlowers event (see step 3 earlier). Now what's left to do is to write an event handler for the SendFlowers event.

8. Select the **clsDispatch** variable from the object drop-down list in the upper-left corner of the Form_frmFlowers Code window. As you make this selection, a template of the event procedure will be inserted into the Code window as shown below:

```
Private Sub clsDispatch_SendFlowers(ByVal strName As String, cancel As Boolean)

End Sub
```

The code that you write within the above procedure stub will be executed when the event is generated by the object.

9. Enter the following statement inside the clsDispatch_SendFlowers procedure stub:

```
MsgBox "Flowers will be sent to " & strName & ".", , "Order taken"
```

Our custom event is not overly exciting but should give you an understanding of how custom events are declared and raised in a standalone class module and how they are consumed in a client application (form class module). The complete code we entered in the form class module is pictured in Figure 27-11.

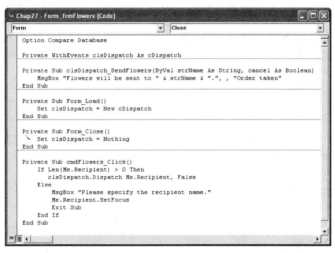

```
Chap27 - Form_frmFlowers (Code)

Form                                              Close

Option Compare Database

Private WithEvents clsDispatch As cDispatch

Private Sub clsDispatch_SendFlowers(ByVal strName As String, cancel As Boolean)
    MsgBox "Flowers will be sent to " & strName & ".", , "Order taken"
End Sub

Private Sub Form_Load()
    Set clsDispatch = New cDispatch
End Sub

Private Sub Form_Close()
    Set clsDispatch = Nothing
End Sub

Private Sub cmdFlowers_Click()
    If Len(Me.Recipient) > 0 Then
        clsDispatch.Dispatch Me.Recipient, False
    Else
        MsgBox "Please specify the recipient name."
        Me.Recipient.SetFocus
        Exit Sub
    End If
End Sub
```

Figure 27-11: The form class module shows code that uses a custom object with its events.

10. Save the changes you made in the Code window by clicking the **Save** button on the toolbar.

11. To test the code, open the **frmFlowers** form in Form view, type any name in the Recipient text box, and click the **Send Flowers** button. You should see the message generated by the SendFlowers custom event. Also see what happens when you type my name (Julitta) in the text box.

 Note: If you need more practice declaring and raising custom events, there's an additional example in the C:\Acc07_HandsOn\Chap_27.mdb database. You will find there the default Class1 class module with the Splash event that displays a splash screen when a form is loaded. Also, be sure to try out the example provided in the online help for the RaiseEvent statement topic. The quickest way to find this example is by positioning the cursor in the RaiseEvent statement (located in the cDispatch class module) and pressing F1.

Chapter Summary

In this chapter, you were introduced to advanced concepts in event-driven programming. You learned how you can make your code more manageable and portable to other objects by responding to events in class modules other than form modules. This chapter has also shown you the process of creating your own events for a class and raising them from a public method by calling the RaiseEvent statement with the arguments defined for the event. The important thing to understand is that while events happen all the time whether you respond to them or not, you are the one to decide where to respond to the built-in events. And, if you ever find yourself short of an event, with the knowledge acquired in this chapter, you can always create one that does exactly what you need. Now that you know the power tools, it's up to you to use them.

This chapter concludes Part IV of this book, which focused on writing event procedures for forms, reports, and controls. In the next chapter, you learn how to use your Access VBA skills to build Internet applications.

PART V

Taking Your VBA Programming Skills to the Web

Gone are the times when working with Access required the presence of the Microsoft Access application on a user's desktop. Thanks to the development of Internet technologies, you can publish both static and dynamic Access data to the web.

In this part of the book, you learn how Active Server Pages (ASP) and Extensible Markup Language (XML) are used with Microsoft Access to develop database solutions for the World Wide Web.

Access and Active Server Pages

In today's world, everyone wants to be able to access data via the company intranet or the World Wide Web. This book would not be complete without showing you how to take your skills where the demand is. So, how can you make the information stored in your Access database available for others to view or query in a web browser? By adding some HyperText Markup Language (HTML) and Microsoft Visual Basic Scripting Edition (VBScript) to your current VBA skill set, you can start making your applications web-ready. Microsoft Access 2007 allows you to save tables, queries, and forms to the web as HTML or XML documents; however, the Microsoft Active Server Pages file format (*.asp) that is used to create dynamic web content off the database data is no longer offered in this version of Access. But never mind this omission. This chapter focuses on showing you how you can create your own ASP files from scratch so that you will feel comfortable when displaying, querying, inserting, updating, and deleting data stored in a Microsoft Access database from a web browser.

Introduction to Active Server Pages

With Active Server Pages (ASP), a technology developed by Microsoft, you can design and program powerful and dynamic web applications. The current version of ASP is 3.0, and it is available with Internet Information Services (IIS) 5.0 or higher. Active Server Pages are text files with the .asp extension. These files contain standard HTML formatting tags and embedded scripting statements. Because the default scripting language for ASP is VBScript, a subset of Visual Basic and Visual Basic for Applications, you already have many of the skills required to web-enable your Access applications. In addition, the tools you need to make Access work with the intranet or Internet are within your reach. Although most of the examples in this chapter have been prepared using Microsoft Visual InterDev 6.0, you can use Windows Notepad or any other text editor to write your code. So, where do you start? You can start by acquiring some working knowledge of the HyperText Markup Language (HTML). A good place to start is the Internet. For easy, step-by-step tutorials, check out the htmlgoodies.com web site. Because Active Server Pages are a mix of HTML and a programming language such as VBScript or JavaScript, you should learn as much as you can about each component.

To better understand this chapter's topics, here are some terms to get acquainted with:

- **HyperText Markup Language (HTML)** — A simple, text-based language that uses special commands known as *tags* to create a document that can be viewed in a browser. HTML tags begin with a less-than sign (<) and end with a greater-than sign (>). For example, to indicate that the text should be displayed in bold letters, you simply type your text between the <B> and </B> tags like this:

```
<B>This text will appear in bold letters.</B>
```

Using plain HTML you can produce static web pages with text, images, and hyperlinks to other web pages.

- **Dynamic HTML (DHTML)** — Allows the HTML tags to be changed programmatically via scripting. Use DHTML to add interactivity to your web pages.

- **VBScript** — A scripting language based on Microsoft Visual Basic for Applications (VBA). Because this is just a subset of VBA, some of the VBA features have been removed. For example, VBScript does not support data types — every variable is a Variant. Like VBA, VBScript is an event-driven language — the VBScript code is executed in response to an event caused by a user action or the web browser itself.

- **JavaScript** — A compact, object-oriented scripting language invented by Netscape and used for developing client and server Internet applications. This is a cross-platform language that can be embedded in other products and applications, such as web browsers. Use JavaScript instead of VBScript in client-side scripts if you want to support browsers such as Firefox or Safari.

- **Active Server Pages (ASP)** — Also referred to as "classic" ASP (this version of ASP preceded a newer technology known as ASP.NET), Active Server Pages is a web development technology that enables you to combine HTML, scripts, and reusable ActiveX server components to create dynamic web applications. ASP is not limited to a particular language. To create ASP pages, you can use scripting languages such as VBScript, JavaScript, or any language for which you have a third-party ActiveX scripting engine. While HTML pages store the actual data, Active Server Pages only store the information on how to obtain the data. How does this work? Suppose you typed the address of the ASP page in your web browser's address bar and pressed Enter or clicked the Go button. The web server will read the script instructions contained in the ASP page (a file with an .asp extension) and access the specified database. Once the data is obtained, the web server will put this information into an HTML page and return that page to you in the web browser in plain HTML code. Users never see the instructions contained in your ASP file unless they have access to the web server and have been given the appropriate permissions to open these files. Because the web server reads and processes the instructions in the ASP page every time your browser requests the page, the information you receive is highly dynamic. ASP allows the page to be built or customized on the fly before the page is returned to the browser. ASP is platform independent. This means that you can view ASP pages in any browser (Internet Explorer, Netscape Navigator, Firefox, Safari, Opera, and others).

■ **ASP.NET** — (pronounced ASP DOT NET) A newer, more advanced, and feature rich web development technology from Microsoft that requires the Microsoft .NET Framework installed on users' computers. Unlike Active Server Pages (ASP), which is limited to scripting languages, .NET technology provides cross-language support (you can write and share code in many different .NET languages such as Visual Basic .NET, C#, Managed C++, JScript .NET, J#). ASP files prepared in .NET end in .aspx, .ascx, or .asmx. ASP.NET is not an upgrade to the classic ASP; it is an entirely new infrastructure for web development that requires learning new concepts behind building web applications and "unlearning" the concepts learned and utilized in programming classic ASP applications. Because programming in .NET languages is quite different from writing programs in Visual Basic for Applications language, it is not covered here. Instead, this chapter concentrates on ASP classic programming, which is more related to Visual Basic via its subset, VBScript.

Hands-On 28-1 creates an ASP page that retrieves data from the Employees table in the Northwind.mdb database.

ⓒ Hands-On 28-1: Creating an Active Server Page from a Microsoft Access Table

1. Create a new folder named **C:\Learn_ASP_Classic** for this chapter's files.

2. Copy the **C:\Acc07_HandsOn\Northwind.mdb** database to the C:\Learn_ASP_Classic folder.

3. Click the **Start** menu button and choose **Run**. In the Run dialog box, type **notepad** and click **OK**.

4. When the text editor opens, type the following code, or copy and paste this code from **C:\Acc07_HandsOn\Employees.txt**.

```
<% @Language=VBSCRIPT %>
<%


' declare variables
Dim accessDB
Dim conn
Dim rst
Dim sql
```

```
' name of the database
accessDB="Northwind"

' establish connection to the database
conn="DRIVER={Microsoft Access Driver (*.mdb)};"
conn=conn & "DBQ=" & Server.MapPath(accessDB)

' Create a Recordset
Set rst = Server.CreateObject("ADODB.Recordset")

' select all records from Employees table
' for indicated fields only
sql = "SELECT FirstName, LastName, Title, City, Country FROM
Employees"

' Open Recordset (and execute SQL statement above)
' using the open connection
rst.Open sql, conn

%>

<HTML>
<HEAD>
<TITLE>Northwind Employees</TITLE>
</HEAD>
<BODY>
<TABLE Border="1">

    <%
       For Each fld in rst.Fields
    %>
       <TH>
          <% Response.Write fld.Name %>
       </TH>
       <%
          Next
          rst.MoveFirst
       Do While Not rst.EOF
    %>
       <TR>
    <%
    For Each fld in rst.Fields
    %>
       <TD>
          <% Response.Write fld.Value %>
       </TD>
       <% Next %>
       </TR>
       <% rst.MoveNext
       Loop
       %>
</TABLE>
</BODY>
</HTML>
<%
' close the Recordset
```

```
rst.Close
Set rst=Nothing
%>
```

The code shown above begins by specifying a scripting language for the page by using the Active Server Pages directive <% @Language= VBScript %>.

The script contained between the <% and %> delimiters is Visual Basic script code that gets executed on the web server. The <% says that what follows is a server-side script, not HTML. The %> indicates the end of a script segment. The script code between the <% and %> delimiters is executed on the web server as the page is processed. Any values you want returned by the script are placed between the <% and %> delimiters.

Similar to VBA procedures, the first step in scripting is the declaration of variables. Because in VBScript all variables are of the Variant type, you don't need to use the As keyword to specify the type of variable. To declare a variable, simply precede its name with the Dim keyword:

```
Dim accessDB
Dim conn
Dim rst
Dim sql
```

Similar to VBA, you can declare all your variables on one line, like this:

```
Dim accessDB, conn, rst, sql
```

To connect with the Access database, we specify a connection string like this:

```
conn="DRIVER={Microsoft Access Driver (*.mdb)};"
conn=conn & "DBQ=" & Server.MapPath(accessDB)
```

The DRIVER parameter specifies the name of the driver that you are planning to use for this connection (Microsoft Access Driver (*.mdb)). The DBQ parameter indicates the database path. The exact path will be supplied by the MapPath method of the Server object:

```
Server.MapPath(accessDB)
```

You can also connect to your Access MDB database by using the OLEDB data provider as follows:

```
Set conn = Server.CreateObject("OLEDB.Connection")
conn.Open "Provider=Microsoft.Jet.OLEDB.4.0; Data Source=" _
                    & Server.MapPath(accessDB)
```

To connect to an SQL server database, use the following format:

```
Set conn = Server.CreateObject("OLEDB.Connection")
conn.Open "Provider="SQLOLEDB;" & _
"Data Source=YourServerName;" & _
"Initial Catalog=accessDB;" & _
"UID=yourId; Password=yourPassword;"
```

To gain access to database records, we create the Recordset object using the CreateObject method of the Server object:

```
Set rst = Server.CreateObject("ADODB.Recordset")
```

After creating the recordset, we open it using the Open method, like this:

```
rst.Open sql, conn
```

The above statement opens a set of records. The sql variable is set to select all the records from the Employees table for the indicated fields. The conn variable indicates how you will connect with the database.

The %> delimiter indicates the end of the server-side script.

Server-side and Client-side Scripting

- A server-side script is the script code that runs on the web server before the page comes down to the client (the user's machine). This script begins to run when a browser requests an ASP file from your web server. The web server then calls the ASP interpreter (ASP.dll), which processes the blocks of code between the <% and %> delimiter tags. After the script commands are executed, the web page is sent to the browser. Server-side scripts cannot be readily copied because only the result of the script is returned to the browser. Users cannot view the script commands that created the page they are viewing. All they can see is the HTML source code for the page.

- In addition to server-side scripts, an ASP file can contain client scripts. A client script is the script code that is processed by a browser on the user's machine while the page is viewed. Client scripts are enclosed between <SCRIPT> and </SCRIPT> tags. When a browser encounters a <SCRIPT> tag, it sends the script that follows this tag to a scripting engine. A scripting engine is the part of the web browser that processes the scripts. Because not all browsers can process client scripts, comment tags (<!-- and -->) are often used to make browsers that do not recognize the <SCRIPT> tag ignore it.

Notice the many tags between the angle brackets: <HTML>, </HTML>, <HEAD>, </HEAD>, <TITLE>, </TITLE>, <BODY>, </BODY>, <B>, </B>, <TR>, and so on (see Table 28-1). The tags tell the browser how to display the file. For example, the <HTML> tag tells the browser that what follows is an HTML document. The closing </HTML> tag at the end of the file tells the browser that the HTML document is completed. The closing tags are denoted by placing a forward slash before the tag name (for example, </TITLE>, </BODY>, </HTML>). Closing tags cancel the effect of the tag.

The next part of the ASP page contains HTML formatting tags that prepare a table. These tags are summarized in Table 28-1.

The table headings are read from the Fields collection of the Recordset object using the For... Each...Next loop. Notice that all instructions that need to be executed on the server are enclosed by the <% and %> delimiters. To enter the data returned by the server in the appropriate table cell, use the Write method of the ASP Response object:

```
Response.Write fld.Name
```

The above statement will return the name of a table field. Because this instruction appears in the file between the <TH> and </TH> HTML formatting tags, the names of the table fields will be written as headings in bold type.

After reading the headings, the next loop reads the values of the fields in each record:

```
Response.Write fld.Value
```

Because the above statement is located between the <TD> and </TD> formatting tags, the values retrieved from each field in a particular record will be written to table cells.

The script ends by closing the recordset and releasing the memory used by it:

```
rst.Close
set rst = Nothing
```

Because the web server reads and processes the instructions in the ASP page every time your browser requests the page, the information you receive is highly dynamic. ASP allows the page to be built or customized on the fly before the page is returned to the browser.

5. Save the file as **C:\Learn_ASP_Classic\Employees.asp** and exit Notepad.

Table 28-1: Frequently used script delimiters and HTML tags

<% and %>	Beginning and end of the ASP script fragment. The script code between the <% and %> delimiters will be executed on the server before the page is delivered to the user browser.
<HTML> and </HTML>	You should place the <HTML> tag at the beginning of each web page. To indicate the end of a web page, use the closing tag: </HTML>. The HTML document has two main sections: <HEAD> and <BODY>.
<HEAD> and </HEAD>	The <HEAD> section contains information about the document such as its title, keywords, description, and stylesheet. Often Java scripts are placed in the <HEAD> section.
<TITLE> and </TITLE>	Place the text you want to display in the window title bar between these HTML tags. The <TITLE> tag always appears within the <HEAD> section.
<BODY> and </BODY>	The text you want to display on the web page should be placed between these tags.
<TABLE> and </TABLE>	Beginning and end of a table.
<TABLE Border = "1">	The Border parameter specifies the width of the table border.
<TH> and </TH>	Place table headings between <TH> and </TH> tags. They will be automatically displayed in bold font.
<TR> and </TR>	<TR> tag begins a new row in a table. Each table row ends with the </TR> tag.
<TD> and </TD>	Each table data item starts with the <TD> tag and ends with the </TD> tag.

We are not ready yet to view the data. Before you can view the Employees data in a browser, we need to perform the following tasks:

- Install the Microsoft Internet Information Services (IIS) 5.0 or a newer version.

- Create a virtual folder.

The ASP Object Model

ASP has its own object model consisting of the objects shown in Table 28-2.

Table 28-2: The ASP Object Model

ASP Object Name	Object Description
Request	Obtains information from a user
Response	Sends the information to the client browser
Application	Shares information for all the users of an application
Server	Creates server components and server settings
Session	Stores information pertaining to a particular visitor

The ASP objects have methods, properties, and events that can be called to manipulate various features. For example, the Response object's Write method allows you to write text to the client browser. The CreateObject method of the Server object is required to create a link between a web page and your Access database. Although this chapter does not introduce you to all of the available ASP objects, properties, methods, and events, you will learn how to use the objects and methods required for performing a specific task related to displaying or manipulating Access data from the web browser.

Installing Internet Information Services (IIS)

To perform all the examples in this chapter, let's proceed to Hands-On 28-2, which will walk you through setting up Internet Information Services (IIS) on your computer if you are using Windows 2000 or Windows XP.

Hands-On 28-2: Installing Internet Information Services (Windows 2000/ Windows XP)

1. Insert the Windows 2000 or XP Professional CD-ROM into a drive.
2. Click **Start**, select **Settings**, and click **Control Panel**.
3. Double-click **Add/Remove Programs**.
4. Click the **Add/Remove Windows Components** button in the left-hand panel.
5. Click the box beside **Internet Information Services (IIS)**.
6. Click **Next** to start the installation.

7. When the installation is complete, click **Finish** to close the wizard.

Figure 28-1: After completing the Internet Information Services installation steps in Hands-On 28-2, you should see the Inetpub folder on your computer. The \Inetpub\wwwroot folder is automatically set as the home directory for IIS.

Creating a Virtual Directory

The default home directory for the World Wide Web service is \Inetpub\ wwwroot. Files located in the home directory and its subdirectories are automatically available to visitors to your site. You can create virtual directories to make web pages that are not stored in the home directory or its subdirectories available for viewing. A virtual directory appears to client browsers as if it were physically contained in the home directory.

For the purposes of this chapter, you created a directory called Learn_ ASP_Classic on your computer (see Hands-On 28-1). In Hands-On 28-3 we will set up the Learn_ASP_Classic folder as a virtual directory.

◎ Hands-On 28-3: Creating a Virtual Directory

1. Open **Windows Explorer** and right-click the **Learn_ASP_Classic** folder you created in Hands-On 28-1. Select **Properties** from the shortcut menu.

2. In the Learn_ASP_Classic Properties window, click the **Web Sharing** tab (Figure 28-2). This window may look slightly different if you are using Windows 2000.

3. Click the **Share this folder** option button. The Edit Alias window will appear, as shown in Figure 28-3.

Figure 28-2: You can use the Properties window to quickly set up an alias users will use to access pages in the specified directory.

A virtual directory has an *alias*, a name that client browsers use to access that directory. An alias is often used to shorten a long directory name. In addition, an alias provides increased security. Because users do not know where your files are physically located on the server, they cannot modify them.

Figure 28-3: The Edit Alias window can be accessed from the Properties window by choosing the Share this folder button (see Figure 28-2). The directory name is automatically entered as the suggested name for the virtual directory (alias).

4. Enter **NorthDB** in the Alias box, as shown in Figure 28-4. In the Access permissions area, make sure that the **Read** permission is selected. In the Application permissions area, make sure that the **Scripts** option button is selected. Click **OK** to close the window.

When you set up a virtual directory, it is important to specify the access permissions for that directory. The Read permission allows users to access web pages. The Read permission is turned on by default. In addition, the Scripts permission should be turned on for virtual directories that will contain ASP pages.

Figure 28-4: You can change the suggested name of the virtual directory by typing your own entry in the Alias box.

5. When you click **OK**, you will see the alias NorthDB listed in the Aliases box (see Figure 28-5).

Figure 28-5: NorthDB is the name your browser will use to access files in the Learn_ASP_Classic folder while working with this chapter.

6. Click **OK** to close the Learn_ASP_Classic Properties window.

Now let's proceed to the next section where we access the employee data from a web browser by requesting in a browser the Active Server Page (Employees.asp) that we prepared in Hands-On 28-1.

◎ Hands-On 28-4: Requesting an ASP Page

This hands-on exercise requires completion of Hands-On 28-1 through 28-3.

1. Launch **Internet Explorer** and type **http://localhost/NorthDB/Employees.asp** in the address box. Press **Enter** to execute the Active Server Pages (ASP) file or click the **Go** button. The contents of the Employees table should appear in your browser as shown in Figure 28-6.

➡ **Important Note:** If you are using Windows XP and you receive an error page with the "access denied" message, be sure to give permissions to your user account on the Learn_ASP_Classic folder. Follow these steps:

1. Click **Start**, and then click **My Computer**.
2. Choose **Tools | Folder Options** and click the **View** tab.
3. In the Advanced Settings section, clear the **Use simple file sharing (Recommended)** check box.
4. Click **OK**.
5. Right-click the **Learn_ASP_Classic** folder and select **Properties**.
6. Click the **Security** tab and select your user account. Give yourself full control to the folder and click **OK**.

Figure 28-6: You can request the ASP page by typing its URL in the web browser's address bar.

2. Right-click anywhere in the browser window and select **View Source** to view the source code.

The View Source command uses Windows Notepad to display a source file. Because the script commands contained in the ASP file are evaluated on the server before the browser receives the page, the resulting page in the browser is 100% pure HTML code. Notice that the browser does not display any of your ASP code that was surrounded by the <% and %> delimiters. The scripting code is evaluated on the server and only the resulting HTML is passed to the browser!

3. Close Notepad and exit Internet Explorer.

Retrieving Records

In the preceding sections of this chapter we worked with the ASP page that retrieved records from the Employees table. Let's get more practice in data retrieval by creating another ASP page. The example ASP code in Hands-On 28-5 retrieves only customer names from the Customers table.

◎Hands-On 28-5: Creating an ASP File to Retrieve Records

This hands-on exercise requires completion of Hands-On 28-1.

1. Start **Windows Notepad** and enter the ASP code as shown below, or copy and paste this code from the **C:\Acc07_HandsOn\GetCustomers.txt** file.

```
<%@ Language=VBScript %>
<HTML>
<HEAD>
<TITLE>Retrieving a Recordset</TITLE>
</HEAD>
<BODY>
<%
Set conn = Server.CreateObject("ADODB.Connection")
```

```
conn.Open "DRIVER=Microsoft Access Driver (*.mdb);DBQ=" & _
        "C:\Learn_ASP_Classic\Northwind.mdb"
Set rst = conn.Execute("SELECT CompanyName FROM Customers")
    Do While Not rst.EOF
        Response.Write rst("CompanyName") & "<BR>"
        rst.MoveNext
    Loop
%>
</BODY>
</HTML>
```

The code shown above begins by specifying a scripting language for the page by using the ASP directive <%@ Language= VBScript %>. Recall that the script contained in the <% and %> is Visual Basic script. This script performs the following actions:

▪ Creates an instance of the ADO Connection object

▪ Opens the connection to the Northwind.mdb database using the Microsoft Access driver (this is the DSN-less connection)

The SQL SELECT statement retrieves the values in the CompanyName field from the table named Customers into a Recordset object named rst. The SELECT statement is executed with the Execute method of the Server Connection object. Notice that the instance of the Recordset object is created implicitly when the SQL statement is executed.

The Do While loop is used to output all the rows from the recordset to the browser. The Write method of the Response object outputs the value of a specific string or expression to the browser. The HTML <BR> tag is used to produce a carriage return after the value of the CompanyName field is output to the browser. Thanks to this tag, all company names are displayed on separate lines. Here, the value of the CompanyName field and a line break (
 tag) is written to the browser with the Response.Write statement like this:

```
Response.Write rst("CompanyName") & "<BR>"
```

The rst("CompanyName") retrieves the value of the CompanyName field from the Recordset object. You can output the values from the Recordset object by using any of the following statements:

```
Response.Write rst.Fields("CompanyName")
Response.Write rst.Fields("CompanyName").Value
Response.Write rst.Fields(1)
Response.Write rst.Fields(1).Value
Response.Write rst(1)
Response.Write rst("CompanyName")
```

Because the Fields collection is the default collection of the Recordset object, you can omit the word Fields. The MoveNext method moves to the next record in the recordset.

2. Save the file as **C:\Learn_ASP_Classic\GetCustomers.asp.**

3. Close Notepad.

Now that you know what the code does, let's proceed and request this ASP page in the browser.

4. Open your web browser and type **http://localhost/NorthDB/GetCustomers.asp** in the address bar.

5. Press **Enter** or click **Go**. When you request the GetCustomers.asp file in the browser, you get the results shown in Figure 28-7.

Figure 28-7: The ASP page created in Hands-On 28-5 displays the names of customers from the Customers table in the Northwind database.

Breaking Up a Recordset When Retrieving Records

In the preceding section, you worked with the ASP page that retrieved 91 records from the Customers table in the Northwind.mdb database. When you need to display more than a few records, it is a good idea to break up the recordset by dividing the list into multiple pages. This allows the user of your application to view a limited number of records at a time.

In Hands-On 28-6 you will create an ASP page that displays 12 customer names per page. The user will be able to move between the pages of data by clicking on the appropriate page number listed at the bottom of the page. To make the ASP page more useful, you will display the customer names as hyperlinks. Clicking on the customer name will call another ASP page displaying the customer's address as listed in the Customers table.

Hands-On 28-6: Creating a Multi-Page ASP File

1. Start **Windows Notepad** and enter the ASP code as shown below, or copy and paste this code from the **C:\Acc07_HandsOn\PageMe.txt** file.

```
<%@ Language=VBScript %>
<HTML>
<HEAD>
<TITLE>View Few at a Time</TITLE>
</HEAD>
<BODY>
```

```
<%
Dim conn, rst, mySQL, currPage, rows, counter
Set conn = Server.CreateObject("ADODB.Connection")
conn.Open "DRIVER=Microsoft Access Driver (*.mdb);DBQ=" & _
          "c:\Learn_ASP_Classic\Northwind.mdb"
Set rst = Server.CreateObject("ADODB.Recordset")

rst.CursorType = 3 'adOpenStatic
rst.PageSize = 12

mySQL= "SELECT * FROM Customers ORDER BY CompanyName"
rst.Open mySQL, conn
If Request.QueryString("currPage")="" Then
    currPage=1
Else
    currPage=Request.QueryString("currPage")
End If

rst.AbsolutePage=currPage
rows = 0

Response.Write "<H2>Northwind Customers</H2>"
Response.Write "<I>Displaying page" & currPage & " of "
Response.Write rst.PageCount & "</I>"
Response.Write "<HR>"


Do While Not rst.EOF And rows < rst.PageSize
    Response.Write "<A HREF=""Address.asp?CustomerID=" & _
       rst("CustomerID") & """>"
    Response.Write rst("CompanyName") & "</A><BR>"
    rows = rows + 1
    rst.MoveNext
Loop

Response.Write "<HR>"
Response.Write "<B>Result Pages: </B>"

For counter = 1 To rst.PageCount
    Response.Write "<A HREF=""PageMe.asp?currPage=" & counter & """>"
    Response.Write counter & "</A>"
    Response.Write Chr(32)
Next
rst.close
Set rst = Nothing
conn.Close
Set conn = Nothing
%>
</BODY>
</HTML>
```

The scripting section begins with the declaration of variables. Because all variables are Variants in Active Server Pages, it is convenient to list them on one line:

```
Dim conn, rst, mySQL, currPage, rows, counter
```

Following the declaration of variables, the Connection object is created and the connection to the Northwind database is opened using the Microsoft Access driver.

Next, the Recordset object is created. For Recordset paging to work properly, the CursorType must be set to adOpenStatic. Notice that the script uses the literal value (3) instead of the constant name adOpenStatic. By default, ADO enumerated constants are not defined in VBScript. However, a list of constants used with ADO is defined in the Adovbs.inc file (for VBScript) or in the Adojavas.inc file (for JScript). These files are installed in the \Program Files\Common Files\System\ado folder. To use constant names instead of their values, you can add a reference to the Adovbs.inc file at the top of your ASP page by using the #INCLUDE FILE directive, as shown below:

```
<%@ Language=VBScript %>
<!-- #INCLUDE FILE="adovbs.inc" -->
<HTML>
```

For the #INCLUDE FILE directive to work, you must copy the Adovbs.inc file to the Learn_ASP_Classic folder. When you add the above directive, you will be able to use the ADO constants instead of literal values in your VBScript. Using the enumerated constants will make your code easier to understand.

Use the PageSize property of the Recordset object to specify how many records are to be displayed on a page. The page is set to display 12 records:

```
rst.PageSize = 12
```

The SQL SELECT statement retrieves all the records in the Customers table into the recordset. We store this statement in the mySQL variable and proceed to open the recordset using the connection that we set up earlier:

```
rst.Open mySQL, conn
```

Next, the script retrieves the page you are currently on. If the contents of the currPage variable is an empty string (""), then you are on the first page.

The AbsolutePage property of the Recordset object is used to move to a particular page after opening the recordset. The AbsolutePage property identifies the page number on which the current record is located. AbsolutePage equals 1 when the current record is the first record in the recordset.

Next, the rows variable is initialized to zero (0). This variable limits the number of records that are displayed on a particular page.

Next, we use the Write method of the Response object to write a little HTML code that formats the page. For example, to format the page title we use the HTML second-level heading tag <H2> and its ending companion tag </H2> like this:

```
Response.Write "<H2>Northwind Customers</H2>"
```

The next two Response.Write statements inform the user about the page number being displayed and the total number of available pages:

```
Response.Write "<I>Displaying page" & currPage & " of "
Response.Write rst.PageCount & "</I>"
```

The HTML <I> tag will cause the text to appear in italics. You get the page number from the currPage variable and obtain the total number of pages from the PageCount property of the Recordset object.

Before we display the data, we want to draw a horizontal line on the page. This is done with the HTML <HR> tag.

Now comes the Do While loop that iterates through the recordset, counting the rows (records) as they are being retrieved and making sure that the number of records displayed per page is less than the specified page size. Company names are written to each page as hyperlinks using the HTML <A> anchor tag. The anchor tag uses the HREF attribute to designate a target page and forwards data to the target page when the user clicks the company name link:

```
Response.Write "<A HREF=""Address.asp?CustomerId=" & rst("CustomerId") & """>"
Response.Write rst("CompanyName") & "</A><BR>"
```

The target page (Address.asp) is created in the next hands-on exercise in this chapter. A question mark (?) separates the target page from the data. The data attached to the hyperlink is a field name followed by an equal sign and the field value. When you use Response.Write to write the links you must pay attention to the quotes. Notice the pairs of double quotes inside the string. Each pair of double quotes ("") can be replaced with a single quote (') to make it easier to read, like this:

```
Response.Write "<A HREF='Address.asp?CustomerId='" & rst("CustomerId") & ">"
Response.Write rst("CompanyName") & "</A><BR>"
```

The HTML <BR> tag ensures that each company name appears on a separate line.

When the value of the rows variable is greater than the page size, the records are output to the next page.

After all records are retrieved and placed on appropriate pages, a horizontal line is placed on the page using the HTML <HR> tag. Following the horizontal line, a list of links to the individual pages appears with the text "Result Pages:" formatted in bold (notice the <B> and </B> HTML tags). Again, to write those page links we use the HTML <A> tag with the HREF attribute:

```
Response.Write "<A HREF=""PageMe.asp?currPage=" & counter & """>"
Response.Write counter & "</A>"
```

The next statement uses the Chr(32) function to put a space between the page links:

```
Response.Write Chr(32)
```

Finally, the script segment ends by closing all objects and releasing the memory used. We announce the end of the file by writing two ending HTML tags:

```
</BODY>
</HTML>
```

Now that you know what the code does, let's proceed to request this page in the browser.

2. Save the file as **C:\Learn_ASP_Classic\PageMe.asp**.

3. Close Notepad.

4. Open your browser and type **http://localhost/NorthDB/PageMe.asp** in the address bar. Press **Enter** or click **Go**. You should see the listing of Northwind customers spanning multiple pages (Figure 28-8).

5. Navigate to different pages by clicking on the page links.

➔ **Note:** Clicking on the company name does not work yet. You must create another ASP page to display the selected customer's address (see Hands-On 28-7).

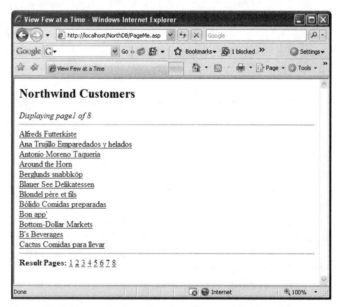

Figure 28-8: The result of running the ASP page titled PageMe.asp is a list of Northwind customers that is both easy to examine and use.

◉ Hands-On 28-7: Creating an ASP File for Loading from a Hyperlink

This hands-on exercise is required for using the company name hyperlinks in the PageMe.asp file created in Hands-On 28-6.

1. Start **Windows Notepad** and enter the ASP code as shown below, or copy and paste this code from the **C:\Acc07_HandsOn\Address.txt** file.

```
<%@ Language=VBScript %>
<HTML>
<HEAD><TITLE>Lookup Results</TITLE></HEAD>
<BODY>
<%
    Dim mySQL, myPath
    CustomerID = TRIM(Request.QueryString("CustomerID"))
    myPath = "C:\Learn_ASP_Classic\Northwind.mdb"
    Set conn = Server.CreateObject("ADODB.Connection")
    conn.Open "Provider=Microsoft.Jet.OLEDB.4.0;Data Source=" & myPath
    Set rst = Server.CreateObject("ADODB.Recordset")
    rst.CursorType = 3 'adOpenStatic
    mySQL= "SELECT * FROM Customers WHERE CustomerID='" & CustomerID & "'"
    rst.Open mySQL,conn
%>
    <H1>Address Lookup</H1>
    <I>Displaying address for <B><%=rst("CompanyName")%></B></I>
    <HR>
    <TABLE colspan=2 align="Center">
    <TR>
        <TD>Customer Id:</TD>
        <TD><input type="text" name="CustomerID"
            value="<%=rst("CustomerID")%>" size="5">
        </TD>
    </TR>
    <TR>
        <TD>Street:</TD>
        <TD><input type="text" name="Address"
            value="<%=rst("Address")%>" size="60">
        </TD>
    </TR>
    <TR>
        <TD>City:</TD>
        <TD><input type="text" name="City"
            value="<%=rst("City")%>" size="15">
        </TD>
    </TR>
    <TR>
        <TD>Region:</TD>
        <TD><input type="text" name="Region"
            value="<%=rst("Region")%>" size="15">
        </TD>
    </TR>
    <TR>
        <TD>Country:</TD>
        <TD><input type="text" name="Country"
            value="<%=rst("Country")%>" size="15">
        </TD>
```

```
</TR>
<TR>
  <TD>Zip:</TD>
  <TD><input type="text" name="PostalCode"
    value="<%=rst("PostalCode")%>" size="10">
  </TD>
</TR>
<TR>
  <TD>Phone:</TD>
  <TD><input type="text" name="Phone"
    value="<%=rst("Phone")%>" size="24">
  </TD>
</TR>
<TR>
  <TD>Fax:</TD>
  <TD><input type="text" name="Fax"
    value="<%=rst("Fax")%>" size="24">
  </TD>
</TR>
</TABLE>
<BR>
<BR>
<CENTER>[ <A HREF="VBScript:history.back(1)">Go Back </A> ]</CENTER>
<%
  rst.close
  Set rst = Nothing
  conn.Close
  Set conn = Nothing
%>
</BODY>
</HTML>
```

The first VBScript code segment between the <% and %> delimiters connects to the sample Northwind.mdb database using the native OLEDB Provider. The SQL SELECT statement retrieves the record for the selected
customer, and the information is output to the page. First, the internal title
is written out and formatted using the HTML level 1 heading tag <H1>.
The user is informed about the name of the customer whose information he
or she is viewing. Next follows the horizontal line (see the <HR> tag) and
the table structure that displays the customer information. The HTML tag
<TABLE> denotes the beginning of a table. <TR> starts a new row, and
<TD> indicates the table cell (where the data is displayed). Each of these
tags is closed with an ending tag (</TD>, </TR>, and </TABLE>). Using
a table to format the results is more pleasing to the eye.

Once the data is written to the page, you should provide the user with a
way to return to the previous page so that another customer record can be
requested. The Go Back hyperlink at the bottom of the page performs the
same action as clicking the Back button in the browser's toolbar:

```
<CENTER>[ <A HREF="VBScript:history.back(1)">Go Back </A> ]</CENTER>
```

The HTML <CENTER> tag positions the hyperlink centered between the
page margins.

Now that you know what the code does, let's proceed to request this page in the browser.

2. Save the file as **C:\Learn_ASP_Classic\Address.asp**.

3. Close Notepad.

4. In your browser's address bar, type **http://localhost/NorthDB/ PageMe.asp** and Press **Enter** or click **Go**. You should see the listing of Northwind customers spanning multiple pages.

5. Click a company name of your choice to view its address information. When you click a company name in the browser, the Address Lookup screen appears as illustrated in Figure 28-9.

Figure 28-9: When you click the company name on the PageMe.asp page (see Figure 28-8), you are presented with the web page that displays the selected company's address.

Retrieving Records with the GetRows Method

Instead of looping through a recordset to retrieve records, you can use the GetRows method of the Recordset object to retrieve records into a two-dimensional array. You've already seen examples of using the GetRows method earlier in this book. Hands-On 28-8 uses the GetRows method to move the records from the Shippers table into an array. Once in the array, the records are written out to a table and displayed in a client browser. When you place records into an array, you can free up the Recordset and Connection objects earlier than in a loop, thus releasing valuable server resources.

◎ Hands-On 28-8: Quick Data Retrieval

1. Start **Windows Notepad** and enter the ASP code as shown below, or copy and paste this code from the **C:\Acc07_HandsOn\FastRetrieve.txt** file.

```
<%@ Language=VBScript %>
<HTML>
<HEAD><TITLE>Fast Retrieve</TITLE></HEAD>
<BODY>
<%
    Dim conn, rst, strSQL, myPath, fld, allShippers, RowCounter, ColCounter
    Dim NumOfCols, NumOfRows, currField
    strSQL = "SELECT * FROM Shippers ORDER BY ShipperId"
    myPath = "C:\Learn_ASP_Classic\Northwind.mdb"
    Set conn = Server.CreateObject("ADODB.Connection")
    conn.open "Provider=Microsoft.Jet.OLEDB.4.0;Data Source=" & myPath
    Set rst = conn.Execute(strSQL)

    Response.Write "<TABLE Border=1><TR>" & VbCrLf
        For Each fld In rst.Fields
            Response.Write "<TD><B>" & fld.name & "</B></TD>" & VbCrLf
        Next
    Response.Write "</TR>" & VbCrLf
    allShippers = rst.GetRows

    rst.Close
    Set rst = Nothing
    conn.Close
    Set conn = Nothing

    NumOfCols = UBound(allShippers, 1) 'columns returned
    NumOfRows = UBound(allShippers, 2) 'rows returned
    For RowCounter = 0 To NumOfRows
        Response.Write "<TR>"& VbCrLf
        For ColCounter = 0 To NumOfCols
            currField = allShippers(ColCounter, RowCounter)
            If IsNull(currField) Then
                currField = currField & "<BR>"
            ElseIf currField= "" Then
                currField="."
            End If
            Response.Write "<TD Valign=Top>"
            Response.Write currField
            Response.Write "</TD>" & VbCrLf
        Next
        Response.Write "<TR>" & VbCrLf
    Next
    Response.Write "</TABLE>"
%>
</BODY>
</HTML>
```

The VBScript code above uses the OLEDB Provider to connect to the Northwind database. After executing the SQL statement, the Write method of the Response object is used to create a table:

```
Response.Write "<TABLE Border=1><TR>" & VbCrLf
```

The VbCrLf constant denotes a carriage return/linefeed combination. Because this constant is built into VBScript, you don't need to define it before using it. The HTML <TR> tag is used for adding a table row.

Next, the For Each...Next loop retrieves the fields from the recordset and places the field names as table headings in the first table row. Notice how the HTML tags are embedded within the VBScript code segment. After the headings are filled in, the procedure uses the GetRows method of the Recordset object and places all the fetched records in the variable named allShippers. Because we already have all the data that we need, we close the recordset and the connection to the database. At this point the records are in a two-dimensional array. Prior to writing them into table cells, you can use the VBA UBound function to check how many rows and columns were retrieved. The data is placed into table cells by using the For...Next loop. Because some fields in a retrieved recordset may not have any data in them, you can end up with some missing HTML table cells. To avoid blank spaces in a table, the VBScript code places the HTML
 (break) tag in a table cell if the field contains a Null value:

```
currField = currField & "<BR>"
```

You can also use a non-breaking space (nbsp;) for this purpose:

```
currField = currField & " "
```

The above statement will make the cell border show up when the cell is empty. You can also write the following statement to ensure that there are no gaps in your table:

```
Response.Write "<TD>" & currField & " </TD>"
```

In addition, if a field contains a zero-length string (""), the VBScript procedure places a dot in a table cell, so that you not only keep the structure of the table intact, but also differentiate between information that does not exist (zero-length) and information that may exist (Null). Recall that by setting the Allow Zero Length property of a table field to Yes and the Required property to No, you can enter two double quotation marks to indicate that the information does not exist. Leaving the field blank by not entering any data in it indicates that the information may exist but is not known at the time of entry.

2. Save the file as **C:\Learn_ASP_Classic\FastRetrieve.asp**.

3. Close Notepad.

4. In your browser's address bar, type **http://localhost/NorthDB/Fast-Retrieve.asp** and press **Enter** or click **Go**. You should see the listing of three shipping companies placed in a table (see Figure 28-10).

Figure 28-10: The FastRetrieve ASP page fetches records from the Shippers table using the GetRows method.

5. Open the **Northwind.mdb** database located in the Learn_ASP_Classic folder and open the **Shippers** table in Design view. Click in the **Phone** field and change the Required property of this field to **No** and the Allow Zero Length property to **Yes**.

6. Save the Shippers table and open it in Datasheet view. Add **Airborne Express** as a new shipping company. Leave the Phone field for Airborne Express empty. Add **DHL** as a new shipping company. Enter two double quotation marks and a space (" ") in the **Phone** field for DHL. Upon saving the record, the quotation marks will disappear.

7. Close the Shippers table and exit Microsoft Access.

8. Return to your browser and press **F5** to refresh the window or click the **Go** button to update the display. Notice that the Phone cell is empty for Airborne Express and there is a dot in the Phone cell for DHL.

Database Lookup Using Drop-Down Lists

Access forms often use a combo box to look up information in a database. When you use a drop-down box, the available choices are limited, so you don't need to worry that the user will enter incorrect information. Hands-On 28-9 illustrates how you can display a drop-down list box in a browser, load it with the product names, and return product information formatted in a table.

Hands-On 28-9: Creating a Web Page with a Drop-Down List Box

1. Start **Windows Notepad** and enter the ASP code as shown below, or copy and paste this code from the **C:\Acc07_HandsOn\ProductLookup.txt** file.

```
<%@ Language=VBScript %>
<%
Dim conn, rst, strSQL
Set conn = Server.CreateObject("ADODB.Connection")
```

```
conn.ConnectionTimeout = 15
conn.CommandTimeout = 30
conn.Open "Driver={Microsoft Access Driver (*.mdb)}; DBQ=" & _
        Server.MapPath("Northwind.mdb") & ";"
Set rst = Server.CreateObject("ADODB.Recordset")
If Len(Request.QueryString("ProductID")) <> 0 Then
    strSQL="SELECT * FROM Products WHERE ProductID="
    rst.Open(strSQL & Request.QueryString("ProductID")), conn, 0, 1
    If Not rst.EOF Then
        rst.MoveFirst
        Response.Write "<TABLE Border=1>"
        Response.Write "<TR>"
        Response.Write "<TD><B>Product ID</B></TD>"
        Response.Write "<TD><B>Product Name</B></TD>"
        Response.Write "<TD><B>Quantity Per Unit</B></TD>"
        Response.Write "<TD><B>Units in Stock</B></TD>"
        Response.Write "<TD><B>Unit Price</B></TD>"
        Response.Write "</TR>"
        Response.Write "<TR>"
        Response.Write "<TD Align='Center'>"
        Response.Write rst.Fields("ProductID") & "</TD>"
        Response.Write "<TD Align='Left'>"
        Response.Write rst.Fields("ProductName") & "</TD>"
        Response.Write "<TD Align='Left'>"
        Response.Write rst.Fields("QuantityPerUnit") & "</TD>"
        Response.Write "<TD Align='Center'>"
        Response.Write rst.Fields("UnitsInStock") & "</TD>"
        Response.Write "<TD Align='Right'>"
        Response.Write FormatCurrency(rst.Fields("UnitPrice"),2) & "</TD>"
        Response.Write "</TR>"
        Response.Write "</TABLE>"
    End If
    rst.Close
End If
rst.Open "Products", conn, 0, 1
If Not rst.EOF Then
    rst.MoveFirst
    Response.Write "<FORM Action='./ProductLookup.asp' Method='GET'>"
    Response.Write "<B>Select a Product:</B><BR>"
    Response.Write "<SELECT Name='ProductID'>"
    Response.Write "<OPTION></OPTION>"
    Do While Not rst.EOF
        Response.Write "<OPTION value=" & rst.Fields("ProductID") & ">"
        Response.Write rst.Fields("ProductName") & "</OPTION>"
        rst.MoveNext
    Loop
    Response.Write "</SELECT>"
    Response.Write "<INPUT Type='Submit' Value='Get Product Details'>"
    Response.Write "</FORM>"
End If
rst.Close
Set rst = Nothing
conn.Close
Set conn = Nothing
%>
```

The VBScript code segment above begins with establishing a connection with the data source. Instead of using a fully qualified path to the Northwind database, the code shows you how to use the MapPath method of the ASP Server object to retrieve the path to the database. The statement Server.MapPath("Northwind.mdb") will return the following path: Learn_ASP_Classic\Northwind.mdb. In fact, if you add the statement:

```
Response.Write Server.MapPath("Northwind")
```

to the code above, the filename with its path will appear in the browser. It is not difficult to guess that using Server.MapPath generates an additional request for the server to process. Therefore, when deploying your web site, you should replace Server.MapPath with a fully qualified path to get a better performance (see the previous hands-on examples for how this is done).

Notice that before the connection to the database is opened, the following statements are used:

```
conn.ConnectionTimeout = 15
conn.CommandTimeout = 30
```

The first statement instructs the Connection object's ConnectionTimeout property to wait 15 seconds before abandoning a connection attempt and issuing an error message. In the second statement above, the Command-Timeout property of the Connection object specifies how long to wait while executing a command before terminating the attempt and generating an error. The default for the ConnectionTimeout and CommandTimeout properties is 30 seconds. Using ConnectionTimeout and CommandTimeout in this example procedure is optional. Before utilizing these properties in your own database applications, make sure that the data source and the provider you are using support them.

Next, the script instantiates a Recordset object and opens it using the open connection. The recordset is opened as forward-only (0 = adOpen-ForwardOnly) and read-only (1 = adLockReadOnly). As mentioned earlier in this chapter, to use enumerated ADO constants, you need to add the #INCLUDE FILE directive at the beginning of the Active Server Pages file.

The SQL SELECT statement contains the WHERE clause that will only pull record for a selected product ID if the user makes a selection from the drop-down box. The data available for the selected record is then placed in a table. In this example, the table headings are hard-coded. If you don't want to hard-code the headings, you could loop through the recordset to read the field names (see the FastRetrieve.asp file created earlier for an example). After writing out the table headings, the procedure fills the table cells with data. The table will contain only one row of data because the recordset is limited to one product selected from the drop-down list. After the data is presented in a table, the Recordset object is closed.

Next, another recordset is opened. This time the code opens the entire Products table. We loop through the recordset to build a drop-down list box. For each record, an <OPTION> tag is created, its value is set to the ProductID field, and the text is set to the ProductName. The first entry in the drop-down list is a blank line. This effect is achieved by omitting the value and text attributes inside the HTML <OPTION> tag:

```
<OPTION></OPTION>
```

The drop-down list box is part of a form. The <FORM> tag is used to generate an HTML form.

Forms allow user input into the browser and act as a container for ActiveX controls. Forms can be processed via two methods: GET and POST. This example uses the GET method to send information. (See Hands-On 28-11 for an example of processing form input with the POST method.) Within a <FORM> and </FORM> block, you can insert tags representing various HTML controls. In this example, the form contains the list box produced by the <SELECT> tag and a command button produced by the <INPUT> tag. When the user clicks a submit form button labeled "Get Product Details," the data gathered from the drop-down list box is passed to the Active Server Pages file specified within the <FORM> statement by the Action parameter.

2. Save the file as **C:\Learn_ASP_Classic\ProductLookup.asp**.

3. Close Notepad.

4. In your browser's address bar, type **http://localhost/NorthDB/Product-Lookup.asp** and press **Enter** or click **Go**. The web page displays a drop-down box and a button as shown in Figure 28-11.

5. Open the drop-down list. When you open a drop-down list box, the list of products appears. Notice that the first entry in the list is a blank line.

6. Select a product from the drop-down list and click the **Get Product Details** button. The product details appear in a table, as shown in Figure 28-12.

Figure 28-11: By using a drop-down box in a web page, you can provide a user-friendly interface for selecting records.

Figure 28-12: When you select a product from the drop-down list and click the Get Product Details button, the selected product information is presented at the top of the web page.

When you use the form with the GET method to send the information, the data is appended to the request for the processing page. The data being passed is visible in the address bar in your browser (see the figure above). Because the data is visible, you can easily troubleshoot any problems by looking at the address bar. The drawback of using the GET method for sending information is that the data is not secure and it is limited in size to the maximum length of the request string.

Database Lookup Using a Multiple-Selection List Box

In the previous section, you saw an example of looking up product information by selecting a product name from a drop-down list. At times, however, a user may want to view several products at once. To meet this requirement, you will need to create a multiple-selection list box and process the user's selections.

Hands-On 28-10 illustrates how you can display a multiple-selection list box in a browser, load it with the product names, and return product information formatted in a table.

Hands-On 28-10: Creating a Web Page with a Multiple-Selection List Box

1. Start **Windows Notepad** and enter the ASP code as shown below, or copy and paste this code from the **C:\Acc07_HandsOn\MultiProduct-Lookup.txt** file.

```
<%@ Language=VBScript %>
<HTML>
<HEAD><TITLE>Select Multiple Products</TITLE></HEAD>
<BODY>
<%
    Dim conn, rst, strSelect, strWhere, strSQL, totalItems, fld

    Set conn = Server.CreateObject("ADODB.Connection")
    conn.ConnectionTimeout = 15
    conn.CommandTimeout = 30
```

```
            conn.Open "Driver={Microsoft Access Driver (*.mdb)}; DBQ=" & _
                Server.MapPath("Northwind.mdb") & ";"
            Set rst = Server.CreateObject("ADODB.Recordset")

    If Len(Request.QueryString("ProductID")) <> 0 Then
        strSelect="SELECT ProductID AS [ID], ProductName AS [Product Name], " & _
                "QuantityPerUnit AS [Qty/Unit], UnitsInStock AS Stock, " & _
                "UnitPrice AS [Unit Price] FROM Products "
        strWhere = "WHERE ProductID="
        strSQL = strSelect & strWhere

        totalItems = Request.QueryString("ProductID").Count
        myValues = Request.QueryString("ProductID").Item

        Response.Write "<P><H5><I>The following SQL statement was used:</I>"

        If totalItems = 1 Then
            rst.Open(strSQL & Request.QueryString("ProductID")), conn, 0, 1
        %>
            <PRE><%= strSQL & Request.QueryString("ProductID") %></PRE>
        <%
        Else
            strWhere = "WHERE ProductID IN ("

            strSQL = strSelect & strWhere
            rst.Open(strSQL & myValues & ")"), conn, 0, 1
        %>
            <PRE><%= strSQL & myValues & ")" %></PRE>
        <%
        End if

        ' get table headings
        Response.Write "</H5><P><TABLE Border=1>"
        Response.Write "<TR>"
        For Each fld in rst.Fields
            Response.Write "<TH>" & fld.Name & "</TH>"
        Next
        Response.Write "</TR>"

        ' get the data
        Do While not rst.EOF
        Response.Write "<TR>"

            For Each fld in rst.Fields
                Response.Write "<TD>"
                If fld.Name = "UnitPrice" Then
                    Response.Write FormatCurrency(fld.value,2)
                Else
                    Response.Write fld.value
                End If
                    Response.Write "</TD>"
            Next
            Response.Write "</TR>"
            rst.MoveNext
        Loop
        Response.Write "</TABLE>"
```

```
      rst.Close
End If

rst.Open "Products", conn, 0, 1
If Not rst.EOF Then
    rst.MoveFirst
%>
    <FORM Action="MultiProductLookup.asp" Method="GET">
    <B><I><FONT Size=2 Face=Tahoma>Hold down CTRL or SHIFT <BR>
        to select multiple products:</FONT></I></B><BR>
    <SELECT Name="ProductID" MULTIPLE Size=8>
<%
    Do While Not rst.EOF
%>
    <OPTION Value="<%=rst.Fields("ProductID")%>">
    <%=rst.Fields("ProductName")%></OPTION>
<%
    rst.MoveNext
    Loop
%>
    </SELECT>
    <INPUT Type="Submit" Value="Get Product(s) Details">
    </FORM>
<%
End If
rst.Close
Set rst = Nothing
conn.Close
Set conn = Nothing
%>
</BODY>
</HTML>
```

The VBScript code segment above establishes a DSN-less connection to the Northwind database by using the Microsoft Access driver and instantiates a Recordset object. Refer to the previous hands-on exercise for an explanation of the Connection object's ConnectionTimeout and CommandTimeout properties and the Server object's MapPath method.

The code proceeds to check whether the user has selected any items in the list box. If at least one product was picked from the list, the procedure defines the SQL SELECT statement and uses the QueryString method of the Request object to retrieve the total number of selected products. This number is then stored in the totalItems variable. The next Request.Query-String statement retrieves the IDs of the selected items and places them in the myValues variable. The next statement announces that the line that follows is the SQL statement the user has selected. This statement is formatted with the HTML <H5> and <I> tags. This will make the enclosed text an italicized heading of size 5 (the largest heading is 1 and the smallest is 6). The <P> tag designates the text as a plain paragraph. The ending </P> tag is optional.

If one product was selected in the list box, a recordset is opened using the following statement:

```
rst.Open(strSQL & Request.QueryString("ProductID")), conn, 0, 1
```

Recall that 0 and 1 at the end of this statement indicate a forward-only and read-only recordset.

The statement:

```
<PRE><%=strSQL & Request.QueryString("ProductID") %></PRE>
```

will write the complete SQL statement to the browser for the user to see. When you use the HTML <PRE> and </PRE> tags, the text between these tags is formatted exactly as it is typed. Spaces and carriage returns are preserved. If more than one product was selected in the list box, we need to change the contents of the strWhere variable to include the IN keyword in the WHERE clause. The IN keyword restricts the rows being selected to those rows where the column values are in the list presented in the SQL statement. Assuming that the user selected products with IDs of 1, 3, and 6 in the list box, the following SQL statement will be generated:

```
SELECT ProductID AS [ID], ProductName AS [Product Name], QuantityPerUnit AS
    [Qty/Unit], UnitsInStock AS Stock, UnitPrice AS [Unit Price] FROM Products
    WHERE ProductID IN (1, 3, 6)
```

The remaining code segment in the code above creates a table in a browser. We use the For Each...Next loop to write out the column names to the browser:

```
For Each fld in rst.Fields
    Response.Write "<TH>" & fld.Name & "</TH>"
Next
```

The <TH> tag makes a cell a table heading. This automatically makes the text bold. After populating the table with the headings, we use the Do While loop to write out the table rows until the end of the recordset is encountered. We must obtain field values for each column in a row. This is done with the For Each... Next loop like this:

```
For Each fld in rst.Fields
    Response.Write "<TD>"
    If fld.Name = "UnitPrice" Then
        Response.Write FormatCurrency(fld.value,2)
    Else
        Response.Write fld.value
    End If
        Response.Write "</TD>"
Next
```

Notice the conditional statement within the above code segment. We use it to perform an additional operation on the UnitPrice field. We format this field as currency using the FormatCurrency function. When all the table rows are written to the browser, the table is closed with the HTML table close tag </TABLE>, and the recordset itself is closed.

Next, the VBScript code continues by opening the recordset based on the Products table and cycling through this recordset to retrieve the product IDs and product names for inclusion in the list box. The HTML form section contains the MULTIPLE keyword in the <SELECT> tag to indicate that the list box should be created. The size of the list box is set to display eight products like this:

```
<FORM Action="MultiProductLookup.asp" Method="GET">
  <B><I><FONT Size=2 Face=Tahoma>Hold down CTRL or SHIFT <BR>
    to select multiple products:</FONT></I></B><BR>
  <SELECT Name="ProductID" MULTIPLE Size=8>
```

Notice that the above code is a client-side script. This code appears outside the VBScript <% and %> delimiters. To make this code a part of the VBScript you may want to rewrite it as follows:

```
Response.Write "<FORM Action=""MultiProductLookup.asp"" Method=""GET"">"
Response.Write "<B><I><FONT Size=2 Face=Tahoma>Hold down CTRL or SHIFT <BR>"
Response.Write "to select multiple products:</FONT></I></B><BR>"
Response.Write "<SELECT Name=""ProductID"" MULTIPLE Size=8>"
```

Once we have defined the list box we can populate it with product names using a Do While loop. We use the <OPTION> tag with the Value attribute <OPTION Value=" "> to specify items in the list:

```
Do While Not rst.EOF
%>
    <OPTION Value="<%=rst.Fields("ProductID")%>">
    <%=rst.Fields("ProductName")%></OPTION>
<%
    rst.MoveNext
Loop
```

Notice again that we set the list values outside the VBScript. For better understanding, and to practice various methods of coding, you can rewrite this code like this:

```
Do While Not rst.EOF
    Response.Write "<OPTION Value="
    Response.Write rst.Fields("ProductID") & ">"
    Response.Write rst.Fields("ProductName") & "</OPTION>"
    rst.MoveNext
Loop
```

To allow the user to submit selections to the server, the form contains the submit button titled "Get Product(s) Details." When the user presses this button, the form data will be submitted using the GET method.

The procedure ends by closing both the Recordset and Connection objects and freeing up memory.

Let's go on to test our work in the browser.

2. Save the file as **C:\Learn_ASP_Classic\MultiProductLookup.asp**.

3. Close Notepad.

4. In your browser's address bar, type **http://localhost/NorthDB/MultiProductLookup.asp** and press **Enter** or click **Go**.

5. The browser will display a list box. Select the items as shown in Figure 28-13 and press the **Get Product(s) Details** button.

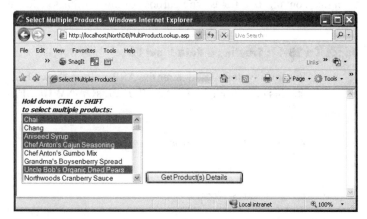

Figure 28-13: You can allow users to filter the data by using a multiple-selection list box.

Figure 28-14: After selecting the products in the list box (see Figure 28-13) and clicking on the Get Product(s) Details button, your browser displays data as shown here.

Adding Data into a Table

You may want to use a web page to collect data from a user and save it in Microsoft Access. The following hands-on exercise creates a simple data entry form that contains two fields. The purpose of this form is to allow users to enter new shippers into the Northwind database Shippers table.

⊚ Hands-On 28-11: Creating a Data Input Page

1. Start **Windows Notepad** and enter the ASP code as shown below, or copy and paste this code from the **C:\Acc07_HandsOn\NWDataEntry.txt** file.

```
<%@ Language=VBScript %>
<%
Dim conn, strConn, strSQL, name, phone, goAhead
name=Request("txtCompanyName")
phone=Request("txtPhone")

For Each key In Request.Form
    If Request.Form(key) = "" Then
    If key = "txtCompanyName" Then
        Response.Write "<FONT Color = 'Blue'>Please enter the Shipper name.
</FONT>"
    Else
        Response.Write "<FONT Color = 'Red'>Please enter the Phone number.
</FONT>"
    End If
    goAhead = False
    Exit For
    End If
    GoAhead=True
Next
If goAhead = True Then
    name=Replace(Request("txtCompanyName"),"'","''")
        If Len(name) <> 0 Or _
                Len(phone) <> 0 Then
        Set conn = Server.CreateObject("ADODB.Connection")
        strConn="Provider=Microsoft.Jet.OLEDB.4.0;Data Source="
        strConn=strConn & server.MapPath("Northwind.mdb") & ";"
        strConn=strConn & "User ID=; Password=;"

        strSQL = "INSERT INTO Shippers (CompanyName, Phone)"
        strSQL = strSQL & "Values ('" & name & "'"
        strSQL = strSQL & ",'" & phone & "')"
        With conn
        .Mode = 3
        .Open strConn
        .Execute(strSQL)
        End With
        Response.Write "<I><FONT Color = 'Green'>" & _
                        "Successfully added the following data:</I></FONT><HR>"

' get the ShipperID (the autonumber field in the Shippers table)
```

```
                strSQL = "SELECT MAX(ShipperID) AS lastID FROM Shippers;"

                Set rst = conn.Execute(strSQL)
                Response.Write "Shipper ID: <B>" & rst("lastID")& "</B><P>"

                rst.close
                Set rst = Nothing
                conn.Close
                Set conn = Nothing

                Response.Write "Company Name: <B>" & Request("txtCompanyName") & _
                        "</B></P>"
                Response.Write "Phone Number: <B>" & phone & "</B>"

                ' clear the Shipper Name and Phone input boxes
                name = ""
                phone = ""
            End If
        End If
        %>
        <HTML>
        <HEAD>
        <TITLE>Data Entry Screen</TITLE>
        </HEAD>
        <BODY>
        <FORM Name="form1" Action="NWDataEntry.asp" Method="POST" >
            <P>
                Shipper Name: <INPUT Type="text" Name="txtCompanyName"
                    Value="<%=name%>" Size= "30" > 
                Phone: <INPUT Type="text" Name="txtPhone" Value="<%=phone%>"></P>
            <P>
        <INPUT Type="Submit" Name="cmdSubmit" Value="Add Data"></P>
        </FORM>
        </BODY>
        </HTML>
```

The VBScript segment shown above assigns values to the name and phone variables. These values are collected from the text fields located on the HTML form. To collect information from a form, use the Request.Form("name") command, where name is the name of the form field (text box, check box, etc.). The VBScript above uses the abbreviated form of the Request.Form command:

```
Request("txtCompanyName")
```

To remove leading and trailing spaces that users often enter in text fields, use the TRIM function as follows:

```
name =TRIM(Request("txtCompanyName")
```

The For Each...Next loop validates user input prior to sending information to the server. It's a good idea to write validation scripts to check for such things as whether the user entered a valid number or whether a text box was left empty. This example only checks if any of the text fields are empty. Data validation should be performed on the client side to reduce

server loads and improve response time. Notice how we check the values
of the form elements with the For Each...Loop:

```
For Each key In Request.Form
    If Request.Form(key)= "" Then
    If key = "txtCompanyName" Then
       Response.Write "<FONT Color = 'Blue'>Please enter the Shipper name.
</FONT>"
    Else
       Response.Write "<FONT Color = 'Red'>Please enter the Phone number.
</FONT>"
    End If
    goAhead = False
    Exit For
    End If
    GoAhead=True
Next
```

The code above iterates through the Forms collection to check whether the
user has entered any data in the CompanyName and Phone fields and displays a message in a different color if any of the text fields were left blank.
If both text fields were filled in, the goAhead variable is set to True, and
the procedure continues.

Because the company name that the user entered may contain an apostrophe, an error could occur when the value is inserted into the SQL statement. To avoid the error, the procedure uses the Replace function to
replace one apostrophe with two apostrophes in the user-supplied text:

```
name=Replace(Request("txtCompanyName"),"'","''")
```

Provided that the length of the strings contained in the name or phone variables is not equal to zero (0), the connection is established to the
Northwind database, and the SQL INSERT INTO statement is executed.
This statement inserts a new record into the Shippers table and places the
contents of the name or phone variables into the CompanyName and Phone
fields. Next, the procedure uses the green font color to inform the user
about the successful addition of the data. Another SQL statement is executed to retrieve the ID of the newly added record, and the Response.Write
statement displays the ShipperID for the user to see in the browser.

After retrieving the value of the ShipperID field, the Recordset and
Connection objects are closed. Next, we write out the user-supplied shipper
name and phone number to the browser, and clear the name and phone
variables so that the form's input boxes display no data.

The remaining section of the ASP page contains HTML tags that generate a form where the user can enter the shipping company and phone number, and includes a button for submitting information to a web server.
Notice that the form's Action argument refers to the file named
NWDataEntry.asp. When the user submits data that he or she entered in the
form's text fields by clicking the Add Data button, the browser will use the
POST method to send the information to the ASP file on the server, in this
case NWDataEntry.asp.

An ASP file can create a form that posts information to itself (as shown in this example) or to another ASP file. By using the POST method, you can send an almost unlimited number of characters to the web server. The POST method is also more secure than the GET method because the information passed to the server does not appear in the browser's address bar. (Refer to the previous hands-on exercise for an example of processing form input with the GET method.) Notice how the values of the name and phone variables are retrieved:

```
Value = "<%=name%>"
Value = "<%=phone%>"
```

2. Save the file as **C:\Learn_ASP_Classic\NWDataEntry.asp**.

3. Close Notepad.

4. In your browser's address bar, type **http://localhost/NorthDB/NWData-Entry.asp** and press **Enter** or click **Go**.

5. Enter the data as shown in Figure 28-15 and press the **Add Data** button.

Figure 28-15: When you request the ASP page prepared in Hands-On 28-11, you are presented with the data entry screen for the Northwind database Shippers table.

When you enter data in the Shipper Name text box and click the Add Data button, the browser displays the data that was inserted into the Shippers table and allows you to make more additions by clearing out previous values from input boxes (Figure 28-16).

Figure 28-16: Notice that the browser displays the Shipper ID of the newly added record as well as the data entered in the text boxes prior to pressing the Add Data button (see Figure 28-15). You can continue adding new data by typing new values into the text boxes and clicking the Add Data button.

Modifying a Record

You can display a record in a browser and allow the user to edit the data. Changes made to the data can then be submitted to the server for processing. The easiest and quickest way to modify a record is by executing the SQL UPDATE statement.

The following hands-on exercise creates an ASP page where the user can select a product to update from a drop-down list. After clicking on the Retrieve Data button, the selected product's current price and units in stock are retrieved from the Products table. The retrieved data is placed in text boxes inside a table structure. The user can edit the data in the retrieved fields and insert the changes to the database table by clicking the Update Data button.

⊚ Hands-On 28-12: Creating a Page for Data Modification

1. Start **Windows Notepad** and enter the ASP code as shown below, or copy and paste this code from the **C:\Acc07_HandsOn\UpdateProduct.txt** file.

```
<%@ Language=VBScript %>
<HTML>
<HEAD><TITLE>Update Product Information</TITLE></HEAD>
<%
Set conn = Server.CreateObject("ADODB.Connection")
    conn.Open "DRIVER=Microsoft Access Driver (*.mdb);DBQ=" & _
        "C:\Learn_ASP_Classic\Northwind.mdb"
set rst = Server.CreateObject("ADODB.Recordset")
If Len(Request.QueryString("ProductID")) <> 0 Then
    strSQL="SELECT * FROM Products WHERE ProductID="
    rst.Open(strSQL & Request.QueryString("ProductID")), conn, 0, 1
    If Not rst.EOF Then
        rst.MoveFirst
%>
<BODY>
<FORM ACTION="UpdateProduct.asp" METHOD="POST" id=form2 name=form2>
<INPUT Type=hidden Name=txtProductID Value="<% =rst("ProductID") %>">
<INPUT Type=hidden Name=txtProductName Value="<% =rst("ProductName") %>">

<CENTER><H4><% =rst("ProductName") %>
     (Product ID=<%=rst("ProductID")%>)</H></CENTER><P>
<TABLE BORDER=0 CELLSPACING=4 CELLPADDING=4>
    <TR>
        <TD WIDTH=200 COLSPAN="2"><FONT COLOR=Blue>Unit Price ($):</FONT></TD>
        <TD BGCOLOR="#00FF00">
        <INPUT TYPE="text" NAME="UnitPrice" VALUE="<% =rst("UnitPrice") %>"</TD>
    </TR>
    <TR>
        <TD COLSPAN="2"><FONT COLOR=Blue>Units In Stock:</FONT></TD>
        <TD BGCOLOR=#00FF00">
        <INPUT TYPE="text" NAME="UnitsInStock" VALUE="<%=rst("UnitsInStock")
%>"</TD>
    </TR>
    <TR>
        <TD COLSPAN="2"></TD>
```

```
        <TD><INPUT type="submit" value="Update Data" id=submit2
name=submit2></TD>
        </TR>
    </TABLE><HR>
</FORM>
<%
    End If
    rst.Close
End If
If Not IsEmpty(Request.Form("submit2")) Then
    If Request.Form("UnitPrice")= "" or _
        Request.Form("UnitsInStock") = "" Then
        Response.Write "<B><Font Color=Red>You cannot leave any fields blank." _
            & "Please Try Again</B></FONT>"
    Else
        strSQL = "UPDATE Products SET " _
            & "UnitPrice = '" & Request.Form("UnitPrice")& "', " _
            & "UnitsInStock = '" & Request.Form("UnitsInStock")& "' " _
            & "WHERE ProductID = " & Request.Form("txtProductID")
        conn.Execute strSQL
        Response.Write "The following Update statement was executed for <B>" _
            & Request.Form("txtProductName") &"</B><BR>"
        Response.Write "<PRE>" & strSQL & "</PRE><BR>"
        End If
End If
    strSql = "SELECT * FROM [Products] ORDER BY [ProductName]"
    Set rst = conn.Execute (strSql)
    If Not rst.EOF Then
        rst.MoveFirst
%>
<FORM ACTION="UpdateProduct.asp" METHOD="GET" >
<TABLE>
<TR>
    <TD><B>Select a Product to Update</B></TD>
    <TD><SELECT Name="ProductID">
    <OPTION></OPTION>
<%
    Do While Not rst.EOF
    Response.Write "<OPTION Value='" & rst("ProductID") & "'> " & _
        rst("ProductName") & "</OPTION>"
    rst.MoveNext
    Loop
    End If
    rst.Close
    set rst = Nothing
    conn.Close
    set conn = Nothing
%>
<TD><INPUT type="submit" value="Retrieve Data" id=submit1 name=submit1></TD>
</SELECT></TD>
</TR>
</TABLE><HR>
</FORM></BODY>
</HTML>
```

Notice that the ASP page shown above contains two HTML forms: Form1 and Form2.

Form1 (whose code appears at the bottom of the ASP page) displays a drop-down list of products for the user to select. This form uses the GET method to send data to the server. This means that you will see the query string in the browser's address bar once you click the Retrieve Data button (see Figures 28-17 and 28-18).

Form2 (whose code appears higher in the ASP page) displays two text boxes with Unit Price and Units in Stock values for the product that was selected from the drop-down list on Form1. The user can modify the data in these text boxes. This form uses the POST method to send the information to the server. The submitted information will not be visible in the browser's address bar. This form will be submitted to itself after the user clicks the Update Data button. Two hidden text fields are placed on Form2 to store information about the retrieved Product ID and Product Name:

```
<INPUT Type=hidden Name=txtProductID Value="<% =rst("ProductID") %>">
<INPUT Type=hidden Name=txtProductName Value="<% =rst("ProductName") %>">
```

In this example, the information stored in hidden fields is used by the VBScript code later in the ASP file to create an SQL UPDATE statement and write an information message in the browser. Hidden form fields are often used with the POST method to hide information from the user.

The first VBScript code segment establishes a connection to the Northwind database and creates an instance of the Recordset object. Next, we check if a selection was made from the drop-down list. If the user made a product selection and clicked the Retrieve Data button, we open the recordset:

```
rst.Open(strSQL & Request.QueryString("ProductID")), conn, 0, 1
```

The Open method of the Recordset object is used to issue an SQL SELECT statement with the WHERE clause that specifies which record should be retrieved. We placed the SELECT statement in the strSQL variable. The Open method also specifies the connection to the database (conn), the cursor type (adOpenForwardOnly = 0), and the lock type (adLockReadOnly = 1). The recordset is opened to retrieve only the data that the user is allowed to modify. The data is placed in a table (see the HTML code segment). Once the data is retrieved, the recordset is closed.

The next VBScript code segment runs after the user clicks the Update Data button on Form2. When the form is posted, all controls, including the command buttons, are posted with it. Using the IsEmpty function you can find out if the user clicked the command button:

```
If Not IsEmpty(Request.Form("submit2")) Then
```

Prior to submitting the data to the server for insertion into the Products table, the code checks whether the Unit Price and Units in Stock text boxes contain any data. If either of these fields is empty (the user may have erased the data completely), a validation message is sent to the browser and the user must request the product again from the drop-down list if he or she wants to continue. On the other hand, if there is data in both text fields (even if the user has not made any changes to the original data), clicking the Update button on the form will send the SQL UPDATE statement to the server. As a result, the user will see the name of the product he or she updated together with the SQL UPDATE statement that was executed.

The last code segment creates a recordset to populate a drop-down list with product names. You should already be familiar with this code as it was demonstrated in the previous hands-on exercise.

2. Save the file as **C:\Learn_ASP_Classic\UpdateProduct.asp**.

3. Close Notepad.

4. In your browser's address bar, type **http://localhost/NorthDB/UpdatePro-duct.asp** and press **Enter** or click **Go**.

5. Select the product as shown in Figure 28-17 and click the **Retrieve Data** button.

Figure 28-17: When you request the UpdateProduct.asp file in your browser, a screen appears with a drop-down list where you can select a product you want to update.

Figure 28-18: When you select a product from the drop-down list and click the Retrieve Data button, the selected product's unit price and units in stock data are retrieved from the Products table and placed at the top of the page.

The user can modify the original data in the text boxes and click the Update Data button. If the user clicks the Update Data button when information is missing in the Unit Price or Units In Stock text boxes, he is advised to enter the data and try again. If the user clicks the Update Data button while the Unit Price and Units In Stock text boxes are not empty, the UPDATE statement is executed on the server and the submitted changes are inserted in the Products table. The user sees the page shown in Figure 28-19 in confirmation of the update request.

Figure 28-19: After submitting the product modification, the user sees the confirmation page with the UPDATE statement that was executed and is given an opportunity to continue by retrieving other products for modification.

Deleting a Record

When you need to delete a record, you can use the SQL DELETE statement. When writing a VBScript to handle the delete request, it's always a good idea to check for the following conditions:

- Did the user specify a record to delete? The user may have pressed the submit button without typing the record ID in the provided text box.

- Does the provided record ID exist in the table? This question is particularly important when the user is expected to type the record ID in a text box instead of selecting it from the drop-down list.

- What happens when the record the user wants to delete has related records in other tables? As you know, Microsoft Access will not allow you to delete records when the referential integrity rules are enforced.

The next hands-on exercise demonstrates how to delete a shipper from the Shippers table.

⊚ Hands-On 28-13: Creating Pages that Allow Record Deletions

This hands-on exercise uses two files for performing the delete operation. The first file is the HTML form that will submit the data to the second file, which is the ASP page.

1. Start **Windows Notepad** and enter the ASP code as shown below, or copy and paste this code from the **C:\Acc07_HandsOn\DeleteShipper.txt** file.

```
<HTML>
<HEAD>
<TITLE>DELETE DEMO</TITLE>
</HEAD>
<BODY>
<FORM Name=DeleteShipperForm Method=GET Action="DeleteShipper.asp"
<INPUT Type="Hidden" Name="Action" Value="Delete">
Please enter the Shipper ID you want to delete
<INPUT Type="Text" Size="6" Name="ShipperID">
<INPUT Type="Submit" Name="Delete" Value="Submit">
</FORM>
</BODY>
</HTML>
```

In the above HTML page, the form's Action argument will call the ASP page named DeleteShipper.asp when the user clicks the Submit button (see Figure 28-20).

2. Save the file as **C:\Learn_ASP_Classic\DeleteShipper.html**.

3. Close Notepad.

4. Start **Windows Notepad** and enter the ASP code shown below, or copy and paste this code from **C:\Acc07_HandsOn\DeleteShipper2.txt**.

```
<%@ Language=VBScript %>
<%
    Set conn = Server.CreateObject("ADODB.Connection")
    mydbFile=Server.MapPath("Northwind.mdb")
    conn.Open "Driver={Microsoft Access Driver (*.mdb)}; DBQ=" & mydbFile & ";"
    myShipper = Cstr(Request.QueryString("ShipperID"))
    If myShipper <>"" Then
        Set rst = Server.CreateObject("ADODB.Recordset")
        rst.Open "Shippers", conn, 3
        rst.Find "ShipperID = " & myShipper
        If rst.EOF Then
            Response.Write "The Shipper ID" & myShipper & " does not exist."
        Else
            On Error Resume Next
            conn.Execute "DELETE * FROM Shippers WHERE ShipperID = " & _
                        myShipper
            If conn.Errors.Count > 0 Then
            Response.Write "Error Number: " & err.Number & "<P>"
            Response.Write "Error Description: " & err.Description _
                        & "<P>"
            Else
            Response.Write "<H2>The Shipper ID " & myShipper & _
                        " was deleted.</H2>"
            End If
            rst.close
            Set rst = Nothing
        End If
    Else
            Response.Write "The Shipper ID was not supplied. Cannot Delete."
```

```
    End If
%>
<HTML>
<HEAD><TITLE>DELETE SHIPPER</TITLE></HEAD>
<BODY>
<HR>
<A HREF="DeleteShipper.html">Please click here to return.</A>
</BODY>
</HTML>
```

The VBScript code segment shown above establishes a connection to the data source and stores the ShipperID value in the myShipper variable. If the variable is not empty, then the code proceeds to create an instance of the Recordset object and opens the Shippers table. The recordset is opened using the static cursor (adOpenStatic) represented by the value of 3 in the following statement:

```
rst.Open "Shippers", conn, 3
```

Recall that the static cursor retrieves all the data as it was at a point in time and is particularly desirable when you need to find data. The next statement uses the Find method to check if the supplied ShipperID exists in the Shippers table:

```
rst.Find "ShipperID = " & myShipper
```

Next, the If...Then...Else statement decides what information should be returned to the browser. When the EOF property of the Recordset object is True, the recordset contains no records. In this situation you want to tell the user that there is no such record in the table. However, if the record is found in the Shippers table, the SQL DELETE statement is executed:

```
conn.Execute "DELETE * FROM Shippers WHERE ShipperID = " & myShipper
```

As noted at the beginning of this section, a user may enter a ShipperID that has related records in other tables. Because this situation will certainly result in an error, the VBScript is instructed to ignore the error and continue with the next line of code:

```
On Error Resume Next
```

The next line of code is another If...Then...Else block statement that sends a different text message to the browser depending on whether or not the error was generated. You will know this by checking the contents of the Errors collection of the Connection object. The code displays the error number and description if the user picked a ShipperID that cannot be deleted. You may want to replace this code section with a more user-friendly message. If there is no error, then the browser will display a message that the record was deleted. The text of this message is formatted in large letters using the HTML level 2 heading tag <H2>.

Next, the Recordset object is closed. And now we are back at the first If...Then...Else statement block where the Else part is executed if the user happened to click the Submit button without first typing in the ShipperID to delete.

The final part of the ASP page shown above creates a hyperlink to allow the user to navigate back to the HTML form (DeleteShipper.html). To create a hyperlink, use the following format:

```
<A HREF="address">displaytext</A>
```

where *address* is the name of the HTML file you want to activate and *displaytext* is the text that the user should click on.

5. Save the file as **C:\Learn_ASP_Classic\DeleteShipper.asp**.

6. Close Notepad.

7. In your browser's address bar, type **http://localhost/NorthDB/DeleteShipper.html** and press **Enter** or click **Go**. Your screen should resemble Figure 28-20.

Figure 28-20: This HTML page is used for submitting information to an ASP page.

8. Click the **Submit** button without typing anything in the provided text box. You should see a message informing you that the ShipperID was not supplied. Also, there is a link to allow you to return to the previous page.

9. Click the hyperlink to return to the previous page and enter **999** in the text box, then click the **Submit** button. Because this ShipperID does not exist in the Shippers table, you are again informed about the problem and provided a way to return to the previous page.

10. Click the hyperlink to return to the previous page. Enter the ShipperID that you inserted into the Shippers table in Hands-On 28-11 and click the **Submit** button. If you don't have a shipper record to delete, add a new record to the Shippers table and delete it using this process. When you type in a ShipperID that exists in the Shippers table but is not referenced in other tables, you get the screen that confirms the deletion (Figure 28-21).

Figure 28-21: This screen announces a deletion of the shipper record having the ID of 4.

When you enter a ShipperID that is referenced in other tables, Access will not allow you to delete that Shipper's record:

Error Number: –2147467259
Error Description: [Microsoft][ODBC Microsoft Access Driver]

The record cannot be deleted or changed because table 'Orders' includes related records.

To see this error in action, try to delete the shipper with an ID of 1.

You can trap the error –2147467259 in your VBScript code to display a user-friendly message.

Creating a Web User Interface for Database Access

Now that we've developed some sample ASP pages, let's see how you can put them together so that they can be easily accessed from a web browser. Instead of typing the appropriate ASP filename in the browser's address bar every time you want to perform a particular operation, you can use hyperlinks and frames to organize the data. For example, take a look at Figure 28-22, which displays the Internet Explorer window divided into three areas. You can navigate between individual hands-on examples created in this chapter by clicking on the text in the left pane. When you click the hyperlink, the main portion of the window on the right-hand side will fill with the data retrieved from a database or display an interface to obtain the data (see Figure 28-23).

Taking Your VBA Programming Skills to the Web

Figure 28-22: This page allows easy access to the hands-on examples on ASP programming introduced in this chapter.

Hands-On 28-14 walks you through the steps required to create the user interface shown in Figure 28-22.

⊚ Hands-On 28-14: Providing Easy Access to Data with Frames

This hands-on exercise creates and uses the following four HTML files: Review.html, Logo.html, Examples.html, and Results.html (see Table 28-3).

Table 28-3: HTML files used in Hands-On 28-14

File Name	Purpose
Review.html	Creates a page containing two frames and breaks one frame into two rows (resulting in three areas visible on the screen). Specifies what should be displayed within each frame and tells browsers that do not support frames to ignore them.
Logo.html	Places a company logo and a hyperlink to navigate to the company web site.
Examples.html	Creates jumps to this chapter's hands-on examples.
Results.html	Used for dumping information from the database or displaying the interface to obtain the data. Displays an information message to the user when the page is first opened.

1. Start **Windows Notepad** and enter the HTML code as shown below, or copy and paste this code from **C:\Acc07_HandsOn\Review.txt**.

```
<HTML>
<FRAMESET COLS="290,*">
    <FRAMESET ROWS="110,*">
        <FRAME SRC="Logo.html">
        <FRAME SRC="Examples.html">
    </FRAMESET>
    <FRAME SRC="Results.html" Name="myDisplay">
</FRAMESET>
```

```
<NOFRAMES>
This page requires frames to be viewed.
</NOFRAMES>
</HTML>
```

The HTML code shown above demonstrates how to divide a page into several areas by using frames. Each frame is controlled by its own HTML file.

You create a frame by using the HTML <FRAMESET> and <FRAME> tags with various parameters. A frame can contain other frames. The page shown in Figure 28-22 has two frames. The left frame is broken into two rows.

The statement:

```
<FRAMESET COLS="290",*">
```

divides the page into two columns. The left-hand column is 290 pixels wide, and the right-hand column occupies the remainder of the screen (denoted by the asterisk). A frameset can contain both frames and other framesets.

Next, the left-hand column is divided into two rows, like this:

```
<FRAMESET ROWS="110",*">
```

The top row is 110 pixels high, and the bottom row occupies the remaining portion of the frame. The top frame points to the Logo.html file. The source file for the lower frame is Examples.html:

```
<FRAME SRC="Logo.html">
<FRAME SRC="Examples.html">
```

The two <FRAME> tags provide the information about each frame. The SRC attribute defines the source data for the frame.

Next, we define the source data for the frame on the right-hand side:

```
<FRAME SRC="Results.html" Name="myDisplay">
```

The Results.html file is created later in this hands-on exercise. We use the Name attribute to define the frame's name so that we can refer to this frame later.

Each frameset ends with the </FRAMESET> tag. Browsers that do not support frames will display an information message located between the <NOFRAMES> and </NOFRAMES> tags:

```
<NOFRAMES>
    This page requires frames to be viewed.
</NOFRAMES>
```

2. Save the file as **C:\Learn_ASP_Classic\Review.html**.

3. Choose **File | New** to create a new document in Notepad.

4. Enter the HTML code as shown below, or copy and paste this code from the **C:\Acc07_HandsOn\Logo.txt** file.

```
<HTML>
<BODY>
```

```
<IMG ALIGN="Middle" WIDTH="127" HEIGHT="99" ALT="Visit us today!"
SRC="Wordware.gif">
    <FONT Color="Blue"><A HREF="http://www.wordware.com">ordware
    Publishing</A></FONT>
</BODY>
</HTML>
```

The HTML code above places an image (Wordware.gif, available in the downloadable files) in the top row of the frame on the left-hand side using the <IMG> tag. The ALIGN parameter tells the browser to position the text that follows in the middle. The WIDTH and HEIGHT parameters determine the size of the image in pixels. These measurements can be easily obtained by opening the image in the Windows Paint program and choosing Attributes from the Image menu. The text placed to the right of the image is a hyperlink. Clicking on it will jump to the Wordware Publishing web site.

5. Save the file as **C:\Learn_ASP_Classic\Logo.html**.

6. Choose **File | New** to create a new document in Notepad.

7. Enter the HTML code as shown below, or copy and paste this code from the **C:\Acc07_HandsOn\Examples.txt** file.

```
<HTML>
<HEAD>
<BASE Target ="myDisplay">
</HEAD>
<BODY>
<H4>Chapter 28 - ASP Examples</H4>
<P>
<FONT Size="-1">
<A HREF="GetCustomers.asp" Target=myDisplay>
Hands-On 28-5 (Retrieve records)
</A><BR>
<A HREF="PageMe.asp">
Hands-On 28-6, 28-7 (Limit records per page)
</A><BR>
<A HREF="FastRetrieve.asp">
Hands-On 28-8 (Retrieve records using GetRows)
</A><BR><P>
<A HREF="ProductLookup.asp">
Hands-On 28-9 (Use a drop-down box)
</A><BR>
<A HREF="MultiProductLookup.asp">
Hands-On 28-10 (Use a multiple selection list box)
</A><BR><P>
<A HREF="NWDataEntry.asp">
Hands-On 28-11 (Add a new record)
</A><BR>
<A HREF="UpdateProduct.asp">
Hands-On 28-12 (Modify a record)
</A><BR>
<A HREF="DeleteShipper.html">
Hands-On 28-13 (Delete a record)
</A>
```

```
</FONT></P>
</BODY>
</HTML>
```

The code in the Examples.txt file is straightforward. It contains a set of jumps to different hands-on examples. Each of these examples has a corresponding ASP file in the Learn_ASP_Classic folder. To control where the requested information should be displayed, use the <BASE> tag:

```
<BASE Target="myDisplay">
```

The Target attribute is set to the name of the frame where the information should appear. When you place the <BASE Target> tag at the beginning of the file, all of the links will display in the same frame.

Here's how we create the first hyperlink:

```
<A HREF="GetCustomers.asp" Target=myDisplay>
    Hands-On 28-5 (Retrieve records)
</A><BR>
```

The <A> tag defines a hypertext link. The HREF attribute specifies the associated URL. In other words, when the user clicks on the "Hands-On 28-5 (Retrieve records)" hyperlink, the GetCustomers.asp file will be requested and its output will be placed in the specified target (right-hand frame).

8. Save the file as **C:\Learn_ASP_Classic\Examples.html**.

9. Choose **File | New** to create a new document in Notepad.

10. Enter the HTML code as shown below, or copy and paste this code from the **C:\Acc07_HandsOn\Results.txt** file.

```
<HTML>
    Please select an option from the menu.
</HTML>
```

11. Save the file as **C:\Learn_ASP_Classic\Results.html**. The Results.html file will display the information text when the Review.html file is first opened in the browser (refer to Figure 28-22 at the beginning of this section).

12. Close Notepad.

You now should have four HTML files as outlined at the beginning of this hands-on exercise. Let's test out our user interface.

13. In your browser's address bar, type **http://localhost/NorthDB/Review.html** and press **Enter** or click **Go**. Your screen should resemble Figure 28-22, shown earlier in this chapter.

14. Verify the results of each hands-on exercise by clicking on its link.

Figure 28-23: When you click a hyperlink on the left-hand side, the right-hand frame will display the requested information as illustrated here.

Chapter Summary

This chapter has introduced you to the world of web development by using a server-side scripting technology from Microsoft known as Active Server Pages (ASP). You learned how by using a subset of VBA, VBScript, you can quickly extract data from a database and present it to a user in a standard HTML page. You also learned how to submit Action queries to insert, update, and delete a database record. You've seen two coding styles: one that mixes HTML and script commands, and one that returns HTML text to the browser by using the ASP built-in Response object and its Write method. By working through several hands-on examples, you've seen that making your application web-ready is not rocket science. ASP scripts are quite easy to write if you understand VBA statements and have already worked with ActiveX Data Objects (ADO). Although it was easy to get started, this chapter did not attempt to teach you all there is to know about HTML, ASP, or VBScript. If you decide to move into the lucrative and exciting world of web development, you should learn more about these subjects. Numerous books and articles have been written on the topics we've only touched on in this chapter, as well as many other topics that are necessary to create truly functional Internet applications.

In the next chapter, you explore another Internet technology known as Extensible Markup Language (XML) and learn how it is integrated with Microsoft Office Access 2007.

Chapter 29

XML Features in Access 2007

If you need to deliver information over the web or you want to store, share, and exchange data between different applications regardless of the operating system or programming language used, you need to become familiar with Extensible Markup Language (XML). Imagine these two scenarios where your combined knowledge of Access and XML will come in handy:

- You have just received a file in XML format and you need to merge its data with an existing Access table, or perhaps create a new table.

- You have been asked to provide a data dump from your Access database in XML format.

XML is a complex language that cannot be covered within the pages of one chapter; however, this single chapter will get you started using XML with Access 2007.

What Is XML?

In the previous chapter you learned how HTML (HyperText Markup Language) uses tags to format data on a web page. Like HTML, Extensible Markup Language uses markup tags; however, its tags serve a different purpose — they are used to describe data content. HTML uses fixed, non-customizable tags to provide formatting instructions that should be applied to the data. XML is *extensible*, which means that it is not restricted to a set of predefined tags. XML allows you to invent your own tags in order to define and describe data stored in a wide range of documents. The XML parser does not care what tags you use; it only needs to be able to find the tags and confirm that the XML document is well formed. When a document is well formed, it follows the formatting rules for XML (see "What Is a Well-Formed XML Document?" below).

What Is a Parser?

If you want to read, update, create, or manipulate any XML document, you will need an XML parser. A parser is a software engine, usually a dynamic-link library (DLL), which can read and extract data from XML. Microsoft Internet Explorer 5 and above have a built-in XML parser (MSXML.DLL, MSXML2.DLL, MSXML3.DLL, MSXML4.DLL, MSXML5.DLL, and MSXML6.DLL) that is capable of reading well-formed documents and detecting those that are not. MSXML has its own object model, known as DOM (Document Object Model), that you can use from VBA to quickly and easily extract information from an XML document. The Microsoft XML parser has been renamed Microsoft XML Core Services (MSXML).

To ensure that you are working with the most recent XML parser, check out the following link:

http://www.microsoft.com/downloads/details.aspx?FamilyID= 993C0BCF-3BCF-4009-BE21-27E85E1857B1&displaylang=en

An XML document must also be valid. When a document is *valid*, it follows the predefined rules for valid data. These rules are defined in a Document Type Definition (DTD) or a schema. Schemas are written in XML and define the rules that make an XML document valid. DTD is an old method of data validation. Later in this chapter you will see how Access uses a schema to determine the type of elements and attributes an XML document should contain, how these elements and attributes should be named, whether they're optional or required, their data types and default values, and the relationship between the elements.

Because of its extensibility, XML makes it easy to describe any data structure (structured or unstructured) and send it anywhere across the web using common protocols such as HTTP (HyperText Transfer Protocol) or FTP (File Transfer Protocol). Although XML was designed specifically for delivering information over the World Wide Web, it is being utilized in other areas, such as storing, sharing, and exchanging data. Because XML is stored in plain text files, it can be read by many types of applications, independent of the operating system or hardware.

What Is a Well-Formed XML Document?

An XML document must have one root element. While in HTML the root element is always <HTML>, in the XML document you can name your root element anything you want. Element names must begin with a letter or underscore character. The root element must enclose all other elements, and elements must be properly nested. The XML data must be hierarchical; the beginning and ending tags cannot overlap.

```
<Employee>
    <Employee ID>090909</Employee ID>
</Employee>
```

All element tags must be closed. A beginning tag must be followed by an ending tag:

```
<Sessions>5</Sessions>
```

You can use shortcuts, such as a single slash (/), to end the tag so you don't have to type the full tag name. For example, if the current Sessions element is empty (does not have value), you could use the following tag:

```
<Sesssions />.
```

Tag names are case-sensitive: The tags <Title> and </Title> aren't equivalent to <TITLE> and </TITLE>.
For example, the following line:

```
<Title>Beginning VBA Programming</Title>
```

is not the same as:

```
<TITLE>Beginning VBA Programming</TITLE>
```

All attributes must be inside quotation marks:

```
<Course ID="VBAEX1"/>
```

You cannot have more than one attribute with the same name within the same element. If the <Course> element has two ID attributes, they must be written separately, as shown below:

```
<Course ID="VBAEX1"/>
<Course ID="VBAEX2"/>
```

The main goals of XML are the separation of content from presentation and the portability of the data. It is important to understand that XML was designed to address the limitations of HTML and not to replace it. One of these limitations is the inability of HTML to identify data. By using XML tags you can give meaning to the data in the document and provide a consistent way of identifying each item of data. By separating content from presentation and structuring data based on its meaning, we are finally able to create documents that are easy to reuse, manipulate, and search.

XML Support in Access 2007

Microsoft Access has supported XML since its 2002 version. In Access 2007 you can export and import XML data by using buttons available in the Import and Export areas on the External Data tab or you can do this programmatically with VBA. Additionally, Access 2007 has the capability to export related tables to a single XML file. When importing XML data, you can create multiple tables from a single XML document and schema. Unfortunately, the parent-child relationships between the tables are not maintained; you must create them yourself. You can also specify a custom schema during the export or import of XML data.

Exporting XML Data

You can export tables, queries, forms, and/or reports to XML files from an Access database (MDB or ACCDB) file or an Access project (ADP) file. There is no XML support for macros and modules. When you export a form or report, you actually export the data from the form or report's underlying table or query.

Access uses a special XML vocabulary known as ReportML for representing its objects as XML data. *ReportML* is an XML file that contains tags describing properties, methods, events, and attributes of the Access object being exported. This file is generated automatically by Access when you begin the export process and is used by Access to generate the final output files.

To allow XML data to be viewed in browsers in a user-friendly format, ReportML relies on the RPT2HTML4.xsl file, which is located in the \Program Files\Microsoft Office\Office12\AccessWeb folder. This file is a rather complicated stylesheet that contains formatting instructions. We examine stylesheets later in this chapter.

After the formatting instructions contained in the stylesheet have been applied to the XML file, the ReportML file is automatically deleted.

> **Note:** If you'd like to take a look at the content of the ReportML file, you must tell Access not to delete it by default. This requires that you add the following entry to the Windows Registry:
>
> `HKEY_CURRENT_USER\Software\Microsoft\Office\12.0\Access\ReportML`
>
> Unless you are very familiar with using RegEdit to edit registry settings, do not attempt this task on your own. Once you make the Registry setting and complete the export to XML, you can open the ReportML file and look at its contents. This file should have the name of the Access object you exported, followed by an underscore and the word "report." For example, if you exported the Shippers table to an XML file, the ReportML name is Shippers_report.xml.

No matter what Access object you need to export to XML, you always follow the same procedure:

- To export all the data, select the appropriate object (table, query, report, or form) in the database window and choose External Data | More | XML File, or right-click the object name in the Navigation pane and select Export | XML File from the shortcut menu.

- To export a single record or a filtered or sorted set of records, open the appropriate object and follow the steps outlined below:

You want to...	Step 1	Step 2
Export a single record	Select that record	Choose External Data | More | XML File, specify the name of the export file you want to create, and click OK. Click the More Options button and in the Records to Export area, select Current Record.
Export filtered records	Apply a filter to the records	Choose External Data | More | XML File and select the appropriate options.
Export records in a predefined order	Arrange records in the order you want	Choose External Data | More | XML File and select the appropriate options.

The following hands-on exercise demonstrates how to use the Export command to save the Access Shippers table in XML format.

⊚ Hands-On 29-1: Exporting an Access Table to an XML File

1. Use Windows Explorer to create a new folder named **C:\Learn_XML** for this chapter's practice files.

2. Right-click the **Learn_XML** folder and choose **Sharing and Security**. You will now set the Learn_XML folder as a virtual directory. Click the **Web Sharing** tab in the Learn_XML Properties dialog box. Select the **Share this folder** option button and click **Add**. In the Edit Alias dialog box, replace the suggested name Learn_XML with **xml** and click **OK**. The Aliases list box in the Learn_XML Properties dialog box should now list the xml alias. Click **OK** to close this dialog box.

3. Open the sample **C:\Acc07_HandsOn\Northwind 2007.accdb** database.

4. In the Navigation pane, select the **Shippers** table, and choose **External Data | More | XML File**.

5. In the File name box, enter C:**Learn_XML\Shippers.xml** and click **OK**.

   In the Export XML dialog box that appears, two check boxes — Data (XML) and Schema of the data (XSD) — are already selected (see Figure 29-1). These options will create two files: an XML file that will contain the data from the Shippers table and an XSD file that will contain the definition of the data.

Figure 29-1: The Export XML dialog box displays three check boxes; the first two are selected by default. The More Options button allows for more customization.

6. Select the **Presentation of your data (XSL)** check box to tell Access to generate HTML and XSL files for presentation of the data in the web browser. With all three check boxes selected in the Export XML dialog box, click **OK** to proceed with the export.

7. When the export operation completes, Access displays the Export - XML File window where you are given a chance to save the export steps so that you can repeat them in the future without using the wizard. Click **Close** to exit the Export - XML File window without saving the export steps.

Understanding the XML Data File

In Hands-On 29-1 we prepared the Shippers.xml file. Let's switch to Windows Explorer and examine the contents of our Learn_XML folder.

◎ Hands-On 29-2: Examining the Contents of an XML Data File

1. Open **Windows Explorer** and switch to the **C:\Learn_XML** folder. Figure 29-2 displays the contents of the Learn_XML folder after exporting the Shippers table to XML in Hands-On 29-1.

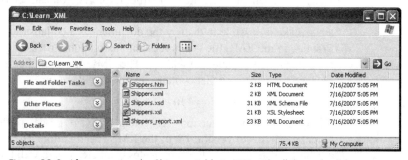

Figure 29-2: After exporting the Shippers table to XML with all three check boxes selected in the Export XML dialog box, Access creates four files. The fifth file is the ReportML file. If you didn't make changes in the Registry as mentioned in the Note at the beginning of this chapter, your Learn_XML directory listing will not contain the Shippers_report.xml file.

➡ **Note:** To have the file extensions displayed, choose Tools | Folder Options, click the View tab, and clear the check box next to Hide extensions for known file types.

2. Highlight the Shippers XML document (**Shippers.xml**) and choose **Open With** from the File menu. Select **Internet Explorer**. Access displays the Shippers data in XML format as shown in Figure 29-3.

Figure 29-3: The tree-like structure of the XML document.

When you open an XML file in Internet Explorer, you can see the hierarchical layout of an XML document very clearly. The plus and minus (+/–) signs make it possible to display the document as a collapsible tree. The first line in the XML file is a processing instruction. Processing instructions begin with <? and end with ?>. The XML document begins with a processing instruction that contains an XML declaration:

```
<?xml version="1.0" encoding="UTF-8" ?>
```

The version attribute (version="1.0") tells the XML processor that the document conforms to version 1.0 of the XML specification. The encoding attribute (encoding="UTF-8") indicates character sets to web browsers. By default, XML documents use the UTF-8 encoding of Unicode.

Character Encodings in XML

The encoding declaration in the XML document identifies which encoding is used to represent the characters in the document. UTF-8 encoding allows the use of non-ASCII characters, regardless of the language of the user's operating system and browser or the language version of Office. When you use UFT-8 or UTF-16 character encoding, an encoding declaration is optional. XML parsers can determine automatically if a document uses UTF-8 or UTF-16 Unicode encoding.

The second line in the XML document is a dataroot element:

```
<dataroot xmlns:od="urn:schemas-microsoft-com:officedata"
xmlns:xsi="http://www.w3.org/2001/XMLSchema-instance"
xsi:noNamespaceSchemaLocation="Shippers.xsd" generated="2007-07-16T17:05:42">
```

The dataroot element tag defines two namespaces:

```
xmlns:od="urn:schemas-microsoft-com:officedata"
xmlns:xsi="http://www.w3.org/2001/XMLSchema-instance"
```

A *namespace* is a collection of names in which each name is unique. The XML namespaces are used in XML documents to ensure that element names do not conflict with one another and are unique within a particular set of names (a namespace).

For example, the <TITLE> tag will certainly have a different meaning and content in an XML document generated from the Books table than the <TITLE> element used to describe the courtesy titles of your customers. If the two XML documents containing the <TITLE> tag were to be merged, there would be an element name conflict. Therefore, in order to distinguish between tags that have the same names but need to be processed differently, namespaces are used.

The attribute "xmlns" is an XML keyword for a namespace declaration. The namespace is identified by a Uniform Resource Identifier (URI) — either a Uniform Resource Locator (URL) or a Uniform Resource Name (URN). The URI used as an XML namespace name is simply an identifier; it is not guaranteed to point to anything. Most namespaces use URIs for the namespace names because URIs are guaranteed to be unique. The use of a namespace is identified via a name prefix. The prefix is mapped to a URI to select a namespace.

For example, in the context of the Shippers.xml document, the od prefix is associated with the urn:schemas-microsoft-com:officedata namespace and the xsi prefix identifies the http://www.w3.org/2001/XMLSchema-instance namespace. These prefixes may be associated with other namespaces outside of this particular XML document. Notice that the prefix is separated from the xmlns attribute with a colon and the URI is used as the value of the attribute.

In addition to namespaces, the dataroot element specifies where to find the schema. This is done by using two attributes: the location of a schema file that defines the rules of an XML document and the date the file was generated.

```
xsi:noNamespaceSchemaLocation="Shippers.xsd" generated="2007-07-16T17:05:42"
```

An XML document's data is contained in elements. An element consists of the following three parts:

- Start tag — Contains the element's name (e.g., <ID>)
- Element data — The representation of actual data (e.g., 1)
- End tag — Contains the element's name preceded by a slash (e.g., </ID>)

If you click on the minus sign in front of the dataroot element, you will notice that the dataroot element encloses all the elements in the Access XML file. Each element in a tree structure is called a *node*.

The dataroot node contains child nodes for each row of the Shippers table. Notice that the table name is used for each element representing a row. You can expand or collapse any row element by clicking on the plus or minus sign (+/−) in front of the element tag name.

Within row elements, there is a separate element for each column (ID, Company, and so on). Notice that each XML element contains a start tag, the element data, and the end tag:

```
<Shippers>
    <ID>1</ID>
    <Company>Shipping Company A</Company>
    <Address>123 Any Street</Address>
    <City>Memphis</City>
    <State_x002F_Province>TN</State_x002F_Province>
    <ZIP_x002F_Postal_x0020_Code>99999</ZIP_x002F_Postal_x0020_Code>
    <Country_x002F_Region>USA</Country_x002F_Region>
</Shippers>
```

The ID, Company, Address, City, State_x002F_Province, Zip_x002F_Postal_x0020_Code, and Country_x002F_Region elements are children of the Shippers element. In turn, each Shippers element is a child of the dataroot element. XML documents can be nested to any depth as long as each inner node is entirely contained within the outer node.

3. Close the browser containing the Shippers.xml file.

Understanding the XML Schema File

Now that you have familiarized yourself with the structure of an XML document, let's look at another type of XML file that was created by Access during the export to XML process — the XML schema file (XSD).

Schema files describe XML data using the XML Schema Definition (XSD) language and allow the XML parser to validate the XML document. An XML document that conforms to the structure of the schema is said to be *valid*.

Here are some examples of the type of information that can be found in an XML schema file:

■ Elements that are allowed in a given XML document

■ Data types of allowed elements

■ Number of allowed occurrences of a given element

■ Attributes that can be associated with a given element

■ Default values for attributes

■ Child elements of other elements

■ The sequence and number of child elements

◉ Hands-On 29-3: Examining the Contents of an XML Schema File

1. Open **Windows Explorer** and switch to the **C:\Learn_XML** folder containing the files generated in Hands-On 29-1 (see Figure 29-2).

2. Use **Windows Notepad** to open the **Shippers.xsd** file located in the Learn_XML folder. Access displays the contents of the Shippers.xsd file as shown in Figure 29-4.

```
Shippers.xsd - Notepad
File  Edit  Format  View  Help
<?xml version="1.0" encoding="UTF-8"?>
<xsd:schema xmlns:xsd="http://www.w3.org/2001/XMLSchema"
xmlns:od="urn:schemas-microsoft-com:officedata">
<xsd:element name="dataroot">
<xsd:complexType>
<xsd:sequence>
<xsd:element ref="shippers" minOccurs="0" maxOccurs="unbounded"/>
</xsd:sequence>
<xsd:attribute name="generated" type="xsd:dateTime"/>
</xsd:complexType>
</xsd:element>
<xsd:element name="shippers">
<xsd:annotation>
<xsd:appinfo>
<od:index index-name="City" index-key="City " primary="no" unique="no" clustered="no" order="asc"/>
<od:index index-name="Company" index-key="Company " primary="no" unique="no" clustered="no"
order="asc"/>
<od:index index-name="First Name" index-key="First_x0020_Name " primary="no" unique="no"
clustered="no" order="asc"/>
<od:index index-name="Last Name" index-key="Last_x0020_Name " primary="no" unique="no" clustered="no"
order="asc"/>
<od:index index-name="Postal Code" index-key="ZIP_x002F_Postal_x0020_Code " primary="no" unique="no"
clustered="no" order="asc"/>
<od:index index-name="PrimaryKey" index-key="ID " primary="yes" unique="yes" clustered="no"
order="asc"/>
<od:index index-name="State/Province" index-key="State_x002F_Province " primary="no" unique="no"
clustered="no" order="asc"/>
<od:tableProperty name="Orientation" type="2" value="0"/>
<od:tableProperty name="OrderByOn" type="1" value="0"/>
<od:tableProperty name="DefaultView" type="2" value="2"/>
<od:tableProperty name="WSSTemplateID" type="3" value="105"/>
<od:tableProperty name="TotalsRow" type="1" value="0"/>
<od:tableProperty name="FilterOnLoad" type="1" value="0"/>
<od:tableProperty name="OrderByOnLoad" type="1" value="1"/>
<od:tableProperty name="DisplayViewsOnSharePointSite" type="2" value="1"/>
<od:tableProperty name="StartColumnHidden" type="1" value="0"/>
<od:tableProperty name="HideNewField" type="1" value="0"/>
```

Figure 29-4: The schema file shown here defines the data in the Shippers.xml document.

If you take a look at the Shippers.xsd file currently open in Notepad, you will notice a number of XSD declarations and commands that begin with the <xsd> tag followed by a colon and the name of the command. You will also notice the names of the elements and attributes that are allowed in the Shippers.xml file as well as the data types for each element.

The names of the data types are preceded with the od prefix followed by a colon. For example:

od:jetType="text"	Defines the Jet data type for an element
od:sqlSType="nvarchar"	Defines the Microsoft SQL Server data type for an element
od:autounique="yes"	Defines a Boolean data type for an auto-incremented identity column
od:nonNullable="yes"	Indicates whether or not a column can contain a Null value

The schema file also specifies the number of times an element can be used in a document based on the schema. This is done via the minOccurs and maxOccurs attributes.

3. Close Notepad and the Shippers.xsd file.

 Note: To find out more about XML schemas, check out the following links:

http://www.w3.org/TR/xmlschema-0/
http://www.w3.org/TR/xmlschema-1/
http://www.w3.org/TR/xmlschema-2/

Understanding the XSL Transformation Files

When you examined the contents of the Shippers.xml document earlier in this chapter you may have noticed that the file did not contain any formatting instructions. Although it is easy to display the XML file in the browser, end users expect to see documents nicely formatted. To meet their expectations, the raw XML data is formatted with the Extensible Stylesheet Language (XSL).

When you exported the Shippers table to XML and selected the Presentation of your data (XSL) check box in the Export XML dialog box (see step 5 in Hands-On 29-1), Access generated an XSL file. Extensible Stylesheet Language is a transformation style language that uses XSL Transformations (XSLT) to create templates that are applied to the source document data to create the target document. The target document can be another XML document, an HTML page, or even a text-based file.

XSL files include all the XSLT transforms that are needed to define how the data is to be presented. Transformations allow you to change the order of elements and selectively process elements. Later in this chapter you will learn how to create XSL files with XSLT transforms to display only selected fields from the Access-generated XML documents. There is no limit to the number of stylesheets that can be used with a particular XML document. By creating more than one XSL file, you can present different formats of the same XML document to various users.

Hands-On 29-4: Examining the Contents of an XSL File

1. Double-click the **Shippers.xsl** file located in the **C:\Learn_XML** folder. Access displays the contents of the Shippers.xsl file as shown in Figure 29-5.

Figure 29-5: The XSL stylesheet document is just another XML document that contains HTML formatting instructions and XSLT formatting elements for transforming raw XML data into HTML.

When you scroll down through the contents of the Shippers.xsl file you will notice a number of XSLT formatting elements such as <xsl:template>, <xsl:for-each>, and <xsl:value-of>. You will also find in it many HTML formatting instructions such as <head>, <title>, <body>, <table>, <colgroup>, <col>, <tbody>, <tr>, <td>, <div>, and <strong>.

The first line of the stylesheet code declares that this is an XML document that follows the XML 1.0 standard (version). An XSL document is a type of XML document. While XML documents store data, XSL documents specify how the data should be displayed.

The second line declares the namespace to be used to identify the tags in the XSL document. (See the "Understanding the XML Data File" section earlier in this chapter for more information about namespaces.) The third line specifies that HTML should be used to display the data.

The next line is the beginning of the formatting section. Before we look at the XSLT tags, you need to know that XSL documents use templates to perform transformations of XML documents. The XSL stylesheet can contain one or more XSLT templates. You can think of templates as special blocks of code that apply to one or more XML tags. Templates contain rules for displaying a particular branch of elements in the XML document. The use of templates is made possible via special formatting tags.

Notice that the Shippers.xsl file contains the <xsl:template> tag to define a template for the entire document. The <xsl:template> element has a match attribute. The value of the match attribute indicates the nodes (elements) for which this template is appropriate.

For example, the special pattern "//" in the match attribute tells the XSL processor that this is the template for the document root:

```
<xsl:template match="//dataroot"
xmlns:xsl="http://www.w3.org/1999/XSL/Transform">
```

The template ends with the </xsl:template> closing tag. Following the definition of the template, standard HTML tags are used to format the document. Next, the XSLT formatting instruction <xsl:for-each> tells the XSL processor to do something every time it finds a pattern. The pattern follows the select attribute.

For example:

```
<xsl:for-each select="Shippers">
```

tells the XML processor to loop through the <Shippers> elements. The loop is closed with a closing loop tag:

```
</xsl:for-each>
```

The XSLT formatting instruction <xsl:value-of> tells the XSL processor to retrieve the value of the tag specified in the select attribute. For example:

```
<xsl:value-of select="ID">
```

tells the XML processor to select the ID column. Because this formatting instruction is located below the <xsl:for-each> tag, the XSL processor will retrieve the value of the ID column for each Shippers element. The select attribute uses the XML Path language (XPath) expression to locate the child elements to be processed.

If you scroll down the Shippers.xsl file, you will also notice that Access has generated a number of VBScript functions to evaluate expressions. To prevent the XSL processor from parsing these functions, the function section is placed within the CDATA directive.

2. Close the browser containing the Shippers.xsl file.

What Exactly Is XPath?

XPath is a query language used to create expressions for finding data in the XML data file. These expressions can manipulate strings, numbers, and Boolean values. They can also be used to navigate an XML tree structure and process its elements with XSLT instructions. XPath is designed to be used by XSL Transformations (XSLT). With XPath expressions, you can easily identify and extract from the XML document specific elements (nodes) based on their type, name, values, or the relationship of a node to other nodes. When preparing stylesheets for transforming your XML documents into HTML, you will often use various XPath expressions in the select attribute.

 Note: For more information about Extensible Stylesheet Language (XSL), visit the following link: http://www.w3.org/TR/xsl/.

Viewing XML Documents Formatted with Stylesheets

When you exported the Shippers table to XML format, Access applied XSLT transforms to turn the XML data into an HTML file so that you can view formatted data in the browser (see Figure 29-6). To display the Access-generated Shippers.htm file in your browser, simply type http://localhost/xml/Shippers.htm and press Enter.

Figure 29-6: This HTML file was created from XML data by using XSLT.

To display only the fields containing the data, export data to the XML file based on a query. For example, the following SQL statement can be used to create the Shippers query:

```
SELECT Shippers.[ID], Shippers.[Company], Shippers.[Address],
Shippers.[State/Province], Shippers.[ZIP/Postal Code],
Shippers.[Country/Region]
FROM Shippers;
```

You can then right-click the Shippers query in the Navigation pane and choose Export | XML File.

The resulting HTML file based on the Shippers query is shown in Figure 29-7.

ID	Company	Address	City	State/Province	ZIP/Postal Code	Country/Region
1	Shipping Company A	123 Any Street	Memphis	TN	99999	USA
2	Shipping Company B	123 Any Street	Memphis	TN	99999	USA
3	Shipping Company C	123 Any Street	Memphis	TN	99999	USA

Figure 29-7: This HTML file was created from XML data by using XSLT.

Advanced XML Export Options

When you exported the Shippers table to XML format, you may have noticed the More Options button in the Export XML dialog box (see Figure 29-1 at the beginning of this chapter). Pressing this button opens a window with three tabs as shown in Figure 29-8. Each tab groups options for the types of XML objects that you can export. The Data tab contains options for the XML document, the Schema tab list options for the XSD document, and the Presentation tab provides options for generating the XSL document.

Data Export Options

The options shown on the Data tab (see Figure 29-8) control the data that is exported to the XML documents. These options are grouped into three main areas.

The Export Data section displays data that you may want to export. In this particular scenario I requested to export the Customers table. Because this table is directly related to the Orders table in the Northwind 2007 database, the Orders table is displayed as a child node of Customers. The Orders table is related to the Order Details table and so on. If you click on the plus sign in front of the [Lookup Data] node, you will see the names of tables that provide lookup information for the main tables. By clicking on the check box you may export just the table that you originally requested or you can export the customers' data along with all the orders, and perhaps include lookup information.

Below the Export Data section is the Export Location area that shows the filename for the XML document that will be created when you click the OK button. You can change the location of this document by using the Browse button. Simply navigate to the folder where you want to save the XML file. You can also change the name of the document by replacing the name shown in the text box with another name.

The area to the right of the Export Data section allows you to specify which records you want to export. This area contains three option buttons that allow you to export all records, filtered records, or the current record. Notice that only one option is enabled in Figure 29-8.

Figure 29-8: Use the Data tab in the Export XML window to set advanced data options.

If you highlight the table to export in the database window and then choose the Export command on the File menu, only the All Records option button will be enabled in the Records To Export section. Opening the table prior to choosing the Export command tells Access to enable the All Records and Current record option buttons. And if you open the table and apply a filter to the data, then select the Export command, Access will enable the Apply existing filter option button in addition to the other two buttons.

The other options on the Data tab are Apply Existing Sort, Transforms, and Encoding. The Apply Existing Sort check box is enabled if the exported object is open and a sort is applied. Access will export the data in the specified order. By clicking on the Transforms button you can select a custom XSL transform file to apply to the data during export. You can choose from the transforms you have written or received with the XML data. Use the Encoding drop-down list to select UTF-8 or UTF-16 encoding for the exported XML. The default is UTF-8.

When you export an object from an Access database file, Access exports static data. This means that the exported object is not automatically updated when the data changes. If the data in the Access database has changed since you exported an Access object to an XML data file, you will need to re-export the object so the new data is available to the client application.

Exporting live data is supported by Access data projects. If the underlying data in the database changes, the client application will receive the updated data automatically when it connects to the SQL Server database. If you are exporting an object from an Access Data Project (ADP) file that connects to the SQL Server database, the Data tab will contain the Live Data check box and the Virtual Directory text box above the Export Location section. The Virtual Directory text box holds the URL of the folder on the server that the export process should use. When exporting live data you must export the entire Access object (you cannot select individual records). The Live Data option also does not allow you to apply a transform during the export.

Schema Export Options

The options shown on the Schema tab (see Figure 29-9) control the way the schema file for the object is exported. Advanced schema options are presented in two sections: Export Schema and Export Location.

The Export Schema section has two check boxes. By selecting the Export Schema check box you indicate that you want to export the object's schema as an XSD file. This selection is the same as choosing the Schema of the data (XSD) option in the first Export XML dialog box (see Figure 29-1). The check boxes under Export Schema allows you to specify whether you want to include or ignore primary key and index information in the XSD schema file, and whether to export all table and field properties (this is a new feature in Access 2007).

The Export Location section has two option buttons that allow you to specify whether you want the schema information to be embedded in the exported XML data document or stored in a separate schema file. You can enter the filename in the provided text box and specify the location of the schema file by clicking the Browse button.

Figure 29-9: Use the Schema tab in the Export XML dialog box to set advanced schema options.

Presentation Export Options

The selections on the Presentation tab (see Figure 29-10) specify available options for the XSL files. The Export Presentation (HTML 4.0 Sample XSL) check box allows you to indicate whether you want to export the object's presentation. Choose the Client (HTML) option in the Run from section if you want the presentation to run on the client. Access will create an HTML file with the script necessary to perform the transform. The script will be executed on the client machine. While this selection reduces the load on the server, a client application will need to download a couple of files (HTML document, XML data file, and XSD schema file) to present the data in the browser. If the XSL file is going to be placed on the web server and called from an ASP page, choose the Server (ASP) option. By choosing this option, only the final HTML is downloaded to the client.

Figure 29-10: Use the Presentation tab in the Export XML dialog box to set advanced presentation options.

If the exported presentation includes pictures, you can indicate whether to include them in the output by clicking the appropriate option button in the

Include report images section. If you choose to include the images, Access will create separate image files and link them with the HTML file. By default, the image files are stored in the Images folder of the main export folder. To place them in another location, click the Browse button to specify the folder name.

The Export Location section allows you to specify the name and location of the export files. When you export a presentation file, Access creates two files: an XSL file that includes all the XSLT transforms needed to define how the data is presented, and a simple HTML file that contains properly formatted data from the exported object and not the raw data with XML tags. The HTML file contains a snapshot of the data as it existed during the export process.

Applying XSLT Transforms to Exported Data

When exporting Access data to XML format, you can use custom transformation files (XSL) to modify the data after you export it. Hands-On 29-5 demonstrates how to create a custom stylesheet for use after export. This stylesheet assumes that for each customer in the Customers table we want to display only selected columns from the Orders table. You learn how to apply this custom stylesheet in Hands-On 29-6. Take a quick look at Figure 29-13 later in this chapter to see the final outcome.

⊚ Hands-On 29-5: Creating a Custom Transformation File

1. Open **Notepad** and enter the statements as shown below, or copy and paste this code from **C:\Acc07_HandsOn\ListCustOrders.txt**.

```
<?xml version="1.0" encoding="UTF-8"?>
<xsl:stylesheet version="1.0" xmlns:xsl="http://www.w3.org/1999/XSL/Transform">
<xsl:output method="html" version="4.0" indent="yes"/>

<xsl:template match="dataroot">
  <html>
  <body>
    <h2><font name="Verdana">Orders by Customer</font></h2>
    <p></p>
      <xsl:apply-templates select="Customers"/>
  </body>
  </html>
</xsl:template>

<xsl:template match="Customers">
<table>
  <tr>
    <td BgColor="#FFCC33">
      <font color="#000000">
        <xsl:value-of select="CustomerID"/>
      </font>
    </td>
    <td><b>
      <xsl:value-of select="CompanyName"/>
    </b></td>
```

```
      </tr>
   </table>
   <table cellpadding="5" cellspacing="5">
      <tr BgColor="black">
         <td bgcolor="black" width="10px"></td>
         <td><font color="white" size="1">Order ID</font></td>
         <td><font color="white" size="1">Order Date</font></td>
         <td><font color="white" size="1">Shipped Date</font></td>
         <td><font color="white" size="1">Required Date</font></td>
         <td><font color="white" size="1">Freight</font></td>
      </tr>
      <xsl:apply-templates select="Orders"/>
   </table>
</xsl:template>

<xsl:template match="Orders">
   <tr>
      <td bgcolor="black" width="10px"></td>
      <td><xsl:value-of select="OrderID"/></td>
      <td><xsl:value-of select="substring(OrderDate, 1, 10)"/></td>
      <td><xsl:value-of select="substring(ShippedDate, 1, 10)"/></td>
      <td><xsl:value-of select="substring(RequiredDate, 1, 10)"/></td>
      <td>$<xsl:value-of select="format-number(Freight,'####0.00')"/></td>
   </tr>
</xsl:template>

</xsl:stylesheet>
```

2. Save the file as C:\Learn_XML\ListCustOrders.xsl. You must type the file extension to ensure that the file is not saved as text.

3. Close Notepad.

Let's now proceed to analyze the contents of the ListCustOrders.xsl file that will be used to transform XML to HTML in our next hands-on exercise. Notice that because the XSLT stylesheet is an XML document, we started out with a standard XML declaration:

```
<?xml version="1.0" encoding="UTF-8"?>
```

Next, we defined the namespace for the stylesheet and declared its prefix like this:

```
<xsl:stylesheet version="1.0" xmlns:xsl="http://www.w3.org/1999/XSL/Transform">
```

On the third line we indicated that XSLT should transform the XML into HTML by using the <xsl:output> tag as follows:

```
<xsl:output method="html" version="4.0" indent="yes"/>
```

In the above XML, the <xsl:output> tag has three attributes: method, version, and indent. The method attribute specifies the format of the output. This can be XML, HTML, or text. The version attribute sets the version number for the output format. The indent attribute, which is set to "yes" in this example, indicates that the XML should be indented. This will make the final XML document more readable when viewed in the browser.

The remaining part of the XSL file contains transformation instructions for the XML document element nodes. We begin by creating the root template. The <xsl:template> tag initiates a template within a stylesheet. Because a template must indicate which nodes you want to use, we supplied the node information by using the tag's match attribute, like this:

```
<xsl:template match="dataroot">
```

This tells the XSLT processor to extract the XML document's root node. The root node provides a base node upon which we will build our web page. Notice that in the root template we included the <html> and <body> tags to create the structure of the final document and used HTML tags such as <h2>, <font>, and <p> to add the required formatting to our web page. In the root template we are also telling the XSLT processor that it should apply the template rules found in the Customers template (defined further down):

```
<xsl:apply-templates select="Customers"/>
```

When the XSLT processor encounters the <xsl:apply-templates> instruction, it will proceed to the following line:

```
<xsl:template match="Customers">
```

This line marks the beginning of the Customers template rule. Within it there are HTML tags as well as other XSLT processing instructions. For example, to output the CustomerID we use the <xsl:value-of> tag with the select attribute like this:

```
<xsl:value-of select="CustomerID"/>
```

Because the <xsl:value-of> tag does not have any content, you must end it with the forward slash (/). Notice that we placed the value of the CustomerID field in a table cell. Using the same approach we output the CompanyName:

```
<xsl:value-of select="CompanyName"/>
```

Next, we defined the column headings for the Orders table. For a special effect, we added to the output a 10-pixel-wide dummy column with a black background:

```
<td bgcolor="black" width="10px"></td>
```

We also told the XSLT processor to apply the Orders template:

```
<xsl:apply-templates select="Orders"/>
```

The Orders template rules indicate how to extract values for each of the defined column headings. This is done by using the <xsl:value-of> tag with the select attribute, like this:

```
<td><xsl:value-of select="OrderID"/></td>
<td><xsl:value-of select="substring(OrderDate, 1, 10)"/></td>
<td><xsl:value-of select="substring(ShippedDate, 1, 10)"/></td>
<td><xsl:value-of select="substring(RequiredDate, 1, 10)"/></td>
<td>$<xsl:value-of select="format-number(Freight,'####0.00')"/></td>
```

To obtain only the date portion from the OrderDate, ShippedDate, and RequiredDate columns, we use the XPath substring function in the select attribute. This function has the same syntax as the VBA Mid function, allowing you to extract a specified number of characters from a string starting at a specific position. The format of the substring function is shown below:

```
substring(string, startpos, length)
```

startpos is the position of the first character to extract, and *length* represents the number of characters to be returned from *string*. Therefore, the expression

```
<xsl:value-of select="substring(OrderDate, 1, 10)"/>
```

tells the XSLT processor to retrieve only the first 10 characters from the value found in the OrderDate column.

Notice also that to correctly format the Freight column we used the format-number XPath expression like this:

```
<xsl:value-of select="format-number(Freight,'####0.00')"/>
```

This tells the XSLT processor to format the value found in the Freight column as a number using two decimal places. Notice that the dollar sign cannot be a part of the XPath expression. It is appended to the final output as shown below:

```
<td>$<xsl:value-of select="format-number(Freight,'####0.00')"/></td>
```

Notice that each of the defined template rules ends with the </xsl:template> ending tag and the stylesheet itself ends with the </xsl:stylesheet> tag.

This concludes our hands-on example of how you can make your own custom stylesheets. While this is a basic stylesheet to get you started, in real life you will probably want to create stylesheets that allow:

■ Batch-processing nodes (<xsl:for-each> tag with the select attribute)

■ Conditional processing of nodes (<xsl:if> tag with the test attribute)

■ Decisions based on conditions (<xsl:choose> tag and <xsl:when> tag with the test attribute)

■ Sorting nodes before processing (<xsl:sort> tag with the select attribute)

 Note: For more information about XSL Transformations (XSLT), visit the following link: http://www.w3.org/TR/xslt#section-Applying-Template-Rules.

Now that you have a custom stylesheet, what do you do with it? Hands-On 29-6 demonstrates how to export data from an Access table directly to an HTML file and apply a custom transform so that only certain columns are displayed in the browser.

Hands-On 29-6: Exporting Data and Applying a Custom XSL File

1. Open the **Northwind.mdb** database.

2. In the Navigation pane, right-click the **Customers** table and choose **Export | XML File**.

3. In the File name box, enter **C:\Learn_XML\ListCustOrders.xml**, and click **OK**.

4. In the Export XML dialog box, the first two check boxes should be selected. Click the **More Options** button.

5. In the Data to Export area, the Customers table is automatically selected. Click the check box next to the **Orders** table to include it in the export.

6. Click the **Transforms** button.

7. In the Export Transforms window that appears, click the **Add** button.

8. Access displays the Add New Transform window. Switch to the **C:\Learn_XML** folder and select the **ListCustOrders.xsl** file that you created in the previous hands-on exercise. Click the **Add** button to add this file to the list of transforms. The transformation file appears in the list as shown in Figure 29-11.

Figure 29-11: Use this window to indicate a transformation file (stylesheet) to be used after export.

9. In the Export Transforms window, click **OK**.

10. Back in the Export XML dialog box, change the file extension from xml to **html** as shown in Figure 29-12.

Figure 29-12: To export XML data directly to the HTML file, you must choose the transformation file using the Transforms button, and change the file extension from xml to html.

11. Click the **OK** button to begin the export.

12. Upon successful export operation, click **Close**.

➔ **Note:**   If the selected transformation file is invalid, you will see an error message. Access will prompt you to save the data for troubleshooting and will bring up the Export XML dialog box. At this time you may want to open the transformation file in Notepad and make appropriate corrections. Once you save the corrected XSL file you should return to the Export XML dialog to try the export again. Before you click the OK button in the Export XML dialog box, ensure that the appropriate tables are selected.

13. Close the Northwind database and exit Microsoft Access.

14. In your browser's address bar, type **http://localhost/xml/ListCust-Orders.html** and press **Enter**. The final result of applying the custom transformation file is shown in Figure 29-13.

15. Close the browser window.

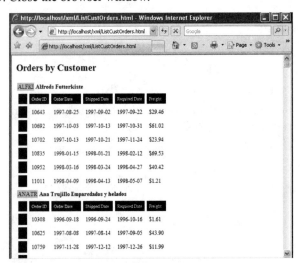

Figure 29-13: XML data can be formatted any way you like by applying a custom transform (see Figures 29-11 and 29-12).

Importing XML Data

You can use the Access built-in Import command to import an XML data or XML schema document to a database. When you import structure or data from an XML file, Access assigns the Text data type to all the fields in a table. However, when you import structure from an XSD schema file, each field is assigned a data type that closely matches the data type specified in the schema. You can change the data types after importing data or a table structure as long as the fields' data allows such a change.

When you import a schema, Access creates a new empty table with the structure of the imported schema. Earlier in this chapter, when you exported the Shippers table to XML format, Access also created the schema of that table. Hands-On 29-7 shows how to import this schema document to a new Access database.

◎ Hands-On 29-7: Importing a Schema File (XSD) to an Access Database

1. Create a new Access database named **C:\Acc07_ByExample\ Chap29.accdb**.

2. In the Access window, choose **Get External Data | XML File**.

3. In the Get External Data - XML File window, type **C:\Learn_XML\Shippers.xsd** in the File name box and click **OK**. Access displays the Import XML dialog box as shown in Figure 29-14.

Figure 29-14: When importing a schema file to an Access database, the Import XML dialog box displays the table name and its columns as defined in the schema.

Notice that you cannot indicate which columns you would like to import. Access always imports the entire XSD file.

4. Click **OK** to perform the import. When the import operation is completed, click **Close**. The Shippers table appears in the Navigation pane of the Access window. Figure 29-15 shows this table opened in Design view.

5. Close the Chap29.accdb database.

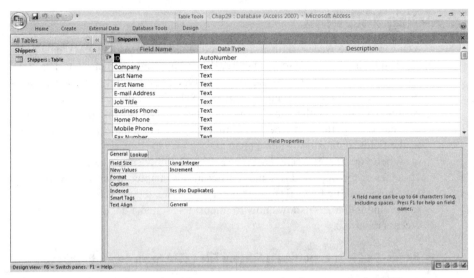

Figure 29-15: The Shippers table was created by importing the Shippers.xsd schema file.

When importing an XML data file to an Access database, you can use Import Options buttons to specify whether you want to import structure only, import structure and data, or append data to an existing table (see Figure 29-16). When you append data to an existing table, Access compares the structure of the imported table with the table structures that are already in the database. If Access cannot find a table structure matching the imported table, the data is placed in a new table; otherwise, it is appended to the existing table. You can also click the Transform button in the Import XML dialog box to specify a transformation file that you want to apply when the XML data is imported.

Figure 29-16: When importing an XML data file, you can use the options buttons in the Import XML dialog to specify the import options. Use the Transform button to apply a transform to the data when it is imported.

It is important to point out that when XML data is imported to an Access database, it is not linked with the original XML file. This means that to refresh the data in the table, you need to repeat the import process.

The following project demonstrates how to import XML data to an Access database and modify the data before import using a transformation file. We will perform the tasks as outlined below:

■ Create a custom transformation file to be used after the XML data import

■ Export the Customers table and the related Orders table to an XML file

■ Import to an Access database only two columns from the Customers table and five columns from the Orders table

◎ Custom Project 29-1: Importing XML Data to an Access Database and Applying a Transform

Part 1: Create a Custom Transformation File to Be Used after the XML Data Import

1. Open **Notepad** and enter the statements as shown below, or copy and paste the code from **C:\Acc07_HandsOn\CustomerOrders.txt**.

```
<?xml version="1.0" encoding="UTF-8"?>
<xsl:stylesheet version="1.0" xmlns:xsl="http://www.w3.org/1999/XSL/Transform">
<xsl:output method="html" version="4.0" indent="yes"/>

<xsl:template match="dataroot">
    <html>
        <body>
            <table>
                <xsl:apply-templates select="Customers"/>
            </table>
            <table>
                <xsl:apply-templates select="Customers/Orders"/>
            </table>
        </body>
    </html>
</xsl:template>
<xsl:template match="Customers">
    <Customer>
        <CustomerID>
            <xsl:value-of select="CustomerID"/>
        </CustomerID>
        <CompanyName>
            <xsl:value-of select="CompanyName"/>
        </CompanyName>
    </Customer>
</xsl:template>

<xsl:template match="Customers/Orders">
    <Order>
        <OrderID>
            <xsl:value-of select="OrderID"/>
        </OrderID>
        <OrderDate>
            <xsl:value-of select="substring(OrderDate, 1, 10)"/>
```

```
        </OrderDate>
        <ShippedDate>
          <xsl:value-of select="substring(ShippedDate, 1, 10)"/>
        </ShippedDate>
        <RequiredDate>
          <xsl:value-of select="substring(RequiredDate, 1, 10)"/>
        </RequiredDate>
        <Freight>
          <xsl:value-of select="format-number(Freight,'####0.00')"/>
        </Freight>
      </Order>
    </xsl:template>

  </xsl:stylesheet>
```

2. Save the file as **C:\Learn_XML\CustomerOrders.xsl**. You must type the file extension to ensure that the file is not saved as text.

3. Close Notepad.

Since you've already created a similar stylesheet in Hands-On 29-5, the contents of the CustomerOrders.xsl file should be recognizable. All that's different here are the <Customer> and <Order> tags that specify the names of Access tables where we want to place our XML data. When importing data, tables are named according to the name of the XML element being imported. If the Access database already has a table with the specified name, a number is appended to the name.

Part 2: Export the Customers and Related Orders Tables to an XML File

1. Open the **C:\Acc07_HandsOn\Northwind.mdb** database. In the Navigation pane, right-click the **Customers** table and choose **Export | XML File**.

2. In the Export - XML File window, type **C:\Learn_XML\Customer-Orders.xml** in the File name box and click **OK**.

3. Access displays the Export XML dialog box with three check boxes; the first two check boxes should be selected. Click the **More Options** button.

4. In the Data to Export area of the Export XML dialog, select the check box next to the **Orders** table. The Customers and Orders tables should both be selected.

5. Click **OK** to perform the export of all the records in the selected tables. When the export operation is completed, click **Close**.

6. Close the Northwind.mdb database file.

Part 3: Import to an Access Database Only Two Columns from the Customers Table and Five Columns from the Orders Table

1. Open the **C:\Learn_XML\Chap29.accdb** database file that you created in Hands-On 29-7.

2. In the Access window, choose **Get External Data | XML File**.

3. In the Get External Data - XML File window, type **C:\Learn_XML\ CustomerOrders.xml** in the File name box and click **OK**.

   Access displays the Import XML window with the file's Customers and Orders tables listed. By expanding nodes in the tree structure you can see the columns in each table, but you cannot indicate which columns to import, as Access always imports the entire file by default. You can, however, tell Access to perform a custom XSLT transform to import only the columns needed.

4. In the Import XML window, click the **Transform** button.

5. In the Import Transforms window that appears, click the **Add** button to apply a transform before importing.

   Access displays the **Add New Transform** window. Switch to the **Learn_XML** folder and select the **CustomerOrders.xsl** file that you created in Part 1 of this project. Click the **Add** button to add this file to the list of transforms.

6. In the Import Transforms window, click **OK**.

7. Back in the Import XML window, make sure that the **Structure and Data** option button is selected under Import Options and click **OK**. When Access finishes importing the C:\Learn_XML\CustomerOrder.xml document, click **Close**.

8. In the Navigation pane of the Access window, notice the appearance of two new tables: Customer and Order. Open both tables and check their contents. As you can see, Access has applied the custom stylesheet before importing the data and only the columns specified in the stylesheet were imported (see Figure 29-17).

9. Open the **Order** table in Design view. Notice that all the fields in this table have been assigned the Text data type. After importing data or table structure you can change the data type of fields.

10. Change the data type of the OrderDate, ShippedDate, and RequiredDate columns to **Date/Time** and the Freight column's data type to **Currency** to match the original Orders table.

11. Save the modified Order table and close the Chap29.accdb database file.

Figure 29-17: Applying a custom transformation file before XML data import to limit the number of columns of data imported to Access database tables.

Exporting to and Importing from XML Programmatically

Now that you've mastered the use of Microsoft Office Access 2007 built-in commands for exporting and importing XML data, let's look at what tools are available for programmers who want to perform these XML operations via code. In the following sections of this chapter you will learn how to work with XML using:

- The ExportXML and ImportXML methods from the Microsoft Office Access 12.0 Object Library

- The TransformXML method

Exporting to XML Using the ExportXML Method

Use the Microsoft Office Access 12.0 Object Library ExportXML method of the Application object to export XML data, schemas (XSD), and presentation information (XSL) from a Microsoft Access database, Microsoft SQL Server 2000 Desktop Engine (MSDE 2000), or Microsoft SQL Server 6.5 or later.

The ExportXML method takes a number of arguments, which are shown in Table 29-1.

Table 29-1: Arguments of the ExportXML method (in order of appearance)

Argument Type	Data Type	Description
ObjectType (required)	AcExportXMLObjectType Use one of the following constants: Constant Value acExportDataAccessPage 6 acExportForm 2 acExportFunction 10 acExportQuery 1 acExportReport 3 acExportServerView 7 acExportStoredProcedure 9 acExportTable 0	Specifies the type of Access object to export. The constant values 10, 7, and 9 are only used with Microsoft Access projects.
DataSource (required)	String	Indicates the name of the Access object specified in the ObjectType argument.
DataTarget (optional)	String	Specifies the path and filename for the exported data. Omit this argument only if you don't want the data to be exported.
SchemaTarget (optional)	String	Specifies the path and filename for the exported schema information. Omit this argument only if you don't want the schema to be exported to a separate file.
PresentationTarget (optional)	String	Specifies the path and filename for the exported presentation information. Omit this argument only if you don't want the presentation information to be exported.
ImageTarget (optional)	String	Specifies the path for the exported images. Omit this argument if you don't want to export images.
Encoding (optional)	AcExportXMLEncoding Use one of the following constants: Constant Value acUTF16 1 acUTF8 0 The default is acUTF8.	Specifies the text encoding for the exported data.

Argument Type	Data Type	Description
OtherFlags (optional)	AcExportXMLOtherFlags Use one or more of the following constants: Constant Value acEmbedSchema 1 acExcludePrimaryKeyAndIndexes 2 acExportAllTableAndFieldProperties 32 acLiveReportSource 8 acPersistReportML 16 acRunFromServer 4	Specifies behaviors associated with exporting to XML. Values can be added to specify a combination of behaviors. Here is the meaning of the constants: (1) Write schema information into a separate document specified by the DataTarget argument. This value takes precedence over the SchemaTarget argument. (2) Does not export primary key and index schema properties. (32) The exported schema contains properties of the table and its fields. (8) Used only when exporting reports bound to SQL Server 2000. Will create a live link to a Microsoft SQL Server database. (16) Persists the exported object's ReportML file. (4) Used only when exporting reports. Creates an Active Server Pages (ASP) or HTML wrapper. The default is HTML.
WhereCondition (optional)	String	Specifies subset of records to export.
AdditionalData (optional)	AdditionalData AdditionalData is an Access object that represents the collection of tables and queries that will be included with the parent table that is exported by the ExportXML method (see Hands-On 29-8).	Specifies additional tables to export. This argument is ignored if the OtherFlags argument is set to acLiveReportSource (8).

In its simplest form, the ExportXML method looks like this:

```
Application.ExportXML ObjectType:=acExportTable, _
        DataSource:="Customers", _
        DataTarget:= "C:\Learn_XML\North_Customers.xml"
```

The above statement, when typed on a single line (without the underscore characters) in the Visual Basic Editor's Immediate window or inside a VBA procedure stub in a Visual Basic module, will render the Customers table in the XML format in the North_Customers.xml file.

Using the arguments described in Table 29-1, you can easily write the command to export the XML Products table with its schema and presentation information placed in separate files:

```
Application.ExportXML ObjectType:=acExportTable, _
        DataSource:="Products", _
        DataTarget:= "C:\Learn_XML\North_Products.xml", _
        SchemaTarget:= "C:\Learn_XML\North_ProdSchema.xsd", _
        PresentationTarget:= "C:\Learn_XML\North_ProdReport.xsl"
```

To export a specific customer's data to an XML data file, use the following statement:

```
Application.ExportXML ObjectType:=acExportTable, _
        DataSource:="Customers", _
        DataTarget:="C:\Learn_XML\OneCustomer.xml", _
        WhereCondition:="CustomerID = 'GROSR'"
```

➡ **Note:**   To try the above statements, open the Northwind.mdb database, switch to the Visual Basic Editor window, type each statement in the Immediate window, and press Enter to execute. Recall that you must not type the underscore characters (type the entire statement on one line with arguments separated by commas). After the export, locate the newly created XML files in your C:\Learn_XML folder.

Hands-On 29-8 demonstrates how to export to XML three tables: Customers, Orders, and Order Details.

◎ Hands-On 29-8: Exporting Multiple Tables to an XML Data File

1. Open the **C:\Acc07_ByExample\Chap29.accdb** database and switch to the Visual Basic Editor window.

2. In the Visual Basic Editor window, choose **Insert | Module** to add a standard module to the current VBA project.

3. In the module's Code window, enter the **Export_CustomerOrderDetails** procedure as shown below, or copy the procedure code from **C:\Acc07_HandsOn\Chap29.txt**.

```
Sub Export_CustomerOrderDetails()
    Dim objAppl As New Access.Application
    Dim objOtherTbls As AdditionalData
    Dim strDBName As String

    strDBName = "C:\Acc07_HandsOn\Northwind.mdb"

    On Error GoTo ErrorHandler
    objAppl.OpenCurrentDatabase (strDBName)

    Set objOtherTbls = objAppl.CreateAdditionalData

    ' include the Orders and OrderDetails tables in export
    objOtherTbls.Add "Orders"
    objOtherTbls.Add "Order Details"
```

```
' export Customers, Orders, and Order Details table into
' one XML data file

objAppl.ExportXML ObjectType:=acExportTable, _
    DataSource:="Customers", _
    DataTarget:="C:\Learn_XML\CustomerOrdersDetails.xml", _
    AdditionalData:=objOtherTbls

MsgBox "Export operation completed successfully."

Exit_Here:
    On Error Resume Next
    objAppl.CloseCurrentDatabase
    Set objAppl = Nothing
    Exit Sub
ErrorHandler:
    MsgBox Err.Number & ": " & Err.Description
    Resume Exit_Here
End Sub
```

The Application object refers to the active Microsoft Access application, which in this case is the Chap29.accdb database where you wrote the procedure code shown above. Because this database does not contain the tables we want to export, we used the New keyword to create a new instance of the Microsoft Access Application object and then opened another Access database (Northwind.mdb) using the OpenCurrentDatabase method. You can use the OpenCurrentDatabase method to open an existing Microsoft Access database as the current database.

Using the AdditionalData object, you can export any set of Access tables to an XML data file. To use this object, perform the following:

- Declare an object variable as AdditionalData:

```
Dim objOtherTbls As AdditionalData
```

- Create the AdditionalData object using the CreateAdditionalData method of the Application object and set the object variable to the newly created object:

```
Set objOtherTbls = objAppl.CreateAdditionalData
```

- Use the AdditionalData object's Add method to add table names to the object:

```
objOtherTbls.Add "Orders"
objOtherTbls.Add "Order Details"
```

- Pass the AdditionalData object to the ExportXML method:

```
objAppl.ExportXML ObjectType:=acExportTable, _
    DataSource:="Customers", _
    DataTarget:="C:\Learn_XML\CustomerOrdersDetails.xml", _
    AdditionalData:=objOtherTbls
```

4. Place the insertion point anywhere within the Export_CustomerOrder-Details procedure code and choose **Run | Run Sub/UserForm**. Access executes the procedure code and displays a message.

5. Click **OK** to clear the informational message.

6. Switch to Windows Explorer and locate and open the **C:\Learn_XML\ CustomerOrdersDetails.xml** file. Notice that all the requested data was placed into one file.

7. Exit Windows Explorer.

Now that you know how to use VBA to export Access tables to XML, let's see how Access handles other objects. Custom Project 29-2 demonstrates how to export the Invoice report from the Northwind.mdb database to an XML file together with the presentation information and images.

◎ Custom Project 29-2: Exporting an Access Report to an XML Data File with ASP

This project requires prior completion of the Hands-On 29-1 exercise.

Part 1: Creating a VBA Procedure to Export Invoice Data

1. In the Visual Basic Editor window, choose **Insert | Module** to add a standard module to the current VBA project.

2. In the module's Code window, enter the **Export_InvoiceReport** procedure as shown below, or copy the procedure code from **C:\Acc07_HandsOn\ Chap29.txt**.

```
Sub Export_InvoiceReport()
    Dim objAppl As New Access.Application
    Dim strDBName As String

    strDBName = "C:\Acc07_HandsOn\Northwind.mdb"

    On Error GoTo ErrorHandler
    objAppl.OpenCurrentDatabase (strDBName)

    objAppl.ExportXML ObjectType:=acExportReport, _
        DataSource:="Invoice", _
        DataTarget:="C:\Learn_XML\Invoice.xml", _
        PresentationTarget:="C:\Learn_XML\Invoice.xsl", _
        ImageTarget:="C:\Learn_XML", _
        WhereCondition:="OrderID=11075"

    MsgBox "Export operation completed successfully."

Exit_Here:
    On Error Resume Next
    objAppl.CloseCurrentDatabase
    Set objAppl = Nothing
    Exit Sub
ErrorHandler:
    MsgBox Err.Number & ": " & Err.Description
    Resume Exit_Here
End Sub
```

Take a look at the last two arguments of the ExportXML method used in the procedure above. ImageTarget specifies that images displayed on the Invoice report are to be placed in the Learn_XML folder. The WhereCondition argument specifies that we want only the data for Order 11075.

Part 2: Executing the VBA Code to Export Data

1. Place the insertion point anywhere within the Export_InvoiceReport procedure code and choose **Run | Run Sub/UserForm**. Access executes the procedure code and displays a message.

2. Click **OK** to clear the informational message.

3. Switch to Windows Explorer and open the **C:\Learn_XML** folder.

4. Notice that Access has created a number of files: Invoice.xsl (stylesheet), Invoice.xml (XML document), Invoice.htm (HTML document), and two image files (PictureLogo.bmp and NameLogo.bmp).

Part 3: Viewing the Invoice Page in the Browser

1. In the browser's address bar, type **http://localhost/xml/Invoice.htm** and press **Enter**.

2. If you are using Internet Explorer, the file opens up as shown in Figure 29-18. When you compare this output with the original Access invoice report, you will notice that the invoice displayed in the browser is an exact image of the report displayed in the Access user interface.

3. Close the browser.

Figure 29-18: Viewing the exported invoice report in Internet Explorer.

Taking Your VBA Programming Skills to the Web

Part 4: Examining the Content of the Invoice.htm File

1. In Windows Explorer, right-click the **Invoice.htm** file and choose **Open With | Notepad**. The content of the Invoice file is shown below:

```
<HTML xmlns:signature="urn:schemas-microsoft-com:office:access">
<HEAD>
<META HTTP-EQUIV="Content-Type" CONTENT="text/html;charset=UTF-8"/>
</HEAD>
<BODY ONLOAD="ApplyTransform()">
</BODY>
<SCRIPT LANGUAGE="VBScript">
    Option Explicit

    Function ApplyTransform()
        Dim objData, objStyle

        Set objData = CreateDOM
        LoadDOM objData, "Invoice.xml"

        Set objStyle = CreateDOM
        LoadDOM objStyle, "Invoice.xsl"

        Document.Open "text/html","replace"
        Document.Write objData.TransformNode(objStyle)
    End Function

    Function CreateDOM()
        On Error Resume Next
        Dim tmpDOM

        Set tmpDOM = Nothing
        Set tmpDOM = CreateObject("MSXML2.DOMDocument.5.0")
        If tmpDOM Is Nothing Then
            Set tmpDOM = CreateObject("MSXML2.DOMDocument.4.0")
        End If
        If tmpDOM Is Nothing Then
            Set tmpDOM = CreateObject("MSXML.DOMDocument")
        End If

        Set CreateDOM = tmpDOM
    End Function

    Function LoadDOM(objDOM, strXMLFile)
        objDOM.async = False
        objDOM.Load strXMLFile
        If (objDOM.ParseError.ErrorCode <> 0) Then
            MsgBox objDOM.ParseError.Reason
        End If
    End Function

</SCRIPT>
</HTML>
```

Notice that when the HTML page loads, it executes the VBScript ApplyTransform function:

```
<BODY ONLOAD="ApplyTransform()">
```

The VBScript code uses a software component called the XML Document Object Model (DOM). The DOM offers methods and properties for working with XML programmatically, allowing you to output and transform the XML data. The XML DOM is automatically installed by Internet Explorer, as well as by Windows 2000/XP and Internet Information Services (IIS) 5.0 or higher.

The DOMDocument object is the top level of the XML DOM hierarchy and represents a tree structure composed of nodes. You can navigate through this tree structure and manipulate the data contained in the nodes by using various methods and properties. Because every XML object is created and accessed from the DOMDocument, you must first create the DOMDocument object in order to work with an XML document.

The ApplyTransform function above begins by setting an object variable (objData) to an instance of the DOMDocument that's returned by a custom CreateDOM function:

```
Set objData = CreateDOM
```

If you take a look at the CreateDOM function that appears at the bottom of the VBScript code, you will notice that a reference to the DOMDocument is set via the CreateObject method of the Server object. Because different versions of the MSXML parser may be installed on a client machine (DOMDocument5, DOMDocument4, DOMDocument, etc.), the function attempts to instantiate the DOMDocument object using the most recent version. If such a version is not found, it looks for older versions of the MSXML parser that may exist. It is extremely important that only one version of the DOMDocument is used, since mixing DOMDocument objects from different versions of the MSXML parser can cause ugly errors.

Once the DOMDocument object has been instantiated, the LoadDOM function listed at the bottom of the page is called. This function expects two parameters: objectDOM, which is the objData variable referencing the DOMDocument, and strXMLFile, which is the name of the file to load into the DOMDocument object. To ensure that Internet Explorer waits until all the data is loaded before rendering the rest of the page, the Async property of the DOMDocument is set to False:

```
objDOM.async = False
objDOM.Load strXMLFile
```

The Load method is used to load the supplied file into the objData object variable. This method returns True if it successfully loaded the data and False otherwise. If there is a problem with loading, a description of the error is returned in a message box.

The Document object of XML DOM exposes a parseError object that allows you to check whether there was an error when loading the XML file or stylesheet. The ParseError object has the properties listed in Table 29-2.

Table 29-2: The ParseError object properties

Property	Description
errorCode	Error number of the error that occurred.
filepos	Character position within the file where the error occurred.
line	Line number where the error occurred.
linepos	Character position within the line where the error occurred.
reason	Text description of the error.
srcText	The source (text) of the line where the error occurred.
url	URL or path of the file that was loaded.

After loading the Invoice.xml data file into the DOM software component, the ApplyTransform function repeats the same process for the Invoice.xsl file. After both files are successfully loaded, the transform is applied to the data using the TransformNode method:

```
Document.Write objData.TransformNode(objStyle)
```

The TransformNode method performs the transformation by applying the XSL (Extensible Stylesheet Language) stylesheet to the XML data file. The result is the HTML document displayed in the browser as shown in Figure 29-18 earlier in this chapter.

2. Close the Invoice.htm file and exit Notepad.

Transforming XML Data with the TransformXML Method

So far you've learned how to use stylesheets to transform XML data files to HTML format to create a web page. While rendering XML files into HTML for display in a web browser is the most popular use of stylesheets, XML data files can also be transformed into other XML files using the XSLT transforms.

In this section we will learn how to use the TransformXML method to apply an XSL stylesheet to an XML data file and write the resulting XML to another XML data file.

The TransformXML method takes a number of arguments, which are presented in Table 29-3. In its simplest form, the TransformXML method looks like this:

```
Application.TransformXML DataSource:="C:\Learn_XML\InternalContacts.xml",
        TransformSource:="C:\Learn_XML\Extensions.xsl", _
        OutputTarget:="C:\Learn_XML\EmpExtensions.xml"
```

The above statement can be used inside a VBA procedure stub to programmatically apply the specified stylesheet.

Table 29-3: Arguments of the TransformXML method (in order of appearance)

Argument Type	Data Type	Description
DataSource (required)	String	Specifies the full path of the XML data file that will be transformed.
TransformSource (required)	String	Specifies the full path of the XSL stylesheet to apply to the XML data file specified in the DataSource argument.
OutputTarget (required)	String	Specifies the full path of the resulting XML data file after applying the XSL stylesheet.
WellFormedXMLOutput (optional)	Boolean	Set this argument to True to create a well-formed XML document. Set this argument to False to encode the resulting XML file in UTF-16 format. The default is False.
ScriptOption (optional)	AcTransformXMLScriptOption Use one of the following constants: Constant Value acDisableScript 2 acEnableScript 0 acPromptScript 1	Use this argument to specify the action that should be taken if the XSL file contains scripting code. acPromptScript is the default.

Custom Project 29-3 demonstrates how to transform an XML data file into another XML file. We will start by creating a custom stylesheet named Extensions.xsl that will transform the InternalContacts.xml file (generated from the Northwind.mdb database Employees table) into an XML file named EmpExtensions.xml. Next, we will write a VBA procedure that exports the XML source file and performs the transformation. Finally, we will import the resulting XML data file into Access.

◎ Custom Project 29-3: Applying a Stylesheet to an XML Data File with the TransformXML Method

Part 1: Creating a Custom Stylesheet for Transforming an XML Source File into Another XML Data File

1. Open **Notepad** and enter the statements as shown below, or copy the code from **C:\Acc07_HandsOn\Extensions.txt**.

```
<?xml version="1.0"?>
<xsl:stylesheet version="1.0" xmlns:xsl="http://www.w3.org/1999/XSL/Transform">
<xsl:output method="xml" indent="yes"/>
<xsl:template match="/">
<dataroot>
<xsl:for-each select="//Employees">
<Extensions>
  <LastName>
```

```
      <xsl:value-of select="LastName" />
    </LastName>
    <FirstName>
      <xsl:value-of select="FirstName" />
    </FirstName>
    <Extension>
      <xsl:value-of select="Extension" />
    </Extension>
  </Extensions>
  </xsl:for-each>
  </dataroot>
  </xsl:template>
  </xsl:stylesheet>
```

Take a look at the stylesheet shown above and notice that we have asked the XSL processor to produce the output in XML format:

```
<xsl:output method="xml" indent="yes"/>
```

Next, we used the following instruction:

```
<xsl:template match="/">
```

This instruction defines a template for the entire document. The special pattern "/" in the match attribute tells the XSL processor that this is a template for the document root. Because each XML document must have a root node, we proceeded to define <dataroot> as the document root. You can use any name you want for this purpose. Next, we told the XSL processor to get all the Employees nodes from the source XML data file:

```
<xsl:for-each select="//Employees">
```

The first forward slash in the above instruction represents the XML document root. This is the same as:

```
<xsl:for-each select="dataroot/Employees">
```

Next, we proceed to extract data from the required nodes. We are only interested in three columns from the source XML data file: FirstName, LastName, and Extension. We create the necessary elements using the <xsl:value-of> tag with the select attribute specifying the element name:

```
<LastName>
  <xsl:value-of select="LastName" />
</LastName>
<FirstName>
  <xsl:value-of select="FirstName" />
</FirstName>
<Extension>
  <xsl:value-of select="Extension" />
</Extension>
```

We tell the XSL processor to place the defined elements under the <Extensions> node. When importing the resulting XML file to Access, Access will create an Extensions table with three columns: LastName, FirstName, and Extension. You can use any name you want when specifying the container node for your elements.

To finish off the stylesheet, we must write the necessary closing tags:

```
</xsl:for-each>
</dataroot>
</xsl:template>
</xsl:stylesheet>
```

2. Save the file as **C:\Learn_XML\Extensions.xsl**. You must type the .xsl file extension to ensure that the file is not saved as text.

3. Close Notepad.

Now that we've got the stylesheet for our transformation, you can write a VBA procedure to actually export the source data and perform the transformation.

Part 2: Writing a VBA Procedure to Export and Transform Data

1. In the Visual Basic Editor window of the Chap29.accdb database, choose **Insert | Module** to add a standard module to the current VBA project.

2. In the module's Code window, enter the **Transform_Employees** procedure as shown below, or copy the procedure code from **C:\Acc07_HandsOn\ Chap29.txt**.

```
Sub Transform_Employees()
    ' use the ExportXML method to create a source XML data file

    Application.ExportXML ObjectType:=acExportTable, _
            DataSource:="Employees", _
            DataTarget:="C:\Learn_XML\InternalContacts.xml"

MsgBox "The export operation completed successfully."

    ' use the TransformXML method to apply the stylesheet that transforms
    ' the source XML data file into another XML data file
    Application.TransformXML DataSource:="C:\Learn_XML\InternalContacts.xml", _
            TransformSource:="C:\Learn_XML\Extensions.xsl", _
            OutputTarget:="C:\Learn_XML\EmpExtensions.xml", _
            WellFormedXMLOutput:=False

    MsgBox "The transform operation completed successfully."
End Sub
```

The first part of the above procedure exports the Employees table from the Northwind database to an XML file named InternalContacts.xml. The second part of this procedure applies the Extensions.xsl stylesheet prepared in Part 1 of this custom project to the InternalContacts.xml data file. The resulting XML document after the transformation is named EmpExtensions.xml. A portion of this file is shown in Figure 29-19.

3. Run the **Transform_Employees** procedure.

Figure 29-19: Partial
contents of the
EmpExtensions.xml file.

After transforming our source XML data file into another XML document, you can bring it into Access with the External Data | Import command (see Part 3 below).

Part 3: Importing the Transformed XML Data File to Access

1. In the database window, choose **External Data | Import**.

2. In the File name box, type **C:\Learn_XML\EmpExtensions.xml** and click **OK**. Access displays the Import XML dialog box.

3. In the Import XML dialog box, click **OK** to perform the import.

4. Click **Close** to exit the Import XML window.

5. In the Navigation pane of the Access window, notice the appearance of the Extensions table. Open the **Extensions** table to view the following contents:

Extensions		
LastName	FirstName	Extension
Davolio	Nancy	5467
Fuller	Andrew	3457
Leverling	Janet	3355
Peacock	Margaret	5176
Buchanan	Steven	3453
Suyama	Michael	428
King	Robert	465
Callahan	Laura	2344
Dodsworth	Anne	452

6. Close the Extensions table.

A nice thing about XSLT transformations is that you can apply different stylesheets to the same XML data file to create and view the resulting document in different formats.

For example, let's assume that in the Extensions table you'd like to combine the LastName and FirstName columns into one column and sort the data by last name. You could create and apply the following Extensions_SortBy-Emp.xsl stylesheet to the InternalContacts.xml file to get the desired XML output:

```
<?xml version="1.0"?>
<xsl:stylesheet version="1.0" xmlns:xsl="http://www.w3.org/1999/XSL/Transform">
<xsl:output method="xml" indent="yes"/>
 <xsl:template match="/">
  <dataroot>
   <xsl:apply-templates select="dataroot/Employees">
     <xsl:sort select="LastName" order="ascending" />
   </xsl:apply-templates>
  </dataroot>
 </xsl:template>

 <xsl:template match="//Employees">
  <Extensions>
   <FullName>
     <xsl:value-of select="LastName" />
     <xsl:text>, </xsl:text>
     <xsl:value-of select="FirstName" />
   </FullName>
   <Extension>
     <xsl:value-of select="Extension" />
   </Extension>
  </Extensions>
 </xsl:template>

</xsl:stylesheet>
```

The above stylesheet uses the <xsl:apply-templates> tag to tell the XSL processor to select the child elements of the dataroot/Employees node and, for each child element, find in the stylesheet the matching template rule and process it:

```
<xsl:apply-templates select="dataroot/Employees">
   <xsl:sort select="LastName" order="ascending" />
</xsl:apply-templates>
```

The <xsl:sort> tag specifies how the resulting XML document should be sorted. The select attribute of this tag is set to LastName, indicating that the file should be sorted by the LastName element. The order attribute defines the sort order as ascending.

Next, in this stylesheet you can see the template rule that begins with the <xsl:template> tag. Its match attribute specifies which nodes in the document tree the template rule should process:

```
<xsl:template match="//Employees">
```

The //Employees expression in the match attribute is equivalent to
dataroot/Employees.

Next, you need to define the document node in the output file as Extensions, and proceed to define its child elements as FullName and Extension:

```
<Extensions>
  <FullName>
    <xsl:value-of select="LastName" />
    <xsl:text>, </xsl:text>
    <xsl:value-of select="FirstName" />
  </FullName>
  <Extension>
    <xsl:value-of select="Extension" />
  </Extension>
</Extensions>
```

Because the FullName element should include the last name of the employee
followed by a space and the first name, you can obtain the values of these
fields with the <xsl:value-of> tag and use the <xsl:text> </xsl:text> tag pair to
output a comma followed by a space between the last name and first name.
Since there is nothing special about the Extension element, you can simply use
the <xsl:value-of> tag to obtain this element's value.

Finally, complete the template and the stylesheet with the required closing
tags:

```
  </xsl:template>

</xsl:stylesheet>
```

To apply the above stylesheet to the source XML file, you could write the following VBA procedure:

```
Sub Transform_ContactsSort()
    Dim objAppl As New Access.Application
    Dim strDBName As String

    strDBName = "C:\Acc07_HandsOn\Northwind.mdb"

    On Error GoTo ErrorHandler
    objAppl.OpenCurrentDatabase (strDBName)

    ' use the ExportXML method to create a source XML data file
    objAppl.ExportXML ObjectType:=acExportTable, _
            DataSource:="Employees", _
            DataTarget:="C:\Learn_XML\InternalContacts.xml"

    MsgBox "The export operation completed successfully."

    ' use the TransformXML method to apply the stylesheet that transforms
    ' the source XML data file into another XML data file

    objAppl.TransformXML DataSource:="C:\Learn_XML\InternalContacts.xml", _
            TransformSource:="C:\Learn_XML\Extensions_SortByEmp.xsl", _
```

```
                    OutputTarget:="C:\Learn_XML\EmpExtensions.xml", _
                    WellFormedXMLOutput:=False

            MsgBox "The transform operation completed successfully."

    Exit_Here:
            On Error Resume Next
            objAppl.CloseCurrentDatabase
            Set objAppl = Nothing
            Exit Sub
    ErrorHandler:
            MsgBox Err.Number & ": " & Err.Description
            Resume Exit_Here
        End Sub
```

After importing the EmpExtensions.xml file to Access, you should see the
Extensions1 table in the database window. When opened, this table displays a
sorted list of employees with their extensions:

Extensions1	
FullName	Extension
Buchanan, Steven	3453
Callahan, Laura	2344
Davolio, Nancy	5467
Dodsworth, Anne	452
Fuller, Andrew	3457
King, Robert	465
Leverling, Janet	3355
Peacock, Margaret	5176
Suyama, Michael	428

Importing to XML Using the ImportXML Method

Use the ImportXML method to programmatically import an XML data file
and/or schema file. The ImportXML method takes two arguments, as shown in
Table 29-4.

Table 29-4: Arguments of the ImportXML method (in order of appearance)

Argument Type	Data Type	Description
DataSource (required)	String	Specifies the full path of the XML file to import.
ImportOptions (optional)	acImportXMLOption Use one of the following constants: Constant Value acAppendData 2 acStructureAndData 1 acStructureOnly 0	Specifies whether to import structure only (0), import structure and data (1) (default), or append data (2).

The following procedure will import the structure of the Extensions table from the EmpExtensions.xml file:

```
Sub Import_XMLFile()
    Application.ImportXML DataSource:="c:\Learn_XML\EmpExtensions.xml", _
        ImportOptions:=acStructureOnly

    MsgBox "The import operation completed successfully."

End Sub
```

Manipulating XML Documents Programmatically

You can create, access, and manipulate XML documents programmatically using the XML Document Object Model (DOM). The DOM has objects, properties, and methods for interacting with XML documents.

To use the XML DOM from your VBA procedures, take a few minutes now to set up a reference to the MSXML Object Library using the following steps:

1. Switch to the Visual Basic Editor window in Chap29.accdb and choose **Tools | References**.

2. In the References window, select **Microsoft XML, v6.0** (see Figure 29-20) and click **OK**.

   If you don't have version 6.0 installed, select the lower version of this object type library or upgrade your browser to the higher version so that the most recent library is available.

Figure 29-20: To work with XML documents programmatically, you need to establish a reference to the Microsoft XML object type library.

3. Now that you have the reference set, open the Object Browser and examine XML DOM's objects, methods, and properties (see Figure 29-21).

Figure 29-21: To view objects, properties, and methods exposed by the XML DOM (Document Object Model), open the Object Browser after setting up a reference to the Microsoft XML object type library (see Figure 29-20).

4. Close the Object Browser window.

As mentioned earlier in this chapter (see Part 4 of Custom Project 29-2), the DOMDocument object is the top level of the XML DOM object hierarchy. This object represents a tree structure composed of nodes. You can navigate through this tree structure and manipulate the data contained in the nodes by using various methods and properties. The hands-on exercises in the following sections demonstrate how to read and manipulate XML documents by using VBA procedures.

Loading and Retrieving the Contents of an XML File

Hands-On 29-9 shows how to open an XML data file and retrieve both the raw data and the actual text stored in nodes.

◎ Hands-On 29-9: Loading and Retrieving the Contents of an XML File

1. In the Visual Basic Editor window of the Chap29.accdb database, choose **Insert | Module** to add a new standard module to the current VBA project.

2. In the module's Code window, enter the **ReadXMLDoc** procedure shown below, or copy the procedure code from **C:\Acc07_HandsOn\Chap29.txt**.

➔ **Note:** For this procedure to work correctly, you must set up the reference to the Microsoft XML object type library as instructed at the beginning of this section.

```
Sub ReadXMLDoc()
    Dim xmldoc As MSXML2.DOMDocument60
    Set xmldoc = New MSXML2.DOMDocument60

    xmldoc.async = False
    If xmldoc.Load("C:\Learn_XML\Shippers.xml") Then
        Debug.Print xmldoc.XML
```

```
    ' Debug.Print xmldoc.Text
    End If
End Sub
```

To work with an XML document, we begin by creating an instance of the DOMDocument object as follows:

```
Dim xmldoc As MSXML2.DOMDocument60
Set xmldoc = New MSXML2.DOMDocument60
```

MSXML uses an asynchronous loading mechanism by default for working with documents. Asynchronous loading allows you to perform other tasks during long database operations, such as providing feedback to the user as MSXML parses the XML file or giving the user the chance to cancel the operation. Before calling the Load method, however, it's a good idea to set the Async property of the DOMDocument object to False to ensure that the XML file is fully loaded before other statements are executed. The Load method returns True if it successfully loaded the data and False otherwise. Having loaded the XML data into a DOMDocument object, you can use the XML property to retrieve the raw data or use the Text property to obtain the text stored in document nodes.

3. Position the insertion point anywhere within the code of the ReadXMLDoc procedure and choose **Run | Run Sub/UserForm**. The procedure executes and writes the contents of the XML file into the Immediate window as shown in Figure 29-22.

```
<?xml version="1.0"?>
<dataroot xmlns:od="urn:schemas-microsoft-com:officedata" xmlns:xsi="http://www.w3.org/:
    <Shippers>
        <ID>1</ID>
        <Company>Shipping Company A</Company>
        <Address>123 Any Street</Address>
        <City>Memphis</City>
        <State_x002F_Province>TN</State_x002F_Province>
        <ZIP_x002F_Postal_x0020_Code>99999</ZIP_x002F_Postal_x0020_Code>
        <Country_x002F_Region>USA</Country_x002F_Region>
    </Shippers>
    <Shippers>
        <ID>2</ID>
        <Company>Shipping Company B</Company>
        <Address>123 Any Street</Address>
        <City>Memphis</City>
        <State_x002F_Province>TN</State_x002F_Province>
        <ZIP_x002F_Postal_x0020_Code>99999</ZIP_x002F_Postal_x0020_Code>
        <Country_x002F_Region>USA</Country_x002F_Region>
    </Shippers>
    <Shippers>
        <ID>3</ID>
        <Company>Shipping Company C</Company>
        <Address>123 Any Street</Address>
        <City>Memphis</City>
        <State_x002F_Province>TN</State_x002F_Province>
        <ZIP_x002F_Postal_x0020_Code>99999</ZIP_x002F_Postal_x0020_Code>
```

Figure 29-22: By using the XML property of the DOMDocument object you can retrieve the raw data from an XML file.

4. In the code of the ReadXMLDoc procedure, comment the first Debug.Print statement and uncomment the second statement that reads **Debug.Print xmldoc.Text**.

5. Run the ReadXMLDoc procedure again. This time the Immediate window shows the entry as one long line of text:

```
1 Shipping Company A 123 Any Street Memphis TN 99999 USA 2 Shipping Company B
123 Any Street Memphis TN 99999 USA 3 Shipping Company C 123 Any Street Memphis
TN 99999 USA
```

Working with XML Document Nodes

As you already know, the XML DOM represents a tree-based hierarchy of nodes. An XML document can contain nodes of different types. For example, an XML document can include a document node that provides access to the entire XML document or one or more element nodes representing individual elements. Some nodes represent comments and processing instructions in the XML document, and others hold the text content of a tag. To determine the type of node, use the nodeType property of the IXMLDOMNode object. Node types are identified either by a text string or a constant.

For example, the node representing an element can be referred to as NODE_ELEMENT or 1, while the node representing the comment is named NODE_COMMENT or 8. See the MSXML2 Library in the Object Browser for the names of other node types.

In addition to node types, nodes can have parent, child, and sibling nodes. The hasChildNodes method lets you determine if a DOMDocument object has child nodes. There's also a childNodes property, which simplifies retrieving a collection of child nodes. Before you start looping through the collection of child nodes, it's a good idea to use the length property of the IXMLDOMNode object to determine how many elements the collection contains.

The following hands-on exercise uses the Shippers.xml file to demonstrate how to work with XML document nodes.

⊚ Hands-On 29-10: Working with XML Document Nodes

1. In the same module of the Visual Basic Editor window where you entered the ReadXMLDoc procedure in the previous hands-on exercise, enter the **LearnAboutNodes** procedure as shown below, or copy the procedure code from **C:\Acc07_HandsOn\Chap29.txt**.

```
Sub LearnAboutNodes()
    Dim xmldoc As MSXML2.DOMDocument60
    Dim xmlNode As MSXML2.IXMLDOMNode

    Set xmldoc = New MSXML2.DOMDocument60
    xmldoc.async = False

    xmldoc.Load ("C:\Learn_XML\Shippers.xml")
    If xmldoc.hasChildNodes Then
        Debug.Print "Number of child Nodes: " & xmldoc.childNodes.length
        For Each xmlNode In xmldoc.childNodes
            Debug.Print "Node name:" & xmlNode.nodeName
            Debug.Print vbTab & "Type:" & xmlNode.nodeTypeString _
                            & "(" & xmlNode.nodeType & ")"
```

```
        Debug.Print vbTab & "Text: " & xmlNode.Text
    Next xmlNode
    End If
    Set xmlDoc = Nothing
End Sub
```

Notice that the above procedure uses the hasChildNodes property of the DOMDocument object to check whether there are any child nodes in the loaded XML file. If child nodes are found, the length property of the childNodes collection returns the total number of child nodes found. Next, the procedure loops through the childNodes collection and retrieves the node name using the nodeName property of the IXMLDOMNode object.

The nodeTypeString property returns the string version of the node type (for example, processing instruction, element, text, etc.) and the nodeType property is used to return the enumeration value. Finally, the Text property of the IXMLDOMNode object retrieves the node text.

2. Position the insertion point anywhere within the code of the LearnAboutNodes procedure and choose **Run | Run Sub/UserForm**. The result of running the LearnAboutNodes procedure is shown below:

```
Number of child Nodes: 2
Node name:xml
    Type:processinginstruction(7)
    Text: version="1.0" encoding="UTF-8"
Node name:dataroot
    Type:element(1)
    Text: 1 Shipping Company A 123 Any Street Memphis TN 99999 USA 2 Shipping
Company B 123 Any Street Memphis TN 99999 USA 3 Shipping Company C 123 Any
Street Memphis TN 99999 USA
```

Retrieving Information from Element Nodes

Let's assume that you want to read the information from only the text element nodes. Use the getElementsByTagName method of the DOMDocument object to retrieve an IXMLDOMNodeList object containing all the element nodes. This method takes one argument specifying the tag name for which to search. To search for all the element nodes, use "*" as the tag to search for.

The following hands-on exercise demonstrates how to obtain data from XML document element nodes.

◎ Hands-On 29-11: Retrieving Information from Element Nodes

1. In the Visual Basic Editor Code window, enter the following **IterateThru-Elements** procedure below the last procedure code you entered in Hands-On 29-10, or copy the procedure code from **C:\Acc07_HandsOn\ Chap29.txt**.

```
Sub IterateThruElements()
    Dim xmldoc As MSXML2.DOMDocument60
    Dim xmlNode As MSXML2.IXMLDOMNode
    Dim xmlNodeList As MSXML2.IXMLDOMNodeList
```

```
Dim myNode As MSXML2.IXMLDOMNode

Set xmldoc = New MSXML2.DOMDocument60
xmldoc.async = False
xmldoc.Load ("C:\Learn_XML\Shippers.xml")
Set xmlNodeList = xmldoc.getElementsByTagName("*")
For Each xmlNode In xmlNodeList
    For Each myNode In xmlNode.childNodes
        If myNode.nodeType = NODE_TEXT Then
            Debug.Print xmlNode.nodeName & "=" & xmlNode.Text
        End If
    Next myNode
Next xmlNode
Set xmlDoc = Nothing
End Sub
```

The IterateThruElements procedure retrieves the XML document name and the corresponding text for all the text elements in the Shippers.xml file. Notice that this procedure uses two For Each...Next loops. The first one (the outer loop) iterates through the entire collection of element nodes. The second one (the inner loop) uses the nodeType property to find only those element nodes that contain a single text node.

2. Position the insertion point anywhere within the code of the IterateThru-Elements procedure and choose **Run | Run Sub/UserForm**. The result of running the IterateThruElements procedure is shown below:

```
ID=1
Company=Shipping Company A
Address=123 Any Street
City=Memphis
State_x002F_Province=TN
ZIP_x002F_Postal_x0020_Code=99999
Country_x002F_Region=USA
ID=2
Company=Shipping Company B
Address=123 Any Street
City=Memphis
State_x002F_Province=TN
ZIP_x002F_Postal_x0020_Code=99999
Country_x002F_Region=USA
ID=3
Company=Shipping Company C
Address=123 Any Street
City=Memphis
State_x002F_Province=TN
ZIP_x002F_Postal_x0020_Code=99999
Country_x002F_Region=USA
```

Retrieving Specific Information from Element Nodes

You can list all the nodes that match a specified criterion by using the selectNodes method. The following hands-on exercise prints to the Immediate window the text for all Company nodes that exist in the Shippers.xml file. The

//Company criterion of the selectNodes method looks for the element named Company at any level within the tree structure of the nodes.

◎ Hands-On 29-12: Retrieving Specific Information from Element Nodes

1. In the Visual Basic Editor Code window, in the same module where you entered previous procedures, enter the **SelectNodesByCriteria** procedure as shown below, or copy the procedure code from **C:\Acc07_HandsOn\ Chap29.txt**.

```
Sub SelectNodesByCriteria()
    Dim xmldoc As MSXML2.DOMDocument60
    Dim xmlNodeList As MSXML2.IXMLDOMNodeList
    Dim myNode As MSXML2.IXMLDOMNode

    Set xmldoc = New MSXML2.DOMDocument60
    xmldoc.async = False
    xmldoc.Load ("C:\Learn_XML\Shippers.xml")
    Set xmlNodeList = xmldoc.selectNodes("//Company")
    If Not (xmlNodeList Is Nothing) Then
        For Each myNode In xmlNodeList
            Debug.Print myNode.Text
            If myNode.Text = "Shipping Company A" Then
                myNode.Text = "Airborne Express"
                xmldoc.Save "C:\Learn_XML\Shippers.xml"
            End If
        Next myNode
    End If
    Set xmldoc = Nothing
End Sub
```

The SelectNodesByCriteria procedure creates the IXMLDOMNodeList object that represents a collection of child nodes. The selectNodes method applies the specified pattern to this node's context and returns the list of matching nodes as IXMLDOMNodeList. The expression used by the selectNodes method specifies that all the CompanyName element nodes should be included in the node list.

You can use the Is Nothing conditional expression to find out whether a matching element was found in the loaded XML file. If the matching elements were found in the IXMLDOMNodeList, the procedure iterates through the node list and prints each element node text to the Immediate window. In addition, if the node element's text value is Shipping Company A, the procedure replaces this value with Airborne Express. The Save method of the DOMDocument is used to save the changes in the Shippers.xml file.

2. Position the insertion point anywhere within the code of the SelectNodes-ByCriteria procedure and choose **Run | Run Sub/UserForm**. The result of running the SelectNodesByCriteria procedure is shown below:

```
Shipping Company A
Shipping Company B
Shipping Company C
```

Note: When you run this procedure again, you should see the following output:

```
Airborne Express
Shipping Company B
Shipping Company C
```

Retrieving the First Matching Node

If all you want to do is retrieve the first node that meets the specified criterion, use the SelectSingleNode method of the DOMDocument object. As the argument of this method, specify the string representing the node you'd like to find. For example, the following procedure finds the first node that matches the criterion //Company in the Shippers.xml file:

```
Sub SelectSingleNode()
    Dim xmldoc As MSXML2.DOMDocument60
    Dim xmlSingleNode As MSXML2.IXMLDOMNode

    Set xmldoc = New MSXML2.DOMDocument60
    xmldoc.async = False
    xmldoc.Load ("C:\Learn_XML\Shippers.xml")
    Set xmlSingleNode = xmldoc.SelectSingleNode("//Company")
    If xmlSingleNode Is Nothing Then
        Debug.Print "No nodes selected."
    Else
        Debug.Print xmlSingleNode.Text
    End If
    Set xmlDoc = Nothing
End Sub
```

The XML DOM provides a number of other methods that make it possible to programmatically add or delete elements in the XML document tree structure. Covering all of the details of the XML DOM Object Model is beyond the scope of this chapter. When you are ready for more information on this subject, visit the following web link: http://www.w3.org/DOM/.

Using ActiveX Data Objects with XML

In Chapter 16 you learned how to save ADO Recordsets to disk using the Advanced Data TableGram (adPersistADTG) format. This section expands on what you already know about the ADO Recordsets by showing you how to use ADO with XML. Since the release of ADO version 2.5 (in 2000), you can save all types of recordsets to disk as XML using the Extensible Markup Language (adPersistXML) format.

Saving an ADO Recordset as XML to Disk

To save an ADO Recordset to a disk file as XML, use the Save method of the Recordset object with the adPersistXML constant. Hands-On 29-13 demonstrates how to create an XML file from ADO.

◎ Hands-On 29-13: Creating an XML Document from ADO

1. In the Visual Basic Editor window of the Chap29.accdb database, choose **Insert | Module** to add a new standard module to the current VBA project.

2. Choose **Tools | References** to open the References dialog box. Check the box next to **Microsoft ActiveX Object Library 2.8** (or a lower version) and click **OK**.

3. In the module's Code window, enter the **SaveRst_ToXMLwithADO** procedure as shown below, or copy the procedure code from **C:\Acc07_HandsOn\Chap29.txt**.

```
Sub SaveRst_ToXMLwithADO()
    Dim rst As ADODB.Recordset
    Dim conn As New ADODB.Connection

    Const strConn = "Provider=Microsoft.Jet.OLEDB.4.0;" _
        & "Data Source=C:\Acc07_HandsOn\Northwind.mdb"

    ' open a connection to the database
    conn.Open strConn

    ' execute a select SQL statement against the database
    Set rst = conn.Execute("SELECT * FROM Products")

    ' delete the file if it exists
    On Error Resume Next
    Kill "C:\Learn_XML\Products_AttribCentric.xml"

    ' save the recordset as an XML file
    rst.Save "C:\Learn_XML\Products_AttribCentric.xml", adPersistXML

    ' cleanup
    Set rst = Nothing
    Set conn = Nothing
End Sub
```

The above procedure begins by establishing a connection to the sample Northwind database using the ADO Connection object. Next, it executes an SQL SELECT statement against the database to retrieve all of the records from the Products table. Once the records are placed in a recordset, the Save method is called to store the recordset to a disk file using the adPersistXML format. If the disk file already exists, the procedure deletes the existing file using the VBA Kill statement. The On Error Resume Next statement allows bypassing the Kill statement if the file you are going to create does not yet exist.

4. Position the insertion point anywhere within the code of the procedure and choose **Run | Run Sub/UserForm**.

5. Open the C:\Learn_XML\Products_AttribCentric.xml file created by the SaveRst_ToXMLwithADO procedure and examine its content.

The web browser displays the raw XML as shown in Figure 29-23. Notice that the content of this file looks different from other XML files you generated in this chapter. The reason for this is that XML that is persisted from ADO Recordsets is created in attribute-centric XML. Microsoft Office Access supports only element-centric XML. Therefore, in order to import to Access an XML file created from ADO, you must first create and apply an XSLT transformation to the source document. The stylesheet you create should convert the attribute-centric XML to element-centric XML that Access can handle (see Hands-On 29-14).

Figure 29-23: Saving a recordset to an XML file with ADO produces an attribute-centric XML file.

Attribute-Centric and Element-Centric XML

If you take a look at the XML file generated in Hands-On 29-13 (see Figure 29-23 above), you will notice that below the XML document's root tag there are two child nodes: <s:Schema> and <rs:data>.

The schema node describes the structure of the recordset, while the data node holds the actual data. Inside the <s:Schema id="RowsetSchema"> and </s:Schema> tags, ADO places information about each column: field name, position, data type and length, nullability, and whether the column is writable. Each field is represented by the <s:AttributeType> element. Notice that the value of the name attribute is the field name. The <s:AttributeType> element also has a child element, <s:datatype>, which holds information about its data type (integer, number, string, etc.) and the maximum field length.

Below the schema definition, you can find the actual data. The ADO schema represents each record using the <z:row> tag. The fields in a record are expressed as attributes of the <z:row> element. Every XML attribute is assigned a value that is enclosed in a pair of single or double quotation marks; however, if the value of a field in a record is Null, the attribute on the <z:row> is not created. Notice that each record is written out in the following format:

```
<z:row ProductID='1' ProductName='Chai' SupplierID='1' CategoryID='1'
    QuantityPerUnit='10 boxes x 20 bags' UnitPrice='18' UnitsInStock='39'
    UnitsOnOrder='0' ReorderLevel='10' Discontinued='False'/>
```

The code fragment above is attribute-centric XML that Access cannot import. To make the XML file compatible with Access, you should have each record written out as follows:

```
<Product>
    <ProductID>1</ProductID>
    <ProductName>Chai</ProductName>
    <SupplierID>1</SupplierID>
    <CategoryID>1</CategoryID>
    <QuantityPerUnit>10 boxes x 20 bags</QuantityPerUnit>
    <UnitPrice>18</UnitPrice>
    <UnitsInStock>39</UnitsInStock>
    <UnitsOnOrder>0</UnitsOnOrder>
    <ReorderLevel>10</ReorderLevel>
    <Discontinued>False</Discontinued>
</Product>
```

The code fragment above represents element-centric XML. Each record is wrapped in a <Product> tag, and each field is an element under the <Product> tag.

Changing the Type of an XML File

Because it is much easier to work with element-centric XML files (and Microsoft Access does not support attribute-centric XML), you must write an XSL stylesheet to transform the attribute-centric XML file to an element-centric XML file before you can import an XML file created from an ADO Recordset to Access.

The following hands-on exercise demonstrates how to write a stylesheet to convert an XML document from attribute-centric to element-centric.

Hands-On 29-14: Creating a Stylesheet to Convert Attribute-Centric XML to Element-Centric XML

1. Open **Notepad** and type the stylesheet code as shown below, or copy the code from **C:\Acc07_HandsOn\AttribToElem.txt**.

```
<xsl:stylesheet version="1.0"
    xmlns:xsl="http://www.w3.org/1999/XSL/Transform"
    xmlns:rs="urn:schemas-microsoft-com:rowset">
<xsl:output method="xml" encoding="UTF-8" />
```

```
<xsl:template match="/">

<!-- root element for the XML output -->
<Products xmlns:z="#RowsetSchema">

    <xsl:for-each select="/xml/rs:data/z:row">
      <Product>
        <xsl:for-each select="@*">
          <xsl:element name="{name()}">
            <xsl:value-of select="."/>
          </xsl:element>
        </xsl:for-each>
      </Product>
    </xsl:for-each>
</Products>

  </xsl:template>
</xsl:stylesheet>
```

2. Save the above stylesheet as **C:\Learn_XML\AttribToElem.xsl**. Make sure to type the .xsl extension so the file is not saved as text. We will use this stylesheet for the transformation in the next hands-on exercise.

Notice that in the above stylesheet, the "@*" wildcard matches all attribute nodes. Each time the <z:row> tag is encountered, an element named <Product> will be created. And for each attribute, the attribute name will be converted to the element name using the built-in XPath name( ) function. Expressions in curly braces are evaluated and converted to strings. The select="." returns the current value of the attribute being read.

See the next section on how to apply this stylesheet to the XML document.

Applying an XSL Stylesheet

Now that you've created the stylesheet that can be used to transform an attribute-centric XML file into an element-centric file, you can use the transformNodeToObject method of the DOMDocument object to apply the stylesheet to the Products_AttribCentric.xml file created in Hands-On 29-13. The hands-on exercise that follows demonstrates how to do this. In addition, the procedure in this exercise will import the converted ADO XML file to Access.

◉ Hands-On 29-15: Applying a Stylesheet to an ADO XML Document and Importing It to Access

1. Enter the following procedure below the procedure code you created in Hands-On 29-13, or copy the procedure code from **C:\Acc07_Hands-On\Chap29.txt**.

```
Sub ApplyStyleSheetAndImport()
    Dim myXMLDoc As New MSXML2.DOMDocument60
    Dim myXSLDoc As New MSXML2.DOMDocument60
```

```
Dim newXMLDoc As New MSXML2.DOMDocument60

myXMLDoc.async = False
If myXMLDoc.Load("C:\Learn_XML\Products_AttribCentric.xml") Then
    myXSLDoc.Load "C:\Learn_XML\AttribToElem.xsl"

    ' apply the transformation
        If Not myXSLDoc Is Nothing Then
            myXMLDoc.transformNodeToObject myXSLDoc, newXMLDoc

            ' save the output in a new file
            newXMLDoc.Save "C:\Learn_XML\Products_Converted.xml"

            ' import to Access
            Application.ImportXML "C:\Learn_XML\Products_Converted.xml"
        End If
    End If

    ' cleanup
    Set myXMLDoc = Nothing
    Set myXSLDoc = Nothing
    Set newXMLDoc = Nothing
End Sub
```

The above procedure begins by loading both the Products_AttribCentric.xml file (created in Hands-On 29-13) and the AttribToElem.xsl stylesheet (created in Hands-On 29-14) into the DOMDocument object. Next, the stylesheet is applied to the source file by using the transformNodeToObject method. This method is applied to a node in the source XML document's tree and takes two arguments. The first argument is a stylesheet in the form of a DOMDocument node. The second argument is another DOMDocument node that will hold the result of the transformation. Next, the result of the transformation is saved to a file (Products_Converted.xml) and the file is imported to Access using the ImportXML method, which was introduced earlier in this chapter.

2. Run the ApplyStyleSheetAndImport procedure.

3. Open the **C:\Learn_XML\Products_Converted.xml** file. Notice that the Products_Converted.xml file content is now element-centric XML (see Figure 29-24).

4. In the Access window, locate and open the table named **Product**.

The Product table was created by the ImportXML method in the ApplyStyleSheetAndImport procedure.

Figure 29-24: This element-centric XML file is a result of applying a stylesheet to the attribute-centric ADO Recordset that was saved to an XML file.

The original XML file is shown in Figure 29-23, and the stylesheet used in the transformation can be found in Hands-On 29-14.

Transforming Attribute-Centric XML Data into an HTML Table

As you've seen in earlier examples, after creating an XML file from an ADO Recordset, the generated output contains attribute-centric XML. To import this type of output to Access you had to create a special stylesheet and apply the transformation to convert the attribute-centric XML to the element-centric XML that Access supports. But what if you simply want to display the XML file created from an ADO Recordset in a web browser? You can create a generic XSL stylesheet that draws a simple HTML table for the users when they open the XML attribute-centric file in their browser.

Hands-On 29-16 demonstrates how to create a stylesheet to transform the attribute-centric XML file that we created in Hands-On 29-13 into HTML. The hands-on exercise that immediately follows performs the transformation by inserting a reference to the XSL stylesheet into the XML document.

◎ Hands-On 29-16: Creating a Generic Stylesheet to Transform an Attribute-Centric XML File into HTML

1. Open **Notepad** and type the stylesheet code as shown below, or copy the code from **C:\Acc07_HandsOn\AttribToHTML.txt**.

```xml
<?xml version="1.0"?>
<xsl:stylesheet version="1.0"
  xmlns:xsl="http://www.w3.org/1999/XSL/Transform"
  xmlns:s='uuid:BDC6E3F0-6DA3-11d1-A2A3-00AA00C14882'
  xmlns:dt='uuid:C2F41010-65B3-11d1-A29F-00AA00C14882'
  xmlns:rs='urn:schemas-microsoft-com:rowset'
  xmlns:z='#RowsetSchema'
  xmlns:html="http://www.w3.org/TR/REC-html40">

<xsl:template match="/">
<html>
<head>
<title>Using Stylesheet to convert attribute based XML to HTML</title>
<style type="text/css">
.myHSet { font-Family:verdana; font-Size:9px; color:blue; }
.myBSet { font-Family:Garamond; font-Size:8px; }
</style>
</head>

<body>
  <table width="100%" border="1">

    <xsl:for-each select="xml/s:Schema/s:ElementType/s:AttributeType">
      <th class="myHSet">
          <xsl:value-of select="@name" />
      </th>
    </xsl:for-each>

    <xsl:for-each select="xml/rs:data/z:row">
    <tr>
       <xsl:for-each select="@*">
          <td class="myBSet" valign="top">
              <xsl:value-of select="."/>
          </td>
       </xsl:for-each>
    </tr>
    </xsl:for-each>
  </table>
</body>
</html>
</xsl:template>
</xsl:stylesheet>
```

The above stylesheet uses the feature known as Cascading Stylesheets (CSS) to format the HTML table. A style comprises different properties — bold, italic, font size and font weight, color, etc. — that you want to apply to particular text (titles, headers, body, etc.) and assigns a common name to these properties. Thus, in the above stylesheet, two styles are defined. A style named myHSet is applied to the table headings, and a style named myBSet is used for formatting the text in the body of the table. Using styles is very convenient. If you don't like the formatting, you can simply change the style definition and get a new look in no time. Notice that to define a style, you must type a period and a class name. Using letters and numbers, you can define any name for your style class. After the class name, you need to type the definition for the class between curly brackets { }.

```
<style type="text/css">
  .myHSet { font-Family:Verdana; font-Size:9px; color:blue; }
  .myBSet { font-Family:Garamond; font-Size:8px; }
</style>
```

Notice that the definition of the class includes the name of the property followed by a colon and the property value. Properties are separated by a semicolon. A semicolon is also placed before the ending curly bracket (}). A style class can be applied to any HTML tag.

The example stylesheet shown above uses template-based processing. The following instruction defines a template for the entire document:

```
<xsl:template match="/">
```

The code between the initial and closing tags will be processed for all tags whose names match the value of the attribute "match." In other words, you want the pattern matching that follows to be applied to the entire document (/).

Next, a loop is used to write out the column headings. To do this, you must move through all the AttributeType elements of the root element, outputting the name attribute's value like this:

```
<xsl:for-each select="xml/s:Schema/s:ElementType/s:AttributeType">
 <th class="myHSet">
  <xsl:value-of select="@name" />
 </th>
</xsl:for-each>
```

An attribute's name is always preceded by @.

Next, another loop runs through all the <z:row> elements representing actual records:

```
<xsl:for-each select="xml/rs:data/z:row">
```

All the attributes of any <z:row> element are enumerated:

```
<xsl:for-each select="@*">
   <td class="myBSet" valign="top">
     <xsl:value-of match="." />
   </td>
</xsl:for-each>
```

The string "@*" denotes any attribute. For each attribute found under the <z:row> element, you need to match the attribute name with its corresponding value. Notice the period in the <xsl:value-of> tag. The period represents the node that XSLT is currently working with. In summary, the above code fragment tells the XSLT processor to display the value of the current node during the iteration of the <z:row> attributes.

2. Save the above stylesheet as **AttribToHTML.xsl**. Be sure to type the .xsl extension so the file is not saved as text.

3. Close Notepad.

4. Open the **AttribToHTML.xsl** file in the browser to test whether it is well formed. If you made any errors while typing the stylesheet code, you must correct the problems before going on to the next section.

5. Close the browser.

Now that you are finished with the stylesheet, you need to link the XML and XSL files. You can do this by adding a reference to a stylesheet in your XML document as shown in Hands-On 29-17.

⊚ Hands-On 29-17: Linking the Attribute-Centric XML File with the Generic Stylesheet and Displaying the Transformed File in a Web Browser

1. Save the Products_AttribCentric.xml file as **Products_AttribCentric_ 2.xml**.

2. Open the **Products_AttribCentric_2.xml** file with Notepad.

3. Type the following definition in the first line of this file:

```
<?xml-stylesheet type="text/xsl" href="AttribToHTML.xsl"?>
```

The above instruction establishes a reference to the XSL file.

4. Save the changes made to the Products_AttribCentric_2.xml file and close Notepad.

5. Open the **Products_AttribCentric_2.xml** file in your browser. You should see the data formatted in a table (see Figure 29-25).

Figure 29-25: You can apply a generic stylesheet to an XML document generated by the ADO to display the data in a simple HTML table.

Loading an XML Document in Excel

After saving an ADO Recordset to an XML file on disk (see Hands-On 29-13 earlier in this chapter), you can load it into a desired application and read it as if it were a database. To gain access to the records saved in the XML file, use the Open method of the Recordset object and specify the filename, including its path and the persisted recordset service provider as Provider=MSPersist. The following hands-on exercise demonstrates how to open a persisted recordset and write its data to an Excel workbook.

◎ Hands-On 29-18: From Access to Excel: Loading an XML File into an Excel Workbook

1. In the Visual Basic Editor window, choose **Insert | Module** to add a new standard module to the current VBA project.

2. Choose **Tools | References** and click the check box next to the **Microsoft Excel 12.0 Object Library**, and then click **OK** to exit the References dialog box.

3. In the module's Code window, enter the **OpenAdoFile** procedure as shown below, or copy the procedure code from **C:\Acc07_HandsOn\Chap29.txt**.

```
Sub OpenAdoFile()
    Dim rst As ADODB.Recordset
    Dim objExcel As Excel.Application
    Dim wkb As Excel.Workbook
    Dim wks As Excel.Worksheet
    Dim StartRange As Excel.Range
    Dim h as Integer

    Set rst = New ADODB.Recordset

    ' open your XML file and load it
    rst.Open "C:\Learn_XML\Products_AttribCentric.xml", "Provider=MSPersist"

    ' display the number of records
    MsgBox "There are " & rst.RecordCount & " records " & _
        "in this file."

    Set objExcel = New Excel.Application

    ' create a new Excel workbook
    Set wkb = objExcel.Workbooks.Add

    ' set a reference to the ActiveSheet
    Set wks = wkb.ActiveSheet

    ' make Excel application window visible
    objExcel.Visible = True
```

```
' copy field names as headings to the first row of the worksheet
For h = 1 To rst.Fields.Count
    wks.Cells(1, h).Value = rst.Fields(h - 1).Name
Next

' specify the cell range to receive the data (A2)
Set StartRange = wks.Cells(2, 1)

' copy the records from the recordset beginning in cell A2
StartRange.CopyFromRecordset rst

' autofit the columns to make the data fit
wks.Range("A1").CurrentRegion.Select
wks.Columns.AutoFit

' save the workbook
wkb.SaveAs "C:\Learn_XML\ExcelReport.xls"

Set objExcel = Nothing
Set rst = Nothing
End Sub
```

The above procedure is well commented, so we will skip its analysis and proceed to the next step.

4. Run the **OpenAdoFile** procedure.

When the procedure is complete, the Excel application window should be visible with the ExcelReport.xls workbook file displaying products retrieved from the XML file (see Figure 29-26).

5. Close the Excel workbook and exit Excel.

Figure 29-26: An ADO Recordset persisted to an XML file is now opened in Excel.

Chapter Summary

This chapter has shown you that Microsoft Access 2007 makes it easy to work with XML files. Using Access built-in commands or programming code, you can both export Access data to an XML file and import an XML file and display the file as an Access table. You learned here what XML is and how it is structured. After working through the examples in this chapter, it's easy to see that XML supplies you with numerous ways to accomplish a specific task. Because XML is stored in plain text files, it can be read by many types of applications, independent of the operating system or hardware. You learned how to transform data from XML to HTML and from one XML format to another. You explored the ADO Recordset methods suitable for working with XML programmatically. You were introduced to XSL stylesheets and XSLT transformations. All of these new methods and techniques you've studied here will need time to sink in. XML is not like VBA. It is not very independent. It needs many supporting technologies to assist it in its work. So don't despair if you don't understand something right away. Learning XML requires learning many other new concepts (like XSLT, XPath, schemas, etc.) at the same time. Take XML step by step by experimenting with it. The time that you invest studying this technology will not be wasted. XML is here to stay. Here are three main reasons why you should really consider XML:

- *XML separates content from presentation.*

  This means that if you are planning to design web pages, you no longer need to make changes to your HTML files when the data changes. Because the data is kept in separate files, it's easy to make modifications.

- *XML is perfect for sharing and exchanging data.*

  This means that you no longer have to worry if your data needs to be processed by a system that's not compatible with yours. Because all systems can work with text files (and XML documents are simply text files), you can share and exchange your data without a headache.

- *XML can be used as a database.*

  This means that you no longer need a database system to have a database. What a great value!

This chapter concludes Part V of this book, which focused on working with an Access database over the Internet by writing Active Server Pages and XML files. In the next chapter, you learn how to work with and customize the new user interface introduced in Access 2007.

PART VI

Working with New Features in Access 2007

Whether you have used Access for years, or you are just starting to use Access with this version, this part of the book introduces you to what's new in Access 2007 in areas such as the user interface, tables, forms, reports, templates, and macros.

Chapter 30

Programming the User Interface

The user interface (UI) in Microsoft Office Access 2007 has been designed from the ground up to improve user interaction with the product. The menu bar and toolbars in previous versions have been replaced with new components that allow easier access to and grouping of related commands. This chapter provides an overview of the new interface elements in Office Access 2007 and shows you how you can customize the UI in your Access database applications.

The Getting Started with Microsoft Office Access Window

When you launch Access from the Start menu or a desktop shortcut, you are greeted with the Getting Started with Microsoft Office Access window (Figure 30-1).

Figure 30-1: Office Access 2007 startup screen.

The middle part of the window provides a button to create a new blank Access database and offers you a selection of prebuilt templates so that you can get a head start on your Access database project. These templates come with ready-to-use tables, forms, reports, queries, relationships, and macros and can be modified as needed. You can organize the templates by category by using category listings in the left pane. The lower part of the window provides quick access to many Office Access 2007 resources such as training, user guides, and downloads. The right pane of the getting started window offers quick access to Access databases that were recently opened and the More hyperlink to browse for a database on your computer or on the network.

The Office Button

In the top left-hand corner of the window you will notice the big, round Office button (🔘). This button opens the Office menu, which provides many options (see Figure 30-2) that were found on the File menu and Database Utilities submenu of Access 2003. When the button is clicked while the getting started window is open, the only available options are for creating a new blank database, opening an existing database, and managing your database by compacting and repairing it. While the Office button itself cannot be customized, you can change the contents of the Office menu as described in the last section of this chapter (see "Customizing the Office Button Menu").

Figure 30-2: Use the Office button to open the Office menu.

When you install the Access Developer Extensions (ADE) add-in you will gain access to additional tools via the Developer option (see Figure 30-3). The Microsoft Office Access 2007 Developer Extensions are used for easy deployment and management of Microsoft Access database solutions. You can download the ADE free of charge from http://www.microsoft.com/downloads/details.aspx?familyid=d96a8358-ece4-4bee-a844-f81856dceb67&displaylang=en.

Figure 30-3: The Developer option in the Office menu is available after installing the ADE add-in.

The Office button also provides access to two command buttons: Access Options and Exit Access. Many options previously set via the Options command on the Tools menu can now be accessed and managed from the Access Options command.

The Quick Access Toolbar

To the right of the Office button is a special tool area known as the Quick Access toolbar. From here you can quickly access the most frequently used commands. You can add other Access built-in commands to the Quick Access toolbar by using any of the following methods:

- Click on the drop-down arrow in the Quick Access toolbar and select a command you want to add or click More commands.

- Right-click on the Quick Access toolbar and choose Customize Quick Access Toolbar.

- Click the Access Options button at the bottom of the window (after clicking the Office button) and choose Customize.

The Quick Access toolbar will expand to accommodate as many commands as you wish to add. Together with the title bar and the Office button, the Quick Access toolbar belongs to a large rectangular area called the Ribbon. This area is positioned at the top of the UI window. The Quick Access toolbar was designed for the convenience of end users, and developers should not alter this toolbar. However, if you have a valid reason to hide the contents of this toolbar or add other buttons to it, you can do this by customizing the Ribbon, which is covered in detail later in this chapter.

Customizing the Navigation Pane

When an Access database is opened, you can easily access all of your objects via the Navigation pane on the left side of the window (see Figure 30-4). The Navigation pane replaces the database window from earlier versions of Access. If you need more screen real estate, you can hide the Navigation pane by clicking on the Shutter Bar Open/Close button (the double arrow at the top of the pane) or by pressing F11.

Figure 30-4: The Navigation pane in Office Access 2007.

Use the Navigation pane to organize your objects by type, date created or modified, or related table, or create your own custom groups of objects. By clicking on the down arrow button at the top of the Navigation pane, you can define how you view and manage database objects (see Figure 30-5).

To sort and filter your database objects, activate the Search Bar, or gain access to the navigation options, right-click the top bar of the Navigation pane (Figure 30-6).

Figure 30-5: Grouping options in the Navigation pane.

Figure 30-6: Objects in the Navigation pane can be easily categorized, sorted, and filtered. You can also locate a hard-to-find object via the Search Bar. Use the Navigation Options tool to create custom groups of objects.

The Navigation Options dialog (see Figure 30-7) allows you to create any number of custom groups for organizing your objects according to specific database needs. The exercise in Hands-On 30-1 will walk you through the process of creating a custom group to track your development efforts.

◎ Hands-On 30-1: Adding a Custom Group to the Navigation Pane

1. Open the **C:\Acc07_ByExample\Northwind 2007.accdb** database. Make sure you cancel the login box.

2. Right-click the top bar of the Navigation pane and choose **Navigation Options**.

3. Click the **Add Item** button and type a new name for the category: **Objects in Development**.

4. While the new Objects in Development category is selected, click the **Add Group** button and enter **Dev Tables** for the new group name.

5. Click the **Add Group** button again to add another group named **Dev Queries**.

6. Add two more groups under Objects in Development named **Dev Forms** and **Dev Reports**. See Figure 30-7 for the final output.

7. Click **OK** to close the Navigation Options dialog.

8. Click on the down arrow button at the top of the Navigation pane and choose **Objects in Development** (Figure 30-8).

Figure 30-7: The Navigation Options dialog.

Figure 30-8: Displaying a custom group in the Navigation pane.

The next logical step is placing some database objects into your custom groups. Let's continue with Hands-On 30-2.

Hands-On 30-2: Assigning Objects to Custom Groups in the Navigation Pane

1. In the Northwind 2007.accdb database that you opened in Hands-On 30-1, right-click the **Customers** table and choose **Copy**.

2. Right-click anywhere in the Navigation pane and choose **Paste**. In the Paste Table As dialog, enter **Companies** for the new name of the table and select the **Structure Only** option button. Click **OK** to exit the dialog box.

3. Drag the **Companies** table from the Unassigned Objects group to the **Dev Tables** group.

When you place a database object into a custom group in the Navigation pane, Access creates a shortcut to this object (see Figure 30-9). You can rename your shortcut by right-clicking its name and choosing Rename Shortcut. You can also hide the shortcut in the group or remove it from the group, provided the Navigation pane has not been locked (this is discussed in the next section). In addition to the Hidden attribute, each shortcut has a Disable Design View shortcuts attribute you can set to prevent users from switching to Design view when using the shortcut. You must restart your Access database for this property change to take effect. To display the shortcut properties as shown in Figure 30-9, right-click on the Companies shortcut under the Dev Tables group and choose Table Properties. You can drag any object listed in the Unassigned Objects group into your custom groups.

Figure 30-9: Navigation pane with custom groupings.

Using VBA to Customize the Navigation Pane

You can lock down and customize the Navigation pane programmatically by using the following methods of the DoCmd object: LockNavigationPane, NavigateTo, and SetDisplayedCategories. There are also two methods of the Application object (ExportNavigationPane and ImportNavigationPane) that enable you to quickly apply the same Navigation pane customization to any other Access database.

Locking the Navigation Pane

To prevent users from deleting database objects that are displayed in the Navigation pane, use the following statement:

```
DoCmd.LockNavigationPane True
```

The LockNavigationPane method of the DoCmd object requires a Lock argument. Use the Boolean value of True to lock the Navigation pane, and False to unlock it.

Controlling the Display of Database Objects

To automatically navigate to a specific category in the Navigation pane upon startup of your Access database or to display only certain objects in the category, use the NavigateTo method of the DoCmd object. This method takes two arguments: Category (required) and Group (optional). The Category argument specifies the category you want to navigate to. The Category argument can be the name of your custom category, such as the Objects in Development category that you created in Hands-On 30-1, or a constant representation of the Object Type, Tables and Views, Created Date, and Modified Date categories (see Table 30-1). The Group argument is optional. If you omit it, the Navigation pane will display all database objects arranged by the criteria specified in the Category argument. See Table 30-1 for valid Group arguments for the various Category arguments.

Table 30-1: Category and Group arguments used in the NavigateTo method

Category Argument	Category Argument Constant	Group Argument	Group Argument Constant
Object Type	acNavigationCategoryObjectType	Tables	acNavigationGroupTables
		Forms	acNavigationGroupForms
		Reports	acNavigationGroupReports
		Queries	acNavigationGroupQueries
		Pages	acNavigationGroupPages
		Macros	acNavigationGroupMacros
		Modules	acNavigationGroupModules
Tables and Views	acNavigationCategoryTablesAndViews	Name of a specific table or view in your database.	
Modified Date	acNavigationCategoryModifiedDate	Today	acNavigationGroupToday
		Yesterday	acNavigationGroupYesterday
		Last Month	acNavigationGroupLastMonth
		Older	acNavigationGroupOlder
Created Date	acNavigationCategoryCreatedDate	Today	acNavigationGroupToday
		Yesterday	acNavigationGroupYesterday
		Last Month	acNavigationGroupLastMonth
		Older	acNavigationGroupOlder
Custom	Name of your custom category	Name of one of the custom groups you have created for the specified custom category.	

Let's get some practice with the NavigateTo method.

◎ Hands-On 30-3: Using the NavigateTo Method to Control the Display of Database Objects in the Navigation Pane

1. In the Northwind 2007.accdb database, press **Alt+F11** to switch to the Visual Basic Editor window. Press **Ctrl+G** (or choose **View | Immediate Window**) to open the Immediate window.

2. In the Immediate window, type each of the DoCmd.NavigateTo statement examples as shown below, pressing **Enter** to execute each statement. After the execution of each statement, check the resulting display in the Navigation pane of the Access main window (see Figure 30-10).

```
DoCmd.NavigateTo "acNavigationCategoryCreatedDate"
```

(The above statement will navigate to the Created Date category and display all database objects.)

```
DoCmd.NavigateTo "acNavigationCategoryObjectType", "acNavigationGroupForms"
```

(The above statement will navigate to the Object Type category and select the Forms group.)

```
DoCmd.NavigateTo "acNavigationCategoryTablesAndViews", "Invoices"
```

(The above statement will navigate to the Invoices table in the Tables and Views category.)

```
DoCmd.NavigateTo "Objects in Development", "Dev Forms"
```

(The above statement will navigate to the Dev Forms group objects in the Objects in Development category that was created in Hands-On 30-1.)

```
DoCmd.NavigateTo "acNavigationCategoryModifiedDate", "acNavigationGroupOlder"
```

(The above statement will navigate to the Modified Date category and display all the database objects beginning with a date later than last month.)

Figure 30-10: Testing out the NavigateTo method of the DoCmd object in the Immediate window. Notice how the main Access window and the Microsoft Visual Basic Editor window are positioned so that the Navigation pane stays in view as you execute each statement.

3. Press **Ctrl+G, Ctrl+A**, and then the **Delete** key to remove the contents of the Immediate window.

Setting Displayed Categories

The SetDisplayedCategories method of the DoCmd object is used to specify which categories should be displayed under Navigate to Category in the title bar of the Navigation pane. Use this method to show and hide groups from the top bar of the Navigation pane. For example, the following statement will remove the custom category Objects in Development from the Navigation pane title bar's drop-down list:

```
DoCmd.SetDisplayedCategories False, "Objects in Development"
```

Notice that the SetDisplayedCategories method uses two arguments. The first argument specifies whether to show or hide the category. Use the Boolean value of False to hide the category specified in the second argument of this method, or True to show the category. The second argument denotes the name of the category you want to show or hide. To show or hide all categories, do not specify this argument.

Saving and Loading the Configuration of the Navigation Pane

The configuration of the Navigation pane can be saved at any time with the ExportNavigationPane method of the Application object. This method requires one argument — the path and the name of the XML file to which you want to save the configuration of the Navigation pane. For example, the following statement will save the current configuration of the Navigation pane to North2007NavConfig.xml in the C:\Acc07_ByExample folder:

```
Application.ExportNavigationPane "C:\Acc07_ByExample\North2007NavConfig.xml"
```

To load a saved Navigation pane configuration from the XML file, use the ImportNavigationPane method of the Application object:

```
Application.ImportNavigationPane "C:\Acc07_ByExample\North2007NavConfig.xml",
False
```

Notice that the ImportNavigationPane method used in the statement above has two arguments. The first one specifies the path and name of the XML file that contains the Navigation pane configuration to load. The second argument is optional. When set to True, the imported categories would be appended to the existing categories. The default value is False.

Hands-On 30-4 demonstrates how to save the current configuration of the Navigation pane and then load it into another Access database.

◎ Hands-On 30-4: Saving and Loading the Configuration of the Navigation Pane

1. In the Visual Basic Editor window of the Northwind 2007.accdb database, type the following statement in the Immediate window and press **Enter** to execute:

```
Application.ExportNavigationPane "C:\Acc07_ByExample\North2007NavConfig.xml"
```

2. Switch to Windows Explorer and check that the North2007NavConfig.xml file is present in the Acc07_ByExample folder.

3. Double-click the filename to open it in the browser. Figure 30-11 displays the partial content of the configuration file.

The XML file contains the objects and structure of the Access Navigation pane. Included in this file is information about the contents of the Navigation pane system tables: MSysNavPaneGroupCategories, MSysNavPane-Groups, MSysNavPaneGroupToObjects, and MSysNavPaneObjectIDs.

Figure 30-11: The current configuration of the Navigation pane is saved in this XML file.

4. Close the Explorer window.

5. Close the Northwind 2007.accdb database.

6. Create a new Access database named **Load_North2007NavConfig.accdb** in your C:\Acc07_ByExample folder.

7. Click the top bar of the Navigation pane and view the Navigation pane title bar's drop-down list before we proceed to import the saved configuration file.

8. Press **Alt+F11**, and then press **Ctrl+G** to activate the Immediate window. Type the following statement and press **Enter** to execute:

```
Application.ImportNavigationPane "C:\Acc07_ByExample\North2007NavConfig.xml",
False
```

9. Press **Alt+F11** to switch back to the Access application window.

10. Click the top bar of the Navigation pane and display the Navigation pane title bar's drop-down list again (see Figure 30-12).

Notice the presence of the additional entries in the drop-down list: Northwind Traders and Objects in Development.

Figure 30-12: The Navigation pane can be easily modified using the external XML file containing the custom configuration settings.

Now that you know how to manually and programmatically control the Navigation pane, you should find it easy to provide users with the needed customization of this new Access database navigation system. The next section will expand your knowledge of the Access user interface by introducing you to the Ribbon, which is new to Office 2007.

A Quick Overview of Access 2007 Ribbon Interface

All Office Access 2007 program commands can be accessed from the Ribbon (see Figure 30-13). The Ribbon replaces the system of menus and toolbars found in earlier versions of Access. The Ribbon contains the title bar, the Office button, the Quick Access toolbar, and the tabs. Each tab on the Ribbon provides access to features and commands related to a particular database task. For example, you can use the Create tab to quickly create new tables, forms, reports, queries, macros, modules, and Microsoft Windows SharePoint Services lists (see Figure 30-14). Related commands within a tab are organized into groups. For example, the Create tab divides its commands into four groups: Tables, Forms, Reports, and Other. This type of organization makes it easy to locate a particular command.

Figure 30-13: The rectangular area at the top of the Microsoft Access 2007 window is called the Ribbon.

Figure 30-14: All Access commands related to creating various database objects are grouped on the Create tab.

Various program commands are displayed as large or small buttons. A large button denotes a frequently used command, while a small button shows a specific feature of the main command that you may want to work with. For example, in the Forms group there is a large Form button and a small Blank Form button. Some large and small command buttons include drop-down lists of other specialized commands. For example, the small More Forms button drop-down contains additional methods of creating a form: Form Wizard, Datasheet, Modal Dialog, and PivotTable (Figure 30-15).

Figure 30-15: Additional commands can be accessed by clicking on the down arrow to the right of the button control.

Some controls that you find on the Ribbon do not display commands. Instead, they provide a visual clue of the output you might expect when a specific option is selected. These types of controls are known as galleries. The gallery control is often used to present various formatting options, such as the margin settings shown in Figure 30-16.

Figure 30-16: Clicking on the Margins button on the Print Preview tab displays a gallery of different margin settings.

As mentioned earlier, the commands on the Ribbon tabs are organized into groups for easy browsing. Some tab groups have dialog box launchers in the right-hand corner (see Figure 30-17) that display a dialog box where you can set several advanced options at once.

Figure 30-17: The dialog box launcher button in the bottom corner of the Font group on the Home tab will display the Datasheet Formatting dialog box.

In addition to main Ribbon tabs, there are also contextual tabs that contain commands that apply to what you are doing. When a particular object is selected, the Ribbon displays a contextual tab that provides commands for working with that object. For example, when a table is opened in Datasheet view, the Ribbon displays a contextual tab called Table Tools (see Figure 30-12 earlier). Clicking on the Table Tools tab activates the Datasheet tab that has commands for dealing with a Datasheet object. The contextual tab disappears when you cancel the selection of the object. In other words, close the datasheet and the Table Tools tab will be gone.

When you open an earlier version database that contains menu or toolbar customizations, the changes made in the user interface appear on an Add-Ins tab in the Ribbon (see Figures 30-18 and 30-19). Only toolbars that are visible in the legacy database will appear on the Add-Ins tab. The tooltips of the controls display the name of the control, the control keyboard shortcut, and the name of the legacy toolbar in which they are located (Figure 30-19). The buttons on the Add-Ins tab behave in the same way as they were programmed in the legacy database.

Figure 30-18: A Microsoft Access 2003 database with a custom toolbar named Main Tools.

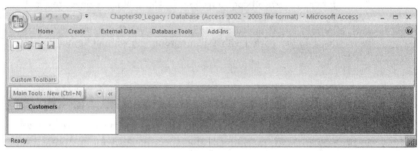

Figure 30-19: In Access 2007, the Add-Ins tab shows the Custom Toolbars group with custom controls that were added to the custom Main Tools toolbar in Access 2003.

Now that you've reviewed the main features of the new Ribbon interface, let's look at how you can extend it with your own tabs and controls. The next section introduces you to Ribbon programming with XML. The XML skills you acquired in the previous chapter should come in handy here.

Ribbon Programming with XML, VBA, and Macros

The components of the Ribbon user interface in the Microsoft Office 2007 system can be manipulated programmatically using Extensible Markup Language (XML) or other programming languages. All Office 2007 applications that use Ribbons rely on the new programming model known as Ribbon extensibility, or *RibbonX*.

This section introduces you to customizing Access 2007 Ribbons by using XML markup. No special tools are required to perform these customizations. XML is plain text; therefore, you can use any text editor to create your customization files. In the examples that follow we'll be using the simple Windows Notepad.

In Access 2007 your Ribbon customizations can be stored in a special Access table, in a VBA procedure, or in another Access database, or they can be linked to from an Excel spreadsheet. When storing your customizations in a location other than the Access table, you must call the LoadCustomUI method of the Application object to load your XML markup manually and then set the Ribbon name in your program at run time. In Access 2007, Ribbon customizations can be applied to the entire application or to specific forms and reports.

 Note: Simple text editors such as Notepad do not provide tools for validating your XML markup. You must be extra careful to write well-formed XML or your code will fail (see Chapter 29 for an introduction to XML terms and markup). If you have access to a copy of Visual Studio 2005, you can use its editor to perform the XML validation based on the XSD schema file. You can download this file (customUI.xsd) from the following web site: http://msdn.microsoft.com/office/tool/ribbon. And, if you'd like to work with the XML in a tree-based format, you may want to download free of charge the Microsoft XML Notepad 2006 at: http://microsoft.com/downloads/. None of these advanced tools are necessary for the completion of this chapter's Ribbon customizations. Each new tool, especially an advanced one, requires that you first familiarize yourself with its interface. To get started with XML programming without further delays, Notepad will do.

Creating the Ribbon Customization XML Markup

To make custom changes to the Ribbon user interface in Access 2007 you need to prepare an XML markup file that specifies all your customizations. The XML markup file that we will use in the hands-on exercise in this section is shown in Figure 30-20 and the resulting output in Figure 30-21.

Figure 30-20: This XML file defines a new tab with two groups for the existing Access 2007 Ribbon. See the output this file produces in Figure 30-21.

Figure 30-21: The custom Edu Systems tab is based on the XML markup file shown in Figure 30-20.

◉ Hands-On 30-5: Creating an XML Document with Ribbon Customizations

1. Open **Windows Notepad** and type the XML markup file as shown below, or copy the code from **C:\Acc07_HandsOn\EduSystems_01.txt**.

```
<customUI xmlns="http://schemas.microsoft.com/office/2006/01/customui">
  <ribbon startFromScratch="false">
    <tabs>
      <tab id="custTabEdu" label="Edu Systems">
        <group id="StudGroup" label="Students">
          <button id="btnNewStud" imageMso="RecordsAddFromOutlook"
            size="large" label="Add Student" screentip="Add Student"
            supertip="Enter new student information"
            onAction="OpenStudentDetails" />
          <button id="btnViewAllStud" imageMso="ShowDetailsPage"
            size="large" label="View Students" screentip="View Students"
            supertip="View Current Students" onAction="OpenStudentList" />
        </group>
        <group id="ToolsGroup" label="Special Commands">
          <button idMso="FilePrintQuick" size="normal" />
          <button idMso="FileSendAsAttachment" size="normal" />
        </group>
      </tab>
    </tabs>
  </ribbon>
</customUI>
```

Let's go over the contents of this XML file. After studying Chapter 29, you know that every XML document consists of a number of elements, called nodes. In any XML document there must be a root node, or a top-level element. In the Ribbon customization file, the root tag is <customUI>. The root's purpose is to specify the Office 2007 RibbonX XML namespace:

```
<customUI xmlns="http://schemas.microsoft.com/office/2006/01/customui">
```

The xmlns attribute of the <customUI> tag holds the name of the default namespace to be used in the Ribbon customization. Notice that the root element encloses all other elements of this XML document: ribbon, tabs, tab, group, and button. Each element consists of a beginning and ending tag. For example, <customUI> is the name of the beginning tag and </customUI> is the ending tag.

The actual Ribbon definition is contained within the <ribbon> tag:

```
<ribbon startFromScratch="false">
[Include xml tags to specify the required ribbon customization]
</ribbon>
```

The startFromScratch attribute of the <ribbon> tag defines whether you want to replace the built-in Ribbon with your own (true), or add a new tab to the existing Ribbon (false).

Hiding the Elements of the Access User Interface

Setting startFromScratch="true" in the <ribbon> tag will hide the default Ribbon as well as the contents of the Quick Access toolbar. The Office menu will be left with only four commands: New, Open, Save As, and Close Database. Use this setting to allow an add-in to place custom buttons in the Quick Access toolbar.

To create a new tab set in the Ribbon, use the <tabs> tag. Each tab element is defined with the <tab> tag. The label attribute of the tab element specifies the name of your custom tab. The name in the id attribute is used to identify your custom tab:

```
<tabs>
<tab id="custTabEdu" label="Edu Systems">
```

Ribbon tabs contain controls organized in groups. You can define a group for the controls on your tab with the <group> tag. The example XML markup file defines the following two groups for the Edu Systems tab:

```
<group id="StudGroup" label="Students">
<group id="ToolsGroup" label="Special Commands">
```

Similar to the tab node, the group nodes of the XML document contain the id and label attributes. Placing controls in groups is easy. The group labeled Students has two custom button controls, identified by the <button> elements. The group labeled Special Commands also contains two buttons; however, unlike the Students group, the buttons placed here are built-in Office System controls rather than custom controls. You can quickly determine this by looking at the id attribute for the control. Any attribute that ends with Mso refers to a built-in Office item:

```
<button idMso="FilePrintQuick" size="normal" />
```

You can download the 2007 Office System lists of control IDs from the following web site: http://www.microsoft.com/downloads/details.aspx?familyid=4329d9e9-4d11-46a5-898d-23e4f331e9ae&displaylang=eng.

As mentioned earlier in this chapter, buttons placed on the Ribbon can be large or small. You can define the size of the button with the size attribute set to "large" or "normal." Buttons can have additional attributes:

```
<button id="btnNewStud" imageMso="RecordsAddFromOutlook"
size="large" label="Add Student"
screentip="Add Student" supertip="Enter new student information"
onAction="OpenStudentDetails" />
```

The imageMso attribute denotes the name of the existing Office icon. You can use images provided by any Office application. To provide your own image, you must use the getImage attribute in the XML markup (see more information in the section "Using Images in Ribbon Customization" later in this chapter).

The screentip and supertip attributes allow you to specify the short and longer text that should appear when the mouse pointer is positioned over the button.

The controls that you specify in the XML markup perform their designated actions via *callback procedures*. For example, the onAction attribute of a button control contains the name of the callback procedure that is executed when the button is clicked. When that procedure completes, it calls back the Ribbon to provide the status or modify the Ribbon. You will write the callback procedures for the onAction attribute in the next section (see Custom Project 30-1).

Buttons borrowed from the Office system do not require the onAction attribute. When clicked, these buttons will perform their default built-in action.

Before finishing off the XML Ribbon customization document, always make sure that you have included all the ending tags:

```
</tab>
</tabs>
</ribbon>
</customUI>
```

2. Save the file as **C:\Acc07_ByExample\EduSystems_01.xml**. By entering the XML extension, the text file is saved as an XML document.

3. To ensure that this XML document is well formed (it follows the formatting rules for XML), open it in a browser. If the browser can read the document, then its output should match Figure 30-20. If the browser finds problems with the document, it will show you the incorrect statement. It is up to you to figure out what correction is required. Open the file in Notepad, correct the erroneous code, save the file, and test it again by loading it in the browser.

4. Close the browser.

At this point, I assume you have a well-formed XML document with Ribbon customizations.

Now that you know how to structure an XML document for Ribbon customizations, you should find it straightforward to add on other features to the Access Ribbon as they are discussed later in the chapter.

Loading Ribbon Customizations from an External XML Document

Since your first Ribbon customization is already in an external XML document, we will go ahead and load it into Access using the combination of VBA and macros. In a later section of this chapter, you will learn how to load the same XML markup into a local Access table and have Access take care of the Ribbon modifications at startup.

Custom Project 30-1 walks you through the steps required to integrate Ribbon customizations into your database application.

◎ Custom Project 30-1: Applying Ribbon Customizations from an External XML File

This custom project depends on the XML document prepared in Hands-On 30-5.

Part 1: Creating an Access Database and Setting Access Options

1. Create a new Access database named **EduSystems1.accdb** based on the **Students** template and save it in your **C:\Acc07_ByExample** folder (Figure 30-22).

    For your convenience this file is included in the Acc07_HandsOn folder in the companion files. Before using this database, please copy it to your C:\Acc07_ByExample folder.

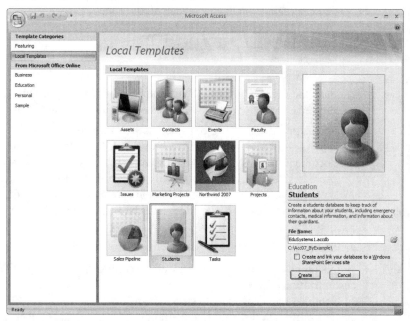

Figure 30-22: The EduSystems1 database is used in Custom Project 30-1 for loading Ribbon customizations.

2. When the EduSystems1 database finishes loading, click the **Microsoft Office** button, click **Access Options**, and then click the **Advanced** tab.

3. In the General section, enable the **Show add-in user interface errors** option (Figure 30-23).

When you enable this option, you will be able to see error messages if errors are encountered when you load your Ribbon customizations.

Figure 30-23: When you check Show add-in user interface errors, Access will notify you about any problems in the Ribbon XML.

4. Click **OK** to close the Access Options dialog.

Part 2: Setting Up the Programming Environment

1. Press **Alt+F11** to switch to the Visual Basic Editor window.

2. Choose **Tools | References**. In the References dialog box, add the reference to the following two libraries: **Microsoft Office 12.0 Object Library** and **Microsoft Scripting Runtime** (Figure 30-24).

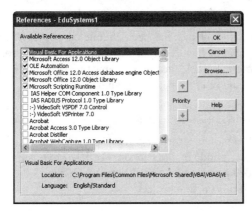

Figure 30-24: To avoid compile errors, you must set library references as shown here.

3. Click **OK** to close the References dialog box.

4. Choose **Insert | Module**.

5. In the Properties window, change the Name property of the module to **RibbonModification**.

Part 3: Writing VBA Code

1. In the RibbonModification Code window, enter the following VBA procedures, or copy and paste the VBA code from **C:\Acc07_HandsOn\ RibbonVBA.txt**.

```
Sub OpenStudentDetails(ByVal control As IRibbonControl)
    DoCmd.OpenForm "Student Details", acNormal, , , acFormAdd
End Sub

Sub OpenStudentList(ByVal control As IRibbonControl)
    DoCmd.OpenForm "Student List", acNormal
End Sub
```

Notice that both procedures shown above open the specified Access forms. In addition, the OpenStudentDetails procedure opens the Student Details form in Add mode. You may recall that these procedures (OpenStudentDetails and OpenStudentList) are the names of the callback procedures that were specified in the onAction attribute of the button XML:

```
<button id="btnNewStud" imageMso="RecordsAddFromOutlook"
    size="large" label="Add Student"
    screentip="Add Student" supertip="Enter new student information"
    onAction="OpenStudentDetails" />
<button id="btnViewAllStud" imageMso="ShowDetailsPage"
    size="large" label="View Students"
    screentip="View Students"
    supertip="View Current Students"
    onAction="OpenStudentList" />
```

As mentioned earlier, a callback procedure executes some action and then notifies the Ribbon that the task has been completed. In Access 2007, the onAction callback can be handled by a VBA procedure, a macro, or an expression. When using VBA, the callback must include the IRibbonControl parameter and return type, as shown below:

```
Sub OpenStudentDetails(ByVal control As IRibbonControl)
Sub OpenStudentList(ByVal control As IRibbonControl)
```

The IRibbonControl parameter is the control that was clicked. This control is passed to your VBA code by the Ribbon. For VBA to recognize this parameter, we added a reference to the Microsoft Office 12.0 Object Library in Part 2 of this custom project.

The IRibbonControl Properties

You can view the properties (Context, Id, and Tag) of the IRibbonControl object in the Object Browser. The Context property returns the active window that contains the Ribbon interface, in this case Microsoft Access. The Id property contains the ID of the control that was clicked. The Tag property can be used to store additional information with the control. To use this property, you need to add the tag attribute to the XML markup. Using the Tag property you can write a more generic procedure to handle the callbacks. For example, instead of writing a separate procedure to open the Student Details and Student List forms as we did in Custom Project 30-1, you could write a single procedure like this:

```
Sub OpenFrm(ByVal control AS IRibbonControl)
    Select Case control.Id
        Case "btnNewStud"
            DoCmd.OpenForm "Student Details", acNormal, , , acFormAdd
        Case "btnViewAllStud"
            DoCmd.OpenForm "Student List", acNormal
    End Select
End Sub
```

Next, you would need to add the tag attribute to the XML markup and change the onAction callback to the OpenFrm procedure name:

```
<button id="btnNewStud" imageMso="RecordsAddFromOutlook"
    size="large" label="Add Student"
    screentip="Add Student" supertip="Enter new student information"
    onAction="OpenFrm" tag="Student Details" />
<button id="btnViewAllStud" imageMso="ShowDetailsPage"
    size="large" label="View Students"
    screentip="View Students"
    supertip="View Current Students"
    onAction="OpenFrm" tag="Student List" />
```

You can see the implementation of the above technique in the EduSystems2.accdb database and EduSystems_02.xml document located in the Acc07_HandsOn folder. Be sure to copy these files to your C:\Acc07_ByExample folder prior to opening them.

2. In the **RibbonModification** Code module, enter the **LoadRibbon** function procedure as shown below, or copy and paste the procedure code from **C:\Acc07_HandsOn\RibbonVBA.txt**.

```
Public Function LoadRibbon()
    Dim strXML As String
    Dim oFso As New FileSystemObject
    Dim oTStream As TextStream

    ' Open the file containing the Ribbon customizations
    ' and return a TextStream object that will be used
    ' for reading from the file
    Set oTStream = oFso.OpenTextFile("C:\Acc07_ByExample" & _
        "\EduSystems_01.XML", ForReading)
```

```
' Read the entire stream into a string variable
strXML = oTStream.ReadAll

' Close the TextStream object
oTStream.Close

' Free up resources
Set oTStream = Nothing
Set oFso = Nothing

' load XML markup that represents a customized Ribbon
Application.LoadCustomUI "EduTabR", strXML

End Function
```

The above procedure uses the LoadCustomUI method of the Application object to load into Access the XML markup that contains your Ribbon customizations. To use this method you must pass in the name of the Ribbon and the XML code that defines the customized Ribbon. In this example, EduTabR is the name of our customized Ribbon. You can name your Ribbon anything you want. The strXML variable contains the XML markup. Because the XML markup must be passed as a text string, the procedure begins by accessing the FileSystemObject from the Microsoft Scripting Runtime (see Part 2 above) and reading the contents of the XML file using the ReadAll method of the TextStream object.

In Part 4 of this custom project you will create an AutoExec macro to call the LoadRibbon function and make the custom Ribbon available to the database application on startup.

3. Click the **Save** button to save changes in the RibbonModification module.

4. Choose **Debug | Compile EduSystems1** to ensure that the VBA code does not contain spelling and other errors. If errors are found, correct them before proceeding to the next step.

5. Press **Alt+Q** to close the Visual Basic Editor window and return to Microsoft Access.

Part 4: Creating an Autoexec Macro

1. In the Access window, click on the **Create** tab, and then click the **Macro** button located in the Other group at the very end of the Ribbon.

2. In the Macro Design window, set the Action to **RunCode**, and type **LoadRibbon()** in the Function Name text box. The function name should automatically appear in the Arguments column (see Figure 30-25).

3. Press **Ctrl+S** or click the **Save** icon on the Quick Access toolbar. Enter **AutoExec** for the macro name.

An Access macro named AutoExec runs automatically each time you open the database. If you need to open a database without running this macro or to bypass other startup options, hold down the Shift key when opening the database. For more information about using macros in Access 2007, refer to Chapter 33.

4. To run the AutoExec macro right now, click on the **Design** tab, and then click the **Run** button.

   If you clicked the Run button and received no error, the macro has run successfully and your Ribbon customization (EduTabR) has been loaded. For the changes in the Ribbon to become visible, you must complete the steps in Part 5 of this custom project.

5. Close the Macro Design window.

Figure 30-25: Creating an AutoExec macro for loading Ribbon customizations via the LoadRibbon() function.

Part 5: Applying the Customized Ribbon

1. Click the **Microsoft Office** button, and then click **Access Options**.

2. Click the **Current Database** option. In the Ribbon and Toolbar Options section, choose **EduTabR** from the Ribbon Name list (Figure 30-26).

Figure 30-26: Enabling a customized Ribbon in the current database.

3. Click **OK** to close the Access Options window.

   Microsoft Access displays a message informing you that you must close and reopen the current database for the specified option to take effect.

4. Click **OK** to the message. Then close and restart the **EduSystems1** database.

   When the database reopens, you should see in the default database Ribbon your custom tab named Edu Systems (see Figure 30-21 earlier in this chapter). Before going on to the next section, allow some time for testing the controls placed in this custom tab.

5. Close the EduSystems1.accdb database.

Embedding Ribbon XML Markup in a VBA Procedure

In Custom Project 30-1, you saw how to load a Ribbon customization from an external XML document. Because the name and path of this document are hard-coded in the LoadRibbon function, prior to loading the database you must make sure that the XML markup file exists in the specified folder or Access will welcome you with one or more error messages. If you don't want to worry about the location of the XML markup file, you can place the XML markup directly inside the VBA function procedure that loads the Ribbon, as shown in Figure 30-27. While the formatting of the XML string is more time consuming than referencing the file directly, it will ensure that your Ribbon markup travels with the database. Placing Ribbon XML markup inside a VBA procedure is not recommended if you plan on using the same Ribbon customizations in more than one database. If the Ribbon needs to be modified, you would need to make changes in several places, which can become confusing.

Figure 30-27: Ribbon XML markup can be embedded inside the procedure.

Storing Ribbon Customization XML Markup in a Table

If you store your Ribbon customization XML markup in a local database table, your XML code will be loaded automatically at startup and you won't need to write a special VBA function to load your markup as you did in Custom Project 30-1. To store your XML in a table, you must create a system table named USysRibbons. This table must include two fields: a text field named

RibbonName and a memo field named RibbonXML. Access expects these specific column names and data types to read your Ribbon customizations. Any additional fields you may add to this table will be ignored. In the RibbonName field, enter a unique name that identifies your custom Ribbon. The RibbonXML field must contain the XML customization markup to be applied to the Ribbon. Please note that the USysRibbons table is a hidden system table. To show this table in the Navigation pane you must tell Access to show hidden objects (see the next hands-on exercise). You can define multiple Ribbons in your database application by adding a new record to the USysRibbons table.

Let's now proceed to Hands-On 30-6 in which you create the USysRibbons table to store the Ribbon customization prepared earlier in this chapter.

◎ Hands-On 30-6: Creating a Local System Table to Store Ribbon Customization

This hands-on exercise depends on the XML document prepared in Hands-On 30-5.

1. Create a new Access database named **EduSystems_Local.accdb** based on the **Students** template and save it in your **C:\Acc07_ByExample** folder.

   For your convenience this file is included in the Acc07_HandsOn folder. Before using this database, please copy it to your C:\Acc07_ByExample folder.

2. In the EduSystems_Local.accdb database, click the **Create** tab, and then click the **Table Design** button.

3. In Table Design view, enter the table structure as shown in Figure 30-28. To make the RibbonName field the primary key, select this field and click the **Primary Key** button in the Tools group of the Design tab.

4. Save the table as **USysRibbons**. (Press **Ctrl+S** or click the **Save** button on the Quick Access toolbar to open the Save As dialog.)

Figure 30-28: USysRibbons is a special system table used for storing Ribbon customizations.

5. In the Design tab, click the **View** button and open the table in the Datasheet view.

6. In the RibbonName field, enter **TestRibbonTab**. Paste the entire contents of the **C:\Acc07_ByExample\EduSystems_01.xml** document into the RibbonXML field. Make changes in the onAction attribute of the buttons as shown in Figure 30-29. In the onAction attribute for btnNewStud, enter **RibbonLib.OpenStudentDetails**. In the onAction attribute for btnViewAllStud, enter **RibbonLib.OpenStudentList**.

Figure 30-29: The USysRibbons table with a record defining Ribbon customization. To define multiple Ribbons in your application, simply add a new record to this table.

7. Save and close the USysRibbons table.

Showing System Objects in the Navigation Pane

By default, system tables do not show in the Navigation pane. If you need to open the USysRibbons table to correct any errors or add a new record, you must enable the system objects in the Navigation Options dialog box.

1. Click the **Microsoft Office** button, and then click **Access Options**.
2. Click **Current Database**, and then in the Navigation section click the **Navigation Options** button.
3. Select **Show System Objects** and click **OK** to close the Navigation Options dialog box.
4. Click **OK** to exit the Access Options dialog.

The next step is to enter the callbacks that are needed for the button actions. In Custom Project 30-1 you wrote VBA callback procedures for the btnNewStud and btnViewAllStud buttons. Instead of a VBA callback, the onAction attribute of the button control can invoke a macro. Macro callbacks do not require that you return a value to the Ribbon. Also, your

Ribbon customization can be functional even in safe mode (when code is not enabled for the database). It is up to you to decide whether to write VBA callbacks or create simple macro actions for your custom Ribbon controls. This hands-on exercise demonstrates the implementation of macros in the onAction attribute for controls.

8. In the database window, click the **Create** tab, and in the Other group, click the **Macro** button.

9. In the Macro Design window, click the **Design** tab, and then click the **Macro Names** button to add a column for a macro name.

10. Add actions for the buttons as shown below and compare with Figure 30-30:

Macro Name: **OpenStudentDetails**
Action: **OpenForm**
Arguments: **Student Details, Form, , , Add, Normal**

Macro Name: **OpenStudentList**
Action: **OpenForm**
Arguments: **Student List, Form, , , , Normal**

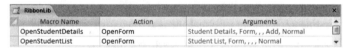

Figure 30-30: Macro callbacks to be used by your Ribbon customization markup.

11. Press **Ctrl+S** to invoke a Save As dialog box. Enter **RibbonLib** for your macro name.

12. Close the Macro Design window.

Now that your macro callbacks are ready, you must tell Access to read your Ribbon definition from the USysRibbons system table. To do this, you must close and then restart the application.

13. Close and then reload the **EduSystems_Local.accdb** database.

When the application starts, Access looks for the USysRibbons system table. If the table exists, Access proceeds to read the data. If any errors are encountered in the Ribbon definition and you have set the option to Show add-in user interface errors (see Figure 30-23 earlier), you will see error messages similar to the one shown in Figure 30-31. Needless to say, you must correct all the errors before Access can display your customization in the Ribbon.

Figure 30-31: Upon loading the database, if errors are found in the Ribbon customization markup, Access displays an error message.

If there are no errors, Access loads your customization; however, before you can see the Ribbon you need to tell Access to apply your Ribbon customization when the application is started.

14. Click the **Microsoft Office** button, and then click **Access Options**.

15. Click **Current Database**. In the Ribbon and Toolbar Options section, choose the name of your customized Ribbon from the Ribbon Name list: **TestRibbonTab**.

16. Click **OK** to close the Access Options window.

   Access will advise you that you must close and restart the application before the changes take effect.

17. Close and restart the database.

   When the EduSystems_Local database is loaded, it should see your custom Ribbon tab named Edu Systems. Take the time to test the controls placed on this tab to make sure that the macro actions are invoked correctly.

18. Close the **EduSytems_Local.accdb** database.

 Note: If you don't want Access to automatically load Ribbon customizations from the USysRibbons table, simply rename this table.

Assigning Ribbon Customizations to Forms and Reports

In addition to customizing the main database Ribbon, Access allows you to create Ribbons that are associated with a particular form or report. To display Ribbon content for forms and reports you can use a contextual tabset called AccessFormReportExtensibility. This tabset is hidden by default; however, it will become visible when it has controls to display. You will insert some commands into this contextual tabset in Custom Project 30-2. Because the contextual tabset takes focus when the form or report is first opened, your users will be able to see right away the special controls you've made available for them. These controls can include built-in icons from other Access tabs or your own custom buttons and other types of controls as discussed later in this chapter.

   Keep in mind that Ribbon customizations for forms and reports are only displayed when a form or report is loaded or activated, and they are removed when the object is closed or deactivated. While a specific form or report is in use, you may also hide other built-in Ribbon items. You can do this by setting the visible attribute of a Ribbon item to False. This will prevent users from using features of the program that you don't want to be available for whatever reason.

To assign a custom Ribbon to a form or report, you need to open a form or report in Design or Layout view, and on the Other tab of the property sheet, choose the Ribbon you want to apply from the Ribbon Name list.

⊚ Custom Project 30-2: Creating and Assigning Ribbon Customization to a Report

This custom project requires access to the EduSystems_Local.accdb database and the USysRibbons table that was created in Hands-On 30-6.

Part 1: Creating Ribbon Customization for a Report Using a Local System Table

1. Open the C:\Acc07_ByExample\EduSystems_Local.accdb database.

   This database will display a custom tab named Edu Systems. Recall from the previous hands-on exercise that the XML markup for this customization is stored in the local system table named USysRibbons. In this exercise, you will add another record to this table to specify a Ribbon customization for an Access report. Before you proceed to the next step, make sure that the USysRibbons table is displayed in the Navigation pane. To unhide the table, follow the steps outlined in the sidebar "Showing System Objects in the Navigation Pane" in the previous section.

2. Open the **USysRibbons** table and enter a new record for the Ribbon named **AlergMedRpt** as shown in Figure 30-32. You can copy the XML markup file from **C:\Acc07_HandsOn\ EduSystems_04.xml**.

Figure 30-32: Entering Ribbon customization for a report.

The RibbonXML field contains the XML markup you want to apply to a report. The RibbonName can be any name you want to use to identify this customization. To have Access use the special contextual tabset that is available for forms and reports, you must use the <contextualTabs> XML tag. Within this tag, use the <tabSet> tag. Because this tabset is defined by Access, you must specify TabSetFormReportExtensibility in the idMso attribute:

```
<contextualTabs>
<tabSet idMso="TabSetFormReportExtensibility">
```

In the next statement, assign a custom ID and a name to the tab that will contain your customization:

```
<tab id="rptTools" label="Report Tools">
```

The above XML statement tells Access to place the focus on the Report Tools tab when the report is opened.

The next two XML statements define the controls you want to display:

```
<group idMso="GroupSortAndFilter" />
<group idMso="GroupFindAccess" />
</tab>
```

In this example, you are telling Access to simply add the Sort and Filter and Find groups from its library of built-in controls. As mentioned earlier, you can download the list of control IDs from the Microsoft web site. Since at this time you are not defining other customizations to appear on this tab, you need to close this XML group by including the closing tags:

```
</tabSet>
</contextualTabs>
```

When the report is loaded, you also want to make unavailable certain built-in features such as controls to collect data and use SharePoint lists. This can be done by setting the visible attribute of the named built-in control groups to false:

```
<tabs>
<tab idMso="TabExternalData" visible="true">
<group idMso="GroupCollectData" visible="false" />
<group idMso="GroupSharepointLists" visible="false" />
</tab>
</tabs>
```

To finish off the customization markup, you need to include the ending tags:

```
</ribbon>
</customUI>
```

3. Press **Ctrl+S** to save changes to the USysRibbons table.

4. Close the USysRibbons table.

Part 2: Making Access Aware of the New Customization

Remember that the Ribbon customization cannot be displayed until you close and reopen the database.

1. Close and reopen the **EduSystems_Local.accdb** database.

   When Access loads, it will read the Ribbon customizations from the USysRibbons table. Now is the time to tell Access to load the customized Ribbon for a specific report.

Note: You should follow the same steps for creating and assigning Ribbon customizations for a form. Of course, your XML markup for a form ought to include the features related to forms and not reports.

Part 3: Assigning a Ribbon Customization to a Report

1. In the Navigation pane, right-click the **Allergies and Medications** report and then choose **Design View**.

2. If the property sheet is not displayed, press **Alt+Enter** to display it. Make sure **Report** is selected in the selection list at the top of the property sheet.

3. In the property sheet, click the **Other** tab, click the down arrow next to the **Ribbon Name** property, and choose **AlergMedRpt** from the drop-down list (see Figure 30-33).

4. Press **Ctrl+S** to save the changes.

5. Close the Allergies and Medications report and then reopen it.

   Notice that when the report opens, the focus is on your custom Ribbon tab named Report Tools (Figure 30-34).

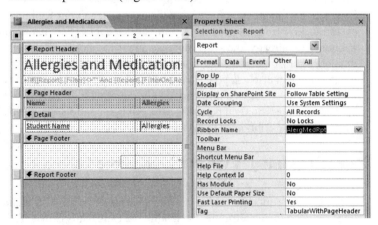

Figure 30-33: Use the Ribbon Name property of the report to assign your Ribbon customization to the active report.

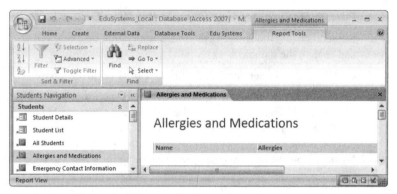

Figure 30-34: The custom Report Tools tab appears in the Access Ribbon when the Allergies and Medications report is opened.

6. Click the **External Data** tab and notice that only two control groups are shown: Import and Export. The other two default groups that normally appear for reports (Collect Data and SharePoint Lists) are removed from the Ribbon. These report groups are made invisible when the Allergies and Medications report is active, and appear on the External Data tab when any other report is open.

7. Close the Allergies and Medications report when you are finished viewing Ribbon customizations.

8. Close the EduSystems_Local.accdb database.

Using Images in Ribbon Customizations

So far in this chapter you have learned how to use in your Ribbon customizations images provided by any Office application that implements the Ribbon. You already know that to reuse an Office icon you must use the imageMso attribute of a control. However, instead of using built-in Office images you can also use your own BMP, GIF, and JPEG image files. These images can be stored in a directory on your computer or a network drive, or in an Access table, and then passed to your Ribbon controls via the loadImage callback for the Ribbon or the getImage callback for a control.

Requesting Images via the loadImage Callback

You can specify the name of a custom image file to be loaded for a specific control on the Ribbon by using the image attribute. When you request the image via the image attribute, the loadImage callback is called. To load images dynamically with one procedure call, define the callback procedure name in the loadImage attribute of the customUI node. Here's a fragment of the XML markup file that we'll use in Custom Project 30-3 to implement this method of loading images:

1. In the first line of your Ribbon customization markup (inside the <customUI> tag), use the loadImage attribute and specify the name of the callback procedure:

```
<customUI xmlns="http://schemas.microsoft.com/office/2006/01/customui"
loadImage="OnLoadImage">
```

2. When defining your Ribbon controls, use the image attribute and specify the name of the image file:

```
<group id="ImagesGroup" label ="Special Features">
<button id="btnNotes" label="Open Notepad"
image="Note.gif" size="large" onAction="OpenNotepad" />
<button id="btnComputer" label="Computer folder"
image="MyFolder.gif" size="normal" />
</group>
```

3. Write the loadImage callback procedure (OnLoadImage) in a VBA module:

```
Public Sub OnLoadImage(imgName As String, ByRef image)
    Dim strImgFileName As String
    strImgFileName = "C:\Acc07_ByExample\images\" & imgName

    Set image = LoadPicture(strImgFileName)
End Sub
```

Notice that to load a picture from a file, you need to use the LoadPicture function. This function is a member of the stdole.StdFunctions library. The library file, which is called stdole2.tlb, is installed in the System or System32 folder on your computer and is available to your VBA procedures without setting additional references. The LoadPicture function returns an object of type IPictureDisp that represents the image. You can view objects, methods, and properties available in the stdole library by activating the Object Browser in the Visual Basic Editor window.

4. Write the callback procedure for the button labeled Open Notepad:

```
Public Sub OpenNotepad(ctl As IRibbonControl)
    Shell "Notepad.exe", vbNormalFocus
End Sub
```

The OpenNotepad procedure tells Access to use the Shell function to open Windows Notepad. Notice that the name of the program's executable file is in double quotes. The second argument of the Shell function is optional. This argument specifies the window style, that is, how the program will appear once it is launched. The vbNormalFocus constant will open Notepad in a normal size window with focus. If the window style is not specified, the program will be minimized with focus (vbMinimizedFocus).

Let's now proceed to Custom Project 30-3, which adds two new buttons with custom images to the Ribbon.

⊚ Custom Project 30-3: Loading Custom Images Using the loadImage Callback

This project requires access to the EduSystems_Local.accdb database and the USysRibbons table that was created in Hands-On 30-6. To use custom images, copy the **Images** folder from the **C:\Acc07_HandsOn** folder to your **C:\Acc07_ByExample** folder.

Part 1: Creating Ribbon Customization for Loading Custom Images

1. Open the **C:\Acc07_ByExample\EduSystems_Local.accdb** database.

2. In the Navigation pane, double-click the **USysRibbons** table to open it. If you cannot find this table, refer to Part 1 in Custom Project 30-2.

3. Enter a new record for the Ribbon named **CustomImage1** as shown in Figure 30-35. You can copy the XML markup from **C:\Acc07_HandsOn\ EduSystems_05.txt**.

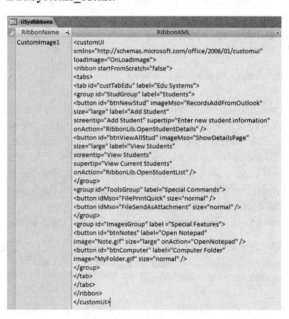

Figure 30-35: Entering Ribbon customization for loading custom images.

In the first line of the Ribbon customization markup (inside the <customUI> tag), notice that we've added the loadImage attribute. This attribute specifies the name of the callback procedure, OnLoadImage, that will handle loading the custom images included in the Special Features group.

The Special Features group contains two images to be loaded from the C:\Acc07_ByExample\Images folder. Notice that the names of these images are specified in the image attribute of each button control in this group. You do not need to specify the file path; the OnLoadImage procedure will contain this information. For the button to perform some action you need to include the onAction attribute with the name of the macro, VBA procedure, or expression to be executed. This example does not define the onAction callback for the button named Computer Folder. To test your skills, you can add your own action for this button when you have completed this project.

4. Press **Ctrl+S** to save changes to the USysRibbons table.

5. Close the USysRibbons table.

Part 2: Setting Up the Programming Environment

1. Press **Alt+F11** to switch to the Visual Basic Editor window.

2. Choose **Tools | References**. In the References dialog box, add the reference to the following library: **Microsoft Office 12.0 Object Library**.

3. Click **OK** to close the References dialog box.

Part 3: Writing the VBA Callback Procedures

1. Choose **Insert | Module**.

2. In the module Code window, enter the following VBA procedures, or copy and paste the VBA code from **C:\Acc07_HandsOn\Chap30.txt**.

```
Public Sub OnLoadImage(imgName As String, ByRef image)
    Dim strImgFileName As String
    strImgFileName = "C:\Acc07_ByExample\images\" & imgName

    Set image = LoadPicture(strImgFileName)
End Sub

Public Sub OpenNotepad(ctl As IRibbonControl)
    Shell "Notepad.exe", vbNormalFocus
End Sub
```

 Note: For the explanations of these procedures, please refer to the beginning of this section.

3. Press **Ctrl+S** to save changes in the Code module window. When asked to name your module, enter any name you want.

4. Choose **File | Close and Return to Microsoft Office Access**.

Part 4: Making Access Aware of the New Customization

Remember that the Ribbon customization cannot be displayed until you close and reopen the database.

1. Close and reopen the **EduSystems_Local.accdb** database.

   When Access loads, it will read the Ribbon customizations from the USysRibbons table.

2. Click the **Microsoft Office** button, and then click **Access Options**.

3. Click the **Current Database** option. In the Ribbon and Toolbar Options section, choose **CustomImage1** from the Ribbon Name list.

4. Click **OK** to close the Access Options window.

Microsoft Access displays a message informing you that you must close and reopen the current database for the specified option to take effect.

5. Click **OK** to the message. Then close and restart the **EduSystems_Local** database.

When the database reopens, you should see in the default database Ribbon your custom tab named Edu Systems (Figure 30-36).

Figure 30-36: The Ribbon customization as defined in Custom Project 30-3.

6. Try out one of the buttons by clicking the **Open Notepad** button to open Windows Notepad. Then close Notepad.

Before going on to the next section, take time to modify the Ribbon XML to include the onAction callback for the button labeled Computer Folder and write your own custom VBA procedure to execute when this button is clicked. For example, you can make this button display a dialog box asking the user for the name of the folder to create and then use the VBA built-in function MkDir to create it. Use the Object Browser to locate this function. Remember that you will have to close and reopen the database for Access to recognize your Ribbon changes.

Requesting Images via the getImage Callback

Custom images can also be loaded to the Ribbon using the getImage attribute of a control. The procedure you specify in this attribute will get the correct image from the specified location using the same LoadPicture function you worked with in the previous section. The following XML markup adds two new controls with custom images to the Special Features group that was defined in Custom Project 30-3:

```
<customUI xmlns="http://schemas.microsoft.com/office/2006/01/customui"
loadImage="OnLoadImage">
 <ribbon startFromScratch="false">
  <tabs>
   <tab id="custTabEdu" label="Edu Systems">
   <group id="StudGroup" label="Students">
    <button id="btnNewStud" imageMso="RecordsAddFromOutlook"
      size="large" label="Add Student"
      screentip="Add Student" supertip="Enter new student information"
      onAction="RibbonLib.OpenStudentDetails" />
     <button id="btnViewAllStud" imageMso="ShowDetailsPage"
```

```
              size="large" label="View Students"
              screentip="View Students"
              supertip="View Current Students"
              onAction="RibbonLib.OpenStudentList" />
          </group>
          <group id="ToolsGroup" label="Special Commands">
            <button idMso="FilePrintQuick" size="normal" />
            <button idMso="FileSendAsAttachment" size="normal" />
          </group>
          <group id="ImagesGroup" label="Special Features">
            <button id="btnNotes" label="Open Notepad"
              image="Note.gif" size="large"
              onAction="OpenNotepad" />
            <button id="btnComputer" label="Computer Folder"
              image="MyFolder.gif" size="normal" />
            <button id="btnRedStar" label="Honor Student"
              getImage="OnGetImage" size="large" />
            <gallery id="glHolidays" label="Holidays" columns="3" rows="4"
              getImage="OnGetImage" getItemCount="OnGetItemCount"
              getItemLabel="OnGetItemLabel" getItemImage="OnGetItemImage"
              getItemID="onGetItemID" onAction="onSelectedItem" />
          </group>
        </tab>
      </tabs>
    </ribbon>
  </customUI>
```

In the above Ribbon customization markup, we are using all the controls that were added thus far in this chapter's hands-on exercises and projects. In addition, the Special Features group now includes a new button labeled Honor Student and a gallery control labeled Holidays:

```
<button id="btnRedStar" label="Honor Student"
  getImage="OnGetImage" size="large" />
<gallery id="glHolidays" label="Holidays" columns="3" rows="4"
  getImage="OnGetImage" getItemCount="OnGetItemCount"
  getItemLabel="OnGetItemLabel" getItemImage="OnGetItemImage"
  getItemID="onGetItemID" onAction="onSelectedItem" />
```

In the above XML markup, the gallery control will perform the action specified in the onSelectedItem callback procedure. To specify your own callback procedure for the Honor Student button, you must add the onAction attribute to this button, and then write the appropriate VBA code. Notice that the gallery control has many attributes that contain static text or define callbacks. We will discuss them later. Right now, let's focus on the image loading process. Both the button and the gallery controls use the getImage attribute with the OnGetImage callback procedure. This procedure will tell Access to load the appropriate image to the Ribbon for each of these controls:

```
Public Sub OnGetImage(ctl As IRibbonControl, ByRef image)
  Select Case ctl.id
    Case "btnRedStar"
      Set image = LoadPicture("C:\Acc07_ByExample\images\redstar.gif")
    Case "glHolidays"
      Set image = LoadPicture("C:\Acc07_ByExample\images\Square0.gif")
```

```
    End Select
  End Sub
```

Notice that the decision as to which image should be loaded is based on the ID of the control in the Select Case statement. The gallery control also uses the OnGetItemImage callback procedure (defined in the getItemImage attribute) to load custom images for its drop-down selection list (see Figure 30-37).

Use the columns and rows attributes to specify the number of columns and rows in the gallery when it is opened. If you need to define the height and width of images in the gallery, use the itemHeight and itemWidth attributes (not used in this example due to the simplicity of the utilized images). The getItemCount and getItemLabel attributes contain callback procedures that provide information to the Ribbon on how many items should appear in the drop-down list and the names of those items. The getItemImage attribute contains a callback procedure that specifies the images to be displayed next to each gallery item. The getItemID attribute specifies the onGetItemID callback procedure that will provide a unique ID for each of the gallery items.

Now that we've discussed the Ribbon customization markup, let's go over the VBA callbacks that are referenced in it. The following procedures need to be added to the VBA module for the above XML markup to work:

```
Public Sub OnGetItemCount(ctl As IRibbonControl, ByRef count)
  count = 12
End Sub
```

In the above procedure we use the count parameter to return to the Ribbon the number of items we want to have in the gallery control.

```
Public Sub OnGetItemLabel(ctl As IRibbonControl, _
                          index As Integer, _
                          ByRef label)
  label = MonthName(index + 1)
End Sub
```

The above procedure will label each of the gallery items. The VBA MonthName function is used to retrieve the name of the month based on the value of the index. The initial value of the index is zero (0). Therefore, index + 1 will return January. To display the month's name abbreviated (Jan, Feb, etc.), specify True as the second parameter to this function:

```
label = MonthName(index + 1, True)
```

If you are using a localized version of Microsoft Office (French, Spanish, etc.), the MonthName function will return the name of the month in the specified interface language.

The next callback procedure shows how to load images for each gallery item:

```
Public Sub OnGetItemImage(ctl As IRibbonControl, _
                          index As Integer, _
                          ByRef image)
```

```
Dim imgPath As String

imgPath = "C:\Acc07_ByExample\images\square"
Set image = LoadPicture(imgPath & index + 1 & ".gif")
End Sub
```

Each item in the gallery must have a unique ID, so the onGetItemID callback uses the MonthName function to use the month name as the ID:

```
Public Sub onGetItemID(ctl As IRibbonControl, _
                       index As Integer, ByRef id)

    id = MonthName(index + 1)

End Sub
```

The last procedure you need to write for the gallery control should define the actions to be performed when an item in the gallery is clicked. This is done via the following onSelectedItem callback that was specified in the onAction attribute of the XML markup:

```
Public Sub onSelectedItem(ctl As IRibbonControl, _
                          selectedId As String, _
                          selectedIndex As Integer)

Select Case selectedIndex
    Case 6
        MsgBox "Holiday 1: Independence Day, July 4th", _
            vbInformation + vbOKOnly, _
            selectedId & " Holidays"

    Case 11
        MsgBox "Holiday 1: Christmas Day, December 25th", _
            vbInformation + vbOKOnly, _
            selectedId & " Holidays"
    Case Else
        MsgBox "Please program holidays for " & selectedId & ".", _
            vbInformation + vbOKOnly, _
            " Under Construction"
    End Select
End Sub
```

In the above callback procedure the selectedId parameter returns the name that was assigned to the label, while the selectedIndex parameter is the position of the item in the list. The first item in the list (January) is indexed with zero (0), the second one with 1, and so forth. In the above procedure we have just coded two holidays: one for the month of July (selectedIndex=6), and one for December (selectedIndex=11). The Case Else clause in the Select Case statement provides a message when other months are selected.

Figure 30-37: Customized Ribbon with the gallery control.

To implement the above Ribbon customization, follow the steps as outlined in Hands-On 30-7.

Hands-On 30-7: Loading Custom Images Using the getImage Callback

This hands-on exercise requires access to the EduSystems_Local.accdb database and the USysRibbons table that was created in Hands-On 30-6. This exercise assumes that you have also completed Custom Project 30-3, which presented a method of loading images via the loadImage callback. Because by now you should be very familiar with the Ribbon customization process, this exercise outlines only the main steps you need to take to complete it.

For a detailed explanation process, refer to the previous exercises and projects. The images used in this example are located in the C:\Acc07_ByExample\Images folder.

1. In the **USysRibbons** table of the **EduSystems_Local** database, add a new record. In the RibbonName field, enter **CustomImage2** for the name of the new Ribbon customization. In the RibbonXML field, enter the following Ribbon XML markup (also shown at the beginning of this section), or copy and paste the XML from **C:\Acc07_HandsOn\EduSystems_05.txt**. Press **Ctrl+S** to save the changes, and then close the **USysRibbons** table.

```
<customUI xmlns="http://schemas.microsoft.com/office/2006/01/customui"
loadImage="OnLoadImage">
 <ribbon startFromScratch="false">
  <tabs>
   <tab id="custTabEdu" label="Edu Systems">
    <group id="StudGroup" label="Students">
     <button id="btnNewStud" imageMso="RecordsAddFromOutlook"
       size="large" label="Add Student"
       screentip="Add Student" supertip="Enter new student information"
       onAction="RibbonLib.OpenStudentDetails" />
     <button id="btnViewAllStud" imageMso="ShowDetailsPage"
       size="large" label="View Students"
       screentip="View Students"
       supertip="View Current Students"
       onAction="RibbonLib.OpenStudentList" />
    </group>
    <group id="ToolsGroup" label="Special Commands">
     <button idMso="FilePrintQuick" size="normal" />
     <button idMso="FileSendAsAttachment" size="normal" />
```

```
        </group>
        <group id="ImagesGroup" label="Special Features">
          <button id="btnNotes" label="Open Notepad"
            image="Note.gif" size="large"
            onAction="OpenNotepad" />
          <button id="btnComputer" label="Computer Folder"
            image="MyFolder.gif" size="normal" />
          <button id="btnRedStar" label="Honor Student"
            getImage="OnGetImage" size="large" />
          <gallery id="glHolidays" label="Holidays" columns="3" rows="4"
            getImage="OnGetImage" getItemCount="OnGetItemCount"
            getItemLabel="OnGetItemLabel" getItemImage="OnGetItemImage"
            getItemID="onGetItemID" onAction="onSelectedItem" />
        </group>
      </tab>
    </tabs>
  </ribbon>
</customUI>
```

2. Press **Alt+F11** to switch to the Visual Basic Editor window. You should see one module with VBA procedures that were added in Custom Project 30-3. You do not need to create a new module for this customization. Simply enter in the existing module Code window the VBA procedures discussed earlier in this section (**OnGetImage, OnGetItemCount, OnGetItem-Label, OnGetItemImage, onGetItemID,** and **onSelectedItem**). Press **Ctrl+S** to save the changes in your module and exit Visual Basic Editor. The procedure code can also be copied from **C:\Acc07_HandsOn\ Chap30.txt.**

3. Close and restart the EduSystems_Local database. When the database is reloaded, click the **Access Options** button in the Office menu. In the Access Options window, click **Current Database**, and select your new Ribbon (**CustomImage2**) from the Ribbon Name list in the Ribbon and Toolbar Options section. Click **OK** to close the Access Options window. Microsoft Access will display a message informing you that you must close and reopen the current database for the specified option to take effect. Click **OK** to the message. Then close and restart the **EduSystems_Local** database.

The customized Ribbon should appear as shown earlier in Figure 30-37. Test the gallery control by clicking on some of the month items.

> **Note:** Instead of loading custom images from a computer folder, you can create an Access table to store your images and then use the Recordset object in the getImage callback to read the images from the table. This table should contain at least two fields: the ControlID field with the name of the control, and ImageFileName specifying the name of the image file for the control. Custom images can also be stored and loaded from an Attachment field, which is available in Access databases created in the ACCDB file format. Please refer to Chapter 31 for more information regarding the Attachment data type.

Understanding Attributes and Callbacks

Ribbon controls have properties defined by attributes, such as id, label, enabled, screen tip, and so on. By using a specific attribute you can modify the appearance of a control either at design time or at run time. To define a control attribute at run time, simply set it to the allowable value right in the Ribbon customization XML markup. For example, you can provide the name for your control in the label attribute. The control label can contain as many as 1,024 characters.

If the attribute value is unknown at design time, add the prefix "get" to the design-time attribute name and specify the name of the callback procedure or macro as the attribute value. For example, if the control's label needs to be defined at run time, use the getLabel attribute and specify the name of the callback procedure:

```
<group id="Today's Events" getLabel="getEventDate">
```

When the Ribbon is loaded, the procedure in the getLabel attribute will run and provide the actual value of the attribute:

```
Public Sub getEventDate(ctl As IRibbonControl, _
                ByRef ReturnValue As Variant)

    ReturnValue = "Events for " & Format(Now(), "mm/dd/yyyy")
End Sub
```

The above procedure will display the current date in the name of the group label. Although many times you will see the callback procedure name prefixed by "get" or "onGet", keep in mind that you do not have to name the callback procedure as the attribute it is used with. Use any name that makes sense to you. The only requirement is that the callback procedure matches a particular *signature*, which is the declaration of the procedure, the parameters, and return types. For example, the callback for the onAction attribute of a button control has the following signature:

```
Public Sub NameOfCallback(control As IRibbonControl)
```

As mentioned in Hands-On 30-6, IRibbonControl is the control that was clicked. This control is passed to your procedure by the Ribbon. You can specify your own name for the control parameter. For example:

```
Public Sub NameOfCallback(ctl As IRibbonControl)
```

Prior to using the IRibbonControl you need to add a reference to the Microsoft Office 12.0 Object Library in your VBA project. The onAction attribute is a special type of attribute that does not need to be prefixed by the word "get" to point to a callback procedure.

Using Various Controls in Ribbon Customizations

Now that you know how to go about creating the XML markup for your Ribbon customizations and loading and applying the custom Ribbon to a database, form, or report, let's look at other types of controls you can show in the Ribbon to give your database application a more polished and professional look. You can reuse the EduSystems_Local database used in the earlier examples to create additional Ribbon customizations that utilize the controls discussed in this section.

Creating Toggle Buttons

A *toggle button* is a button that alternates between two states. Many formatting features such as Bold, Italic, or Format Painter are implemented as toggle buttons. When you click a toggle button, the button stays down until you click it again. To create a toggle button, use the <toggleButton> XML tag as shown below:

```
<toggleButton id="tglNewStudent" label="New Student Questionnaire"
size="normal" getPressed="OnGetPressed" onAction="ShowHideQ" />
```

You can add a built-in image to the toggle button with the imageMso attribute, or use a custom image as discussed earlier in this chapter. To find out whether or not the toggle button is pressed, include the getPressed attribute in your XML markup. The getPressed callback procedure provides two arguments: the control that was clicked and the pressed state of the toggle button:

```
Sub OnGetPressed(control As IRibbonControl, _
                 ByRef pressed)

    If control.id="tglNewStudent" then
        pressed = False
    End if
End Sub
```

The above callback routine will ensure that the specified toggle button is not pressed when the Ribbon is loaded.

To perform an action when the toggle button is clicked, set the onAction attribute to the name of your custom callback procedure. This callback also provides two arguments: the control that was clicked and the state of the toggle button:

```
Sub ShowHideQ(control As IRibbonControl, pressed As Boolean)
    If pressed Then
        MsgBox "The toggle button is pressed."
    Else
        MsgBox "The toggle button is not pressed."
    End If
End Sub
```

If the toggle button is pressed, the value of the pressed argument will be True; otherwise, it will be False.

Creating Split Buttons, Menus, and Submenus

A *split button* is a combination of a button or toggle button and a menu. Clicking the button performs one default action, and clicking the drop-down arrow opens a menu with a list of related options to select from. To create the split button, use the <splitButton> tag. Within this tag, you need to define a <button> or a <toggleButton> control and the <menu> control, as shown in the following XML markup:

```
<group id="OtherControlsGroup" label="Other Controls" >
<splitButton id="btnSplit1" size="large" imageMso="ImportAccess" >
  <button id="btnImport" label="Import More" />
  <menu id="mnuImport" label="More Import Formats" itemSize="normal" >
    <menuSeparator id="mnuDiv1" title="Other Databases" />
    <button id="btnImportODBC" label="ODBC database" imageMso=
            "ImportOdbcDatabase" />
    <button id="btnImportDbase" label="Dbase file" imageMso="ImportDBase" />
    <button id="btnImportParadox" label="Paradox file" imageMso=
            "ImportParadox" />
    <menuSeparator id="mnuDiv2" title="Spreadsheet Files" />
    <button id="btnImportExcel" label="Excel file" imageMso="ImportExcel" />
    <button id="btnImportLotus" label="&Lotus 1-2-3 file" imageMso=
            "ImportLotus" />
    <menuSeparator id="mnuDiv3" title="Other Files" />
    <button id="btnText" label="Text file" imageMso="ImportTextFile" />
    <button id="btnXML" label="XML file" imageMso="ImportXmlFile" />
    <button id="btnHTML" label="HTML file" imageMso="ImportHtmlDocument" />
    <button id="btnOutlook" label="Outlook folder" imageMso="ImportOutlook" />
    <button id="btnSharepoint" label="SharePoint List" imageMso=
            "ImportSharePointList" />
  </menu>
</splitButton>
</group>
```

You can specify the size of the items in the menu using the itemSize attribute. To display a description for each menu item below the item label, set the itemSize attribute to large (itemSize="large") and use the description attribute to specify the text. The <menuSeparator> tag can be used inside the menu node to break the menu into sections. Each menu segment can then be titled using the title attribute, as shown in the above example. You can add the onAction attribute to each menu button to specify the callback procedure or macro to execute when the menu item is clicked. In addition to button controls, menus can contain toggle buttons, check boxes, gallery controls, split buttons, other menus, and dynamic menus. Figure 30-39 displays a split button control with a menu and a submenu consisting of check boxes.

Figure 30-38: This custom split button control uses the built-in Office images.

Figure 30-39: A custom split button control with a menu and a submenu consisting of check boxes.

The XML markup for the split button displayed in Figure 30-39 is shown below:

```
<group id="OtherControlsGroup" label="Other Controls" >
<splitButton id="btnSplit1" size="large" imageMso="ImportAccess" >
  <button id="btnImport" label="Import More" />
  <menu id="mnuImport" label="More Import Formats" itemSize="normal" >
    <menuSeparator id="mnuDiv1" title="Other Databases" />
    <button id="btnImportODBC" label="ODBC database" imageMso=
            "ImportOdbcDatabase" />
    <button id="btnImportDBase" label="Dbase file" imageMso="ImportDBase" />
    <button id="btnImportParadox" label="Paradox file" imageMso=
            "ImportParadox" />
    <menuSeparator id="mnuDiv2" title="Spreadsheet Files" />
    <menu id="mnuExcel" label="Excel File Formats" imageMso="ImportExcel"
          itemSize="normal" >
      <checkBox id="xlsFormat" label="xls file" />
      <checkBox id="xlsxFormat" label="xlsx file" />
    </menu>
```

```
    <button id="btnImportLotus" label="&Lotus 1-2-3 file" imageMso=
        "ImportLotus" />
    <menuSeparator id="mnuDiv3" title="Other Files" />
    <button id="btnText" label="Text file" imageMso="ImportTextFile" />
    <button id="btnXML" label="XML file" imageMso="ImportXmlFile" />
    <button id="btnHTML" label="HTML file" imageMso="ImportHtmlDocument" />
    <button id="btnOutlook" label="Outlook folder" imageMso="ImportOutlook" />
    <button id="btnSharepoint" label="SharePoint List" imageMso=
        "ImportSharePointList" />
  </menu>
 </splitButton>
 </group>
```

> **Note:** The <checkBox> tag used in the above example XML is discussed in detail in the next section.

Creating Check Boxes

The check box control is used to show the state true (on) or false (off). It can be included inside of a menu control as you've seen demonstrated in the previous section, or used as a separate control on the Ribbon. To create a check box, use the <checkBox> tag, as shown in the following XML:

```
<separator id="OtherControlsDiv1" />
<labelControl id="TitleForBox1" label="Areas of Interest (please
            check below)" />
<box id="boxLayout1">
<checkBox id="chkSafety" label="School Safety"
  enabled="true" visible="true"
  onAction="DoSomething" />
<checkBox id="chkHealth" label="Health" enabled="false" />
<checkBox id="chkSportsMusic" getLabel="onGetLabel" />
</box>
```

In the above XML markup, the <separator> tag will produce the vertical bar that visually separates controls within the same Ribbon group (see Figure 30-40). The <labelControl> tag can be used to display static text anywhere in the Ribbon. In this example, we use it to place a header over a set of controls. To control the layout of various controls (to display them horizontally instead of vertically), use the <box> tag. You can define whether a check box should be visible or hidden by setting the visible attribute to true or false. To disable a check box, set the enabled attribute to false; this will cause the check box to appear grayed out. Notice that the check box labeled Health is not active (it is grayed out).

Figure 30-40: These check box controls are laid out horizontally.

Similar to other controls, labels for check boxes can contain static text in the label attribute, or they can be assigned dynamically using the callback procedure in the getLabel attribute:

```
<checkBox id="chkSportsMusic" getLabel="onGetLabel" />
```

The getLabel attribute points to the onGetLabel callback procedure, which needs to be added to your VBA module:

```
Public Sub onGetLabel(ctl As IRibbonControl, ByRef label)
    If ctl.id = "chkSportsMusic" And _
        Weekday(Now(), vbWednesday) Then
        label = "Sports"
    Else
        label = "Music"
    End If
End Sub
```

The above procedure will run automatically upon loading of the Ribbon. If today happens to be Wednesday, you will see a check box for Sports; otherwise, it will be Music.

The action of the check box control is handled by the callback procedure in the onAction attribute:

```
<checkBox id="chkSafety" label="School Safety"
    enabled="true" visible="true"
    onAction="DoSomething" />
```

The DoSomething procedure needs to be added to the VBA module for the School Safety check box to respond to a user's click:

```
Public Sub DoSomething(ctl As IRibbonControl, _
                        pressed As Boolean)
    If ctl.id = "chkSafety" And pressed Then
        MsgBox "Safety is our number one concern."
    Else
        MsgBox "Sorry to hear that safety is not your concern."
    End If
End Sub
```

To get the checked state for a check box, point to your callback procedure in the getPressed attribute, similar to what we've done earlier with the toggle button. The default VBA syntax for this callback is shown below:

```
Sub GetPressed(control As IRibbonControl, ByRef return)
```

➡ **Note:** As mentioned earlier, callback procedures don't need to be named the same as the attribute they are used with. Also, you may change the callback's argument names as desired.

Creating Edit Boxes

Use the <editBox> tag to provide an area on the Ribbon where users can type
text or numbers:

```
<editBox id="txtFullName" label="First and Last Name:"
sizeString="AAAAAAAAAAAAAAAA" maxLength="25"
onChange="onFullNameChange" />
```

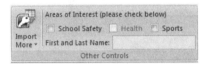

Figure 30-41: An edit box
control allows data entry
directly on the Ribbon.

The sizeString attribute specifies the width of the edit box. Set it to a string that
will give you the width you want. The maxLength attribute allows you to limit
the number of characters and/or digits that can be typed in the edit box. If the
text entered exceeds the specified number of characters (25 in this case),
Access automatically displays a balloon message on the Ribbon: "The entry
may contain no more than 25 characters."

When the entry is updated in an edit box control, the callback procedure
specified in the onChange attribute is called:

```
Public Sub onFullNameChange(ctl As IRibbonControl, _
                            text As String)
    If text <> "" Then
        MsgBox "Is '" & text & _
        "' your real name?"
    End If
End Sub
```

When the user enters text in the edit box, the procedure will display a message
box.

Creating Combo Boxes and Drop Downs

There are three types of drop-down controls that can be placed on the Ribbon:
combo box, drop down, and gallery.

These controls can be dynamically populated at run time by writing
callbacks for their getItemCount, getItemID, getItemLabel, getItemImage,
getItemScreentip, or getItemSupertip attributes. The combo box and drop
down controls can also be made static by defining their drop-down content
using the <item> tag, as shown below:

```
<separator id="OtherControlsDiv2" />
<comboBox id="cmbLang" label="Languages" supertip="Select Language Guide"
    onChange="OnChangeLang" >
        <item id="English" label="English" />
        <item id="Spanish" label="Spanish" />
        <item id="French" label="French" />
        <item id="German" label="German" />
        <item id="Russian" label="Russian" />
</comboBox>
```

To separate the combo box control from other controls in the same Ribbon group, the above example uses the <separator> tag. Notice that each <item> tag specifies a new drop-down row.

 Note: A combo box is a combination of a drop-down list and a single-line edit box, allowing the user to either type a value directly into the control or choose from the list of predefined options. Use the sizeString attribute to define the width of the edit box.

The combo box control does not have the onAction attribute. It uses the onChange attribute that specifies the callback to execute when the item selection changes:

```
Public Sub OnChangeLang(ctl As IRibbonControl, _
                        text As String)

    MsgBox "You selected " & text & " language guide."
End Sub
```

Notice that the onChange callback provides only the text of the selected item; it does not give you access to the selected index. If you need the index of the selection, use the drop down control instead, as shown below:

```
<dropDown id="drpBoro" label="City Borough"
    supertip="Select School Borough"
    onAction="OnActionBoro" >
        <item id="M" label="Manhattan" />
        <item id="B" label="Brooklyn" />
        <item id="Q" label="Queens" />
        <item id="I" label="Staten Island" />
        <item id="X" label="Bronx" />
</dropDown>
```

The onAction callback of the drop down control will give you both the selected item's ID and its index:

```
Public Sub OnActionBoro(ctl As IRibbonControl, _
                        ByRef SelectedID As String, _
                        ByRef SelectedIndex As Integer)

    MsgBox "Index=" & SelectedIndex & " ID=" & SelectedID

End Sub
```

Figure 30-42: The Languages combo box and City Borough drop down controls look the same on the Ribbon.

 Note: The gallery control was introduced earlier in this chapter in the section titled "Requesting Images via the getImage Callback." This control cannot be static; it must be dynamically populated at run time.

Creating a Dialog Box Launcher

On some Ribbon tabs you can see a small dialog launcher button at the bottom-right corner of a group (see Figure 30-17 earlier). You can use this button to open a special form that allows the user to set up many options at once, or you can display a form that contains specific information. To add a custom dialog launcher button to the Ribbon, use the <dialogBoxLauncher> tag, as shown below:

```
<dialogBoxLauncher>
    <button id="Launch1"
        screentip="Show Product Key"
        onAction="OnActionLaunch" />
</dialogBoxLauncher>
```

The dialog box launcher control must contain a button. The OnAction attribute for the button contains the callback procedure that will execute when the button is clicked:

```
Public Sub OnActionLaunch(ctl As IRibbonControl)
    ' open the About Microsoft Office Access box
    DoCmd.RunCommand acCmdAboutMicrosoftAccess
End Sub
```

Figure 30-43: A dialog box launcher control on the Ribbon.

The dialog box launcher control must appear as the last element within the containing group element, as shown in the XML below. This XML code contains the entire definition of the custom Edu Systems Ribbon tab created in this chapter and depicted in Figure 30-43:

```
<customUI xmlns="http://schemas.microsoft.com/office/2006/01/customui"
    loadImage="OnLoadImage">
<ribbon startFromScratch="false">
<tabs>
<tab id="custTabEdu" label="Edu Systems" >
<group id="StudGroup" label="Students">
<button id="btnNewStud" imageMso="RecordsAddFromOutlook"
    size="large" label="Add Student"
    screentip="Add Student" supertip="Enter new student information"
    onAction="RibbonLib.OpenStudentDetails" />
<button id="btnViewAllStud" imageMso="ShowDetailsPage"
    size="large" label="View Students"
    screentip="View Students"
    supertip="View Current Students"
    onAction="RibbonLib.OpenStudentList" />
</group>
```

```
<group id="ToolsGroup" label="Special Commands">
<button idMso="FilePrintQuick" size="normal" />
<button idMso="FileSendAsAttachment" size="normal" />
</group>
<group id="ImagesGroup" label="Special Features">
<button id="btnNotes" label="Open Notepad"
   image="Note.gif" size="large"
   onAction="OpenNotepad" />
<button id="btnComputer" label="Computer Folder"
   image="MyFolder.gif" size="normal" />
<button id="btnRedStar" label="Honor Student"
   getImage="OnGetImage" size="large" />
<gallery id="glHolidays" label="Holidays" columns="3" rows="4"
   getImage="OnGetImage" getItemCount="OnGetItemCount"
   getItemLabel="OnGetItemLabel" getItemImage="OnGetItemImage"
   getItemID = "onGetItemID" onAction="onSelectedItem" />
</group>
<group id="OtherControlsGroup" label="Other Controls" >
<splitButton id="btnSplit1" size="large">
<button id="btnImport" label="Import More" imageMso="ImportAccess" />
<menu id="mnuImport" label="More Import Formats" itemSize="normal" >
<menuSeparator id="mnuDiv1" title="Other Databases" />
<button id="btnImportODBC" label="ODBC database" imageMso=
           "ImportOdbcDatabase" />
<button id="btnImportDBase" label="Dbase file" imageMso="ImportDBase" />
<button id="btnImportParadox" label="Paradox file" imageMso="ImportParadox" />
<menuSeparator id="mnuDiv2" title="Spreadsheet Files" />
<menu id="mnuExcel" label="Excel File Formats" imageMso="ImportExcel"
           itemSize="normal" >
<checkBox id="xlsFormat" label="xls file" />
<checkBox id="xlsxFormat" label="xlsx file" />
</menu>
<button id="btnImportLotus" label="Lotus 1-2-3 file" imageMso="ImportLotus" />
<menuSeparator id="mnuDiv3" title="Other Files" />
<button id="btnText" label="Text file" imageMso="ImportTextFile" />
<button id="btnXML" label="XML file" imageMso="ImportXmlFile" />
<button id="btnHTML" label="HTML file" imageMso="ImportHtmlDocument" />
<button id="btnOutlook" label="Outlook folder" imageMso="ImportOutlook" />
<button id="btnSharepoint" label="SharePoint List" imageMso=
           "ImportSharePointList" />
</menu>
</splitButton>
<separator id="OtherControlsDiv1" />
<labelControl id="TitleForBox1" label="Areas of Interest (please check
                below)" />
<box id="boxLayout1">
<checkBox id="chkSafety" label="School Safety"
   enabled="true" visible="true"
   onAction="DoSomething" />
<checkBox id="chkHealth" label="Health" enabled="false" />
<checkBox id="chkSportsMusic" getLabel="onGetLabel" />
</box>
<editBox id="txtFullName" label="First and Last Name:"
   sizeString="AAAAAAAAAAAAAAA" maxLength="25" onChange="onFullNameChange" />
<separator id="OtherControlsDiv2" />
<comboBox id="cmbLang" label="Languages"
```

```
        supertip="Select Language Guide"
        onChange="OnChangeLang" >
<item id="English" label="English" />
<item id="Spanish" label="Spanish" />
<item id="French" label="French" />
<item id="German" label="German" />
<item id="Russian" label="Russian" />
</comboBox>
<dropDown id="drpBoro" label="City Borough"
    supertip="Select School Borough"
    onAction="OnActionBoro" >
        <item id="M" label="Manhattan" />
        <item id="B" label="Brooklyn" />
        <item id="Q" label="Queens" />
        <item id="I" label="Staten Island" />
        <item id="X" label="Bronx" />
</dropDown>
<dialogBoxLauncher>
<button id="Launch1"
    screentip="Show Product Key"
    onAction="OnActionLaunch" />
</dialogBoxLauncher>
</group>
</tab>
</tabs>
</ribbon>
</customUI>
```

 Note: The above XML code can be copied from the C:\Acc07_HandsOn\ FinalRibbon.txt file to the RibbonXML field in the USysRibbons table in your C:\Acc07_ByExample\EduSystems_Local.accdb database. In the RibbonName field, enter any name you want to use. The VBA callback procedures for this XML code can be entered in the same VBA module. This VBA code can also be copied from the C:\Acc07_HandsOn\FinalRibbonVBA.txt file. Refer to Hands-On 30-6 earlier in this chapter for creating a local system table to store Ribbon customization and using macro callbacks.

Disabling a Control

You can disable a built-in or custom Ribbon control by using the enabled or getEnabled attribute. Here's how we disabled our custom check box control earlier by using the enabled attribute:

```
<checkBox id="chkHealth" label="Health" enabled="false" />
```

Use the getEnabled attribute to disable a control based on some conditions or simply display a "not authorized" message. The following XML code shows how to disable the built-in Relationships button on the Ribbon's Database Tools tab:

```
<!-- Built-in commands section -->
<commands>
    <command idMso="DatabaseRelationships" onAction="DisableRelations" />
</commands>
```

To make your XML code more readable, you can include comments between the <!-- and --> characters. The <command> tag can be used to refer to any built-in command. This tag must appear in the <commands> section of the XML code. To see how this works, simply add the code fragment above the XML code shown in the previous section just before the line:

```
<ribbon startFromScratch="false">
```

The onAction attribute contains the following callback procedure that will display a message when the Relationships button is clicked:

```
Sub DisableRelations(ctl As IRibbonControl, _
                     ByRef cancelDefault)

    MsgBox "You are not authorized to use this function."
    cancelDefault = True
End Sub
```

You can add more code to the above procedure if you need to cancel the control's default behavior only when certain conditions have been satisfied.

Repurposing a Built-in Control

It is possible to change the purpose of a built-in Ribbon button. For example, when the user clicks the DatabaseDocumentor button while the Student List form is open you could display a Database Properties dialog box instead of the default Documentor dialog:

```
<command idMso="DatabaseDocumentor" onAction="ShowDbProperties" />

Public Sub ShowDbProperties(ctl As IRibbonControl, _
                            ByRef cancelDefault)

    If CurrentProject.AllForms("Student List").IsLoaded Then
        ' display Database Properties dialog box instead
        DoCmd.RunCommand acCmdDatabaseProperties
    Else
        cancelDefault = False
    End If
End Sub
```

Only simple buttons that perform an action when clicked can be repurposed. You cannot repurpose advanced controls such as combo boxes, drop downs, or galleries.

Refreshing the Ribbon

So far in this chapter you've seen how to use callback procedures to specify the values of control attributes at run time. But what if you need to update your custom Ribbon or the controls placed in the Ribbon based on what the user is doing in your application? The good news is that you can change the attribute values at any time by using the InvalidateControl method of the IRibbonUI object. To use this object, start by adding the onLoad attribute to the customUI element in your Ribbon customization XML:

```
<customUI xmlns="http://schemas.microsoft.com/office/2006/01/customui"
    loadImage="OnLoadImage" onLoad="RefreshMe">
```

The onLoad attribute points to the callback procedure that will give you a copy of the Ribbon that you can use to refresh anytime you want. In this example, the onLoad callback procedure name is RefreshMe.

Let's say you have a check box that is disabled when the Ribbon is first loaded and you would like to enable it when the user enters text in an edit box. Also, upon entry you want the text of the edit box to appear in uppercase. To implement the onLoad callback, start by declaring a Public module-level variable of type IRibbonUI;

```
Public objRibbon As IRibbonUI
```

The above statement should appear in the declaration section at the top of the VBA module. To keep track of the state of the two Ribbon controls we are interested in, declare two Private module-level variables:

```
Private strUserTxt As String
Private isCtlEnabled As Boolean
```

Next, enter the callback procedure that will store a copy of the Ribbon in the objRibbon variable and assign an initial value to the isCtlEnable variable:

```
' callback for the onLoad attribute of customUI
Public Sub RefreshMe(ribbon As IRibbonUI)
    Set objRibbon = ribbon
    isCtlEnabled = False
End Sub
```

When the Ribbon loads, the check box control will be disabled. You will also have a copy of the IRibbonUI object saved for later use. Now, let's take a look at the XML markup used in this scenario:

```
<checkBox id="chkHealth" label="Health" getEnabled="onGetEnabled_Health" />
<editBox id="txtFullName" label="First and Last Name:"
    sizeString="AAAAAAAAAAAAAAAAAA" maxLength="25"
    getText="getEditBoxText" onChange="onFullNameChangeToUcase" />
```

These check box and edit box controls were introduced earlier in this chapter (see Figure 30-41). In order to change the enabled state of the check box control based on the user action, the getEnabled attribute must be used. The callback procedure for this attribute is shown below:

```
Public Sub onGetEnabled_Health(control As IRibbonControl, _
                                ByRef enabled)
    enabled = isCtlEnabled
End Sub
```

When the Ribbon is loaded, the onGetEnabled_Health procedure will provide the value for the getEnabled attribute. The Health check box will be displayed in the Ribbon in its disabled mode because we have set the value of the isCtlEnabled variable to False in the RefreshMe procedure.

The edit box control contains two attributes that require callback procedures. The getText attribute points to the following callback:

```
Public Sub getEditBoxText(control As IRibbonControl, _
                          ByRef text)
    text = UCase(strUserTxt)
End Sub
```

The above callback uses the VBA built-in UCase function to change the text that the user entered in the edit box to uppercase letters. When text is updated in the edit box, the procedure in the onChange attribute is called:

```
Public Sub onFullNameChangeToUcase(ByVal control As IRibbonControl, _
                                   text As String)

    If text <> "" Then
        strUserTxt = text
        objRibbon.InvalidateControl "txtFullName"
        isCtlEnabled = True
    Else
        isCtlEnabled = False
    End If
    objRibbon.InvalidateControl "chkHealth"
End Sub
```

The above callback begins by checking the value of the text parameter provided by the Ribbon. If this parameter contains a value other than an empty string (""), the text the user entered is stored in the strUserTxt variable. Before a change can occur in the Ribbon control, you need to mark the control as invalid. This is done by calling the InvalidateControl method of the IRibbonUI object that we have stored in the objRibbon variable:

```
objRibbon.InvalidateControl "txtFullName"
```

The above statement will tell the txtFullName control to refresh itself next time it is displayed. When the control is invalidated, it will automatically call its callback functions. The getEditBoxText callback procedure in the onChange attribute will execute, causing the text entered in the txtFullName edit box control to appear in uppercase letters.

The second action that we want to perform is to enable the chkHealth check box control when the user enters text in the edit box control and keep this button disabled when the edit box control is empty. This is done by setting the isCtlEnabled Boolean variable to True or False, and invalidating the chkHealth check box control. When the chkHealth control is marked as invalid, it will call its callback functions. The onGetEnabled_Health callback procedure in the getEnabled attribute will execute, causing the control to appear in the enabled state if the txtFullName edit box control contains any text.

Figure 30-44: The Ribbon controls are shown here after the Ribbon refresh. The Health check box is enabled upon entry of any text in the First and Last Name edit box, and disabled when the entry in the edit box is deleted. The XML markup for this Ribbon customization is contained in the C:\Acc07_HandsOn\FinalRibbon_WithRefresh.txt file.

Note: The IRibbonUI object has only two methods: InvalidateControl and Invalidate. Use the InvalidateControl method to refresh an individual control. Use the Invalidate method to refresh all controls in the Ribbon.

The CommandBars Object and the Ribbon

You can make your custom Ribbon button match any built-in button by using the CommandBars object. In Office 2007, this object has been extended with several get methods that expose the state information for the built-in controls: GetEnabledMso, GetImageMso, GetLabelMso, GetPressedMso, GetScreentipMso, GetSupertipMso, and GetVisibleMso. Use these methods in your callbacks to check the built-in control's properties. For example, the following statement will return False if the Ribbon's built-in Cut button is currently disabled (grayed out), and True if it is enabled (ready to use):

```
MsgBox Application.CommandBars.GetEnabledMso("Cut")
```

Notice that the GetEnabledMso method requires that you provide the name of the built-in control. To see the result of the above statement, simply type it in the Immediate window and press Enter.

The GetImageMso method is very useful if you'd like to reuse any of the built-in button images in your own controls. This method allows you to get the bitmap for any imageMso tag. For example, to retrieve the bitmap associated with the Cut button on the Ribbon, enter the following statement in the Immediate window:

```
MsgBox Application.CommandBars.GetImageMso("Cut", 16, 16)
```

The GetImageMso method above uses three arguments: the name of the built-in control, and the width and height of the bitmap image in pixels. Because this method returns the IPictureDisp object, it is very easy to place the retrieved bitmap onto your own custom Ribbon control by writing a simple VBA callback for your control's getImage attribute.

In addition to the methods that provide information about the properties of the built-in controls, the CommandBars object also includes a handy ExecuteMso method that can be used to trigger the built-in control's default action. This method is quite useful when you want to perform a click operation for the user from within a VBA procedure or want to conditionally run a built-in feature.

Let's take a look at the example implementation of the GetImageMso and ExecuteMso methods. Here's the XML definition for a custom Ribbon button:

```
<button id="btnRptWizard" label="Use Report Wizard" size="normal"
    getImage="onGetBitmap" onAction="DoDefaultPlus" />
```

The above XML code can be added to any of the custom Ribbon definitions you've already defined in the USysRibbons table. Now let's look at the VBA part. You want the button to use the same image as the built-in button labeled Report Wizard. When the button is clicked, you'd like to display the built-in

Report Wizard dialog box only when a certain condition is true. Here is the code you need to add to your VBA module:

```
Sub onGetBitmap(ctl As IRibbonControl, ByRef image)

    Set image = Application.CommandBars. _
        GetImageMso("CreateReportFromWizard", 16, 16)
End Sub
```

When the Ribbon is loaded, the onGetBitmap callback automatically retrieves the image bitmap from the Report Wizard button's imageMso attribute and assigns it to the getImage attribute of your button. When your button is clicked and the Student List form is open, the Report Wizard dialog box will pop up; if the specified object is not open, the user will see a message box:

```
Sub DoDefaultPlus(ctl As IRibbonControl)
    If Application.CurrentObjectName = "Student List" Then
        Application.CommandBars.ExecuteMso "CreateReportFromWizard"
    Else
        MsgBox "To run this Wizard you need to open " & _
            " the Student List Form", _
            vbOKOnly + vbInformation, "Action Required"
    End If
End Sub
```

Figure 30-45: The custom Use Report Wizard button in the Special Features group of the Edu Systems tab uses a built-in image and runs a built-in Access feature based on the condition specified in the callback assigned to its onAction attribute.

Customizing the Office Button Menu

While the Office Button menu cannot be removed, it can be easily customized. You can show, hide, add, or reposition any commands in the menu by preparing Ribbon customization markup. Your menu customization must appear between the <officeMenu> and </officeMenu> tags, as shown in the following XML:

```
<customUI xmlns="http://schemas.microsoft.com/office/2006/01/customui"
    loadImage="OnLoadImage" onLoad="RefreshMe" >
    <!-- Built-in commands section -->
    <commands>
    <command idMso="DatabaseRelationships" onAction="DisableRelations" />
    <command idMso="DatabaseDocumenter" onAction="ShowDbProperties" />
    </commands>
    <ribbon startFromScratch="false" >
    <!-- Office Button Menu section -->
    <officeMenu>
        <control idMso="MenuPublish" visible="false" />
```

```
        <control idMso="FileSendAsAttachment" visible="false" />
        <menu idMso="FileManageMenu">
          <button idMso="ManageReplies" />
        </menu>
        <button id="btnNotes1" label="Open Notepad"
          image="Note.gif" insertBeforeMso="FileSave"
          onAction="OpenNotepad" />
      </officeMenu>
    </ribbon>
  </customUI>
```

In the above XML, we hide two default commands in the Office Button menu
by setting the value of their visible attribute to False. We also add a new option
to the Manage menu command:

```
    <menu idMso="FileManageMenu">
      <button idMso="ManageReplies" />
    </menu>
```

You can also include your own custom buttons as commands in the Office Button menu:

```
    <button id="btnNotes1" label="Open Notepad"
      image="Note.gif" insertBeforeMso="FileSave"
      onAction="OpenNotepad" />
```

You can control the position of your custom commands with respect to other
built-in commands by using the insertBeforeMso and insertAfterMso
attributes.

The customized Office Button menu is shown in Figure 30-46.

Figure 30-46: The custom-
ized Office Button menu.

Chapter Summary

This chapter introduced you to using and customizing the new user interface in Access 2007. After a short overview of the initial Microsoft Office Access screen, Office button, and Quick Access toolbar, we looked at numerous features of the Access Navigation pane. You learned how to use the Navigation pane to access and organize your database objects by using both manual techniques and VBA code. Next, we briefly covered the Ribbon interface to get you warmed up and ready for the Ribbon customization exercises. You learned how to create XML Ribbon customization markup and load it in your database by using the LoadCustomUI method of the Application object or via a special Access system table called USysRibbons. You also learned how Ribbon customizations can be assigned to forms or reports. You spent quite a bit of time in this chapter familiarizing yourself with various controls that can be added to the Ribbon and writing callback procedures in order to set your controls' attributes at run time. In addition to Ribbon customizations, you learned how to modify the Office Button menu.

While this chapter covered many controls and features of the Ribbon, it did not attempt to cover all there is to know about this interface. After all, this book is about VBA programming in Access in general, not just the Ribbon. The knowledge and experience you gained in this chapter can be applied to customizing the Ribbon and the Office Button menu in all of the Microsoft Office 2007 applications.

In the next chapter, we focus on working with the new features introduced in Access 2007 tables, forms, and reports.

Chapter 31

Tables, Forms, and Reports

If you are creating an Access database in the ACCDB file format, then you can take advantage of all the new features introduced in Access 2007 by using the provided built-in tools or programmatically by writing code. This chapter focuses on important new features and enhancements that apply to Access tables, forms, and reports. A number of new features were introduced to make it easier for beginner end users to get started designing and working with Access databases; others were added with the purpose of making Access compatible with the Windows SharePoint Server lists. As an Access programmer, you need to know what is possible with all the new features, regardless of their intended audience.

New Features in Tables

One of the first things everyone notices when creating a new Access database or opening an existing database is how easy it is to create tables. Access 2007 comes with a much improved Datasheet view that allows creating tables on the fly. Simply use the new Add New Field column in this view and start typing in your data (Figure 31-1). Access will automatically recognize whether it's Text, Date, Currency, or another data type. If you'd like to change the field's data type, you can do this easily with buttons provided on the Ribbon. You can rename the default field names (Field1, Field2, and so on) by double-clicking the column heading and typing the new name for the column. While creating table columns in this fashion can be useful for someone who just needs a quick structure to collect data and may not have an understanding of what a data type is, you will be more in control of Access by performing table design in the Design view or writing code using any of the methods introduced earlier in this book.

Figure 31-1: You can create a quick Access table by simply typing in the values for each column; Access will automatically determine the data type for each field.

Another improvement in the table design process is the addition of field templates for creating new fields (see Figure 31-2). You can simply drag onto a datasheet a predefined field from the Basic Fields list in the Field Templates pane. You can also use fields from other table templates such as Assets, Contacts, Tasks, Issues, and Events. The fields available from the Field Templates pane have been preset with specific names, data types, length, and other properties, so that users can get through the table design phase quicker. To display the Field Templates pane, choose Datasheet | New Field. When designing or modifying a table, you can also include fields from other tables. Access 2007 offers the Field List pane (Figure 31-3) that you can access by choosing Datasheet | Add Existing Fields. Simply drag the required field from the Field List pane and Access will either automatically create a relationship between tables or walk you through the process.

Figure 31-2: You can quickly add new fields to a table by using field templates.

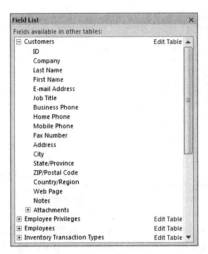

Figure 31-3: Use the Field List pane to quickly add to datasheet fields from other tables in your database. This is the Field List pane as it appears in the Northwind 2007 database.

When designing tables in Access 2007, you will notice the addition of new field data types (see Figure 31-4). The Access ACCDB file format enables new field types such as attachments and multi-value fields. By using the Attachment data type, it is now possible to attach one or more documents, spreadsheets, images, or other files to a table record. Multi-value fields allow you to store more than one value in a field. For example, if you want to assign a task to more than one person, you can use the Lookup Wizard to create a field that contains a drop-down list from which you can select multiple values. You will learn about these new data types later in this chapter.

Figure 31-4: Rich Text fields are memo fields that have the Text Format property set to Rich Text in the table design. They are discussed in detail later. The Data Type drop-down list includes two new data types introduced in Access 2007 that can be created via the Attachment and Lookup Wizard options.

The following table describes 10 different field data types that are supported in Access 2007 when creating tables.

Working with New Features in Access 2007

Table 31-1: Access 2007 data types

Data Type	Description
Text	Stores up to 255 characters. Text fields can contain text, numeric values, or a combination of both. You can change the field length in the Field Size property for the field.
Memo	Stores up to 2 GB of text data. Only the first 255 characters of the memo field can be searched or indexed. Using the table datasheet or text box controls placed on a form, users can work with the first 63,999 characters in memo fields; if your memo field is larger than that, the remaining characters must be accessed programmatically. Memo fields now support rich text formatting, meaning that the formatting options you applied to the text (bold, italic, fonts and colors, numbering, bullets, text highlighting, etc.) will be stored in the database. Memo fields in previous versions of Access could only use plain (unformatted) text.
Number	Stores numeric values up to 16 bytes of data. It can be an integer or a floating type number. The Field Size property of the Number data type can have one of the following values: Byte (1-byte integer), Integer (2-byte integer), Long (4-byte integer), Single (2-byte scaled floating point), Double (4-byte scaled floating point), Replication ID (16-byte GUID), and Decimal (12-byte scaled floating point).
Date/Time	Stores date and time information. Allows a date range of 1 January 100 to 31 December 9999; the time value range is 0:00:00 to 23:59:59. This field provides a new auto calendar feature via its Show Date Picker property.
Currency	Stores monetary values as 8-byte numbers with precision to four decimal places.
AutoNumber	Automatically creates a unique value for a new record. Used for primary keys in Access.
Yes/No	Stores Boolean data of true/false values. Can also be formatted as Yes/No and On/Off. The size of this data type is 1 byte.
OLE Object	Stores up to 2 GB of OLE object data (documents, spreadsheets, images, and other binary files). Storing very large files in the OLE Object will slow down a database. In Access 2007, the Attachment data type is a replacement data type for the OLE Object.
Hyperlink	Stores web addresses. Can store up to 1 GB of data.
Attachment	Stores images, spreadsheets, documents, and other files in table records. Replaces the OLE Object data type used in earlier versions of Access. The Attachment data type is a complex data type that allows multiple values.

Entering dates in a datasheet has become easier as Access 2007 now offers a calendar for picking dates. The Calendar button automatically appears to the right of a column defined with the Date/Time data type (see Figure 31-5). The calendar can be suppressed in the Table Design view via the Show Date Picker property of the Date/Time field.

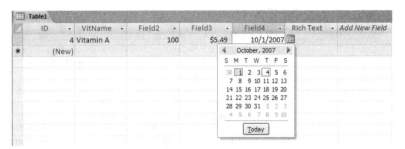

Figure 31-5: You can quickly find and choose a date with the Calendar control.

You can now filter or sort a datasheet by clicking the drop-down arrow in the column header (see Figure 31-6).

To indicate that the datasheet includes only a partial set of data, changes have been made to the Record Navigator at the bottom of the datasheet. Notice the addition of the Filtered button. This button works as a toggle. Click it to clear the filter, and its label will change to "Unfiltered." Click it again, and you again will be viewing filtered data. When the table is not filtered, this button's label will read "No Filter." Another new feature in the Record Navigator is the Search box, which allows you to quickly find data. Simply enter in the Search edit box the string you are looking for and press Enter. Access will move the record selector to the first row that meets your search criteria. Press Enter again to find the next record, and so on. To quickly move the focus to the Search box, press Ctrl+Shift+F. Press Esc to cancel the search. Use the quick search to quickly locate the record you want to edit.

Figure 31-6: Datasheets in Access 2007 offer enhanced sorting and filtering.

Another new and welcome feature of the datasheet is the addition of the Totals row where you can use various functions (Sum, Average, Count, Maximum, Minimum, etc.) to calculate values (see Figure 31-7). To add a Totals row, click the Totals button in the Records group on the Home tab. In the Totals row, click the field you want to add the calculation to, and select one of the aggregate functions from the drop-down list. If the field is too narrow to display all the digits, Access 2007 will display pound signs (#) to indicate that the size of the column should be increased. This new behavior is controlled via the Check for truncated number fields check box in the Application Options section of the current database in the Access Options dialog box (click the Office menu button and choose Access Options).

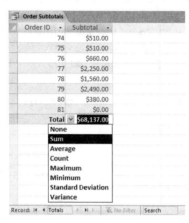

Figure 31-7: Before Access 2007, you could calculate totals in a query, form, or report view. Now you can also add a Totals row to datasheets.

Datasheet rows can now be shaded with alternating colors. This feature is available by clicking the Alternate Fill/Back Color button in the Font group on the Home tab.

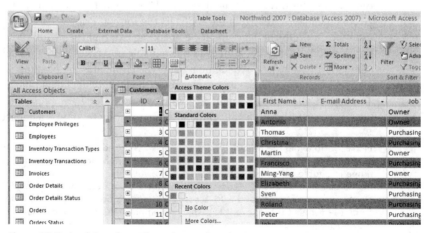

Figure 31-8: Applying alternating colors to datasheet rows.

Saving Tables as Queries

A nice enhancement to Access 2007 datasheets is the ability to save all your customizations as a query. Say you opened an Employee table in Datasheet view and filtered it to display only employees who live in Redmond. You also hid certain fields that you didn't care to see. To have Access create a query based on this modified dataset, click the Office menu button, and choose Save As. Type a name for your query and choose Query from the drop-down in the Save As dialog box. Access will recognize that you have made changes to the datasheet and will advise you that you must save the table before you can create an object based on it. Click Yes to the message. Access saves the table and creates a query in which the filter you applied is preserved and the hidden columns are not included:

```
SELECT Employees.ID, Employees.[Last Name], Employees.[First Name],
       Employees.[E-mail Address], Employees.[Job Title],
       Employees.[Business Phone], Employees.City
FROM Employees
WHERE (((Employees.City)="Redmond"));
```

In earlier versions of Access, any customizations of the datasheet would be lost; Access would create a query based on the entire table and not the modified dataset.

Working with Attachment Data Type Fields

The Access 2007 Attachment data type makes it possible to store various types of external files directly in the database. This new data type is only available in Access databases created in the ACCDB file format. Prior versions of Access used the OLE Object data type for embedding external files within MDB databases, and this format continues to be available in Access 2007 for backward compatibility. The new Attachment data type eliminates the bloating issues that plagued Access MDB databases whenever the OLE Object data type was used. To keep ACCDB files as small as possible, Access 2007 compresses the uncompressed files in the attachments before storing them in a database.

Note: To avoid the bloating issue in Access 2003 and earlier, do not embed external files directly in the Access MDB database. Simply store the external filename in a table using the Text data type. Store your files in the same folder as the database and write VBA code to retrieve the files as needed. The sample Northwind.mdb file included with Access 2003 and earlier has VBA code in the Employee form's Current event to display an employee picture as the user moves through the form.

The Attachment data type allows you to add multiple attachments to a single record; however, keep in mind that the maximum size of an attached data file cannot exceed 256 megabytes. You can store as many external files as you want as long as you stay within 2 gigabytes of data, which is the maximum size of an Access database. You cannot restrict how many attachments are allowed in a database field. Also, some attachment file types are not supported (see Figure 31-9).

Figure 31-9: The unsupported attachment file types.

You can work with attachments manually via the Attachments dialog box (see Figure 31-10), or programmatically using the new Attachment object.

To attach a file or to view a list of attachments, double-click the paper clip icon in a database record. This will open the Attachments dialog box as shown in Figure 31-10. Notice that you can use this dialog box for all your attachment needs.

To add a new attachment, click the Add button. Access will display the Choose File dialog box where you can browse to a file you want to attach and click OK. The selected file will appear in the Attachments list in the Attachments dialog box.

To delete an attachment, select the attachment in the Attachments list and click the Remove button.

To open an attachment, select the attachment in the Attachments list and click the Open button. You can open the attachment to view its contents or to edit it. If you edit the file, Access will update the attachment automatically. Be sure to close the attachment file before closing the Attachments dialog box so Access can reflect your updates in the database.

You can also save a copy of an attachment to any folder on your computer or a network drive by clicking the Save As button. To save all the attachments from a database field, click the Save All button.

You can show the attached data in forms and reports with the new Attachments control that is available in the toolbox. You will see this control at work later in this chapter when we discuss new features in Access 2007 forms.

Figure 31-10: Working with attachments in Access 2007.

Adding Attachments Using the Attachments Dialog Box

Let's start out by adding some attachments to the Attachments column in the Customers table in the Northwind 2007.accdb database. Hands-On 31-1 shows how to store attachments in a database without writing VBA code. Further hands-on exercises will manipulate these attachments programmatically.

◎ Hands-On 31-1: Adding Attachments to Database Records

1. Open the **C:\AccBy_Example\Northwind 2007.accdb** database. Click **Cancel** in the Login dialog box.

2. In the Navigation pane, double-click the **Customers** table.

3. Double-click on the paper clip icon for the third record, as shown in Figure 31-10 earlier. You should see an empty Attachments dialog box. To add the files listed in Figure 31-10 (**California1.jpg** and **California2.jpg**), click the **Add** button. Switch to the **C:\Acc07_HandsOn\External Docs** folder, select the two California JPG images and click **Open**. The names of the selected files are now listed in the Attachments dialog box. Click **OK** to close the dialog box and press **Ctrl+S** to save the record. Notice that the paper clip column now displays the number of attached files in parentheses next to the paper clip icon for the record.

4. Double-click the paper clip icon for the 11th record (FL) and add the **Florida1.jpg** and **Florida2.jpg** files from the **C:\Acc07_HandsOn\External Docs** folder. Close the Attachments dialog box when finished and be sure to save the record.

5. Add the **C:\Acc07_HandsOn\External Docs\Mass1.jpg** image file as an attachment to the 18th record. Close the Attachments dialog box when finished and be sure to save the record.

Working with New Features in Access 2007

Using an Access Query to Return Rows with Attachments

After completing the Hands-On 31-1 exercise, the Customers table should contain five attachment files in three different records. You can find out what records contain attachments by running a query, as shown in the next hands-on exercise. The files attached to database records are stored in a hidden complex data table. While this table is not available for Access users to see, the query designer reveals three columns that are stored in that table: FileData, File-Name, and FileType (see Figure 31-12). FileData is the attachment file itself stored as binary data, FileName is the name of the attachment file, and FileType is the file extension.

➔ **Note:** When you define a complex data type such as an attachment, Access stores this information in the MSysComplexColumns system table. Figure 31-11 shows the contents of this table for the Northwind 2007 database.

ColumnName	ComplexID	ComplexTypeObjectID	ConceptualTableID	FlatTableID
Attachments	1	39	745	77
VersionHistory_F5F8918F-0A3F-4DA9	2	619	659	101
Supplier IDs	3	27	689	94
Attachments	4	39	689	84
Attachments	5	39	64	105
Attachments	6	39	728	110
Attachments	7	39	46	89

Figure 31-11: The MSysComplexColumns system table stores information about the complex data types you have defined in an Access database. The table shown here refers to the data in the Northwind 2007 database.

ColumnName is the name of the complex column. ComplexID is a primary key for the system table. ComplexTypeObjectID stores the ID of the complex data type; 39 is the ID for attachments, 619 is the ID for memo fields with the enabled version history, and 27 is the ID for multi-value fields based on a table or query. The two last columns in the MSysComplexColumns table (Conceptual-TableID and FlatTableID) refer to a hidden system table that is not exposed for anyone to see.

◎ Hands-On 31-2: Using an Access Query to Return Rows with Attachments

This hands-on exercise requires the completion of Hands-On 31-1.

1. Click the **Query Design** button in the Other group of the Create tab.

2. In the Show Table dialog box, select **Customers** and click **Add**. Click **Close** to dismiss the Show Table dialog.

3. Drag **ID**, **Last Name**, **First Name**, and **Attachments.FileName** to the Query grid. In the Criteria row of the Attachments.FileName column, enter **Is not Null** to ensure that only records with attachments are shown (see Figure 31-12).

Figure 31-12: Creating a query to retrieve a list of records with attachments.

4. To run the query, click the **Run** button in the Results section of the Design tab. Access shows the records that meet the criteria.

ID	Last Name	First Name	Customers.Attachments.FileName
3	Axen	Thomas	California2.jpg
3	Axen	Thomas	California1.jpg
11	Krschne	Peter	Florida2.jpg
11	Krschne	Peter	Florida1.jpg
18	Autier Miconi	Catherine	Mass1.jpg
* (New)			

Figure 31-13: Results of running the query in Hands-On 31-2.

5. Press **Ctrl+S** to save the query. In the Save As dialog box, type **qryGetCust_Attachments** for the query name, and click **OK**.

6. Close the qryGetCust_Attachments window.

Working with Attachments Using VBA

To work with Attachment fields in VBA, you need two recordsets: a table recordset that represents the main table data and a child recordset used for accessing and manipulating the Attachment data type. Both recordsets should be declared as Recordset2 objects.

The Recordset2 object represents the records in the main (base) table and the records obtained by running a query. The Recordset2 object was added to the Access 2007 DAO Object Library to support multi-value lookup fields and attachments. If you open the Object Browser and search for the Recordset and Recordset2 objects, you will notice that the Recordset2 object contains the same methods and properties as the Recordset object. The only difference is that the Recordset2 object has a ParentRecordset property, which is very handy in determining if the specified recordset represents a multi-value field.

Similar to the Recordset2 object, the Field2 object has been added to Access 2007 to support multi-value fields and attachments. In DAO, both Field and Field2 objects represent a column of data. The Field2 object exposes special methods and properties for dealing with multi-value fields and attachments. For example, you can use the Field2 object's LoadFromFile and SaveToFile methods to programmatically add and save attachments, and you can use the IsComplex property of the Field2 object to determine whether the specified field is a multi-value lookup or attachment field.

Listing Attachments

Hands-On 31-3 demonstrates how to use new DAO objects (Recordset2, Field2) to retrieve filenames that are attached to records in the Customers table.

◉ Hands-On 31-3: Using DAO to Retrieve the List of Attachments

This hands-on exercise requires the completion of Hands-On 31-1.

1. Press **Alt+F11** to switch to the Visual Basic Editor window.

2. Choose **Insert | Module** to add a new module to the current VBA project.

3. In the module's Code window, enter the following **GetAttachmentNames** procedure, or copy the procedure code from **C:\Acc07_HandsOn\ Chap31.txt**.

```
Sub GetAttachmentNames()
    Dim db As DAO.Database
    Dim rst As DAO.Recordset2
    Dim rstChild As DAO.Recordset2
    Dim fldAttach As DAO.Field2

    Dim strCustName As String

    Set db = CurrentDb
    Set rst = db.OpenRecordset("Customers")
    rst.MoveFirst

    Do Until rst.EOF
        strCustName = rst("Last Name").Value

        'open a recordset for the attachment field
        Set rstChild = rst!Attachments.Value

        Do Until rstChild.EOF
            rstChild.MoveFirst
            Set fldAttach = rstChild.Fields("FileName")
            Do Until rstChild.EOF
                Debug.Print strCustName & Chr(0) & _
                    Chr(45) & Chr(0) & fldAttach.Value
                rstChild.MoveNext
            Loop
        Loop
    Loop
```

```
    rst.MoveNext
Loop

rst.Close
db.Close
fldAttach = Nothing
Set rstChild = Nothing
Set rst = Nothing
Set db = Nothing
End Sub
```

In the above procedure, we open the recordset to access data in the Customers table. For each record in this recordset, we store the customer's last name in the strCustName variable. As we move through each record of the main recordset (rst), we open the child recordset using the following statement:

```
Set rstChild = rst!Attachments.Value
```

In the above statement, Attachments is the name of the attachment field. This statement, which instantiates the child recordset, can also be written as follows:

```
Set rstChild = rst.Fields("Attachments").Value
```

Because a record could contain one or more attached files, we need to iterate through the child recordset to find out whether it contains any attachments. We can get the Attachment field values by accessing the Value property of the Field2 object. We instantiate the field object with the following statement:

```
Set fldAttach = rstChild.Fields("FileName")
```

Recall from the earlier discussion that FileName is the name of the attached file. If the field in the child recordset contains at least one attachment, the procedure writes the customer's last name and the attachment's filename to the Immediate window. Chr(0) will generate a space and Chr(45) a dash; these will separate the customer's last name from the filename, as in the following:

```
Axen - California1.jpg
Axen - California2.jpg
Krschne - Florida1.jpg
Krschne - Florida2.jpg
Autier Miconi - Mass1.jpg
```

After the data is retrieved, we perform the usual resource cleanup:

```
rst.Close
db.Close
Set fldAttach = Nothing
Set rstChild = Nothing
Set rst = Nothing
Set db = Nothing
```

4. Position the insertion point anywhere within the GetAttachmentNames procedure and press **F5** to run it.

5. Press **Ctrl+G** to activate the Immediate window. You should see the names of the five files that were added to three customer records in Hands-On 31-1.

Retrieving the Fields Defined by the Attachment Data Type

Access 2007 stores information about the attached files in different fields of the child recordset. To generate the listing of the fields defined by the Attachment data type, you could write the following VBA procedure:

```
Sub FieldNamesInAttachments()
    Dim db As DAO.Database
    Dim rst As DAO.Recordset2
    Dim fldMain As DAO.Field2
    Dim fldChild As DAO.Field2
    Dim fldItem As DAO.Field2

    Set db = CurrentDb
    Set rst = db.OpenRecordset("Customers")

    For Each fldMain In rst.Fields
        If fldMain.IsComplex Then
            Set fldChild = rst.Fields(fldMain.Name)
            For Each fldItem In fldChild.ComplexType.Fields
                Debug.Print fldItem.Name
            Next
        End If
    Next
    rst.Close
    db.Close
    Set fldItem = Nothing
    Set fldChild = Nothing
    Set fldMain = Nothing
    Set rst = Nothing
    Set db = Nothing
End Sub
```

The above procedure iterates through all the fields in the Customers table and uses the IsComplex property of the Field2 object (fldMain) to determine whether the particular field is a multi-value or attachment field. Once the complex data type field is found, a child recordset is opened for that field. The ComplexType property of the Field2 object (fldChild) is then used to access the collection of fields defined for the complex data type:

```
For Each fldItem In fldChild.ComplexType.Fields
    Debug.Print fldItem.Name
Next
```

The above statement prints to the Immediate window the names of six fields defined by the Attachment data type:

```
FileData
FileFlags
FileName
FileTimeStamp
```

```
FileType
FileURL
```

Three of these fields (FileData, FileName, and FileType) were mentioned earlier in this chapter.

The FileFlags and FileTimeStamp fields are reserved for future use. The
FileURL field stores the URL for a linked SharePoint list. The value of this
field is Null for Access tables.

Saving Attachments

Files attached to database records can be stored in any location on disk using
the SaveToFile method of the Recordset2 object.

Hands-On 31-4 creates a new folder named Collect Attachments on your
disk drive and saves to this folder all attachments found in the Customers table.

⊚ Hands-On 31-4: Using DAO to Save Attachments to Disk

This hands-on exercise requires the completion of Hands-On 31-1.

1. In a Visual Basic module, enter the following **SaveAttachmentsToDisk**
   procedure, or copy the procedure code from the **C:\Acc07_HandsOn\
   Chap31.txt** file. You can enter the code in the same module where you
   entered the procedure in Hands-On 31-3, or you can create a new module
   for this code.

```
Sub SaveAttachmentsToDisk()
    Dim db As DAO.Database
    Dim rst As DAO.Recordset2
    Dim rstChild As DAO.Recordset
    Dim fldAttach As DAO.Field2
    Dim strFile As String

    Const dirName = "C:\CollectAttachments"
    Set db = CurrentDb

    ' Open the recordset for the Customers table
    Set rst = db.OpenRecordset("Customers")
    rst.MoveFirst

    Do Until rst.EOF
        'open a recordset for the attachment field
        Set rstChild = rst!Attachments.Value

        Do Until rstChild.EOF
            If Dir(dirName, vbDirectory) = "" Then MkDir dirName
            rstChild.MoveFirst
            ' get the binary data of the attachment file
            Set fldAttach = rstChild.Fields("FileData")
                Do Until rstChild.EOF
                    strFile = dirName & "\" & rstChild.Fields("FileName").Value
                    If Dir(strFile) = "" Then
                        fldAttach.SaveToFile strFile
                    End If
```

```
            rstChild.MoveNext
        Loop
    Loop
    rst.MoveNext
Loop

    Set rstChild = Nothing
    rst.Close
    Set rst = Nothing
    Set db = Nothing
End Sub
```

The above procedure iterates through all the records in the Customers table and copies all found attachment files to the directory specified in the constant dirName. Notice that the procedure uses the VBA Dir function to determine if the specified directory already exists on the computer. If the directory does not exist, the VBA MkDir function is used to create a new folder with the specified name:

```
    If Dir(dirName, vbDirectory) = "" Then MkDir dirName
```

The Dir function is also used to find out if the attachment file already exists in the specified directory. If the file does not exist, then we pass the name of the file to the SaveToFile method of the fldAttach object variable. The SavetoFile method is exposed in DAO by the new Field2 object. Notice that to save the attachment you need to get the binary data of the attached file. This is done by accessing the FileData field in the child recordset:

```
    Set fldAttach = rstChild.Fields("FileData")
```

2. Run the SaveAttachmentsToDisk procedure.

3. Check the contents of the C:\CollectAttachments folder. You should see the five image files that you added to the Customers table via the Attachments dialog box in Hands-On 31-1.

Adding Attachments

In Hands-On 31-1, you used the Attachments dialog box to add external files to records in the Customers table. Hands-On 31-5 demonstrates how to add attachment files programmatically.

◎ Hands-On 31-5: Using DAO to Add an Attachment to a Table Record

1. In a Visual Basic module, enter the following **AddAttachmentToRecord** procedure, or copy the procedure code from the **C:\Acc07_HandsOn\ Chap31.txt** file. You can enter the code in the same module where you entered the procedure in Hands-On 31-4, or you can create a new module for this code.

```
Sub AddAttachmentToRecord()
    Dim db As DAO.Database
    Dim rst As DAO.Recordset2
    Dim rstChild As DAO.Recordset2
    Dim addFlag As Boolean

    Const dirName = "C:\Acc07_HandsOn\External Docs\"
    Const fileN = "California3.jpg"

    Set db = CurrentDb

    ' Open the recordset for the Customers table
    Set rst = db.OpenRecordset("Customers")

    'move to the 16th customer (count records from 0)
    rst.Move 15

    ' initialize child recordset
    Set rstChild = rst.Fields("Attachments").Value

    If rstChild.RecordCount > 0 Then
    'check if the specified file is already attached
        Do Until rstChild.EOF
            If rstChild.Fields("FileName").Value = fileN Then
                addFlag = True
                Exit Do
            End If
        Loop
    End If
    If addFlag Then MsgBox "The specified file " & fileN & _
                " is already attached to this record."
    If Not addFlag Then
        ' put the parent recordset in Edit mode
        rst.Edit
        ' add a new record to the child recordset
        rstChild.AddNew
        ' load the attchment file
        rstChild.Fields("FileData").LoadFromFile dirName & fileN
        ' update both the child and parent recordsets
        rstChild.Update
        rst.Update

        MsgBox "Successfully attached " & fileN & " to " & _
                rst.Fields(1).Value & " record."
    End If

    rstChild.Close
    Set rstChild = Nothing
    rst.Close
    Set rst = Nothing
    Set db = Nothing
End Sub
```

The above procedure adds an attachment to the 16th record in the Customers table. This is a record for Company P. Prior to adding a record to the child recordset that holds the records for the Attachment field, the procedure checks the RecordCount property of the child recordset to see if the specified file is already attached.

If RecordCount is greater than zero (0), then the addFlag Boolean variable is set to True and the user will see a message that the file is already attached. The procedure will then end. If the addFlag Boolean variable is False, then we know that it is okay to add the file. Note that before adding a new record to the child recordset you must put the parent recordset in Edit mode using the Edit method of the Recordset object. Next, call the AddNew method of the child recordset to add a new child record, and use the LoadFromFile method to load the new attachment file. To finish off, be sure to update both the child and parent recordsets.

2. Run the AddAttachmentToRecord procedure.

3. Press **Alt+F11** to switch to the Microsoft Access main window.

4. In the Navigation pane, double-click the **Customers** table. Find the 16th record in this table and check out the paper clip column. It should indicate that one record is attached.

5. Close the **Customers** table and press **Alt+F11** to return to the Visual Basic Editor window.

6. Run the AddAttachmentToRecord procedure again to test the condition when the attachment file already exists for the specified record.

Deleting Attachments

The following hands-on exercise uses the Delete method of the Recordset2 object to delete an attachment from a table record.

⦿ Hands-On 31-6: Using DAO to Delete an Attachment from a Table Record

This hands-on exercise requires the completion of Hands-On 31-5.

1. In a Visual Basic module, enter the following **RemoveAttachmentFrom-Record** procedure, or copy the procedure code from the **C:\Acc07_HandsOn\Chap31.txt** file. You can enter the code in the same module where you entered the procedure in Hands-On 31-5, or you can create a new module for this code.

```
Sub RemoveAttachmentFromRecord()
    Dim db As DAO.Database
    Dim rst As DAO.Recordset2
    Dim rstChild As DAO.Recordset2
    Dim removeFlag As Boolean

    Const dirName = "C:\Acc07_HandsOn\External Docs\"
    Const fileN = "California3.jpg"

    Set db = CurrentDb

    ' Open the recordset for the Customers table
```

```
Set rst = db.OpenRecordset("Customers")

'move to the 16th customer
rst.Move 15

' get the child recordset for the Attachment field
Set rstChild = rst.Fields("Attachments").Value

' search for the attachment file and remove it if found
Do Until rstChild.EOF
   If rstChild.Fields("FileName").Value = fileN Then
      rstChild.Delete
      removeFlag = True
   End If
   rstChild.MoveNext
Loop
' display a message
If Not removeFlag Then
   MsgBox "The specified file " & fileN & _
         " is not attached to this record.", _
         vbOKOnly + vbInformation, "Nothing to Remove"
Else
   MsgBox "The specified file " & fileN & _
         " was deleted from this record.", _
         vbOKOnly + vbInformation, "Attachment Removed"
End If

' cleanup code
rstChild.Close
Set rstChild = Nothing
rst.Close
Set rst = Nothing
Set db = Nothing
End Sub
```

2. Run the RemoveAttachmentFromRecord procedure.

3. Press **Alt+F11** to switch to the Microsoft Access main window.

4. In the Navigation pane, double-click the **Customers** table. Find the 16th record in this table and check out the Attachment field. It should indicate that there are no attachments.

5. Close the **Customers** table and press **Alt+F11** to return to the Visual Basic Editor window.

6. Run the RemoveAttachmentFromRecord procedure again to test the condition when the attachment file for the specified record does not exist.

Now that you've learned about using and programming the Attachment data type, let's proceed to the next complex data type that the new Access 2007 ACCDB format provides — multi-value fields.

Working with Multi-value Fields

Thanks to the introduction of the complex multi-value data type in the ACCDB file format, table columns can store more than one value. This makes it easy for any Access user to create a lookup field without knowing much about setting table relationships. Access will automatically store the values entered in multi-value fields in hidden system tables and create proper table relationships if necessary. The source data for a multi-value field can be one of the following: Value List, Field List, or Table/Query. To have Access guide you in the creation of a multi-value field, choose Lookup Wizard in the Data Type column of the table's Design view.

The following hands-on exercise demonstrates how to use the Access user interface to add a multi-value field named Literature Sent to the Northwind 2007 database's Customers table.

⊚ Hands-On 31-7: Creating a Multi-value Lookup Field

1. Open the **Customers** table in the **Northwind 2007.accdb** database in Design view.

2. Type **Literature Sent** in the Field Name column of the first empty row. In the Data Type column, select **Lookup Wizard** from the drop-down list.

3. Access will display the first screen of the Lookup Wizard. Click the second option button, which is labeled "I will type in the values that I want." Then click **Next** to continue.

4. Access displays the second Lookup Wizard screen, where you specify the values you want to store. Type the values shown in Figure 31-14 and press **Next** when done.

Figure 31-14: Values entered in each column cell will appear in the lookup list.

5. Access displays the next Lookup Wizard screen (Figure 31-15). Make sure that the **Allow Multiple Values** check box is selected, and click **Finish**.

When you click Finish, you are returned to the table's Design view. Notice that Access has entered Text as the data type for the Literature Sent field. The Field Properties Lookup tab shows properties that were automatically set to enable the lookup feature (see Figure 31-16). Setting the Allow Multiple Values property to Yes indicates that Access should create a field that accepts more than one value.

Figure 31-15: To have Access create a multi-value field, be sure to check the Allow Multiple Values check box.

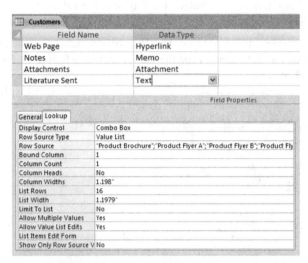

Figure 31-16: The Field Properties Lookup tab contains numerous properties that tell Access how to display values in the Literature Sent field.

6. Press **Ctrl+S** to save the changes in the Customers table, and then close the table.

7. Open the **Customers** table in Datasheet view, and click the drop-down arrow in the **Literature Sent** field of the first record. Access displays a

drop-down list that contains check boxes allowing you to select one or more values. Make your selections as shown in Figure 31-17 and click **OK**.

Customers						
ZIP/Postal C ▾	Country/Reg ▾	Web Page ▾	Notes ▾	ⓘ	Literature Sent	▾
⊞ 99999	USA			ⓘ(0)		
⊞ 99999	USA			ⓘ(0)	☐ Product Brochure	
⊞ 99999	USA			ⓘ(2)	☑ Product Flyer A	
⊞ 99999	USA			ⓘ(0)	☐ Product Flyer B	
⊞ 99999	USA			ⓘ(0)	☑ Product Flyer C	
⊞ 99999	USA			ⓘ(0)	☐ Sales Agreement	
⊞ 99999	USA			ⓘ(0)	☑ Company Portfolio	
⊞ 99999	USA			ⓘ(0)	[OK] [Cancel]	
⊞ 99999	USA			ⓘ(0)		

Figure 31-17: Literature Sent is a multi-value field that can store one or more values. The values are shown in the order they were entered.

When you click OK, Access displays the chosen values separated by commas and in alphabetical order — Company Portfolio, Product Flyer A, Product Flyer C.

8. Close the **Customers** table.

Editing Values in a Multi-value Field

Users can edit the list of values that are displayed in the multi-value fields if the Allow Value List Edits property is set to Yes on the Lookup tab in the Field Properties area of the table's Design view (see Figure 31-16 earlier). When this property is set to Yes, Access displays a small Edit button below the drop-down box that users can click to add a new item to the list (see Figures 31-18 and 31-19). This button is hard to spot when it first appears but becomes more obvious when you move the mouse over it. To display the Edit List Items dialog, you can also right-click the drop-down list and choose Edit List Items.

Figure 31-18: You can add a new item to the list by clicking the edit button that appears when you open the drop-down.

Figure 31-19: When the RowSourceType property of the multi-value lookup field is set to Value List (Figure 31-16), and the user clicks the button shown in Figure 31-18, Access displays an Edit List Items dialog where list items can be modified or added. After closing the dialog, the updated values immediately appear in the drop-down list.

If the drop-down values are provided by a table or query, you must specify the form Access should open in order for users to add new values to the table. This is done by selecting the form name in the List Items Edit Form property on the Lookup tab in the Field Properties area of the table's Design view. The Northwind 2007 database contains the Products table with a multi-value field named Supplier IDs. The RowSource property of this lookup field has the following SQL statement:

```
SELECT [Suppliers Extended].[ID], [Suppliers Extended].[Company]
FROM [Suppliers Extended]
ORDER BY [Suppliers Extended].[Company];
```

If you set the List Items Edit Form property to Supplier List, users will be able to add a new value to the Supplier IDs field by entering a new record in the Supplier List table. Access will open this table when a user clicks on the Edit button that appears below the drop-down list.

Using an Access Query to Return Rows with Multi-value Fields

You can find out what records contain multiple values by running a query, as shown in the next hands-on exercise. The Query Designer reveals a Value field that Access uses to store the values entered in a multi-value field (see Figure 31-21 in Hands-On 31-8). As with the other complex data types, Access stores the information about the multi-value fields in its system table — MSysComplexColumns (see Figure 31-20).

ColumnName	ComplexID	ComplexTypeObjectID	ConceptualTableID	FlatTableID
Attachments	1	39	745	77
VersionHistory_F5F8918F-0A3F-4DA9-AE71-184EE5012880	2	619	659	101
Supplier IDs	3	27	689	94
Attachments	4	39	689	84
Attachments	5	39	64	105
Attachments	6	39	728	110
Attachments	7	39	46	89
Literature Sent	8	37	46	210

Figure 31-20: MSysComplexColumns is a system table updated by Access each time you create a complex data type. The table shown here refers to the data in the Northwind 2007 database after the addition of the Literature Sent field in Hands-On 31-7.

As noted earlier in this chapter, ComplexTypeObjectID stores the ID of the complex data type — 39 is the ID for attachments, 619 is the ID for memo fields with the enabled version history, 27 is the ID for multi-value fields based on a table or query, and 37 is the ID for multi-value fields based on a value list. The last two columns in the MSysComplexColumns table (ConceptualTableID and FlatTableID) refer to a hidden system table that is not exposed for anyone to see.

Working with New Features in Access 2007

⊚ Hands-On 31-8: Using an Access Query to Return Rows with Multi-value Fields

This hands-on exercise requires the completion of Hands-On 31-7.

1. Click the **Query Design** button in the Other group of the Create tab.

2. In the Show Table dialog box, select **Customers** and click **Add**. Click **Close** to dismiss the Show Table dialog.

3. Drag **ID**, **Company**, **Last Name**, and **Literature Sent.Value** to the Query grid. In the Criteria row of the Literature Sent.Value column, enter **Is Not Null** to ensure that only records with multiple values are shown (Figure 31-21).

Figure 31-21: Creating a query to retrieve a list of records with multi-value fields.

4. To run the query, click the **Run** button in the Results section of the Design tab. Access shows the records that meet the criteria.

ID	Company	Last Name	Customers.Literature Sent.Value
1	Company A	Bedecs	Product Flyer A
1	Company A	Bedecs	Product Flyer C
1	Company A	Bedecs	Company Portfolio
*	(New)		

Figure 31-22: Results of running the query in this hands-on exercise.

5. Press **Ctrl+S** to save the query. In the Save As dialog box, type **qryGetCust_MultiValues** for the query name, and click **OK**.

6. Close the qryGetCust_MultiValues window.

Working with Multi-value Fields Using VBA

As with the Attachment data type, you will need a child recordset to manipulate multi-value fields in DAO. Hands-On 31-9 demonstrates how to retrieve literature items that were sent to a customer.

◉ Hands-On 31-9: Using DAO to Manipulate Multi-value Fields

This hands-on exercise requires the completion of Hands-On 31-7.

1. In the Visual Basic Editor window, choose **Insert | Module** to add a new module to the current VBA project (Northwind 2007).

2. In the module's Code window, enter the following **RetrieveMultiValues** procedure, or copy the procedure code from the **C:\Acc07_HandsOn\ Chap31.txt** file.

```
Sub RetrieveMultiValues()
    Dim db As DAO.Database
    Dim rst As DAO.Recordset2
    Dim rstChild As DAO.Recordset2
    Dim strCustName As String

    Set db = CurrentDb
    Set rst = db.OpenRecordset("Customers")
    rst.MoveFirst

    ' open the parent recordset
    Do Until rst.EOF
        strCustName = rst![Last Name].Value

        ' open the child recordset
        Set rstChild = rst![Literature Sent].Value
        If rstChild.RecordCount > 0 Then Debug.Print strCustName
        Do Until rstChild.EOF
            Debug.Print Chr(0) & Chr(45) & Chr(0) _
                & rstChild!Value.Value
            rstChild.MoveNext
        Loop
        rst.MoveNext
    Loop

    ' cleanup
    rst.Close
    db.Close
    Set rstChild = Nothing
    Set rst = Nothing
    Set db = Nothing
End Sub
```

The above procedure iterates through the parent recordset and its child recordset that contains the multi-value field named Literature Sent. To instantiate the child recordset, the Value property of the multi-value field is used:

```
Set rstChild = rst![Literature Sent].Value
```

If a customer record contains at least one value in the Literature Sent column, the customer name will be printed to the Immediate window. To retrieve the field values, the procedure iterates through the child recordset.

3. Run the RetrieveMultiValues procedure.

Afer you run the procedure, you should see the following output in the Immediate window:

```
Bedecs
 - Company Portfolio
 - Product Flyer A
 - Product Flyer C
```

Adding Values to Multi-value Lookup Fields

You can add a new value to a multi-value field by modifying its RowSource propery when the RowSourceType property is set to Value List. The function procedure in the next hands-on exercise adds a new value named "Dinner Invitation" to the Literature Sent multi-value field in the Customers table

◎ Hands-On 31-10: Using DAO to Add Values to a Multi-value Field

1. In the Visual Basic Editor window, in the same module where you entered the procedure in Hands-On 31-9, enter the following **AddToMulti-ValueList** function procedure, or copy the procedure code from the **C:\Acc07_HandsOn\Chap31.txt** file.

```
Function AddToMultiValueList(strTblName As String, _
                            strMultiFldName As String, _
                            strNewVal As String)
        Dim db As DAO.Database
        Dim tdf As DAO.TableDef
        Dim fld As DAO.Field2
        Dim prp As DAO.Property

        On Error GoTo ErrorHandler

        Set db = CurrentDb
        Set tdf = db.TableDefs(strTblName)
        Set fld = tdf.Fields(strMultiFldName)

        If fld.Properties("RowSourceType").Value = "Value List" Then
            Set prp = fld.Properties("RowSource")
            Debug.Print prp.Value

            If InStr(1, prp.Value, strNewVal) = 0 Then
                prp.Value = prp.Value & Chr(59) & Chr(34) _
                    & strNewVal & Chr(34)
                Debug.Print prp.Value
            End If
        End If

ExitHere:
        Set prp = Nothing
```

```
    Set fld = Nothing
    Set tdf = Nothing
    Set db = Nothing
Exit Function

ErrorHandler:
    MsgBox Err.Number & ":" & Err.Description
    GoTo ExitHere
End Function
```

The above function procedure takes three arguments — the strTblName argument specifies the name of a table where a multi-value field is located, the strMultiFldName argument specifies the name of a multi-value field, and the strNewVal argument specifies the value you want to add to the list. To work with the specified table, we begin by setting the tdf object variable to point to our table:

```
    Set tdf = db.TableDefs(strTblName)
```

The DAO TableDefs collection contains TableDef objects, which are table definitions. Each TableDef object contains a Fields collection. We set up the fld object variable to gain access to the specified multi-value field via the Fields collection of the TableDef object:

```
    Set fld = tdf.Fields(strMultiFldName)
```

The Field object has a collection of properties. Before we do any work, we check that the RowSourceType property is set to Value List. If this test is True, we need to get the current value of the RowSource property. We set up the prp object variable to point to this property and write the property value to the Immediate window:

```
Set prp = fld.Properties("RowSource")
Debug.Print prp.Value
```

Because we only want to have unique values in the multi-value lookup field, we need to check if the value passed in the strNewVal parameter is already in the value list. To do this, you can use the VBA InStr function:

```
If InStr(1, prp.Value, strNewVal) = 0 Then
```

The InStr function returns the position of the first occurrence of one string within another. The first parameter is optional. It indicates the character position where the search should start. Obviously, we want to start at the first position so that we can examine the entire value list string. The second parameter is the string to search in. The value of the prp variable contains the following string when the function is called:

```
"Product Brochure";"Product Flyer A";"Product Flyer B";"Product Flyer C";
    "Sales Agreement";"Company Portfolio"
```

The third parameter of the InStr function is the string you want to find. We will specify this string when we call the function procedure in the next step. The InStr function also has an optional fourth argument that specifies the type of string comparison. When omitted, Access performs a binary comparison where each character matches only itself. This is the default. The InStr function will return a zero (0) when the string you are looking for was not found in the string you searched in. We will then add the new item to the current RowSource value list:

```
prp.Value = prp.Value & Chr(59) & Chr(34) _
            & strNewVal & Chr(34)
```

To add a new value to the list, we use the concatenation character (&). The Chr(59) function will give us the required semicolon; the Chr(34) is for the double quotes. The underscore character (_) simply breaks the long code line into two lines.

Notice that the procedure uses the Error Handler code to trap errors that may result from entering a nonexistent table or column name.

2. Run the AddToMultiValueList function procedure by typing the following statement in the Immediate window and pressing **Enter** to execute:

```
AddToMultiValueList "Customers", "Literature Sent", "Sales Contract"
```

After you execute the function procedure, the Immediate window should display the original value of the RowSource property and the new updated value:

```
"Product Brochure";"Product Flyer A";"Product Flyer B";"Product Flyer C";
    "Sales Agreement";"Company Portfolio"

"Product Brochure";"Product Flyer A";"Product Flyer B";"Product Flyer C";
    "Sales Agreement";"Company Portfolio";"Sales Contract"
```

3. Run the AddToMultiValueList function procedure again by typing the following statement in the Immediate window and pressing **Enter** to execute:

```
AddToMultiValueList "Customers", "Literature Sent", "Dinner Invitation"
```

You should now see in the Immediate window the following two strings:

```
"Product Brochure";"Product Flyer A";"Product Flyer B";"Product Flyer C";
    "Sales Agreement";"Company Portfolio";"Sales Contract"

"Product Brochure";"Product Flyer A";"Product Flyer B";"Product Flyer C";
    "Sales Agreement";"Company Portfolio";"Sales Contract";
    "Dinner Invitation"
```

4. Press **Alt+F11** to switch to the Microsoft Access window and double-click the **Customers** table in the Navigation pane.

5. Open the **Literature Sent** drop-down list in any record and notice the two new entries that were added by the VBA code in this hands-on exercise: Sales Contract and Dinner Invitation.

6. Close the **Customers** table.

Working with Append Only Memo Fields

Another type of complex multi-value field introduced in the Access 2007 ACCDB file format is the Append Only memo field. What this means is that the memo field now has a new property called Append Only (see Figure 31-23). When set to Yes, you can append data to the field, but you are not allowed to change the data that has been previously entered into this field. This feature is useful for keeping track of the changes made to the field. Let's say you want to preserve the history of problems submitted by users. Every time you edit the data in the Append Only memo field, the date and time stamp and your changes are automatically saved to the version history of the field (see Figure 31-24). You can view the history of an Append Only memo field by right-clicking a value in the field, and selecting Show column history from the shortcut menu.

Figure 31-23: To collect history on a memo field you must set the field's Append Only property to Yes.

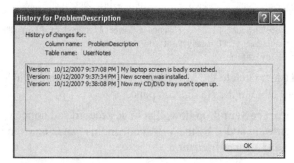

Figure 31-24: To access the memo field's history, right-click the field and select "Show column history" from the shortcut menu.

Working with New Features in Access 2007

 Important Note: The Append Only feature comes with a warning from Microsoft. If you are tracking the history of changes in the memo field and then for some reason you or someone else decides to change the Append Only property to No, Access will erase the field value's history without asking you to confirm.

Working with Append Only Memo Fields Using VBA

You can get the history of values that have been stored in a memo field by using the ColumnHistory method of the Application object. For example, the following statement:

```
Debug.Print Application.ColumnHistory("UserNotes", "ProblemDescription",
    "UID=1")
```

will print to the Immediate window the Problem Description history of a user whose UID equals 1 (see Figure 31-25).

```
Immediate
Debug.Print Application.ColumnHistory("UserNotes", "ProblemDescription", "UID=1")
[Version:  10/12/2007 9:37:08 PM ] My laptop screen is badly scratched.
[Version:  10/12/2007 9:37:34 PM ] New screen was installed.
[Version:  10/12/2007 9:38:08 PM ] Now my CD/DVD tray won't open up.
```

Figure 31-25: Retrieving the history of values stored in a memo field.

Notice that the ColumnHistory method requires three parameters: the name of the table that contains the Append Only memo field, the name of the memo field, and a string used to locate a record in the table.

Let's begin by creating a new table with an Append Only memo field. After entering some sample data in this table, we will run a procedure that retrieves the history data into three separate items: MemoDate, MemoTime, and MemoText.

◎ Custom Project 31-1: Working with Append Only Fields

While this project does not depend on the data in the Northwind 2007 database, we will use this database since it's already open.

Part 1: Writing a VBA Procedure to Create a Table with an Append Only Memo Field

1. In the Northwind 2007 database, switch to the Visual Basic Editor window and choose **Insert | New Module**.

2. In the module's Code window, enter the **CreateTblUserNotes** procedure as shown below, or copy the procedure code from the **C:\Acc07_HandsOn\Chap31.txt** file.

```
Sub CreateTblUserNotes()
    Dim db As DAO.Database
    Dim tdf As DAO.TableDef
    Dim fld As DAO.Field2
```

```
Dim idx As DAO.Index

On Error GoTo ErrorHandler

Set db = CurrentDb

' create UserNotes table
Set tdf = db.CreateTableDef("UserNotes")

' create an AutoNumber field
Set fld = tdf.CreateField("UID", dbLong)
fld.Attributes = dbAutoIncrField
tdf.Fields.Append fld

' create the Primary Key on UID field
Set idx = tdf.CreateIndex("PrimaryKey")
With idx
    .Primary = True
    .Fields.Append tdf.CreateField("UID")
End With

'append the index
tdf.Indexes.Append idx

' create a text field
Set fld = tdf.CreateField("UserName", dbText, 50)
tdf.Fields.Append fld

' create a memo field
Set fld = tdf.CreateField("ProblemDescription", dbMemo)
tdf.Fields.Append fld

' set the memo field to track version history
fld.AppendOnly = True

' append table to the database
db.TableDefs.Append tdf

Application.RefreshDatabaseWindow

ExitHere:
    ' cleanup
    Set idx = Nothing
    Set fld = Nothing
    Set tdf = Nothing
    Set db = Nothing
Exit Sub

ErrorHandler:
    MsgBox Err.Number & ": " & Err.Description
    Resume ExitHere
End Sub
```

The code in the above procedure should already be familiar to you. You've used DAO to create new tables and set up indexes in Part II of this book. Notice that after creating the ProblemDescription field, we set the

AppendOnly property of this field to True to ensure that Access keeps the history of changes for this field.

3. Run the CreateTblUserNotes procedure.

After running this procedure, Access creates a new table called UserNotes. This table contains the Append Only memo field that will store the history of text entries in this field together with the date and time stamp.

Part 2: Entering Data in the Table

Before you can continue, you must enter some data in one or two records so you have something to work with in the next part of this project.

1. Switch to the Microsoft Office Access window, and double-click the **UserNotes** table in the Navigation pane.

2. In the UserName field, type any name. Press **Tab** to move to the ProblemDescription column and type **My laptop screen is badly scratched**. Click on the next record and type any name in the UserName field. Press **Tab** to move to the ProblemDescription column and type **The keyboard is broken**. Press **Ctrl+Enter** to start a new line and type **All the function keys fell out**. Press the **up arrow** until the text in the ProblemDescription column in the first record is selected. Type **New screen was installed**. Continue to enter more data in the first two records of the UserNotes table so that you can build up some history in the memo field.

3. After you are done with the data entry, right-click on the ProblemDescription field in each record to check out the version history.

4. Close the UserNotes table.

Part 3: Writing a VBA Procedure to Retrieve the History Data from the Memo Field

1. Press **Alt+F11** to switch to the Visual Basic Editor window.

2. In the same module where you entered the previous procedure in this project, enter the **RetrieveMemoHistory** procedure as shown below, or copy the procedure code from the **C:\Acc07_HandsOn\Chap31.txt** file.

```
Sub RetrieveMemoHistory()
    Dim arrayString() As String
    Dim MemoText As String
    Dim i As Integer
    Dim strSearch As String
    Dim startPos As Integer
    Dim EndDatePos As Integer
    Dim EndTimePos As Integer
    Dim MemoDate As Date
    Dim MemoTime As Date

    arrayString = Split(Application.ColumnHistory("UserNotes", _
            "ProblemDescription", "UID=1"), "[Version:  ")
    If UBound(arrayString) = -1 Then
```

```
    MsgBox "There is no history data for this field."
    Exit Sub
  End If

  For i = 1 To UBound(arrayString)
    startPos = 1
    strSearch = arrayString(i)
    EndDatePos = InStr(startPos, strSearch, " ")
    MemoDate = CDate(Left(strSearch, EndDatePos - 1))

    startPos = EndDatePos + 1
    EndTimePos = InStr(startPos, arrayString(i), "]") - 3
    MemoTime = CDate(Mid(strSearch, startPos, EndTimePos - startPos))

    startPos = EndTimePos + 3
    strSearch = Trim(Replace(strSearch, vbCrLf, ""))
    MemoText = Right(strSearch, Len(strSearch) - startPos)
    Debug.Print MemoDate, MemoTime, MemoText
  Next
End Sub
```

As mentioned earlier, the Application object's ColumnHistory method is used in VBA to retrieve memo column history data. Because Access returns this data in a single string and we want to have it as separate items, we use the Split function. This function is ideal for breaking a long string into an array of substrings based on a specified delimiter. The Split function returns a zero-based, one-dimensional array where each substring is an element. To hold the result of this function, the above procedure defines an array variable of the String data type named arrayString. The first argument of the Split function specifies the string expression you want to split. The string that will be returned by the ColumnHistory method of the Application object is shown below.

```
    arrayString = Split(Application.ColumnHistory("UserNotes", _
                "ProblemDescription", "UID=1"), "[Version:  ")
```

The second argument of the Split function specifies a string that is used to identify substring limits. You can split a string on a single character, a space, or a group of characters. Because each history item is separated by a line feed and a carriage return (vbCrLf), you might think that it's a good idea to break the Access-generated history string into separate lines by using the vbCrLf delimiter. Well, it isn't, simply because memo fields allow carriage returns. A better delimiter is something that does not conflict with anything the user may enter into the memo field. You should be able to use the "[Version: " string that Access adds to each line of the history string without having to worry about unexpected results. Notice that there are two spaces after the colon that we also want to include in the delimiting string.

Now that we have eliminated from the history string extraneous text ([Version:), we need to iterate through the array elements using the For...Next loop. However, there is no point of doing this if the arrayString variable does not contain any elements. To check this out we can use the UBound function, which will return –1 when the array is empty.

While enumerating the history data, the procedure uses several variables to determine the character position where the date and time strings end (EndDatePos, EndTimePos). We also use the startPos variable to specify at which position in the search string the search should begin. Before extracting the date and time strings, we find the end character positions for these strings using the InStr function, which was discussed earlier in this chapter. We also use two other text functions (Right, Left) to extract a specified number of characters from the string. Because we defined the MemoDate and MemoTime variables as Date, after extracting the date and time strings from the searched string, we use the CDate function to convert them into the Date format.

3. Run the RetrieveMemoHistory procedure. The procedure prints to the Immediate window the history string broken into three columns as shown below:

```
10/12/2007    9:37:08 AM    My laptop screen is badly scratched.
10/12/2007    9:37:34 AM    New screen was installed.
10/12/2007    9:38:08 AM    Now my CD/DVD tray won't open up.
```

While the text in your output might be different, the layout of the data should match the above example.

It is a good idea to run this procedure again in Step mode (F8) to see the values of variables during the procedure run. Use the debugging tools you learned about in Chapter 9 to help you understand the parsing process.

 Note: As an additional exercise, you could now modify the RetrieveMemo-History procedure to write the date, time, and the memo text to a table instead of to the Immediate window.

Rich Text Memo Fields

The Access 2007 ACCDB file format introduces the Rich Text feature in memo fields. In a datasheet, you can now format your memo fields with the bold, italics, underline, and other formatting options that are available via the new Ribbon. To enable the Rich Text feature, you need to open a table in Design view and under the field properties for the selected memo field, set the Text Format property to Rich Text (see Figure 31-26). When you use the Rich Text feature in a memo field, Access stores the data in HTML format.

 Note: You cannot use rich text formatting in Append Only memo fields. Even if you set the Text Format property of this field to Rich Text, Access will disregard it and use its Plain Text format. In other words, the text will be saved unformatted.

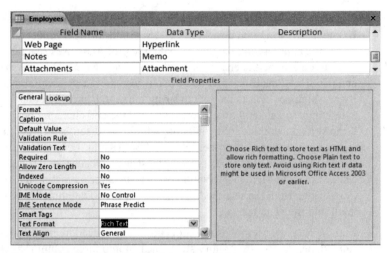

Figure 31-26: Enabling Rich Text for a memo field.

Last Name	State/	ZIP/F	Country/Re	Web Page	Notes	
⊞ Cencini	WA	99998	USA	http://northwi ndtraders.com	Joined the company as a sales representative, was promoted to sales manager and was then named vice president of sales.	(0)
⊞ Kotas	WA	99998	USA	http://northwi ndtraders.com	Was hired as a sales associate and was promoted to sales representative.	(0)

Figure 31-27: Memo text in a datasheet with rich text formatting.

New Features in Forms

Access 2007 brings many enhancements and a new set of features to the form design area. For example, with the new Layout view you can see what you get. The form interface is now a true WYSIWYG; you can see the live data as you design your form without the need of constant switching between the Design and Form views. The new form features include various methods of creating forms, the split form, bound image controls, the Attachments control, new styles and AutoFormats, and rich text support as well as new ways of grouping controls by using the layouts. Some of the new form features also apply to datasheets and were discussed earlier in this chapter. These include the Date Picker, alternating row colors, the Totals row, truncated number displays, sorting and filtering, and an easy way to add new list items to combo boxes.

Many Ways to Create Access Forms

The form buttons on the Ribbon's Create tab enable users to create both simple and more advanced forms (see Figure 31-28). The standard Access form can be created by clicking the Form button. Access creates the form based on the object selected in the Tables, Queries, or Reports sections of the Navigation pane. Split Form is a new type of form introduced in Access 2007 that contains a datasheet and a standard Access form (see Figure 31-29). The datasheet displays multiple records. Simply click on the record in the datasheet and the form will change to show the details for this record. Access can create these types of forms with ease without asking you a single question. The Multiple Items form is a standard continuous form used in earlier versions of Access. This form displays multiple records in a datasheet, with one record per row (see Figure 31-30).

Figure 31-28: The Create tab on the Ribbon provides many ways of creating forms in Access 2007.

Figure 31-29: Split Form is a new type of form available in Access 2007.

Figure 31-30: The Multiple Items form in Access 2007 is the standard continuous form used in earlier versions of Access.

The PivotChart form is a Pivot table-type chart based on the selected data source. Access provides you with the layout for your data and you fill it in with data elements. Figure 31-31 shows the completed PivotChart form included in the Northwind 2007 database.

Figure 31-31: PivotChart form in Access 2007.

The Blank Form button on the Ribbon can be used to create a custom form from scratch. As in earlier versions of Access, this form is not connected to any data source and can be used to create any form you want.

The More Forms button on the Ribbon provides additional types of forms users can create in Access: Datasheet, Modal Dialog, and PivotTable. The Datasheet form organizes data like the Multiple Items form but looks more like an Excel spreadsheet (see Figure 31-32). The Modal Dialog form opens a form that functions like a modal window. What this means is that the user will not be able to activate any other object before closing that form. Modal Dialog forms are very useful when you need to gather specific information from the users before allowing them to perform other actions. There is also an option for launching the Form Wizard used in earlier versions of Access. When you use the Form Wizard, Access allows you to specify which fields to include from which table or query and makes it easy to choose from a variety of AutoFormats. Using the wizard you get only the fields you want. When using other form buttons, Access creates forms that include all the fields, so you need to spend extra time deleting the fields you don't want and repositioning the remaining fields.

ID	Company	Last Name	First Name	E-mail Address	Job Title	Business
1	Company A	Bedecs	Anna		Owner	(123)555
2	Company B	Gratacos Solso	Antonio		Owner	(123)555
3	Company C	Axen	Thomas		Purchasing Representat	(123)555
4	Company D	Lee	Christina		Purchasing Manager	(123)555
5	Company E	O'Donnell	Martin		Owner	(123)555
6	Company F	Pérez-Olaeta	Francisco		Purchasing Manager	(123)555

Figure 31-32: The Datasheet form in Access 2007 resembles an Excel spreadsheet.

Grouping Controls Using Layouts

Access 2007 introduces a new way of grouping controls through a feature known as Layouts. Layout view allows working with entire groups of controls. You no longer need to guess if the controls are properly sized and positioned. Take a look at Figure 31-33 and notice the Selector widget. When you click on the widget, you will see which controls are included in that layout. Using the Layout view you can easily move controls around in the form and resize them. To control the layouts, use the buttons in the Control Layout section of the Ribbon's Arrange tab (see Figure 31-34).

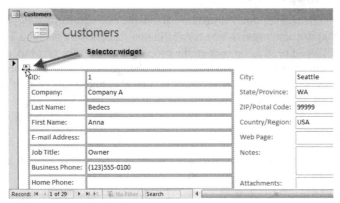

Figure 31-33: A group of controls on the form can be moved easily by using the anchor point (Selector widget).

Figure 31-34: The Form Layout Tools section provides numerous options for controlling the layout of the controls placed on the form.

Groups of controls can be moved to a new layout in one step. The tabular layout makes it easy to group the controls similar to a spreadsheet, with labels positioned across the top and data displayed in columns below the labels. To do this quickly, select the control group you want to reposition by clicking the anchor (Selector widget), and then click the Tabular button on the Ribbon. The Stacked button can be used to create a layout similar to a paper form with labels to the left of data. Removing entire groups of controls is also easy with the Control Layout section's Remove button.

You can use anchoring to tie a control or a group of controls to a section or another control so it moves into place in accordance with the parent. The Anchoring options in Figure 31-34 show various positions where controls can be moved and ways they can be stretched to maximize the use of the space available on the form.

To keep users from making changes to the form, you can disallow the Layout view in the property sheet for the form.

Rich Text Support in Forms

Earlier in this chapter you learned how to enable rich text formatting in memo fields. You can also use rich text formatting on Access forms via the Text Box control. All you need to do is open the property sheet for the text box and set its Text Format property to Rich Text. This change will enable text formatting tools on the Ribbon. At run time, users will be able to change the font style and color, add bold, italics, and highlighting, and apply other formatting.

AutoFormats

Access 2007 provides a gallery of 25 new themes that you can use to give your forms a pleasing and consistent look.

To preview these new designs, switch to the Form Layout view and click on the Gallery control in the AutoFormat section of the Format tab.

Figure 31-35: The Quick Format gallery in
Microsoft Access 2007.

Using Images in Access Forms

Access 2007 comes with better image support. Earlier versions of Access converted the images from their native format and stored them as bitmaps (BMP). This format caused a significant increase in the size of the database because bitmap files are not compressed. Also, during the conversion process, if the image had a transparency feature, this would also be lost. In Access 2007 if you use the Image control and specify the image in the Picture property, Access will store the image in its native format with no conversion. Images with transparency work just fine. You can see examples of transparent buttons and pictures in the Northwind 2007 database's forms (see Figure 31-36).

Figure 31-36: Transparent images and buttons work very well with Access 2007.

Because some people are still using the older MDB databases that do not support saving images in the native format, there is a new database property that lets you choose whether the images should be converted to DIB (device independent bitmap) or stored in their native format. The default setting in Access 2007 is to store images in their native format and convert them to bitmaps for MDB and ADP databases. If you want your images to be displayed in previous versions of Access, choose the second option button under the Picture Property Storage Format setting (see Figure 31-37).

Figure 31-37: To tell Access how to store images in Access 2007 and earlier, use the options under the Picture Property Storage Format. The Access Options window can be accessed by clicking the Microsoft Office button and then selecting Access Options.

Also new to Access 2007 is a bound Image control. Earlier versions of Access needed lots of VBA code to display images on forms and reports when the images were stored in the directories on disk. The Image control can now be bound to the image path. To add an image to your form, place the form in Design view and click the Image button in the Controls group of the Ribbon's Design tab. When you click the form grid, Access displays the Insert Picture dialog box where you can browse to your picture location on disk. When you click OK, the selected picture is placed in the Image control on the form. If you activate the property sheet for the Image control, you will see that Access has placed the filename in the Picture property. If you don't like the picture you've chosen, you can simply click the Browse button next to the Picture property and choose another image.

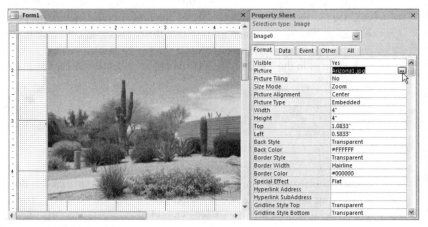

Figure 31-38: The picture is shown here using the Image control placed on an Access 2007 form.

Using the Attachments Control

In the Controls group of the Design tab you will find a new Attachments control (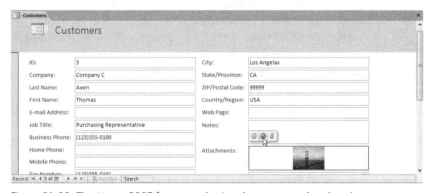) that enables you to attach a file or a collection of files to any database record. We've worked with the Attachment data type earlier in this chapter and have seen how to use it both manually and programmatically.

When you click on the Attachment field on the form, Access displays a small toolbar with three buttons (see Figure 31-39 in Custom Project 31-2). The Forward and Backward buttons allow you to move through the attached files, and the third button opens the Attachments dialog box. You can also right-click the Attachment field and choose the same options from the shortcut menu.

Recall that we've added several attachments to the Customers table in the Northwind 2007 database. Let's now see how you can work with the attachments in an Access form.

⊚ Custom Project 31-2: Working with the Attachments Control

This project depends on the data that was added to the Customers table in the Northwind 2007 database in Hands-On 31-1.

Part 1: Generating an Access Form

1. In the Northwind 2007 database, highlight the **Customers** table in the Navigation pane, and then click the **Form** button in the Forms group on the Ribbon's Create tab.

    Access will display a form as shown in Figure 31-39.

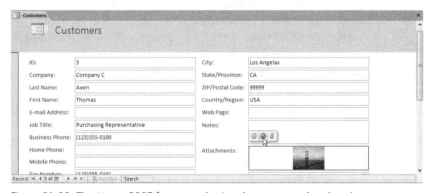

Figure 31-39: The Access 2007 form uses the Attachments control to show images attached to a record.

2. Be sure to activate the record for the third customer.

3. On the Customers form, click the Attachments control next to the Attachments label and notice a small toolbar with three buttons. Scroll through the attached files by clicking the Forward and Backward buttons.

Part 2: Modifying the Form to Display Additional Information about the Attachments

1. Switch to the Design view of the Customers form and use the **Text Box** control in the Controls group of the Design tab to add two text boxes to the form as shown in Figure 31-40. Change the labels of the text boxes to match the figure.

Figure 31-40: Placing unbound text box controls on the form.

2. Click the first unbound text box next to the Number of Attached Files label, and in the property sheet for this text box, click the **All** tab and type **txtNumOfFiles** in the Name property. Click the **Format** tab and change the Back Color property to any color you like.

3. Click the second unbound text box next to the Current File Name label, and in the property sheet for this text box, click the **All** tab and type **txtCurrentFileName** in the Name property. Click the **Format** tab and change the Back Color property to any color you like.

Part 3: Writing an Event Procedure to Display Information about Attachments in the Text Boxes

1. In the form grid, click the **Attachments** control. In the property sheet for this control, click the **Event** tab and click the **Browse** button next to the On Attachment Current property. In the Choose Builder dialog box, select **Code Builder** and click **OK**.

   Access will write for you the stub of the Attachments_AttachmentCurrent event procedure.

2. Complete the code of the **Attachments_AttachmentCurrent** procedure as shown in Figure 31-41, or copy the procedure code from the **C:\Acc07_ HandsOn\Chap31.txt** file.

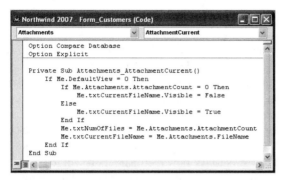

Figure 31-41: Use the AttachmentCurrent event procedure for the Attachments control to retrieve information about attachments and load it into your form's controls.

The Attachments control comes with special properties that apply to working with the Attachment data type. The FileName property returns the name of the attachment file. If you need to display the file extension, use the FileType property. The AttachmentCount property returns the number of attachments stored for the record.

The Attachments control has a special event called AttachmentCurrent. This event is similar to the form's OnCurrent event. It is triggered when you move the focus from one attachment to another. The code shown in Figure 31-41 begins by checking if the form's default view is set to Single Form (0). If DefaultView is set to display other types of Access forms, this code in the event procedure will not run. The procedure then hides the txtCurrentFileName text box if the record does not have any attachments. This is done by setting the Visible property of the text box to False. Next, the procedure fills in the text boxes with the values retrieved from the AttachmentCount and FileName properties.

3. Press **Alt+F11** to return to the Microsoft Office Access window and activate the **Customers** form in Form view. Notice that for the first record, the first text box you added displays 0 and the second text box is empty because the record does not have any attachments.

4. Scroll to the third customer record and click on the **Attachment** field. Next, click the **Forward** button, and notice that when the new file loads into the Attachments control the Current File Name box displays the name of the file being viewed (see Figure 31-42).

5. Press **Ctrl+S** to save changes to the Customers form, and then close this form.

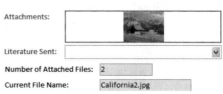

Figure 31-42: The text boxes added to the form provide information about the attachments stored in a record.

New Features in Reports

Many of the new features that were introduced in Access 2007 forms are also available for reports. For example, to make long tabular reports easier to read, you can apply alternating row shading just by changing the Alternate Back Color property in the report's Detail section. Like forms, reports can utilize bound Image controls, rich text formatting, and new filtering and sorting features. The new Layout view makes it easier to design reports; since in Layout view you are working with the live data, you no longer need to switch between Design and Report views to see how the final report will look. The Layout view allows formatting report sections and controls, adding new fields, applying AutoFormats, grouping and sorting data, and changing many of the report's properties. As with the Layouts feature in forms, layouts can be used in reports for resizing and moving groups of controls together, or adding grid lines that grow or shrink with the data. You no longer need to spend time creating lines the way you did in earlier versions of Access. In addition to the Layout view, Access 2007 introduces a new view for reports called Report view in which you can easily perform data searches, as well as sorting and filtering. You can even copy the data. This is a big improvement over the Print Preview that only displays the data image. Another big improvement for reports is in the area of their distribution. You can now save your reports in portable document format (PDF) or XML Paper Specification (XPS) format.

Using the Report View

Reports have a new interactive view called Report view. This is the default view for all new reports created in Access 2007. In this view you can easily copy data by selecting it and clicking the Copy button in the Clipboard group of the Home tab, or simply press Ctrl+C. If you need to find particular data in the report, use the Find button in the Find group of the Home tab or simply press Ctrl+F. Access will pop up the standard Find dialog box in which you can enter your search criteria. Filtering and sorting is also enabled for the Report view via the buttons located in the Filter & Sort section of the Home tab. The report open in the Report view isn't divided into pages; it is one big page. If you have any calculations that depend on the Page or Pages properties of the report, they may not return the correct results. Certain report events, such as Print and Format, will not be triggered when the report is displayed in the Report view. The Report view has its own new event called Paint that is used with sections in Report view. This event fires whenever a section needs to be drawn on the screen. Use this event to conditionally format controls in that view, as shown in Hands-On 31-11.

➡ **Note:** The Paint event fires multiple times for each section of the report because Access paints various elements of the given section separately at different times. The calculated controls are painted separately, and so are the items that require a change in background or foreground colors.

Figure 31-43: Access 2007 reports offer users four different views.

◎ Hands-On 31-11: Conditionally Formatting a Control in the Report View

1. In the Northwind 2007 database, right-click the **Customer Address Book** report in the Navigation pane and choose **Design view**.

2. Click the **Detail** section and activate the property sheet.

3. In the property sheet of the Detail section, click the **Event** tab, and then click the **Browse** button next to the Paint property. In the Choose Builder dialog box, select **Code Builder** and click **OK**.

   Access will write for you the stub of the Detail_Paint event procedure.

4. Complete the code of the **Detail_Paint** procedure as shown below, or copy the procedure code from the **C:\Acc07_HandsOn\Chap31.txt** file.

```
Private Sub Detail_Paint()
    If Me.City.Value = "Chicago" Then
        Me.City.ForeColor = vbBlue
    Else
        Me.City.ForeColor = vbBlack
    End If
End Sub
```

   The above procedure will set the ForeColor property for a control called City to blue when the City name is Chicago, and display the names of all other cities in black. This procedure will be triggered when you open the report in Report view.

5. Press **Ctrl+S** to save the changes in the Report module.

6. Press **Ctrl+F11** to return to the Microsoft Office Access window.

7. Click the **View** button in the Views group of the Design tab.

8. Access displays the report in its default Report view. Press **Ctrl+F** to activate the Find dialog box. Enter **Chicago** and click **Find Next**. Access locates the first customer who lives in Chicago. Click **Find Next** again to

locate the next customer. Notice that all the Chicago names are shown in blue.

9. Close the Customer Address Book report.

Sorting and Grouping Data

Access 2007 has a new interface for grouping data, adding totals, and filtering. These features are now available from a separate Group, Sort, and Total pane as shown in Figure 31-44. To work with this pane, open the report in the Layout view, click the Format tab, and select the Group & Sort button in the Grouping & Totals section. When you click on the Add a Group or Add a Sort buttons in the pane at the bottom of the report, Access will walk you through the steps required to create new report groups, add totals, or perform sorting.

Figure 31-44: The new Group, Sort, and Total pane provides a quick way to add calculations in Access 2007 reports.

Saving Reports in the PDF or XPS File Format

Access 2007 reports can now be saved to the PDF or XPS format. The portable document format (PDF) preserves document formatting and makes files easy to distribute and print. Reports distributed as PDF files will retain their format and can be protected so that the data may not be copied or changed. To view and print PDF files you need to download a free Adobe Acrobat Reader from the Adobe web site. Another format that you can use for your report distribution is the XML Paper Specification (XPS) format. This file format also retains the format of the original document. Currently you need Windows Vista to view XPS files. In order to save your Access reports in PDF or XPS file format, you need to download and install a free add-in from Microsoft. You will find more information on this subject in the Access online help (see Figure 31-45).

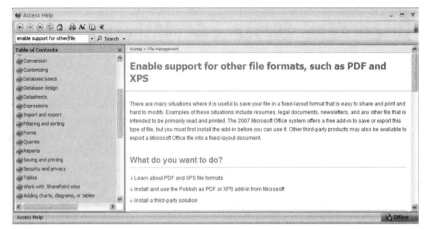

Figure 31-45: See the online help for how to get the free add-in from Microsoft for saving your reports to PDF and XPS file formats.

Chapter Summary

This chapter introduced you to the important new features in Access 2007 tables, forms, and reports. Some features were just highlighted, while others were covered in more detail, showing you how to use the feature both manually and with VBA. After working through this chapter's examples, you should feel comfortable using the new complex data types in your Access 2007 database and the many new tools provided by the user interface in the design of your forms and reports. If you have used prior versions of Access, it may take a while for you to get used to all the new features. It's always easier to learn something new than it is to unlearn the thing that we've been using for years.

In the next chapter, we will take a look at other important additions and changes introduced in Access 2007 that apply to working with templates and macros.

Chapter 32

Macros and Templates

While programming Access applications there are two other areas of Access that you need to be acquainted with: macros and templates. Macros in Access have been around longer than the Visual Basic for Applications language. When Access 2 came out in 1992, it included a macro language called Access Basic that contained a subset of Visual Basic 2.0's core syntax. Access 95 replaced Access Basic with Visual Basic for Applications, but up until Access 97, macros were the most common means of automating database tasks. When Access 2000 came out, many successful macro users had already moved to the new programming platform to take advantage of the language model that offered more control over Access. In fact, in versions 2000 through 2003, Microsoft recommended VBA to automate Access applications, and macros were supported mainly for backward compatibility.

The outlook on macros has changed again with the release of Access 2007. After performing some extensive research, Microsoft found out that many users are intimidated by the programming environment that Access provides but are quite successful at creating macros. It seems that it is much simpler to pick a macro action and set a couple of parameters than it is to write VBA code. Since most of the Access applications created by end users are loaded with macros, Microsoft decided to improve the "macro experience" in Access 2007 by adding event handling, temporary variables (TempVars), better error handling, and a new type of macros called embedded macros. Another new macro feature is a Macro sandbox, which is related to the new security model introduced in the 2007 release.

This chapter focuses on the new macro features in Access 2007. After we've looked at macros, we will take a look at the new ACCDT file format used with Access templates.

New Features in Macros

You can use both VBA and macros to automate your Microsoft Access applications. While macros in Access 2007 are more powerful than those in earlier versions of Access, whether you use macros or VBA will depend on what you want to do. Macros can perform just about any task you can do with the Access user interface by using the keyboard or the mouse. They provide an easy way of opening and closing various Access objects (tables, queries, forms, and reports). You can also use them to automate repetitive tasks, execute commands on the Access Ribbons, set values for form and report controls, import and export spreadsheet and text files, display informative messages, or even sound a beep. These are just a few examples of what macros can do.

What macros cannot do is create and manipulate database objects the way we did in VBA earlier in this book by using DAO or ADO, or step through the records in a recordset and perform an operation on each record. You need to write VBA code to perform these types of operations. You must also use VBA when you need to pass parameters to your Visual Basic procedures, call dynamic link libraries (DLLs), create custom functions, or find out if a file exists on the system. Even if you don't want to get started with macros now that you know how to write code in VBA, you still need to understand how macros are used in Access 2007 as Microsoft makes extensive use of macros in their templates and the built-in Button Wizard creates embedded macros.

Access 2007 Macro Security

In Microsoft's documentation, the term "macro security" applies to macros and VBA, as well as other executable content that could be harmful when allowed to run. In Chapter 1 of this book (see Hands-On 1-4) we specified that Access should trust any database file opened from the C:\Acc07_ByExample folder. This enabled you to work with this book's examples without having to constantly deal with the Access 2007 security warning (see Figure 32-1).

Figure 32-1: Security Warning message bar in Access 2007.

If, however, a file you are attempting to open contains macros and that file does not reside in a trusted location, Access determines whether to display a security alert by checking your macro settings (see Figure 32-2). You can change your macro settings at any time by following these steps:

1. Click the Microsoft Office button, and then click Access Options.

2. In the Access Options dialog box, click the Trust Center tab, and then click Trust Center Settings.

3. In the Trust Center dialog box, select Macro Settings.

Figure 32-2: The Macro Settings options allow you to specify whether the macros should be disabled or allowed to run and whether you should see a notification when macros are disabled.

If the Disable all macros with notification option is selected, you may want to leave it at that. This option allows you to enable the disabled content for this session only by clicking the Options button in the Security Warning message bar and clicking the Enable this content option in the Microsoft Office Security Options dialog box (see Figure 32-3).

Figure 32-3: The Microsoft Office Security Options dialog box allows you to temporarily enable disabled programming content.

If you select the first option button in the above figure, Access will open the database in disabled mode, meaning it will turn off all executable content, as shown in Figure 32-4.

Figure 32-4: The Access online help lists the components that Access 2007 disables.

If you plan on distributing your Access database in the new ACCDB file format, you can use the IsTrusted property of the CurrentProject object to test on loading whether your application has its executable content disabled. This is a new property in Access 2007. Use this property in an AutoExec macro to check whether your application can load (see the next section).

Note: Notice that the disabled mode, as described in the Access online help, disables only so-called unsafe actions in macros. Many other macro actions that are not labeled as unsafe will function even with the macro security enabled. This is what Microsoft calls a Macro sandbox, as explained later in this chapter.

Using the AutoExec Macro

The most important macro that every Access programmer needs to be familiar with is the AutoExec macro. This macro is not new in Access 2007; it's been with Access since the very beginning. An AutoExec macro in your Access application will automatically run when the database is opened. This is very convenient, especially when you need to check whether the rest of your application will load. Let's see how Microsoft does this in the Northwind 2007 database.

Hands-On 32-1: Understanding and Using the AutoExec Macro

1. Copy the **C:\Acc07_ByExample\Northwind 2007.accdb** database to your desktop or any other new folder that you want to create for this hands-on exercise.

2. Double-click the copied database file to open it.

    Access starts with the screen shown in Figure 32-5. Notice the Security Warning message bar with the Options button, and the startup screen that tells you exactly what you should do to use this database.

3. Click the **Options** button, choose the **Enable this content** option button (see Figure 32-3 earlier in this chapter), and click **OK**.

4. Dismiss the Login dialog by clicking the "X" in the upper-right corner.

5. In the Navigation pane, locate the Macro group. Right-click the **AutoExec** macro name and choose **Design View**.

Figure 32-5: Startup screen in the Microsoft Northwind 2007 sample database. This screen tells the user what to do to run the application.

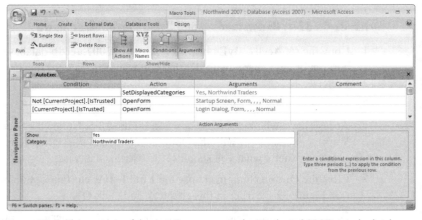

Figure 32-6: The contents of the AutoExec macro in the Northwind 2007 sample database.

6. Close the AutoExec macro in the same way you close any other Access window. You can click the "X" button in the window's upper-right corner or right-click the **AutoExec** tab and choose **Close**.

Understanding Macro Actions, Arguments, and Conditions

A macro can have one or more actions. The Action column is the only required column when creating macros. However, if the task you are trying to perform is based on a condition, then use the optional Condition column as well. Your condition could test a value in a field or evaluate the result of a function. You can use any expression that evaluates to True/False (Yes/No) in the Condition column. If there is an expression in a macro's Condition column, the action specified in that row will execute if the condition is true. If the condition is not true, the action will be skipped, and the macro control will move to the next row. The actions that should not be executed when the condition is true are preceded with Not. If the Condition column is not visible in the Macro Design view, click the Conditions button in the Show/Hide group of the Design tab. Macro actions can be picked from the drop-down list that appears when you click in the Action column. Access 2007 includes 70 macro actions to pick from. If the macro action requires arguments, you enter them in the Action Arguments area at the bottom of the Macro Design screen. Your choices will be automatically reflected by Access in the Arguments column. Arguments are separated by commas, which are also used to indicate empty arguments. You will find documentation on all macro actions and their arguments in the Access online help. The AutoExec macro in the Northwind 2007 database uses the following macro actions:

- **SetDisplayedCategories** — This action is used to specify which categories are displayed under Navigate to Category in the title bar of the Navigation pane. This action has two arguments. The Show argument can be set to Yes to show the category name or No to hide it. The Category argument specifies the name of the category you want to show or hide. The Northwind 2007 database contains a custom category named Northwind Traders, and the first macro line simply says to display this category in the Navigation pane.

- **OpenForm** — This action is used to open any form. The form can be selected from a drop-down list when you click the Form Name box in the Action Arguments section of the Macro Design view. All forms in the current database will be shown. You can also specify the view in which the form will open. The default view is Form; you can select the view from the drop-down box once you click the View box in the Action Arguments section. Not all arguments need to be filled in. You can easily look up arguments that a particular action can take by clicking on any line in the Action Arguments section and pressing the F1 key. The second macro action in the AutoExec example shown in Figure 32-6 tells Access to open the startup screen in Form view using the Normal window. Notice that the arguments that were not provided are shown as commas in the Arguments column:

```
Startup Screen, Form, , , , Normal
```

The first comma after Form is an argument separator; the other three commas are placeholders for the arguments that were not provided: Filter Name, Where Condition, and Data Mode.

Whether a form opens can depend on a certain condition being met; in this example, the Condition column has the following statement:

```
Not [CurrentProject].[IsTrusted]
```

This statement tells Access to show the startup screen only if the current project (the database) is not trusted. Notice the use of the IsTrusted property of the CurrentProject object to test whether your application has its executable content disabled. You saw this line of macro code execute when you opened the Northwind 2007 database, as shown in Figure 36-5.

The next line of macro code loads the login dialog if [CurrentProject].[IsTrusted] is true. This line was executed when you told Access to "Enable this content" in the Microsoft Office Security Options dialog box (see steps 3-4 in the hands-on exercise).

A macro executes until it encounters a blank line. Therefore, never use blank lines to separate your macro actions.

 Note: To open an Access database without running the AutoExec macro, hold down the Shift key while opening the database.

Creating Macros in Access 2007

Access 2007 supports two types of macros: standalone macros used in earlier versions of Access and embedded macros introduced in Access 2007. Standalone macros are visible in the Navigation pane under Macros; embedded macros are part of the object in which they are embedded (form, report, or control) and therefore are not visible in the Navigation pane.

Creating and Using Standalone Macros

The AutoExec macro we looked at in the previous section is a standalone macro. Once created, this macro appears in the Navigation pane.

The general steps to create a standalone macro are as follows:

1. Click **Macro** in the Other group of the Create tab (Figure 32-7).

Figure 32-7: Creating a standalone macro.

Note that a macro consists of macro actions that are carried out in the order you list them in the Macro Design view.

2. To add an action to the macro, click the first empty cell in the Action column. Type the action name or select the action from the Action drop-down list. The Action list displays all the available macro actions when the Show All Actions button is selected. When this button is not selected, you will see a shorter list of actions that are allowed to run even if the database is not trusted.

3. In the Arguments column, specify arguments for the selected action, if required. If you click in the text box next to the Argument name in the Action Arguments section of the Macro Design view, you will see a short description in the box to the right.

4. If the macro action should be conditionally executed, type an expression in the Condition column. If this column is not visible, click the **Conditions** button in the Show/Hide group of the Design tab.

    If there is an expression in the Condition column of a macro, the action in that row will execute if the condition is true. If the condition is not true, the action will be skipped. Instead of repeating the same condition in line after line, use an ellipsis (...) as shown in Figure 32-8. When a line has an ellipsis in the Condition column, the condition from the previous line continues to apply. If the action on the ellipsis line is StopMacro, then the macro will end without executing the next lines.

5. To make your macro actions easy to understand for yourself and others, type a comment in the Comments column. Comments are optional.

6. To add another action to your macro, type or select an action in the next row's Action column, and repeat steps 3-5 above.

    To add an action row in between the actions you've already entered, simply right-click where you want to add a new row and select **Insert Row** from the shortcut menu, or click the **Insert Rows** button in the Rows group of the Design tab.

    To delete a row, right-click the row and choose Delete Row from the shortcut menu, or click the Delete Rows button in the Rows group of the Design tab.

7. When you are done entering all actions for your macro, press **Ctrl+S** to save your macro, or click the **Save** button on the Quick Access toolbar. Enter the macro name in the Save As dialog box and click **OK**.

8. Close the Macro Design view.

Using Macro Groups

Instead of having a large number of standalone macros listed in the Navigation pane, consider storing related macros together in a macro group. Figure 32-8 shows macros that can be attached to the Suppliers form in the Northwind.mdb database. Notice how this single macro object named Suppliers stores all related macros in a macro group. To create a macro group, you must give each macro a unique name.

Macro Name	Condition	Action	Comment
			The macros in this group could be attached to the Suppliers form in place of the code in the form's
			Attached to the Add Products button of the Suppliers form.
Add Products		Echo	Freeze screen while macro is running (Echo off).
		Close	Close Product List form.
		OpenForm	Open the Products form.
		SetValue	Set the SupplierID to the current supplier on the Suppliers form.
		GoToControl	Go to the CategoryID control.
			Attached to the Review Products button of the Suppliers form.
Review Products		Echo	Freeze screen while macro is running (Echo off).
	IsNull([SupplierID])	MsgBox	If no current supplier on Suppliers form, display a message...
	...	GoToControl	...go to the CompanyName control...
	...	StopMacro	...and stop the macro.
		OpenForm	Open the Product List form and show current supplier's products.
		MoveSize	Postion the Product List form in the lower right of the Suppliers form.
			Attached to the OnCurrent property of the Suppliers form.
Show Related Products	IsNull([SupplierID])	StopMacro	If no current supplier on Suppliers form, stop the macro.
	IsLoaded("Product List")	OpenForm	If the Products form is open, bring it to the top and show the current supplier's products.
			Attached to the OnClose property of the Suppliers form.
Close	IsLoaded("Product List")	Close	If Product List form is open, close it.
	IsLoaded("Products")	Close	If Products form is open, close it.

Figure 32-8: The Suppliers macro group in the sample Northwind.mdb database included with previous versions of Access contains macros that can be used in the Suppliers form. The yellow warning sign in the record selector indicates that the specified action will not execute if the database is not trusted.

The general steps to create a macro group are as follows:

1. Click the **Macro** button in the Other group of the Create tab (see Figure 32-7 earlier).

2. Make sure the Macro Name column is displayed by clicking the **Macro Names** button in the Show/Hide group of the Design tab.

3. Type the macro name in the Macro Name column in the same row where you want the macro to begin.

4. Specify your first macro action in the same row where you entered the macro name.

5. Follow steps 3-6 as outlined in the procedure for creating standalone macros.

6. Save the macro group by pressing **Ctrl+S** and typing the name for the group. The name you specify is the name of the group of macros. This name will appear in the Navigation pane under Macros.

7. Close the Macro Design view.

Macro groups work great for creating modular macros. Instead of a longer macro with many conditions, simply create a small macro that calls other small macros.

Running Standalone Macros

You can run standalone macros from the Design view, from the Navigation pane, from another macro, from a VBA procedure, or in response to an event on a form, report, or control.

- **Run a macro from the Design view** — If the standalone macro is open in the Design view, you can click the Run button in the Tools group of the Design tab to run the macro. To run a macro in the macro group, click the macro name and then click the Run button.

> **Note:** You can also run your macro one action at a time by selecting the Single Step button and then clicking the Run button (see "Error Handling in Macros" later in this chapter).

- **Run a macro from the Navigation pane** — A standalone macro can also be run directly from the Navigation pane. Simply right-click the macro name and choose Run from the shortcut menu, but make sure you know what the macro will do before you run it. A badly designed macro could wipe out all the data in your database without asking you if you want to proceed.

> **Note:** If the macro contains macro groups and you right-click the macro in the Navigation pane and choose Run, only the first macro in the group will execute.

- **Run a macro from another macro** — To run a macro from another macro, you must create at a minimum two macros. The main macro should include the RunMacro action. Set the Macro Name argument of this action to the name of the macro you want to run. When you run the main macro, both macros will execute.

- **Run a macro from a VBA procedure** — The RunMacro method of the DoCmd object carries out the RunMacro action in VBA.

  - To run a standalone macro, use the following statement:

```
DoCmd.RunMacro "YourMacroName"
```

Optionally, you may specify how many times the macro should be run:

`DoCmd.RunMacro "YourMacroName", 2`

■ To run a particular macro in a macro group, use the name of the group followed by a period and the name of the macro:

`DoCmd.RunMacro "Sales.AddProducts"`

■ **Run a macro in response to an event on a form, report, or control** — A standalone macro can be bound to events for forms, reports, or controls. For example, if your form contains a button that needs to open another form and you have previously created a macro that performs this action, you can specify the macro name in the OnClick property of the button, as shown in Figure 32-9. To do this you must open the form in Design or Layout view, click the Button control on the form, and open the property sheet. On the property sheet for the button, click the Event tab, and then click the event property for the event you want to trigger. The macro will run when you return to Form view and click the button. Notice that Access lists all the available macros when you open a drop-down list next to an event property. Macros that appear in macro groups are listed in two parts — the name of the standalone macro and the name of the macro in a macro group.

Figure 32-9: Binding a standalone macro to an event property. Shown here is the Suppliers form in the sample Northwind.mdb database from an earlier version of Access.

Creating and Using Embedded Macros

New to Access 2007 are macros that can be embedded in any of the events provided by a form, report, or control. As mentioned earlier, these embedded macros are not visible in the Navigation pane.

The general steps to create an embedded macro are as follows:

1. Open a form or report in Design or Layout view.

2. Select an object to which you want to assign an embedded macro (a form, report, or control).

3. Activate the property sheet. In Design view, the Property Sheet button is located in the Tools group of the Design tab. In Layout view, you will find this button in the Tools group of the Arrange tab.

4. In the property sheet, click the **Event** tab, and then click the **Build** button (...) next to the desired property.

5. In the Choose Builder dialog box, select **Macro Builder**, and then click **OK**. Access will open the same Macro Design view that you use for creating standalone macros.

6. Choose the actions for your macro, and specify the arguments and conditions if required.

7. Press **Ctrl+S** to save your macro, and click the **Close** button in the Close group of the Design tab. Access closes the Macro Design view and enters [Embedded Macro] in the event property (see Figure 32-10).

➔ **Note:** To modify the embedded macro, click on the Build button (...) next to the property with [Embedded Macro], and Access will open the Macro Builder (Design view) where you can make the required modifications.

Keep in mind that you cannot reference an embedded macro from other macros. To reference a macro from another macro, you must create a standalone macro.

Figure 32-10: Assigning an embedded macro to the event property of a form's command button.

Copying Embedded Macros

Because embedded macros are part of the object in which they were created, the macro behind the control is also copied when you copy the form, report, or control.

You can also copy an embedded macro from one event property to another. This is possible thanks to so-called "shadow properties." What this means is that for each event property of a control, form, or report there is a "shadow" event property that contains the embedded macro for that property. For example, if your form's On Load event property is set to [Embedded Macro], then the shadow property called On Load Macro contains its embedded macro. The

On Click event property has the On Click Macro property if you are using the embedded macro to trigger the On Click event. If the event property is empty, then there is no shadow property.

Hands-On 32-2 demonstrates how to use VBA to copy an embedded macro from the Shipper Details form to the Supplier List form in the Northwind 2007.accdb database.

◎ Hands-On 32-2: Copying Embedded Macros

1. In the **Northwind 2007. accdb** database, open the **Supplier List** form in Design view. You may use the same version of the database that you opened in Hands-On 32-1.

2. In the Form Header section, right-click the **Home** button and choose **Copy**.

3. Right-click anywhere in the empty area of the Form Header section and choose **Paste**. The copied button appears in the upper-left corner of the Form Header section. Leave the button in this location right now until we change some of its properties. The button has the same label as the original button and a default name, such as Command232. You need to change the button's Name and Caption properties.

4. While the button is selected, click the **Property Sheet** button in the Tools group of the Design tab. Click the **All** tab and change the button's Name property to **cmdClose** and the Caption property to **&Close**. The ampersand in front of the letter "C" assigns a keyboard shortcut to the button.

5. Position the Close button to the left of the Home button as shown in Figure 32-11.

Figure 32-11: Use the property sheet to change the Name and Caption properties of the Close command button.

6. Press **Ctrl+S** to save the changes to the form.

7. While the Close button is selected, click the **Event** tab in the property sheet.

Notice that when you copied the Home button, Access also copied the embedded macro attached to the On Click event property (see Figure 32-12). At this point, you could simply click the Builder button (…) to modify this macro to have it close the Supplier List form instead of opening the Home form. However, the purpose of this exercise is to show you how to use VBA to copy an embedded macro from one property to another. We will overwrite this embedded macro with a different one by writing a VBA procedure in the next steps.

Figure 32-12: When you copied the Home button the new button, inherited the embedded macro assigned to the On Click event property.

8. Press **Alt+F11** to activate the Visual Basic Editor window, and choose **Insert | Module**.

9. In the module's Code window, enter the following **Copy_OnClickMacro** procedure as shown below, or copy the procedure code from **C:\Acc07_ HandsOn\Chap32.txt**.

```
Sub Copy_OnClickMacro()
    Dim ctl As Control

    ' open in the Design view the Supplier List form
    DoCmd.OpenForm "Supplier List", acDesign

    ' only run the code if the specified control
    ' exists on the form
    For Each ctl In Forms("Supplier List").Controls
        If TypeOf ctl Is CommandButton Then
            If StrComp(ctl.Name, "cmdClose", vbTextCompare) = 0 Then

                ' open in the Design view the Shipper Details form
                ' this form contains an embedded macro in the OnClick
                ' event of cmdClose button

                DoCmd.OpenForm "Shipper Details", acDesign

                ' copy macro from the OnClick event property of the
                ' cmdClose button on the Shipper Details form
                ' to the OnClick event property of the cmdClose button
                ' on the Supplier List form

                Forms("Supplier List").Controls("cmdClose").OnClickMacro = _
                    Forms("Shipper Details").Controls("cmdClose").OnClickMacro
                DoCmd.Save acForm, "Supplier List"
                DoCmd.Close acForm, "Shipper Details"
                MsgBox "The embedded macro was successfully copied."
                Exit Sub
            End If
        End If
    Next

    MsgBox "Operation could not be performed. " & vbCrLf & _
        "Ensure that the specified control exists."

End Sub
```

In the above procedure, we begin by opening the Supplier List form in Design view and iterate through the form's controls to find out whether the form contains the control named "cmdClose." We use the TypeOf...Is expression to specifically look for the CommandButton control. Because the Supplier List form contains several buttons, we can use the StrComp function to determine if we found the correct button. This function will tell us if the string specified in the second argument is found in the string specified in the first argument of this function. The third argument of the StrComp function tells Access to perform the comparison of the two text strings. If the StrComp function returns zero (0), then we found the control we were looking for and we can proceed to open the Shipper Details form and copy the embedded macro assigned to the On Click event property of this form's cmdClose button to the On Click event property of the Supplier List's equivalent button. The following statement copies the embedded macro from the On Click event property to another On Click event property:

```
Forms("Supplier List").Controls("cmdClose").OnClickMacro = _
            Forms("Shipper Details").Controls("cmdClose").OnClickMacro
```

Once we are finished copying, we can simply exit the procedure using the early exit expression Exit Sub.

If the Supplier List form does not contain the button with the specified name, we display a message.

10. Run the **Copy_OnClickMacro** procedure.

If you followed all the steps of this hands-on exercise, you should see a message stating that the embedded macro was successfully copied. Click **OK** to close the message box. If you got a different message, check the code for any errors and ensure that the Supplier List form has the cmdClose button. Then rerun the procedure.

11. Press **Ctrl+S** to save changes in the module. Access will ask you to assign a new name to the module. Click **OK** to accept the default name.

12. Press **Alt+F11** to return to the Microsoft Office Access window.

13. In the property sheet for the cmdClose button, click the **Macro Builder (...)** button next to the On Click event property (Event tab). Access opens the Macro Builder Design view, as shown in Figure 32-13. This macro will close the form when the user clicks the Close button on the Supplier List form.

Figure 32-13: Examining an embedded macro after it's been copied from another event property.

14. Click the **Close** button to close the Macro Builder Design view.

15. Right-click the **Supplier List** tab, and choose **Form View**.

16. Click the **Close** button in the Header section of the Supplier List form to close this form.

You can see the contents of the OnClickMacro shadow property by typing the following statement in the Immediate window and pressing Enter (the form must be open for this to work):

```
?Forms("Supplier List").Controls("cmdClose").OnClickMacro
```

You should see the output as shown below:

```
Version =196611
ColumnsShown =8
Begin
    Action ="Close"
    Argument ="-1"
    Argument =""
    Argument ="0"
End
```

Access has a large number of hidden properties that make it possible to get and set embedded macros. The property name begins with the name of the event property and ends with "EmMacro," such as OnClickEmMacro, AfterUpdateEmMacro, and so on. Try out the following statement in the Immediate window (the form must be open for this to work), and notice that it produces the same output as the statement you tried earlier:

```
? Forms("Supplier List").Controls("cmdClose").Properties
        ("OnClickEmMacro").Value

Version =196611
ColumnsShown =8
Begin
    Action ="Close"
```

```
      Argument ="-1"
      Argument =""
      Argument ="0"
    End
```

With this knowledge, it is easy to create a standalone macro from an embedded macro. Here's an example VBA procedure that does just that:

```
Sub SaveEmToStandalone()
    Dim strMacro As String
    Dim objFileSys As Object
    Dim objFile As Object
    Dim strFileName As String

    ' open in the Design view the form that contains
    ' the embedded macro
    DoCmd.OpenForm "Login Dialog", acDesign

    ' to write an embedded macro to a file use the Value property
    strMacro = Forms("Login Dialog"). _
        Controls("cboCurrentEmployee"). _
        Properties("AfterUpdateEmMacro").Value

    ' close the form
    DoCmd.Close acForm, "Login Dialog"

    ' Create a text file
    strFileName = "C:\Acc07_ByExample\AfterUpdate for combo.txt"

    Set objFileSys = CreateObject("Scripting.FileSystemObject")
    Set objFile = objFileSys.CreateTextFile(strFileName, True)

    ' Write strMacro to the text file
    objFile.Write strMacro
    ' Close the file
    objFile.Close

    ' Use the undocumented LoadFromText method
    ' of the Application object to create a standalone macro
    ' from the text file
    Application.LoadFromText acMacro, "Cbo Employee After Update", _
            strFileName

End Sub
```

The LoadFromText method of the Application object makes it possible to create various Access database objects (including macros) from information that was previously saved to a text file. The LoadFromText method requires that you specify the object type, the object name, and the name of the text file.

After running the above procedure, you should see the Cbo Employee After Update macro listed in the Navigation pane under Macros.

Working in Sandbox Mode

By default Access 2007 runs in Sandbox mode, which means that the program blocks all the expressions in field properties and controls that are considered unsafe. A *safe expression* is one that does not use functions that could be used to access drives or other resources on a user's computer to damage data or files. When Access is running in Sandbox mode, any expressions that use unsafe macro actions are marked with a yellow warning sign, as shown earlier in Figure 32-8.

Access allows you to disable Sandbox mode by setting the macro security level to low; however, for security reasons this setting is not recommended. If you trust the database and want to run unsafe expressions that the Sandbox mode blocks without having to change your current macro security, you can disable Sandbox mode by changing a Registry key. Modifying the Registry is beyond the scope of this chapter.

Error Handling in Macros

Access 2007 adds three new macro actions that give macros the capability to handle errors: OnError, ClearMacroError, and SingleStep. There is also a new MacroError object that you can use to obtain information about the error received and create user-friendly error messages. The OnError action is similar to the On Error statement in VBA. The OnError action specifies how errors should be handled when a run-time error occurs. This action has two arguments, as shown in the table below.

Table 32-1: OnError action arguments

Arguments	Description
Go To (This argument is required)	Specifies how macro should handle errors. The Go To argument can be set to: Next, Macro Name, or Fail. **Next** — The error is recorded in the MacroError object and the execution of the macro moves to the next macro action. *This is similar to the On Error Resume Next statement in VBA.* **Macro Name** — The macro execution is passed to the macro that is named in the Macro Name argument. *This is similar to the On Error GoTo statement in VBA.* **Fail** — Access will stop the execution of the macro and display an error. *This is similar to On Error GoTo 0 in VBA.*
Macro Name (This argument is optional)	If the Go To argument is set to Macro Name, the name of the macro in the current macro group will handle the error.

The OnError action suppresses standard error messages displayed by Access when an error occurs. If you use the OnError action in your macro, then you should use the error information saved in the MacroError object to display a user-friendly message about the error.

The MacroError object has the following properties: ActionName, Arguments, Condition, Description, MacroName, and Number. You can check the MacroError object's Number property to find out if an error occurred, as shown in Figure 32-14. If there was no error, the Number property will return zero (0). However, if [MacroError].Number <> 0, then you should handle the error right away.

By default, the MacroError object is cleared at the end of the macro execution; however, you can clear it right after the error has been handled by using the ClearMacroError action. This action will reset the error number in the MacroError object back to zero and clear other information stored in the object such as macro name, action name, condition, arguments, and description. The MacroError object contains information about only one error at a time; if more than one error occurred, only the error information about the last error can be retrieved. Therefore, when writing longer macros use the ClearMacroError action right after handling the first error so the ErrorObject will be able to capture information about the next error that might occur.

Use the StopMacro action to stop the currently running macro. In Figure 32-14 the StopMacro action is run right after the user receives the message about the macro error.

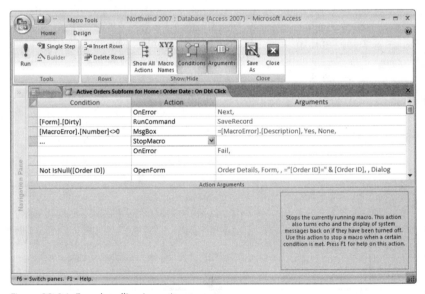

Figure 32-14: Error handling in an Access macro.

To debug a macro that is not working properly, you can click the Single Step button in the Tools group of the Design tab and then click the Run button, or you can use the SingleStep macro action just before an action that you suspect is causing a problem. The SingleStep macro action is new to Access 2007. This action pauses the macro and opens the Macro Single Step dialog box (see Figure 32-15), which displays information about the current macro action (macro name, condition, action name, arguments, and error number). The Macro Single Step dialog box contains the following three buttons:

Table 32-2: Macro Single Step dialog buttons

Button Name	Description
Step	Move to the next macro action.
Stop All Macros	Stop the current macro and any other macros that may be running.
Continue	Use this button to exit the Single Step mode and continue the normal execution of the macro.

Figure 32-15: Debug your macros using the Macro Single Step dialog box.

 Note: If you started the Macro Single Step dialog box using the Single Step button on the Ribbon, you must click this button again when you are done debugging your macro or the next macros that you run will also be run using the Single Step mode.

Using Temporary Variables in Macros

A new functionality in Access 2007 that applies both to VBA and macros is temporary variables (TempVars). You've seen the VBA side of using the TempVar object earlier in this book in Chapter 3. Recall that the TempVar object of the TempVars collection allows you to get or set a value for a variable. Each TempVar object has a name and value property. In macros, there are three new macro actions that relate to TempVars:

■ **SetTempVar**(*name, expression*) — This macro action is used to create a new temporary variable. This variable can then be used as a condition or argument in subsequent macro actions. Temporary variables are global; therefore, you can use them in another macro, in an event procedure, or on a form or report. The first argument of the SetTempVar macro action assigns a name to the temporary variable. The second argument is the expression that Access should use to set the value for this temporary variable. You can define up to 255 temporary variables at one time.

■ **RemoveTempVar**(*name*) — This macro action is used to remove the temporary variable. Use the *name* argument to provide the name of the variable to remove. It is recommended that you remove the temporary variable once you've finished working with it. If you don't remove your temporary variables, they will be removed automatically when you close the database.

■ **RemoveAllTempVar** — This macro action is used to remove all temporary variables from the TempVars collection.

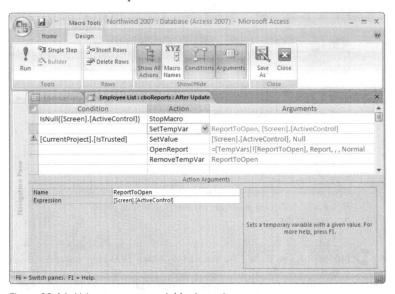

Figure 32-16: Using temporary variables in an Access macro.

> **Note:**   Because both macros and VBA use the same TempVars collection, it is now easy to share data between your macros and VBA procedures.

Converting Macros to VBA Code

The ability to convert standalone macros to VBA code has been available since Access 97. With the introduction of embedded macros, Access 2007 also provides a button to convert to VBA code macros stored in an event property of a form, report, or control (Figure 32-20).

Converting a Standalone Macro to VBA

To convert a standalone macro to VBA, select the macro in the Navigation pane under Macros and click the Convert Macros to Visual Basic button in the Macro group of the Database Tools tab (see Figure 32-17). Access will display a dialog box asking whether you want to include error handling and comments in the code (see Figure 32-18). To keep your code very simple, you can clear both check boxes. Start the conversion process by clicking the Convert button.

Figure 32-17: Converting a standalone macro to Visual Basic for Applications code.

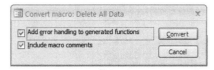

Figure 32-18: Access displays this dialog box when you click the Convert Macros to Visual Basic button (see Figure 32-17).

Upon completion of the macro conversion process, Access displays a message stating that the conversion is finished. Click OK to the message, and review the Modules group in the Navigation pane. You should see a separate module for the converted macro. The name of the module is Converted Macro followed by a dash and the name of the macro you converted. For example, after converting the Delete All Data macro, the name of the VBA module is Converted Macro – Delete All Data. To view the converted macro, double-click the converted module's name. This will open the Visual Basic Editor window, as shown in Figure 32-19.

```
Option Compare Database

'----------------------------------------------------------
' Delete_All_Data
'
'----------------------------------------------------------
Function Delete_All_Data()
On Error GoTo Delete_All_Data_Err

    If (Eval("7=MsgBox(""Do you really want to delete all data in the database?"""",260)
        Exit Function
    End If
    DoCmd.RunSQL "Delete * from [Invoices]", -1
    DoCmd.RunSQL "Delete * from [Order Details]", -1
    DoCmd.RunSQL "Delete * from [Orders]", -1
    DoCmd.RunSQL "Delete * from [Purchase Order Details]", -1
    DoCmd.RunSQL "Delete * from [Purchase Orders]", -1
    DoCmd.RunSQL "Delete * from [Inventory Transactions]", -1


Delete_All_Data_Exit:
    Exit Function

Delete_All_Data_Err:
    MsgBox Error$
    Resume Delete_All_Data_Exit

End Function
```

Figure 32-19: This VBA code was generated by Access from a standalone macro.

Note: You can modify the code generated by the macro conversion process to suit your needs.

Converting Embedded Macros to VBA

To convert embedded macros, open the form or report in Design view and click the Database Tools tab. If you opened a form, you should see the button named Convert Form's Macros to Visual Basic in the Macro group, as shown in Figure 32-20.

Figure 32-20: Converting embedded macros to VBA code.

After clicking the Convert Form's Macros to Visual Basic button, Access displays the same dialog box as was shown earlier in the conversion process for standalone macros (see Figure 32-18). When you click the Convert button, Access begins the conversion process, and when this process completes you will see a message about the successful completion of the conversion. Click OK to the message. Next, activate the property sheet, and notice that form and control event properties that have previously been set to [Embedded Macro] now display [Event Procedure]. You can click the Builder button (…) to view the VBA code. The following VBA event procedures were generated for the embedded macros found in the Shipper List form:

```
Option Compare Database

'----------------------------------------------------------
' cmdNew_Contact_Click
'
'----------------------------------------------------------
Private Sub cmdNew_Contact_Click()
On Error GoTo cmdNew_Contact_Click_Err
```

```
        DoCmd.OpenForm "Shipper Details", acNormal, "", "1=0", , acDialog
        On Error Resume Next
        DoCmd.Requery ""
        DoCmd.SearchForRecord , "", acFirst, "[ID]=" & Nz(DMax("[ID]",
        Form.RecordSource), 0)


cmdNew_Contact_Click_Exit:
    Exit Sub

cmdNew_Contact_Click_Err:
    MsgBox Error$
    Resume cmdNew_Contact_Click_Exit

End Sub



'------------------------------------------------------------
' cmdAddFromOutlook_Click
'
'------------------------------------------------------------
Private Sub cmdAddFromOutlook_Click()
On Error GoTo cmdAddFromOutlook_Click_Err

    On Error Resume Next
    DoCmd.RunCommand acCmdAddFromOutlook


cmdAddFromOutlook_Click_Exit:
    Exit Sub

cmdAddFromOutlook_Click_Err:
    MsgBox Error$
    Resume cmdAddFromOutlook_Click_Exit

End Sub



'------------------------------------------------------------
' cmdEmailList_Click
'
'------------------------------------------------------------
Private Sub cmdEmailList_Click()
On Error GoTo cmdEmailList_Click_Err

    On Error Resume Next
    DoCmd.SendObject acForm, "", "", "", "", "", "", "", True, ""


cmdEmailList_Click_Exit:
    Exit Sub

cmdEmailList_Click_Err:
    MsgBox Error$
```

```
        Resume cmdEmailList_Click_Exit

End Sub


'-------------------------------------------------------------
' cmdCollectDataviaEmail_Click
'
'-------------------------------------------------------------
Private Sub cmdCollectDataviaEmail_Click()
On Error GoTo cmdCollectDataviaEmail_Click_Err

    DoCmd.OpenQuery "Shippers Extended", acViewNormal, acEdit
    DoCmd.RunCommand acCmdCollectDataViaEmail
    DoCmd.Close acQuery, "Shippers Extended"


cmdCollectDataviaEmail_Click_Exit:
    Exit Sub

cmdCollectDataviaEmail_Click_Err:
    MsgBox Error$
    Resume cmdCollectDataviaEmail_Click_Exit

End Sub


'-------------------------------------------------------------
' cmdHome_Click
'
'-------------------------------------------------------------
Private Sub cmdHome_Click()
On Error GoTo cmdHome_Click_Err

    DoCmd.OpenForm "Home", acNormal, "", ""


cmdHome_Click_Exit:
    Exit Sub

cmdHome_Click_Err:
    MsgBox Error$
    Resume cmdHome_Click_Exit

End Sub


'-------------------------------------------------------------
' Last_Name_DblClick
'
'-------------------------------------------------------------
Private Sub Last_Name_DblClick(Cancel As Integer)
On Error GoTo Last_Name_DblClick_Err
```

```
    On Error Resume Next
    If (Form.Dirty) Then
        DoCmd.RunCommand acCmdSaveRecord
    End If
    If (MacroError.Number <> 0) Then
        Beep
        MsgBox MacroError.Description, vbOKOnly, ""
        Exit Sub
    End If
    On Error GoTo 0
    If (Not IsNull(ID)) Then
        DoCmd.OpenForm "Shipper Details", acNormal, "", "[ID]=" & ID, , acDialog
    End If


Last_Name_DblClick_Exit:
    Exit Sub

Last_Name_DblClick_Err:
    MsgBox Error$
    Resume Last_Name_DblClick_Exit

End Sub



'------------------------------------------------------------
' First_Name_DblClick
'
'------------------------------------------------------------
Private Sub First_Name_DblClick(Cancel As Integer)
On Error GoTo First_Name_DblClick_Err

    On Error Resume Next
    If (Form.Dirty) Then
        DoCmd.RunCommand acCmdSaveRecord
    End If
    If (MacroError.Number <> 0) Then
        Beep
        MsgBox MacroError.Description, vbOKOnly, ""
        Exit Sub
    End If
    On Error GoTo 0
    If (Not IsNull(ID)) Then
        DoCmd.OpenForm "Shipper Details", acNormal, "", "[ID]=" & ID, , acDialog
    End If


First_Name_DblClick_Exit:
    Exit Sub

First_Name_DblClick_Err:
    MsgBox Error$
    Resume First_Name_DblClick_Exit

End Sub
```

```
'-----------------------------------------------------------
' Company_DblClick
'
'-----------------------------------------------------------
Private Sub Company_DblClick(Cancel As Integer)
On Error GoTo Company_DblClick_Err

    On Error Resume Next
    If (Form.Dirty) Then
        DoCmd.RunCommand acCmdSaveRecord
    End If
    If (MacroError.Number <> 0) Then
        Beep
        MsgBox MacroError.Description, vbOKOnly, ""
        Exit Sub
    End If
    On Error GoTo 0
    If (Not IsNull(ID)) Then
        DoCmd.OpenForm "Shipper Details", acNormal, "", "[ID]=" & ID, , acDialog
    End If


Company_DblClick_Exit:
    Exit Sub

Company_DblClick_Err:
    MsgBox Error$
    Resume Company_DblClick_Exit

End Sub


'-----------------------------------------------------------
' E_mail_Address_DblClick
'
'-----------------------------------------------------------
Private Sub E_mail_Address_DblClick(Cancel As Integer)
On Error GoTo E_mail_Address_DblClick_Err

    On Error Resume Next
    If (Not IsNull(Screen.ActiveControl)) Then
        DoCmd.SendObject , "", "", Screen.ActiveControl, "", "", "", "", True, ""
    End If


E_mail_Address_DblClick_Exit:
    Exit Sub

E_mail_Address_DblClick_Err:
    MsgBox Error$
    Resume E_mail_Address_DblClick_Exit

End Sub
```

Working with New Features in Access 2007

```
'-----------------------------------------------------------
' ID_Click
'
'-----------------------------------------------------------
Private Sub ID_Click()
On Error GoTo ID_Click_Err

    On Error Resume Next
    If (Form.Dirty) Then
        DoCmd.RunCommand acCmdSaveRecord
    End If
    If (MacroError.Number <> 0) Then
        Beep
        MsgBox MacroError.Description, vbOKOnly, ""
        Exit Sub
    End If
    On Error GoTo 0
    DoCmd.OpenForm "Shipper Details", acNormal, "", "[ID]=" & Nz(ID, 0), ,
acDialog
    If (Not IsNull(ID)) Then
        TempVars.Add "CurrentID", "[ID]"
    End If
    If (IsNull(ID)) Then
        TempVars.Add "CurrentID", "Nz(DMax(""[ID]"",[Form].[RecordSource]),0)"
    End If
    DoCmd.Requery ""
    DoCmd.SearchForRecord , "", acFirst, "[ID]=" & TempVars!CurrentID
    TempVars.Remove "CurrentID"


ID_Click_Exit:
    Exit Sub

ID_Click_Err:
    MsgBox Error$
    Resume ID_Click_Exit

End Sub
```

> ➲ **Note:** If after the conversion process you still want to keep the [Embedded
> Macro] setting in the event properties of a form, report, or control, perform
> these steps:
>
> 1. Save the VBA code generated by the macro conversion to a file by choosing
>   File | Export in the Visual Basic Editor window. Access will create a file with
>   the .cls extension. To view the contents of this file, right-click its name in
>   Windows Explorer and choose Open With | Choose Program. Select Note-
>   pad and click OK.
> 2. In Access, close the form and answer No when prompted for changes.
>   Access will revert the [Event Procedure] setting in the event properties back
>   to [Embedded Macro].

New Features in Templates

As stated in Chapter 30, Access 2007 comes with several prebuilt templates that give users a head start with various types of Access database projects. The template files can be easily recognized by their .accdt file extension. By default, Access stores the prebuilt template files in the C:\Program Files\ Microsoft Office\Templates\1033\Access folder, as shown in Figure 32-21. Access will also look for template files in the user's application data directory, which is hidden by default. On computers with Windows Vista, this folder is named: C:\Users\<user name>\AppData\Roaming\Microsoft\Templates. On computers with Windows XP and Windows 2000, the user's template folder is: C:\Documents and Settings\<user name>\Application Data\Microsoft\ Templates.

Figure 32-21: Template files included in Access 2007. The templates that are used to create an entire database use the .accdt file extension. The ACCFL and ACCTB files store information about field and table templates that you can see in the Field Templates pane when you click the New Field button in the Fields & Columns group of the Datasheet tab (see Chapter 31, Figure 31-2).

The remaining sections of this chapter focus on the new template format introduced in Access 2007.

Creating a Custom Blank Template

When you click the Blank Database button in the Getting Started screen (see Chapter 30, Figure 30-1), Access provides you with an empty database that you can customize to suit your specific needs. If you are like many users, you start your next database project by again clicking the Blank Database button and proceed to implement many of the same customizations that you applied to the previous database project. If you have been working like this, however, you are not taking advantage of the startup template — Blank.accdb. Instead of customizing each new blank database, simply create a new database called Blank.accdb in the \Program Files\Microsoft Office\Templates\1033\Access folder and customize it to include specific database properties, VBA references and custom functions, Ribbon customizations, default forms and reports, and customized controls, as well as any other special configuration settings that you normally use in your database applications. The next time you click the Blank Database button in the Getting Started screen, Access will make a copy of your Blank.accdb database so you won't need to start from scratch. Your new database will already contain the common settings that you saved in the Blank.accdb file. Moreover, if your database requirements have changed, you can create a new Blank.accdb database with settings that conform to these new requirements.

 Note: If you already have a database that you want to use as the starting point for your new Access databases, click the Microsoft Office button, and choose Save As. Under Save the database in another format, click the file format you want for the template. In the Save As dialog box, browse to the system template folder (C:\Program Files\Microsoft Office\Templates\1033\Access) or the user template folder as discussed in the previous section. In the File name box, type Blank.accdb or Blank.mdb, and click Save.

Understanding the ACCDT File Format

The ACCDT file format that Access 2007 uses for its database templates is based on the new Microsoft Office Open Packaging Convention (OPC) file format. This file format is based on the XML and ZIP archive technologies. The OPC file format is also used by the new .docx, .xlsx, and .pptx file formats introduced for Word 2007, Excel 2007, and PowerPoint 2007. The OPC format makes it possible to store a number of text, image, and .xml/.xsd files in a single compressed file. The OPC files can be easily opened and examined. Before you can open an Access template file (.accdt) and examine its structure, you need to add the .zip extension at the end of the filename as shown in the following steps:

1. Locate the Northwind.accdt file in your Program Files\Microsoft Office\ Templates\1033\Access folder and rename it **Northwind.accdt.zip**.

2. When the Rename dialog box appears, click **Yes** to confirm that you want to change the filename extension. The file format changes to the zip archive.

3. To open the Northwind.accdt.zip file, right-click the filename and choose **Open With | Compressed (zipped) Folders**. The folders that make up the document are shown in Windows Explorer (see Figure 32-22).

    If you are using Windows Vista, right-click the filename and choose **Extract All**. In the Extract Compressed (Zipped) Folders dialog box,

accept the default location or choose a new location, and then click
Extract.

Figure 32-22: The directory structure of an Access template file.

Notice that the archive file contains the following three folders: _rels,
docProps, and template. The _rels folder contains one XML file with the
extension .rels that defines the relationships between various files included in
the file package (see Figure 32-23). Access uses this file to find out information about the template and the database.

```xml
<?xml version="1.0" encoding="UTF-8" standalone="yes" ?>
- <Relationships xmlns="http://schemas.openxmlformats.org/package/2006/relationships">
    <Relationship Target="docProps/core.xml" Id="CoreDocumentProperties"
      Type="http://schemas.openxmlformats.org/package/2006/relationships/metadata/core
      -properties" />
    <Relationship Target="template/preview.jpg" Id="PreviewImage"
      Type="http://schemas.microsoft.com/office/access/2005/04/template/preview-
      image" />
    <Relationship Target="template/template.xml" Id="Template"
      Type="http://schemas.microsoft.com/office/access/2005/04/template/start" />
  </Relationships>
```

Figure 32-23: The contents of the .rels XML file in the _rels folder.

You can modify the contents of the .rels file to, for example, have Access load
a different preview image.

The docProps folder contains the core.xml file that describes the core document properties such as creator name, identifier, title, description, keywords,
category, version, and lastModifiedBy (see Figure 32-24).

```xml
<?xml version="1.0" encoding="UTF-8" standalone="yes" ?>
- <cp:coreProperties
    xmlns:cp="http://schemas.openxmlformats.org/package/2006/metadata/core-properties"
    xmlns:dc="http://purl.org/dc/elements/1.1/" xmlns:dcterms="http://purl.org/dc/terms/"
    xmlns:dcmitype="http://purl.org/dc/dcmitype/"
    xmlns:xsi="http://www.w3.org/2001/XMLSchema-instance">
    <dc:creator>Microsoft Corporation</dc:creator>
    <dc:identifier>TC012289971033</dc:identifier>
    <dc:title>Northwind 2007</dc:title>
    <dc:description>Northwind Sample</dc:description>
    <cp:keywords>Sample, Northwind</cp:keywords>
    <cp:category>Sample</cp:category>
    <cp:version>1.0</cp:version>
    <cp:lastModifiedBy>Template Creator</cp:lastModifiedBy>
  </cp:coreProperties>
```

Figure 32-24: The contents of the core.xml file in the docProps folder.

When you double-click the template folder, you will see two subfolders named _rels and database, as well as the preview.jpg file of the Northwind image and a template.xml file (Figure 32-25).

Figure 32-25: The contents of the template folder.

The template.xml file contains information about the format of the template file.

You can find out a lot of information about the contents and the structure of the .accdt file by opening the database folder (Figure 32-26).

Figure 32-26: The contents of the database folder.

The databaseProperties.xml file in the database folder stores various database settings and properties. You can modify this file to include additional properties that need to be set by adding new nodes to the file.

The navpane.xml file contains information about the structure of the Navigation pane. It also contains the data for the Navigation pane system tables: MSysNavPaneGroupCategories, MSysNavPaneGroups, MSysNavPaneGroupToObjects, and MSysNavPaneObjectIDs.

The relationships.xml file contains the contents of the MSysRelationships system table.

The vbaReferences.xml file contains all VBA project references that Access needs to set.

If you take a look at the objects folder you will find a whole bunch of other files that describe different database objects (Figure 32-27).

Name	Type	Packe...	Has ...	Size	R...	Date
_rels	File Folder	0 KB		0 KB	0%	10/4/2006 6:34 PM
properties	File Folder	0 KB		0 KB	0%	10/4/2006 6:34 PM
sampleData	File Folder	0 KB		0 KB	0%	10/4/2006 6:33 PM
formActiveOrdersSubformforHome.txt	Text Document	5 KB	No	57 KB	92%	10/4/2006 6:34 PM
formCustomerDetails.txt	Text Document	44 KB	No	371 KB	89%	10/4/2006 6:34 PM
formCustomerDetailsAddFurigana.txt	Text Document	45 KB	No	395 KB	89%	10/4/2006 6:34 PM
formCustomerDetailsFlipAddress.txt	Text Document	45 KB	No	379 KB	89%	10/4/2006 6:34 PM
formCustomerDetailsFlipName.txt	Text Document	44 KB	No	378 KB	89%	10/4/2006 6:34 PM
formCustomerList.txt	Text Document	24 KB	No	197 KB	89%	10/4/2006 6:34 PM
formCustomerListAddFurigana.txt	Text Document	25 KB	No	214 KB	89%	10/4/2006 6:34 PM
formCustomerListFlipAddress.txt	Text Document	24 KB	No	203 KB	89%	10/4/2006 6:34 PM
formCustomerListFlipName.txt	Text Document	24 KB	No	203 KB	89%	10/4/2006 6:34 PM
formCustomerOrdersSubform.txt	Text Document	7 KB	No	83 KB	93%	10/4/2006 6:34 PM
formEmployeeDetails.txt	Text Document	45 KB	No	368 KB	88%	10/4/2006 6:33 PM
formEmployeeDetailsAddFurigana.txt	Text Document	46 KB	No	391 KB	89%	10/4/2006 6:33 PM
formEmployeeDetailsFlipAddress.txt	Text Document	45 KB	No	376 KB	89%	10/4/2006 6:34 PM
formEmployeeDetailsFlipName.txt	Text Document	45 KB	No	376 KB	89%	10/4/2006 6:34 PM
formEmployeeList.txt	Text Document	25 KB	No	203 KB	89%	10/4/2006 6:33 PM
formEmployeeListAddFurigana.txt	Text Document	26 KB	No	221 KB	89%	10/4/2006 6:33 PM
formEmployeeListFlipAddress.txt	Text Document	25 KB	No	210 KB	89%	10/4/2006 6:33 PM
formEmployeeListFlipName.txt	Text Document	25 KB	No	210 KB	89%	10/4/2006 6:33 PM
formEmployeeOrdersSubform.txt	Text Document	7 KB	No	94 KB	93%	10/4/2006 6:33 PM
formHome.txt	Text Document	35 KB	No	207 KB	84%	10/4/2006 6:33 PM
formInventoryList.txt	Text Document	21 KB	No	131 KB	85%	10/4/2006 6:33 PM
formInventorytoreorderSubformforHom...	Text Document	4 KB	No	46 KB	92%	10/4/2006 6:33 PM
formLoginDialog.txt	Text Document	54 KB	No	231 KB	77%	10/4/2006 6:33 PM
formOrderDetails.txt	Text Document	34 KB	No	256 KB	88%	10/4/2006 6:33 PM
formOrderList.txt	Text Document	22 KB	No	166 KB	87%	10/4/2006 6:33 PM
formOrderSubformforOrderDetails.txt	Text Document	7 KB	No	70 KB	91%	10/4/2006 6:33 PM
formProductCategorySalesbyMonth.txt	Text Document	6 KB	No	82 KB	94%	10/4/2006 6:33 PM
formProductDetails.txt	Text Document	40 KB	No	287 KB	87%	10/4/2006 6:33 PM
formProductSalesbyCategoryChart.txt	Text Document	6 KB	No	68 KB	92%	10/4/2006 6:33 PM
formProductSalesbyTotalRevenueChart...	Text Document	6 KB	No	65 KB	92%	10/4/2006 6:33 PM
formProductSalesQtybyEmployeeChart....	Text Document	6 KB	No	70 KB	92%	10/4/2006 6:33 PM

Figure 32-27: Files in the objects folder contain information about different database objects in the template file as well as information about sample data and properties for each object included in the template.

You can open any of the files listed in the above figure to find out what type of information is stored. Since this chapter covered macros, take a look at the SupplierList.txt file to find out how Access stores the embedded macros.

 Note: When you are done viewing the files, rename the Northwind.accdb.zip file back to its original name — Northwind.accdb.

Chapter Summary

This chapter introduced you to the new features in Access 2007 macros. We took a detailed look at macro security, created standalone and embedded macros, saw examples of temporary variables (TempVars), and examined the new error-handling actions in macros. We also learned how standalone and embedded macros can be converted to Visual Basic code. Because Access 2007 uses embedded macros extensively in its templates, we examined the structure and contents of the new ACCDT file format. If you need to create template files yourself, I recommend that you download from the Microsoft web site the Access Developer Extensions (ADE) for Microsoft Access 2007. This tool is absolutely free for you to use and explore.

Index

Public keyword, 55
public variables, *see* global variables

Q

queries, 350
 deleting, 384-386
 determining if updatable, 386-387
 listing, 383-384
 non-row-returning, 372
 opening ADO recordset based on, 308-309
 retrieving properties for, 382-383
 row-returning, 358, 366
 saving tables as, 846
 temporary, 356
 using to return rows, 849-850, 862-864
Query event, 593-595
QueryDef object, 204, 354-355
Quick Access toolbar, 781
Quick Format gallery, 878-879
Quick Info feature, 31
Quick Watch dialog box, 180
 using, 180-181

R

RaiseEvent statement, 639, 653
records,
 adding to table, 327, 328-329
 archiving, 433-436
 cloning, 407-412
 copying, 336-344
 counting, 309, 324-325
 deleting, 334-336, 702-706
 determining position of, 313-314
 discarding changes to, 332
 fetching, 304
 filtering, 323-324, 344-348
 finding, 295-298, 317-321
 inserting, 431-433
 marking with bookmark, 322-323
 modifying, 329-332, 698-702
 moving between, 292-293
 navigating, 312-313
 retrieving, 672-674, 681-684
 saving to disk, 394-395
 sort order of, 354
 sorting, 348-349
 updating, 332-334
 using stored procedures to modify, 560
Recordset object, 204, 212-213, 269, 287, 298
 see also ADO Recordsets *and* DAO
 Recordsets

recordsets,
 breaking into multiple pages, 674-678
 checking for records in, 310
 child, 413, 417
 creating, 389-392
 determining if in other recordset, 418
 disconnected, 392-393
 hierarchical, 422-430
 navigating, 288
 opening, 288-289
 parent, 413
 persisted, 394, 397
 shaped, 413, 415-417
 working with shaped, 418-422
Recordsets collection, 204
ReDim statement, 133, 135
reference,
 creating for ADO Object Library, 206-207
 setting to MSXML Object Library, 757-758
REFERENCES clause, 523
References dialog box, 201-202
referential integrity, 523
RefreshDatabaseWindow method, 502
RELATE command, 413
Relation object, 204
relational operators, 94
relationship-based filters, 479
relationships, creating between tables, 523-525
RemoveAllTempVar macro action, 908
RemoveTempVar macro action, 908
Replica object, 475
replicas, 475
 creating, 477-481
 properties of, 486
 retrieving properties of, 486-488
 synchronizing, 485-486, 488-491
 types of, 475
Replication Conflict Viewer window, 490-491
replication, database, 474
report events, 611-617
report modules, 12-13
report section events, 617-623
Report view, 884-885
 formatting control in, 885-886
ReportML, 715
reports,
 Access 2007 updates to, 884
 assigning Ribbon customizations to,
  808-812
 saving in PDF format, 886-887
 saving in XPS format, 886-887